45131

4
77
53

Ideals and Self-Interest
in America's Foreign Relations

THIS BOOK HAS BEEN PREPARED UNDER THE AUSPICES OF THE CENTER FOR THE STUDY OF AMERICAN FOREIGN POLICY AT THE UNIVERSITY OF CHICAGO

ROBERT ENDICOTT OSGOOD

Ideals and Self-Interest
in America's Foreign Relations

THE GREAT TRANSFORMATION
OF THE TWENTIETH CENTURY

THE UNIVERSITY OF CHICAGO PRESS

CHICAGO & LONDON

Library of Congress Catalog Card Number: 53-10532

THE UNIVERSITY OF CHICAGO PRESS, CHICAGO 60637
The University of Chicago Press, Ltd., London W.C. 1

For

GRETCHEN

FOREWORD

THE Center for the Study of American Foreign Policy was established in 1950. Its general purpose is to contribute to a better understanding of the principles, objectives, and probable results of American foreign policy and to investigate possible alternatives to current policies in the light of these principles and objectives.

Three areas of research have thus far been mapped out: the foreign policies of American statesmen, the development and principles of United States foreign policy, and contemporary problems of United States foreign policy. Dr. Osgood's book belongs to the second area of research. Of the studies of American statesmen which are in preparation, a study by Gerald Stourzh of Benjamin Franklin's conception of foreign policy is in preparation.

HANS J. MORGENTHAU
Director

PREFACE

IN THIS book I have sought to present a thesis about America's foreign relations which will have a useful application to contemporary circumstances. The historical material is developed at considerable length in the belief that this thesis requires a rather extensive illustration and documentation if the reader is to appreciate the full meaning of its generalizations and to judge their validity with relative objectivity. While I hope that this approach will be thorough enough to avoid some of the evils of oversimplification that inevitably occur when one organizes any mass of historical detail according to a particular scheme of analysis, I have not attempted to set forth a definitive or comprehensive interpretation of any particular man or event. In my research I have relied chiefly upon published material, of which there is a vast accumulation relating to the period since the turn of the century. At the same time, from consulting those who are thoroughly familiar with all the relevant historical material, including the many unpublished manuscripts and private papers, I have reason to think that an exhaustive investigation of these sources would not significantly modify my central thesis.

In so far as *Ideals and Self-Interest in America's Foreign Relations* succeeds in presenting an interpretation of America's past foreign relations that contributes to an understanding of the problems of power and moral purpose underlying her present position in world politics, it will be due, in large measure, to the encouragement and wisdom of men who know far more than I about international relations and American foreign policy. In so far as the book fails, it will be partly due to my own limitations and partly due to the substantial limitations imposed by the inordinate complexity of the problems themselves. Where fundamental principles of international relations are concerned there are no pat answers, no unambiguous generalizations, no final solutions, but only educated guesses about cause and effect and rough approximations to the impenetrable truth.

I owe a special debt of gratitude to McGeorge Bundy, of Harvard University, for devoting such great care and understanding to this work in its original form as a doctoral dissertation; to Hans J. Morgenthau, of the University of Chicago, whose interest in my manuscript led to its revision and publication; to Richard W. Leopold and Arthur S. Link, of Northwestern University, who gave me the benefit of their extraordinary historical scholarship; and to William Yandell Elliott, of Harvard, and Edward Mead Earle, of the Institute for Advanced Study at Princeton, who gave me discerning advice on matters of emphasis and scope. My research was made easier and more profitable by the intelligent guidance of the late Nora Cordingley, custodian of the Roosevelt Memorial Association Collection in Widener Library, Harvard University. Academic and nonacademic readers alike should be as thankful as I that my wife found time to read the manuscript with the exacting eye of a shrewd nonexpert.

The following publishers have granted permission to quote material from the books indicated: Charles Scribner's Sons, from Reinhold Niebuhr, *Moral Man and Immoral Society;* Harper & Brothers, from Robert E. Sherwood, *Roosevelt and Hopkins;* Houghton Mifflin Company, from Claude G. Bowers, *Beveridge and the Progressive Era;* Harcourt, Brace and Company, from Lewis Mumford, *Men Must Act;* The Macmillan Company, from Charles and Mary Beard, *America in Midpassage.*

CONTENTS

INTRODUCTION

1. The Problem of Self-Interest and Ideals

ACCORDING to Thucydides, Pericles proclaimed in his Funeral Oration that Athens was the school of Hellas, because only Athens obeyed the dictates of the highest morality, because "we alone do good to our neighbors not upon a calculation of interest, but in the confidence of freedom and in a frank and fearless spirit."[1] But during fifteen years of the Peloponnesian War the Athenians saw their ideal of a great movement of liberation transformed into a mere struggle for power, and when their ambassadors approached the magistrates of Melos, it was expediency, not morality, that ruled the nation.

> But you and we should say what we really think, and aim only at what is possible, for we both know that into the discussion of human affairs the question of justice only enters where the pressure of necessity is equal, and that the powerful exact what they can, and the weak grant what they may
>
> .   .   .   .
>
> For of the Gods we believe, and of men we know that by a law of their nature wherever they can rule they will. This law was not made by us, and we are not the first to have acted upon it: we did but inherit it, and shall bequeath it to all time, and we know that you and all mankind, if you are as strong as we are, would do as we do.[2]

Thus Thucydides, himself the child of an age in which the imperatives of survival had darkened man's outlook, gave classic expression to the eternal conflict between ideal principles and sheer power in the service of self-interest. The conflict between ideals and self-interest is as much a part of the international life of the United States as it was of Athens. It is, in fact, a fundamental part of all human relations, whether among individuals or groups of individuals, for man's conscience is geared to ideal aspirations which his innate selfishness prevents him from attaining. Yet because man's conscience, as well as his ego, demands satisfaction, the reconciliation of ideals with self-interest is one of the central problems of all human experience and philosophical speculation. It is, of course, the kind of problem men are forever trying to solve but never solving; and yet those who would preserve the highest values of civilization cannot afford to abandon the attempt to unreasoning impulse or the blind rush of events. The problem of reconciling national self-interest with universal ideals transcending the interests of particular nations forms a central theme of this study of America's foreign relations.

A problem which involves so many intangible elements capable of so many different meanings demands, at the outset, an attempt to define terms and objectives and underlying assumptions. However, the reader should be warned that the process of definition, although essential for analytical purposes, necessarily distorts the infinite complexities of a nation's thoughts and actions by lending them a precision and logical simplicity which they could never possess in reality. The full significance of ideals and self-interest in America's foreign relations can be discovered only amid the concrete historical details of the nation's experience in world politics. The general statements in this introductory chapter are merely a rough guide for that discovery.

2. THE SOURCES OF AMERICAN CONDUCT

This book is, primarily, a historical interpretation of the evolution of the American attitude toward world politics since the turn of the century. However, in its broadest aspect it is concerned with two more general areas of inquiry, which are essential parts of this interpretation. On the one hand, it inquires into the nature of some of the underlying sources of America's international conduct as they bear upon the nation's adaptation to its status as a world power; on the other hand, it seeks to develop and apply to specific historical situations in terms of this analysis some basic principles of conduct that ought to guide the United States in its foreign relations. Both the sources and the principles of America's foreign relations are examined in terms of the relation between universal ideals and national self-interest.

With respect to the guiding principles of American conduct, this study is concerned with the conditions under which the nation can hope to reconcile its self-interest with transcendent ideals. With respect to the sources of American conduct, it analyzes the relation between ideals and self-interest in three different ways: first, the role of these two ends in shaping America's international conduct and the conduct of nations in general; secondly, the role which Americans believe these ends ought to play in international relations; and, thirdly, the role which Americans believe these ends do, as a matter of fact, play in their own conduct and the conduct of other nations.

These three ways of looking at the relation between universal ideals and national self-interest are considered as sources of America's international conduct in that they are basic ways in which Americans orient themselves to their international environment. Obviously, they are interrelated, and it is their interrelation which determines their total significance in shaping the course of America's foreign relations.

Stated abstractly, this proposition may seem obscure, but in practice we commonly recognize its truth in the sphere of personal relations. Thus we recognize that there is a certain relationship between a man's estimate of human nature, the quality of his ideal aspirations, and his conduct toward his fellowmen. For example, if a man believes that human beings are basically selfish and mean, then he might well conclude that reform has very narrow limits and that it behooves him to bend his efforts toward furthering his own interests lest he lose out in the competition for survival. But if, on the other hand, a man believes that his fellowmen are basically unselfish and good, then he will expect them to respond to appeals of reason and moral suasion, and duty beckons him to strive toward the finest aspirations the imagination can construct. It need hardly be remarked that what a man believes to be the facts of human nature may be just as important as the actual facts themselves. At the same time, we expect a stable individual to hold beliefs that correspond fairly closely to reality; otherwise, he will be constantly acting upon unrealistic expectations and committing himself to aspirations which are bound to be disappointing.

In a general way, the same considerations apply to national conduct. If the estimate which Americans make of the existing ends and motives of nations —of their ability, for example, to transcend their selfish interests for the sake of ideal principles—does not bear a certain correspondence to the actual ends and motives of nations, including their own, then one might say that the American people were maladjusted with respect to their international environment—maladjusted, that is, in the same sense as one who is out of harmony with his environment from failure to reach a satisfactory and stable adjustment between his desires and his condition of life. For unrealistic expectations concerning human conduct encourage extravagant aspirations; and among nations, as among individuals, the result is apt to be disillusionment and an erratic fluctuation from one extreme in conduct to another. A maladjusted nation is not likely to achieve its international ends; for, in the long run, it will lack the poise and maturity to reconcile its self-interest with its ideals.

It should be stated here that the attribution of thought and behavior to nations is simply a convenient manner of speaking about significant ways in which large numbers of individual citizens think about their nation with respect to other nations. The basic unit of analysis here is not any mystical "group person" but the individual citizen as he orients himself to his international environment by identifying himself with his nation-state and projecting upon this personified group of individuals his own thoughts and emotions.

It should also be stated that this study is not concerned with the relation between an individual and his nation. How individuals reconcile their private interests with their devotion to the nation is another matter and an important one, but in an age in which the value of patriotism is taken for granted and one of the central features of human relations is the close personal identification of individuals with their national groups, it is even more important to examine the ways in which citizens think about their own nation's conduct in relation to international society.

3. SELF-INTEREST AND IDEALS DEFINED

It should not be supposed that the analysis of the role of ideals and national self-interest as sources of America's international conduct and the problem of reconciling these two ends in America's foreign relations can be approached with anything like mechanical precision or scientific objectivity. Obviously, these ends are not simple, tangible entities with self-evident meanings. Nevertheless, the very vagueness of the terms makes it necessary, for the sake of clarity in the body of the historical interpretation that follows this introduction, to give national self-interest and universal ideals more exact meanings than they possess in ordinary usage.

National self-interest is understood to mean a state of affairs valued solely for its benefit to the nation. The motive of national egoism, which leads men to seek this end, is marked by the disposition to concern oneself solely with the welfare of one's own nation; it is self-love transferred to the national group. An ideal is a standard of conduct or a state of affairs worthy of achievement by virtue of its universal moral value. The motive of national idealism is the disposition to concern oneself with moral values that transcend the nation's selfish interests; it springs from selflessness and love.*

Of course, these ends and motives are not nearly so distinct as their definitions imply. In neither personal nor international relations does one find pure idealism or pure self-interest but only a strange mingling of ambiguous and contradictory ends and motives. One can never be sure whether selfishness belies some subtle compassion or whether altruism is the guise of a secret anticipation of self-satisfaction or the approbation of others. And even if idealism or egoism were pure and distinct, one would never find either of them perfectly embodied in a single individual—certainly never in an entire nation. Indeed the popular view encourages no such expectation but rather

---

* Throughout this study an end is defined as the object, result, or effect aimed at; it is a state of affairs one seeks. A motive is defined as a consideration, idea, need, or emotion that induces a choice or excites the will; it is a state of mind one experiences. Obviously, ends and motives are intermingled and indistinct; nevertheless, as the following discussion and the body of the historical narrative should show, an analysis of national conduct must take both ends and motives into account.

holds that individuals should achieve some sort of equilibrium between the two qualities. It is, in fact, the fusion of these ends and motives in men's minds that creates the really significant consequences in personal relations and, more particularly, in the international relations with which this essay is concerned.

Nevertheless, the lack of rigid distinctions between these two basic categories of ends and motives does not obviate the fact that there are basic differences; and for the purposes of analysis it is necessary not only to define ideals and self-interest but also to distinguish among different kinds of idealistic and self-interested ends and motives, for it is quite misleading to speak of either category as though it referred to a uniform entity. The following elaboration of ends and motives does not pretend to be exhaustive or universally applicable. It is intended simply as a useful scheme for generalizing the international ends and motives of Americans, while, at the same time, taking account of the fact that all modern nationalism has a good deal in common.

Basic to all kinds of national self-interest is survival or self-preservation, for upon national survival depends the achievement of all other self-interested ends. The exact nature of the national self that must be preserved at all costs is open to various interpretations, but, above all, it is the nation's territorial integrity, political independence, and fundamental governmental institutions. National security is a related but broader end, since it embraces not only survival but the nation's ability to survive. Security, in its broadest sense, is subjective; it is an absence of fear. The distinguishing motives associated with national self-preservation are the will to live and the fear of death.

One of the most commonly avowed and vaguest kinds of national self-interest is that nebulous catch-all "vital interests," which includes a wide range of ends believed to be more or less important for the nation's welfare—and there may be considerable disagreement about the importance of some vital interests—but not essential for its survival. In this category one might place equal commercial opportunity, the protection of citizens and property outside the nation's territorial limits, or the control of immigration.

Another important category of national self-interest might be called self-sufficiency, or the conduct of foreign relations without reference to other nations or to matters beyond unilateral national control. When self-sufficiency is motivated by a passive egoism, by an urge to withdraw and a longing to be left alone, it is commonly known as isolation. To be sure, isolationism may also spring, in part, from idealistic motives, but historically its determining aspect has always been a conception of national self-interest. On the other hand, self-sufficiency may be motivated by a more aggressive egoism, by an urge to assert the national will on one's own nation's terms without regard for the will of other nations. This state of affairs is also called isolation in common usage, but its real significance might better be distinguished from the passive kind of isolation by noting that it is sought out of an urge for national self-assertion and not simply out of a passive yearning for withdrawal.

In any analysis of national ends and motives one must also take into account the desire for national prestige. Prestige includes national honor; that is, the respect of other nations for one's own nation by virtue of its reputation as a proud and self-reliant state. But it may also refer to the nation's reputation for virtue, to the admiration of other nations for one's own nation's moral excellence. The egoism in the pursuit of this form of prestige is more subtle; certainly it consists in a peculiar kind of vanity when it leads a nation to covet the approbation of other nations in order that it may exercise over them the power of "moral force." Admittedly, this is a sublimated form of self-interest, which must be sustained, in part, by genuine idealism; but it is self-interest nevertheless, and it has played a vital part in America's recurring assertions of moral purpose.

Finally, there is national aggrandizement or the increase of national power, wealth, or prestige. This kind of self-interest is readily identifiable by virtue of the vehement motives which lead to its pursuit: ambition, militancy, the urge to dominate, the will-to-power.

The ideal ends with which this study is concerned are by no means shared by all nations. They are, in fact, either largely unknown or seriously challenged by a great portion of humanity. Nevertheless, considering the diversity of social and cultural traditions in this world, it is remarkable to what extent modern nations profess their allegiance to these ideals, either from conviction or from expediency. I refer to the ideals derived from the Christian-liberal-humanitarian tradition of Western civilization.

According to these ideals, the ultimate moral value is the innate dignity and worth of every human being. From this principle it follows that every individual has certain inalienable rights of self-protection and self-expression so that he may fulfil his potentialities as a rational being. It also follows that he has certain obligations to respect the rights and dignity of other individuals by treating them as ends and never as means so that they too may fulfil their potentialities. In practice, the realization of these ideals may require various degrees of subordination of the individual to a larger group, but always the ultimate moral standard remains the individual's welfare. Idealists must recognize as a basic condition for the realization of the liberal and humane values the creation of a brotherhood of mankind in which all men, regardless of physiological, social, religious, or political distinctions, will have equal partnership and in which human conflicts will be settled by reason, morality, and law rather than by physical power, coercion, or violence. And idealists must seek, as an integral part of this brotherhood, a progressive command over nature, to the end that every individual may share the material benefits essential to a full and happy existence on earth.

Most commonly professed among the national ends related to these fundamental ideals of Western civilization are those principles of right conduct which apply to personal relations; I mean those ethical restraints upon egoism —honesty, truthfulness, fidelity to obligations, kindness, fair play, lawfulness, nonintervention in other people's affairs, and all the rest—which operate by force of conscience, custom, or law. Obviously, this sort of idealism is frequently associated with a prudent recognition of the practical advantages of peace and orderliness.

Another kind of ideal, almost as frequently avowed by nations but of an exceedingly indefinite nature, expresses allegiance to a universal goal, that is, to some state of international affairs believed to be of benefit to all mankind, such as peace, good will, and justice among nations, or freedom and a decent standard of living for all men.

The pursuit of a universal goal may demand the practice of that extreme form of idealism, national altruism, according to which men dedicate themselves to the welfare of other nations and peoples without regard for their own nation's welfare. But the ultimate form of idealism is national self-sacrifice, which demands the deliberate surrender of one's own nation's self-interest for the sake of other nations and peoples or for the sake of some moral principle or universal goal. Every ideal demands that nations place some restraints upon egoism and renounce the more extreme forms of self-interest, but the ideal of self-sacrifice must countenance even the surrender of national survival itself.

4. Egoists and Idealists; Realists and Utopians

In order to appreciate the significance of national self-interest and universal ideals as sources of America's international conduct it is necessary to consider these ends as they relate to the three principal ways, mentioned previously, in which individual citizens orient themselves to their international environment. In the evolution of the American attitude toward the outside world certain distinct attitudes toward the relation between self-interest and ideals stand out as having had a peculiar significance in shaping America's foreign relations. Because they recur time and again in the body of this historical interpretation it is necessary to take the inevitable risk of distorting human thought and motivation by giving these attitudes and their proponents distinguishing names. This is doubly necessary because current discussions of international politics are full of references to "realists" and "idealists" but almost devoid of attempts to define these words. Unfortunately, the English language does not readily supply, for the purposes of such discussions, nouns which are free of moral and emotional connotations, but it is, nevertheless, the author's duty to disclaim such connotations.

In so far as individuals, thinking and acting in their capacity as members of a nation, are governed in their attitude toward other nations by self-interest, they may be called egoists; and in so far as they are governed by ideals transcending the national interest, they may be called idealists. Necessarily, these terms, like the terms that follow, refer to matters of degree, not absolute distinctions; it should be stressed that there is no such thing as a pure egoist or a perfect idealist in the sphere of national thought and action, any more than in the sphere of individual relations.

In so far as men believe that nations ought to conduct themselves—in practice, not just theoretically—in accordance with transcendent ideals, they are idealists; and in so far as they believe that nations ought to pursue only their own self-interest, they are national egoists. Of course, men may be thoroughgoing national egoists in their actual ends and motives and, at the same time, idealists in their desires; and they may erect a different standard of conduct for other nations than for their own, although the appeal of moral consistency usually forbids a frank acknowledgment of this enormity. Moreover, because of the force of ideals in the civilized world, national egoists are usually moved to rationalize their actions either in terms of ideal principles or circumstances beyond human control. These are just a few of the subtleties and qualifications that the reader must bear in mind when he measures these generalities against historical detail.

Finally, in so far as individuals believe that nations, as a matter of fact, are moved by self-interest, we shall call them Realists; and in so far as they believe that nations conduct themselves according to idealistic ends and motives that transcend their selfish interests, we shall call them utopians. This terminology is in accord with the common-sense distinction between a skeptical and an optimistic view of human nature. There is no implication that the skeptical view is necessarily the true view of the realities of international relations—hence the use of a capital "R"—nor is there any implication that an idealist must be a utopian or that a Realist is necessarily a national egoist.

It should be observed that the important criterion of the Realist's and the utopian's view of national conduct is not so much what a man may believe to be the ends and motives of particular nations at particular points in history but rather what he believes to be the potentialities of national conduct—in other words, the ends and motives that nations are capable of acting upon. We apply a similar criterion to individual relations when we recognize, for example, that a man may acknowledge the existence of evil individuals and still entertain a utopian view of man's ability to overcome evil.

The issue between the Realist and the utopian is fully joined in their views about the role of power in international relations. The Realist, because he is skeptical of the ability of nations to transcend their self-interest, sees the struggle for national power as the distinguishing characteristic of international relations. He tends to view international conflict as an inevitable state of affairs, issuing from man's tenacious patriotic instincts and conditioned by relatively immutable influences, such as geography or some primordial urge, like the drive to dominate. Consequently, he is skeptical of attempts to mitigate international conflict with appeals to sentiment and principle or with written pledges and institutional devices unless they express the existing configuration of national interests or register the relative power among nations. He believes that if power conflicts can be mitigated at all, they can be mitigated only by balancing power against power and by cultivating a circumspect diplomacy that knows the uses of force and the threat of force as indispensable instruments of national policy.

The utopian, on the other hand, believes that the essence of international relations is spiritual power, which springs from the impact of thoughts and actions upon the supreme arbiter of all human affairs, the individual conscience. Because he is convinced that man's conscience is progressively attuned to immutable principles transcending particular selfish interests, he tends to regard national egoism as a transient phenomenon, and he looks upon the struggle for national power as a kind of social aberration—the consequence of ignorance, unenlightened guidance, the exceptional selfishness of the few, the suppression of the public voice, or faulty institutional arrangements. Therefore, he has an abiding faith in man's ability to direct his conscience and reason toward restraining, controlling, or overcoming the self-seeking and aggressive impulses that foul national sentiment and conduct. Through appeals to the common interest of all men in peace and justice, through sublimating selfish interests and channeling them toward social goals, and through declarations, agreements, laws, and institutional devices, the utopian believes that nations can subordinate their interests to universal moral precepts. Men who approach international relations in this manner naturally tend to distrust the devious art of diplomacy and the inscrutable machinations of those who are absorbed in the narrow pursuit of national self-interest or are preoccupied with the prerogatives and instruments of national power. They tend to deprecate the calculation of power and the pursuit of strategic advantage as the manifestations of a sordid and anachronistic game played by evil leaders at the expense of the multitude.

5. The Realities of International Politics

In the course of explaining and elaborating the meaning of self-interest and ideals in this study of America's attitude toward international relations, it was suggested that unrealistic expectations concerning the role of self-interest and ideals in national conduct are apt to render a nation's adjustment to its international environment erratic and ineffective and to prevent it from achieving its ends through a satisfactory reconciliation of its self-interest with universal moral principles. But what is a realistic view of the ends and motives of nations? In general, realism—with a small "r"—is used in this book to refer to an accurate assessment of the ends and motives that determine the conduct of nations; it implies a disposition to perceive and act upon the real conditions under which a nation may achieve its ends in international society. Therefore, in order to make explicit a major premise underlying the historical interpretation that follows, it is essential that the author set forth his view of the real conditions of international politics, however oversimplified and pretentious any short statement must be.

If this interpretation of the realities of international relations seems to underestimate the role of ideals in shaping national conduct, that is because of my belief that in the historical circumstances with which it deals the American people have been prone to overestimate the role of ideals and underestimate the role of national power and self-interest. We may be reaching a stage in which the reverse will be true, but that stage has not yet arrived. Nevertheless, in view of the peculiar stresses exerted upon the American outlook by the present unprecedented international tension, a balanced account of the real conditions under which the nation may hope to achieve a sound adjustment to its international environment calls for specific recognition of the interdependence of national self-interest with ideal ends transcending self-interest. That recognition is implicit in the body of this study; it is made explicit in the conclusion, in which the last half-century of America's foreign relations is surveyed with an eye to its lessons for the future.

The most important reality of international politics is the fact that nation-states are the major units of political life, which command the supreme loyalty and affection of the great mass of individuals in the civilized world. More than ever, since the rise of modern nations several centuries ago, the great mass of citizens feel that their personal welfare, both spiritually and materially, depends absolutely upon the welfare of the nation to which they owe allegiance; and this is true regardless of divergent views about the

proper scope of state intervention in private affairs. This situation is not immutable, but neither is it likely to change in the foreseeable future, for such
major transformations in man's outlook occur only in the course of centuries.

A citizen's dependence upon his nation assumes a distinct intimacy because
he confers upon the object of his allegiance the attributes of a person so closely
identified with his own personality that he virtually acquires a second self, in
whose behalf he can feel friendly, hostile, generous, selfish, confident, afraid,
proud, or humiliated almost as poignantly as he would feel these emotions for
himself in his relations with other individuals. However, the conscience of this
vicarious personality, unlike the private conscience, is relieved by the sanction
of patriotism, so that a citizen can manage with a sense of complete moral
consistency to combine lofty altruism toward his own nation with extreme
egoism toward other nations and thereby actively support a standard of ethics
in foreign relations which he would not dream of tolerating in his private
dealings. It is to this explosive combination of altruism and egoism, satisfying
two profound impulses in one great emotional coalescence, that modern nationalism owes its peculiar intensity.

We are seldom fully conscious of the intensity of our allegiance to the nation because we are so profoundly under its spell. But how many other loyalties do we willingly permit to claim our very lives? Carlton Hayes suggests
that national loyalty is nothing less than the latest expression of that mysteri-
ous, instinctive "religious sense" which has inspired man from the dawn of his
history.[3] Like medieval religion, the faith of nationalism has its saints, shrines,
hymns, rituals, symbols, catechism, holy scripture, and sacred traditions. Like
the medieval church, the nation grants grace, receives prayers, promises salvation, punishes heresy, inspires sacrifice, and promotes its ideal mission and
destiny. Moreover, national faith has a way of absorbing all other faiths and
loyalties and turning them to its own use. It is significant that the traditional
repositories of worship, though theoretically committed to the brotherhood
of man without regard to national boundaries, have been, in reality, formidable propagators of exclusive national loyalties, especially in times of crisis.

Clearly, the intensity of national sentiment imposes narrow limits upon
the extent to which a nation can be expected to transcend its own self-interest
in the service of universal principles or the welfare of others. This is not
to deny that idealism works a great influence among nations, as among individuals; it is a potent influence, for example, in moderating the more aggressive manifestations of self-interest. However, it seldom overrules fundamental aspects of national self-interest. On the contrary, the moral force of
supranational principles would seem to be most compelling when the pursuit
of ideals coincides with the national advantage.

The primacy of self-interest among national ends can take many forms, depending upon the kind of egoism that moves men to act upon it; but it is pre-eminently an expression of the most fundamental end of all, national survival, for upon survival depends a nation's ability to achieve all other ends.

In an age in which national survival is in constant jeopardy it is not necessary to belabor its obvious egoistic value, but it is worth noting that the compelling character of national survival is derived from high moral values as well. So intimate is man's identification with his national group that national extinction, like the murder of one's family, would be equivalent to a direct depredation of the dignity of the individual personality, since it would destroy a virtually indispensable source of personal security and happiness, as well as the sum of all those personal satisfactions derived from the nation's "way of life." For this reason, those responsible for the nation's course in international affairs, although they may rightly feel the obligation to sacrifice their own lives, are no more justified morally than they are justified on grounds of expediency in committing national suicide.

But the pursuit of national self-preservation can take many shapes. It has a way of merging into a wide range of national interests, conferring upon them something of its own sanctity, since every end that seems to promote and assure survival assumes a part of its supreme importance. Thus national security becomes virtually as compelling as self-preservation because it implies the ability to survive. National security, in turn, demands a constant vigilance over the nation's vital interests, its honor and prerogatives, and its ability to make decisions on its own terms, for a nation cannot afford to minimize the scope of its security when the very anarchy of international relations places its ability to survive under a constant shadow of doubt. Security is a state of mind as well as a state of affairs, and a nation can never feel certain of its ability to survive, in the absence of some universal arbiter of national conflicts, when it is inevitable that some nations must seek security at the disadvantage of others. The very recognition among nations of the crucial importance of survival to each of them creates the fear that other nations will pursue security to the detriment of their own. Thus suspicion begets suspicion, and the resort to violence is never excluded.

Of course, this description of national ends and motives is not universally applicable. For some nations and some periods of history it is, perhaps, an understatement—notably those periods, like our own, in which international relations have been thrown into chaos by nations not content to seek self-preservation but determined to pursue a course of aggrandizement. For other times, during which there was general satisfaction with the international status quo, this description is an overstatement. Nevertheless, since the United

States became an independent nation—and certainly since the turn of this century—the periods have been few and fleeting in which the great powers have not been actively engaged in what could be accurately described as a struggle for survival; and with the emergence of total war in recent decades this struggle has assumed a new urgency, for the failure to survive approaches the point of utter humiliation and virtual physical extinction.

Because of the crucial importance of national security, national egoism enjoys a rational and moral justification which renders the primacy of self-interest among national ends an indisputable and unavoidable reality of international politics. In practice, this means that the exercise of independent national power—power being understood as the ability of one nation to influence others to do its will—is the most important means of achieving national ends. It means that international relations are bound to be characterized by a competition for power, more or less severe, among nations wedded to their own interests above all other ends. This competition for power may be mitigated by a variety of restraints upon rampant egoism—by ideals, sentiment, international law, collective power, mutual self-interest, etc.—but it will never be abolished or even transformed into orderly procedures enforced impartially by reference to custom or law until men undergo a psychological revolution that will permit them to owe their primary allegiance to some community greater than their nation-state; and this revolution does not seem likely to occur in the foreseeable future.

This situation has a profound bearing upon the conditions under which a nation can hope to achieve its ends by reconciling its self-interest with its ideals; for it means that nations are not likely to achieve their ends, in the long run, unless they choose the most effective means to an end, even though the means fall far short of moral perfection, and then support their choice with national power, exercised wisely and rationally on the basis of an objective calculation of the configuration of international power.

Of course, the exercise of national power can take many forms, ranging from moral and rational persuasion to physical coercion; but because of the relative weakness of supranational mores, laws, and ideals, the chief measure of national power is, ultimately, the ability to deprive other nations of their self-interest, including their very survival as a last resort. Therefore, coercion or the threat of coercion is an indispensable instrument of national policy. This does not mean that an overt threat of physical force is necessarily wise statesmanship; the power of coercion is, in fact, most effective when it is used with restraint and circumspection and in conjunction with noncoercive measures. It is the task of diplomacy, the "brains of power," to employ coercion or the threat of coercion with its maximum effectiveness.

It follows from these realities that a nation that hopes to achieve any end, from security to international reform, must, inevitably, be involved in a continual series of moral compromises, for the requirements of power seldom conform perfectly to ideal standards. In this sense, every effective national policy must be tinged with the sin of selfishness. However, an ineffective policy, regardless of the purity of its motives, can no more escape these moral compromises than an effective one, if one judges a nation's actions by consequences as well as by motives. As long as the effective means to a national end remains, essentially, the exercise of independent national power, it is folly to expect national selflessness or sheer impulse, however high-minded, to promote ideal goals. On the contrary, selflessness or impulsiveness, by blinding reason to the practical consequences of national actions, may work untold international mischief and even jeopardize a nation's survival.

But these are not the only compromises nations must make. A nation's adjustment to its international environment and a nation's ability to achieve its ends in international society depend not only upon reconciling its self-interest with its ideals but also upon reconciling one self-interested end with another, and one ideal end with another. Contradictions among ends in the latter sphere are as inevitable—and, hence, compromises are as necessary—as between ideals and national self-interest; for just as national survival may not always permit the maintenance of peace, so a rash attempt to vindicate the national honor may jeopardize the nation's security, and the principle of nonintervention in other nations' affairs may preclude the defense of international decency and humanitarianism. At the root of this situation is the fact that man is entangled in such a complex environment that he cannot possibly achieve all his goals simultaneously; therefore, the pursuit of one goal must frequently conflict with the attainment of another. Thus in personal relations, truth may conflict with kindness, and the single-minded pursuit of either end without compromising in terms of the other will probably result in vitiating both. Because of the greater complexity of international relations, the contradictions among national ends are correspondingly numerous and perplexing.

These inevitable contradictions among ends can never be perfectly resolved, but neither can any nation concerned with universal ideals or its own self-interest afford to ignore them or leave them to resolve themselves. If there were a formula for resolving such contradictions, it might prescribe that men compromise with perfection by choosing among various ends according to a scale of priorities consistent with a well-established hierarchy of value-preferences and then, on the basis of an objective calculation, apply the means most likely to translate this choice among ends into concrete results. Stated abstractly in a single sentence, this prescription is ludicrously mechanical.

Intangible values cannot be arranged with neat, mathematical precision in a comprehensive formula applicable to every relevant situation; and even if they could be, who would adhere to such a formula? Yet the fact remains, if men were to act with complete indifference to consistent criteria for choosing and compromising among various ends and means, human relations would be characterized by far more irresponsibility and chaos than actually exists. The complexity of human society precludes perfectly consistent discrimination among ends; but to the extent that a nation's pursuit of idealistic and self-interested ends is without any relation to a general pattern of preferences transcending the particular situation, its actions are bound to be arbitrary and unduly inconsistent. It will apply one standard of judgment to one situation and a totally different standard to another, and its enthusiastic pursuit of a particular end at one time will be the source of deep regret and disillusionment later. Too much of America's experience in international relations confirms this proposition.

Therefore, with due regard for the above reservations, a general scheme for analyzing the sources of America's international conduct should present at least the principal characteristics of a scale of priorities among self-interested and idealistic ends which expresses the broad value-preferences of the American people and others who share the traditions of Western culture. This too is a part of the realities of international politics upon which stable and effective foreign relations must be based.

Among the ends of national self-interest, survival, of course, must be rated the most compelling. However, this is an end that commands active attention only when it is joined by the catalyst of fear, as when the nation perceives a clear threat to its self-preservation. Therefore, a nation may not always, in concrete situations, take into account the full value of its survival, which in any theoretical scale of values it would unquestionably award top priority. This becomes an important consideration in the case of the United States, whose relative physical isolation, almost up to World War II, encouraged a complacency toward its security permitted to few other nations.

Self-sufficiency must also be placed high in the scale of priorities among self-interested ends, since the desire for an untrammeled national will is at the heart of the sense of national distinctness and is, therefore, an integral part of man's outlook in this nationalist age. In the long run it would seem that no nation willingly entangles itself with other nations except on its own terms, unless some more compelling interest, such as national self-preservation, demands it.

As for the self-assertive and aggressive manifestations of national self-interest, nations with liberal traditions surround these more obtrusive aspects of egoism with a host of moral inhibitions. Hence their great ingenuity in lending them the guise of idealism. However, in spite of these inhibitions—and probably because of them—conscience-bound nations, like the United States, occasionally indulge in great bursts of intense aggressive egoism, leading even to aggrandizement, which are inconsistent with their basic hierarchy of values and their long-run scale of priorities and which are, therefore, usually a source of self-recrimination, disillusionment, and apathy in the aftermath.

The scale of priorities among idealistic ends is more difficult to discern. In spite of the weakening of ethical restraints under the strain of recent decades of international revolution and upheaval, certain minimum standards of decency in international relations probably remain the least debatable and most compelling ideal ends.

The traditional universal goals embody powerful and abiding aspirations of all men of good will, even in an era when international strife has dissipated confidence in their fulfillment; but these goals are so vague in content and so remote from the practical day-to-day imperatives of international politics that they have less tangible effect upon national conduct except as a rationalization of more compelling ends. Their greatest impact is registered in outbursts of crusading ardor, when the nation temporarily abandons its general scale of priorities and soars into new realms of idealism, including altruism and even self-sacrifice. But, like the vehemence aroused by extreme forms of national egoism, the intensity of the crusading urge is not matched by its stability; and its inconsistency with the nation's general hierarchy of values is finally revealed in the reaction that follows.

With regard to the scale of priorities between self-interested and idealistic ends, this outline of the realities of international politics has already set forth the proposition that, owing to the peculiar force of national loyalty, egoism has a higher priority among nations than among individuals and that, accordingly, the pursuit of ideals is, in the long run, contingent upon their compatibility with the most compelling ends of national self-interest. Nevertheless, this reality should not obscure the fact that national egoism, especially in its more aggressive manifestations, is restrained by idealism, just as, to a greater extent, national idealism is limited by self-interest. Liberal and democratic nations are not completely heedless of moral restraints, even when the most compelling national interests are at stake. It is true that the reconciliation of national self-interest with ideal principles takes place more readily on a verbal level than in the sphere of national conduct, but the common hypocrisy of nations is a tribute to the force of ideals as well as a mark of the primacy of national self-interest.

In its broadest aspect, the interdependence of universal ideals and national self-interest is simply a reflection of the fact that man has a moral sense as well as an ego and that both parts demand satisfaction. Consequently, nations act with the greatest consistency and stability when their actions are based upon a balance of egoism and idealism. For this reason the most compelling national ends are those self-interested ends, like survival, which are most easily reconciled with idealistic ends, and those idealistic ends, like the minimum standards of international decency, which are most compatible with national self-interest. By the same token, the instability of self-assertive egoism and altruistic idealism can be attributed, in large part, to the incompatibility of the former with fundamental ideals and of the latter with the most basic national interests.

6. Summary of America's Adjustment to Its International Environment

The full significance of the foregoing attempt to define the terms and clarify the assumptions underlying this interpretation of America's attitude toward foreign relations can be discerned only when these terms and assumptions are applied to the actual details of America's experience in world politics. Their general application is indicated in the following summary description of America's adjustment to its international environment since the turn of the century.

From the Spanish-American War to World War II the United States largely failed to make a mature adjustment to its international environment because it failed, as a whole, to understand or act upon a realistic view of international relations. In other words, because Americans were largely ignorant of the actual ends and motives of nations, including their own, they failed to govern their foreign relations in the light of the actual political conditions under which they might hope to achieve their national ends.

Because the United States was relatively isolated from the pressures of world politics by virtue of its geographical and economic position, the American people were spared the necessity of testing their assumptions about American conduct and the conduct of other nations against the unpleasant realities of international relations. Consequently, they were encouraged to believe that the realities were perfectly consistent with their ideals; that standards of personal conduct, including even altruism, were entirely applicable to national conduct; and that these standards were quite compatible with national self-interest. With a mixture of self-righteousness and genuine moral fervor they interpreted their own history as the prime example of this truth and based their assertion of the American mission upon a faith that their lofty example would shed enlightenment abroad. At the same time, seeing no reason why other nations should not follow America's exalted standards of conduct, they tended to regard the society of foreign nations, which were preoccupied with the toils of power politics, as something either to be avoided or to be uplifted rather than to be understood and lived with. Nevertheless, the American nation demonstrated by its actions that, while it was indeed inspired by an unusual degree of idealism, it was also strongly motivated by egoism and was, in fact, no more capable of completely transcending its self-interest than other nations.

Because the American people held an unrealistic view of the conditions under which they might reconcile their ideals with their national self-interest, their foreign relations from the turn of the century to the 1930's were marked by impulsiveness, instability, and ineffectiveness. Americans entertained ideal expectations that could not be fulfilled. With extravagant enthusiasm they undertook commitments which they repudiated later. Their maladjustment to the international environment manifested itself in drift, bewilderment, improvisation, and disillusionment. These characteristics were conspicuous in two great mass fluctuations—coinciding with the Spanish-American War and World War I—between intervention in international politics and withdrawal, each fluctuation being accompanied by an outburst of militant crusading and followed by a lapse into reaction and disillusionment.

Underlying America's lack of political realism was the absence of an incentive for the mass of the populace to confront the harsh and complex conditions of international relations. The nature of America's response to world politics suggests that the only end sufficiently compelling to have induced the nation to confront these conditions would have been a self-interested end higher in the scale of priorities than self-sufficiency, which—especially in the form of isolation—exerted a powerful influence among the mass of Americans. Only fear for survival could have taken priority over isolation in the long run. However, an active concern for America's survival simply did not exist, for the nation as a whole, until it was created by the intense international struggle for power preceding America's entrance into World War II and continuing to the present time.

Two crusades, one against Spain and one against Germany, were sustained during hostilities by an explosive combination of altruism and self-assertive national egoism;* but after the immediate object of victory was achieved, these motives seemed inadequate and misguided compared to traditional and

* The word "crusade," which is used in this book simply to refer to a moral enterprise undertaken with great zeal, was not, so far as I know, applied to either the war against Spain or the war against Germany at the time. It first came into general use after World War I as a term of opprobrium.

more compelling conceptions of self-interest and idealism; and the reasons for which the nation had fought and entered the wars seemed contrary or irrelevant to the practical consequences. As a result, both crusades produced a significant reaction—the first crusade, a reaction against the aggressive egoism of the imperialists; the second, a reaction against the altruism of the internationalists. Both reactions militated against a more realistic and widespread recognition of the conditions for a stable and effective foreign policy.

Although both crusades were accompanied by an upheaval in international politics which turned the minds of an important group of statesmen, scholars, politicians, military officials, and publicists toward the imperatives of power politics, the realism of these groups was sustained chiefly by a romantic, aggressive egoism that ran counter to America's fundamental hierarchy of values and the dominant trend of her outlook upon international relations. Consequently, egoistic Realists, frustrated in their attempts to lead the nation, were increasingly distracted from the rational dictates of expediency by the mutual antagonism between them and their adversaries, the idealistic utopians. As a result of the intensity of these antagonisms, the great debates on foreign relations were diverted from the practical task of reconciling ideals with self-interest by a conflict between irreconcilable temperamental antipathies. In the struggle between the two principal factions contending for the leadership of American public opinion, it was the utopians who largely succeeded in capturing the conscience of the nation, while the Realists sank constantly into lower repute. Consequently, idealism was championed by those least disciplined by the actual conditions of world politics, while concern for the exigencies of power politics remained largely the province of those least inhibited by moral restraints.

Although America's second crusade produced disillusionment, not realism, by depreciating altruism it did create a climate of opinion conducive to a recognition of the primacy of national self-interest and the necessity for an objective calculation of the configuration of national power. That climate of opinion, combined with the threat to American survival imposed by the circumstances preceding World War II, set the stage for a new widespread consciousness of the dependence of America's security upon the course of events beyond the Western Hemisphere. This new consciousness constitutes a major transformation in America's adjustment to her international environment, for it is the necessary basis for the growth of political realism, the vital balance wheel needed to restrain and give direction to the nation's egoistic and idealistic impulses. Even before World War II the impact of world politics evoked in some sectors of the citizenry that objective political realism and steady posture of enlightened self-interest which alone can enable the nation to reconcile its ideal mission with its selfish advantage in the long run.

However, apprehension of national insecurity is only the precondition for a widespread realism; it is not realism itself. Although the current trend of world politics makes calm realism indispensable, it also raises grave obstacles to the achievement of such an outlook. The growing fear of insecurity is not the least of these obstacles. Moreover, the same emotional and intellectual antipathies which have so conspicuously confounded a realistic approach to foreign policy since the turn of the century will persist, even though they manifest themselves in the form of arguments about national security.

7. Ethical Assumptions

Implicit in all the foregoing description and analysis is the premise that nations ought to strive to reconcile their selfish interests with certain ideal principles transcending their self-interest. If this were not the premise, there would be no particular reason to be concerned about the conditions under which America can hope to achieve this goal. There is no virtue in a nation's being able to achieve its ends if those ends are not worth achieving. Obviously, I am not just interested in the stability and effectiveness of America's foreign relations as one might be interested in the adjustment of the Hopi Indians to their social and physical environment, without passing any judgment on the moral purpose and consequence of such an adjustment. This study is concerned with what ought to have been and what ought to be as well as with what has been and what is.

Therefore, it should be acknowledged that I accept the Christian-liberal-humanitarian ideals referred to in the body of this analysis, recognizing, at the same time, that there is no fundamental justification for these ideals beyond the ideals themselves; they are matters of faith, not empirical propositions; they are either self-evident or not evident at all.

On the same grounds, I judge the morality of an action by its consequences as well as its motives. This judgment is not in accord with some of the deepest religious insights, but it represents the view of the overwhelming majority of mankind. On the other hand, the majority are not so commonly aware that this view involves them in an unavoidable moral dilemma. For if men are morally responsible for the consequences as well as the motives of their actions or their failure to act, they are thereby obligated to use their reason to calculate the best means to achieve a given ideal end; but because of the complexity of the human environment the best means to an end will seldom conform perfectly to ideal standards. Moreover, in international relations the best means must be consistent with the nation's security, especially because national survival is itself a high moral value; but the imperatives of national security are frequently incompatible with the dictates of supranational ideals and almost always inconsistent with the highest moral values of self-abnegation. Therefore, in international relations, even more than in personal relations, moralists must be involved in continual compromises with selfishness and sin.

I have suggested the necessity of attempting to resolve or mitigate the inevitable contradictions among national ends by choosing means and ends according to a consistent scale of priorities based upon a fundamental hierarchy of values. Some of the characteristics of the scale of priorities that actually exists among nations sharing the Christian-liberal-humanitarian tradition have been set forth. This is no place to undertake the monumental task of expounding in detail what the scale of priorities ought to be. It is enough to state that the general ethical approach of this essay is that men ought to seek to reconcile their national self-interest with supranational ideals in such a way as to maximize ideal values within the conditions established by the realities of international relations, providing that they never lose sight of the imperfection of this conditional ethics in comparison to the ultimate ideals of a liberal and humane civilization. I do not mean that men should accept the realities as immutable but simply that they should seek to alter them by the painful processes of mitigation rather than by futile attempts at abolition. The real moral task facing the American people is to fix their eyes upon the ultimate ideals without losing their footing on the solid ground of reality. This is not a perfect ethical standard, but it is probably the highest standard men are capable of acting upon.

Therefore, I am content that moralists should not exhort nations to depart drastically from the scale of priorities already described as expressing the enlightened citizenry's basic hierarchy of values. It is enough for men of good will to attempt to mitigate the extreme forms of egoism and idealism by bringing reason and imagination to bear upon the task of stabilizing the existing pattern of national ends and motives. By the same token, I believe that as long as men owe their supreme loyalty to nation-states, nations ought to act upon idealistic ends only in so far as they are compatible with the most fundamental ends of national self-interest, leaving to idealism the role of enlightening and civilizing the pursuit of self-interest and keeping self-interest in the perspective of ultimate moral principles.

However, it should be understood that general principles like this do not begin to comprehend all the moral complexities that confront nations. Thus it would be a mistake to maintain that all kinds of ideals ought to be contingent upon all kinds of national self-interest. Certainly, the extreme manifestations of national egoism, such as aggrandizement, ought not to take priority over the most basic tenets of idealism; and there are some moral principles which are so essential to the preservation of liberal and humane values that they ought not to be subordinated to any self-interested end, except, perhaps, survival itself; moreover, there is a place for the most extreme forms of idealism, even for altruism and self-sacrifice, providing they do not jeopardize national security.

Beyond recognizing the primacy of national self-interest, the value of a balance between egoism and idealism, and the limitations upon the extreme forms of idealism and self-interest, it is much less important, from the standpoint of maximizing ideals, to attempt to arrange the infinite moral complexities into a comprehensive scale of priorities than to recognize that the complexities exist; for man's willingness to believe that moral contradictions either do not exist or else are easily reconcilable must certainly be one of the greatest sources of international sin. It is man's reluctance to face the inevitable moral dilemmas of social existence that robs him of his moral perspective and leads him into an easy identification of his own nation's self-interest with high moral purpose and the welfare of mankind. It is this common conceit that persuades men to view the inevitable moral compromises of international relations as good things in themselves rather than as unfortunate expedients designed to maximize ideal values in a society where partial morality is the best morality attainable. It is this moral corruption that encourages both egoists and idealists to satisfy their emotional predispositions by confusing what is with what ought to be, so that egoists persuade themselves that the unpleasant realities of national egoism are a positive good, and idealists are content merely to deprecate them as an unmitigated evil, which can be easily exorcized by virtuous men.

Recognition of the moral complexities and incongruities of international existence does not imply a relativistic or nihilistic view of human conduct. On the contrary, it implies a firm allegiance to ultimate principles of moral perfection, even though these principles remain forever beyond human attainment; for how can a man know the moral imperfection of his actions unless he has an ideal standard of judgment? In this sense, the ultimate ideals of the Christian-liberal-humanitarian tradition are an indispensable source of that humility and critical self-appraisal which is the lifeblood of true idealism and the only antidote to national self-righteousness.

Although it is morally imperative that men should not minimize the contradictions between national self-interest and universal ideals, it is equally imperative that they should not exaggerate the contradictions by positing a rigid antithesis between these two ends. The utopian, anxious to assert the claims of idealism and impatient with reality, or the Realist, exasperated by the inability of utopians to perceive the reality of national egoism, may be tempted to simplify the troublesome moral dilemma of international society by declaring that ideals and self-interest are mutually exclusive or that one end is the only valid standard of international conduct. But neither view does much to illuminate reality or advance the cause of idealism. In very few situations are statesmen faced with a clear choice between ideals and national self-interest; in almost all situations they are faced with the task of reconciling the two. If they succeed in reconciling them so as to maximize ideal values, they will come as near to moral perfection as anyone can reasonably hope. But they will surely fail unless the nation as a whole understands the wisdom of combining realism with idealism.

To recognize the points of coincidence between national self-interest and supranational ideals is one of the highest tasks of statesmanship. The last half-century of Anglo-American relations demonstrates that men can recognize and even multiply the points of coincidence by patiently building upon a foundation of mutual self-interest to enlarge the area of international confidence and respect. It seems likely that the greatest advances in international morality in the foreseeable future will be brought about by men with enough vision and good will to temper the more immediate or extreme demands of national self-interest with the superior demands of a long-run interest in international compromise and the rational, peaceful settlement of differences. In this imperfect world it is neither too much nor too little to expect that man's recognition of the coincidence of ideals with national self-interest may mitigate and enlighten the thrust of national egoism.

PART I

SUMMARY

T HE American people arrived at the center of the stage of world politics by entering a war to free Cuba and vindicate the national honor, fighting a victorious crusade for Manifest Destiny and the American mission, acquiring a far-flung empire, and then forgetting about it. Thereby the nation unwittingly exerted a major impact upon the world competition for power and inextricably involved its destiny in the course of politics across the seas and yet remained, on the whole, as attached to its isolation and as contemptuous of the changing imperatives of international power as before the war.

The nation entered and fought the war with Spain out of a combination of self-assertive egoism and altruistic idealism which was inconsistent with its long-run scale of priorities among national ends and motives. Consequently, this combination of extreme egoism and idealism, although sustaining an intense enthusiasm for winning the war, soon dissipated after victory was attained. In the aftermath of their crusade Americans were unwilling to make good their claims to altruism, since the imperial responsibilities of ruling over an alien people seemed incompatible with traditional isolationist self-interest and contrary to the democratic and humanitarian values for which they had entered the war.

The instability of America's crusading ardor reflected the lack of a balance wheel to restrain and give direction to egoistic and idealistic impulses; in other words, the lack of a realistic view of the conditions under which nations can achieve their ends and reconcile their ideals with their self-interest. Consequently, America's adjustment to its status as a world power was, to a large extent, placed at the mercy of popular impulses undisciplined by an objective calculation of their practical consequences.

America's lack of realism and her indifference toward the shifting currents and alignments of national interests can be explained by the absence of a sufficiently strong motive to counteract isolationist predispositions and induce a widespread concern for the effect of the configuration of world power upon her self-interest. Only an active fear for American security could have turned American minds toward the real political conditions of the international environment. But the circumstances of international relations did not create this fear; instead they increased America's sense of self-sufficiency and reinforced her complacent assurance of physical insulation from the toils of world politics.

A group of American Realists, led by Alfred Thayer Mahan and Theodore Roosevelt, was absorbed in the study and pursuit of power politics; and this group exerted a powerful influence upon America's foreign relations. But its concern for the realities of world politics was motivated by an aggressive national egoism and a romantic attachment to national power rather than by any fear for American security. For a short while this group captured popular leadership under the banner of a missionary imperialism, but it never succeeded in breaking down isolationism or creating a concern in the general populace for the imperatives of power. Actually, it hindered the achievement of these objectives by associating with them a kind of egoism not in accord with America's basic hierarchy of values and thereby attaching to some valid realistic insights the stigma of a discredited imperialist élan.

In the popular reaction against imperialism, born, in part, by the frustration of extravagantly high expectations, idealistic utopians largely replaced the Realists as spokesmen for the American mission. Their vigorous repudiation of the Realists' leadership, at first in the anti-imperialist movement and then in the peace movement, enhanced the appeal of utopian assumptions about international conduct and rendered realism less attractive than ever. In the struggle for popular favor between egoistic Realists and idealistic utopians the exacerbation of underlying temperamental antipathies further obscured the common ground of enlightened self-interest, upon which both groups might have met and compromised constructively.

CHAPTER I

MAHAN AND PREMONITIONS OF WORLD POWER

I. The Initial Impact of World Power

FOR many Americans who witnessed the dramatic events of the Spanish-American War, the end of the nineteenth century seemed to mark the beginning of a new era. And they were right, for by the end of that war the United States had become a world power. Of course, no nation achieves world power in the span of a few years; but the important transformation that did take place was the sudden awareness among many Americans, and Europeans as well, that the United States was in fact a world-wide power, not simply a hemispheric power, which was bound to exert a mighty influence upon the destinies of all peoples and play a major role in the calculations of every other great nation.

This new consciousness of American power coincided with widespread forebodings of some great upheaval in international relations. The most powerful industrial nations were swept up in a wild competition for industrial wealth, foreign markets, and colonies in Asia, Africa, and the Pacific. Great shifts were taking place in the relative strength and prestige of nations. Coalitions were forming. Naval rivalry was growing intense. Everywhere the instruments of power were bulging ominously behind the curtain of diplomacy. For the Realist who surveyed the international scene, there was much to confirm the view that the quest for national self-interest and power is the moving force in the world.

Even before the Spanish-American War there were signs that the United States was entering the strife of world politics, making new friends and acquiring new rivals, and restlessly shifting her weight in the scales of international power. In the second half of the nineteenth century two nations were conspicuous for their ambitious development of industry and military potential. One was Germany, which achieved unification and set out in systematic fashion to consolidate and increase its gains. The other was the United States, which completed its continental expansion, preserved its unity, and began to feel the itch of destiny. Even before the turn of the century a few sensitive observers of world affairs—navalists, statesmen, and academic men—read these signs of their time with alarm. Casting a wary eye upon Bismarck's thriving project, they proposed shoring up America's vulnerable position with an Anglo-American naval and political understanding in the Atlantic, in the Pacific (where they proposed the annexation of Hawaii), and in the Central American isthmus (where they advocated a canal under exclusive American construction and control).

However, it would be a mistake to suppose that the American public at large shared this intimation of America's participation in a world-wide struggle for power. As a matter of fact, until after the Samoan affair of 1888 Americans, generally, looked with favor upon the German Empire. They remembered German opposition to arrogant British sea power. American liberals admired German liberals. American intellectuals respected the great German university system. The overwhelming German victory in the Franco-Prussian War not only failed to arouse American apprehensions but was widely hailed as a blow for liberalism and national unification, another nail in the coffin of despotism.[1]

That the Samoan affair should have been the turning point in German-American relations is a revealing indication of the extremely devious impact of the shifting alignments of power upon the American mind. The United States' interest in Samoa originated soon after the Civil War in the minds of naval officers, who were impressed with its usefulness as a coaling station athwart the ocean lanes of the South Pacific.[2] However, it was not considerations of grand strategy that attracted public attention to that remote archipelago.

Probably few Americans had even heard of the island before 1878, when the majestic "tattooed Prince," Le Mamea, arrived in Washington and concluded a treaty granting the United States naval rights at Pago Pago. But within a decade this hapless potentate's realm was a seething center of national animosities. When Great Britain and Germany also acquired rights, in 1879, the drowsy paradise became alive with the rival ambitions and suspicions of naval officers, consuls, missionaries, commercial agents, and land-grabbers. In 1888 a three-way adjustment of interests collapsed in a torrent of consular intrigue and dissension among the natives. Then the jingoes began to get the public ear, and soon there was serious talk of war. Although a devastating hurricane, which destroyed the German and American vessels in Apia Harbor, somewhat sobered human enmities, and although a conference in Berlin succeeded in re-establishing American rights in a condominium, the end result was a legacy of suspicion toward Germany. The United States and Germany never quite regained their cordial relationship, and in the next decade Germany replaced Great Britain and France as the chief American rival.

Some American navalists and imperialists looked upon this transformation as a manifestation of great, imponderable shifts of national power. They beheld a global struggle for national strength and wealth and urged Americans to pay heed to their strategic interests. But it is safe to say that the average American's concern with the Samoan incident was inspired by a chauvinistic desire to keep "Old Glory" unsullied rather than by a concern for the commercial and military advantages of a remote spot in the Pacific Ocean. The excitement which the Samoan controversy aroused is best understood as a manifestation of the quickening national consciousness of the eighties, which had already found its prophets of national destiny in men like Josiah Strong, John W. Burgess, and John Fiske. It was a rehearsal for the full-blown imperialism of the nineties.

2. The Sense of Security and Isolation

Before the turn of the century Americans were feeling the urge to assert their national power, but they were not, in general, concerned with the impact of world politics upon their national self-interest. Why should they bother about world politics when they were convinced that America's progress was the result of keeping aloof from its toils?

Some expansionists replied that it was time that the United States take a realistic view of its power position in the world because the ruthless struggle among nations impinged upon the most basic of all national interests, self-preservation. This opinion was frequently espoused by the advocates of military preparedness. The promoters of America's expanding navy constantly stressed the defenseless condition of the American coastline—so constantly that there was considerable panic along the eastern seaboard when the Spanish-American War began.[3]

However, in the 1890's national security was a thin reed for supporting a preparedness movement of the dimensions envisioned by America's most vocal nationalists. And, as a matter of fact, the most persuasive arguments for military and naval expansion were directed toward such emotionally charged goals as the propagation of American ideals, the salvation of Anglo-Saxon civilization, and the fulfilment of Manifest Destiny. Indeed, in the decade preceding the war with Spain it was obvious to most of the populace, whether expert or untutored, that the United States was in an enviable defensive military position. Her rapidly growing navy seemed to assure dominance in the Western Hemisphere. She was favored with abundant resources, a highly developed technology, diversified industry, and great accumulated wealth. With no strong military powers to threaten the nation's frontiers or seaports, with miles of ocean separating her from Europe and Asia, and with European discord increasingly preoccupying potential aggressors, it would have been extremely difficult to convince Americans that their confidence in the absolute security of the United States was misplaced.

The opponents of naval and military expansion, such as Senator Arthur P. Gorman, Representative William S. Holman, and Carl Schurz, never failed to poke the preparedness advocates in their most vulnerable spot by challenging them to point out exactly from what quarter they expected danger to come.[4] It was a challenge that was reiterated time and again after the war with Spain and, especially, during World War I. However, this group's strongest argument was simply the American tradition of isolation, which had developed into a cardinal tenet of the national creed in the course of three quarters of a century of relative freedom from the threat of foreign intervention. The typical American outlook upon world politics combined a fierce national pride, a sense of moral superiority, and an aversion to foreign institutions with a conviction that the United States could not be seriously affected by events outside her hemisphere. Why, then, erect a costly military establishment, contrary to democratic principles and destructive of republican institutions, unless to suck the American people into the vortex of power politics and foreign entanglements? And since when did the nation that had subjugated a continent and defied interference from the great powers of the world need to resort to the toils and trappings of Old World diplomacy in order to protect itself? It would take powerful arguments to counteract this sort of reasoning.

3. The Reputation of a Realist

A realistic view of international politics was not likely to flourish in a nation so complacent about the security of its own power. And yet it was in the 1890's that political Realism found one of its most influential advocates in all American history. From his vantage point as president of the naval war college at Annapolis, Captain Alfred Thayer Mahan became America's most illustrious philosopher of world politics and one of the world's most influential exponents of sea power. Everyone who examines America's adjustment to the status of a world power must reckon with Mahan, for his was a seminal mind in the theory of international relations, and against his teachings one can measure the evolution of America's attitude toward the outside world.

Less than a decade before the United States acquired an empire, Mahan launched his life's campaign to educate the American people in the lessons of national greatness. Although he first gained public recognition as a naval historian on the basis of his classic studies, *The Influence of Sea Power upon History, 1660–1783* (1890) and *The Influence of Sea Power upon the French Revolution and Empire, 1793–1812* (1892), these histories were no mere chronicles of naval events, for Mahan was pre-eminently a student and a teacher of world politics; and the message he conveyed was that a nation needed a large merchant marine protected by a navy with battle-fleet supremacy in order to compete successfully in the world-wide struggle for overseas markets and colonies.[5] In elaborating this theme, Mahan analyzed the grand strategy of world power with an unrivaled clarity, calmness, and breadth of vision. But he was by no means impartial toward the facts he observed. Sometime between 1885 and 1890 he became a convert from anti-expansionism to the cause of expansion;[6] from that time on, his larger motive in all his books and articles was to educate his countrymen to appreciate the need for power in international relations; that is, the need for colonies, a merchant marine, strategic bases, and a massed fleet of line-of-battle ships.

Mahan's conversion proved timely, for soon after the publication of his first book he became the high priest of expansionism among naval men, diplomats, and scholars; and through the devoted labors of two apostles in particular, Senator Henry Cabot Lodge and Theodore Roosevelt, then Assistant Secretary of the Navy, he exerted an influence upon the course of history that was the envy of many statesmen.

Nevertheless, in the long run, it is doubtful whether Mahan's gospel took root in the minds of his countrymen at large. It is significant that, although he preached from an American pulpit, his largest and most responsive congregation was across the oceans.[7] *The Influence of Sea Power upon History, 1660–1783* was for three years rejected by publishers in the United States, while its author was being acclaimed an authority and a genius in England. Mahan's study became a campaign handbook for British navalists. In 1894 he was dined by the Queen, the Prime Minister, and the First Lord of the Admiralty; and Oxford and Cambridge conferred degrees upon him.

Some of Mahan's popularity in Great Britain can be attributed to the fact that his work admirably substantiated the contentions of British navalists and imperialists. British naval officers were understandably enthusiastic about an interpretation of history which so neatly generalized the phenomenon of the simultaneous rise of the British Navy and the British Empire. But, perhaps, the greater receptiveness of the British as compared to the Americans should also be ascribed to their greater familiarity with the elements of power in world politics. It has been said that Mahan really organized into a philosophy the strategic principles which the British Admiralty had been following more or less blindly for over two hundred years.[8] Thus the British were in the position of Molière's *Bourgeois Gentilhomme,* who suddenly discovered he had been speaking prose all his life.

A striking indication of the universality of Mahan's doctrine was its enthusiastic reception in Germany, which was fast becoming England's chief naval rival. The Kaiser, with the encouragement of his imperial-minded naval chief, Alfred Von Tirpitz, was so taken with *The Influence of Sea Power upon History* that he made it an official textbook of the German Navy; and in order to make the German people naval-minded, he had the complete sea-power series supplied to public institutions, libraries, and schools at government expense.

According to Mahan, more of his writings were translated into Japanese than into any other language. Japanese naval and military colleges adopted his first history of sea power as a textbook, and the government placed translations of both histories and of other works by Mahan in all the schools. In Japan, as in England and Germany, Mahan's reputation soared because his works spoke the universal language of power politics and provided a persuasive rationale for resurgent imperialism.

Thus, in spite of his ambition to educate his countrymen in the lessons of Realism, Captain Mahan found his most enthusiastic audience in military and naval circles abroad and, to a lesser extent, at home. Yet he was not entirely a prophet without honor among the general American public, for when the expansionist mood caught fire, he gathered a substantial following through his articles in the *Atlantic Monthly,* the *North American Review, Forum, McClure's,* and *Harper's New Monthly Magazine.* His arguments were frequently voiced on the floor of Congress. As he rode the flood tide of imperialist sentiment during the approach of the war with Spain, he reached what was probably the peak of his popularity.

However, an author's popularity is not necessarily based upon the message he intends to popularize. In order to assess the significance of Mahan's reputation with respect to America's outlook upon world politics, one should first examine his message and then observe the way it was received by the citizenry at large.

4. IDEALS AND SELF-INTEREST IN MAHAN'S MESSAGE

Mahan deserves the reputation of a realist because he analyzed the self-interested basis of national conduct with a more piercing and candid vision than the cloak of sentiment and custom permit to ordinary eyes. He has earned the reputation of an extreme national egoist because he preached the doctrine of imperialism with a force and candor unequaled by most Americans who shared his views. But he would be far less deserving of his reputation as a perceptive thinker if he had not understood the power of ideals as well as self-interest. And his appeal to his contemporaries would certainly have been insignificant had he failed to combine idealism with egoism, for that was a popular blend which proved irresistibly intoxicating to the conscience-bound Americans during their imperialist adventure. Mahan's message cannot be understood in terms of any simple antithesis between national self-interest and supranational ideals. The essence of his doctrine is the particular way in which it combined both elements of thought.

All of Mahan's essays bespeak an awareness of the profound influence of ideals upon national behavior. Although he held that the citizenry's solid grasp of enduring national interests was the only stable foundation for a provident foreign policy, he never ignored the part of moral sentiment in leading men to act upon their perception of interest.

> The sentiment of a people is the most energetic element in national action. Even when material interests are the original exciting cause, it is the sentiment to which they give rise, the moral tone which emotion takes, that constitutes the greater force. Whatever individual rulers may do, masses of men are aroused to effective action—other than spasmodic—only by the sense of wrong done, or right to be vindicated.[9]

As if in direct response to this perception, Mahan's writings resounded with the tones of a crusade. His language was Biblical; the righteous quality of his expression arose from intense spiritual beliefs and a profound knowledge of the Scriptures. Nations, he was accustomed to saying, like religions, decay if they neglect their missionary enterprises. To him, American expansion was more than national expediency, it was a moral duty; and he was confident that the extension of American influence in the world would enlighten backward races and confer upon them the blessings of Christianity and Anglo-Saxon political genius.

Mahan's idealism was endowed with the force of sincere conviction; yet it was fused with motives of extreme national egoism, which clearly confined it to a secondary role. This egoism was rationalized by a consistent depreciation of the ability of ideal principles to alter the thrust of national self-interest. Thus Mahan combined Realism and egoism in the same breath: "It is vain to expect governments to act continuously on any other ground than national interest. They have no right to do so, being agents and not principals."[10]

Mahan's doctrine was distinguished by the way in which the imperatives of national power constantly obtruded upon matters of the spirit. He never repudiated ideal ends, but his belief in the imperfection of humanity led him to place a low estimate on the efficacy of moral principles unsupported by force. Therefore, it made no difference from what ideal point he started an argument; it always ended in a lesson on the need for military preparedness.

For example, as he took a long view into the twentieth century, it seemed to him as though he were witnessing the opening of a period in which it would be decided whether the spiritual ideas of the East or those of the West would dominate the world. Therefore, the great mission before civilized Christianity was "to receive into its own bosom and raise to its own ideals those ancient and different civilizations by which it is surrounded and outnumbered."[11] Yet Mahan sensed the turbulence and latent power of the East and prophesied that the assimilation of Western aspirations and Western technological progress would cause the peoples of the East to rouse from their long sleep, and then the two great civilizations of the East and the West would close together in a struggle for survival. "Our material advantages," Mahan noted, "will be recognized readily and appropriated with avidity; while the spiritual ideas which dominate our thoughts . . . will be rejected for long." Therefore, in the interval caused by the imperfection of man's moral sense, "force must be ready to redress any threatened disturbance of an equal balance between those who stand on divergent planes of thought, without common standards."[12]

Clearly, for Mahan the distinctive feature of international politics was not ideological conflict but the struggle for power. Everywhere he looked he saw strife, everywhere nation arrayed against nation. And this was no transient phenomenon. Conflict was the condition of all life, in Mahan's view. He looked upon the struggle for colonies and commerce among nations as a manifestation of the inexorable Darwinian law of nature, which decreed a struggle for survival and survival of the fittest. Under these circumstances he held that it would be folly for a nation to drop behind in the race or to trust national security to the benevolence of its rivals. The efforts of the increasingly articulate peace advocates to limit the instruments of national power and compose national conflict with arbitration treaties and other artificial contrivances excited only contempt in Mahan, for it was his conviction that such measures were futile and dangerous unless moral forces should come to weigh heavier with mankind than material desires; and should this remote contingency occur, then these idealistic devices would be superfluous anyway.

It is true that Mahan sometimes urged the subordination of national self-interest to universal moral principles, but in these instances he always found that the dictates of morality coincided with national self-assertion as opposed to a passive form of national self-interest. Thus he was accustomed to exhorting his countrymen to subordinate the ignoble desire for mere ease and comfort and survival to the heroic moral duty of upholding Christianity and the American mission throughout the world.

Believing as he did in man's innate selfishness and in the incurably predatory nature of nations, Mahan was understandably fickle in his advocacy of ideal goals. Thus after arguing that an understanding between the two great Anglo-Saxon nations would greatly increase the world's sum of happiness, he threw aside moral pretensions: "But if a plea of the world's welfare seem suspiciously like a cloak for national self-interest, let the latter be accepted frankly as the adequate motive which it assuredly is."[13] Self-interest was always an adequate motive in Mahan's scheme of values. Idealism was adequate only when it did not interfere with the vigorous assertion of national self-interest.

5. SELF-PRESERVATION OR SELF-ASSERTION?

In his concern for the self-interest of the United States, Mahan had a great deal to say about national defense, but if one is to understand the nature of the Realism of the imperialists, it is important to recognize that the national interest he invoked in the name of defense was nearer aggrandizement than self-preservation.

In the 1890's Mahan did not seriously contend that the United States was unable to protect its existing territory, wealth, or rights from foreign attack or the threat of attack. In 1896 he wrote, "Of invasion, in any real sense of the word, we run no risk."[14] But was there danger of invasion in another sense, requiring a different kind of defense? Mahan expressed the hope that "the United States would never seek war except for the defense of her rights, her obligations, or her necessary interests," and he protested that he wanted a navy only for defense, not aggression. However, he also insisted that defense be construed to include all national interests.[15] Therefore, his statement of principles was scarcely a limitation upon national action, for, after all, Mahan maintained that one of the nation's most vital interests was the relentless search for world markets. His naval policy was designed to defend the merchant shipping and strategic outposts which this search required. Since competing nations could be expected to resist American commercial and territorial expansion, America's control of the seas could readily be interpreted as a defense of vital national interests.

Certainly, this sort of reasoning strained the word "defense" to its bursting point, for in Mahan's terms the requirements of defense could increase indefinitely in a sort of chain reaction. Thus, while he argued that an Isthmian canal was essential for the defense of America's coastal and Pacific trade routes, he also contended that the United States needed Caribbean bases, because the construction of the canal would induce a great increase of foreign commercial and naval activity throughout the Caribbean Sea and thereby imperil the peace of this strategic region.[16] At the same time, the enhanced commercial and military value of the Pacific trade routes, which would result from the construction of a canal, led Mahan to urge the annexation of Hawaii as an indispensable key to their defense.[17] And to make the circle complete, he argued that the acquisition of Hawaii would render the construction of an Isthmian canal imperative as a means of facilitating the naval defense of that outpost. And, of course, a greatly expanded battle fleet, with suitable naval bases, was essential to defend the canal, the Caribbean bases, the strategic commercial lanes, and Hawaii.

Although motives are never unmixed, it seems evident from the content and context of these imperialist arguments, from their phrasing and tone, and, above all, from their consequences, that the imperialists' pleas of self-defense were sustained by motives more akin to ambition, pride, or covetousness than to fear or apprehension. Mahan's own writings clearly demonstrate that this observation applies to him.

Mahan was a publicist, but if on that account he sought to make his writings palatable to his American audience, he never concealed his deepest beliefs. And so when he protested that military training and naval expansion were the best assurance of national security, as well as of harmony and peace in the world, he was rather obviously parrying the thrusts of the peace advocates; but when he frankly proclaimed preparedness as an elemental virtue, a good thing in itself, he spoke with conviction and passion. Then national defense seemed merely incidental to national self-assertion. Indeed, in view of his belief that nations must either expand or retrogress, Mahan could not logically reduce self-preservation to mere protection of the status quo.

The first law of states, as of men, is self-preservation—a term which cannot be narrowed to the bare tenure of a stationary round of existence. Growth is a property of healthful life, which does not, it is true, necessarily imply increase in size of nations . . . but it does involve the right to insure by just means whatsoever contributes to national progress, and correlatively to combat injurious action taken by an outside agency, if the latter overpass its own lawful sphere.[18]

No yearning for a peaceful and isolated national existence troubled Mahan's breast. He considered peace the false idol of a civilization grown fat and soft on the sterile pursuit of material pleasures and the senseless amassing of wealth. "Ease unbroken, trade uninterrupted, hardship done away, all roughness removed from life—these are our modern gods."[19] Away with them! True salvation lies in cultivating the masculine, combative instincts. When these instincts lie dormant, nobility atrophies and civilization degenerates.

In the rivalries of nations, in the accentuation of differences, in the conflict of ambitions, lies the preservation of the martial spirit, which alone is capable of coping finally with the destructive forces that from outside and from within threaten to submerge all the centuries have gained.

. . . Not in universal harmony, nor in fond dreams of unbroken peace, rest now the best hopes of the world, as involved in the fate of European civilization. Rather in the competition of interests, in that reviving sense of nationality . . . in the jealous determination of each people to provide first for its own . . . in these jarring sounds which betoken that there is no immediate danger of the leading peoples turning their swords into ploughshares—are to be heard the assurance that decay has not touched yet the majestic fabric erected by so many centuries of courageous battling.[20]

These words make somber reading in the middle of the twentieth century. It is difficult to imagine men of good will avowing them; and, as we shall see, there were many who disavowed them. Nevertheless, to Americans on the brink of a great national awakening, stirring martial phrases did not bear the connotations they have acquired in the course of a half century of the "accentuation of differences." Then war could be faced with a certain lightheartedness and bravado. Mahan was not so far from the common view when he wrote in 1897, "War now not only occurs more rarely, but has rather the character of an occasional excess, from which recovery is easy."[21] Remember that this was the era of the daring, manly, adventurous Richard Harding Davis, who made his fame by dashing from war to war across the face of the globe, glorifying the risk and heroism of physical combat. In so far as Mahan's view of national self-interest moved the American people, it moved them in the spirit of Richard Harding Davis, not in the spirit of self-defense.

6. MAHAN AND THE AMERICAN PUBLIC

Undoubtedly, Americans, in general, did not go so far as to agree with Mahan about the beneficent influence of international conflict upon human society; but they were, nevertheless, in harmony with the sort of nationalistic bluster and pugnacity which make international conflict almost inevitable. Yet because Americans shared something of Mahan's national egoism, it does not follow that they subscribed to his rationale of national self-interest. They recognized the tune, but few caught the words. Beneath Mahan's aggressive nationalism, his glorification of the military virtues, and his idealization of international strife there was a solid substratum of realism in his perception of the role of self-interest and power in national conduct. Americans skimmed the surface, but there was no inducement to penetrate beyond. Mahan's panoramic vision and prophetic tone lent an intellectual respectability to nationalistic fervor, but patriotism is a notorious parasite upon the intellect. The public took of Mahan what they wanted and left the rest for professional navalists and power politicians.

One clue to America's indifference toward the realism in Mahan's message is contained in his mounting despair over the state of public opinion. Mahan wrote for the general reader as much as, if not more than, for the navalists and scholars like himself. He hoped that he might thereby persuade enough people throughout the country to make them "rallying points for the establishment of a sound public opinion."[22] He was bound to be gratified by the wave of crusading ardor that surged through the American people and lifted them to the undisputed heights of world power, but his gratification was short-lived. After spending a decade expounding the cold, practical lessons of world politics, he spent the rest of his life deploring American indifference to them; and he died, a little over a decade after America's first crusade, thoroughly distressed over the public's lack of realism.

Disregard and distortion of doctrine is part of the price prophets pay for public esteem, but Mahan's popularity faded soon enough to spare his doctrine distortion. This is not difficult to understand, for there was much in his preaching that was unwelcome to an American congregation, even before the first flush of expansionism died out. He was outspoken in his disparagement of the hoary maxims about foreign entanglements and alliances. He repeatedly pointed to the practical implications of America's status as a world power; in calm and realistic analyses he explained the nation's inextricable involvement in world politics. But Americans saw no reason for renouncing the sacred tradition of isolation, which had apparently served them so well; and the reasons which Mahan gave were not designed to win converts. He decried isolation primarily because it was inconsistent with American expansion and an active role in world politics. Isolation, he felt, was a policy which might have befitted the United States in its infancy, but it was a serious impediment in its maturity, when destiny beckoned outward. No fear of embroilment in the nefarious schemes of foreign diplomats encumbered Mahan's analysis of the prospects of entanglement. He yearned for entanglement. And so he had a strong incentive for turning his mind toward the esoteric details of the configuration of national interests. No emotional antipathies or moral scruples inhibited Mahan's perception of the intricate, inscrutable workings of the international competition for power. It was with the pleasure of anticipation that he fixed his analytical eye upon the iron compulsions of national self-interest and plotted the course of history.

Mahan foresaw that expansion would radically change America's relation to the rest of the world. He reasoned that, although the United States had thus far escaped the toils of world politics, the geographical basis of her relative immunity would disappear with the extension of her political and economic commitments and with the rapid spread of technological advancements in transportation and communication. Then not only as a moral responsibility but as a practical national interest Americans would be forced to assume their share of the travail of Europe. This, he asserted, was the inevitable consequence of the "enduring principle of necessary self-interest" which gave the Monroe Doctrine its vitality.

namely, that not merely the interest of individual citizens, but the interests of the United States as a nation, are bound up with regions beyond the sea, not part of our own political domain, in which, therefore, under some imaginable circumstances, we may be forced to take action.[23]

Mahan would have been more accurate had he expressed his opinion about the American outlook as a wish rather than as a prophecy. He overestimated the impact of a changing distribution of world power upon the American attitude toward world politics. Or perhaps he just underestimated the lag between stimulus and response. It is interesting to note that in the past decade or so American scholars and publicists have granted Mahan's teachings some of the esteem men commonly bestow upon prophets who die too soon. Yet what endures of his teaching is not its militant nationalism or its strident militarism but the central trunk of realism, which these emotional and philosophical outgrowths concealed from his contemporaries.

CHAPTER II

THE FIRST CRUSADE

1. THE CAPRICIOUS CRUSADE

I T WAS the Spanish-American War which brought the American people to the full consciousness of their power in the world. For a decade before that event Mahan and his followers had been realistically charting the shifting currents of international politics and setting the course of national aggrandizement accordingly. But there was little in the impact of power politics upon the lay mind to suggest that the general public respected Mahan's chart, no matter how keenly they shared his eagerness for the voyage. That the American people were off on a great adventure was clear to all, but whether they knew where they were going or would understand where they were when they had arrived seemed doubtful, if one could judge from the complacency, the capricious nationalism, and the lighthearted moral assurance of the nineties.

When one realizes how little relation the origin of America's war with Spain had with its consequences, it is easy to understand how historians conclude that an Unseen Hand or some great impersonal force, like geography or economics, determines the course of nations. Indeed, the United States displayed much of the facility of the mother country for acquiring an empire in a fit of absent-mindedness. Americans began the war not out of a realistic calculation of national advantage but largely as an idealistic crusade to free the Cubans from Spain's imperial shackles. Yet they ended it with a far-flung empire of their own from the Philippines to Hawaii to Puerto Rico. They undertook the war as a local action, but their victory affected the relations among all the great powers of the world.

As in all crusades, idealism was not unmixed with other motives. Not before or since the Spanish-American War have the American people experienced such a paroxysm of national pride and chauvinism. Clearly, they were ripe for the event. The United States had had no foreign war since 1848. It had fully recovered from the Civil War and just surmounted the panic of 1893. The mighty nations of the world were restless, and Americans were anxious to have a suitable role in the world drama that seemed about to commence. America had stuck her toe into the turbulent waters of imperialism during the Samoan adventure, had taken a hasty dip when the Harrison administration just missed annexing Hawaii, and had boldly splashed Great Britain with Cleveland's ultimatum during the Venezuela crisis. In 1898 she was ready to take the big plunge.

However, the public as a whole, as distinguished from its more nationalistic, navy-minded, or power-conscious members, was not ready to take the plunge just for the sheer joy of getting wet. That would have been inconsistent with the American tradition of refraining from intervention in other people's affairs, of decrying aggression and acquisitiveness. But the pitiful plight of the Cuban revolutionists was a different matter. A war to free Cuba from Spanish despotism, corruption, and cruelty, from the filth and disease and barbarity of General "Butcher" Weyler's reconcentration camps, from the devastation of haciendas, the extermination of families, and the outraging of women; that would be a blow for humanity and democracy. No one could doubt it if he believed—and skepticism was not popular—the exaggerations of the Cuban *Junta's* propaganda and the lurid distortions and imaginative lies purveyed by the "yellow sheets" of Hearst and Pulitzer at the combined rate of two million a day.

Yet it took the melodramatic explosion of the American battleship *Maine* in Havana Harbor with the loss of 260 American seamen to precipitate war. Although succeeding years have yielded little credible evidence that the Spanish were responsible for the sinking, Americans were in no mood for sifting evidence at the time. The public pressure generated by the ensuing emotional outburst swept away all reason and hesitation. Apparently, the incident ignited the spark of chauvinism that was needed to fire humanitarian sentiment to war heat.

However, it was not humanly possible for the excitement of that fateful spring of 1898 to last long once war had set in. As passion waned, outraged humanitarianism gave way to a broader idealism, and frenzied jingoism was supplanted by a general sense of national power and destiny. Yet when the war of liberation assumed the proportions of extensive conquest, an increasing number of Americans found that even this milder combination of moral enthusiasm and national self-assertiveness failed to recommend itself to reason or conscience. The Spanish-American War was, as wars go, remarkably brief and painless, and many enjoyed it almost as much as Theodore Roosevelt; but even before it ended, voices of doubt and dissent were raised. Less than a decade later, Americans had lost interest in the plight of the Cubans and all the other alien peoples for whose regeneration the nation had fought; and a great many citizens, especially those devoted to the growing peace movement, looked upon Hay's "splendid little war" as the very antithesis of idealism. They were inclined to agree with the anti-imperialists of 1900 that the nation's better instincts had fallen prey to sheer power lust, that its profession of an ideal mission had been the hypocritical pretense of individual and collective greed or, at best, a transparent rationalization of national aggressiveness. And the fact that some of the most critical anti-imperialists, like William Jennings Bryan, had been in the vanguard of the crusaders added the poignancy of disillusionment to the passion of self-righteousness.

2. America Enters the War Idealistically

The animadversions of anti-imperialists notwithstanding, there was nothing cynical about the way America embarked cn its capricious crusade. McKinley was very much the voice of the people when he said of Cuba in his annual message of 1897, "I speak not of forcible annexation, for that can not be thought of. That by our code of morality would be criminal aggression."[1] The joint resolution which declared that the United States would free Cuba also disclaimed, in the Teller Amendment, any intention of annexing Cuba. This provision was unanimously approved in Congress, and so far as anyone has been able to tell, approved by the great majority of the public as well.[2]

According to a popular assumption in the years following the war, America was drawn into the war by businessmen in search of new markets and investment opportunities. But, actually, businessmen, far from perpetrating the war, were, except for a few who made a living off Cuban investment and trade, generally more reluctant than most citizens to disturb the ordinary pattern of peace and commerce; they were largely opposed or indifferent to the selfish, material aspects of the enterprise until the acquisition of the Philippines raised great hopes of new markets. If any interest group, aside from the Navy, can be singled out for its special enthusiasm for going forth to battle, it is Protestantism, which was deeply impressed by Spanish inhumanity and the opportunities for missionary activity in the Orient.[3]

It may be that moral principles were espoused, in part, as a rationalization of nationalistic conceit and avarice. But idealistic professions were no flimsy fabrication or afterthought; they were the product of a compelling conviction, rooted solidly in American character and tradition. It was a combination of idealism and egoism, of knight-errantry and national self-assertiveness, that moved the American people to support military action; and one motive was as important as the other.

3. The Egoism of Imperialists

It cannot be doubted that some highly articulate publicists saw in a war to liberate Cuba a providential opportunity to enact their program of national glory. These men composed that small coterie of nationalist politicians, naval strategists, and scholars who, for a decade or more, had led the preparedness and expansionist movements. Sea power, new markets, new investment opportunities, protection of trade routes, territorial expansion—all these objects were bound up with a genuine missionary zeal, but, as far as Mahan, Roosevelt, Lodge, and Albert J. Beveridge were concerned, they were probably sufficient reasons in themselves for meeting the moribund Spanish Empire in battle. Mahan saw the Spanish-American War as "something of a side issue." Theodore Roosevelt thought it would be "good for the Navy."* The war looked like a magnificent opportunity to gain popular support for the powerful fleet essential to a larger commercial and political future.[4] Mahan and Beveridge were about the only expansionists who advocated intervention as a means of commercial development, but economic considerations were an integral part of the gospel of naval strength, strategic territories, and the extension of American influence in the world. All these objects of national aggrandizement had been in the forefront of ultranationalist minds during the abortive attempt to annex Hawaii;[5] the same men looked forward to a war with Spain as another chance to make good. They welcomed the Spanish-American War as a supreme opportunity to enact Mahan's whole strategic program of dominant bases in the Caribbean, an Isthmian canal, and the development of a Pacific frontier.

To be sure, the men who composed the nucleus of the expansionist agitation yielded to no one in their affirmation of moral purpose. Several months before the sinking of the *Maine,* Roosevelt privately advocated a war to lift the burden from the wretched Cubans, and even when urging this project before naval men, he did not fail to place considerations of humanity ahead of naval and strategic considerations.[6] However, it is significant that this undoubtedly sincere idealism was not the kind that called for a restraint upon national egoism but rather the kind that demanded a vigorous assertion of the national will; and the closer to war Roosevelt came, the less he restrained his self-assertive egoism. In his private correspondence just before the outbreak of war he gave humanitarian and broad idealistic considerations about equal weight with arguments for the national self-interest, which called for avenging American honor and establishing American bases in the Caribbean;[7] but by the time he was on board the ship off Florida that would carry him and his Rough Riders to high adventure in Cuba, he was urging Lodge to prevent

* Roosevelt wrote Hermann Speck Von Sternburg, January 17, 1898, "Between ourselves I have been hoping and working ardently to bring about our interference in Cuba. If we could get the seven Spanish ironclads together against our seven seagoing ironclads on this coast we would have a very pretty fight; and I think more could be learned from it than from the Yalu [battle of the Yalu River, Sino-Japanese War, 1894]." Elting E. Morison, ed., *The Letters of Theodore Roosevelt* (Cambridge, 1951), I, 763–64.

any talk of peace until the United States got Manila, Hawaii, Puerto Rico, and the Philippines.[8]

When Roosevelt sent Admiral Dewey to the little-known Philippine Islands, and Dewey dramatized the sudden extension of the conflict by annihilating a decrepit Spanish fleet in Manila Harbor, the expansionists' humanitarian exertions began to embrace more ambitious goals, their missionary fervor converged with a swelling urge for national power, their idealism merged with bellicosity. Albert J. Beveridge struck this note early in his famous imperialist pronouncement before the Middlesex Club of Boston, in which, just two days after the formal declaration of war, he proclaimed its objectives as expansion. The acquisition of new markets and new lands, Beveridge said, was "part of the Almighty's infinite plan, the disappearance of debased civilizations and decaying races before the higher civilization of the nobler and more virile types of men." He was frank in his avowal of material self-interest: "American factories are making more than the American people can use; American soil is producing more than they can consume. Fate has written our policy for us; the trade of the world must and shall be ours." But he did not neglect the missionary aspects of expansion: "And American law, American order, American civilization, and the American flag will plant themselves on shores hitherto bloody and benighted, but by those agencies of God henceforth to be made beautiful and bright."[9]

It is important to recognize the pugnacious instincts which underlay the exhortations of these nationalistic spokesmen, because the aggressive quality of their imperialism explains much about the popular reception of their views in the years that followed the war with Spain. Beveridge, like Mahan, believed in the beneficent influence of national aggressiveness upon the progress of civilization. He decried the loss of moral fiber that comes from the sterile pursuit of material pleasures. Through great deeds, he proclaimed, the nation must evoke a sense of religious dedication in its citizens, lest it spawn a generation of self-centered weaklings and spineless money-grubbers. Strong nations make strong men. The qualities Beveridge admired in men were the qualities he admired in nations: courage, energy, masterfulness. He was "obsessed with the thought of empire building, of redeeming waste places, of subduing inferior peoples to the will of the master nations, of maintaining order, setting up the machinery of civilization."[10]

Theodore Roosevelt made himself a living example of the virile, fighting qualities, the martial virtues, the strenuous life. And as he despised "mollycoddles," so he abhorred timidity in nations. A nation, like an individual, he believed, must always deal squarely and champion righteousness; but, above all, it must be saturated with a fierce concern for its rights and its honor; and

just as an honorable man must on occasion resort to fisticuffs, so an honorable
nation must go to war. War held no horrors for Roosevelt. In 1886 he was
elated by the prospect of a good scrap in Mexico and offered to organize his
Medora ranch hands into a cavalry battalion.[11] In 1892 he dreamed of leading
a cavalry charge to enforce the United States demands that Chile pay an indemnity for injuries American sailors had incurred in a Valparaiso brawl.[12]
In 1895 he welcomed a war with Great Britain in defense of America's right
to demand arbitration of the Venezuela boundary dispute, and he thought
that the United States might well conquer Canada while it was about it.[13]
When the Spanish-American War erupted, Roosevelt was haunted by the fear
that it might end before he got into it.[14]

Although love of violence may be one incentive for seriously regarding the
imperatives of national power, it can be readily seen that there was much in
the imperialist and expansionist rationale, especially in its martial code of
virility and honor, which had no logical relation to a realistic view of world
politics. This rationale would seem to have been chiefly the product of a
strong temperamental or emotional bias against idealism and its values of
love, reason, humility, and self-denial. In many respects American imperialism of the 1890's echoed the yea-saying of the nineteenth-century romantic
rebellion against the tame virtues of utilitarianism and individualism, against
the Age of Enlightenment and its middle-class values. The spirit of imperialism was an exaltation of duty above rights, of collective welfare above individual self-interest, the heroic values as opposed to materialism, action instead of logic, the natural impulse rather than the pallid intellect. This
romantic Weltanschauung, which possessed Mahan and Roosevelt and other
egoistic Realists, goes a long way to explain the unfriendly reception which
the American public accorded their views on foreign relations after the war.

4. The Growth of Anti-Imperialism

Undoubtedly, combative instincts were less highly developed in the general
American public than in Roosevelt or Beveridge. Few could have been so
eager to save their manliness at the risk of losing their lives at this juncture
in the history of warfare. Yet something of the imperialists' truculence did
seize the American people and fill them with a desire to show the world that
the United States had come into its own. A perceptive editorial in the *Washington Post* described the new sensation:

> A new consciousness seems to have come upon us—the consciousness of strength—
> and with it a new appetite, the yearning to show our strength. It might be compared with
> the effect upon the animal creation of the taste of blood.
> Ambition, interest, land hunger, pride, the mere joy of fighting, whatever it may be,
> we are animated by a new sensation. We are face to face with a strange destiny.

The taste of empire is in the mouth of the people even as the taste of blood in the jungle. It means an imperial policy, the Republic renascent, taking her place with the armed nations.[15]

The United States was not long in tasting its first imperial blood, but the after-taste was not so pleasant as the first sampling; for when hostilities ended, less than four months after they had begun, the American people suddenly found themselves arguing about what they should do with the Philippines and its liberated inhabitants. Once the fighting was over, most Americans, having an ordinary susceptibility to the temptations of peace and harmony, found less incentive for bellicosity; and some began to wonder if national glory were sufficient compensation for the unwonted task of supervising an alien people on the other side of the Pacific Ocean, especially at the risk of embroiling the nation in the quarrelsome arena of world politics.

To be sure, imperialists advanced weighty moral reasons for assuming the burden of empire. They argued that the United States had a solemn obligation to sustain the liberating and civilizing mission it had set out to fulfil. And even when this mission encountered the armed resistance of its beneficiaries, the advocates of empire, confirmed in their opinion that the Filipinos were incapable of self-government, urged Americans, in the words of Kipling's timely poem, to "take up the white man's burden" for the sake of the true interests of the misguided heathens.

But, as the war spirit abated, the imperialists' interpretation of ideals became less and less persuasive. Their willingness to govern an alien people without its consent and then to meet its dissent with bullets; their unwillingness to renounce permanent sovereignty or even to establish a protectorate; the contrast between the original aims of the war and these practical consequences, together with their openly avowed predilections toward violence; these circumstances suggested to those with less aggressive temperaments and more sensitive consciences that the promoters of American destiny were guilty of flagrant inconsistency, if not outright deceit, in their professions of altruism.

By the time the debate on the disposition of the Philippines reached its peak, the imperialist assertion of a Manifest Destiny which mere mortals were powerless to resist had begun to sound less like the rallying cry for a crusade than the whimpering alibi for a morally dubious venture. The growth of anti-imperialist sentiment among political leaders as well as among literary figures, journalists, social reformers, and intellectuals promised at least to embarrass Destiny even if it could not halt it.

The anti-imperialist movement, in its inception, was pre-eminently a moral protest. Focusing upon America's rule—and, later, subjugation—of alien peoples against their will and contrary to the principles upon which the nation was founded, the anti-imperialists drew upon all the hallowed principles of liberty and humanitarianism for which Americans prided themselves in order to expose imperialism as an evil distortion of the original purpose of the war and a travesty upon the national mission. America, they protested, had undertaken the war as a liberator, not as a conqueror. As for her mission of regenerating the world, which the imperialists invoked, they insisted that its achievement depended upon the power of example, not the might of the sword. In fact, they regarded imperialism as the very denial of America's mission, for how could the nation exemplify love and justice while it engaged in aggrandizement and coercion? "No, do not deceive yourselves," cried Carl Schurz.

If we turn that war which was so solemnly commended to the favor of mankind as a generous war of liberation and humanity into a victory for conquest and self-aggrandizement, we shall have thoroughly forfeited our moral credit with the world. Professions of unselfish virtue and benevolence, proclamations of noble humanitarian purposes coming from us will never, never be trusted again.[16]

Although Carl Schurz and his fellow anti-imperialists were, at first, but a narrow protest group sniping at the moral outposts of entrenched imperialism, they fought with the complete assurance that they were on the side of the Lord and the Declaration of Independence; and, in the end, the imperialists proved no match for the spiritual might of their zealous adversaries. Indeed, the superior moral confidence of the anti-imperialists was not misplaced, for they were squarely in line with America's deep-rooted liberal and humane tradition. They took as their text the American Creed, the whole heritage of Enlightenment embodied in American nationalism, the ingrained pattern of idealism permeating the national thought and speech, the pervasive belief in the dignity and perfectibility of man, the sacred postulates of freedom and justice enshrined in the maxims of the national gods and heroes. In the light of these principles, the imperialist fulminations about virility, destiny, and the white man's burden seemed like a reversion to the discredited doctrines of militarism and acquisitiveness, which America had renounced when she severed her ties with the Old World and established a better way of life in the New.

These moral protestations struck some Realists as the product of an extremely silly view of international relations. What could one expect from war? In their minds there was something incongruous about playing the devil's game for heavenly stakes. Yet some of the prominent "ultrapacifists," whom Mahan and Roosevelt denounced, had been the strongest advocates of a holy war. Perhaps the anti-imperialists, and the American people in general, had set the stakes of war too high; but they were new to the game, and once they were in it, it was too late to renege.

In retrospect it seems evident that this war could have retained the support of American idealists and anti-imperialists only if it could have been reconciled with traditional principles of progress and the national mission, principles for which men like Bryan had supported the crusade in the first place. Unlike the imperialists, these men could reconcile themselves to the violence of war only through the highest moral expectations. But could any war possibly fulfil such expectations? For that matter, could any national policy, violent or peaceful, effective or ineffective, avoid the contradictions and compromises with perfection which the idealists of 1898 chose to ignore?

The impact of the Spanish-American War upon sensitive consciences is more comprehensible when one realizes the abhorrence with which many idealists in the nineties—particularly the evangelical pacifists, liberal intellectuals, and reformers—looked upon war itself. It was a singular circumstance that at the very time the nation thrilled to its greatest surge of aggressive nationalism it was also feeling a new hopefulness and enthusiasm for the abolition of war. The growing number of international conferences, arbitrations, conciliations, and mediations throughout the world, the beginnings of a democratic renaissance at home, and the spread of humanitarianism and social reform suggested to the more progressive elements of society that a new day was dawning in international relations. The growing power of the people was believed to guarantee the ultimate triumph of justice over greed and special privilege, among nations as well as among classes, while the spread of humanitarianism and the increasing tendency to resolve social conflicts by reason instead of force seemed to presage the gradual disappearance of armaments, secret diplomacy, and all the other sources of national conflict dividing man from man. Some were even permitted to hope that in their lifetimes the scourge of war would follow the anachronistic practice of the duel into oblivion.

For those who shared these high hopes and ideals, the only compelling justification, other than self-defense, for the United States, of all nations, to resort to war was the advancement of Christianity, democracy, and humanitarianism. Consequently, when their crusade degenerated into conquest, the indignation which moral optimists poured upon the imperialists reflected the bitterness of remorse as well as the consciousness of thwarted expectations.

5. SELF-INTEREST IN THE DEBATE OVER EMPIRE

As the great debate over imperialism reached its climax in the Presidential campaign of 1900, it clearly revealed its origin in basically conflicting attitudes toward international relations. The trend of that debate shows that the controversy between imperialists and anti-imperialists turned as much upon differing conceptions of national self-interest as upon divergent interpretations of the American mission.

In the course of the struggle the imperialists met their antagonists' moral assault by falling back upon more familiar positions. As the force of circumstances and the growing opposition of the anti-imperialists began to cast doubt upon the idealistic professions of imperialism, the proponents of expansion and empire shifted the emphasis of their arguments toward the selfish national advantage.[17] They began to say more about evidence of the islands' economic and strategic value, about their vital function in preserving a foothold in the highly competitive markets of the Far East, and about the folly of abandoning them to the predatory instincts of Japan and Germany.

Indeed there were valid considerations of political and strategic advantage which weighed heavily in the decision to keep all the Philippines. That decision cannot be understood solely in terms of President McKinley's famous account of divine guidance, which he delivered to a group of visiting clergymen.[18] At the end of the war the configuration of international power in the world and the alignment of national interests in the Pacific were such that, had the United States given the Filipinos immediate independence, with the great risk of plunging them into anarchy, the great powers—particularly Germany, Japan, England, and Russia—would almost certainly have been tempted to intervene. This would have touched off a scramble for position that might well have precipitated a world war, from which the United States could hardly have remained isolated.[19]

However, these strategic considerations actually played a small role in the public arguments of the imperialists. That Realists, who certainly appreciated them privately, should have given them so little publicity is, perhaps, an indication of their recognition of the American public's indifference or antipathy toward power politics. Instead, they presented their self-interested arguments for empire in terms of emotional appeals to American prestige and honor. The thought of surrendering a prize of war was obviously repugnant to the imperialists' sense of national self-exaltation. Such a sacrifice of patent self-interest for the sake of a dubious moral gesture struck the nationalistic mind as a futile and dangerous species of unrealism and softness. And so President McKinley, Senator Lodge, Whitelaw Reid, ex-Minister Charles Denby, and others fervently warned against hauling down the flag and rendering Americans an object of derision among the power-wise nations of the world.

What the imperialists were saying, fundamentally, was that national idealism was contingent; that it was valid only as long as it was not inconsistent with national self-interest. And in their view America's self-interest inhered chiefly in her reputation amid the society of great nations for excelling in the competitive struggle for military strength and commercial predominance. There was no need for making this hard-headed premise of international politics explicit as long as America's crusading ardor was at a high pitch, but when it showed signs of faltering, imperialists felt that it was necessary to elucidate the more compelling bases of national conduct.

Thus in the early stages of the debate over Philippine independence Senator Lodge was willing to meet idealists on their own ground. "The opponents of the treaty have placed their opposition on such high and altruistic grounds that I have preferred to meet them there."[20] But as imperialists and anti-imperialists marshaled their forces for the election campaign of 1900, he made it clear that, in his mind, national interest would always take precedence over conflicting international altruism. Philanthropy was all right, but philanthropy at the expense of American power and prestige was akin to suicide, in Lodge's opinion. In a speech before the Republican National Convention he stated the case for hardheadedness very simply: "We make no hypocritical pretense of being interested in the Philippines solely on account of others. While we regard the welfare of these people as a sacred trust, we regard the welfare of the American people first."[21]

In the same year Richard Olney, formerly Secretary of State under President Cleveland and an astute observer of the changing scene, published an article in the *Atlantic Monthly,* which, although it turned Lodge's argument back upon the imperialists by criticizing the purchase of the Philippines as contrary to the national interest, nevertheless succeeded in expressing the realistic view of the relation of idealism and self-interest more succinctly than the imperialists themselves. Olney deprecated the sickly sentimentality that had led the United States to regard the acquisition and pacification of the Philippines as a humanitarian enterprise. The paramount duty of a government, he declared, is to its own subjects; benevolence and charity are simply incidental and subsidiary. This was in the nature of things, and must be the policy of every power.

None can afford not to attend strictly to its own business and not to make the welfare of its own people its primary object—none can afford to regard itself as a sort of missionary nation charged with the rectification of errors and the redress of wrongs the world over. Were the United States to enter upon its new international role with the serious purpose of carrying out any such theory, it would not merely be laughed at but voted a nuisance by all other nations—and treated accordingly.[22]

The difference between Olney and the imperialistic Realists lay not in their understanding of the role of self-interest in national conduct but in their conceptions of what kind of self-interest America ought to pursue. Olney argued that the acquisition of the Philippines was contrary to American self-interest because it would unnecessarily entangle the nation in the world struggle for commercial and political supremacy, enfeeble it with the burden of defending an immense, remote, and vulnerable area, and bring no material benefits in return; but the imperialists were not content to define national self-interest as mere material welfare, comfort, and security; they were thinking in bolder terms of self-assertion and self-aggrandizement.

Yet it is significant that, as it rapidly became evident after the acquisition of the Philippines that America's new charges might be a literal and not just a romantic burden, some of the leading imperialists seem to have been troubled with doubts about the priority of their heroic conception of self-interest over Olney's more prosaic view. These doubts could be only partially resolved by devotion to the moral responsibility and duty of fulfilling the American mission.[23] Thus Roosevelt, who less than a decade later was calling the Philippines America's "achilles heel," wrote to Frederic Coudert in 1901,

> While I have never varied in my feeling that we had to hold the Philippines, I have varied very much in my feelings whether we were to be considered fortunate or unfortunate in having to hold them, and I most earnestly hope that the trend of events will as speedily as may be justify us in leaving them. . . . Sometimes I feel that it is an intensely disagreeable and unfortunate task which we cannot in honor shirk. At other times I am tempted to think that the whole business fits in with my favorite doctrine, and that we should count ourselves fortunate in having a great work to do.[24]

Roosevelt's doubts were but a pale reflection of the doubts that seized the nation as a whole. They foreboded the collapse of the imperialist counterattack. To the majority of Americans the imperialists' appeal to national self-interest seemed increasingly dubious on both ethical and practical grounds.

If opponents of expansion and empire were more sensitive to the moral issue than imperialists, their position was no less governed by a conception of national interest.[25] They charged that annexation of the Philippines would be contrary not only to democratic principles and international ethics but also to the American tradition of noninterference and nonentanglement in world politics. They were afraid that the acquisition of an empire would not only destroy the United States' moral position in the world but would also expose Americans to endless foreign wars and saddle them with the loss of liberty and the expense that would accompany the maintenance of a large military establishment. As the distinguished Yale scholar William Graham Sumner expressed it in his powerful indictment, *The Conquest of the United States by Spain,* "Expansion and imperialism are at war with the best traditions, principles, and interests of the American people, and . . . they will plunge us into a network of difficult problems and political perils, which we might have avoided, while they offer us no corresponding advantage in return."[26]

Political and social reformers, like Carl Schurz, Moorfield Storey, and E. L. Godkin, and liberal-minded intellectuals, like David Starr Jordan, William James, Charles Eliot Norton, Mark Twain, and William Dean Howells, attributed America's moral prestige, the progress of her democratic government, and her marvelous material development in large part to her relative isolation from the turbulent affairs of European nations.[27] These men were not impressed by Mahan's prophecies of economic and strategic advantages. To them the white man's burden meant the ordeal of governing an ignorant and hostile people, while embroiling the nation in a contest for foreign markets, territorial aggrandizement, and ever larger armaments.

6. THE RATIONALIZATION OF SELF-INTEREST

In some respects the great debate over imperialism sounded like *Alice in Wonderland*. Both sides used the same words, but the words seemed to mean different things. Imperialists and anti-imperialists alike proclaimed, with equal sincerity no doubt, their faith in America's mission, the spread of liberty, and the regeneration of mankind. Yet, although both groups had generally supported America's crusade at its inception, each later charged the other with subverting it, while asserting that it alone remained true to the national ideals.

The pervasiveness and uniformity of the idea of the American mission suggest that divergent attitudes toward national self-interest were the controlling factor in the conflict between imperialists and their antagonists, even when the controversy was cast in ideal terms. In the imperialist view the self-interest of the nation lay in a positive assertion of national power in accordance with a Manifest Destiny of world dominion. This view was consistent with a pugnacious, aggressive attitude and a temperamental bias toward heroic action and the military virtues. Anti-imperialists, on the other hand, conceived of national self-interest as the preservation of the status quo in accordance with the wisdom of the Forefathers, a conception which was consonant with a more pacific disposition, an exaltation of reason and love, and an aversion toward violence.

In response to a primary characteristic of national sentiment, not to say the propensity of all human beings for rationalizing their self-interest, patriots of both imperialist and anti-imperialist persuasion sought to identify the selfish interest of the nation, as they saw it, with ideal purposes. Consequently, their particular views of national interest and their emotional proclivities somewhat colored their interpretations of the traditional American mission. Thus imperialists found that commercial and territorial expansion, no matter how the consequences might affect its alleged beneficiaries, were truly instruments of civilization and democracy; and they were confident that the full exercise of man's combative instincts in the competitive struggle of nations was the best assurance of America's moral fiber and the vitality of American principles. Anti-imperialists, on the other hand, asserted that the fulfillment of America's exalted mission depended upon her continued isolation from the vicissitudes of world politics, since only by remaining politically detached from the controversies and combinations of European powers could the nation remain faithful to Washington's advice and "give to mankind the magnanimous and too novel example of a people always guided by an exalted justice and benevolence."

As might be expected, each side charged the other with selfishness. Imperialists asserted that the tradition of isolation was selfish because it thwarted the moral ambition of the nation out of a mean and narrow concern for mere safety from the hazards of international politics. Anti-imperialists denounced their antagonists for abandoning principle in the service of greed, for sacrificing America's moral reputation to an inordinate lust for power. But, actually, neither the imperialist nor anti-imperialist view was wholly selfish or wholly idealistic. The important difference between the two camps lay, first, in their conception of national self-interest and, secondly, in the way they combined self-interest with ideal purpose.

Obviously, aggressive national egoism is more likely to conflict with the interests of other peoples than passive national egoism. Therefore, an attitude of self-assertiveness, unlike an attitude of self-denial, tends to become incongruous with liberal and humane principles. It is in this situation that patriots are confronted with the problem of consciously reconciling national self-interest with supranational ideals. American imperialists solved the problem, to their own satisfaction, not by disavowing ideals but by relegating them to a secondary status. When the vicissitudes of empire and the moral strictures of anti-imperialists centered public attention upon the growing incompatibility of a robust national egoism with international altruism, some of the imperialists frankly acknowledged the primacy of self-interest and sought to turn an apparent vice into a virtue.

If the imperialist conception of national self-interest had been more in accord with traditional attitudes, Americans might have overlooked ethical incongruities; but time and public inertia absorbed the imperialist impulse, and self-interest reverted to its defensive posture. For a brief moment in history, when traditional self-interest was overwhelmed by a nationalistic urge for power and prestige, the proponents of expansion were able to capture the moral leadership of America; but when the aggressive conception of national self-interest subsided, imperialist idealism had to commend itself to the public on its own merits, and it suffered in the comparison of pretense with practice.

On the other hand, idealists, unlike egoists, were largely able to ignore the problem of reconciling national self-interest with missionary fervor, since they were in the enviable position of critics who did not have to test their own assumptions. They had no cause to doubt their major premise that, as long as the United States remained aloof from the political affairs of other nations, its self-interest would always be in perfect harmony with ideal principles. Whereas imperialists, unwilling to rely upon the Manifest Destiny they avowed, were actively engaged in the business of putting their ambitious conception of self-interest into practice, proponents of the status quo were inclined to take their view of self-interest for granted, in the comforting belief that America's prosperity and the progress of her institutions were assured, almost automatically, by the nation's adherence to the alleged dicta of isolation set down for all time by the Forefathers.

The importance of this utopian assumption lies in the fact that it was, in large measure, common to all Americans. Many of the supporters of imperialism were as oblivious of the necessity of reconciling ideals with self-interest as the anti-imperialists. They were merely more naïve and less candid than Roosevelt, Mahan, and Lodge, and more insensitive to the demands of conscience than were the anti-imperialists. Few who embraced expansionism as a kind of nationalistic orgy comprehended the practical results of their ambition. In general, ultranationalists were no more burdened than the extreme idealists with the facts of world politics as they impinged upon American security. America's egoistic and altruistic impulses were equally free of a sense of the limitations prescribed by the realities of world politics. Accordingly, national self-assertiveness and national idealism displayed the same propensity for extravagance; and one impulse was as fickle as the other.

On the whole, America's first crusade gave little evidence of that steadiness of national purpose one associates with the mature possession of world power. On the eve of the war with Spain Richard Olney had warned that an irresponsible idealism threatened not only to render Americans contemptible in the eyes of the world, as a "nation of sympathizers and sermonizers and swaggerers," but also to involve the United States in situations that would be positively detrimental to its self-interest; and he had pleaded that American idealism be tempered with a realistic appraisal of the nation's position in world politics.[28] Whether or not his warning was premature would depend, to a large extent, upon circumstances beyond American control, but by the turn of the century his assessment of the American approach to international relations seemed only too accurate; for although the nation had tasted the first fruits of world power, most Americans lingered in the age of innocence, naïve and scornful witnesses of the unsentimental calculation of national advantage which preoccupied the minds of military men and power-conscious statesmen and scholars.

CHAPTER III

THE REALISTIC RESPONSE TO WORLD POWER

1. Shifts in America's Political Environment

WILLIAM JENNINGS BRYAN, who supported the war as a humanitarian crusade but opposed it as an imperialist adventure, took a dim view of the expansionist cry of Manifest Destiny. "Destiny," he said, "is the subterfuge of the invertebrate, who, lacking the courage to oppose error, seeks some plausible excuse for supporting it."[1] But imperialists and Realists, surveying their success in leading into the arena of world politics a nation which scarcely comprehended its own actions, could be pardoned for agreeing with McKinley that the "march of events rules and overrules human action."[2] For Americans, quite apart from their original intentions and contrary to their traditional aspirations, had somehow acquired strategic commitments thousands of miles from home and altered the whole distribution of power in the world. Now, for better or for worse, the United States, whether willing or not, was involved in the toil of the leviathans.

As we shall see in this chapter, the nation's new international position instantly impressed itself upon the consciousness of a number of statesmen, philosophers, politicians, and publicists, notably those whose concentrated efforts, in accordance with the gospel of Mahan, happened to coincide with the course of history. How the great mass of Americans would respond to the new pattern of international relations was another question. Would they deliberately seize the direction of their destiny or would they remain unwitting agents of history, blindly drifting about on strange currents of world politics? At least it can be said that some Americans were determined that the nation should not be without a chart and compass.

Whether or not the American people understood their new position in the world, the rulers and statesmen of the other great nations of the earth were quick to feel the force of a new weight in the scales of international power; and their adjustment to the altered balance exerted an immediate impact upon the conditions of America's international environment. These conditions, in turn, were the stark facts which no realistic chart could ignore. The disciples of Mahan were eager to acknowledge the facts and make the best of them.

Great Britain was the first to react to the new balance of power. Faced with the decline of her historic naval superiority in the narrow seas of Europe and in the eastern Atlantic and finding her foreign holdings threatened by late-comers on the scene of colonial aggrandizement, she could ill afford another competitor but sorely needed a partner. France had designs on the Nile Valley. Germany was fast becoming a major naval and colonial rival. Russia menaced the Indian frontier and England's spheres of influence in China. Consequently, when British statesmen failed to stabilize conditions in the Far East by converting Russia into an ally, they sought counterpoises in Japan and the United States. The Japanese counterpoise was effected through the Anglo-Japanese alliance of 1902.

Led by Joseph Chamberlain, the Colonial Secretary, British statesmen systematically cultivated America's good will by a variety of official acts and private assurances.[3] Their benevolent neutrality during the Spanish-American War left no doubt about England's new direction in world politics. The press echoed official sympathy for the American cause, and the Foreign Office made no secret of its desire to have the United States annex the entire Philippine Islands.[4] Sir Cecil Spring-Rice, a life-long friend and counselor of influential Americans, kept Secretary of State Hay informed of Germany's designs on the archipelago, designs which counted heavily in Hay's and McKinley's decision to retain the entire group of islands.[5]

Undoubtedly, German officials also welcomed American good will, but being under the strain of Anglo-German rivalry, they were in no mood to encourage the ambitions of a nation bound so closely by ties of sentiment and interest to the Ruler of the Seas. It was England's general purpose to preserve the existing distribution of power in the world in order to protect her dominant position, but Germany had set out to destroy that distribution in order to make up for a late start in the race for power. The United States, which was far behind in the business of grabbing up the spoils of East Asia, had the same interest in stabilizing the status quo as Great Britain, which was so far ahead as to be satiated. But the ambitious German Emperor despised the Asiatic status quo and dreamed of capturing the markets of the Far East with the aid of the equally ambitious Czar of Russia.

Moreover, quite apart from the factor of Great Britain or the Far East in the power equation, the simultaneous ascendance of Germany and the United States in industrial development, military might, and nationalistic spirit was bound to breed suspicion and rivalry. It is not strange that suspicion and rivalry turned into hostility when America thrust its domain to the very door of China. Germany's official attitude toward the United States during the war was governed by a desire to prevent any blow to the monarchical principle or any adverse change in the balance of colonial power. There may never have been any danger of war, since neither Germany, Austria, nor France was willing to take the first step in a concerted intervention, and Germany was unwilling to intervene unilaterally. Nevertheless, the tempers of the German and American people were dangerously roused.[6] The German people and the German press, in striking contrast to the British, displayed outspoken sympathy for the Spanish cause.[7] American jingoes had some cause for sounding alarms over the presence of a large German squadron in Philippine waters, for if the United States had abandoned the Philippines, Germany might well have snatched a naval base, at the least.[8] The menace of Von Diederich's squadron convinced Admiral Dewey, for one, that America's next war would be fought against the Kaiser's navy. After the war Dewey became head of the General Board of the Navy, and for sixteen years he was a key man in the determination of American naval policy.

2. HAY AND THE ANGLO-AMERICAN RAPPROCHEMENT

One of the most striking features of the first decade of the twentieth century was the rapprochement between England and the United States. England's partiality during the war was very gratifying to a number of prominent Senators, such as William Frye, John Morgan, Cushman Davis, and Lodge, who had not previously wasted any love on the mother country. A group of outward-looking officials and politicians, with Roosevelt, Hay, Lodge, Whitelaw Reid, W. W. Rockhill, Elihu Root, and Henry White in the vanguard, accompanied by Mahan, as chief strategist, and Henry Adams, as "stable-companion to statesmen," was so elated by the new pattern of world politics that it constituted itself a sort of special committee for the promotion of an Anglo-American entente.

No American was more profoundly dedicated to Anglo-American rapprochement than Secretary of State John Hay. Hay's guiding principle of diplomacy, as he wrote to Henry White, was his unerring belief that "the one indispensable feature of our foreign policy should be a friendly understanding with England."[9] He could not have failed to perceive that British distress in Europe, Africa, and Asia was rapidly conspiring to make that understanding indispensable to England. The acceleration of German fleet expansion, Great Britain's embroilment in the Boer War, the Kaiser's famous message of sympathy to Oom Paul Kruger, increasing portents of strife on the Continent, Russia's stealthy "peaceful penetration" of Manchuria, the remarkable growth of the United States Navy; these facts, as well as Hay's diplomacy, were leading England to liquidate her disputes with the United States and realize the boast of Canning, three quarters of a century before, that he had brought in the New World to redress the balance of the Old. The compulsion of events, as much as Hay's skill and foresight, laid the foundation for Anglo-American mutual interest and sympathy, which played such a decisive role in the calculations of all the great powers, as, even at the turn of the century, they chose up sides for Armageddon.

Nevertheless, John Hay, never straying from his charted course of Anglo-American unity, shrewdly made the best of the favorable tides of national fortune. Thus while he was Secretary of State he was able to achieve negotiations indispensable to the Alaskan arbitration, which gave the United States an unbroken Alaskan coastline. He gained clear title to the Island of Tutuila, in Samoa, with the excellent harbor of Pago Pago. By the Hay-Pauncefote Treaty he won the right to build and defend an interoceanic canal, thereby fulfilling America's primary postwar strategic requirement, while speeding the withdrawal of the British Navy from the Caribbean and the substitution of uncontested American supremacy.

Through close collaboration with the British, Hay promulgated the famous Open Door notes, which were intended to stabilize the Far East by restricting the great powers' exploitation of China to their respective spheres of influence.* These notes were an extension of America's traditional policy since the beginning of the nineteenth century of insisting on equal commercial opportunity in Asiatic countries, a policy which reflected great expectations of the development of a prosperous trade with China.

This traditional policy had been seriously threatened when Japan's surprisingly easy victory over China in the war of 1895 stimulated the already lively imperialist rivalry of Russia, Germany, France, Japan, and Great Britain and led to a series of treaties in which the beleaguered China granted special commercial privileges to the great powers. Great Britain, which already had extensive interests in Asia, and the United States, which had infinitesimal interests but gargantuan expectations,† had found a common interest in checking the disintegration of China and restricting the imperialistic contest. Largely through the urging of W. W. Rockhill, an American expert on Far Eastern affairs and a close friend of Hay's, and Alfred Hippisley, a British subject formerly in the Chinese customs service, Secretary Hay had been persuaded

* The first Open Door note set forth the doctrine of most-favored-nation treatment in the spheres of influence and the leased areas of China. It was sent in the fall of 1899 in the form of identical notes to Russia, Great Britain, Germany, France, Italy, and Japan. In March, 1900, Hay announced that he had received "final and definitive" acceptances, although all the replies were actually ambiguous. The second circular note, sent in July, 1900, called for the preservation of Chinese territorial and administrative integrity as well as equal trade opportunities. No formal replies were requested.

† America's combined import and export trade with China constituted only 2 per cent of America's total foreign trade. For a typical expression of the extravagant hopes for future trade with China see Senator Jonathan P. Dolliver's article, "Significance of the Anglo-Japanese Alliance," *North American Review*, CLXXIV (April, 1902), 594–605.

to take the initiative in proclaiming the Open Door doctrine. The doctrine as such was scarcely more effective than the power of Great Britain and the United States to back it up, and neither Hay nor any other American official had any intention of enforcing it; nevertheless, it is one of the most significant reflections of the growing coincidence of Anglo-American interests, which was exerting such a powerful influence on the shifting world balance of power at the turn of the century.

To the coterie of Realists and devout expansionists Hay's achievements seemed to be the outward signs of Providence ordaining the lessons of Mahan; for, according to Mahan, one of the primary requirements of a wise foreign policy was a cordial understanding with Great Britain, based on a mutual recognition of the fact that both peoples were dependent on the sea for their national well-being and, by virtue of their geographical severance from rivals, exempt from the burden of great land armies.[10] These two nations, he reasoned, were "so alike in inherited traditions, habits of thought, and views of right, that injury to the one need not be anticipated from the predominance of the other in a quarter where its interests also predominate."[11] Mahan did not favor an immediate alliance, because he thought that Americans were not prepared for this advanced measure; but he was confident that public recognition of the national interest would lead to an equally useful arrangement of mutual advantage. "Let each nation be educated to realize the length and breadth of its own interest in the sea; when that is done, the identity of these interests will become apparent."[12]

Mahan's *The Problem of Asia* (1900), a reprint of articles written in the fall and winter of 1899, expressed the views upon the Far East current in the best-informed circles in Washington and undoubtedly reflected the thinking that led to Hay's promulgation of the Open Door policy.[13] In this book Mahan envisioned a great contest between the land power Russia and the sea powers Great Britain, Germany, the United States, and Japan over a crucial no man's land between the thirtieth and fortieth degrees north latitude and extending from the Mediterranean and the Black Sea to the East China Sea and the Japan Sea. In this middle belt Mahan conceded Manchuria to Russia's sphere of influence and allotted China proper to the "Teutonic" powers as a sphere for general uplift and civilization. In the "Teutonic" sphere he advocated the prevention of the preponderance of any power or group of powers and the maintenance of an open door for commerce and Western thought. He called for a united front against Russian expansion and pointed, especially, to the need of Anglo-American co-operation in the Yangtze Valley.[14]

John Hay's vision of world order really encompassed even more than a world-wide Anglo-American entente. He would have liked to include Germany and Russia in a grand design to stabilize the existing distribution of power, and call a halt to the race for commerce and armaments.[15] But the opportunity to achieve this goal steadily slipped away as Anglo-German relations hardened into hostility. By the end of the Spanish-American War Kaiser Wilhelm II seemed determined to make "a place in the sun" for his empire, and the British Navy was the chief obstacle in his way. By the end of 1901 negotiations on an Anglo-German defensive alliance had ceased, and Lord Landsdowne had concluded that British and German interests were antithetical and that the United States was the one power whose hostility Great Britain was bound not to incur.[16] Already America's role in international politics was being fashioned by the ominous alignments of a worldwide struggle for power.

3. REALISTIC THEORISTS OF AMERICA'S FOREIGN RELATIONS

There was something about America's new problems and responsibilities that stimulated reflective imaginations to take sweeping views of her new position in world politics and formulate the underlying principles of international relations that determined the dramatic shifts in the distribution of power. The views of three theorists of American foreign policy, Henry Adams, his brother Brooks, and H. H. Powers, are of particular interest in illustrating the Realistic response to America's ascendance to world power.

Henry Adams, America's great bemused pessimist of history and literature, brooded upon the imponderable shifts of national power and advised his friend Hay to leave his post before chaos set in.* Living beside Hay in the famous double mansion on Lafayette Square, opposite the White House, which two of his ancestors had occupied, Adams was absorbed in finding order and direction in the diplomacy of the new era. To him it seemed as though history were force; and he tried, perhaps half whimsically, to plot the course of history according to the second law of thermodynamics, which posited the dissipation and ultimate exhaustion of energy. According to his scheme of things, the fate of nations was determined by great impersonal forces. Men were but the creation of power, and the historian's job was "to follow the track of energy." Adams thus left little scope for morality in international relations. "In the struggle of interest or force," he admonished Hay, "it is weight that wins, and we must have the weight."[17]

But weight lay not alone in industrial and military might; it required an international arrangement of power, such as Hay's grand design, for which

---

* Hay did try to resign when the Senate began emasculating the Hay-Pauncefote Treaty in March, 1900, but McKinley dissuaded him. Tyler Dennett, *John Hay* (New York, 1933), p. 210.

Adams coined the term "McKinleyism"; that is, "the system of combinations, consolidations, trusts, realized at home, and realizable abroad." The nucleus of this world order was the Atlantic System, formed by Great Britain and the United States. The task of statesmanship was, first, to bring France into the Atlantic System; then to incorporate Germany into this "coal-power combination," lest it merge with Russia in a "gun-powder combination." Finally, the vast, glacial-like force of Russia would have to be contained somehow in a consolidation of all five powers.[18]

However, the longer Adams trained his Olympian vision upon the trend of world affairs, the more pessimistic he grew. By the end of the Algeciras Conference in 1906, he had lost all hope of chaining the expansive energy of Germany to the Atlantic System, and he had reached the conclusion that the problem of the Far East was resolving itself into a struggle between American intensity and Russian inertia.

Brooks Adams, like his brother and fellow historian, for whom he had an enormous admiration, was also moved by America's entrance into the drama of the great nations to philosophize about the ceaseless, ineluctable flux of force in the affairs of men. In his scheme of world politics the determining forces were economics and geography.[19] The law of history was the concentration of force, rather than its exhaustion. Man was powerless to shape his environment, but man alone of all the animals could consciously adapt himself to the demands of nature.

More specifically, Brooks Adams believed that the whole trend of political organisms was toward combination and concentration. The more vigorous and economical organisms were destroying the less active and more wasteful at such a rapid pace that "the moment seems at hand when two great competing systems will be pitted against each other, and the struggle for survival will begin."[20] As Brooks saw it, the struggle for survival would take place between land-power nations and sea-power nations. He traced this theory back to antiquity and dated the existing period of international conflict from about 1890, when the focus of energy and wealth began shifting from the British Empire toward the United States and Germany. He predicted that, if America's expansion were stopped by the entrenchment of a German and Russian coalition in Eastern Asia, the resulting pressure would shake American society to its foundations, for according to his Weltanschauung and a familiar maxim of imperialism, "not to advance is to recede; and to recede before your competitor is ruin."

Whereas Henry Adams viewed such intimations of chaos with the equanimity of one somewhat amused at the futility of man, Brooks was deadly earnest in his eagerness for the United States to stem the tide of disaster by adapting itself to the law of history and seizing the sources of power. With the outbreak of the Spanish-American War he launched a private campaign to arouse the country to meet its imperial destiny. He reasoned that the American economy would be thrown into chaos if the United States did not sell its surplus manufactures abroad; and the only region that could absorb this surplus was Eastern Asia. Here America's chief rival was Russia; therefore, the United States must get the upper hand of Russia in China, upholding the Open Door, by force if necessary, and taking control of the Chinese market.[21]

But Brooks Adams's prescription for power, like his brother's, required more than one national ingredient. In his mind the salvation of America, and civilization as well, depended upon the closest collaboration with Great Britain. Only an Anglo-Saxon coalition could resist the Continental coalition which threatened the commerce and military security of both nations. As a matter of self-preservation the United States, as senior partner, would soon have to bear the burden England had borne, securing the global seat of wealth and power and assuming the responsibility for world order; for unless the maritime system could absorb and consolidate mankind as energetically as the Continental system, the Anglo-Saxon world would surely be doomed to extinction.

H. H. Powers, a sometime professor of economics, whose chief interest lay in the tranquil field of art, was as preoccupied as the Adamses with the influence of force in international relations. In Powers' theory, force manifested itself in a Darwinian struggle for race supremacy, working out its inexorable logic through the competition of ever larger aggregates of nations, and producing, inevitably, an ultimate synthesis of humanity. In an adaptation of the expansionist rationale provided by John Fiske, Josiah Strong, and others in the early 1890's, Powers maintained that the substitution of more efficient forms for less efficient forms of life was nothing but the necessity of nature and concerned ethics no more than gravitation did.[22] Therefore, men could do little about the course of history. "Our wisdom must consist in an intelligent adaptation of ourselves to conditions which transcend our power and our intelligence."[23]

Chief among these conditions was the disintegration of the balance of power in Europe. This situation, he reasoned, would result eventually in the ascendancy of one power. If the United States remained aloof and isolated, a Continental power, probably under Russian domination, would emerge. This power would dictate terms to the world; its civilization would tend to become universal. Only a policy of "cautious but energetic self-assertion" on the part of the Anglo-Saxon race could prevent this eventuality. "Slav and Saxon, it narrows down to these. . . . Which will rule the world?"[24]

While this momentous threat amused Henry Adams and aroused Brooks, Powers claimed to be consoled by the knowledge that argument and deliberation would have little effect upon the struggle. Reason might determine the details of an Anglo-Saxon coalition, but the laws of force, the irresistible pressure of interest, predestined the amalgamation of the United States and the "order-creating power" of England and assured the extinction of American isolation. "That the ideal of national isolation is a Utopia is due to no accident of mood or circumstance, but to laws as fundamental as the constitution of protoplasm."[25]

It must be admitted that these three theorists are significant as the products rather than the shapers of their international environment. They were not publicists in the same sense that Mahan was a publicist. Their views on world politics were not widely read or widely appreciated. Their greatest influence was on close friends and upon that small group of prominent Realists who were already ardent converts. Yet no important politicians or statesmen would have acted differently if they had been completely ignorant of this triumvirate. However, in that these men gave philosophical expression to the portentous stirrings of national power and to the challenge to American foreign policy posed by the turbulent international environment, their writings are a measure of the impact of momentous events upon sensitive minds. It is significant that their theory of America's vital strategic interests conformed with the practical calculations of Mahan, Hay and Theodore Roosevelt.

4. ROOSEVELT AND THE CHALLENGE TO ISOLATION

Although few observers of the shifting international scene possessed the breadth of imagination of the Adamses or H. H. Powers, many Americans at the turn of the century—and we experience the same phenomenon at the mid-century mark—were in a mood to gauge the trend of history and peer into the future. Human affairs rarely conform to the artificial reckoning of time, but there happened to be a real correspondence between the beginning of the twentieth century and America's emergence as a fully conscious world power; and this coincidence heightened the impression that America was leaving one era and entering another.

In keeping with this impression, a number of Americans—mostly expansionists but also some more impartial students of foreign policy—were moved to re-examine realistically in the light of changing circumstances the traditional relation of the United States to the other great nations. They reached the conclusion that aloofness from world politics was a policy suitable, perhaps, to the nation's infancy and weakness but unworthy of her maturity and strength. Not only duty but self-interest, they argued, demanded that the United States be ready to assume the burdens and reap the advantages of a great nation, a nation cognizant of its weight in the affairs of the world and willing to employ it vigorously to compass national ends.

Richard Olney was one of those who protested against the misconstruction of the Farewell Address as an absolute, eternal dictum of national policy. In his opinion the considerations of national interest which justified Washington's advice no longer existed, and he warned that a policy of isolation which became an ingrained habit of thought, not just a conception of expediency, could be as dangerous to the national interest in the twentieth century as entanglement in the ordinary concerns of European politics would have been in Washington's time.[26]

As fate would have it, while the tradition of isolation was receiving its most serious verbal challenge, the assassination of President McKinley placed at the head of the nation a zealous apostle of the gospel according to Mahan. No President since George Washington had been more sensitive to the factor of power in international relations or more concerned with the impact of the international environment upon the national interest. As one of the nation's most vociferous and colorful exponents of America's active participation in world politics, Theodore Roosevelt was as good as his word, for under his dynamic leadership the United States not only asserted its preponderant authority in relations between the Caribbean area and foreign countries but also intervened decisively in the major controversies of Europe and the Far East.

It was characteristic of Roosevelt's approach to foreign policy that when war broke out between Japan and Russia he immediately set about calculating its relation to the national advantage. At first he was disposed to favor any plan that might weaken Russia's hold on Manchuria and thereby protect the Open Door.[27] This policy reflected his high regard for the potential civilizing influence of a victorious Japan, but it was also inspired by the fears of navalists and experts on oriental affairs concerning Russia's restrictions on American commercial enterprise in Manchuria, which they believed were part of a general aim to dominate all North China.[28] However, Roosevelt came to distrust Japan almost as much as Russia when she began feasting upon the fruits of victory; and from the standpoint of America's long-run interest in preserving a balance of power in Asia, he was as anxious to restrain the former as the latter. In fact, he preferred a long, exhausting war that would leave both powers in the position of mutual antagonists, with neither power able or quite so eager to gain predominance over the other.[29] Therefore, when Japan's unexpectedly decisive victories at Port Arthur and

Mukden raised the prospect of Japanese hegemony, he sought to save the balance of power by bringing the war to an end. With this aim in mind he advised the Japanese that a few months more of warfare would consume far more reserves than they could gain from any indemnity, while he warned the Russians that, if the war continued, they would be driven out of Siberia to the outskirts of Lake Baykal. At the same time, he tried to persuade France, England, and Germany to bring pressure upon the belligerents to sit down at the peace table.[30]

Roosevelt's efforts to induce other nations to play peacemaker were a distinct failure; apparently, he was ignorant of the complex crosscurrents of diplomatic intrigue and strategic design which precluded this arrangement. However, in the end, the exhaustion of both Japan and Russia, coupled with the relative detachment of the United States, disposed the belligerents to accept Roosevelt himself as a peacemaker. And so, reluctantly, he decided to accept the secret invitation of a seemingly victorious Japan that he act as a mediator; and in due time the Rough Rider succeeded in assembling the delegates of the quarreling nations at the Portsmouth Navy Yard, New Hampshire, where he treated his countrymen to the novel spectacle of a crisis in world politics centered on American soil and revolving around the President of the United States.

Unfortunately for Roosevelt's future peace of mind, the balance of power, which excited his interest, proved to be an unstable and complex equilibrium. The Japanese victory created a powerful new threat to America's vulnerable position in the Pacific. After the peace of Portsmouth the patron-and-protegé friendship between the United States and Japan gave way to suspicion, jealousy, and outright hostility; and American diplomats and military men began to recognize in Japan the same nationalistic drive and expanding industrial and military establishment, harnessed to an authoritarian discipline, as they had come to see in that other recent arrival upon the scene of world power, the German Empire. Through treaties with Russia, Japan achieved a rapprochement with her recent adversary which tended to nullify the restraining effect of a pattern of mutual antagonism and which virtually excluded the United States from Manchuria, where Americans had enjoyed a dominant position.[31] At the same time, the United States could hardly expect British co-operation in restraining the Nipponese, because England and Japan were allies, and England was increasingly preoccupied with the threat of Germany in Europe.

The developments surrounding this Russo-Japanese crisis were a significant forecast of the difficulty of maintaining the Open Door in China. However, it should be noted that Roosevelt did not regard that policy as an absolute doc-

trine to be pursued with inflexible purpose as a matter of principle. He regarded it, as did Hay, as an expedient aimed at preserving an opportunity
for American commercial expansion.[32] Therefore, China's territorial integrity
notwithstanding, he was quite willing to recognize the inevitable and grant
Japan a free hand in Korea as long as Japan did not interfere with America's
private concessions;* and, as he stated repeatedly in private letters, his objection to Russia's refusal to open Manchurian ports was not based upon any
high-minded opposition to Russia's acquisition of political control in Manchuria but only upon his desire that Russia should not prevent China from
granting the United States commercial rights.[33]

The headaches of the Portsmouth Conference were enough to discourage
a less ardent practitioner of the strenuous life from assuming the burdens of
active intervention in world politics; but Roosevelt, still in hot pursuit of the
elusive national interest, was soon to accept another opportunity to play the
arduous role of honest broker among nations. Even before one crisis had
ended in the Far East another was gathering steam on the northern coast of
Africa. Russia's involvement in the disastrous war with Japan encouraged the
German Imperial Chancellor von Bülow to take a bolder stand in opposing
the efforts of Russia's ally, France, to close the open door in Morocco. When
the Kaiser proceeded to touch off a full-scale crisis with a saber-rattling speech
at Tangier, the British, sensing a German scheme to break up the newly
formed Anglo-French entente, rallied to France's side. Roosevelt, undaunted
by his previous entanglement, consented once more to act as peacemaker in a
foreign dispute, this time at the Kaiser's request. Once more he played an
important part in shaping the terms of a settlement.

Roosevelt's chief motive in intervening seems to have been a desire to
prevent a European war, which he believed would jeopardize America's
world leadership, possibly endanger her peace, and quite probably destroy his
plans for a balance of power in the Far East, where both British and German
support of a moderate peace were essential.[34] We know from Secretary of
State Root's instructions to the chief American delegate, Henry White, that a
major American goal during the Algeciras Conference was the prevention of
any weakening of the Anglo-French entente, such as might have resulted if a
diplomatic defeat had induced France to join her Russian ally in Kaiser
Wilhelm's anti-British league.[35] At any rate, it is clear that the signing of the
Algeciras Convention in April, 1906, signalized the high point of America's
deliberate involvement in the toils of international politics until the war

* Tyler Dennett, *Roosevelt and the Russo-Japanese War* (New York, 1925), p. 110. By the
terms of the Taft-Katsura memorandum, negotiated by Secretary of War Taft in July, 1905, the
United States approved Japan's suzerainty over Korea in return for Japan's disavowal of aggressive designs on the Philippines. *Ibid.*, pp. 112–14.

which Roosevelt was instrumental in preventing broke out in full fury eight years later and converted the United States into an armed associate of the Anglo-French entente, which Root had sought to preserve.

There is room for argument about the wisdom of Roosevelt's diplomacy, but the really significant thing about his intervention in both the European and Far Eastern crises is that an American President took a serious interest in the manifestations of sheer power and self-interest in international relations and acted vigorously upon the principle that the national advantage was bound up with regions beyond the sea, where, under certain circumstances, the United States might properly take action.

CHAPTER IV

THE POPULAR RESPONSE TO WORLD POWER

1. The Anglo-American Entente: Sentiment Above Realpolitik

IN THE formative years of world power between the Spanish-American War and World War I it is certain that America's fortunes were being mightily shaped by the shifting coalitions of national power. And some Americans, more attuned to the cold calculation of national self-interest than others, were aware of the naked facts of international life. But what of the great body of the American people? Clearly, they were imbued with a new consciousness of might; but the nature of the popular response to world power suggests that their emotional appreciation of the national position far exceeded their intellectual grasp. The general public gave little indication of approaching the tasks of world power with the realist's instinct. Although the nation's first crusade involved it in the *Realpolitik* of Europe and Asia as surely as though it had deliberately contrived the situation, Americans had not consulted the vicissitudes of world politics when they undertook their war and they did not intend to do so after they had won it.

It was the misapprehension of a melodramatic incident, not the reckoning of strategic advantage, that induced America's war-born friendship for Great Britain. The popular belief in British benevolence was based upon the impression that on the day Manila fell the commander of the British flotilla had averted a German attack by running his ships in front of Diederich's squadron. Captain Chichester had, indeed, maneuvered his ships between the German and American squadrons, but only to afford his officers a better view of the proceedings.[1]

It would be a mistake to interpret even the efforts of that self-constituted committee for an Anglo-American entente, led by John Hay, solely as a response to the exigencies of *Realpolitik,* for admiration of British culture and institutions and a strong feeling of racial kinship were powerful motives in the hearts of some of the staunchest American nationalists. Hay poured forth his deepest beliefs in his address "A Partnership in Beneficence," delivered at the Lord Mayor's dinner in 1898, in which he conjured a vision of a Pax Americana, which would extend to Cuba, Hawaii, and the Philippines the same blessings of freedom and civilization that Pax Britannica had brought to India, Egypt, and South Africa. He even composed a sonnet to express his feelings of kinship:

> To thee, the cradle of our race, we come—
> Not breaking fealty to a dearer home—
> To warm our hearts by ancient altar-fires;
> Thy children's children, from whatever skies;
> Greet the high welcome of thy deathless eyes,
> Thou fair and mighty mother of our sires![2]

Such sonnets are not written out of a calculation of power politics.

One did not need to be an Anglophile—although it helped—in order to appreciate the practical basis of mutual self-interest that underlay an Anglo-American understanding; Roosevelt's regard for the British Empire was considerably cooler than Hay's. But by the same token, one did not need to have Hay's concern for power politics in order to embrace the new amity among the English-speaking peoples.

Accordingly, Anglo-American friendship won quite as much support among idealists and anti-imperialists—Andrew Carnegie, for instance—as among Realists and imperialists.[3] Carl Schurz, writing in the *Atlantic Monthly* in 1898, rejoiced over the new friendship with England because it meant the passing of the old-style jingo who played upon national antipathies. But he could see no common interests that called for a co-operative policy. In his opinion the only common interest binding America and Great Britain was an interest in the advancement of civilization. But each nation could best promote that goal in its own way. In fact, as if to refute Mahan, Schurz contended that any undertaking of a common enterprise or any dependence of these two nations upon each other for the maintenance of their interests or their position in the family of nations would engender suspicion and enmity. In other words, the less the United States needed British friendship, the more enduring it would be. And as a clincher to his argument, Schurz repeated the commonplace assurances of America's unique situation in the world, her vast resources and population, her ample domestic opportunities for engaging in missionary efforts and perfecting democracy, and her unassailable continental position.[4]

Although there was a great deal of talk among expansionists and imperialists about the unity of the English-speaking peoples, actually, few imperialists were any more inclined than the anti-imperialists to regard such unity as essential to the nation's self-interest. The arch-imperialist Beveridge, in his April, 1898, address before the Middlesex Club of Boston, evoked visions of an "English-speaking people's league of God for the permanent peace of this war-worn world."[5] Yet he was foremost among those who aroused the Senate to oppose the first Hay-Pauncefote Treaty, displaying that very brand of jingoism which Schurz had expected the new Anglo-American friendship to eradicate.

Beveridge admired the British Empire and hoped that the United States would emulate its Anglo-Saxon brother. He was fired with a mystic enthusiasm for a joint Anglo-American enterprise to redeem waste places, subdue inferior peoples, and organize the world. But the very spirit of intense, blindly aggressive national egoism, which was the substance behind his vague talk of an English-speaking people's league, precluded any specific and practical collaboration with Great Britain or any other nation. Beveridge exulted in a passionate national self-assertiveness, but, fundamentally, he was no more concerned with the requirements of *Realpolitik* than Schurz. In common with many strong nationalists, he was eager to play the game of power politics, but, like the great majority of Americans, he was ignorant of the rules and averse to playing with a partner.

It is true that Beveridge, like Roosevelt and Hay, expressed contempt for the isolationist shibboleths, but isolation had a special meaning in the context of his imperialist exhortations. "There is no such thing as isolation in the world today," he wrote to George Perkins in May, 1898. But then he added, "They say that Cuba is not contiguous . . . that the Philippines are not contiguous. They are contiguous. Our navy will make them contiguous."[6] In Beveridge's mind, abandonment of isolation meant the extension of American power, influence, and trade; but his vehement assertion of national self-sufficiency was not moderated by any of the realism that enabled Roosevelt to see that America's interests were bound up with the political relations of nations beyond the sea. Like most nationalists, Beveridge regarded that conception as inconsistent with traditional American pride, strength, and self-reliance.

Plotting mutual self-interest was an agreeable task when interest coincided with such felicitous sentiments as Hay expressed in his sonnet to England. But the great majority of Americans, while pleased with England's benevolent neutrality during the war, were not prepared to embrace an ancient rival so readily; and they were far from accepting the mother of their sires, or any other nation as a partner in beneficence. As a matter of fact, America still harbored a stubborn tradition of Anglophobia, and politicians had lost none of their zest for the old game of twisting the lion's tail, especially when it could be twisted before the large and appreciative audiences of Irish extraction in the great cities. Professional Hibernians gained considerable support from German-American groups and even from some of the blue-blooded members of the Anti-Imperialist League, such as Moorfield Storey, Charles F. Adams, and Senator George F. Hoar.

The millstone of Anglophobia was an especially cruel burden around John Hay's fine Anglo-Saxon neck. No statesman was ever more profoundly frustrated and exasperated by public and Senatorial caprice than he. Chafing under the "mad-dog hatred of England" and the "diseased state of the public mind," which prevented him from securing a frank understanding with Great Britain in the Far East, Hay burst out, "All I have ever done with England is to have wrung great concessions out of her with no compensation, and yet these idiots say I am not an American because I don't say 'To hell with the Queen' at every breath."[7]

Although Anglophobia and the impetuous spirit of national swagger that frequently accompanied it obviously militated against the sort of diplomatic give-and-take by means of which Hay hoped to enact his co-operative policy, yet, ironically enough, it was sheer, blind national egoism and pugnacity, as much as Hay's diplomacy, that quickened the pace of the Anglo-American rapprochement. It was rampant jingoism, more than Hay's sagacious designs, that hastened the departure of the British fleet from the Caribbean and the substitution of an exclusive American sphere of influence. It was public eagerness and Congressional readiness to defy the Clayton-Bulwer Treaty that prompted England to sign the first Hay-Pauncefote Treaty (1900), permitting the United States to construct, own, and neutralize an Isthmian waterway. It was the shrill voices of jingoism, mingling with the familiar cry of the Irish, joined now by the discordant imprecations of German-Americans indignant over the Boer War, and not Hay's sweet melody of reasonable compromise which moved the Senate, always attuned to election-year themes, to demand the right to fortify the proposed Isthmus canal, and which thereby forced Hay to negotiate a second treaty with Pauncefote expressly superseding the fifty-year old Clayton-Bulwer arrangement. There was more of the spirit of ultimatum than of rapprochement in these negotiations.

The public was equally deaf to the overtones of world politics in the promulgation of the Open Door notes. Otherwise John Hay would probably have been eternally damned instead of lionized. Fortunately for him, the American and British representatives involved in the formulation of the Open Door principle took the precaution of presenting it as coming entirely from American initiative. As far as the American people were concerned, the beloved author of *Jim Bludso,* like his rugged hero, had "seen his duty a dead sure thing and went for it thar and then"; and with a single stroke of his pen he had saved China from exploitation and forced the great nations of the world to observe American treaty rights.[8] Because there was obviously nothing the United States could do about it if the predatory nations continued to scorn the principle of commercial equality and the territorial integrity of China,

Hay's announcement escaped the stigma of an international commitment or an entanglement in the sordid concerns of power politics. Instead, it appeared to be simply the brave deed of a strong and independent nation, acting in accordance with the long-standing concern of missionary and religious groups for Chinese welfare. The public did not suspect that Hay had so little regard for his pronouncement as a principle of beneficence that in November, 1900, under pressure from the War and Navy departments, he directed the American minister at Peking to seek free and exclusive use of Samsah Bay— a project that was defeated only by Japanese objections.[9] Quite understandably, no one was more thoroughly amazed than Hay by the magnification of his fame to heroic dimensions at the hands of the public that was his constant vexation. But this was not the first or the last time that the American people so lightly assumed the burden of moral leadership.

2. ROOSEVELT AND THE PUBLIC

Theodore Roosevelt was not plagued, as Hay felt plagued, by a refractory public opinion. He experienced remarkably little difficulty in leading the nation to its most active participation in international affairs since the days of the French alliance. But his success can scarcely be attributed to any sudden burst of realism in the popular attitude toward world politics. Rather it was due to Roosevelt's political genius, his consummate skill in tapping the resources of aroused nationalism and directing them into new channels. By bold deeds, such as "taking" the Canal Zone, composing the famous "Perdicaris alive or Raisuli dead" telegram, and sending the great white fleet around the world, he was able to capture the public imagination and dramatize the emergency of the United States as a great power, capable of inspiring awe and respect in all parts of the world.

The popular response to Rooseveltian diplomacy would have been of quite a different sort had the general public been cognizant of the extent of their President's involvement in what they would have considered strictly European and Asian affairs. But as it was, Americans who looked with favor upon the interventions at Portsmouth and Algeciras beheld fresh examples—like the promulgation of the Open Door notes—of a robust and munificent young nation knocking a few foreign heads together in order to bring peace to less happily situated peoples through the exercise of her commanding moral prestige.

Nevertheless, even Roosevelt could not entirely please the Senate with the Algeciras Convention. After all, Morocco was a remote spot with no direct relation to American welfare. Embarrassing the Kaiser and maintaining world peace were worthy goals but did not strike most Senators as having any practical connection with American interests. Consequently, the Senate approved the Convention only after it had, in effect, affirmed American disinterestedness by appending a reservation disavowing the implication of a departure from "the traditional American foreign policy."[10]

It would be rash to suppose that the general public had any notion of the turbulent undercurrent of power conflict that seethed beneath the surface of the Portsmouth mediation. The American people beamed upon the Japanese people as smart little protégés of American democracy and material progress. During the Russo-Japanese War they sympathized with Japan as an underdog nation whose very existence was threatened by the corrupt and decadent colossus Russia. They welcomed Japan's victory; they were ignorant of the growing fear in American official circles that Japan might become a threat to American possessions and interests in the Far East. They applauded Roosevelt's mediation as an act of pure altruism in the interests of international amity. They praised Japan for her magnanimous surrender of just demands in the peace settlement and generally approved the substantial concessions she gained in Korea, Manchuria, and the Island of Sakhalin as an assurance of peace and order and civilization in Asia, resulting from the wholly beneficent effect of Japanese dominion.[11]

Subsequent American hostility toward Japan in the years before World War I was generated far less by the shifting balance of power in the Orient than by the opposition of West Coast citizens to the influx of Japanese after Japan's destructive war with Russia.* Three times—in Roosevelt's, Taft's, and Wilson's administrations—the attempts of Californians to exclude the prolific Orientals from the enjoyment of white privileges almost precipitated a major crisis. Roosevelt, in common with those who were most conscious of the imperatives of international politics, was disgusted and alarmed by a foolish exhibition of local prejudice, which he believed jeopardized America's amicable trade relations in the Orient, her strategic interest in Chinese territorial integrity, the security of the Philippines, and, in short, the whole *modus vivendi* in the Far East.[12] By the winds of such caprice could the most expedient constructions of national interest be shattered.

3. DECLINE OF THE ZEST FOR POWER

If the great majority of the American people were unmindful of the factor of power in their international environment, if they were indifferent to the

---

* A. Whitney Griswold, *The Far Eastern Policy of the United States* (New York, 1938), pp. 347 ff. On the other hand, the hostile reaction of Japanese jingoists to West Coast jingoists did arouse some fears that Japan would grab the Philippines. American ultranationalists and exclusionists naturally exploited these fears. However, others were not impressed; and, in general, students of international relations believed that Japan did not want the Philippines. Eleanor Tupper and George E. McReynolds, *Japan in American Public Opinion* (New York, 1937), pp. 100–2.

implications of America's new status in the world and heedless of the practical consequences of national conduct, the wonder is that there were so many
prominent dissenting voices. For what incentive was there for men to reverse
the direction of their thoughts? Americans had apparently thrived without
having to worry about power politics; so why should they bother with such
sordid matters when the nation had attained an unprecedented peak of
strength and prestige?

While America was under the spell of expansionism, an inflated national
ego, infused with a crusading ardor, sustained a certain popular interest in the
advantages to be reaped from playing the game of power politics. However,
that interest proved to be insubstantial and largely emotional. It collapsed
when nationalistic exuberance waned and idealistic professions became difficult to reconcile with seamy deeds. Theodore Roosevelt stirred up the ashes
of national self-assertiveness, but he could not revive the flame. To change the
metaphor, his success in prolonging the thrill of imperialism was a tribute to
his preaching rather than his teaching. He carried the national congregation
with him, but he failed to inculcate the basic lessons of international politics.
At that, he dramatized America's enlarged role in world affairs not so much
by an exhibition of aggressive energy as by striking two well-publicized blows
for world peace. It was a sign of the times that the man who had been distinguished for his bellicosity in 1898 was awarded the Nobel Peace Prize in
1906.

American imperialism continued, but it continued because of public apathy,
not because of popular enthusiasm. As high expectations of commercial and
strategic gain failed to materialize, it became increasingly difficult to justify
imperial holdings on grounds of self-interest; and national philanthropism,
unsupported by self-interest or bellicosity, was rapidly absorbed in the inertia
of less extreme and, in the long run, more compelling ends and motives of
national conduct.

By the end of Roosevelt's first term imperialism had lost its claim to moral
leadership and had gone on the defensive. Henceforth the proponents of
empire were to direct their arguments not toward expanding national power
but toward preserving its outward manifestations. The fire had gone out of
the old champions. No one in 1903 was greatly interested in Beveridge's
defense of army conduct in the Philippines, which was currently being investigated; and Beveridge himself now found his crusading energy almost
completely absorbed in promoting a series of domestic reform issues. In less
than a decade after the Spanish-American War, Roosevelt, in a fit of despondency over the lack of public interest in expanding the Navy, was expressing
his wish to give up the Philippines as a troublesome and vulnerable "heel of

Achilles."[13] But the ultimate in despondency was voiced by Henry Adams, who, ever since the Spanish-American War, had been growing increasingly pessimistic about the ability of a benevolent Anglo-American imperialism to stop the headlong rush into chaos resulting from the concentration of power among nations. As early as 1901, in a letter to Brooks, he lamented, with customary exaggeration,

. . . the world will break its damned neck within five and twenty years; and a good riddance. This country cannot possibly run it. I incline now to anti-imperialism, and very strongly to anti-militarism. I incline to let the machine smash, and see what pieces are worth saving afterwards. I incline to abandon China, Philippines and every-thing else. I incline to let England sink; to let Germany and Russia try to run the ma-chine, and to stand on our own internal resources alone.[41]

4. ABSENCE OF THE FEAR OF INSECURITY

The fact is that in these years the American people lacked the only in-centive which, under the circumstances, could have sustained a consistent regard for the nation's position in world politics; and that was the preserva-tion of America's territorial integrity and her fundamental institutions. Self-preservation is the most basic national interest, but it commonly commands attention and compels action only when it is joined with the catalyst of fear. Fear, however, was conspicuously absent from the American outlook. Noth-ing seemed surer than America's continued safety from foreign intervention, nothing more certain than the unimpeded expansion of her wealth and the perfection of her institutions.

But if the American people took their national security for granted, there was, after all, little in the United States' position in the world to disturb their complacency. The conquest of Spain's West Indian islands, the provision for a naval base in Cuba, the retirement of the British fleet from Caribbean waters, and the rapid expansion of the United States Navy, which by 1907 had become second only to England's, made continental impregnability more nearly an accomplished fact than ever before.[15] Great Britain's continued domination of the narrow seas of Europe and her policy of amity with the United States assured the maintenance of the Atlantic Ocean as a major bulwark of defense. The annexation of the Hawaiian Islands at the crossroads of the Pacific and the partition of the Samoan archipelago greatly strengthened America's posi-tion in the Pacific. The development of a base at Pearl Harbor and construc-tion of the Panama Canal, completed in 1914, raised the prospect of a de-fensively invincible naval force.

The threat to American security was potential and remote, not actual and immediate. If Americans would content themselves with protecting their continental position, then the problem of security would be relatively simple, as long as the British Navy retained its control of the Atlantic; but if Americans intended to protect the fruits of their war with Spain and uphold the national honor and prestige by backing up their new commitments, then the United States, as Olney had warned in 1900, would be forced "by the stress of the inexorable facts of the situation" to abandon a good measure of its accustomed independence of action and entangle itself in world politics; for the annexation of the Philippines and Guam vastly complicated the American defense problem. Projected as an indefensible salient into Japan's expanding sphere of power, flanked by islands transferred from Spain to Germany, and left virtually undeveloped and unfortified, these distant possessions were a strategic liability. If the United States expected to keep the spoils of victory and secure its vulnerable line of communications in the Pacific, if it had any notion of enforcing commercial equality in the Far East or of preserving China's territorial integrity in accordance with the Open Door, it would need help. It would have to seek alliances, understandings, or other arrangements of mutual advantage, either to supplement its own power or to fashion a political substitute. It would have to take an active part in shaping the balance of power in both Europe and Asia. However, the anticipation of hypothetical dangers such as these was in a realm of speculation quite incompatible with the widespread public indifference toward matters beyond American shores. Having acquired an empire, the American people were quick to exercise their privilege of ignoring it.

Even among those few who took a consistent interest in events outside the United States and prided themselves in their sensitivity to the currents of international power there was considerable ignorance of the strategic implications of America's new acquisitions. Although one of the reasons for keeping the Philippines had been the threat of the German Navy, German statesmen were amazed and overjoyed to find Americans offering no opposition whatsoever to Germany's acquisition of a whole chain of islands—the Marshall, Mariana (with the exception of Guam), and Caroline archipelagoes—athwart America's vital Pacific line of communications.[16]

The security of America's new position in the world depended upon many contingencies, more or less remote, which, even if they had been absolutely predictable, were scarcely so urgent as to inspire fear. Roosevelt and others were occasionally seized by visions of a German or Japanese naval attack upon the Western Hemisphere when America's relations with those countries were particularly strained; but when the crisis had passed, they soon recovered their accustomed posture of prudent suspicion.[17] In 1900 Mahan himself wrote that the United States need fear no external blow to its lines of communication throughout the world.[18] There is no reason to think that he ever revised this estimate.

Yet there was one area outside the continental United States which was so closely and so obviously related to America's defense that, by the turn of the century, a threat of foreign intervention there would have been generally regarded as tantamount to a threat to the territorial integrity of the United States itself; and that was Latin America—particularly, the area including and bordering upon the Caribbean. America's interest in this quarter stemmed from the tremendous popularity of the Monroe Doctrine, or the policy of "Hands off," as it was commonly conceived. The appeal of the Monroe Doctrine, like that of any tenet of national faith, was enhanced by an aura of patriotic sentiment, but its distinct persuasiveness must be attributed to its solid grounding in a sense of self-preservation. After the United States began building the Panama Canal, Americans were more sensitive than ever to the security of the Caribbean approaches from the menace of European interference. However, it is doubtful whether, as some claimed during World War I and preceding World War II, the popular perception of the strategic foundation of the Monroe Doctrine extended to an appreciation of its dependence upon British sea power in the Atlantic. After all, the doctrine was considered a unilateral pronouncement of a strong and independent nation, and Americans had no reason to take the unflattering view that their country was hiding behind British skirts.

Because the Caribbean area was an integral part of America's defense strategy and yet by no means an exclusive domain, it was the natural center of American anxiety over national security; and, as one might expect from the trend of American friendships and antipathies, the chief source of anxiety in this region was the German Empire. However, as far as the general public was concerned, there was no keen intimation of danger, no well-defined fear of a specific menace, only a vague distrust of German intentions and a growing resolution to keep a potential trouble-maker from expanding its influence in an area so close to home.

As Americans forgot their own imperialist slogans, they were increasingly antagonized by the Kaiser's arrogant declarations of German power, his ominous panegyrics to the German spirit and German destiny. Grotesque allusions to "Me und Gott," his bristling mustache and Prussian regalia, made the German Emperor a caricature of autocracy and militarism and a living symbol of the ideological rift between the American and German nations. In the pernicious atmosphere of mounting German-American antipathy, every German move in the Caribbean was likely to be suspect. Thus, when in December, 1902, Germany and Great Britain, on the latter's initiative, instituted a blockade of Venezuela in order to force the contumacious dictator Castro to arbitrate their financial claims, it was Germany and not England that incurred the wrath of the American public. The German bombardment of Fort San Carlos in January, 1903, touched off a conflagration in the American press which the hasty withdrawal of German and British forces was unable to extinguish. But whereas the British Government consolidated its friendship with the United States by paying public homage to the Monroe Doctrine and disavowing any intention of meddling in an American sphere of influence, Germany's failure to follow suit, plus a good deal of deprecation of Yankee impudence in the German press, only exacerbated America's indignation over Prussian militarism and imperialism.[19]

However, apprehension of a German menace to the Monroe Doctrine, even an indefinite and ill-defined menace, was by no means universal. Those who suspected that the Doctrine was becoming a pretense for imperialism were wont to point out that Germany had enough problems to occupy it in Europe without taking on the Western Hemisphere. Moreover, there was an ample reservoir of good will in America, especially among large groups of German-Americans, which Germany could yet draw upon if she would.

Nevertheless, Ambassador Speck Von Sternburg, who was substituted for Von Holleben in 1903 in an effort to tap this reservoir, felt that fears of a German menace were serious enough to warrant his writing a disavowal in the *North American Review* in 1906. His article refuted the notion that Germany had designs on Denmark or Holland or on their possessions in the Caribbean and went to particular pains to explain that Brazilian colonists were peaceful citizens and not German reservists.[20] As a matter of fact, the ambassador was only reiterating Von Holleben's previous assurances, delivered to the *New York Herald* in January, 1900, and repeated in November, 1901.[21] Sternburg's successors would find it necessary to repeat his disavowal when the German Army swept across the Lowlands. However, this official concern with a minor source of international friction would always reveal more about the German than about the American outlook upon international politics.

5. REALISTS AND THE GERMAN MENACE

It was among the coterie of Realists and quiescent expansionists that the German menace was felt most acutely. American naval advocates did not allow themselves to forget the Samoan incident; they confidently expected the next German challenge to occur in the Caribbean. Their touchiness over this area was increased by the British withdrawal of naval strength from the Western Hemisphere after 1904, which left Germany as America's sole naval rival athwart the approaches to the Panama Canal. Throughout the period between the Spanish-American War and World War I the State Department received reports of German schemes for naval bases in the Danish West Indies, Haiti, the Margarita Islands, the Galapagos, Santo Domingo, and even on the coast of Lower California. Alarming rumors circulated among high officials, more than a few of them being inspired by the fabulous German adventurer Captain Christmas, who, having failed to interest the German Foreign Office in the purchase of the Danish West Indies, hoped to gain his commission by scaring the United States into buying them.[22] In 1900 so moderate and well-informed a man as Secretary of War Elihu Root was moved to warn, "No man who carefully watches the signs of the times can fail to see that the American people will within a few years have to either abandon the Monroe Doctrine or fight for it, and we are not going to abandon it."[23] In 1902 the fear that Germany might buy or grab the strategic Danish West Indies led Secretary of State Hay to conclude a treaty of annexation with Denmark. When the treaty was rejected by the Danish Parliament, influential diplomats and political leaders were convinced that it was due to German pressure. Although competent historians have found nothing in the German archives or in any other documents to substantiate this conviction, the legend was generally accepted as a factual basis for suspicion of German designs.[24]

Even if there had been a serious threat of a seizure of naval bases in the Caribbean, one would suppose that at least American shores were safe from the German menace, in view of the presence of the British Navy in the Atlantic and the immense technical difficulties involved in launching a successful overseas operation. Nevertheless, those who should have known most about the national security professed to take a grave view of the possibility of a German invasion. One basis for perennial premonitions of invasion was the War College studies, which sought to demonstrate that a small standing army and the ineffective state militias would be powerless to stop a determined foe from capturing important East Coast financial and industrial centers.[25] The Office of Naval Intelligence received numerous reports of discussions of such an invasion in German military and naval circles.[26] But the most prolific source of apprehension was the writings of fanatical and militant patriots of the Pan-German League and similar organizations. In the process of elaborating visions of world empire, these writings delineated plans for colonizing southern Brazil and indulged in detailed portrayals of successful German attacks upon American shores. Although the authors of this ultranationalist literature were by no means synonymous with the German Foreign Office, that impression was often conveyed by the *Army and Navy Journal* and some popular periodicals, which gave currency to several of the more sensational military books appearing in Berlin.[27]

There is no evidence that the general public was greatly concerned over Pan-Germanism; indignant, maybe, but not concerned. However, American nationalists took their rabid German counterparts more seriously. Roosevelt and Lodge, although they did not publicize their fears, were well aware of the various German plans of attack and were quite willing to believe that they had official sanction. While they regarded an actual attack on seacoast towns as a hazardous undertaking, they did not discount its possibility, since the Kaiser became rather wild and "jumpy" at times, as Roosevelt put it. The attack, they speculated, would most likely come in stages, with Brazil being the first step.[28]

But this raises an interesting question: If Roosevelt beheld a threat to American security, why did he not inform the public of its existence? He was not a reticent man. As Assistant Secretary of the Navy he had not hesitated to expound upon the menace which the ruthless struggle among nations held for the American position. Yet as President he scarcely mentioned that menace, except, by implication, when urging eternal vigilance and a large navy as the price of liberty. Soon after he exchanged views with Lodge on Germany's most probable line of attack, he announced in his annual message of December, 1902, "There is not a cloud on the horizon. There seems not the slightest chance of trouble with a foreign power."[29]

This discrepancy between Roosevelt's private and public views can be attributed, in part, to the fact that, fortunately, the irrepressible Rough Rider was far more circumspect deliberating within the office of the Presidency than fulminating outside it. His temperament demanded a role of a magnitude commensurate with his boundless energy; when the role was lacking, his exuberance tended to assume a strident quality quite incompatible with the tasks of diplomacy.

But, apart from this consideration, it would seem that Roosevelt was more cautious than anxious concerning America's defensive position. Certainly he did not believe that the threat to America's security was imminent. He regarded the German menace, at the most, as simply one of the rocks and shoals which Realists had to recognize in calculating safe passage for the ship of state. If the United States expected the worst of its potential enemies, expanded the Navy, and remained in constant readiness to meet force with force, then, in his opinion, it need fear no one. Thus in 1905 he confided to his friend Sir Cecil Spring-Rice,

When I first came into the Presidency I was inclined to think that the Germans had serious designs upon South America. But I think I succeeded in impressing on the Kaiser, quietly and unofficially, and with equal courtesy and emphasis, that the violation of the Monroe Doctrine by territorial aggrandizement on his part around the Caribbean meant war, not ultimately, but immediately, and without delay. He has always been as nice as possible to me since and has helped me in every way, and my relations with him and the relations of the two countries have been, I am happy to say, growing more close and more friendly.[30]

6. REALISM DISCREDITED

If diplomatic discretion and the defense problem's lack of urgency ruled out appeals to self-preservation, the old nationalistic allusions to the hazards of the ruthless competition among nations were effectively precluded by the more pacific temper of the times..Power politics assumed a sinister connotation as Americans became disenchanted with the imperialist élan and disillusioned by its consequences.

The leaders of the expansionist and imperialist movement knew the value of an objective calculation of the imperatives of national self-preservation, but their public and private statements left the unavoidable impression that their heed for the practical problems of international politics sprang more from the will-to-power than the will to live, more from the desire to dominate than the fear of being dominated. Indeed, it was not mere preservation of the status quo that had directed the expansionists' attention toward international politics; they needed no such incentive. The game of *Machtpolitik* was worth playing for its own sake; and the fear that, if one did not play it shrewdly, one would suffer the consequences was secondary to the pleasurable sensation of pride and power derived from the playing itself. But the imperialist temper, in the long run, failed to recommend itself to the general public, either on grounds of idealism or America's self-interest. When traditional conceptions of national interest reasserted themselves and when domestic reform and the international peace movement siphoned off America's crusading energy, neither patriotic nor philanthropic fervor sufficed to sustain the leadership of the Realists who had planned and guided America's entrance into the arena of world politics. Moreover, because the Realists' active concern for power politics became associated in the public mind with a discredited militarism and imperialism, a realistic calculation of power politics became synonymous with Machiavellianism. Realism had kept bad company; therefore, it shared the opprobrium.

It was this trend in the popular attitude toward world politics, as much as any other factor, which inhibited Roosevelt from publicly sounding alarms about the strategic dangers to America's position, for although Roosevelt was outspoken, he was also sensitive to the shifting demands in the marketplace of American opinion, and he was too shrewd a leader to try to sell a rejected product.

Roosevelt might rail in private against the "mollycoddles" and the "peace-at-any-price boys," but his public actions and pronouncements were as good a barometer as any of the pacific trend in the public attitude toward international politics. By his mediation in the Portsmouth and Algeciras conferences and his support of the Hague Tribunal he demonstrated his concern for international peace; yet he was silent about the bearing of his actions upon the distribution of world power. Roosevelt's intervention in the Panama revolution in order to acquire the Canal Zone did nothing for the cause of peaceful settlement of international disputes, but he did not fail to square his actions with "the interest of collective civilization."[31] A major motive in his announcement of the so-called Roosevelt Corollary to the Monroe Doctrine, which was intended to sanction American intervention in the foreign debt controversies of Latin American nations, was the forestalling of a situation which might have led to European, and especially German, intervention in a strategic area; but Roosevelt justified his policy as the "exercise of an international police power."[32]

Yet, however much he might covet the role of peacemaker, however adroit his expressions of America's new consciousness of collective civilization, Theodore Roosevelt remained, at heart, a romantic militarist, an aggressive national egoist. And when America's brief surge of imperialism had passed, he was never again reconciled with his times. What disturbed him most as the second decade of the twentieth century began to unfold was the phenomenal growth of the peace movement. What exasperated him about the peace movement was not its objectives but the growing reluctance of its followers to face the facts of international relations realistically, as he saw them. In the end, no sign of the popular response to world power in the years before World War I was more revealing than the mounting despair of Mahan's most active disciple.

CHAPTER V

THE PEACE MOVEMENT

1. Successor to Anti-imperialism

IN THE tide of reaction against imperialism, touched off by the moral disrepute it earned in the Philippines, the advocacy of a variety of measures for the peaceful settlement of international disputes became not only respectable but within the realm of political practicability. Not only pacifists, but wealthy philanthropists, influential politicians, and renowned statesmen swelled the rosters of peace organizations and flocked to hundreds of peace congresses throughout the world. The heads of the great powers of the world vied with one another in pronouncing the death of the old diplomacy of threat and intrigue and in heralding the birth of a new era of disarmament and good will. These sanguine expectations gained an air of plausibility from a growing number of successful conciliations, mediations, adjudications, and arbitrations. If one could believe the signs of the times, international relations would henceforth be governed by the lessons of Christ instead of Machiavelli.

Although the American peace movement embraced a great many schools of thought, from the absolute pacifists to the advocates of a league to enforce peace, it drew its chief inspiration directly from traditional American idealism, from a faith in the indefinite moral and rational perfectibility of mankind and a utopian belief that the spirit of love exemplified in Americans would spread outward, as from the original Christian communities, and eventually pervade all mankind.

As a matter of fact, in its missionary spirit the peace movement was a brother of imperialism. For both movements combined a new-found sense of national power and prestige with an old desire for a world of liberty, brotherhood, and prosperity. Both combined the appeal of universal values with the lure of national destiny. Out of the consciousness that the United States was no longer a weakling among nations and in the knowledge of her superior endowment of Christian ethics and the attributes of civilization, both movements were impressed with America's greatly increased responsibility for extending to the less fortunate peoples of the earth the blessings of democracy, order, and progress.

Consider the following expression of the American mission:

> Before the clock of the century strikes the half-hour the American Republic will be the sought-for arbitrator of the disputes of the nations, the justice of whose decrees every people will admit, and whose power to enforce them none will dare resist. And, to me, the Republic as an active dispenser of international justice is a picture more desirable than a republic as an idle, egotistical example posing before mankind as a statue of do-nothing righteousness. . . . The regeneration of the world, physical as well as moral, has begun, and revolutions never move backward.[1]

This was spoken by Albert J. Beveridge, America's most vociferous imperialist, in a New Year's Eve address in 1901.

Then reflect upon this statement of American idealism:

> Behold a republic increasing in population, in wealth, in strength and in influence, solving the problems of civilization and hastening the coming of a universal brotherhood—a republic which shakes thrones and dissolves aristocracies by its silent example and gives light and inspiration to those who sit in darkness. Behold a republic gradually but surely becoming the supreme moral factor in the world's progress and the accepted arbiter of the world's disputes—a republic whose history, like the path of the just, "is as the shining light that shineth more and more unto the perfect day."[2]

That was spoken by William Jennings Bryan, America's foremost anti-imperialist, in his address at Indianapolis in August, 1900, accepting the Democratic nomination for president.

That both imperialists and anti-imperialists should have cast their appeals in virtually identical terms of idealism is testimony to the pervasive and enduring power of America's faith in the national mission. Indeed, it is the similarities as much as the differences between imperialism and anti-imperialism that place these conflicting views in their true historical light, for much of the otherwise meaningless moral controversy that marks all such great American debates on foreign policy becomes significant only when it is seen as an essential part of the struggle between groups of broadly divergent attitudes toward international politics competing for control of the symbolic spigots of a vast reservoir of popular idealism.

As it was suggested in chapter II, the crux of the difference between the imperialist and anti-imperialist conceptions of America's mission lay not in the content of idealism but in the practical application of idealism; and the practical application depended chiefly upon a conception of national interest and upon the way in which interest was combined with principle. Thus in the imperialist view the dispensation of international justice and the regeneration of the world followed as an incident of the vigorous prosecution of the nation's self-interest, which was conceived as the acquisition of power; whereas the anti-imperialist, conceiving the basis of self-interest as self-preservation rather than self-assertion, was content to trust America's mission to the nation's moral prestige and the efficacy of example, while he denounced the philanthropic venture of the imperialists as contrary to traditional conceptions of national interest and incompatible with liberal and humane principles. Of the two views of America's conduct toward the outside world, imperialism was oriented more toward national egoism, in so far as the drive for national power involved the frank espousal of the primacy of self-interest; whereas anti-imperialism was oriented more toward altruism, since the absence of the same necessity for reconciling ideals with self-interest freed moral enthusiasm from the bondage of expediency. This difference in emphasis was sharpened by both temperamental and philosophical differences: temperamental, in that the imperialist view gained inspiration from the aggressive, combative instincts, while anti-imperialism stressed motives of love and sublimated the urge for power into the drive for prestige and moral influence; philosophical, in that the anti-imperialist view placed a higher estimate on the ability of reason and morality to transcend selfishness, while imperialists were wont to stress the immutable element of self-interest in all human relations.

Generally speaking, the peace movement was sustained by the attitudes exemplified in anti-imperialism. In fact, after anti-imperialism received its political death blow in the election of 1900, its leaders became equally ardent apostles of the peace movement. But where were the successors to the imperialists? They could be found taking a strong nationalist position on a variety of issues, and many were in positions of authority. But as the tide of their times receded, they floundered about in the uncongenial waters of the peace movement in evident frustration, for even while they retained control of the official instruments of foreign policy they were confronted with the loss of their moral leadership and the absence of an issue which could serve as a new rallying point.

2. THEODORE ROOSEVELT'S PHILOSOPHY OF INTERNATIONAL RELATIONS

In the public addresses and private letters of Theodore Roosevelt one can read something of the change in the temper of the times and the emergence of new patterns in the struggle between egoism and idealism, Realism and utopianism—patterns which foreshadowed America's response to World War I and which eventually involved Roosevelt in the bitterest contest of his life. The running controversy between nationalism and internationalism, which had its genesis in the reaction of Realists and national egoists to the peace movement, becomes more intelligible in the light of Roosevelt's philosophy of international relations.

Roosevelt was not so much disturbed by the dramatic rise in the popular enthusiasm for international peace; he could adapt himself to that trend and even encourage it; but he was profoundly agitated by what he believed to be an unrealistic misconception of the nature of international relations, which lay at the basis of the peace movement. He could agree, as he said when speaking of the formation of the international tribunal at the Hague, that "as civilization grows, warfare becomes less and less the normal condition of foreign relations";[3] but he deplored the tendency of peace advocates to assume that war was an anachronism and an absolute evil. He conceded that the world-wide spread of technological progress and democratic institutions was making every part of the globe interdependent and raising the ethical level of all human relations, but he felt that to assume that these developments rendered war obsolete was greatly to exaggerate the capacity of morality, sentiment, or reason to transcend the hard facts of an anarchical society of nations.

Roosevelt was firmly convinced that as long as men owed their primary allegiance to nations—and few of the peace advocates denied that this was the prospect for a long time to come—any common ideals or sentiments had to be strictly subordinate to national interests. Fools might ignore this fact and preach altruism and disarmament as long as their concern for humanity was compatible with the national interest; but when the interests of other nations conflicted with American interests, as inevitably they would, then national power, not humanity, would be the sole arbiter recognized by all. Therefore, to hold that the ultimate resort to war was obsolete and always evil was, in Roosevelt's mind, equivalent to valuing the interests of other nations above American interests; and that was contrary to all manliness and true idealism.

Although Roosevelt's approach to international relations was Realistic, he was far from being a cynic. While recognizing the primacy of self-interest, he did not draw any rigid antithesis between ideals and self-interest as ends of national action. In his sixth annual message to Congress he stated,

It is a mistake, and it betrays a spirit of foolish cynicism, to maintain that all international government action is, and must ever be, based upon mere selfishness, and that to advance ethical reasons for such action is a sign of hypocrisy. This is no more necessarily true of the action of governments than of the action of individuals. . . . It is neither wise nor right for a nation to disregard its own needs, and it is foolish—and may be wicked—to think that other nations will disregard theirs. But it is wicked for a nation only to regard its own interest, and foolish to believe that such is the sole motive that actuates any other nation. It should be our steady aim to raise the ethical standard of national action just as we strive to raise the ethical standard of individual action.[4]

However, as far as Roosevelt was concerned, the inescapable fact that mankind was divided into national groups placed the burden of raising international ethics squarely upon the strong, independent shoulders of each nation. He considered the ultimate absorption of national distinctions by a common brotherhood of mankind as a possibility too remote to have practical consequences; but even if some sort of Parliament of Man were desirable—and Roosevelt never admitted it—that goal could be realized only through the slow accretion of mutual respect and trust among proud, virile nations, which at all times practiced square dealing with their neighbors but which remained eternally ready to strike the necessary blow for their own interests or the obvious interest of humanity.

Roosevelt was convinced that as long as nations existed, the loftiest ideals would be ineffective unless backed by national force. In his opinion nothing was more futile or dangerous than seeking the extension of international morality through national emasculation. But he was afraid that this was just what some "peace demagogues" were preaching. By inhibiting the nation's essential independence and depriving it of military power they would destroy the only practical instruments of benevolence for the sake of a fatuous sentimentality and an irresponsible idealism.

Actually, Roosevelt was in theory closer to the idealists than many of his followers—Henry Cabot Lodge, for example—in that he subscribed to a major tenet of idealism: that the same moral law applies to nations as to individuals. However, he noted that there was no judicial way of enforcing observance of the moral law in international relations and concluded that, although nations should work toward substitutes for war, they were obliged, at the same time, to hold force in readiness to protect their own interests and, in exceptional cases, to enforce the moral law which, in a more advanced stage of human relations, might fall under international jurisdiction.[5] Roosevelt was particularly concerned that the instruments of international enforcement should not extend their jurisdiction to the things that nations were most likely to fight over, comprised in the familiar phrase "honor, territorial integrity, and vital interests." He believed that, until one nation could trust other nations not to encroach upon these basic prerogatives, neither national interest nor the cause of peace would be advanced by pretending that the judgment of some international body could settle disputes over such matters impartially or effectively.

In truth, Roosevelt regarded international society as being in about the same stage of development as the frontier gun-toting community of Dakota cattle-owners, which he admired so extravagantly. Cowpunchers might join together in a rough association for limited and practical purposes, but their best assurance of peace and order remained the readiness of each man to draw his gun and his knowledge that every little quarrel might end fatally. The

fact that international morality was largely at the mercy of national interpretation and national enforcement only magnified each nation's obligation to
conduct itself honorably and see that others did likewise. The standards of
honorable conduct, which the cowpuncher-nations were obliged to uphold,
were summed up in one of Roosevelt's favorite words, "righteousness."

Righteousness decreed that nations should be scrupulously fair in their
dealings with one another but should be quick to reach for their guns if
their own honor or rights were not similarly respected. It is important to
understand that righteousness was not altruism, not a gentle virtue of humility or self-abnegation. It was a fighting word. By imposing positive duties of
gentlemanly conduct, this knightly code sanctioned and even demanded the
bold assertion of national power and prestige, upon suitable provocation.
Righteousness embodied the Christian ethics, but it implied an enlargement
rather than a restriction upon national action. It stressed the duty to enforce
observance of moral standards upon others rather than the obligation to deny
transgression to one's own nation. This was what Mahan meant when he
compared a nation's obligation to repress evil external to its borders to the
responsibility of the rich for the slums.[6] Such an obligation might require a
police action, but it was utterly inconsistent with a reduction of the strength
or sovereignty of the police force. This ethically dubious conception of unilateral police action gained some of the moral prestige of a universal principle
by virtue of the assumption that it was essential to the maintenance of a
system of honor and rights for all nations, upon which international order
and the progress of civilization absolutely depended.

It was this fusion of egoism and idealism, symbolized in "righteousness,"
that constituted the ideological underpinning for the Rooseveltian conception
of just war. Righteousness was Roosevelt's constant rebuttal to the peace
advocates in the years of America's rehearsal for the momentous denial of
peace which remained but an hypothesis up to the very eve of Sarajevo.
"More and more war is coming to be looked upon as in itself a lamentable
and evil thing," Roosevelt observed in his annual message in 1905. He said he
agreed that war was a bad thing, but he added,

We can, however, do nothing of permanent value for peace unless we keep ever clearly
in mind the ethical element which lies at the root of the problem. Our aim is righteousness. Peace is normally the handmaiden of righteousness; but when peace and righteousness conflict then a great and upright people can never for a moment hesitate to follow
the path which leads toward righteousness, even though that path also leads to war.[7]

3. UTOPIAN IDEALISM

Twelve years later many of the strongest peace advocates adopted this
principle as a call to battle, but their conception of righteousness was not

Roosevelt's. Roosevelt's righteousness bore too great a resemblance to its imperialist ancestry, and Americans were no longer in the heroic mood. Just as Roosevelt's appeals to national security were suspect, so were his appeals to idealism. After all, he and the other leading imperialists had glorified the ruthless competition among nations as a boon to civilization and had even acclaimed war itself as a benevolent institution, or, at least, an inevitable one. The decline of the market for imperialist wares was swift and sure. The belligerent connotation of righteousness gave no assurance that its sponsors had changed more than the label on their product.

In the decade after the Spanish-American War the incomparable humorist Mr. Dooley, as well as moral critics like Bryan and David Starr Jordan, greatly deflated the romanticism of that particular war and wars in general. Anti-imperialists, with an assist from the Democratic party, succeeded in fastening the stigma of autocracy, economic self-seeking, and moral turpitude upon the familiar imperialist phrases. These strictures, which before the war were confined chiefly to the protestations of a small group of radicals and reformers, became after the war the common currency of a rising middle-class peace sentiment. But what gave them popular standing was not, primarily, the appeal of anti-imperialism; it was not so much disillusionment with crusading—the war had been too painless for that—as optimism over the prospects of peace.

In America the beginning of the twentieth century was marked by an amorphous but widespread feeling that a different order of society was arising. The popular slogans Square Deal, New Nationalism, and New Freedom were all expressions of a pervasive belief that the deliberate application of good will and reason to human affairs was steadily tempering the struggle for existence with the spirit of co-operation and healing animosities with the spirit of tolerance. Frederick Lynch, who was to become Secretary of the Church Peace Union, founded in 1914 with two million dollars from Andrew Carnegie, observed in 1912, "It looks as though this were going to be the age of treaties rather than the age of wars, the century of reason rather than the century of force. And every treaty is a golden band uniting the nations into one."[8]

Some peace enthusiasts even foresaw the withering away of nations. David Starr Jordan, the eminent head of Leland Stanford University, sounded this note early in his *Imperial Democracy* (1899):

The day of nations is passing. National ambitions, national hopes, national aggrandizement—all these become public nuisances. Imperialism, like feudalism, belongs to the past. The men of the world as men, not as nations, are drawing closer and closer together. The needs of commerce are stronger than the will of nations, and the final guarantee of peace and good will among men will be not "the parliament of nations," but the self-control of men.[9]

No wonder Jordan was the favorite butt of nationalists and ex-imperialists.

The spirit of reform was in the air, and there was a general assumption that in foreign as well as domestic affairs the increasingly effective voice of the people was rapidly overcoming selfishness and raising the ethical level of political action, so that force and violence would soon be things of the past. War is immoral, the people are moral; therefore, give the people more power, and war will vanish. War is wicked, it must be caused by wicked men; therefore, convert the misguided, and peace will reign. It was prescriptions as simple as these that struck common sense as the cure for man's oldest affliction.

These sanguine expectations reflected a tendency to treat war as a moral aberration and peace as a problem for conversion—a natural enough reaction, perhaps, to the religious zeal with which imperialists had glorified war. This attitude found its inspiration in the Christian principle of the supreme power of love. Previously, its most vocal champions had been visionaries and evangelical pacifists, but in the second decade of the twentieth century there seemed to be a real basis in fact for pacifist affirmations, which all could perceive. The very popularity of the peace movement so soon after an equally popular war attested to the power of conversion. The tremendous progress in international as well as domestic reform confirmed the perfectibility of mankind. The whole trend of the postwar period suggested that ideals, by virtue of their rightness, could conquer the world, independently of might.

Thus William Jennings Bryan, although a more thorough-going pacifist than most peace advocates, spoke the mind of the great majority of his countrymen when, in his London speech on the Fourth of July, 1906, he proclaimed the efficacy of moral example as opposed to violence. "Example may be likened to the sun, whose genial rays constantly coax the buried seed into life, and clothe the earth, first with verdure, and afterward with ripened grain; while violence is the occasional tempest, which can ruin, but cannot give life." Could anyone, he asked, doubt the efficacy of example when on every hand lay the evidence that the Christian nations were gradually reforming the world? It was clear to Bryan that the world was on the threshold of a great intellectual and moral awakening, which would supplant the period of aggrandizement with an era in which nations would consider justice more important than physical prowess.[10]

Similar statements were reiterated in more conservative quarters. Charles W. Eliot, the President of Harvard University and one of the earliest advocates of an international police force, in a speech before the Lake Mohonk

Conference on International Arbitration in 1907, stressed, not the application of force through international instruments, but the steady improvement of the "moral climate" in order to bring about a state of public opinion that would render force unnecessary; and he expressed his belief that this goal was not far away, since everywhere good will and the widening of human sympathies were being fostered by the decline in prescriptive force and the increase in comparative teaching in the colleges and universities.[11]

Andrew Carnegie, delivering his rectorial address before St. Andrew's University in Scotland, October 17, 1905, saw the assurance of world peace in the gradual extension of international law. But his conception of the reign of law did not envision enforcement. Far from it. "International Law is unique in one respect. It has no material force behind it. It is a proof of the supreme force of gentleness—the irresistible pressure and final triumph of what is just and merciful."[12]

It is important to notice that the cosmopolitan implications of such expansive thoughts lost none of their appeal by virtue of their association with national pride and conceit; for it was argued that, since America most completely exemplified the new rationality and the new morality, America was surely the chosen instrument of world enlightenment. Thus in *America's Conquest of Europe* (1913) D. S. Jordan, presenting the familiar thesis that the movement toward peace was but part of a greater movement towards democracy, observed that moral standards ranked much higher in America than in any other land because the people had a stronger voice. In America, the people had concluded that all war was wrong—"brutal, wasteful, wild, irrational"—therefore, he reasoned, America must be the instrument for converting the less enlightened peoples of the world.

> The only permanent conquest is that of ideas. America stands, has always stood, for two ideals from which she cannot escape, for they are fundamental in her origin and in her growth. These are internationalism and democracy, and these ideals, being invincible, must conquer America and, through her, conquer Europe. . . . The conquest of the world by the ideals of internationalism and democracy marks the coming of universal peace.[13]

The juxtaposition of conquest with peace, which appears throughout Jordan's book, was a significant feature of the whole peace movement. It suggests William James's theory of the moral equivalent of war, which he expounded in 1910. There is in this idealized notion of national conquest an obvious fusion of aggressive and egoistic impulses with an extravagant moral enthusiasm. It might be said that peace advocates reconciled their belief in American destiny with their antagonism toward imperialism by sublimating the will-to-power and placing their faith in an imperialism of ideas. But however you interpret this militant pacifism, one thing is sure: it was the stuff of which crusades are made.

4. INTERNATIONALISM VERSUS NATIONALISM

In the placid atmosphere of the postwar years the votaries of peace lacked an issue which called for a full-scale crusade, just as the ultranationalists and the ex-imperialists lacked a cause around which they could rally popular enthusiasm again. However, one such issue was foreshadowed in the emerging conflict between nationalism and internationalism.

The two international peace conferences at the Hague, in 1899 and 1907, the increasing number of treaties embodying judicial and other procedures for the peaceful settlement of international disputes, the world-wide disarmament movement, and the growing interest in international organization all testified that pacifist visions were entering the realm of practical politics. Roosevelt himself promoted one of the most advanced programs of internationalism when, in his address at Christiana, Norway, in May, 1910, accepting the Nobel Peace Prize, he advocated a league to enforce peace, as well as arbitration treaties, extension of the Hague Tribunal, and international agreements to check the growth of armaments.[14] In subsequent years, when the controversy between nationalism and internationalism had grown sharper, Roosevelt was reminded of this address and charged with inconsistency in his current opposition to similar programs. But it is important to realize that he delivered his address before interest in the instruments for the peaceful settlement of international disputes was transmuted into a controversy over basic conceptions of international relations and long before that controversy was polarized by the great debate over a specific instrument, the League of Nations. Moreover, Roosevelt was careful to exclude questions of territorial integrity, sovereignty, and honor from international jurisdiction; and he seized the opportunity to distinguish himself from the bulk of the peace movement by repeating his preference for righteousness over peace, saying that peace "becomes a very evil thing if it serves merely as a mask for cowardice and sloth, or as an instrument to further the ends of despotism or anarchy."[15]

The critics of Roosevelt's later opposition to the league idea largely failed to understand that, although his attachment to the cause of international organization sprang, in part, from ideal motives, it was also rooted in a conception of America's long-run self-interest. Like Hay's scheme for stabilizing world politics through a system of combinations and trusts, Roosevelt's league to enforce peace was founded upon the assumption that the maintenance of America's new position in the world depended upon the preservation of a nucleus of Anglo-American power. In such a rabid expansionist's sudden embrace of internationalism there is a suggestion of satiated imperialism. It is clear that Roosevelt's idea of a league with teeth in it was directed toward regularizing and not supplanting the balance of power and the diplomatic processes of power politics. Clearly, his early advocacy of a league to enforce peace, as well as his later opposition, conflicted fundamentally with the internationalism of the peace movement.

A clearer indication of the nature of the emerging conflict between nationalism and internationalism can be found in the controversy surrounding the Taft-Knox arbitration treaties.[16] In August, 1911, the Taft administration signed identical arbitration treaties with Great Britain and France, providing for arbitration of all "justiciable" questions, not excepting "vital interests" or "national honor," the question of justiciability of any particular case to be decided by a joint high commission of inquiry. Although public opinion strongly supported the treaties, Roosevelt, Mahan, and Senator Lodge spearheaded an assault upon these darlings of the peace movement and were largely responsible for their passage in the Senate in such a mutilated form that Taft refused to go through with the ratification. The treatment these treaties received in the Senate can be partially explained by the influence of partisanship, jealousy of Senatorial prerogative, and the desire of Southern and Pacific Coast Senators to exempt Southern bond claims and restrictions on Oriental immigration from arbitration; but it was on more general grounds that Lodge, Roosevelt, and Mahan appealed to the country at large, grounds which revealed a fundamental cleavage between their conception and the peace movement's conception of international relations.

The burden of the nationalist argument was that the arbitration treaties, by including national honor and vital interests and allowing an international commission to determine justiciability, presumed to settle conflicts at the very heart of national existence by mere moral suasion rather than by the only reliable arbiter, the balance of power. They charged that any such agreements, no matter how popular they might be emotionally and in the abstract, would not be lived up to when a decision either contravened America's self-interest or required enforcement; and that, therefore, these impracticable instruments of hypocrisy and wishy-washy sentimentality were vastly more dangerous to both the national welfare and the cause of peace than no treaty at all, since they raised false hopes among the public and led to needless disputation and broken agreements among nations. The nationalists never failed to spice this basic reasoning with an assortment of jibes at "mushy philanthropists," "visionaries," and "mollycoddles"—all expressions of their conviction that the real source of these pacifist misconceptions was a deficiency of red blood.

Roosevelt jumped to the attack before the treaties were even negotiated. In May, 1911, as associate editor of the *Outlook*, he wrote an editorial explaining his opposition on the grounds of impracticability, charging that the nation would repudiate a decision the moment it became necessary to enforce it. He argued that the treaties would be safe only between nations which would not resort to measures harmful to each others' honor, independence, and integrity. But the only nation which he would trust that far was Great Britain. Otherwise, international society was predatory, and the United States had better look to its guns.[17] This view echoed Mahan's opinion that arbitration was dangerous and unworkable between the "have" nations—Great Britain, France, and the United States—and the "have not" nations—Japan, Germany, and Russia.*

In a letter to Arthur Lee, in August, Roosevelt put a somewhat different slant on the argument. Neutral arbitration courts, he explained, follow technical legality and are prone to compromise claims instead of deciding on the basis of "real justice and right." He pointed out that if the United States had lived up to such a treaty it could not have gone to war with Spain nor started building the Panama Canal.[18]

President Taft, for his part, confirmed all the nationalists' fears that he had been captured by the visionaries. Foreshadowing Wilson's course, he set out on a western tour to plead his case before the people, and in a series of public addresses he placed himself in the vanguard of the peace movement. Taft replied to his critics that arbitration treaties which excluded matters of national honor and vital interest failed to serve their purpose of preventing war, since these were the very things that might lead to war. But, not content with this logic, he asserted that he did not believe in the efficacy of war to avenge national honor. He even said that he thought that the war with Spain could have been settled without a fight, and he charged the opposition with a covert love of war and violence.

In the end, Taft lost his fight and refused to ratify the treaties, since they had been amended beyond recognition. But the nationalists, while they had won a battle, had not won the war for the public mind. They were, in fact, very much on the defensive. An all-out battle on the field of internationalism had been deferred for the moment, but internationalism was only a phase of an overall struggle which might erupt in a dozen different sectors. And nationalists of the Rooseveltian variety sensed the mounting threat to their positions, implicit in the formation of a new alignment of public opinion, of which the peace movement was only one manifestation.

* William D. Puleston, *Mahan* (New Haven, 1939), pp. 280–81. This distinction between satiated and unsatiated powers was common among Realists after the Spanish-American War, although it did not come into general use in the United States until the 1930's.

5. REALISM ON THE DEFENSIVE

One of the manifestations of this new alignment which particularly exasperated the nationalists was America's growing indifference toward its political relations with the outside world. The utopian assumptions of the peace movement were but one aspect of the general glow of well-being and security which suffused America as World War I approached. In this tranquil atmosphere, with the postwar surge of nationalism greatly mollified by the progress of the peace movement, Americans had no desire to play an heroic role in the sordid drama of world politics, and they had little interest in observing the antics of others.

It is true that the growing interest in internationalism somewhat mitigated America's traditional provincialism. Never before had the colleges, women's clubs, churches, and journals paid so much attention to events abroad. Never before had Americans shared so many scientific, cultural, and professional contacts with peoples beyond the sea. But these expanding cultural and intellectual horizons were not accompanied by a corresponding alteration in America's political myopia. The day was not far off when circumstances would recruit this new internationalism in the service of a bold attack upon America's political isolation. But that day was scarcely within the scope of popular imagination as the first decade of the twentieth century passed.

Even the students of international relations were less interested in searching world politics and charting the flux of power among nations than in elaborating international law and devising procedures and organizations for the peaceful settlement of international disputes.[19] The exceptions merely emphasize the rule.

Mahan was one such exception. He had achieved fame at a time when the ethical validity of power politics was less questionable, when popular opinion countenanced a vigorous assertion of American power. Writing in 1910, he had softened the aggressiveness of his national egoism and muted the Darwinian overtones of his philosophy of international politics. But he was still hammering away at his campaign to educate the American people to take a realistic view of their national interest.

Mahan published *The Interest of America in International Conditions* (1910) in the hope that it would excite, in the words of his biographer Puleston, "at least a beginning of public interest."[20] This modest hope reflected the book's premise that Americans were still basically provincial in that they lacked a reasoned apprehension and knowledge of the effect of international politics upon their national interest. The central message Mahan wished to convey was the folly, as Washington had said in his Farewell Address, of expecting nations to act consistently from any motive other than self-interest. In Mahan's view sentiment was powerful but fickle. So once more he expounded his lesson of Realism.

It follows from this, directly, that the study of interests, international interests, is the one basis of sound and provident policy for statesmen . . . but for a nation to exert its full weight in the world such knowledge and appreciation must be widespread among its plain people also. So only can the short vision common to most men expand to the prevision of national needs and the timely provision of the necessary means for national self-assertion.[21]

The main body of *The Interest of America in International Conditions* was an analysis of the distribution of world power as it affected America's strategic needs, taking into account not only relative military strength but political, geographical, economic, and psychological factors as well. Mahan's conclusions were not new: America's interest coincided with Great Britain's interest in preserving a balance of power against Germany and Japan. However, Mahan's views on world strategy continued to attract more attention in England than in the United States. His latest effort to educate his countrymen did nothing to elevate his reputation beyond that of a naval strategist among navalists. As a publicist his exhortations struck deaf ears. Mahan was oppressed by the refusal of Congress to expand the Navy according to the General Board's recommendations. In a state of thorough alarm over the threat of an aggressive Germany and Japan, he made his last trip to Europe in 1912 in the hope of gaining some personal tranquility, but there he found only premonitions of a world war. Puleston has written that at this time and, particularly with a Democratic victory approaching, Mahan fully realized that his countrymen were little interested in him or his themes.[22] Theodore Roosevelt, commemorating Mahan's death in the *Outlook* in January, 1915, admitted that the height of Mahan's influence and popularity was reached with his *Life of Nelson,* published in 1897.[23]

David Lewis Einstein—historian, lecturer, and a diplomat with experience in Paris, London, Constantinople, Peking, and Costa Rica—was another student of world affairs who stood out as an exception to the general tendency to ignore the elements of power in international relations. Because of his connection with the diplomatic service, he chose not to acknowledge his authorship of *American Foreign Policy,* which appeared in 1909, signed "By a Diplomatist." Although Einstein started from the imperialist premise of the need for foreign markets, a navy to protect them, and an efficient diplomacy as an adjunct to the navy, his emphasis lay upon an objective analysis of the currents of national interest as they impinged upon America's security. Although he reached the imperialists' conclusion that the United States, because of its interest in the balance of power in Europe and Asia, required a close understanding with Great Britain, his concern, like Richard Olney's, was not with the expansion of American commitments but with the practical requirements of a foreign policy that would conform to the magnitude of the commitments already acquired. Like Mahan, Einstein soft-pedaled the aggressive aspects of national self-interest. His reasoning did not vibrate with overtones of the Darwinian struggle nor resound with the echoes of an imperialist destiny beyond the control of mere mortals. He was content to make the common-sense point that a nation's diplomatic as well as its military resources should be adapted to its commitments, and that, therefore, if the United States intended to keep its present status in the world, it would have to modify its policy of isolation, in order to protect its vital interests.

American Foreign Policy, in common with the writings of Olney, Mahan, and, later, Walter Lippmann, attributed the shortsightedness and immaturity of America's foreign policy to the public's unrealistic attitude toward international politics; and it found the cause of this failing in the fact that, during America's long period of internal development—from 1812 to the war with Spain—relatively free from international strife, the nation had forgotten the bases of its security, with which it had been so actively concerned in the perilous early years of diplomacy. Americans had achieved world power too easily, Einstein thought; as a result, they lacked a corresponding intellectual preparation. It seemed to him that they had been lulled by the precarious luxury of innocence: "We have not experienced the discipline of adversity which has schooled other great states."[24]

Four years later the discipline of adversity was even more remote from American experience, and Einstein's message had exerted as little influence upon his countrymen as Mahan's. In January, 1913, he published an article in the British periodical, *The National Review,* under the pesudonym "Washington," analyzing the effect of Anglo-German rivalry upon American security.[25] He reached the conclusion that a protracted war between Germany and Great Britain would seriously embarrass American neutrality and that a German victory would warrant America's active intervention. But Americans were far from anticipating such dire contingencies, and Einstein recognized this fact. Like Mahan's *The Interest of America in International Conditions,* his article began with the pessimistic premise that, although America had altered its political, strategical, and economic situation so as to make its former isolation untenable, the country as a whole remained unaware that its interests were in any way affected by European problems.

If there was no American audience for even the most moderate counsels of Realism, at least one exposition of power politics enjoyed by virtue of its excesses the momentary attention of outrage. This was *The Valor of Ignorance,* published by Harper's in 1909 and written by the strangest of American prophets, "General" Homer Lea, military adventurer and one-time adjutant to Sun Yat-Sen.[26] This brilliant hunchback with a Napoleonic complex was bolder and more prescient than the Adamses in "following the track of energy" and more savage than Mahan in his indictment of pacifism and isolationism.

Lea's work started with this uncompromising militarist premise: "As physical vigor represents the strength of man in his struggle for existence, in the same sense military vigor constitutes the strength of nations: ideals, laws and constiutions are but temporary effulgences, and are existent only so long as this strength seems vital."[27] However, it was not this premise that makes Lea's book unique but the specific deductions which followed. In amazing detail he described a Japanese attack upon Manila, Hawaii, and the California coast, which thirty-two years later proved frighteningly accurate.

The Valor of Ignorance became a "best seller" in Japan. It attracted a great deal of attention among Japanese, English, German, Italian, and Russian military circles and was made required reading in the military schools of Japan, Germany, and Russia. Its publication in the United States caused a momentary flurry of indignation among peace groups. D. S. Jordan, who had had Lea as a student at Stanford, thought that the book was important enough to pillory several times in print. Hearst exploited its anti-Japanese potentialities for a while. Yet this work was obviously even less congenial to the American mind than Mahan's writings, and it was even more quickly forgotten, although it found a place on the optional list at West Point.

Homer Lea was not daunted. With equal diligence he set to work studying the European power situation, being greatly aided by invitations from the Kaiser and England's Field Marshal Lord Roberts. Several years later he wrote the equally prescient *The Day of the Saxon,* published in 1912 as he lay dying in his California cottage. In this book Lea described the approaching war of Great Britain and the United States against Germany and set forth some of the material which he intended to include in a third book describing a final war between Russia and the West. *The Valor of Ignorance* sold about 18,000 copies in its English edition, but *The Day of the Saxon* sold only 7000. Homer Lea's first work was resurrected after Pearl Harbor fulfilled his predictions. His last work remains virtually unknown.

Homer Lea was an echo from the turn of the century. By the time his first book appeared, most of the imperialists were silent or else they had softened the militant edges of their nationalism. In fact, after Roosevelt's administration Realism went on the defensive. Even Mahan found it necessary to justify national power on ethical grounds almost to the exclusion of self-interest, just as Roosevelt cloaked power in the garb of righteousness. This is illustrated by his controversy with Norman Angell, the English lecturer and author, whose book *The Great Illusion* (1910), which went through many editions and was translated into twenty languages, became a handbook for the peace movement throughout the world and enjoyed a great popularity in the United States.

Although Angell dealt with the specific context of the Anglo-German armaments race, the real significance of his book lay in its argument that wars are undertaken because nations expect commercial advantage; that such advantage is an illusion, since conquest is economically futile; and that, therefore, if potential antagonists will but recognize this fact, war will disappear from the earth.*

Mahan was moved to attack this view in the *North American Review* in March, 1912. Angell replied in the same magazine in June. Then Mahan published his article, with additional comments by way of a rejoinder to Angell's reply, as a chapter in his counteroffensive to the peace movement, *Armaments and Arbitration* (1912).[28] Now Mahan, a life-long exponent of Realism, denied Angell's assumption that the basis of international relations was a concern for material self-interest, and he protested that his hostility to the peace advocates was founded "rather on the basis of altruism than of interest." He did not dispute the contention that war was unprofitable, but he argued that the point was irrelevant, since nations went to war, not from the cold calculation of material self-interest, but because they differed in their sentiment and feeling of right and wrong. Speaking in terms of Rooseveltian righteousness, he asserted that Angell and his fellow pacifists were the truly self-interested ones, since out of a miserly respect for their pocketbooks and a timid regard for mere physical safety they preferred a state of peace to a state of justice.

Angell's popularity soared. Mahan's rejoinders were largely ignored. In the reassuring atmosphere of the second decade after the Spanish-American War even a subdued, defensive, and highly moralized exposition of the elements of national egoism and power in international relations seemed incongruous.

6. Taft: An Interim Figure

Theodore Roosevelt led his assault upon isolation by capturing the imagination of a people moved by a peculiar war-born combination of self-assertive egoism and altruism. But by the end of his administration it was clear that the popular basis of his foreign policy was dissolving and forming into new shapes and alignments of thought and sentiment. When America's moral and

---

* Angell's message was widely misunderstood as an argument that war was impossible. In his autobiography, *After All* (London, 1951), he dwells much on his continual and largely futile efforts to correct this misapprehension, which, be it noted, Mahan did not share.

intellectual energy were recruited again in a challenge to traditional isolationism, it was by a different kind of leader, Woodrow Wilson, leading in a different direction.

In the lull between Roosevelt and Wilson President Taft proved incapable
of leading in either direction. He showed no inclination to repeat his predecessor's dramatic performance when, in 1911, a second Moroccan crisis threatened to produce a general war. He went out of his way in both the Italo-
Turkish War and the Balkan War to announce that the United States had no
interest, direct or indirect, in these strictly European concerns.[29] His major
excursion into world politics was an ill-conceived insistence upon the right of
American capital interests to participate in a three-power consortium to build
the Hukuang railway in China and an even more inept attempt of his Secretary of State, Philander C. Knox, to interest various powers in a financial
scheme to wrest the Manchurian railways from Russian and Japanese control and, ultimately, place Manchuria under an international economic protectorate. In both ventures his administration displayed a vast ignorance of
the *Realpolitik* of the Far East.[30]

Because of its naïve bungling in the Far East and even more because of its
announced policy of inducing American bankers to assume the debts of shaky
Latin American governments, a policy which led to the dispatch of marines to
revolution-ridden Nicaragua in order to secure the payment of an American
loan and protect American interests, the Taft administration was remembered
not for its sincerely idealistic interest in international peace but for its inept
indulgence in Dollar Diplomacy. The principal motive of Dollar Diplomacy
was certainly not to enrich American financiers or even the United States but,
as Knox and Taft declared with respect to Latin America, to reduce the dangers of foreign intervention in a strategic area by stabilizing the political situation. But Americans largely ignored this aspect; instead they turned their
moral indignation upon a policy which bore the sinister mark of imperialism
and power politics.[31]

7. Beginnings of Wilsonian Idealism

Taft succeeded in alienating both nationalists and internationalists, egoists
and idealists. But he did help set the stage for the dramatic entrance of his
successor. Woodrow Wilson lost no time ingratiating himself with the anti-
imperialists and the peace advocates; the nationalists were equally quick
to spot a major antagonist. Although the election of 1912 did not turn on
foreign policy, and although Wilson expected his major contribution to be in
the field of domestic reform, the new Chief Executive entered office with

definite ideas about international politics, in general, and American foreign policy, in particular. Harley Notter has neatly summarized them:

> He entered office with an intention to produce a radical reform of foreign policy which would give America world leadership in standards and policy, lift her diplomacy to the best levels for mankind, cause her to act for the progress of mankind, and advance American ideals rather than the contracts of a narrow circle of financiers. . . . He of course regarded morality as a guide in foreign policy and thought that moral duties between nations were the same as those within a nation, that the United States used moral standards in its judgments, and that all nations were coming to be judged by morality.[32]

Wilson's early acts and pronouncements made it clear that he intended to apply the same moral principles to foreign relations as to the field of industrial and social legislation. The New Freedom was to have its counterpart in the New Diplomacy. On March 5, 1914, he delighted liberals and outraged Rooseveltian nationalists with a novel exhibition of self-denying morality when he dramatically appeared before Congress to ask on grounds of national honor for the repeal of a provision in the Panama Canal Act of August, 1912, which exempted American coastwise shipping from the payment of tolls, contrary to the clear intent of the Hay-Pauncefote Treaty.[33]

Then on March 11, 1913, the President used the unorthodox procedure of a communication to the press in order to proclaim the end of Dollar Diplomacy, saying, "We can have no sympathy with those who seek to seize the power of government to advance their own personal interests or ambition." And a week later he rebuked the vested interests by announcing, through the press again, that American investors in foreign fields could expect no more support from their government,[34] thereby affirming a favorite anti-imperialist thesis, which had grown popular in the Progressive Era: The people are moral; so if they are led into war and imperialism, it is because of the baleful influence of selfish interests.

Next, turning his attention toward America's neighbors to the south, Wilson delivered at Mobile, Alabama, in October, 1913, the most radical exposition of altruism that had ever emanated from a President of the United States. It was no mere rhetoric but the product of a considered philosophy. Predicting that a bond of understanding would tie the United States and the Latin American republics closer together than ever before, he went on to generalize about international relations: "Interest does not tie nations together; it sometimes separates them. But sympathy and understanding does unite them."

> We must prove ourselves their friends and champions upon terms of equality and honor. . . . We must show ourselves friends by comprehending their interest whether it squares with our own interest or not. It is a very perilous thing to determine the foreign policy of a nation in the terms of material interest.
> . . . Human rights, national integrity, and opportunity as against material interests—

that, ladies and gentlemen, is the issue which we now have to face. I want to take this occasion to say that the United States will never again seek one additional foot of territory by conquest.[35]

But if these signs were not enough to arouse egoists and Realists, there was Wilson's appointment of the arch anti-imperialist, ardent pacifist, and Chautauqua lecturer William Jennings Bryan as Secretary of State. After the death of John Hay, Lodge had written Roosevelt about the qualities of a successor: "He must know Europe and understand world politics, the relations of nations and the balance of equilibrium of the powers."[36] Root had measured up to this standard; Knox had fallen sadly short; but Bryan seemed its very antithesis. He soon confirmed the nationalists' contempt and alarm when he negotiated and slipped through the Senate thirty of his beloved "cooling-off" conciliation pacts, providing for the submission of all otherwise insoluble disputes, not excepting questions of national honor, to permanent commissions of investigation, which would make their recommendations only after a year-long period, during which the resort to arms was forbidden. The assumption was that by that time national tempers would have cooled and an omnipotent world opinion would have marshaled reason and morality behind a peaceful solution. Roosevelt never tired of denouncing these pacts as exhibit "A" among the futile attempts of irresponsible idealism and effeminate sentimentality to allay the ineluctable strife of nations.

It may be an indication of the strength of the logic of geography and strategic interest that this moral-minded administration, largely out of solicitude for the security of the Panama Canal, found it necessary to carry out more armed interventions in Latin America than any of its predecessors, to impose upon Haiti and the Dominican Republic prolonged military occupations without treaty sanction and against the protests of the native governments, and almost, but for the Senate's refusal, to convert Nicaragua into a protectorate. Yet it is a suggestion of the power of ideals that Wilson, because of his obviously benevolent intentions and because of his skill in squaring unpleasant facts with tender consciences, remained, through it all, a champion of constitutional government and the friend of backward peoples. And even Latin American people, in general, trusted his professions of good will far more than they had trusted similar protestations of the Roosevelt and Taft administrations.[37]

8. IDEALISM DIVORCED FROM REALISM

Before war seized Europe and galvanized American opinion into new alignments it was clear that the forces of idealism were regrouping and taking direction once more under a leader who could formulate the amorphous thoughts of inarticulate millions and release their hidden springs of moral energy. The reaction to the Spanish-American War had diverted America's crusading energy into new channels but had deprived it of none of its latent vitality. Wilsonian idealism was the moral equivalent of Rooseveltian nationalism.

Clearly, the American mission had found new and powerful sponsors within the peace movement. Yet it was difficult to see from what source there could arise the widespread realism which Mahan and Einstein believed essential to the efficiency of that mission. Realism shared the opprobrium of its self-assertive proponents, while the utopian assumptions of idealists seemed more credible than ever. Both Realists and idealists gratified basic temperamental predispositions by taking an overly simple view of the real conditions for reconciling ideals with national self-interest, convincing themselves that the troublesome contradictions and complexities that beset the pursuit of national ends were either nonexistent or easily surmountable. The Realists, in order to rationalize a self-assertive national egoism, exaggerated the force of aggressive national self-interest in international society and posited the existence of an inexorable struggle for power, which men were incapable of altering, while they interpreted ideals according to a romantic conception of moral duty that sanctioned a free exercise of national power but did little to encourage self-restraint. Idealists, on the other hand, distorted reality to fit their desires by exaggerating the efficacy of supranational ideals in national conduct and belittling the force of national egoism, in Americans as well as nations in general, while they viewed the fulfilment of universal ideals as a task involving no particular political responsibilities or distasteful expediencies but simply the conversion of the unenlightened by means of America's beneficent example. Thus idealism was actively propagated by those most ignorant of the role of national self-interest and power in world politics, while realism remained the province of those least inhibited by ethical restraints upon the assertion of the nation's power and self-interest.

The shifting distribution of world power might refute the complacent assumptions which underlay the American attitude toward international politics, but the national psychology seemed to be every bit as inexorable as the imperatives of power. Since the Spanish-American War there had been a number of voices challenging American isolation and provincialism but very few dispassionately admonishing a realistic heed for national security. Isolation had been assaulted by the strong nationalists, and provincialism had been attacked by devout internationalists; but neither egoistic nor idealistic entreaties had proved conducive to a calm appraisal of the exigencies of sheer survival. Another break with traditional isolation was conceivable. A fusion of nationalistic sentiment and altruistic fervor might again sweep the nation into the stream of world politics. But only a clear threat to the nation's self-preservation seemed likely to bring about any more enduring or substantial modification of its fundamental approach toward international relations than was produced by its haphazard entrance upon world power at the turn of the century.

PART II

SUMMARY

WORLD WAR I is a crucial period in the evolution of America's attitude toward international relations. It provides a highly significant context of events in which to examine the real conditions for reconciling national self-interest with universal ideals.

As we now know, but as few foresaw in 1914, the United States entered World War I on the side of British sea power and played a decisive part in preventing Germany from gaining control of Continental Europe. Twenty-five years later, when Germany had once more swept across the Lowlands and upset the balance of power, some American observers, anxious to support their arguments for intervention with the sanction of history, contended that the nation had joined forces with Great Britain during the previous world conflict because the people and their leaders had perceived America's enduring strategic interest in the preservation of the Atlantic System espoused by Henry Adams.

This contention has very important implications concerning America's outlook upon world politics. If it is a true explanation of American intervention in World War I, it suggests a sharp break with traditional conceptions of national self-interest. If, on the other hand, the explanation is an unwarranted projection of contemporary circumstances upon past history, then it involves a substantial misinterpretation of the whole significance of World War I in the course of America's adaptation to its international environment.

It is true that a number of American publicists, politicians, diplomats, and scholars during 1914–17 believed that a German victory would directly endanger the nation's security. If a German victory had at any time before April, 1917, seemed imminent, their apprehensions might possibly have seized the general public and become a major factor in American intervention; but, actually, this circumstance never developed; and the nation as a whole, even including some of the most prominent Realists, supported America's intervention for reasons quite different from national self-preservation. Because of the inertia of traditional attitudes toward world politics, because of the character of American leadership, and, above all, because of the circumstances of the war itself Americans, as a whole, entered the war without a clear and reasoned perception of any enduring self-interest, such as their national sur-

vival. Instead, they drifted into war, largely oblivious of the practical consequences of momentary impulses, out of an aroused sense of national honor,
combined with a missionary zeal to achieve world peace and democracy.

The practical demands of national self-interest were further obscured by the
exacerbation of an underlying temperamental and ideological conflict, personified in the antipathy of Theodore Roosevelt toward Woodrow Wilson,
between those most conscious of the imperatives of power and those most
anxious to subordinate national egoism to universal moral values. This conflict was suspended momentarily in the common embrace of a new crusade,
but, as in 1898, it flared up with increasing heat as the issues of war aims and
the peace settlement arose. Largely because the circumstances of the war failed
to provide the incentive for subjecting either militant or pacific sentiments to
the test of expediency, the deep-rooted struggle for public opinion between
the Rooseveltians and the Wilsonians, instead of bringing about a fusion of
realism with idealism, actually exacerbated their dissociation.

As it was, neither the egoistic nor the idealistic motives which led the
United States to intervene in the European contest were sufficiently rooted in
a consciousness of compelling self-interest to sustain beyond victory the break
with the nation's pacific ideals and its traditional sense of self-interest in isolation. This fact was concealed during the period of American intervention by
the nation's preoccupation with the overriding object of victory and by President Wilson's success in reconciling even the tenderest consciences to warfare
through the identification of intervention with America's altruistic mission.
However, when victory was achieved, altruism collapsed, and the nation
reverted to its normal isolationist behavior in the society of nations. Those
with the greatest inhibitions toward intervention became impatient with
the frustration of their proportionately lofty expectations; the most militant
interventionists became apprehensive lest idealism get out of hand and ham-
string the nation's power of independent action; and with the immediate
object of winning the war removed, the nation as a whole relaxed its moral
muscles and began comparing the human and material sacrifices of war with
its meager rewards, both tangible and spiritual.

President Wilson appealed for peace, as he had appealed for war, in terms
of the fulfilment of America's service to the rest of the world. But he greatly
overestimated his countrymen's capacity for sustained altruism. The debate
over the League of Nations did not prove that Americans, as a whole, were
opposed to assuming greater international obligations, but it did suggest that
they were not prepared to fulfil such obligations. Consistent with the debate
over intervention, the League controversy was conspicuous for the absence of
considerations of broad self-interest and the practical consequences of inter-

national commitments. Again an underlying struggle between a self-assertive national egoism and a self-denying idealism, encouraged by the moralistic nature of Wilson's leadership, helped obscure a common ground of enlightened self-interest, upon which all factions might reasonably have compromised.

Because the warm sentiments and ideals that sustained a temporary break with traditional isolation were not joined with a cold calculation of national self-interest of more enduring significance than victory for the sake of victory, the nation committed itself to great hopes and noble resolves, which, if they could have been achieved at all, could have been achieved only through sacrifices of national sovereignty and political isolation for which there was no compelling incentive after the war was won. In the long run, Americans, like all peoples, were unwilling to assume international commitments that seemed unrelated to their fundamental self-interest. In the American outlook, political isolation stood for national comfort, ease, and security. Only a broader conception of self-interest could have prevented a reversion to America's traditional habits of conduct.

However, from the nature of the evolution of America's attitude toward foreign relations since the turn of the century, it seems likely that a broader conception of national self-interest, rooted in a sense of political realism, could have arisen only if the pressure of world politics had leavened impulsive idealism and national egoism with the instinct for survival. Because the nation's experience in World War I failed to alter the people's confidence in America's isolated security, the trials of war and the complexities of peace brought disillusionment instead of realism.

CHAPTER VI

FEARS OF A GERMAN VICTORY

1. America's Initial Complacency

THERE was nothing in America's first reaction to the outbreak of war in Europe to indicate that the United States would come to the aid of British sea power and French land power in resisting German domination of the Continent.

Americans were not particularly surprised at the assassination of an obscure archduke in a place called Sarajevo on June 28, 1914. For months their newspapers had been laden with accounts of European intrigue, rivalry, armament races, rumors of war, and similar manifestations of Old World decadence. And Americans certainly were not worried. As the archduke's assassination mushroomed into a mass murder, with one nation after another mobilizing its troops and declaring war, they heaved a universal sigh of relief over the three thousand miles separating them from their ancestors' homes. Even the outspoken nationalists and the eager prophets of perpetual struggle were, at first, more solicitous of the nation's isolation than its virility. To be sure, they regarded President Wilson's appeal to the American people for impartiality as a fatuous counsel of perfection; but, in general, they were no more anxious than he to incur the risk of unneutral action. In this respect they were in accord with the great body of the American people, even though their sympathy for the Allies was more marked.[1]

Few informed Americans expected the European war to affect the United States in any vital way. Among the newspaper editors throughout the country polled by the *Literary Digest* in the middle of August, some foresaw new tensions arising in a nation of immigrants; others were absorbed in predicting the effect of the war on American commerce or the price of imported goods; but all bade their readers rejoice in their unique insulation from the waste and destruction abroad.[2] In the first months of war, Americans could regard the pitiful spectacle of Old World lunacy with amiable contempt. In August the *Boston Transcript,* which was to become one of the most vehement organs of intervention, quipped, "The worst has befallen in this cruel war. The price of beans has risen." In September a newsboy pedaled the late edition of another paper, crying, "Extra! Giants and Germans lose! Extra!"

Yet if the interests of the United States were really as inextricably involved

114

in the distribution of world power as the Realists had been proclaiming for the better part of a quarter of a century, Americans could not long afford the luxury of smugness. If America were not in fact isolated, then no display of good will or pacific intentions, no profession of neutrality nor pretension to exclusiveness, could shelter the nation from the raging storms of world politics.

On the other hand, in gauging America's reaction to the European struggle, one had to take into account the American mind as well as the great impersonal shifts of national power. In fact, the two considerations were inseparable, for, as the years following the Spanish-American War had demonstrated, the nation's response to its international environment might be largely determined by ideals and sentiments which had only an indirect relation to the imperatives of power but which could, nevertheless, shape her international conduct in ways that were the despair of power-conscious Realists.

2. LIPPMANN'S THESIS OF INTERVENTION

The fact that twice in the course of a quarter of a century the United States has entered a world war, contrary to its explicit intention of remaining aloof, and that both times it has entered on the side of British sea power against the aggressive Continental land power of Germany suggests that a disturbance in the balance of power in Europe excites an instinct of self-preservation in the American people that is stronger than the tradition of isolation. Because this interpretation, as applied to American intervention in World War I, played an important role in the debate between isolation and intervention preceding World War II, it has a double significance in the evolution of America's attitude toward international relations. However, in Part Two we are concerned with its historical truth rather than its historical role, for an analysis of the validity of this interpretation is admirably suited to illuminating the impact of World War I upon the American outlook.

Notable among the expounders of the thesis that America intervened in World War I in order to redress the balance of power for the sake of its own security is Walter Lippmann, certainly one of the most widely read and influential journalists in the period between the two world wars. His interpretation is peculiarly significant, for not only was he the chief popularizer of this thesis in the period preceding America's entrance into World War II; he was also one of the most consistent proponents of a Realistic view toward intervention during the period from 1914 until America entered World War I.

In 1941 Lippmann, in affirming the dependence of American security upon the British Navy's control of the Atlantic lines of communication, set forth in a feature article in *Life,* April 7, the view that America had intervened in

World War I "when, and only when, a victorious Germany was threatening to conquer Britain and become the master of the other shore of the Atlantic Ocean."[3] He drew this comparison between the two world wars: "The military and diplomatic advisers of President Wilson knew then and were moved then by the same essential estimate of America's vital interests as are Secretaries Hull, Stimson, and Knox, the advisers of President Roosevelt."[4]

Lippmann gave President Wilson credit for having decided upon intervention on the basis of a reasoned and statesmanlike judgment of what was vital to the defense of America, but he blamed him for having become so fascinated with his vision of world peace that he led the country to regard the war as a philanthropic crusade.

This view was more fully developed in the extremely popular little book *U.S. Foreign Policy,* which appeared in 1943, after the United States had once more become a full-scale belligerent. In this book Lippmann recapitulated the thesis that America had intervened in 1917 for reasons of security, but he added that "because this simple and self-evident American interest was not candidly made explicit, the nation never understood clearly why it had entered the war."[5] Modifying his thesis further, Lippmann conceded that the "occasion" for intervention had been Germany's resumption of unrestricted submarine warfare, but he held that the "substantial and compelling reason for going to war was that the cutting of the Atlantic communications meant the starvation of Britain and, therefore, the conquest of Western Europe by imperial Germany." Unfortunately, Wilson had avoided this explanation, "choosing to base his decision upon the specific legal objection to unrestricted submarine warfare and upon a generalized moral objection to lawless and cruel aggression." But these, Lippmann asserted, were "superficial reasons" and would not have brought the nation to war if "a majority of the people had not recognized intuitively, and if some Americans had not seen clearly, what the threatened German victory would mean to the United States." For it would have meant nothing less than an immense armament program and a perpetual state of military preparedness.[6]

In his *U.S. War Aims* (1944) Lippmann elaborated substantially the same thesis and neatly generalized it in the following rule: "The events leading to two wars with Germany demonstrate that the instinct of national self-preservation is aroused in this country by successful aggression against countries on the opposite shores of the oceans which surround us."[7]

Leaving aside the nuances of Lippmann's thesis, one might fairly paraphrase it in the following manner:

> The predominant American interest in the European war, the interest which the nation could least afford to forfeit, was its own self-defense, which depended upon the

securing of the Atlantic Community through the defeat of Germany. By April, 1917, certain conditions, particularly submarine warfare, confronted America with the alternative of either entering the war on the side of the Allies or else jeopardizing its predominant interest. The majority of the American people understood this alternative intuitively, and many perceived it clearly. Because of this understanding and perception the United States intervened.

This is a plausible explanation of American intervention. As we have seen in the preceding chapters, at the turn of the century and afterward, a number of leaders as well as observers of American foreign policy had concluded that America's fundamental strategic interest lay in the continued predominance of the British Navy athwart the vital lines of communication leading into the Atlantic and in the preservation of a European balance of power to prevent an aggressive Germany from gaining continental hegemony. And with this configuration of national interest in mind, many had warily speculated upon the threat to American security which might follow a relative decrease of British power or an increase of German power. True, this consideration had failed to impress itself upon the general public; but if, in the course of a world war, the hypothetical circumstances which such calculations anticipated were actually to materialize, then the clear threat to national self-preservation might yet induce a widespread awareness of basic strategic interests and generate a popular determination to protect them, even at the cost of intervention.

3. LIPPMANN AS A PUBLICIST

The plausibility of Lippmann's thesis is enhanced by the fact that its view of America's interest in a British victory was actually espoused by a good many Americans while the nation was in the throes of neutrality. As Lippmann indicated in *U.S. Foreign Policy,* he was himself one of those who insisted upon a realistic appraisal of the effect of a German victory upon America's security.

As a brilliant young editor on Herbert Croly's *New Republic,* Lippmann, seeking to explain America's real stake in the European conflict, subordinated issues of international law, honor, and ethics to the one big issue of America's vital interest in the preservation of the Atlantic Community. Placing his beliefs on record before the Academy of Political and Social Science in April, 1916, he argued that the nation's one great interest in international relations was an alliance with Great Britain, since everywhere in the world the United States was in contact with British power, and it therefore had to choose between antagonism and friendship, for its own safety. "The future of America," he asserted, "is bound up with the future of sea power"; and England's command of the sea is gravely threatened by Germany's submarine warfare.

"We are face to face, therefore, with the most serious calamity that could happen to our civilization—the disintegration of sea power."[8]

In an unsigned editorial, entitled "The Defense of the Atlantic World," which appeared in the New Republic of February 17, 1917, Lippmann expressed his mounting impatience with the controversy over neutrality. He thought that the legalism surrounding this technical bone of contention had obscured the real issue, which was keeping the Atlantic highway open to the Allies in order to prevent a German triumph. He made the prophetic observation, "If we put the matter on the basis of neutral rights, we shall never know whether we have vindicated them or not, and our participation in the war would be as futile as a duel of honor." But if the United States were to allow the Atlantic Community to be destroyed, "we should know what we had lost. We should understand then the meaning of the unfortified Canadian frontier, of the common protection given Latin America by the British and American fleets."*

However, it should not be thought that Lippmann was indifferent to America's idealistic interest in a British victory. He shared Woodrow Wilson's liberal and humanitarian sentiments concerning world peace. In common with many Americans in 1917, he coveted for the United States a large role in bringing about the reorganization of the world on an orderly and democratic basis through an association of nations that could enforce peace. But he was far ahead of the majority of Americans in his belief that world organization should be the basis for the abandonment of neutrality and a frank discrimination in favor of England. In a memorandum and a covering letter submitted to President Wilson on March 11, 1917, he set forth the view he had presented in his editorial of February 17. The American people, he wrote, were being confused and misled by pretensions of neutrality, when in fact the United States should enforce its rights against Germany or suspend them against England as it might serve the nation's purpose of bringing about a league of nations against aggression. If this were done, it would be possible to educate American opinion to the truth that the issue with Germany was "not mere legalism or commercialism, but one arising out of America's vital interest in a just and lasting peace."[9]

* "The Defense of the Atlantic World," New Republic, X (February 17, 1917), 59–61. In his article in Life (April 7, 1941), Lippmann quoted from this editorial at considerable length by way of substantiating his thesis of intervention; but the author was not identified. In U.S. Foreign Policy the great body of the same editorial was reproduced in a footnote on pages 33–5 in order to substantiate the same thesis; but this time Lippmann acknowledged that he was the author. Except for this piece of evidence and the mere assertion that the editors of the New Republic, President Wilson, and Wilson's advisers were moved to intervene in order to prevent Germany from wresting control of the other side of the Atlantic from Great Britain, Lippmann has made no attempt to substantiate his historical thesis.

Wilson's War Message on April 2, 1917, bore an obvious resemblance to Lippmann's memorandum, except, of course, that it said nothing about the partiality of American neutrality. If Lippmann thought that the reasons for entering the war which Wilson set forth in this address were inadequate or superficial, he said nothing about it at the time. Addressing the American Academy of Political and Social Science once again in April, 1917, he explained with approval the idealistic purposes espoused in Wilson's message; but he said nothing about America's interest in a favorable balance of power. Reviewing the causes of American intervention, he stated that Germany's submarine warfare had rendered strict neutrality impossible and had confronted the United States with the choice of helping Great Britain or helping Germany. "To such an alternative," he said, "there was but one answer for a free people to make. To become the ally of the conqueror of Belgium against the French and British democracies was utterly out of the question."[10]

In his memorandum to Wilson, Lippmann had set forth the principle, "The only victory in this war that could compensate mankind for its horrors is the victory of international order over national aggression." In his address in April he avowed, "We can win nothing from this war unless it culminates in a union of liberal peoples pledged to co-operate in the settlement of all outstanding questions, sworn to turn against the aggressor, determined to erect a larger and more modern system of international law upon a federation of the world. That is what we are fighting for."[11]

In *U.S. Foreign Policy* Lippmann asserted that, because the nation's simple and self-evident interest in its own security was not candidly made explicit, the American people never understood clearly why they entered the war. If his observation is correct, he might well have included himself in his indictment of Wilson, on the basis of his memorandum to the President and his explanation of the President's War Message.

On the other hand, the written record of Lippmann's thoughts clearly shows that on numerous occasions he did, in fact, unequivocally stress America's selfish advantage in preventing a German victory. Undoubtedly, he held the same view of America's strategic interest in April, 1917. Some of the editorials in the *New Republic* which candidly and explicitly asserted this view during the month preceding intervention bear the unmistakable stamp of his thought.

Then why was Lippmann less explicit on other occasions? Not because he changed his mind about the vital Atlantic lines of communication and the European balance of power but, perhaps, because the possibility of a German victory did not appear to be an immediate problem or because the securing of a league to enforce peace seemed a more compelling basis for intervention.

It should be observed that in Lippmann's own mind a league of nations was never dissociated from America's advantage in the survival of British sea power; he looked upon such a league not merely as a device of pacifism or idealism but as a means of preventing an aggressive nation from upsetting a balance of power favorable to America's position in world politics. This view is clearly presented in the preface he wrote on January 1, 1917, to his second edition of *The Stakes of Diplomacy*. Then why did he not explicitly acknowledge this connection between American security and the ideal of a league in his memorandum? Perhaps the most important reason is expressed in a significant observation about public opinion which appeared in the same preface. The realistic basis for a league had been discussed very little, Lippmann noted, ". . . and on that basis it might never be accepted by the American people. It is not a popular way of stating the theory, and if the plan is to be popular it will not be preached widely as practical world politics."[12]

But an association of free nations to revolutionize diplomacy, with America showing the way, that was an idea that could seize the popular imagination—and Walter Lippmann's too.

In order to understand the vicissitudes of Lippmann's appeals to public opinion, one must realize that Lippmann, like Mahan and Lewis Einstein, was acutely concerned with the attitude of the general public toward international relations; and that, like those two Realists, his greatest desire was to find some way to stabilize public opinion, to give it direction and purpose, to mitigate the curse of caprice, so that a consistent diplomacy, anchored upon a firm foundation of fundamental national interests, might serve the common welfare. It was this desire to order things, to minimize the drift, which pervaded his philosophic inquiry *Drift and Mastery* (1914).

But how could one minimize the drift in America's international conduct by enlightening public opinion with a realistic conception of American foreign policy when the whole pattern of American thought about foreign relations rejected realism? This was the problem that faced Lippmann the publicist. In the first edition of *The Stakes of Diplomacy,* published in 1915, he conceded that ordinary citizens were indifferent to the problems of power which really concerned diplomats. "The stakes of diplomacy figure hardly at all in popular thinking. The big items are frontier disputes, the oppression of kindred people, racial mysticism, and a huge sentimental interest in prestige."[13]

In the light of this view of American opinion one can appreciate the significance of an editorial, entitled "Uneasy America," which Lippmann wrote in late December, 1915, as a commentary on the profound drift in the American attitude toward the war.[14] Taking note of the jerks and jolts in America's relations with the belligerents, the violent oscillations between panic and insensibility, he called these the outward signs of a deep spiritual unrest, the frustrated products of a constricting neutrality. "To feel and feel and feel and never to use that feeling is to grow distracted and worrisome and to no end." In his opinion the situation cried aloud for leadership; yet from the outbreak of the war "the President has never said anything to which the nation might rally. He has been pushed and goaded. He has never led." On a more plaintive note Lippmann observed that, perhaps, it was impossible in the nature of neutrality for Wilson to give the American position a positive meaning.

For the better part of two years Lippmann tried in vain to anchor American policy upon the nation's solid strategic interest in the Atlantic Community by enlightening his readers about the facts of power politics. Then in the last of May, 1916, President Wilson publicly pledged allegiance to the idea of a league to enforce peace. This, finally, was the answer to "Uneasy America" that he had been waiting for. He quit Roosevelt's camp and joined Wilson's bandwagon. In Wilson's exalted moral leadership Lippmann finally beheld the force that could steady the national purpose and surmount the distractions of an uncertain and inconsistent neutrality. In the transcendent issue of a league of free peoples he perceived, at last, the compelling basis for American intervention. In this way he called idealism into the service of realism and cheered Wilson as he rallied the nation to the side of British sea power. Like many Realists, Lippmann was also something of an opportunist when it came to inducing the American people to follow the unfamiliar paths of strategic interest.

4. THE "NEW REPUBLIC"

Walter Lippmann's views about America's relation to the European conflict were reflected in the whole editorial policy of the *New Republic*, which began its experiment in liberal journalism on November 7, 1914.* The influence of this weekly journal of opinion is not adequately measured by its circulation to less than 20,000 subscribers, for it was widely read and commented upon by thinking people everywhere and was closely watched by those who would learn or shape public opinion. There was a general belief among journalists and politicians that the *New Republic* had a direct influence upon President Wilson, although there is no evidence to prove it other

---

* Because the editorial section of the *New Republic* was unsigned and usually a joint product, it is impossible to tell how much of it was written by Lippmann and how much by Herbert Croly or Walter Weyl, the other two editors who wrote about foreign affairs. However, it is safe to say that Lippmann was the chief influence in this area. Weyl retired from the editorial board in August, 1916.

than the close correspondence between many of its positions and Wilson's subsequent announcements and actions.

The *New Republic's* editorial policy during the neutrality years was distinguished by its objectivity, its deliberate calmness, and its sense of balance. These qualities reflected the editors' faith in man's rational and moral faculties, which they hoped to direct toward realizing in international society the material and humanitarian goals embodied in the ideal of the co-operative national commonwealth.

Consistent with its exalted reasonableness, the *New Republic* refused to get excited over Hunnish atrocities or German espionage and sabotage. It deplored the hysteria aroused by the submarine warfare's alleged affront to the national honor, and it repudiated the belief that any one government or people had a monopoly on iniquity in the world. It blamed the war upon conditions more than upon wickedness, and upon the wickedness of human society rather than upon the evil of any particular segment of humanity. It denounced both super-patriotism and sentimental pacifism with a fine, impartial contempt for undisciplined passion. In fact, throughout the war the editors of the *New Republic* seemed to be consciously striving to say nothing that would look foolish in the cold light of reason after the war. They proclaimed Abraham Lincoln as their standard. Surrounded by the immediate obsessions of a desperate war, they would emulate Lincoln's example of first getting all the available facts and then making a cool, disinterested appraisal of the expedient national interest, unbefuddled by irrelevant moral judgments or blind patriotism.

Throughout most of 1915 the *New Republic* supported Wilson's views on neutrality, holding that the country, having taken its stand on legal precedent, should strive to keep alive the continuity of international law, archaic and meaningless as it might be, since that was "the only way we have of showing that we are not satisfied to live in a world where power is the sole arbiter."[15] However, as submarine warfare demonstrated its effectiveness, the *New Republic* began to think more about the destruction of British sea power than about the violation of human decency. It warned that American security depended upon British sea power and the balance of forces in Europe; that submarine warfare had rendered isolation a geographical illusion.

More than any other event, the dramatic torpedoing of the British liner *Lusitania* with a loss of 128 United States citizens awakened the American people to the extent of their involvement in the war; but while the press and platform rang out with indignation against German inhumanity, the *New Republic* spoke only of the incident's larger significance. This disaster, it pointed out in a lead editorial, should serve as a lesson on America's commercial and political dependence upon Great Britain, for if the German submarine campaign should render British sea power ineffective, the United States would in large measure share England's disaster, since her fleet was the only real guarantee for the security of the Monroe Doctrine as well as transoceanic travel and American exports and imports.[16]

However, as the *Lusitania* incident dragged into a diplomatic controversy, the editors of the *New Republic* found themselves in a dilemma. On the one hand, they foresaw that a repetition of the *Lusitania* tragedy might force the United States into the war. Yet they were unwilling to avoid that war at the price of waiving the rights of American citizens to travel on belligerent ships, since that would not only encourage the Germans to press for further concessions but would also destroy the respect for law that lay at the foundation of any enduring international structure. But, on the other hand, they thought that the nation could ill afford to drift into the war merely to assert rights no military action could secure, especially since the American people were neither mentally nor morally prepared to fight on the submarine issue. Moreover, they shared the moral objections of all liberals to entering the war. America would be torn by friction among the various nationality groups. The current intolerance toward nonconformists would ripen into persecution. American democracy would find itself the companion-in-arms of powers with predatory objectives, and it would sacrifice its great opportunity to act as peacemaker and to lend its immense moral prestige and technological skill to the reconstruction of Europe.

The editors were ready to overrule all these objections if the Allies should be in danger of losing the war, but in the summer of 1915 this danger did not loom large in their minds. Consequently, they began to cast about for some new way of securing American interests. Perhaps the solution lay in a scheme such as Norman Angell had suggested for the internationalization of sea power as the first step toward a world organization capable of dealing with recalcitrant members.[17]

The *New Republic's* dilemma was resolved by events. During the fall of 1915 the growing evidence that Germany did not intend to modify its submarine warfare made the editors restive under the confinement, timidity, and inconsistencies of a merely neutral position. The United States, they found, could not be fair to one belligerent without being unfair to the other; and if it came to a choice between the two belligerents, there could be no doubt with which belligerent American interests lay. In November the *New Republic* frankly announced, "The United States is neutral and justifiably neutral, but it is benevolently neutral. So far as we have any discretion, we do not propose seriously to embarrass Great Britain and France during their desperate contest with a ruthless and terrifying enemy."[18] Although the editors believed that an Anglo-American alliance was not immediately practicable, they announced their opinion that the United States should work toward that goal, since American security and international organization as well clearly depended upon it.[19]

Finally, in April, 1916, the *New Republic* printed "An Appeal to the President," urging that the United States abandon neutrality altogether by announcing that it would sever relations with Germany and aid her enemies until she agreed to abandon submarine warfare, evacuate Belgium, France, and Serbia, indemnify Belgium, and accept the principle that in the future all nations would combine against any power refusing to submit a quarrel to international inquiry.[20] This appeal was amply rewarded on May 27 when Wilson announced before the League To Enforce Peace a momentous principle. The United States, he proclaimed, should become a partner in a universal association of nations

. . . to maintain inviolate the security of the highway of the seas for the common and unhindered use of all nations of the world, and to prevent any war begun either contrary to treaty convenants or without warning and full submission of the causes to the opinion of the world—a virtual guarantee of territorial integrity and political independence.[21]

Although Wilson failed to associate this pronouncement with self-preservation or with any alteration in the nation's neutrality policy, the editors of the *New Republic* were exultant in their belief that the President had boldly acknowledged the true bases of American security.[22] And from this time on they pointed to Wilson's speech as the rational basis for armed intervention. The United States, they asserted, would not go to war in order to vindicate obsolete maritime rights or enforce the law of nations, which both belligerents had violated, but in order to range itself with Western sea power against Continental land power; for the triumph of the latter would leave the nation "in imminent danger and in utter spiritual isolation," while the triumph of the former would not only save the nation from these disasters but also provide an opportunity to prevent their recurrence by the internationalization of sea power.[23]

In this manner the *New Republic* combined idealism with realism. Yet, while it had nothing but praise for Wilson's enunciation of moral principles, it displayed considerable dissatisfaction with the tendency of the public and the press to consider this idealism apart from its context of broad national self-interest. Above all, it wanted to emphasize that America's interest in the war had nothing to do with alleged neutral rights. Instead, it kept hammering away at the dire consequences of a German submarine victory. In a prophetic editorial criticizing Wilson's justification of the arming of merchant ships in terms of neutrality, the *New Republic* warned, "By obscuring the issue [of security] in legalism the administration is in the very great danger of making the conflict with Germany sterile and altogether meaningless."[24] One week before America's declaration of war the editors pointed out for the last time the nation's larger strategic interest.

> The first business before us is so clear that it is mere confusion of thought to label it with some moralist's phrase. The United States must insure the communications to France and England.
> This is so obvious that it ought hardly to be necessary to say it. Yet a reading of editorials and speeches by men who are most anxious to have America play a big part discloses no realization of this first principle of sound strategy.[25]

5. REALISTS OF 1914–17

If Realists make realistic estimates about the popularity of their own ideas, the estimates of Lippmann and the *New Republic* indicate that the American people were little concerned with the effect of submarine warfare upon American security. Nevertheless, one cannot ignore the fact that there were many Americans, besides Lippmann and the editors of the *New Republic,* who regarded a British victory as essential to American self-preservation.

As we noted in the last chapter, Lewis Einstein, writing under the pseudonym "Washington" in the British *National Review* of January, 1913, warned that, in the event of a war between Great Britain and Germany, the United States could not afford to stay neutral if it seemed likely that the British might be crushed.[26] In November, 1914, Einstein published a second article in the *National Review,* this time under his own name, setting forth his opinion on what American foreign policy should be now that the war he had foreseen had come about.[27] Again he contended that the United States' relative isolation depended not so much upon her distance from Europe as upon the maintenance of British sea power and a balance of power on the continent of Europe. He thought that America's present policy should be one of watchful neutrality and readiness to seize the opportunity to play a part in peace negotiations; but he urged the nation to prepare its navy as war insurance and as a reinforcement of its diplomacy; and he warned that, while the United States had nothing to fear from an Allied victory, a draw might be dangerous, and a German victory would impose an intense military strain. Therefore, he recommended, as a safeguard, the extension of the Monroe Doctrine to England on the same grounds of self-preservation which made that principle an essential bulwark of the Western Hemisphere.

Similar ideas found support among academic men. The historian George Louis Beer declared that the time had come for the United States to make an unequivocal alliance with England as a logical step toward political union with the Commonwealth, which, incidentally, he had been advocating for almost a decade. He contended that the nation's security depended upon the maintenance of British sea power, that a German victory would seriously threaten the Monroe Doctrine, and that the American people, whether they realized it or not, were confronted with the alternatives of isolation with militarism or alliance with collective security.[28]

George Burton Adams, professor of history at Yale and a former editor of the *American Historical Review,* claimed that Germany's aim was a dictatorship of the world and that she would certainly clash with the United States if she won the war. He was well aware of the opportunity for securing a permanent peace which a British victory would provide, but he did not rest his case for America's interest in a British victory upon any idealistic basis; he took his position solely on the grounds of "political and military expediency." On these grounds he concluded that the United States should declare war on Germany if—but only if—Germany seemed about to gain a final victory.[29]

The famous Harvard historian Albert Bushnell Hart was equally alarmed by the threat to the Western Hemisphere which the destruction of British sea power would pose. America's safety, he warned, was based on a distribution of power in Europe which the war might upset. He considered the invasion of Belgium proof that Latin America and even the East Coast of the United States would be at Germany's mercy in the event of her victory.[30] He admonished the nation to build up a large navy or else prepare for an invasion of the United States by Germany or Japan at the conclusion of the war.[31] In February, 1917, through the columns of the *New York Times* he addressed an urgent appeal to President Wilson to rush military preparedness. "You realize, of course, Mr. President, that if the Germans should by any chance destroy the British fleet New York would be the first objective after London."[32]

Professor Hart was thoroughly indignant over Germany's violation of America's neutrality rights, but, like the *New Republic,* he found it difficult to fight to vindicate rights for which one belligerent showed as little respect as the other; so he concluded, "If we fight, it will be a defensive war, in which national dignity and honor are factors; but the main question is one of national existence on those terms which alone can make a nation powerful."[33]

In 1916 H. H. Powers was moved to go into print again with *The Things Men Fight For.* He, too, pointed out the threat to the United States in a German victory, but his book was so absorbed in the long view of the struggle among nations that the immediate conflict was made to seem like a mere incident in a ceaseless, inexorable process. He explained in his preface that it was impossible to cope with the war unless one viewed it realistically as the consequence of the blind, instinctive drive for national power, not just the product of tyrannical monarchs or capricious nations. In his view, every nation was simply asserting its power according to the stubborn physical facts of its environment and chiefly through the medium of a struggle for sea power. No nation would have acted differently had it been in the other's place. The misunderstandings among rulers, statesmen, and the people of various nations were simply pretexts and occasions for war, the surface phenomena of an underlying struggle for existence. The current struggle, in Powers' opinion, had resolved itself into a fight to the finish between Germany's necessity to expand and England's necessity to protect her supply lines. In such a fight the United States' existence as a free and democratic state, even though it might never be invaded by Germany, clearly depended upon the survival of British sea power.*

A year later, Powers was still impressed by the importance of the cosmic forces of geography and national instinct as compared to the ephemeral issues of international law and morality. In *America Among the Nations,* which he regarded as a sequel to *The Things Men Fight For,* he stressed the point that nations, even more than individuals, act from self-interest, not in response to their sensibilities; that all nations go to war to further their interests, and that every other reason is secondary and superficial. "The great decisions of nations have seemingly been unconscious. Men are free to choose among the alternatives which present themselves, but they have little power to determine what those alternatives shall be. Their choices, even within the limits allowed, have a significant uniformity."[34]

As for the alternatives which confronted the United States in 1917, Powers said there were two: American survival or German victory; but looking beyond the immediate war, he could see the menace of Japan, which, like Germany, was a hungry nation obeying the merciless law of growth. And beyond that, he saw the expansion of Russia in her ceaseless search for access to the sea. In time, he warned, there would be nothing to stop Russia from establishing an empire from the Elbe to the Pacific; and if Russia could control the Eastern Hemisphere, she could control the world. "The world will be as unwilling to be Russianized as to be Germanized, and it will ultimately find it even more difficult to avoid it. . . . The struggle is with Germany today. It will be with Russia tomorrow."[35]

Powers concluded that, if the present war were not to be fought in vain, it should not permanently crush Germany but ought rather to lead to an under-

---

* In the epilogue Powers abandoned objectivity and voiced a passionate plea for the preservation of Anglo-Saxon civilization. However, this sentiment was not introduced into the central argument of the book.

standing between Teuton and Saxon, since only a single authority from Inverness to Bagdad could save the United States and the rest of the West from being engulfed by the swarming East. But, as for the immediate task, he thought that the prerequisite of such an understanding was an overwhelming defeat of Germany in order to chasten her aggressive spirit.

Powers' works, with their sweeping calculations of the pressure of irresistible forces and their forebodings of the inevitable clash of peoples driven by a blind impulse to power, were strong fare for stomachs accustomed to the palatable diet of cooling-off pacts and peace palaces. The liberal-minded, authoritative, matter-of-fact writings of Roland G. Usher, a professor of history at Washington University, in St. Louis, were more convincing and more popular.

Usher gained prominence chiefly because the outbreak of the war seemed to bear out some of the predictions he had made in *Pan-Germanism,* published in 1913. In this book he had set forth in considerable detail and with scholarly detachment the strategic aims of Pan-Germanism and had forecast their precipitation of a clash with Great Britain. However, much of the popularity of this book was a result of the mild furor created by its assertion that the United States and England and France had reached an understanding, probably in the summer of 1897, about the "probable action of the United States in certain contingencies."*

Professor Usher's fame gave him an opportunity to present subsequent reflections upon the European war in several books and in a number of articles in the *Atlantic Monthly, Century,* the *New Republic,* and other periodicals. In these books and articles Usher, like the editors of the *New Republic,* expressed the opinion that the American people's unrealistic view of foreign relations left them ill-equipped to deal with the current upheaval in world politics. On the one hand, Americans cherished a tradition of pacifism and noninterference in the affairs of Europe. Yet, on the other hand, they had assumed foreign commitments and strategic positions in the world which led directly to a policy irreconcilable with traditional attitudes. In Usher's opinion the resulting disinclination or inability of Americans to choose among alternatives and define their preferences was preventing the government from preparing effectively for an emergency of any kind.[36]

In an effort to correct this situation he published *Pan-Americanism* in 1915. Although this work bore the rather sensational subtitle *A Forecast of the Inevitable Clash Between the United States and Europe's Victor,* upon examin-

* Contrary to a popular assumption, Usher did not say that any formal pledges had been exchanged; he simply stated that the understanding in question had grown out of a concurrence of American, French, and British interests in resisting the Pan-Germanic threat. Roland G. Usher, *Pan-Germanism* (2d ed.; New York, 1914), pp. 140–41.

ing the book, one discovered that the inevitable clash was actually contingent upon a number of hypotheses and probabilities, which Usher was at pains to set forth in an objective manner. *Pan-Americanism* was, in fact, a comprehensive and dispassionate analysis of the strategic relation of the Western Hemisphere to the warring nations.

Usher's central conclusion was that the victor in the war, no matter which nation it might be, would upset the balance of power in Europe, upon which American immunity from European interference had largely rested. If the Germans won, they would not be likely to covet Latin America, he calculated, but would turn instead to Pan-Germanic schemes of absorbing India and Africa; but if there were other nations to oppose her there, she might turn toward unexploited Latin America for a solution of her economic problems. However, he could foresee no likelihood of an invasion of the North American continent, and he ascribed any such motion to a "fundamentally incorrect conception of Pan-Germanism." Any war with the European victor, he said, would come as a result of its forcible attempt to exclude South America from United States trade. In the interests of impartiality he also set forth the possibility of English aggression, once the destruction of the balance of power in European waters released her navy for aggressive use. Nor did he rule out the possibility that Japanese expansionists might take advantage of American weakness in the Pacific to perpetrate a war in that quarter.

These potentialities of conflict had become much narrower in scope and had grown into probabilities by the time Usher published his next book in 1916, *The Challenge of the Future*. And yet his air of deliberate objectivity was stronger than ever. He called this book an "essay in expediency" and reproached Americans for thinking sentimentally about international relations and failing to recognize true national interests, which sprang from "fundamental economic disabilities, rooted in economic and geographic phenomena." In this book Usher reached the conclusion that a foreign alliance was essential to American security, and he found that the only possible ally was Great Britain, with whom Americans shared a community of cultural and strategic interests. The trend of events had turned his suspicions into convictions about German territorial expansion in South America in the event of a German victory. He admitted that a German invasion of the Western Hemisphere was incredible, but he insisted that this was precisely the danger: the inability or refusal of the American people to believe the incredible.

Although Roland Usher's writings give no clear indication of his motives for supporting American intervention, they demonstrate that he was quite conscious of the threat to American security in a German victory. However, Usher wrote nothing that would indicate that national expediency played any part in the thinking of the nation as a whole. In fact, his wartime interpretation of American intervention stressed the absence of expediency. In his sequel to *Pan-Germanism,* called *The Winning of the War* (1918), he asserted that the American people had not grasped the fact that their independence was endangered. "They have been and are still moved by a righteous indignation and high moral anger which has in it no admixture whatever of baseness or selfishness."[37] In January, 1919, in a burst of Wilsonian idealism, he proclaimed, "The United States entered the war for reasons the most nearly disinterested and impersonal which any great nation ever possessed for an act of such magnitude."[38] In a chapter in his brief history of the war, *The Story of the Great War* (1919), Usher explained American intervention as a response to the ruthless invasion of Belgium, the sinking of the *Lusitania,* the execution of Nurse Cavell, German espionage and sabotage, and unrestricted submarine warfare.[39]

6. The Alarmists

If the average American, as opposed to the Realist, was skeptical about the possibility of an invasion of the Western Hemisphere, it was in spite of—or perhaps because of—a flood of literature devoted to dramatizing this very invasion in a way far more demanding of credulity than Professor Usher's calm analysis. Disdaining the concise or profound analysis of strategic interests and foregoing any attempt to educate the public in first principles, this lurid literature specialized in arousing Americans to the full magnitude of the foreign menace.

About the only author of this sort of alarmist literature who had any scholarly pretensions was André Chéradame, a French writer—some considered him a propagandist—who wrote a number of articles and books for English and American consumption during the war years. A forceful writer, who revealed his findings with passionate certainty, Chéradame was one of the most insistent exposers of boundless Pan-Germanic ambition. Although he started his study of the Pan-Germanic press before the Spanish-American War, the general American public became familiar with his work chiefly by virtue of two books, *The Pan-German Plot Unmasked* (1916) and *The United States and Pan-Germania* (1917).

In these books Chéradame took it for granted that the German Foreign Office was following to the letter a master plan devised by the country's most extreme militarists, and, particularly in the latter book, he made it clear that this plan included the control of South America, the mastery of Canada, and the domination of the United States itself, should the Allies be defeated in the war.

Paralleling the efforts of Chéradame were the exposés of a score of American journalists and publicists, who, according to a fad of the early neutrality years, set about exhuming the works of otherwise obscure German militarists and ultranationalists with the purpose of conveying to a pleasantly horrified public the boundless ambition of the Kaiser's regime. Although the chief animus of these German works was toward the British Empire, their frank avowal of aggressive intentions, their glorification of national power and the military virtues, and their detailed blueprints for aggrandizement lent an air of credibility to American apprehensions of a postwar German threat to the Western Hemisphere.

Much of the groundwork in translating and disseminating German expansionist literature was accomplished by the British, who, quite naturally, seized upon the outbreak of hostilities as confirmation of the deadly parallel between German precept and practice. British publishers were not lax in communicating their findings to American alarmists.

By all odds the most publicized German militarist, both among the English and Americans, was General Friedrich von Bernhardi. Bernhardi's *Deutschland und der nächste Krieg* (1912) sold poorly in Germany but created a literary sensation in Great Britain and the United States when it was translated into English in 1914, shortly after the outbreak of the European war.[40] A cheap paper edition of this translation appeared at railway newsstands and in hotel lobbies throughout America. Only by a strained interpretation could one discover in *Germany and the Next War* any design for the invasion of the United States, but there were numerous passages plainly proclaiming the patriotic slogan "World power or downfall!" These passages embellished hundreds of American addresses, articles, pamphlets, and books otherwise undistinguished by documentation. They were the chief basis for Bernhardi's sudden notoriety.

Some of the stir over Bernhardi can be attributed to the fact that he was alive and in command of German troops, but he shared his infamy with two countrymen who had been dead since the turn of the century: Nietzsche and Treitschke. These two power-conscious Germans were already familiar to academic circles, but their doctrine was so contrary to enlightened thought that they were scarcely known by the untutored populace until the passions and prejudices of war enables choice passages to be plucked from their context and circulated generously among the tabloid and Sunday-supplement audience. Treitschke's and Nietzsche's ominous fulminations about the will-to-power not only suggested the sinister quality of Germany's vaunted Kultur but also served as documentation of the incurably aggressive nature of German foreign policy, of which Bernhardi was assumed to be only a contemporary exponent.

However, the single most prolific source of downright scare literature was not the Pan-Germanic translaters or the dispensers of Bernhardi, Treitschke, and Nietzche but the advocates of military and naval expansion. Especially during 1915, while the preparedness movement was gathering steam but had not yet come under the sponsorship of the Democratic administration, militarists and navalists were wont to point with alarm to America's defenselessness in the face of a potential German invasion that might follow a British defeat.

Among the preparedness advocates who specialized in alarms of foreign invasion, Hudson Maxim, a munitions inventor and manufacturer, enjoyed the widest sales and attracted the most attention with his *Defenseless America,* published in 1915.[41] As was the case with much of the preparedness literature, *Defenseless America* spent a good many pages denouncing the degenerate, effeminate influence of pacifists and isolationists; that is, those who did not support an adequate military and naval program. It argued that, because of the innate selfishness of human nature, war was inevitable; and it quoted Homer Lea, Theodore Roosevelt, and Mahan to prove it. But, aside from the incidental benefits to the nation's wealth, manliness, and general fitness, Maxim's principal argument for building up the Army and Navy in a hurry was that the United States' wealth combined with its defenselessness was sure to induce an attack by the victor of the European war. The enemy, he predicted, would smash the American fleet and within a few days land an army of 100,000 men, which would capture the rich East Coast industrial targets, commandeer industries and men, levy a crushing tax on the people, and force its victims to furnish the conquerors with wives, daughters, and sweethearts. The invader was not identified, but for those who could not draw their own conclusions, Maxim's later writings dispelled any doubt that it could be anyone but the hated Hun.

This theme was repeated in numerous articles in popular magazines and newspapers, bearing such titles as "The Subjugation of America," "The Writing on the Wall," and "The Invasion of Long Island." In the same year there appeared a dozen or more books and pamphlets depicting similar invasions.[42] Following such a rigid pattern as to appear to be centrally inspired, they began with a disavowal of an attempt to scare the reader and a profession of their purpose to say nothing that was not based on facts long known to responsible officials in the Army and Navy. Then, usually after a short essay on the blindness of "pacifists" and the necessity of remaining constantly vigilant, they entered into an eyewitness account of a German attack on the East Coast several years after a crushing defeat of the British Empire. With considerable detail and, frequently, with the aid of military maps and lurid illustrations the descriptions proceeded through the annihilation of the inadequate American fleet, sometimes aided by the destruction of the Panama Canal, to a devastating bombardment of Boston or New York, followed by a landing of from 80,000 to 500,000 Huns, who within six months succeeded in capturing the principal Eastern industrial centers and holding them for ransom, while extorting foodstuffs, raw materials, and wealth from the conquered population and the helpless American government beyond the Alleghenies.

If these eyewitness accounts were not sufficiently graphic, there were movies and plays to demonstrate just what an invasion would mean to one's family and friends. The best-selling movie was *The Battle Cry of Peace,* based on Maxim's *Defenseless America* with a scenario by Commodore J. Stuart Blackton, president of Vitagraph Company of America. In this film the United States suffered a disastrous and humiliating invasion at the hands of an unidentified enemy, whose soldiers wore helmets closely resembling those of the Kaiser's troops and conducted themselves in an appropriately atrocious manner. A popular play on the same theme was Thomas Dixon's and Victor Herbert's *The Fall of a Nation,* which appeared on the New York stage in June, 1916. It described a gigantic conspiracy, which led to the seizure of New York by 20,000 European-trained aliens, preliminary to the lliquidation of the Atlantic Squadron by an Imperial Navy and the landing of 150,000 troops of an Imperial Army, which promptly subdued the East Coast.

7. A Potential Source of Realism

One did not need to take such sensational hypotheses at face value in order to heed them as warnings of the peril of unpreparedness. One might hesitate to accept these descriptions of conquest in their literal detail but, at the same time, harbor a vague fear of the consequences of a German victory. Historians of World War I have generally overlooked the sedulous cultivation of the twin fears of German victory and American defenselessness; but when one considers the fanciful tales of invasion, along with the popularization of German expansionists, militarists, and philosophers of *Blud und Boden,* and adds to this the calm, intelligent analyses of the Lippmann variety, it becomes clear that there existed during the long prelude to intervention a significant challenge to America's traditional attitude toward national security. And, consequently, one cannot ignore the fact that in the American reaction to the European conflict there was a potential source of a new realism.

Whether this potential source of realism became an actual source is quite a different question. If the thesis is correct that the United States intervened in the war primarily upon a calculation of its own security, that would suggest that by April, 1917, a realistic approach to world politics exerted considerable influence upon the nation. But the thesis is by no means verified by the fear which a number of citizens felt and urged concerning the consequences of a German victory, even though, as in the case of Lippmann, this fear may have been a dominant consideration at the time of intervention. In the eventful years between the summer of 1914 and the spring of 1917 the American people were assaulted by many powerful appeals; in the light of the evolution of the American attitude toward international relations since the war. with Spain, it would seem likely that the general public's response was governed by many factors besides the appeal to national self-preservation.

Just what weight one should assign to the fear of a German victory in the explanation of American intervention can best be determined later in the light of the popular reaction to the shifting circumstances of the war. But if Lippmann's analysis of that reaction is correct, the first place we should expect to find corroborating evidence is among those members of the public who were most conscious of the impact of world politics upon the nation's self-interest. This chapter has suggested that such a course of investigation can yield positive evidence, but none of the men considered above had a large enough public following or exerted a great enough influence upon the political life of the nation to warrant any generalizations about the effect of their views upon the general public's attitude toward intervention. However, if we should find the avowed leaders of public opinion echoing these same views, that would be a more significant piece of evidence in favor of the thesis that self-preservation was a determining motive for America's joining the Allies in battle.

CHAPTER VII

THEODORE ROOSEVELT

1. The Significance of Roosevelt

IN THE years after the Spanish-American War no leader of public opinion was more solicitous of the nation's position in world politics than Theodore Roosevelt. None was more anxious to preserve a favorable world balance of power. By 1914 he was convinced that America's strategic interests were roughly parallel to those of England and France in restraining Germany's aggressive, expansive energy. Undoubtedly, he harbored a suspicion that Germany would make serious trouble for the United States if she should succeed in destroying the British Navy's control of the strategic highways of the Atlantic. He had demonstrated his credulity concerning German schemes of aggrandizement in the Western Hemisphere. If there were any influential Americans who were moved to urge intervention in order to prevent a balance of power inimical to American security, we should expect to find Roosevelt in the vanguard.

It is especially important to examine Roosevelt's reaction to the events of 1914-17 because he played a significant role in bringing Americans to a willingness to enter the war. Among his contemporaries as well as succeeding generations, Roosevelt's detractors as well as his worshippers have agreed that he was the established leader among those urging a militant foreign policy and vigorous intervention in the European struggle for power.

2. From Private Alarm to Public Indignation

The outbreak of war was no great surprise to Roosevelt. Since the Algeciras Conference he had regarded a clash between Germany and England as a definite possibility; and in 1910 he had returned from his visit to Germany and the Kaiser, en route from an African hunting expedition, more convinced than ever of the aggressive intentions of the Prussian military clique.

A number of times before 1914 Roosevelt had clearly expressed his view that a German victory would threaten American security. As recently as 1911, in a letter to his sister Anna, he had predicted that if Germany should ever overthrow England, she would be almost certain to want to try her hand in America.[1] A year later he had told his good friend Baron Hermann Von

Eckhardstein, when the German diplomat called on him at the *Outlook* office,

As long as England succeeds in keeping up the balance of power in Europe, not only in principle but in reality, well and good. Should she, however, for some reason or other fail in doing so, the United States would be obliged to step in, at least temporarily, in order to re-establish the balance of power in Europe, never mind against which country or countries our efforts may have to be directed. In fact, we are becoming, owing to our strength and geographical situation, more and more the balance of power of the whole globe.[2]

At the same time, Roosevelt's public statements about Germany and her leaders were more than tactful. On June 8, 1913, the *New York Times* ran a special section celebrating the twenty-fifth anniversary of the accession of Emperor William II. Roosevelt headed the list of prominent Americans and Englishmen addressing eloquent testimonials to the Kaiser's contributions to civilization and world peace.

Roosevelt continued his discreet silence about German aggressiveness even after her mighty troops had plunged across Belgium in defiance of that country's neutrality treaty, which the blundering German chancellor dubbed a "scrap of paper."* In the September 23 issue of *Outlook* he said he would not pass judgment on Germany. "The rights and wrongs of these cases where nations violate the rules of abstract morality in order to meet their own vital needs," he explained, "can be precisely determined only when men's blood is cool."[3] He could not refrain from saying, somewhat inconsistently, that Belgium had been innocently wronged; but as for America's course, there could be no doubt that she should conserve her influence for helping toward the establishment of a general peace when the time came, for "only the clearest and most urgent national duty would ever justify us in deviating from our rule of neutrality and non-interference."

However, Roosevelt was writing a more alarming message to his friends in the United States and England and to some German acquaintances as well.[4] From the end of August throughout the remainder of 1914 he privately expressed the opinion that the fate of Belgium proved beyond a doubt that if Germany were to subjugate England, it would not be long before she would invade the United States, probably in alliance with Japan, or at least seek a dominant position in Central and South America. He said he had gathered personal knowledge of such plans from frank conversations with Germans in high places.

* Roosevelt's restraint was probably not due to surprise, for as early as September, 1911, he had anticipated a world war and a German attack either through Belgium or Switzerland in violation of solemn treaties. He claimed personal knowledge of such plans. Roosevelt to Lodge, September 12, 1911, Henry C. Lodge, *Selections from the Correspondence of Theodore Roosevelt and Henry Cabot Lodge, 1884–1918* (New York, 1925), II, 409.

Roosevelt was not only alarmed. He was, according to his private letters, prepared for the United States to take strong action. By October he was telling his correspondents that had he been president he would have acted as the head of a signatory of the Hague treaties and summoned the United States and all other neutrals to join in enforcing Belgium's guaranty of neutrality, and he would have been ready to back up his summons with force. He considered the administration's failure to act as he would have acted a shocking dereliction of duty, an outrageous exhibition of timidity, and a demonstration of abominable ignorance of international affairs. He had retained a painful silence on this subject, he explained, only because he thought it would be mischievous for an ex-president to mar the appearance of American unity and useless for him to try to influence the administration, which was struggling to meet its problems in its own way and might yet develop a worthy policy.

Because Roosevelt's public position on Belgium depended as much on his assessment of the American attitude toward international affairs as upon his own opinions, his reasons for withholding his true feelings about America's duty to intervene give a clue to the public's attitude as well as his own. In his letter to Kipling, November 4, 1914, he explained,

> If I should advocate all that I myself believe, I would do no good among our people, because they would not follow me. Our people are short-sighted, and they do not understand international matters. Your people have been short-sighted, but they are not as short-sighted as ours in these matters. The difference, I think, is to be found in the comparative widths of the Channel and the Atlantic Ocean. . . . Thanks to the width of the ocean, our people believe that they have nothing to fear from the present contest, and that they have no responsibility concerning it.

Therefore, Roosevelt would preserve an unruffled composure, forego denouncing the administration, and try patiently to teach the American people to see the true significance of Belgium. In articles written during the fall of 1914 and up to January, 1915, for the Wheeler Syndicate, *Outlook, Everybody's,* and the *Independent,* and in his book *America and the World War* (1915), which was a collection of such articles with some additions and revisions, he stuck to his purpose of refraining from moral judgments concerning the belligerents; instead he hammered out his theme that what happened to Belgium could happen to the United States if, after the war, any of the belligerents should approach the position of predominance in the Old World.

Roosevelt chose not to single out any particular belligerent as a potential menace, although it is safe to say that no reader thought he anticipated an attack by England. In his sixth article for the Wheeler Syndicate series he did express his belief in the validity of recently published plans of operations by Germany in case of war with America, but he denied that they were an expression of hostility or cause for resentment. Bernhardi's books, he explained, did not indicate any aggressive intentions; they merely demonstrated a wise preparation for any eventuality and a willingness to look all possible facts squarely in the face, which, in his opinion, was a realistic approach Americans might well emulate. "I have myself," he revealed, "become personally cognizant of the existence of such plans, and of the larger features of their details in two cases, as regards two different nations"; and he described the familiar plans for seizure of the coastal cities for ransom. However, he drew from this information, not proof of German iniquity, but the lesson of preparedness.[5]

If there was one point in these articles upon which Roosevelt was determined to express his strongest convictions, it was the necessity for military preparedness. Actually, he held that America's duty was not only to prepare itself militarily but also to help secure the conditions after the war that would prevent another world catastrophe; and he even outlined his own plan for a world league to enforce peace. However, he insisted that no hypothetical internationalist device could be a substitute for the nation's immediate readiness to meet force with force. He pointed out that if the world had been properly organized for a peace of righteousness, Belgium's neutrality might have been upheld; but he stressed his conviction that, in the absence of an efficient world league, Belgium's experience proved that America's security depended on its independent military and naval strength and not on moral innocence, all-inclusive arbitration treaties, or visions of the Parliament of Man.

Roosevelt's mounting exasperation and indignation over the frustration of his campaign for military preparedness foreshadowed a basic shift in his public position. His increasingly frequent references to the "peace-at-any-price" advocates, the "flubdubs," "mollycoddles," and "ultra-pacifists," for their failure to urge the expansion of the Navy and the establishment of some system for universal military training testified to his growing realization that in his campaign to teach the American people the bases of their security he was fighting not only public complacency but an even greater adversary, irresponsible idealism.

By the end of November he had satisfied himself that the administration possessed no special information on Belgium that might warrant inaction, and he had become convinced that Wilson and Bryan were temperamentally incapable of developing an honorable policy toward the war. So now his struggle for public opinion shifted to broader grounds and assumed a faster tempo. The evident popularity of Wilson's pious pronouncements of American altruism and his moral strictures upon the instruments of coercion fanned the flame of righteousness within Roosevelt's martial breast. Now it was not just

American security that was at stake. The whole international code of gentle-manly behavior was being mocked by the timid, ignoble prating of milk-and-water pacifists, who flaunted the banner of international morality but declined to do anything practical to defend it. In Roosevelt's mind, Wilson's continued failure to take a strong stand on the violation of Belgian neutrality, while he wrapped himself in the mantle of idealism, seemed like a prime example of an attitude toward international relations which had been a mounting source of exasperation to him ever since he had turned over the helm to Taft. Consequently, righteousness loomed up as an issue transcending even the threat of a German victory to the national security. Finally, in late November, Roosevelt announced that it had become "a duty for self-respecting citizens to whom their country is dear to speak out."[6] But still he did not feel free to proclaim to the whole nation the urgent message he had been conveying in private letters and conversations.

It was Wilson's handling of the problem of Germany's submarine warfare that eventually provoked Roosevelt to make public his irrepressible outrage. On February 4, 1915, the German government announced that it would es-tablish a war zone around the British Isles and try to sink all enemy ships within it. This threat became a reality after the middle of February, when one Allied ship after another fell victim to an unprecedented type of warfare. American passengers, who continued to venture into the war zone on British liners, many of which bore munitions, were not immune to the dramatic death by torpedo which emblazoned the headlines during the spring of 1915.

By April Roosevelt was thoroughly incensed at the destruction of life and property in defiance of established international law, which required warning belligerent ships and providing for the safety of passengers and crew. Ger-many pleaded that conventional practice was inapplicable to the vulnerable submarines as long as British merchantmen remained armed, but Roosevelt agreed with the Allied argument that no special conditions could justify such flagrant inhumanity. In a letter to F. W. Whitridge, April 6, 1915, he ex-pressed his profound agitation: "It is all I can do to control myself in writ-ing." He was for having the United States, as a signatory of the Hague Con-ventions, demand that the submarine sinkings cease and enforce the demand should Germany refuse to yield. Yet he was still reluctant to take a position too far in advance of public opinion.

But inasmuch as I cannot act and as my aim is to get my fellow-countrymen into the proper mental attitude, I continually strive to keep myself in such shape that I won't alienate good uninformed people of slightly timid or sluggish mind, who simply are utterly unable to face the new questions. These people I would tend to lose by a proper violence of statement![7]

However, this self-imposed censorship did not extend to the area of general principles. By April Roosevelt had arrayed his full arsenal of ideological weapons in opposition to the Wilson and Bryan policies. With one verbal volley after another he battered away at the administration's moral façade. It was sheer hypocrisy, he charged, to vociferate high-sounding platitudes about peace and morality in the abstract while shrinking from venturing one word about specific violations of the Hague Conventions. Deification of peace without regard to justice was not virtue; putting peace above righteousness, preaching the gospel of feebleness for the sake of mere safety from violence was utter selfishness and crass materialism; neutrality between right and wrong was sheer poltroonery. He looked upon the opposition to preparedness and the blind adherence to neutrality as varieties of that degenerate doctrine which taught comfort and ease of body above all else. In short, Roosevelt charged that Wilson and Bryan had ignobly failed in their duty toward the nation and humanity and, what was worse, had encouraged, by a shameful exhibition of moral flabbiness, a dangerous deterioration in the American character. As in his fight against the anti-imperialists and, later, against the supporters of the Taft-Knox arbitration treaties, he evoked the hard, virile virtues.

Woe to the nation which practices the peace of cowardice! Woe to the nation which prefers ease, and soft living, and the pleasures of material well-being, and the timid avoidance of danger and hardship and effort, to the exercise of those stern virtues which treat all things, including life itself, as worth nothing when weighed in the balance against fealty to a high ideal! The just war is a war for the integrity of high ideals. The only safe motto for the individual citizen of a democracy fit to play a great part in the world is service—service by work and help in peace, service through the high gallantry of entire indifference to life, if war comes on the land.[8]

3. "MURDER ON THE HIGH SEAS"

Even before the torpedoing of the *Lusitania* on May 7, 1915, Roosevelt had attained that same crusading frame of mind which had animated him during the war with Spain; but it was the terrible fate of that vessel which aroused his latent pugnacity to its full fury. When confronted with such an appalling spectacle of indiscriminate murder, he felt duty-bound to speak out publicly, at last, the full measure of his seething indignation. As a New York reporter read him the details of the tragedy over the telephone, he could scarcely contain himself. "That's murder!" he exclaimed, and in white heat he dictated a statement charging piracy on a vast scale and concluding, "It is inconceivable that we can refrain from taking action in this matter, for we owe it not only to humanity but to our own self-respect."[9] To H. J. Whigham of the *Metropolitan* magazine he expressed his amazement that the government had not already seized all German ships interned in American harbors and stopped all trade with Germany in order to bring her to her senses.[10] In an editorial written especially for the *Metropolitan* on May 9, entitled "Murder on the High Seas," he denounced Germany for barbarism and piracy and castigated the American government for maintaining neutrality between right and wrong.[11]

If President Wilson failed to act now, Roosevelt was prepared to unload his heaviest artillery upon the recreant administration, for in his opinion the injunction "Stand by the President" lost all merit when it violated the clear dictates of national and international duty. But Wilson, envisaging the requirements of America's moral obligations in a different light, only asserted with maddening self-control, "There is such a thing as a man being too proud to fight. There is such a thing as a nation being so right that it does not need to convince others by force that it is right."[12] Although in a series of notes to Germany the President took a firm position—so firm, in fact, that the second note caused his Secretary of State, Bryan, to resign—the advocates of strong action and strong words seized upon the phrase "too proud to fight" as the essence of "Professor Wilson's" disgraceful, emasculated diplomacy. Roosevelt, least of all, could countenance a conception of the national mission which disparaged the role of force in sustaining honor and morality. Such a conception was not only unrealistic; it was cowardly, selfish, and base. He coupled Wilson's failure to protect American lives and property on the high seas with his failure to throw force behind righteousness in Belgium and Mexico.* The situation called for one of his favorite metaphors: If a man slaps your wife, you prove neither your virtue nor your virility by writing notes, offering to arbitrate, or professing to be too proud to fight. The man who habitually submits to insult, Roosevelt asserted, gradually loses all sense of morality and all capacity for manly action. Until the United States finally entered the war this was the strident theme with which Roosevelt sought to rouse the American people from their lethargy.

4. EXPEDIENCY AND PRINCIPLE

In the first four or five months of the war Roosevelt had stressed, with as much impartiality between the belligerents as he could muster, the threat to

---

* Throughout 1914–17 Roosevelt was much exercised over the national humiliation suffered at the hands of Mexican revolutionists, which he attributed to Wilson's inept vacillation and his unwillingness to employ coercion. In an article in June, 1916, he listed the administration's most flagrant derelictions of national duty in descending order of importance as follows: failure in preparedness; failure to protect the lives and property of American citizens on the high seas, in foreign countries, and within the United States; failure to serve righteousness in Mexico; failure to serve righteousness in Belgium. "The Policy of Drift and Danger," *Metropolitan*, XLIV (June, 1916), 8.

American security inherent in the decisive victory of one power over the other. This was his chief argument for preparedness and would certainly have been a major consideration in his urging American intervention, if a German victory had become imminent. But there is no evidence in Roosevelt's public statements or private correspondence that he ever considered a German victory imminent or even probable. Consequently, he centered his fight for public opinion upon an issue more immediate and more convincing than an hypothetical invasion of the Western Hemisphere. This issue was the threat of German submarines to American property, honor, and life on the high seas; but in a more general way the issue was militant righteousness versus timid pacifism. Because Roosevelt found in Wilson's high-flown moral leadership and deprecation of brute physical force the epitome of that pacifist temperament and utopian view of international relations which had been his nemesis for a quarter of a century, he felt compelled to rally all his crusading fervor and high animal spirits behind an appeal to principle, beside which an appeal to mere national expediency paled into insignificance.

In Roosevelt's vigorous assertion of the national honor, the stern virtues, and the martial code of righteousness, in his desperate attempt to counteract the moral appeal of Wilson's leadership, he went so far as to pronounce the superior claim of international morality over a mean concern for physical safety and comfort. However, it should be understood that in his advocacy of universal precepts he was forever cognizant of the fact that their validity depended upon their compatibility with national self-interest. Thus in an article in December, 1916, he reaffirmed the international duty Americans owed to weak nations struggling against strong oppressors. "However," he added, "our duty to others must come second, because it can only be performed as a sequence to the performance of our duty to ourselves."[13] In his philosophy righteousness was not altruism. Idealism was contingent upon national self-interest, and in Roosevelt's view national self-interest consisted, above all, in a militant assertion of national power and prestige.

Because Roosevelt's conception of national self-interest placed a high value upon honor and self-assertiveness, he was willing to risk a bolder course of action than the general public could countenance—at least before a succession of provocations on the high seas largely vitiated the soothing effect of the peace movement upon nationalistic sentiment. On the other hand, his concern for an aggressive assertion of American purpose never extended to a willingness to sacrifice that most basic national interest, self-preservation. His attitude toward national policy was always disciplined by an awareness of the practical consequences of a German victory for America's security.

George Sylvester Viereck, a leading German propagandist, has recalled a conversation early in 1916 in which Roosevelt explained his bitterness toward Germany by drawing out from his papers a copy of a plan of the German General Staff for the invasion of the United States, which he was sure would go into operation should Germany win the war.[14] In July, 1917, Roosevelt had not forgotten this estimate. "If Germany now conquered France and England," he wrote, "we would be the next victim. . . . France and England have been fighting the battle of this nation as certainly as they have been fighting for themselves."[15]

It is reasonable to suppose that Roosevelt's underlying determination that England should not lose the war, lest America's position in the world be destroyed, played a large part in his willingness to press an uncompromising view of national honor and a bold conception of international moral obligation; but it is doubtful whether considerations of national security had a direct influence upon his desire for intervention. As he frequently stated, he had wanted to intervene after the sinking of the *Lusitania* while that crisis was foremost in the public mind. Clearly, it was the inhumanity and humiliation inflicted by Germany's submarine campaign and not its threat to the Western Hemisphere that induced his towering passion during 1917.

Of course, Roosevelt's private motives are a matter of speculation, but it is a fact of public record that for more than two years before the United States entered the war Roosevelt's appeals to the American people were couched in terms of saving civilization and the national honor rather than the United States itself. Whatever the extent of his influence upon public opinion may have been—and it was undoubtedly large in the East and South—it was not, after 1914, directed toward arousing a realistic appraisal of the imperatives of self-preservation.

During 1916 and 1917 the moral and emotional tones of Roosevelt's public pronouncements were more prominent than ever. Each successive sinking that snuffed out an American life elicited a withering barrage of epithets. He was convinced that the Allies were fighting for fundamental democratic and humanitarian principles against the ruthless incursion of Prussian autocracy upon the bastions of modern civilization; and, with characteristic crusading ardor, he anticipated a war to avenge the breach of righteousness. He could concede that there were dangers connected even with a successful war for righteousness, but there were equal dangers in peace, and he warned that the consequences of inaction might be not only danger to the nation's existence but "death of the soul" itself.[16]

Roosevelt's perception of the struggle between Light and Darkness was sharpened by his belief that Germany's war leaders were guided by the gospel of deliberate terror. Before Lord Bryce's famous report on German atrocities in Belgium was opportunely released, one week after the *Lusitania* incident, Roosevelt had minimized these tales of horror; but thereafter he could find no words strong enough to condemn the fiendish wickedness of Germany's military and political leaders. The shooting of Nurse Edith Cavell, the destruction of Louvain and the cathedral in Rheims, the bombardment of unfortified places, the devastation of Poland and Serbia, the Armenian massacres perpetrated by Germany's ally Turkey, the mass deportation of noncombatant civilians from France and Belgium to perform forced labor; Roosevelt regarded all these outrages, along with Germany's submarine warfare, as the products of calculated frightfulness devised by an autocratic regime bent upon undermining the very bases of Anglo-Saxon civilization. It was unthinkable that he should reduce a momentous issue like this to the level of mere national expediency.

5. The Warrior and the Priest

Roosevelt's indignation over Germany's conduct was surpassed only by his anger at Wilson and the pacifists, virtually identical devils in Roosevelt's view. For Germany's outrages against humanity and the national honor the administration and all its peace-at-any-price followers shared a full measure of responsibility with the most brutal militarists, in Roosevelt's opinion. "They represent what has been on the whole the most evil influence at work in the United States for the last fifty years; and for five years they have in international affairs shaped our governmental policy."[17]

To Charles Willis Thompson he expressed the opinion that "Wilson has done more to emasculate American manhood and weaken its fiber than anyone else I can think of. He is a dangerous man for the country, for he is a man of brains and he debauches men of brains."[18]

Germany's cynical contempt for international morality was wicked enough, but at least Prussian militarism betrayed no timidity nor lack of purpose. Even in 1917 Roosevelt could find something to admire in German doctrine when compared with Wilson's policies. He was enough of a militarist himself to believe, as he had written to a friend in December, 1914, "If I must choose between a policy of blood and iron and one of milk and water . . . why I am for the policy of blood and iron. It is better not only for the nation but in the long run for the world."[19]

In some respects Roosevelt comes into sharpest focus when he is placed opposite Wilson, for there was something elemental in his antipathy for that good gentleman. One is reminded of Nietzsche's distinction between the Warrior and the Priest. The Warrior with all his natural strength and virility exults in the free and unabashed exercise of the will-to-power. He is the man of true nobility, the man of honor transcending self-interest, the man of uninhibited action and violence. He hates strongly and loves strongly, and he is contemptuous of those who do not share his code. For the Priest he reserves a special loathing, since he sees that the Priest is also driven by the will-to-power, but in a perverted way that is forever confounding the Warrior, frustrating his manly passion, and denying him his rightful status in society. For the will of the Priest is not the frank, straightforward will of the Warrior but rather the devious influence of a crafty intellect, which compensates the Priest for his physical weakness by investing cowardice with the semblance of morality, by embellishing weakness with the holy glow of enlightenment, self-denial, and the gentle Christian virtues. The Warrior perceives that his rival is incapable of true manly pride, selflessness, and honor, which can come only from the unquestioning acceptance of combat. Instead the Priest must conceal his mean and materialistic soul through the clever manipulation of words and concepts, through the sickly inventions of his own artificial world, which enable him to drug the masses, who worship him as their moral leader.

Of course, the parallel is imperfect, since Roosevelt was forever donning the priestly robe and Wilson was, on occasion, a formidable Scotch Presbyterian Warrior. Nevertheless, as the war progressed, the differences between these two men grew sharper and more strident, and their mutual antipathy came to symbolize a profound temperamental and ideological split-in the nation as a whole, a split which became an increasingly pervasive and conspicuous aspect of the great public controversies over America's relation to the world conflict.

6. The Frustration of Unpopularity

The intensity of Roosevelt's emotional reaction to the war was partly a consequence of the desperation with which he waged his struggle for public opinion. It was bad enough to lack authority in a time of crisis, but it was torture to a man of Roosevelt's fervent energy to fight a losing battle for the public mind. And against such a foe!

Roosevelt had begun his campaign to awaken the American people with more conviction than hope. To Kipling he had confided in October, 1914, "At the moment I think the ideas I hold are only shared by a minority and perhaps only by a small minority of our people." Ten or twelve years ago, he wistfully recalled, he had exercised considerable influence upon his countrymen, but he had no illusions about the present. "It is utterly impossible in a nation like ours to expect that such influence will continue for a very long time. The kaleidoscope has been shaken; my influence has very nearly gone, and the battle I am still waging is not made with the hope of success but because I feel it my duty to make it."[20]

In the months that followed, Roosevelt enjoyed just enough success in his battle to heighten the bitterness of his failure. His chief success was scored among nationalist and pro-Ally groups. In addition, he derived some ironic satisfaction from seeing his preparedness campaign and, eventually, his policy concerning submarine warfare adopted by those who had called him a militarist and a fire-eater for his earlier advocacy of the same programs. But although the American people eventually reached a position concerning national honor and the moral issues of the conflict approximating Roosevelt's, they did so under the auspices of Wilson and only after they were satisfied that Wilson had done everything honorably possible to avoid the active military intervention which Roosevelt said he would have urged when the *Lusitania* went down. Many of those who applauded the Rough Rider's robust nationalism were glad to have a man with a more pacific disposition in the White House. And Roosevelt realized that the administration represented only too well the majority of the nation.

Roosevelt's keenest source of disappointment was the support which Wilson received from liberal, idealistic intellectuals, such as Nicholas Murray Butler of Columbia, D. S. Jordan of Leland Stanford, President Eliot of Harvard, Sherman of Cornell, and Northrop of Minnesota. It is a revealing commentary upon Roosevelt's temperamental and ideological predispositions that nothing aroused his ire more than Wilson's reputation for idealism, for, above all, he coveted the moral leadership of the nation. As he wrote to Frederick Scott Oliver in England, April 7, 1916, the selfish opponents of his views did not bother him; he could appeal to enlightened selfishness; but the men who really aroused his anger were those who claimed to be idealists and denounced him for not being sufficiently altruistic.[21] In his scale of values true idealism was the militant righteousness of the Warrior; the lofty, benign Wilson was a personification of the sham idealism of the Priest. We can judge something of Roosevelt's excruciating frustration over his inability to rival Wilson's popular leadership by the venom which he periodically spewed out upon his antagonist, whom he characterized, at various times, as insincere, shifty, utterly selfish, a physical coward, a "peace prattler," a "Byzantine logothete," and the worst President since Buchanan.

7. THE ISSUE OF INTERNATIONAL ORGANIZATION

If ever two men were temperamentally and ideologically antipathetical, they were Woodrow Wilson and Theodore Roosevelt; yet in their missionary fervor the Warrior and the Priest had more in common than either would admit. Unless one grants the sincerity and the profundity of the idealism of both of these leaders it is impossible to understand the intensity of their differences over a league to enforce peace.

The bitterness of this controversy, which was to ripen into the great debate over the League of Nations, is not accounted for by mere personal and partisan differences. In a very real sense it was a struggle between contrasting philosophies of international relations and, indeed, of life itself, which is inseparable from the personalities involved, but which is inexplicable except in terms of ideals and conceptions of human conduct that transcend individual antipathies. We shall return to this theme when Roosevelt and Wilson meet in their last encounter, on the field of battle over the Treaty of Versailles; but it should be observed here that this final struggle for the American mind had an important rehearsal in the tense months preceding American intervention. And Roosevelt's involvement in this preliminary skirmish further explains the nature of his desperate effort to arouse the people to assume their proper responsibilities in the European conflict. To Roosevelt cold expediency seemed like a colorless and unworthy motive for dealing with the emotion-laden issues of national sentiment and international morality raised by the deep-rooted controversy over America's responsibilities for world peace.

During the latter part of 1914 and the first few months of 1915 Roosevelt clearly advocated some sort of league to enforce peace as a method of preventing the recurrence of another violation of righteousness like the invasion of Belgium.[22] However, he made it equally clear that any such organization should reserve certain attributes of "sovereignty" to its members; namely, matters of national honor, territorial integrity, and vital interest. He stressed his conviction that international organization should supplement military preparedness, not replace it; for in his view the growth of international sympathy and trust was a very gradual thing, which should not be exceeded by the abandonment of the instruments of independent national purpose. Moreover, he believed that the actual arrangement of a world league should conform to the existing power relationships; otherwise, it would be as dangerous as it was impracticable. He assumed that its nucleus would be the common strategic interests of the two great Anglo-Saxon powers, which by the vigor and intelligence of their peoples would guarantee a peace of righteousness and security for all. But he was convinced that, in the last analysis, no league could be more effective than the willingness of its national members to support their international obligations and uphold their national rights and that, therefore, the backbone of any international system was a fierce sense of pride and honor and a manly readiness to back righteousness with force on the part of those who held preponderant power.

In Roosevelt's brand of internationalism it is possible to see the reflection of a satiated imperialism that strives to perpetuate its gains; yet his world league for peace was more than a device for assuring the predominance of Anglo-Saxon power. It was also an expression of his zealous devotion to America's mission of extending the blessings of liberty and civilization to all peoples, a devotion which imperialists and anti-imperialists shared alike. If he had been less of an idealist, he would not have burned so hotly under the strictures of those who condemned him for nationalistic selfishness. If he had been less of a militant national egoist, he would not have been so rash in his denunciation of Wilsonian idealists. But Roosevelt was an inflammable combination of both idealist and egoist, and in the ensuing explosion the delicate balance wheel of dispassionate realism was all but obliterated.

Even before the *Lusitania* incident Roosevelt dissociated himself from those who talked piously of America's mission to bring peace to the world and yet threw up their hands at the thought of military preparedness and turned their heads the other way at the suggestion of any practical action to avenge Germany's violation of Belgian neutrality. Put first things first, he said. The sinking of the *Lusitania* and the failure of the administration and the great majority of the people, for that matter, to support vigorous action to uphold such an immediate and imperative object as American rights convinced him of the futility and wickedness of the growing tendency to rely upon America's support of an hypothetical postwar international organization to solve the world's problems.

This conviction grew apace with the increasing popularity during the latter part of 1915 of the idea of a league to enforce peace. Some prominent idealists were beginning to look upon America's chief responsibility in the war as staying out of it in order to lend the nation's vast moral prestige to the promotion of a world league when hostilities ceased. In Roosevelt's view this sort of thinking put peace above righteousness. Moreover, it represented a cowardly attempt to salve the public conscience with words and visions in order to avoid the effort and risk of undertaking the immediate and practical task of making ideals effective. If this was the sort of thinking which the advocacy of a world league encouraged, he would have none of it.

By August, 1915, Roosevelt was taking the position that the proposal for a world peace of righteousness with force behind it, though valid in itself, was inopportune at that time, when more pressing and immediate duties cried out for action. This agitation for a league, he reasoned, only encouraged escapists to exult in their own beneficence, while they substituted elocution

for action. It distracted men with good intentions from the harsh realities
of their existence and lulled their consciences with the assurance of a remote
heaven. Thus Roosevelt came to believe that a world league was truly the
opiate of the people. The baleful consequences lay all about him. How inconsistent and hypocritical, he thought, for Americans to refuse to assume
the modest risk of protesting the violation of Belgium's neutrality and defending their own rights in order that they might avoid entanglements and
secure a remote peace, while at the same time they swore allegiance to the
greatest of all entanglements, a world league. In his mind there was something ludicrous about promising to undertake war on behalf of others, under
hypothetical conditions, when one was unwilling to undertake a war on
behalf of one's own rights under existing conditions. He expressed this view
succinctly in the *Metropolitan* magazine for August, 1915.

> Every league that calls itself a Peace League is championing immorality unless it clearly
> and explicitly recognizes the duty of putting righteousness before peace and of being pre-
> pared and ready to enforce righteousness by war if necessary; and it is idle to promise to
> wage offensive war on behalf of others until we have shown that we are able and willing
> to wage defensive war on behalf of ourselves. The man who fears death more than dis-
> honor, more than failure to perform duty, is a poor citizen; and the nation that regards
> war as the worst of all evils and the avoidance of war as the highest good is a wretched
> and contemptible nation, and it is well that it should vanish from the face of the earth.[23]

These principles were at the heart of Roosevelt's philosophy of individual
as well as national conduct. Morality, he insisted, was not assured by lofty
intentions, sweet reasonableness, and the construction of logically impeccable
institutions. Morality was a matter of grave danger, grim risks, brave men,
and bold deeds. And, therefore, any movement that sought to persuade good
and honest people that great ends could be secured without arduous labor
and sacrifice was a gigantic fraud.

When such vital principles as these were at stake in the conduct of American foreign policy, a crusader of Roosevelt's caliber could not content himself
with an exposition of the effect of an alteration in the European balance of
power upon American security.

If Roosevelt needed any confirmation of the urgency of his struggle for
righteousness, he got it on May 27, 1916, when President Wilson publicly
committed himself to work for America's partnership in a universal association of nations, which would bring about "a new and more wholesome
diplomacy."[24] Now the personification of cowardly and false idealism had
given his support to this mischievous instrument of escapism.

Roosevelt's anger was compounded when Wilson, in his note of December 18, 1916, appealed to the belligerents to state their war aims as a basis
for settling their differences amicably and accepting American mediation.

In his note President Wilson had taken the liberty of "calling attention to the fact that the objects, which the statesmen of the belligerent nations on both sides have in mind in this war, are virtually the same, as stated in general terms to their people and to the world." To Roosevelt, as to the Allies, this literal statement of fact seemed like neutrality between right and wrong. In a published statement, January 3, 1917, he exclaimed, "The note takes positions so profoundly immoral and misleading that high-minded and right-thinking American citizens, whose country this note places in a thoroughly false light, are in honor bound to protest. For example, the note says that thus far both sides seem to be fighting for the same thing. This is palpably false. Nor is this all. It is wickedly false."[25]

When the President followed up his note with a memorable address to the Senate on January 22, 1917, in which he proposed a league of nations and proclaimed that only a "peace without victory" could bring a permanent settlement, the beleaguered Roosevelt was appalled by the moral blindness of this professorial mollycoddle, who had sold himself to the nation as a supreme idealist. In his eyes Wilson, by his support of a world league and a peace without victory, had become a rallying point for all the pacifists, cowards, and short-sighted fools which had plagued him since the war began. Now he regarded the promotion of a world league as not only inopportune but profoundly immoral as well, and he denounced the project as "a move against international morality, against our own national honor and vital interest, and in the real interest of international barbarity."[26]

8. INTERVENTION

In his desperate attempt to combat Wilson's moral claim upon the American people Roosevelt worked himself into a frenzy asserting his own claim. The vindication of American honor and the absolute victory of Anglo-Saxon civilization over Prussian autocracy became his supreme goal, the measure of all lesser issues. It was with a mixture of righteous indignation, bellicosity, crusading zeal, and an intense antipathy to Wilson that Roosevelt reacted to Germany's submarine warfare in the last few months before the United States finally intervened.

In his final speech of the presidential campaign of 1916, in which he had fought more against Wilson than for Hughes, Roosevelt displayed the full depth of his bitterness. Toward the end of his address he cast aside the manuscript and, trembling with emotion, spoke of Wilson at Shadow Lawn, the summer White House.

There should be shadows enough at Shadow Lawn; the shadows of men, women and children who have risen from the ooze of the ocean bottom and from graves in foreign lands; the shadows of the helpless whom Mr. Wilson did not dare protect lest he might have to face danger; the shadows of babies gasping pitifully as they sank under the waves, the shadows of women outraged and slain by bandits. . . . Those are the shadows proper for Shadow Lawn; the shadows of deeds that were never done; the shadows of lofty words that were followed by no action; the shadows of the tortured dead.[27]

After the United States severed relations with Germany on February 3, 1917, Roosevelt openly urged hostilities, contending that the renewal of unrestricted submarine warfare was in itself a declaration of war.[28] By the time the unarmed American merchantman *Algonquin* was sunk without warning on March 12, 1917, he was in a frame of mind to regard Wilson as nothing short of criminally negligent for failing to call the nation to arms. In a letter to Senator Lodge the next day he spilled forth his enmity: "I regard Wilson as far more blameworthy than the 'wilful' Senators. I am as yet holding in; but if he does not go to war with Germany I shall skin him alive."[29]

And yet was President Wilson so far behind Roosevelt after all? On April 2, 1917, the President finally went before Congress to ask recognition of the fact that Germany was waging war on the nation. He appealed, as Roosevelt had appealed, for the vindication of the principles of peace and justice against selfish and autocratic power. Like Roosevelt, he called Germany's submarine warfare a warfare against mankind and declared that there could be no neutrality where the peace and freedom of peoples were menaced by autocratic government; for "the right," he averred, "is more precious than peace." Americans were fighting, he said, to make the world safe for democracy.[30]

The day after Wilson delivered this stirring message Roosevelt rushed to Washington to offer him his congratulations and his services. Possibly he derived some secret satisfaction from seeing Wilson affirm the principles which he had himself long urged unsuccessfully, even though he considered the President's belated acknowledgment of their validity a terrible indictment of the administration's former position.[31] Indeed, with a remarkable similarity in expression Roosevelt had actually anticipated Wilson's message by more than a week; for in an editorial in the *Metropolitan*, written on March 21, he had said,

We are going to war with Germany because Germany has bitterly wronged us. But there is much more than this at stake. In reality we are not fighting Germany merely in any private quarrel of ours. We are fighting Germany because under its present government, a government of ruthless and despotic militarism, Germany has become the arch foe of international right and of ordered freedom throughout the world. . . . We fight not only to protect ourselves, but to bring nearer the day when justice, and honor, and fair dealing between nation and nation, and man and man shall exist through all continents.[32]

Roosevelt proclaimed the same principles after Wilson's War Message. In the July issue of the *Metropolitan* he explained American intervention in these exalted terms:

We are in this war partly because it had become impossible for a high-minded nation longer to submit to the intolerable outrages and injuries which for two years we had suffered from Germany; and partly because it was—as it long had been—our clear duty to take an active part in the war for democracy against autocracy, for right against wrong, for liberty against militaristic tyranny, for the cause of the free people against the despotic and oligarchic governments which deny freedom to the peoples.[33]

To one who was not a witness of the American scene during 1914 to 1917, to an objective outside observer comparing Roosevelt's statements with Wilson's War Message, it might have seemed that the Warrior and the Priest had finally met on common ground. Indeed, in their belief in the American mission they were closer than either suspected. Yet Wilson was obviously oppressed by the message of death he brought to his countrymen. He had reached his fateful decision only after painful soul-searching and not until he had weighed every alternative with a scrupulous conscience and all the deliberate objectivity of his intellect and had finally been forced to the woeful conclusion that all hope of reason and peace was exhausted. Roosevelt, on the other hand, was tremendously elated by the declaration of war, and his immediate thought was of waging it to a victorious conclusion, which he dearly hoped that he and his four sons might help secure through their efforts on the field of battle. He had answered the call of righteousness without hesitation, with the direct, unquestioning response of the loyal soldier who is ordered into combat. In the white heat of glorious, manly passion he had seen his duty clearly and had set forth to perform it in spite of all obstacles.

Perhaps the difference between Roosevelt's and Wilson's approach to intervention was, in the last analysis, a difference of temperament. At least it can be said that Roosevelt's intense concern for honor and virility, his exuberant militancy, became more and more the dominant feature of his attitude toward the European conflict as American neutrality stumbled on and his antagonism toward Wilson mounted.

However, Roosevelt's visceral reactions cannot be considered apart from his deep-seated ideological and intellectual antipathy toward Wilson's self-denying idealism and the utopian view of international society which accompanied it. In this antipathy there was something of fundamental importance transcending the personalities of Roosevelt and Wilson, for in each man's view of the means and ends of national conduct there were valid insights into the problem of reconciling universal ideals with America's self-interest —insights which the other man lacked. And yet in the heat of public contro-

versy these insights were obscured by the emotional intensity of the antipathies surrounding them.

We shall return to this phenomenon later, but it can be suggested here
that Roosevelt might better deserve the reputation of a realist during 1914–17
had he kept his combative instincts subordinate to his intellect. Lippmann
and other Realistic analysts of American intervention in World War I have
charged Wilson with leading the nation into battle for superficial reasons of
national honor, abstract legality, and international morality, while they have
credited Roosevelt with responding to the true basis of America's interest
in the European conflict, America's self-preservation. The observation about
Roosevelt, at least, is true; but it is only partly true. For Roosevelt was not
only a Realist; he was also a militant idealist and something of an aggressive
national egoist as well, and the emotional fervor generated by these latter
two attributes largely nullified the effect of the former. Under the peculiar
circumstances of America's uneasy period of neutrality it was chiefly the
nation's ideals and her honor, not her security, which he invoked.

CHAPTER VIII

WILSON'S ADVISERS

1. The Significance of Wilson's Advisers

W ALTER LIPPMANN has said that President Wilson's military and diplomatic advisers clearly understood that a German victory over Great Britain would threaten American security, and he has implied that this estimate was the determining factor in their decision that America should enter the war.[1] If this view is correct, it suggests that a realistic appraisal of the nation's interest in the distribution of international power may have played a greater role in America's wartime policy than is generally recognized by historians of World War I.

The opinions of Woodrow Wilson's advisers are not necessarily evidence of either Wilson's or the American people's motives for intervention; but one might reasonably suppose that those closest to the official sources of information and the actual execution of foreign policy exerted as great an influence upon the course of the nation as Theodore Roosevelt and various journalists, publicists, scholars, and politicians. If, on the other hand, Lippmann's view is incorrect, if these military and diplomatic advisers ignored the practical consequences of a German victory in counseling intervention, then it would seem less likely that calculations of America's strategic interest in British survival had a decisive effect upon the official decisions which led to war.

Just a cursory examination of the views of Wilson's official family and his informants in the diplomatic service establishes the fact that a number of these men did, as Lippmann has asserted, look upon the preservation of British sea power and the prevention of German hegemony on the continent of Europe as a primary condition of American security. But a determination of the part which this view of American interest played in their advocacy of American participation in the European conflict requires a closer investigation.

2. Ambassador Page

From the beginning of the war Ambassador Walter H. Page in London was the most outspoken pro-Ally of all American diplomats. Certainly one basis for his position was his conviction that Prussian militarism would not rest until it destroyed all the democracies of the world. He never doubted that the United States was high on Germany's list of prospective victims. If German bureaucratic force could conquer Europe, he wrote to Colonel House in September, 1914, it would presently try to conquer the United States. The Monroe Doctrine "would at once be shot in two, and we should have to get 'out of the sun.'" At the least, an era of big armies and navies would be forced upon all nations, and periodic armed conflicts would shatter world peace.[2] At about the same time Page warned President Wilson against mediation, giving as his reason the opinion that, if Germany were thereby saved from defeat, she would attack the Monroe Doctrine and eventually invade the United States.[3] On other occasions in 1914 he expressed his concurrence with the view then popular in England that, if Germany conquered Great Britain, she would seize the Panama Canal and dominate the Eastern seaboard within a couple of months.[4] He said much less about this threat after 1914, but there is no reason to think that he changed his mind about the consequences of a German victory. As late as the spring of 1916, in a letter to his brother, Henry, he reiterated his belief that the German rulers' aim was to make somebody pay for their vast military machine; that for this reason they intended to bombard New York and hold it for ransom; and that if Germany appeared to yield on the submarine issue, it was only to keep the United States out of the war so that she would be deprived of England's help when the Germans got ready to attack her.[5]

It was Page's firm belief that under no circumstances should England be allowed to suffer a defeat. Consequently, he considered both American and British adherence to the laws of neutrality strictly secondary to the objective of not jeopardizing England's war effort. One of the considerations which led him to this policy was, undoubtedly, his opinion of what Germany would do to the United States if she succeeded in winning. Thus in October, 1914, he advised President Wilson against pressing the British to adhere to the Declaration of London, a codification of international law which would have trammeled England's dominant sea power.

Look a little further ahead. If Germany wins, it will make no matter what position Great Britain took on the Declaration of London. We shall see the Monroe Doctrine shot through. We shall have to have a great army and navy. If England wins, and we have an ugly academic dispute with her because of this controversy, we shall be in a bad position for helping to compose the quarrel or for any other service.

However, Page did not rest his case on considerations of national self-interest alone. He declared that the European war was no war in the ordinary sense but a struggle between English civilization and German autocracy. Moreover, he considered the controversy with Great Britain over shipping as of the smallest consequence compared to the danger of "shutting ourselves off from a position to be of some service to civilization and to the peace of the world."[6]

Actually, Ambassador Page's appraisal of the nation's strategic interest in a British victory was made in the larger context of a well-defined attitude toward America's general role in the world balance of power. Like Theodore Roosevelt, he judged America's relation to the European war according to the broad objective of a Pax Anglo-Americana, a kind of Anglo-Saxon world order, which would safeguard the prestige and power the United States had acquired in her war with Spain. However, in his feeling of kinship with the British Empire, Page resembled John Hay more than Roosevelt. For such an extravagant admirer of the British it was impossible to divorce strategy from sentiment, and Page made no pretensions of doing so. His dearest hope envisioned a great, friendly rivalry between the two great Anglo-Saxon nations, engaged in a joint venture of benevolent imperialism.[7] He devoutly believed that the transcendent issue of the war was English free institutions against German military autocracy; he was convinced that unless the former predominated there could be no hope for the triumph of the Anglo-Saxon mission of spreading the blessings of liberty, constitutional order, and humanitarianism throughout the world.

In Page's mind the triumph of the Anglo-Saxon mission meant more than the triumph of an idea; it meant the preponderance of Anglo-Saxon power; and Page was quite willing to join in an alliance with Great Britain in order to achieve this preponderance. In a letter to Colonel House he let his speculations on this subject run free.

> Suppose there were—let us say for argument's sake—the tightest sort of an alliance, offensive and defensive, between all Britain, colonies and all, and the United States— what would happen? Anything we'd say would go. . . . That might be the beginning of a real world-alliance and union to accomplish certain large results—disarmament, for instance, or arbitration—dozens of good things.

But he added more soberly, "I'm not proposing a programme. I'm only thinking out loud. I see little hope of doing anything so long as we choose to be ruled by an obsolete remark made by George Washington."[8]

As far as the European struggle was concerned, Page saw the single big practical issue as English or German domination in Europe. "For my part," he wrote to House, "I'll risk the English and then make a fresh start ourselves to outstrip them in the spread of well-being. . . . These are *our* world tasks, with England as our friendly rival and helper. God bless us."[9]

Thus Page's attitude toward the war was, in part, an expression of the kind of Anglo-Saxon patriotism manifested by such divergent personalities as John Hay and Andrew Carnegie and, in part, the product of a calculation of strategic interests propounded by Mahan and succeeding American Realists.

At the same time, Page clearly shared the militant national egoism of Roosevelt and other ex-imperialists. In his private correspondence he could be every bit as vehement as the virile Roosevelt in denouncing those elements which seemed to be destroying the moral fiber of the nation. Feminized reformers, visionary cranks, all forms of coddlers, simple-minded faddists, hyphenated degenerates, and just plain damn fools; all these purveyors of silly and sentimental idealism he lumped together with the peacemongers of the Bryan type as the worst influence in the entire nation. He believed that they represented the qualities produced by the softness and materialism of modern civilization, which were preventing the nation from asserting its natural influence in the world. Unless the American people could get back to the self-sacrificing, patriotic outlook of the Founding Fathers he could see no hope for converting the world into American customers, friends, and followers.

Because of his conception of the larger strategy and because of his aggressive nationalism Page was not inhibited in his attitude toward America's participation in the war by the ethical and ideological doubts which plagued the leaders of the peace movement. War was no mental hazard for him. Among the benefits which he thought American intervention might bring were the destruction of traditional isolation, the revival of manhood, the disgrace of mollycoddlers, and the restoration of true nationality. With more enthusiasm than prescience he predicted that the survivors of a war would be "in an heroic mood for the rest of their lives."[10] War would not only invigorate the American people; it would breathe freedom and new hope into the weary populace of the Old World. But, most important, America's entrance into the European conflict would insure the expansion of her own power and influence. If the United States could only get rid of its cranks and throw off its isolation, if it could "get into the world and build ships, ships, ships, ships, and run them to the ends of the seas," Page was confident that Americans could "dominate the world in trade and in political thought."[11]

In view of Page's militant temperament, his Anglo-Saxon imperialism, and his love of the Birtish, it seems likely that he would have favored America's entrance into the war solely to save England and her free institutions from disaster. Undoubtedly, he would also have regarded the threat of a German victory to American self-preservation as in itself a sufficient cause for intervention. But when it comes to explaining why Page actually advocated intervention, it is important to note that there is no evidence that he believed in April, 1917, or any other time that a German victory was imminent or even probable. It is true that some Englishmen were nervously suggesting to him that American intervention would save civilization, but those in authority probably refrained from informing him of the full precariousness of Great Britain's military situation lest they appear overanxious or desperate.[12] Hendrick writes that Page's papers show that as early as February 25, 1917, he understood the proportions of Germany's success. Yet not until Admiral Sims arrived in London a week after the declaration of war did he learn the details of the military situation through Sims's interview with Admiral Jellicoe; and then he was aghast at the magnitude of the British danger.[13]

Undoubtedly, Page's view of America's strategic interest in a British victory was a constant consideration in his diplomacy, but his public and private statements give no basis for concluding that his concern for national self-preservation had a direct effect upon his advocacy of American intervention. It should be noted that on the several occasions when he urged intervention, he did not justify his plea in terms of national security; and it is, perhaps, significant that the longer the war lasted, the less he said about the German threat to the Western Hemisphere. It is not likely that tact or diplomatic strategy governed these omissions, for Page was not fond of mincing words. It is more reasonable to conclude that as the war progressed, other considerations loomed larger.

Chief among these considerations was Germany's submarine warfare—its inhumanity and its affront to national honor. Page was struck numb by the sinking of the *Lusitania*. The historian Hendrick has said that Page was not one of those who thought the United States should declare war immediately after the disaster, since he was willing to give Germany a chance to make amends and disavow the act.[14] However, House recorded in his diary at the time, "Page strongly urges the President to bring us into the struggle upon the side of the Allies, stating that he does not believe we can retain the good opinion of any one if we fail to do so."[15]

A few days after the first *Lusitania* note had been sent to Germany, Page unburdened his emotional tension upon his son, Arthur.

> Nobody knows the day or the week or the month or the year—and we are caught on this island with no chance of escape, while the vast slaughter goes on and seems just beginning, and the degradation of war goes on week by week; and we live in hope that the United States will come in, as the only chance to give us standing and influence when the reorganization of the world must begin. . . . I can see only one proper thing: that all the world should fall to and hunt this wild beast down.[16]

Page was sure that Germany's campaign of frightfulness would eventually drag the nation to war, but he did not want to wait that long. On July 21, 1915, he wrote House,

But looking at the thing in a long-range way, we're bound to get into the war. For the Germans will blow up more American travellers without notice. And by dallying with them we do not change the ultimate result, but we take away from ourselves the spunk and credit of getting in instead of being kicked and cursed in.

And he added, "It's a curious thing to say. But the only solution that I see is another *Lusitania* outrage, which would force war."[17] When on August 19, 1915, the British passenger liner *Arabic* was sunk with the loss of two American lives, Page wrote to his son, "That settles it. They have sunk the *Arabic*. That means that we shall break with Germany and I've got to go back to London."[18] Page underestimated the ability of President Wilson and the American people to forbear the German assaults on the sea; but there can be no doubt that when the United States actually intervened, he regarded intervention as a vindication of American honor and the laws of international decency upon the high seas and not as a measure of self-defense.

Page viewed the submarine issue as the immediate justification for America's entrance into the war. However, he preferred to place intervention on a broader basis as well. In a letter to President Wilson on November 24, 1916, he had outlined this broader basis.[19] The United States, he had written, stands for democracy in the world. For that cause we became a nation. But now the fight for democracy against autocracy is on a much vaster scale. Germany must either "reduce Europe to the vassalage of a military autocracy" or else work its way toward democracy. Only autocracies wage aggressive wars. Therefore, "The defeat of Germany . . . will make for the spread of the doctrine of our Fathers and our doctrine yet." However, we are concerned with the spread of democracy not only for idealistic reasons but "because under no other system can the world be made an even reasonably safe place to live in." Page concluded that for the sake of the nation's duty to democracy and for its own safety the United States should undertake "some sort of active identification with the Allies." He recommended severing relations with Germany and Turkey.* Among the beneficial practical results which he foresaw from such action were the ending of the war and the establishment of a league to enforce peace under the guidance of the Allies and the United States; but, above all, he anticipated

the impressive and memorable spectacle of our Great Democracy thus putting an end to this colossal crime, merely from the impulse and necessity to keep our own ideals and to lead the world right on. We should do for Europe on a large scale essentially what we did for Cuba on a small scale and thereby usher in a new era in human history. . . . The United States would stand, as no other nation has ever stood in the world— predominant and unselfish—on the highest ideals ever reached in human government. It is a vision as splendid as the Holy Grael.

* Turkey was included because of its harsh treatment of the Armenian population that lived on the Russian border.

There is an obvious resemblance between this letter and Wilson's War Message six months later. However, it is also clearly an expression of Page's belief in a Pax Anglo-Americana and his attachment to the idea of an Anglo-Saxon benevolent imperialism. Moreover, it is important to realize that, in Page's mind, the transcendent ideals, for which he urged Wilson to intervene, coincided with America's national interest in preserving the European balance of power.

One indication of the distance between Page and Wilson on the subject of world peace is the contempt with which Page regarded the ideas of perhaps the most influential organization concerned with peace, the League to Enforce Peace. He thought that a world league was a good, though vague, idea; but the main issue was defeating Germany and establishing Anglo-American hegemony, and he was afraid that in its attachment to the former idea the nation would lose sight of the latter objectives. Much more important than a league to enforce peace, in his opinion, was a working understanding between Great Britain and the United States to keep the predatory nations in order.[20] The day before President Wilson delivered his War Message, Page wrote to Secretary of Agriculture Houston, "We musn't longer spin dreams about peace, nor leagues to enforce peace, nor the Freedom of the Seas. These things are mere intellectual diversions of minds out of contact with realities."[21]

Certainly the realities of power politics, as Page saw them, were an underlying factor in his policy toward the European war; but, because he never perceived an actual threat to American security and because he was deeply moved by other compelling issues, he did not stress the realistic basis for intervention. Actually, in his dispatches to President Wilson and the State Department sheer national expediency played a role quite subordinate to other considerations. If one judges Page's influence by the principal character of his advice, one must conclude that it manifested itself far more in indignation over the tactics of submarine warfare and a passionate preference for democracy over autocracy than in an appraisal of the imperatives of self-preservation.

3. Colonel House

Edward M. House, Woodrow Wilson's personal representative and confidant, was closer to the President, both geographically and in his attitude toward foreign policy, than Walter Page; but he shared Page's view of America's strategic interest in a British victory. House never doubted that a victorious Germany might eventually attempt to invade the United States; and he believed that, even if such an invasion proved impractical, the United States would be forced to build up a military machine of vast proportions in order to be prepared for the possibility.[22] Undoubtedly, House was impressed by the danger of a German policy of expansion in South and Central America, and this was one of the reasons for his suggestion to President Wilson in December, 1914, that the United States enter into informal negotiations with the diplomatic representatives of the A.B.C. Powers in order to gain approval of the principle that defense against a possible European attack was the concern of the whole hemisphere. Later House supported preparedness, partly, at least, in order to strengthen hemispheric defenses.[23]

House was determined that the Allies should not lose the war, even if they required American intervention—although he hoped that they would not—for he was convinced that America would be next on Germany's list. It was on this ground that he suggested in a brief conversation with Wilson early in October, 1915, a scheme for ending the war through either diplomatic or military intervention. In his diary House explained that he had presented the plan because he thought that Germany had a better chance than ever of winning,

and if she did win our turn would come next; and we were not only unprepared, but there would be no one to help us stand the first shock. Therefore, we should do something decisive now—something that would either end the war in a way to abolish militarism or that would bring us in with the Allies to help them do it.[24]

Writing the counselor for the Department of State, Frank Polk, about his scheme, House said, "It will not do for the United States to let the Allies go down and leave Germany the dominant military factor in the world. We would certainly be the next object of attack and the Monroe Doctrine would be less indeed than a scrap of paper."[25]

Wilson met House's suggestion with silence, and nothing more came of it at the time. This was the nearest House came to recommending America's entrance into the war as a measure of self-defense. After the fall of 1915 he never seems to have looked upon the war as presenting a clear alternative of American intervention or eventual German invasion of the Western Hemisphere.

When Wilson sent House on a peace mission early in 1916, House and Sir Edward Grey reached agreement on a scheme very similar to the one the President had ignored in October, 1915; but this time House's motives were broader than mere national self-interest. He expressed his general purpose as the achievement of the victory of democracy over autocracy, for, as he had impressed upon Secretary of State Lansing in a conversation at the end of November, 1915, he was convinced of the

necessity of the United States making it clear to the Allies that we considered their cause our cause, and that we had no intention of permitting a military autocracy to dominate the world, if our strength could prevent it. We believed this was a fight between democracy and autocracy and we would stand with democracy. . . . I thought also that unless we did have a complete and satisfactory understanding with the Allies we would be wholly without friends when the war was ended, and our position would be not only perilous but might become hurtful from an economic viewpoint.[26]

In August, 1915, House had written Walter Page of his deep conviction concerning the great moral issue at stake. "Our hopes, our aspirations and our sympathies are closely woven with the democracies of France and England, and it is this that causes our hearts and potential economic help to go out to them and not the fear of what may follow for us in their defeat."[27]

House appears to have agreed with Wilson that intervention solely on the basis of self-interest would have deprived the United States of the moral leadership which they both cherished. "It is impossible," he wrote Wilson on February 9, 1916, "for any unprejudiced person to believe that it would be wise for America to take part in this war unless it comes about by intervention based upon the highest motives."[28] When House talked about the "highest motives," he had in mind not just the victory of democracy over autocracy but, specifically, the consummation of a working agreement between Great Britain and the United States, such as Page advocated. House, like Page, was a strong believer in the advantages and virtues of a Pax Anglo-Americana. In his fanciful romance of a super-reformer, *Philip Dru, Administrator,* published in 1912, he made Dru's supreme achievement the formation of an international league of peace based on the closest co-operation between the two great English-speaking peoples. He was not tormented by the suspicions of Allied motives and the distrust of European power politics that dampened Wilson's enthusiasm for throwing the national weight into the balance of power.

Thus House envisioned his peace mission in 1916, which resulted in the famous House-Grey memorandum, as a means of helping Great Britain win the war—either by calling a peace conference at the opportune moment or by American intervention, should this conference be refused by Germany or fail to secure peace on suitable terms[29]—whereas Wilson was planning for a peace without victory and the exercise of America's *moral* force against Germany if she should refuse to co-operate in this idealistic enterprise.[30]

However, there is no reason to think that House's desire to base American intervention upon the beneficial results of a British victory was inspired by any serious fears of a British defeat. He never seems to have doubted that the Allies would win without American help.* On the other hand, even before

* House did receive some gloomy information from London and Paris during March, 1917; but, like Page, he learned that the Allies were desperate only after America had intervened. Charles Seymour, *The Intimate Papers of Colonel House* (Boston, 1926, 1928), III, 7 ff. Moreover, by March House had already decided that America should enter the war for other reasons.

the United States severed relations with Germany, House did consider the submarine depredations sufficient provocation for American intervention. House was as outraged as Page over the *Lusitania* disaster. In fact, the two were dining together in London when they learned the news. "We shall be at war with Germany within a month," House exclaimed.[31] In a telegram to President Wilson two days later he declared that, if Germany failed to guarantee that another such incident would not occur, she should be informed that the United States intended "to take such measures as were necessary to ensure the safety of American citizens." If war followed, House was consoled by the belief that American intervention would save, rather than increase, the loss of life. He concluded,

America has come to the parting of the ways, when she must determine whether she stands for civilized or uncivilized warfare. We can no longer remain neutral spectators. Our action in this crisis will determine the part we will play when peace is made, and how far we may influence a settlement for the lasting good of humanity. We are being weighed in the balance and our position amongst nations is being assessed by mankind.[32]

With America's honor, her moral reputation, and her whole position after the war, with humanity and civilization itself at stake, House could not possibly remain neutral. He was well aware that the United States' official stand on neutrality favored Great Britain, and that was the way he wanted it. As he told Wilson in April, 1916, the American position meant "freedom of the seas for England and, as far as I can see, not for Germany, for it would merely restrict depredations by submarines, and the nation that controlled the seas would destroy commerce with their other warships."[33]

Certainly one, but only one, of the reasons underlying House's deliberate partiality for the Allies was his apprehension of a German threat to American security should Great Britain go down in defeat. But the war happened to develop in such a way that his anxiety over this hypothetical threat was secondary to his eagerness to strike a blow for civilization and world peace, in accordance with the historic American mission and the mutual interests of the two great English-speaking peoples. House seized upon Germany's submarine campaign as the immediate justification for America's active participation in the war; but what tipped the scales toward intervention in his mind was not that campaign's implied threat to American self-preservation but rather its patent wickedness and its affront to the nation's self-respect.

4. SECRETARY OF STATE LANSING

Perhaps the clearest case for the compelling influence of national self-preservation as a motive for intervention, as far as Wilson's advisers are concerned, can be constructed from the private memoranda of Robert Lansing, who became Secretary of State upon Bryan's resignation in June, 1915.[34] Lansing's logical and incisive mind and his ability to separate his emotions from his intellectual processes enabled him to sustain an unwavering vigilance toward what he regarded as the primary basis of America's interest in the European war: America's own security. Although he tried to maintain the appearance of official neutrality by protesting against both British and German violations of alleged neutral rights, he was never neutral himself, because his view of world politics would not permit him to regard the outcome of the European war with indifference; for he was sure that if Germany won, the Western Hemisphere would be imperiled.

In his *War Memoirs* (1935) Lansing explained that he endeavored to adhere to the laws of neutrality during 1914–17 only because public opinion was not prepared for a war with Germany and because the administration had to be able "to show that everything had been done to avoid war in order to arouse a public demand for war."[35] In a memorandum, dated July 11, 1915, prepared for his own guidance, Lansing set forth his highly unneutral private views. This memorandum recorded his settled conviction that eventually the United States would have to enter the war on the side of the Allies in order to ward off the danger inherent in a German victory.[36] He thought that the German threat to the United States would come either through plots and sabotage within America, should a repetition of the *Lusitania* incident require action, or through actual war upon the nation, should the Allies be defeated. Therefore, he recommended that the following policies be adopted: settlement of the submarine controversy; prosecution of German plots; secret investigations of German activities in Latin America and especially in Mexico; cultivation of Pan-Americanism in order to wean those countries away from German influence; maintenance of friendly relations with Mexico; purchase of the Danish West Indies lest Germany conquer Denmark 'and come into legal title of these strategic islands; the prevention of German influence from becoming dominant in any nation bordering upon the Caribbean or near the Panama Canal; and, finally, "the actual participation of this country in the war in case it becomes evident that Germany will be the victor," or even if the war should become a draw. The memorandum concluded, "American public opinion must be prepared for the time, which may come, when we will have to cast aside our neutrality and become one of the champions of democracy."

Lansing preferred that the government defer casting aside its neutrality and joining the ranks of the democracies until the public should become aware of the menace of a German victory; but it is significant that when he actually did advise intervention, he did so on the grounds of the illegality of submarine warfare and the future position of the United States at the peace table, not on the basis of the German threat to American security. Like Colonel House, he seized upon the torpedoing of the *Arabic* in August, 1915, to urge upon Wilson the advantages of intervention.[37] He argued that, if the United States entered the war, then even though it were on the losing side, it would be included in the peace settlement, and "Germany would be deprived of the free hand she would otherwise have in dealing with us after she had overcome her European adversaries." And if, on the other hand, America should tip the balance toward victory, then she would be in a position at the peace table to establish an ideal settlement by moderating England's demands and, at the same time, regaining Germany's good will through generosity.

Apparently, Lansing was willing to have the United States enter the war at least a year and a half before Wilson broke off diplomatic relations with Germany, but he was constrained from pressing toward this goal by the inability of the American people and President Wilson to understand the nature of Germany's threat to the nation's position in the Western Hemisphere. In another memorandum for his own use, dated January 9, 1916, Lansing indicated that this was a matter of tactics, not overall strategy.

> It is my opinion that the military oligarchy which rules Germany is a bitter enemy to democracy in every form; that, if that oligarchy triumphs over the liberal governments of Great Britain and France, it will then turn upon us as its next obstacle to imperial rule over the world; and that it is safer and surer and wiser for us to be one of many enemies than to be in the future alone against a victorious Germany.
>
> Public opinion is not yet ready to accept this point of view. The American people will have to be educated to a true vision of the menace that Germany is to liberty and democracy in America as well as in Europe.
>
> I believe, therefore, that for the present we must endeavor to keep out of the war and avoid, if we can, being forced by German aggressions to employ severe measures. We must be patient and endure indignities and injustice until the people of this country realize that the German government is the inveterate foe of all the ideals which we hold sacred and for which this Republic stands. When the mass of our people are convinced of the real character of the German government and are awake to its sinister designs, the time for action will have arrived. We must wait patiently for that day and not act before if action can possibly be avoided.[38]

When the unarmed French steamer *Sussex* was torpedoed late in March, 1916, with heavy loss of life and serious injury to several Americans, Lansing evidently concluded that the nation had awaked at least enough to support a diplomatic break with Germany. Like House, he insisted that the time for writing notes had passed; and he recommended an ultimatum stating that, unless Germany admitted the illegality of submarine warfare and paid an indemnity for Americans killed or injured, the United States would sever relations.[39] Yet if the people had truly awaked to the German peril, why was it necessary to base American action on the illegality of submarine warfare? And if the people were not yet sufficiently aware of the threat to their security to support intervention, how could they be enlightened by an appeal to neutral rights? The whole position of neutrality made sense only if the nation had no interest in the outcome of the war; and yet the basic premise of Lansing's policy was that a German victory would seriously threaten America's position in world politics.

Apparently, Lansing was ensnared in the same dilemma that diverted other Realists from the frank pursuit of national expediency. On the one hand, he believed that the United States should intervene on the basis of enduring national interests; but, on the other hand, he perceived that the only way those interests were likely to be served was through the force of popular indignation over submarine warfare. Lansing knew well that the nation's tradition of isolation from power politics would not permit the government to base its policy on political expediency; and he understood the people's desire to have their neutral rights upheld, no matter how this desire might conflict with their distaste for war. And so, regarding himself as a special attorney for the nation rather than as a bold originator of policy, he was willing to drift along with the course of public opinion and make the best of it. But, fundamentally, Lansing was bound to remain dissatisfied with the American attitude toward the war; for, although he had done more than any of Wilson's advisers to build up a legal and ethical case against Germany's submarine campaign, he was probably the least moved by that campaign's purported transgressions of international law and morality. Unlike Page or House, his concern over submarine incidents was limited, largely, by their capacity to arouse the public's humanitarian sentiments and sense of national honor. Something of his impatience and dissatisfaction with the trend of public opinion is revealed in a private memorandum he wrote on January 28, 1917, while contemplating the possibility of a renewal of unrestricted submarine warfare.

If our people only realized the insatiable greed of those German autocrats at Berlin and their sinister purpose to dominate the world, we would be at war today. . . . Sooner or later the die will be cast and we will be at war with Germany. . . . We must nevertheless wait patiently until the Germans do something which will arouse general indignation and make all Americans alive to the peril of German success in this war. . . . The Allies must *not* be beaten. . . . War cannot come too soon to suit me.[40]

Ever since the *Lusitania* incident Lansing had been convinced that American intervention was inevitable, for he believed that the German militarists would surely repeat the incident and that, moreover, the German threat to the Western Hemisphere would eventually arouse America's instinct for self-preservation. However, since there is nothing in his private or public papers

to indicate that he ever believed that the American people reached an awareness of the German threat to their security, one must assume that he relied
exclusively upon submarine incidents to enlighten the nation about its proper
course.

Actually, by starting with the premise that the United States could not
possibly stay out of the war, Lansing avoided the task of spelling out the
precise grounds upon which the nation should intervene; instead, he concentrated his attention upon the problem of determining the most expedient
moment for the step. The premise that war was inevitable underlay all his
recommendations for action during the final months before Wilson proclaimed that a state of war existed. With the renewal of unrestricted submarine warfare, he urged immediate intervention instead of waiting for
further incidents; but among the grounds upon which he based this policy
there was no mention of the German threat to American security.

In a note to President Wilson on February 2, 1917, Lansing stressed the advantages of following up a break in diplomatic relations with the prosecution
of a full-scale effort to chastise Germany. This action, he contended, would
influence neutrals to undertake vigorous action, leave the United States with
some friends after the war, help end the war, give the nation a prominent
place in the peace negotiations, "give tremendous moral weight to the cause
of human liberty and suppression of absolutism," and, finally, satisfy the
American people.[41]

On March 19 Lansing argued once again the advantages of immediate
intervention, giving almost identical reasons and adding two other premises
besides the inevitability of war: "They are that the Entente Allies represent
the principle of Democracy, and the Central Powers, the principle of Autocracy, and that it is for the welfare of mankind and for the establishment
of peace in the world that Democracy should succeed."[42]

We may accept this expression of idealism as sincere, but we should also
observe that in Lansing's mind it coincided with the proper tactics to persuade President Wilson, as well as with Lansing's clear-cut conception of a
particular arrangement of power in the world, which he believed to be essential to American security.

Secretary Lansing, like Lippmann, House, and Page, gave his unqualified
approval to President Wilson's War Message. On April 4 he wrote to House,
"I believe it to be one of the greatest state papers issued by a President of the
United States."[43] Perhaps he preferred to read into this address his own
thoughts. Perhaps, after all, he did not consider the issue of national security
of paramount importance in April, 1917. If he had grown truly apprehensive
over the ability of the British to win the war, one might expect that he would

have included the unfavorable military situation somewhere among his reasons for entering the war immediately.

In any event, judging by his statements soon after America entered the war, it would seem that Lansing felt free to speak his view of national expediency for the first time only when intervention was an accomplished fact. Thus in an article that formed part of a pamphlet entitled *A War of Self-Defense,* published in August, 1917, by the Committee on Public Information, he endeavored to correct some erroneous impressions about the reasons for America's entrance into the war. After paying his respects to the issue of democracy versus autocracy and all but ignoring the submarine issue, he set forth what he regarded as the real reason for the momentous action of April 2: "Let us understand once for all that this is no war to establish an abstract principle of right. It is a war in which the future of the United States is at stake." He apologized for the implausibility of the thesis that America was in potential danger of being attacked, but he observed that impossible things had happened before.[44]

Perhaps, in the last analysis, it was the implausibility of a threat to America's isolated security, more than any other factor, that impeded Lansing's clear and explicit assertion of the realistic basis for American intervention.

5. Ambassador Gerard

Ambassador James W. Gerard in Berlin was a constant source of information concerning Germany's designs upon the Western Hemisphere. Since he had access to German leaders at all times, one would suppose that his alarms and warnings would have carried considerable weight.

Gerard, like Lansing, was quite apprehensive during 1915 over the revolutionary situation in Mexico, since he feared that Germany might take advantage of the unsettled conditions there to establish a beachhead on the Western Hemisphere. In a telegram to Secretary of State Bryan in February, 1915, he indicated his belief in the possibility of German intervention in Mexico if Germany were victorious in the war. He said that he was told by the Foreign Office that "if it were not for the war the European powers would never permit present Mexican conditions to continue," and he implied that the United States should prepare militarily for dire eventualities at the end of the war.[45] In the middle of August, 1915, House transmitted to Wilson a letter, dated August 3, in which Gerard disclosed further information about German ambitions in the chaotic republic to the south. According to this letter, no less a person than the State Secretary of Foreign Affairs, Von Jagow, had told Gerard before the war that the German government had tried to get England to join Germany in interfering in Mexico; "and the Germans 'Gott strafe' the Monroe Doctrine in their daily prayers of Hate."[46]

Gerard's distrust of German intentions was greatly stimulated by an interview with the Kaiser in the fall of 1915. The Kaiser appeared to be dangerously excited, and he repeatedly warned America to watch her step after the war, declaring that he would stand for no nonsense from her.[47] On October 25, 1915, Gerard informed the State Department of his growing apprehension: "I hope we are getting ready for defense. If these people win we are next on the list—in some part of South or Central America which is the same thing."[48] A week later he wrote to Colonel House, "Germany seems to be winning this war, to us here. . . . The military are careless of the public opinion of neutrals; they say they are winning and do not need good opinion. I am really afraid of war against us after this war—if Germany wins."[49]

Gerard entertained a profound distaste for Prussian autocracy and militarism, and he always suspected German leaders of plotting for the world. His suspicions seemed to be largely stimulated by his knowledge of the extreme views of some of Germany's naval and military men. In a telegram to Lansing in late February, 1916, he communicated the substance of a reported interview in the *Frankfurter Zeitung* with a high naval officer concerning the advantages and disadvantages of a war with the United States. According to the interview, German naval officers urged the proposition that, in the event of a war, they could sink without warning any vessels in sight and starve out England within two months. England would surrender her whole fleet, and Germany would then force the United States to return all interned German ships and pay all the costs incurred by Germany and her allies. Gerard added that German statesmen argued against the practicability of this scheme.[50]

On May 7, 1916, he sent another warning telegram: "Military and naval people all hope for revenge on United States later after the war when they can better arrange their hoped-for revolts in our country and incite the Mexicans and others against us."[51] Gerard did not believe that such sentiments were confined to military and naval extremists, for his telegram the next day bore this alarming message:

The widespread sentiment of the German people, especially the ruling class, is that Germany is only waiting until the end of this war to be revenged on the United States for the export of arms and stand on submarine war, and that then with open communication, numbers of its people of the Prussian races can be stirred to revolt . . . and the Mexicans can be armed, drilled, and led to war by German officers. I find this sentiment practically universal.[52]

It was these fears and suspicions which led Gerard, like Lansing, to urge, after the renewal of unrestricted submarine warfare, the advantages of outright war as opposed to mere severance of relations. In a telegram dated February 4, 1917, he advised, "Suggest if you decide make any threats threaten war. Germans not afraid of break of diplomatic relations which simply means they can go ahead and do what they please and attack us if they win. Chancellor spoke of the great hatred the military and naval people have for America."[53]

Clearly, Gerard anticipated German incursions upon the Western Hemisphere should the Allies be defeated; and in his mind the German peril was good cause for American intervention, once it became evident that the nation could no longer tolerate the submarine campaign. On the other hand, there is no indication that in 1917 he believed that a German victory was imminent. On the contrary, his despatches to the State Department during 1916 and 1917 reveal his impression of a steady decline of German morale and military strength.[54]

Shortly after the United States finally entered the war, Gerard wrote that he believed that the nation had intervened because Germany "murdered our citizens on the high seas" and "filled our country with spies and sought to incite our people to civil war." But he added, "We are not only justly in this war but prudently in this war. If we had stayed out and the war had been drawn or won by Germany we should have been attacked . . . through an attack on some Central or South American state."[55]

It was prudence, not fear, which evoked Gerard's concern for American security. But it was fear, not prudence, that was necessary to summon in the general public that instinct for national self-preservation which Lippmann has attributed to the American people. Nevertheless, in considering Woodrow Wilson's response to the European war, one might suppose that, where prudence was so widespread among his advisers in the cabinet and the diplomatic corps, the President of the United States could not afford to ignore it.[56]

6. WILSON'S ADVISERS AND LIPPMANN'S THESIS

If these, then, were the advisers of President Wilson who most nearly conformed to the specifications of Lippmann's thesis about the cause of American intervention, what light do their views throw upon the validity of that thesis?

It is true that these men thought that a German victory would have disastrous consequences for America's security in the Western Hemisphere. Page, House, and Lansing, especially, approached the whole war in terms of the dependence of American prestige and influence upon the preponderance of an Anglo-American nucleus of power. This conception of the arrangement of world power played a large part in their willingness to press a policy which, by its favoritism to the Allies, may have hastened the events that led to America's declaration of war.

Yet the fact remains that Wilson's security-minded advisers did not advocate intervention primarily on the basis of national self-preservation. This was principally because the circumstances of the European conflict were simply never ordered so as to present the plain alternative: either fight Germany now or be attacked by her later. Actually, the circumstances of submarine warfare tended to enhance considerations of international morality and national honor at the expense of cold expediency the nearer America approached belligerency. Moreover, these considerations seemed to form the only convincing basis for an appeal to the American people—and to Wilson —for vigorous national action; therefore, Wilson's power-conscious advisers, accepting the realities of democratic government as well as the realities of international politics, based their appeals upon the existing climate of opinion as the most effective means to the imperative end, the defeat of Germany.

CHAPTER IX

WOODROW WILSON

1. WILSON'S INDEPENDENCE

EVEN if it were true that a number of high officials and advisers to the administration favored America's entrance into the war primarily in order to redress the balance of power and to safeguard the Atlantic lines of communication, it would not follow that their views were a decisive cause of American intervention. That is quite another proposition.

The influence of these men upon the course of the nation during 1914–17 would be difficult to determine with any assurance. However, it is reasonable to assume that a major share of their influence would have had to be transmitted through the thoughts and actions of the nation's Chief Executive, for no President was ever in more complete control of the conduct of the nation's foreign affairs than Woodrow Wilson. Therefore, it is pertinent to inquire about the relation of the President to his advisers.

In the broad outlines of his foreign policy and the principal decisions implementing it, Wilson was remarkably independent of his advisers. These men have testified to their inability to change the President's mind upon important issues. Partly because of his innate stubbornness but largely because of his steadfast resolve to make scholarly and impartial decisions, Wilson was extremely cautious and deliberate in forming his opinions and quite tenacious of them once they were formed. He might listen patiently to a variety of advice, and he often appeared to accept the views of others without question; but because he tended to lose confidence in those who differed with him very often, most members of his cabinet were careful not to dissent too frequently, lest they lose what influence they had; and on crucial issues his seemingly unquestioning acceptance of the views of others was more the pose of impartiality than the reality of acquiescence.

As a matter of fact, Wilson's independence was strongest when the most important issues were at stake, for then he felt the full weight of his responsibility for resolving crises with wise and exalted decisions. Thus when he composed his note of protest over the sinking of the *Lusitania*, he avoided consulting anyone, even the experts of the State Department.[1] When he had completed the draft on his own typewriter, as was his custom, he submitted it to the cabinet, and on May 13 the note was sent to Germany practically as originally drafted.

On numerous occasions Wilson rejected the counsel of his chief advisers when they advocated a tougher stand against Germany or a softer policy toward Great Britain. His distrust of this kind of advice increased as America's relations with Germany grew more critical. He came to regard Ambassador Page as so biased that he refused to read his letters. He was at odds with almost all his advisers during the weeks immediately preceding the severing of diplomatic relations with Germany, since his determination to secure peace between the belligerents was never greater than at that time.

Among all his advisers, the President probably relied most heavily upon the opinions of Colonel House. Although House's papers exaggerate his influence upon the Chief Executive, it is true that Wilson shared many of House's views on international relations. Wilson felt such a deep friendship for his confidant that he was wont to refer to him as an extension of his own personality. When House was in England seeking American mediation, Wilson wrote, "I am of course content to be guided by your judgment as to each step."[2] It was on the assumption that his intimate friend completely understood his mind and agreed with his judgments that Wilson trustingly delegated the solution of such important problems to him.

However, Wilson's trust in House was not always accompanied by a frank meeting of minds. Consequently, it led to some significant misunderstandings —as, for example, over the purposes and terms of American mediation— which left a residue of distrust that could never be dispelled.[3] Wilson was, at times, willing to give his alter ego full rein in exploring possibilities and opening discussions and negotiations; but he never accepted from House or anyone else a concrete and detailed proposal in final form without subjecting it to the scrutiny of his own intellect. Eventually, when Wilson was forced to think out certain vital issues for himself, the assumption that House's mind was as one with his own could no longer be reconciled with his own opinions.

The final word on Wilson's independence was delivered by Secretary of Interior Lane.

> My own ability to help him is very limited, for he is one of those men made by nature to tread the winepress alone. The opportunity comes now and then to give a suggestion or to utter a word of warning, but on the whole I feel that he probably is less dependent upon others than any President of our time. He is conscious of public sentiment—surprisingly so—for a man who sees comparatively few people, and yet he never takes public sentiment as offering a solution for a difficulty; if he can think the thing through and arrive at the point where public sentiment supports him, so much the better.[4]

President Wilson's official biographer, Ray Stannard Baker, has concluded that Wilson "personally dominated, as the head of no other nation perhaps dominated, the international relations of the country."[5] If this is true, the key to American intervention must lie in the thoughts and actions of the Chief Executive more than in the purposes of any other individual or group of individuals.

2. WILSON'S INDIFFERENCE TOWARD POWER AND STRATEGY

Before the war in Europe broke out Wilson had demonstrated, especially in his policy toward Latin America, his profound dedication to America's mission of bringing constitutional and democratic liberty, universal peace, and the Golden Rule to all the peoples of the world. He had proclaimed that Americans were placed on earth as mankind's shining example of the subordination of material and national interests to the highest moral values and the service of humanity. By 1914 Wilson had formulated and had begun to put into practice certain ideal principles of American foreign policy. On the other hand, he had given very little thought to problems of national security and the exigencies of power politics. And as for the balance of power, he abhorred it as a tool of militarists and despots.

Wilson was not blind to America's strategic interests. His policy toward Mexico, Nicaragua, San Domingo, Haiti, and Latin America in general, like the hemispheric policy of his predecessors in office, was motivated, in part, by a desire to safeguard American security by keeping the Western Hemisphere free from opportunities for European interference. Moreover, he seems to have believed at one time that the nation's hemispheric defense would be jeopardized by a German victory in the European war. The British ambassador Spring-Rice, in a letter to Sir Edward Grey early in September, 1914, reported a conversation with the President in which Wilson expressed the opinion that if Prussian militarism won the war, the United States would have to take such measures of defense as would be fatal to its form of government and its ideals.[6] Harley Notter, in a studious examination of the philosophical bases of Wilson's foreign policy, has said that, undoubtedly, an "impelling consideration" in Wilson's desire to purchase the Danish West Indies was the threat to the Monroe Doctrine which would follow transfer of the islands to a Germany victorious in Europe; and that the "dominant factor" in Wilson's policy toward these islands was the general protection of the Canal and America's strategic interests in the Caribbean.[7]

Yet Wilson's private correspondence contains only a hint here and there of any fear of the impact of a German victory upon America's position in world politics, while his public pronouncements are almost totally devoid of strategic considerations. Moreover, on numerous occasions he specifically disavowed the existence of any German threat to the national security. For example, Colonel House records Wilson's opinion in the fall of 1914 that "even if Germany won, she would not be in a condition seriously to menace our country for many years to come. . . . He did not believe there was the slightest danger to this country from foreign invasion, even if the Germans were successful."[8]

After the first half-year of the war Wilson steadfastly maintained that, no matter which side won, the warring nations of the world would be so utterly exhausted that, for a generation at least, they could not possibly threaten the United States, even economically; but that, on the contrary, they would desperately need America's healing influence.[9]

Those who had direct access to the President during the neutrality years have testified to their inability to impress upon him the gravity of the German threat. Thus Lansing in a memorandum to himself early in the summer of 1916 expressed his amazement at Wilson's inability to grasp the real issues of the war: "That German imperialistic ambitions threaten free institutions everywhere apparently has not sunk very deeply into his mind. For six months I have talked about the struggle between Autocracy and Democracy, but do not see that I have made any great impression."[10]

Actually, Wilson was impressed by the struggle between autocracy and democracy; and, eventually, in his War Message he placed American might on the side of democracy; but, far from implying the preservation of a balance of power, as Lansing hoped, Wilson's pronouncement heralded the death of this iniquitous system and the birth of a new order in international relations, in which power politics and the pursuit of selfish national interests would be supplanted by the higher moral standards of personal conduct. In fact, Wilson's conception of foreign relations was remarkable not so much for its neglect of the problems of power as for its conscious subordination of national expediency to ideal goals. Above all, he coveted for America the distinction of a nation transcending its own selfish interests and dedicated in altruistic service to humanity.

3. Wilson's National Altruism

Wilson's national altruism, like Roosevelt's national self-assertiveness, was an integral part of his temperament and his philosophy of life, inseparable from his personality and yet giving universal expression to elemental values of human conduct.

Woodrow Wilson was distinguished from most men by his constant awareness of high motives. Many men strive to subordinate selfish interests to universal ethical principles, and occasionally some succeed. A few act nobly from habit or impulse; but in a world of Woodrow Wilsons, men would scrutinize their every move in accordance with the most rigorous moral standards, deliberately select the highest motive applicable to the situation, and only then act upon it. Wilson did not reach his moral judgments with that simple directness and clear, unquestioning passion characteristic of Theodore Roosevelt. He was determined not to indulge his emotions lest he reach a decision that might seem unworthy in the cool light of history, for his conception of morality was the product of solid intellectual conviction, not a thin rationalization of emotional inclinations. He believed that self-control, not self-assertion, was the first requisite of righteousness, for in his mind morality was not instinctive but rational, and the dictates of this higher reason were revealed only to those who would rid themselves of the animal spirits and exalt the spark of divinity common to all mankind.

Among the animal spirits which Wilson particularly abhorred was the propensity toward violence. He looked upon the organized violence of war as the supreme folly and tragedy of mankind. His whole nature rebelled against the loss of emotional and intellectual discipline, the surrender of love to the instinct of hatred, and the very denial of civilization which were implied in war. However, Wilson was far from being a doctrinaire pacifist. He approved of the war with Spain as a philanthropic crusade, even though he opposed it as a measure of material aggrandizment.[11] There was nothing in his philosophy which prohibited a holy war. In an address in May, 1911, he stated that under some circumstances moral duty might dictate the resort to arms, for

there are times in the history of nations when they must take up the instruments of bloodshed in order to vindicate spiritual conceptions. For liberty is a spiritual conception, and when men take up arms to set other men free, there is something sacred and holy in the warfare. I will not cry "peace" so long as there is sin and wrong in the world.[12]

Many American leaders said the same thing in 1898 and 1917; but, more than most, Wilson said it out of intellectual conviction rather than emotional exultation. The kind of war that he would fight was certainly the most difficult of all wars, requiring the exercise of violence without militancy and the exploitation of combative instincts without loss of self-control; but Woodrow Wilson, imbued as he was with the precepts of eighteenth-century liberalism and fortified by an uncompromising Scotch Presbyterian conscience, was not one to permit the imperfections of human morality to deter him from pursuing an altruistic endeavor.

Just as Wilson subordinated material and selfish interests to universal principles in his conception of individual conduct, so he applied the same standards of self-mastery and altruism to national conduct. He was well aware of past limitations upon American altruism. In an article written in 1901 he observed,

We have become confirmed . . . in the habit of acting under an odd mixture of selfish and altruistic motives . . . we have sympathized with freedom everywhere . . . have pressed handsome principles of equity in international dealings. . . . [But] when issues of our own interest arose, we have shown ourselves kin to all the world, when it came to pushing an advantage.[13]

However, what Wilson proposed to do as President was not to construct a foreign policy upon the frank recognition of this ambivalence but rather to eradicate all selfishness from America's foreign conduct; for he was convinced that only if Americans perfected their own international behavior could they hope to fulfil their mission of uplifting the rest of the world by exemplifying in international relations the ethical standards applicable among individuals.

On the basis of America's duty to uplift the world Wilson was convinced that the United States could no longer live isolated from the rest of mankind. Instead, she was bound to assume the new obligations for neighborliness imposed by the increasing interdependence of the world and by her ascendance to world power. However, he was always careful to point out that the realization of America's mission did not imply an extension of her physical power, for he believed that it was American character and American ideals, not American wealth or military might, that the world so keenly needed.

This view of America's mission can best be understood as an expression of Wilson's conviction that spiritual, not material factors, made a nation great. A nation was strong in so far as it embodied spiritual and moral qualities. What made a nation truly formidable was its "purified purpose" and its "irresistible quality of rectitude." "There is nothing," he avowed, "so self-destructive as selfishness. . . . Whereas the nation which denies itself material advantage and seeks those things which are of the spirit works . . . for all generations, and works in the permanent and durable stuffs of humanity."[14] If America was powerful, Wilson believed that it was not because of her wealth and the extension of her territory but because of the strength of her ideals. America was established to realize a vision. If she were to subordinate her spiritual goals to her material ambitions, she would forsake her national identity.[15] Just as Wilson himself was distinguished for conscious altruism, so he coveted that distinction for America. "There have been other nations as rich as we, there have been other nations as powerful, there have been other nations as spirited; but I hope we shall never forget that we created this Nation, not to serve ourselves, but to serve mankind."[16] Just a month before the

European war broke out Wilson elaborated this theme in his Independence Day speech in Philadelphia.

My dream is that as the years go by and the world knows more and more of America it . . . will turn to America for those moral inspirations which lie at the basis of all freedom . . . and that America will come into the full light of day when all shall know that she puts human rights above all other rights, and that her flag is the flag not only of America, but of humanity.

He concluded with an aspiration that foreshadowed his later adoption of world peace as an American responsibility.

I do not know that there will ever be a declaration of independence and of grievances for mankind, but I believe that if any such document is ever drawn it will be drawn in the spirit of the American Declaration of Independence, and that America has lifted high the light which will shine unto all generations and guide the feet of mankind to the goal of justice and liberty and peace.[17]

Wilson's continual emphasis upon the nation's supreme allegiance to the highest moral purpose, its service to mankind, seemed to his detractors like the rhetorical sermonizing of a sanctimonious intellectual. Indeed, his Olympian prepossession and his addiction to such ghost-like abstractions as Humanity, Justice, and Duty infused his pronouncements with a sort of sterilized, disembodied moral enthusiasm, remote from the flesh-and-blood world. He seemed to be talking over the heads of his contemporaries and addressing himself to the millennium. Nevertheless, Woodrow Wilson meant what he said, and, for the most part, he knew what he meant. The principles of foreign policy which he enunciated may have originated in the scholar's tower, but, as Wilson proceeded to demonstrate, they were intended to apply to the world below in very specific ways.

4. Wilson's Ideal of Neutrality

From the moment President Wilson learned of the outbreak of war in Europe he looked to America to exemplify that self-control and dispassionate idealism which he believed was indispensable for the fulfilment of her historic mission to serve humanity. As the German Army advanced through neutralized Luxemburg he told newspaper correspondents, "I want to have the pride of feeling that America, if nobody else, has her self-possession and stands ready with calmness of thought and steadiness of purpose to help the rest of the world."[18] It was in response to this aspiration, as well as to America's traditional policy toward European belligerents and to the overwhelming weight of public opinion, that he issued a proclamation on August 4, explicitly stating the duties imposed upon Americans as citizens of a neutral nation.[19] Two weeks later he evoked the full measure of self-possession implied in this proclamation by asking Americans not only to observe their legal obligations but to "act and speak in the true spirit of neutrality, which is the spirit of impartiality and fairness and friendliness to all concerned."

> My thought is of America. . . . She should show herself in this time of peculiar trial a Nation fit beyond others to exhibit the fine poise of undisturbed judgment, the dignity of self-control, the efficiency of dispassionate action; a Nation . . . which keeps herself fit and free to do what is honest and disinterested and truly serviceable for the peace of the world.[20]

In accordance with this ideal Wilson rejected all suggestions that he protest Germany's violation of Belgian neutrality. His refusal to pass moral judgment on the belligerents was strengthened by his belief that the whole war was such a tremendous evil that it was the part of discretion to remain impartial until all the pertinent facts were available.

However, as reports of the German invasion of helpless Belgium flowed in and the German Chancellor referred contemptuously to Belgium's treaty of neutrality as a "scrap of paper," Wilson, like the majority of the nation, began to draw a moral distinction between the Allied cause, which was identified in a general way with the cause of democracy, and the cause of the German rulers, who were seen as exhibiting the inevitable wickedness of militarism and autocracy.[21] Wilson's private condemnation of Germany's part in the war was consistent with his early antipathy toward her philosophy of materialism and her political system of military despotism. His general approval of British aims reflected a long-standing preference for Anglo-Saxon philosophy and institutions. Wilson's secretary, Tumulty, writing after the war, reported a conversation in which Wilson, referring to Lord Grey's remark to Page that England was fighting to save civilization, stated, "He was right. England is fighting our fight and . . . I shall not . . . place obstacles in her way. Many of our critics suggest war with England in order to force reparation in these matters. War with England would result in a German triumph."[12] Whether or not one places credence in the absolute accuracy of Tumulty's recollections, one can take the reported conversation as an authentic representation of Wilson's belief, which he reached during the first year of war, that an English victory was desirable, whereas a German victory would be a disaster for civilization.

However, this belief failed to modify the President's public and official neutrality. More than ever, as the trials of neutrality set in, Wilson's old suspicion of British diplomacy, his determination to reserve judgment until all the facts were available, and, above all, his desire to keep America impartial and self-possessed in order that she might reconstruct world peace led him to stress America's independence from the Old World conflict.

We can only speculate about the nature of Wilson's position had he fore-seen the probability of a German victory, but it is clear that, as a matter of fact, he did not feel that he was confronted with the alternative of choosing a British or a German victory. Thus, in spite of his advisers' warnings about the German threat to American security that would follow a British defeat, he reassured the nation in his annual message on December 8, 1914, that there was no need for additional military preparedness, since there was no "reason to fear that . . . our independence or the integrity of our territory is threat-ened. . . ." This was "a war with which we have nothing to do, whose causes cannot touch us."[23] Live and let live, was his motto. Wilson later changed his view on military preparedness, but he changed it in order to prepare the nation for the defense of its rights, not its security. He continued to repeat his assurances that America's interests—aside from its honor and rights, which he interpreted as the larger interests of humanity—were in no way involved.

President Wilson's more bellicose critics denounced his position on neu-trality as a transparent rationalization of timidity and moral myopia, but in Wilson's mind neutrality did not mean simply keeping out of trouble; it meant self-control and service to humanity. As he said in this same message, America's purpose in staying out of the war was to bring peace to the bel-ligerents, for this was a war "whose very existence affords us opportunities of friendship and disinterested service which should make us ashamed of any thought of hostility or fearful preparation for trouble." America, he declared, had been "raised up" to "exemplify the counsels of peace."

Wilson's position appears in its true perspective when it is placed beside his preoccupation during the autumn of 1914 and thereafter with bringing about peace through mediation.

According to Stockton Axson's memorandum of his conversation with the President in August, 1914, Wilson, even at this early date, had definite ideas about the kind of peace the world needed. His plan included prohibition of the acquisition of land by conquest, "a recognition of equal rights between small nations and great," the manufacturing of munitions by public enter-prise only, and, finally, "an association of nations, all bound together for the protection of the integrity of each, so that any one nation breaking from this bond will bring upon herself war; that is to say, punishment, automati-cally."[24] It was such far-sighted visions as these that moved Wilson to seek the role of mediator through the private negotiations of Colonel House with Jusserand, Spring-Rice, and Bernstorff. It was the ideal of world peace which led him to send House to Europe at the end of January, 1915, in order to discover the peace terms upon which the belligerents would accept American mediation.

Nothing concrete came of House's mission, since neither of the belligerents was willing to call a halt to hostilities while the hope of victory remained. But Wilson did not surrender his peace ambitions. Addressing the Associated Press on April 20, 1915, he asserted that the three thousand miles between the United States and Europe gave Americans a unique calm and detachment, and he noted that by force of circumstances the nation was becoming a focus of financial power. "Therefore, is it not likely that the nations of the world will some day turn to us for the cooler assessment of the elements engaged?" He was at pains to assure his audience that America did not assume her isolated position in a mean and petty spirit.

. . . I am not speaking in a selfish spirit when I say that our whole duty, for the present at any rate, is summed up in the motto, "America first." Let us think of America before we think of Europe, in order that America may be fit to be Europe's friend when the day of tested friendship comes. The test of friendship is not now sympathy with the one side or the other, but getting ready to help both sides when the struggle is over. The basis of neutrality, gentlemen, is not indifference; it is not self-interest. The basis of neutrality is sympathy for mankind. . . .

We are the mediating Nation of the world. . . . We are compounded of the nations of the world. . . . We are, therefore, able to understand all nations. . . . It is in that sense that I mean that America is a mediating nation. . . .

My interest in the neutrality of the United States is not the petty desire to keep out of trouble. . . . I am interested in neutrality because there is something so much greater to do than fight; there is a distinction waiting for this Nation that no nation has ever got. That is the distinction of absolute self-control and self-mastery.[25]

Here was the perfect expression of Wilsonian idealism. The principles he voiced in this address formed the core of his whole foreign policy during the neutrality years and, eventually, became the basis for American intervention when neutrality became untenable.

Compared to the goal of world peace and democracy, national self-interest seemed an ignoble consideration. Wilson may have entertained some vague apprehensions of the practical effect of a German victory upon America's strategic position in the world, but these apprehensions were insignificant when measured against his concern for America's moral position. In Wilson's philosophy it was the things of the spirit that counted, and how could America serve as an impartial peacemaker if she placed her own self-interest above the interests of mankind and adopted national expediency rather than Humanity as her guide? Wilson was determined that Americans should not lose sight of their mission in the world by abandoning their self-composure and falling victim to the alarms of German peril sounded by the jingoes and militarists. Americans were different; they created their nation, not to serve themselves, but to serve mankind.

5. Wilson's Practice of Neutrality

In Wilson's view neutrality was never an end in itself. It was the traditional way of getting along with belligerents, and it seemed to be a means of keeping the United States sufficiently aloof to enable it to serve as an impartial mediator. But if neutrality should become incompatible with his ultimate ideal objectives, it was likely that Wilson would abandon its substance, if not its form. The events of 1914–17 rapidly conspired to make this hypothesis a reality.

As long as the war did not vitally concern America's own interests and as long as the ideal objectives of neutrality seemed more important than the victory of one belligerent over the other, Wilson was, apparently, willing to discharge America's obligations under international law impartially, regardless of his preference for British over German culture and institutions. However, the laws of neutrality not only imposed legal obligations upon Americans; they also granted legal rights; and this was where Germany's submarine warfare entered to confound the issue of neutrality as Wilson had conceived it.

Briefly, the confounding circumstances were these: America's merchant marine at the beginning of the war was small, and, after August, 1914, Great Britain was the undisputed ruler of the high seas; consequently, the United States was almost wholly dependent upon British ships and the British Navy for the transportation of its goods and its citizens across the Atlantic. At the same time, the safety of American goods and citizens transported on Allied vessels was seriously jeopardized when, on February 4, 1915, Germany announced that it would sink all enemy ships found within a war zone established around the British Isles, pointing out that neutrals on board enemy merchantmen might incidentally suffer the same fate as enemies. The primacy of the issue of submarine warfare in America's foreign policy became inevitable when, on February 10, 1915, the State Department delivered a note, devised jointly by Wilson and Lansing, strongly protesting Germany's proclamation and solemnly declaring that the German government would be held to "strict accountability" for acts jeopardizing American property and lives by "unprecedented" methods.[26] From this moment on, the relation of the United States to the belligerents was bound to be determined, primarily, by events on the sea, over which Americans had little or no control.

If the American government had had only its neutral obligations to consider, Wilson might have enjoyed a large measure of freedom in choosing

the methods by which he sought his ultimate objectives in the European conflict. In Wilson's view the traditional objectives of the American mission
would have been served best by remaining aloof from the war. But, as long
as the nation was determined to demand observance of its neutral rights, its
freedom of choice was circumscribed by the extent to which the belligerents
chose to conform to America's conception of legal and humanitarian conduct. By holding Germany strictly accountable to a rigid standard of conduct
Wilson greatly increased the difficulty of his problem of reconciling America's
role as a peacemaker with the maintenance of her honor and her rights. From
the first he realized that this difficulty might be insurmountable.[27]

Wilson's dilemma was sharpened by the difficulties of applying the uncertain rules of international law to unprecedented circumstances. The conventional law that forbade a belligerent warship from destroying an enemy
merchantman without first stopping it, ascertaining its identity, and making
adequate provision for the safety of passengers and crew had not anticipated
the predicament of the small and vulnerable submarine. Yet the American
government would not admit that unusual conditions justified a departure
from the rules, especially when that departure involved such gross inhumanity. At the same time, it was unwilling to avoid serious incidents arising
from the loss of American lives at sea at the price of abnegating the legal right
of neutral citizens to take passage on belligerent vessels.

There is a good deal in the record of American diplomacy during 1914–17
to indicate that Wilson's administration met the unprecedented circumstances of submarine warfare by insisting upon the observance of the nation's rights on the high seas with something less than perfect impartiality
or a rigid adherence to the spirit of neutrality. For instance, the government
was certainly on shaky legal and practical ground when it defended the immunity of Great Britain's armed merchantmen by drawing a distinction between defensive and offensive armament and yet, at the same time, denied
Germany the right to attack any armed merchantman without warning.
However, the inconsistencies and incongruities of the government's legal position had much less to do with America's relation to the European conflict
than some postwar critics of intervention claimed. They do explain something
about the way in which the administration chose to rationalize America's fateful course; but that course itself—once the basic decision to hold Germany
strictly accountable had been made—was determined largely by the vicissitudes of submarine warfare.

Germany's policy toward Allied ships was governed by the exigencies of
war rather than by the legality or absence of legality with which the United
States executed its policy toward the belligerents. It was unrestricted sub-

marine warfare against neutral as well as belligerent ships that eventually brought America into the war; and the decision to wage that kind of warfare was made on the basis of a cold military calculation that the advantages of destroying all commerce flowing to Great Britain outweighed the disadvantages of a war with the United States.[28] Under these circumstances the United States could have avoided intervention only if Americans had been willing to accept unparalleled destruction of their lives and property without retaliating or else to renounce the right of all her citizens and ships to travel on the high seas. Americans were unalterably opposed to either course.

6. WILSON'S RATIONALIZATION OF A DILEMMA

The government's original stand on neutral rights and the widespread public support of this stand made America's relation to the European conflict largely dependent upon events beyond American control. However, the grounds upon which the government based its policy toward that conflict were well within President Wilson's power to choose and explain and rationalize. The grounds which Wilson chose were the grounds upon which he eventually led the nation into war. They had a very significant impact upon America's international conduct both during and after the period of intervention. Therefore, it is important to examine their origin in the tortuous process by which Wilson strove to evoke a consistent and high-principled concept of American purpose amid the ironic contradictions between the ideal and the practice of neutrality.

With the sinking of the *Lusitania* Wilson confronted the first great test of his firm resolve to lead the nation to exemplify the reasonableness, nobility, and calm moral courage befitting its world mission. His emotional reaction to the *Lusitania* disaster was in harmony with the reaction of the majority of the American people. He was indignant and deeply shocked, but he was strongly opposed to flying into a rage or resorting to war. His self-control was steeled not only by an aversion toward violence but also by a conviction that the world would need America to mediate for peace. It was with this mission in mind that, three days after the *Lusitania* disaster, addressing a large gathering in Philadelphia, he asserted,

> The example of America must be a special example. The example of America must be the example not merely of peace because it will not fight, but of peace because peace is the healing and elevating influence of the world and strife is not. There is such a thing as a man being too proud to fight. There is such a thing as a nation being so right that it does not need to convince others by force that it is right.[29]

In his Flag Day address on June 15, 1915, Wilson said much the same thing, but more pointedly, as though in answer to those demanding strong action. "I sometimes wonder why men even now take this flag and flaunt it. If I am respected, I do not have to demand respect. If I am feared, I do not have to ask for fear. If my power is known, I do not have to proclaim it." The flag, he asserted, "is henceforth to stand for self-possession, for dignity, for the assertion of the right of one nation to serve the other nations of the world. . . ."[30] In other words, genuine power used for altruistic purposes did not need bluster or force to vindicate it.

The jingoes, the Rooseveltian nationalists, and the pro-Ally patriots largely ignored this latter speech, but they seized upon the phrase "too proud to fight" in the May 10 address and flaunted it across the nation as the motto of a coward and a moral weakling. To anyone sympathetic with Wilson's constant assertion of national self-control this much-distorted statement was, obviously, an expression of the highest idealism, which posited the superior power of justice over force and morality over national self-interest.

Nevertheless, American lives had been lost as the result of a frightful violation of American rights; and the President of a great nation could not honorably dismiss the incident without a protest, no matter how proud and self-possessed he might be, especially since he had taken the position that Germany should be held strictly accountable. Moreover, Wilson's own stiff sense of national honor and self-respect would not permit him to turn the other cheek. Therefore, he also pursued another policy toward the problems of neutrality, and that was forthrightly to condemn any violation of what he considered the nation's just rights and steadfastly to refuse any modification of his original conception of these rights.

In accordance with this policy, the first American note of protest over the *Lusitania* vigorously upheld the right of noncombatants to travel on "unarmed" belligerent merchantmen; demanded disavowal, reparation, and assurance against repetition of the sinking; and declared that the United States would omit no act "necessary to the performance of its sacred duty of maintaining the rights of the United States and its citizens."[31]

But Wilson was not content to meet alleged violations of American rights with a mere assertion of a legal case; for America, as the mediating nation of the world, had more at stake in the war than its own rights and interests. Moreover, he was painfully aware of the uncertainties of interpreting international law under unprecedented circumstances, and he had no desire to base his foreign policy upon complex legal disputation. Consequently, in response to an inveterate proclivity for moralizing national ends, he sought to place American protests on the highest possible ethical ground. He contended that it was not just American rights and honor that were involved but the rights of humanity itself, not just a legal case but a supreme moral issue. In this vein he wrote to Bryan, explaining his position on a note of protest over the death of the American citizen Thrasher on the British ship *Falaba,* sunk on March 28. "My idea, as you will see, is to put the whole note on very high grounds, —not on the loss of this single man's life, but on the interests of mankind which are involved and which Germany has always stood for."[32]

In the series of notes on the *Lusitania* incident Wilson based his case on these lofty grounds. Bryan, who was no mean moralist himself, could see neither principle nor vital interest at stake in taking the risk of plunging the whole nation into war in order to support the right of a few citizens to expose themselves to known dangers by traveling on foreign ships, which might or might not be armed; and, accordingly, he resigned his position as Secretary of State when the second *Lusitania* note, of June 9, 1915, took such a resolute stand as to convince him it would bring war. But Wilson was intent upon the moral issue at stake. Brushing aside German allegations that the *Lusitania* carried contraband, the second note declared,

The sinking of passenger ships involves principles of humanity which throw into the background any special circumstances of detail that may be thought to affect the cases. . . . The Government of the United States is contending for something much greater than mere rights of property or privileges of commerce. It is contending for nothing less high and sacred than the rights of humanity. . . .[33]

While this moralistic position may have helped Wilson reconcile his conscience with the contradictions of neutrality, it did not solve his basic problem of securing the observance of America's rights and still remaining at peace. In fact, it only heightened his dilemma. By generalizing American honor and rights Wilson succeeded in elevating a tenuous legal position and a dubious neutrality into a matter of high principle; but in doing so he, in effect, sublimated his stubborn adherence to a policy which, though seemingly wise and far-sighted at the beginning of the war, now promised to become more and more inconsistent with its original objective of making the United States the world's impartial mediator. For if the administration would not compromise a position which it had erected into a moral issue, and if Germany would not meet the crippling conditions this position imposed, the nation would inevitably drift toward war. In other words, as long as Wilson was honor-bound to pursue the logic of his chosen policy, its ultimate success rested not upon his decisions but upon the fortunes of war and the military calculations of the German leaders. At the same time, the more the United States was forced to defend its policy, the more difficult it became to alter it. And once Wilson had taken his stand on the grounds of international law and humanity, it was natural that he should regard any diminution of American rights as an appeasement of evil leading to the destruction of the whole principle of international morality, since to allow expediency to take the place of principle in one case would only invite further transgression.

Therefore, it is understandable that President Wilson felt bound to oppose the McLemore resolution of early 1916, which would have prohibited American travel on belligerent ships passing through the war zone. On February 24, 1916, he wrote a letter to Senator Stone defending his opposition and admirably expressing his whole philosophy of national honor.

> For my own part, I cannot consent to any abridgement of the rights of American citizens in any respect. The honor and self-respect of the nation is involved. We covet peace and shall preserve it at any cost but the loss of honor. To forbid our people to exercise their rights for fear we might be called upon to vindicate them would be a deep humiliation indeed. . . . It would be a deliberate abdication of our hitherto proud position as spokesmen . . . for the law and right. It would make everything this Government has attempted and everything that it has achieved during this terrible struggle of nations meaningless and futile. . . . Once accept a single abatement of right, and many other humiliations would certainly follow, and the whole fine fabric of international law might crumble under our hands piece by piece. What we are contending for in this matter is of the very essence of the things that have made America a sovereign nation. She cannot yield them without conceding her own impotency as a nation, and making virtual surrender of her independent position among the nations of the world.[34]

In an address before the Gridiron Club at Washington, D.C., two days later, Wilson made it clear that the principles embodied in this letter might logically become the basis for intervention. "America ought to keep out of this war. She ought to keep out at the sacrifice of everything except this single thing upon which her character and history are founded, her sense of humanity and justice."[35]

It was on the same basis that Wilson went before Congress on February 26, 1917, to ask for authority to arm American merchant ships.

> I have spoken of our commerce and of the legitimate errands of our people on the seas, but you will not be misled as to my main thought, the thought that lies beneath these phrases and gives them dignity and weight. It is not of material interests merely that we are thinking. It is, rather, of fundamental human rights, chief of all the right of life itself. . . . I am thinking of those rights of humanity without which there is no civilization.[36]

After the *Lusitania* disaster Wilson fully realized the dilemma which this stand upon fundamental human rights imposed upon him. He confessed, both privately and in public, that he might not be able to grant the "double wish" of the American people that the nation might rigidly maintain its national honor and, at the same time, keep out of the war.[37] Even a highly moralized stand on the laws of neutrality was not easily squared with his vision of an impartial, self-possessed nation, subordinating its own rights and interests to the welfare of humanity in order to bring about a new era of peace and unity. It is probable that Wilson was sensitive to charges by both critics and advocates of neutrality that his policy was not truly neutral but benevolently neutral. At any rate, it was the fear that he might not be able to resolve this dilemma short of war that moved him during 1916 to fall back upon America's ultimate objective, world peace, as the major criterion of the nation's policy toward the belligerents; for as the contradictions between the ideal and the practice of neutrality grew deeper and the incompatibility of American and German policy became manifest, Wilson reached the conclusion that the best way for America to keep out of the European conflict was to bring it to an end.

7. AMERICA'S GOAL: WORLD PEACE

Behind House's famous peace mission in 1916 there was a background of Wilson's growing interest in the bases of a just and lasting peace. During the autumn of 1915 his ideas on this subject matured to the stage of specific provisions, including a league of nations. In January, 1915, as a first step toward permanent peace, he sent House to sound out the belligerents concerning American mediation. House's mission failed, but Wilson continued to ponder the bases of peace. Throughout 1915 his interest in world organization increased, along with the growing concern of a large body of highly educated Americans with such projects as the League to Enforce Peace. He rejected House's advice that the United States discard its neutrality and throw its whole weight behind a demand for a just peace based on a world league; but during the fall of 1915 he did decide that the nation should become a partner in an organization for world peace, and to that end he encouraged House and Sir Edward Grey to develop their ideas on the subject of the formation of a league after the war.

Early in 1916 the mounting hazards of neutrality placed a new urgency upon ending the war, and once more Colonel House went to Europe to work for mediation. This time Wilson authorized him to urge peace negotiations and to promise that America would throw her moral force—he did not say her physical force—against Germany if she should refuse to co-operate. To this extent Wilson expressed his preference for the Allied cause in the war; but he was far from subscribing to House's interpretation of mediation as an adjunct of an Allied victory, for he harbored a lingering distrust of Allied war aims, and he believed that no peace that resulted in the crushing of the vanquished could endure. Moreover, whereas House's version of mediation involved American intervention on the side of the Allies if Germany refused a settlement, Wilson regarded mediation as a means of enabling America to avoid intervention.

As it developed, House's second mission of peace became an imbroglio of misunderstanding between Wilson and House, and House and Grey. But coincident with the rising interest in both England and the United States in linking a peace settlement with a league of nations, the President became more determined than ever to bring about American mediation. This was the period when the *New Republic* issued its appeal to the President to link a peace plan with the breaking of relations with Germany. However, Wilson, who was reaching a peak of exasperation over England's interference with American rights on the high seas, was in no mood to predicate peace upon an Allied victory. He was, if anything, more insistent than ever upon the necessity of American neutrality and impartiality, more firmly convinced that only a settlement that transcended the selfish advantage of all parties concerned could attain the spiritual strength to resolve international dissension. Therefore, mediation was still precluded by Sir Edward Grey's determination to make a settlement contingent upon British victory.

However, Wilson could at least affirm America's moral commitment to an association of nations founded on the principles of self-determination, the equality of small states, and the prevention of aggression. And this he accomplished in his significant address of May 27, 1916, before the League to Enforce Peace.[38] The United States, he announced, was willing to become a partner in a universal association of nations

to maintain the inviolate security of the highway of the seas for the common and unhindered use of all nations of the world, and to prevent any war begun either contrary to treaty covenants or without warning and full submission of the causes to the opinion of the world—a virtual guarantee of territorial integrity and political independence.

Wilson had long been convinced of the interdependence of the peoples of the world. Now, for the first time, he clearly challenged America's political isolation and acknowledged the revolutionary character of the movement for a league to enforce peace. "We are participants, whether we would or not, in the life of the world. The interests of all nations are our own also. . . . What affects mankind is inevitably our affair as well as the affair of the nations of Europe and Asia." But Wilson was referring to moral interdependence, not strategic interdependence. America's mission was conceived in altruism, not self-interest. Americans, he said, wanted to end the war because it affected their rights and interests, but they approached the task of establishing permanent peace as an opportunity to replace the selfish struggle among nations and the balance-of-power system with a "new and more wholesome diplomacy," as an opportunity to realize among nations the same standards of honor and morality that were demanded of individuals. He expected an association of nations to come about as a great moral awakening rather than as a response to new conditions of national security. The war had disclosed "a great moral necessity," but he said nothing about strategic necessity.

As for America's part in bringing about an association of nations, in Wilson's view she remained an impartial, magnanimous bystander, ready to apply her moral weight to the service of humanity whenever the warring nations were willing to accept it. With the "causes" and "objects" of the war she had no concern. "We have nothing material of any kind to ask for ourselves, and are quite aware that we are in no sense or degree parties to the present quarrel. Our interest is only in peace and its future guarantees." This principle of disinterested service to the cause of world peace dominated Wilson's foreign policy thereafter.

Wilson's determination to keep the nation out of war in order that it might fulfill its mission was symbolized by the Democratic campaign slogan "He Kept Us out of War." With this slogan still ringing in his ears the President entered upon one final desperate effort to achieve its implied promise. On December 18, 1916, he sent identical notes to the belligerents asking them to state the terms upon which they would be willing to stop fighting.[39] While his advisers were urging him to align the country on the side of the democracies, and while Roosevelt was fairly apoplectic over his refusal to abandon neutrality, Wilson was more soberly resolute than ever in his determination to refrain from moral judgments that might distract the nation from its goal of impartial mediation. Thus he pointed out in his note that "the objects which the statesmen of the belligerents on both sides have in mind in this war are virtually the same, as stated in general terms to their own people and to the world." America, he said, had no interest in the outcome of the war except the achievement of these objects, including a league of nations "to insure peace and justice throughout the world." But Americans were interested in the immediate ending of the war "lest it should presently be too late to accomplish the greater things which lie beyond its conclusion, lest the situation of neutral nations be rendered altogether intolerable, and lest, more than all, an injury be done civilization itself which can never be . . . repaired."

When this final attempt to achieve a peace based upon the principles proclaimed in the May 27 address failed to elicit a favorable response from the belligerents, Wilson went before the Senate, on January 22, 1917, and in a classic expression of America's moral leadership announced to the peoples of the world his own conception of an enduring peace.[40]

Chief among the indispensable elements of peace which he set forth was a concert of nations to guarantee liberty and justice throughout the world. "It is inconceivable," he said, "that the people of the United States should play no part in that great enterprise." But Wilson did not look upon this concert as an arrangement of power to assure Anglo-American supremacy, nor was he interested in the victory of one belligerent over the other. Quite the contrary. If "the guarantees of a universal covenant" were to result in permanent peace, he believed that the peace terms would have to "win the approval of mankind." Therefore, the settlement should replace the balance of power with a "community of power"; and, lest harsh terms create resentment in the defeated nations, the war should end in a "peace without victory."

Wilson's critics were incensed at this maddeningly exalted assertion of national altruism, but Americans in general welcomed the speech as evidence that the President was doing everything in his power to keep the nation out of the war. Moreover, there were some grounds for confidence that he would succeed. Ever since Germany's so-called *Sussex* pledge of May 4, 1916, diplomatic relations with Germany had been more amicable than with the Allies. By that pledge Germany acceded to the United States' demand that no more merchantmen should be sunk without warning and without humanitarian precautions, even though it qualified its assurance by making it contingent upon the other belligerents' respect for the "laws of humanity."[41] Therefore, on the face of things, the administration had averted war, maintained American prestige, and exacted assurances from Germany that it would perpetrate no further incidents involving innocent neutrals traveling aboard belligerent vessels. And the President himself was, evidently, more determined than at the beginning of the war to enforce the nation's rights impartially. From all appearances, Wilson had succeeded in surmounting the inconsistencies and dangers of his original stand upon neutral rights. He had done so by urging self-restraint and abstention from the war, by sublimating his interpretation of American rights as the cause of humanity, and, above all, by elevating America's neutrality into the instrument of a new world order of peace and brotherhood.

As for the threat of a German victory to American security, this was not a consideration in his mind. His devotion to America's mission of serving humanity led him to minimize such matters of expediency, while his aversion to the balance-of-power system and to all elements of force in international relations caused him to depreciate strategic calculations as a basis for national action. And as long as a German victory did not seem imminent, it remained possible that he might continue to reconcile America's honor and rights with the highest sort of idealism and still keep the nation free from the holocaust of war without jeopardizing American security.

8. INTERVENTION

On January 31, 1917, the foundation of American neutrality collapsed, for on that date the German government announced that U-boat commanders would henceforth sink all ships—neutrals included—within the war zone. Before the American government had extracted the *Sussex* pledge it had unequivocally stated, "Unless the Imperial Government should now immediately declare and effect an abandonment of its present methods of submarine warfare against passenger and freight-carrying vessels, the. Government of the United States can have no choice but to sever diplomatic relations."[42] It was evident that the government could not now consistently or honorably avoid carrying out this threat. Reluctantly, Wilson returned to his dogged defense of American rights. On February 3 he told Congress that the nation was severing relations with Germany. The American people well-nigh unanimously supported him. On February 26, 1917, he asked Congress for authority to provide arms for American merchantmen. The House passed a bill for this purpose, but eleven Senators, whom Wilson branded as "a little group of wilful men," filibustered it to death. Wilson found authority to arm American vessels anyhow, and it then became just a question of time before a German submarine commander would commit an "overt act" that would bring the United States into the war. A number of such acts occurred before the middle of March. By March 21 Wilson had finally made the fateful decision to ask Congress to declare that a state of war existed.

To the last, Wilson was oppressed by the thought of taking America into war. He could find no solace in the ecstasy of patriotism. His bellicosity was too refined. He had reached his decision simply because he could find no alternative. In his final reckoning with the logic of strict accountability, which he had constantly feared but which he was powerless to escape, there is an element of the high tragedy that befalls men who, due to the inevitable choices dictated by their nature, become the victims of events beyond their control.

However, if Wilson could finally choose no other course but intervention, he would, at least, lead America into war upon the highest possible moral ground: the service of others. He had always believed in a holy war to vindicate spiritual conceptions and set men free. For a man with his strong emotional and intellectual revulsion toward international conflict, war had to be holy in order to be justifiable. Wilson was following a higher consistency than his opposition to war when he based his War Message of April 2 on the very principles for which he had sought to keep America a disinterested bystander.[43]

I have exactly the same things in mind now that I had in mind when I addressed the Senate on the twenty-second of January last; the same that I had in mind when I addressed Congress on the third of February and on the twenty-sixth of February. Our object now, as then, is to vindicate the principles of peace and justice in the life of the world as against selfish and autocratic power and to set up amongst the really free and self-governed peoples of the world such a concert of purpose and of action as will henceforth insure the observance of those principles.

He explained that America had taken up arms as a last resort. "We enter this war only where we are clearly forced into it because there are no other means of defending our rights." And he reviewed the events on the high seas that made neutrality untenable, also mentioning the spies and "criminal intrigues" which Germany had set loose upon the nation. But it was not just American rights which he was considering; it was the fundamental rights of all peoples. "The present German submarine warfare against commerce is a warfare against mankind. It is a war against all nations. . . . The challenge is to all mankind."

Wilson further generalized America's cause by presenting it as the cause of democracy against autocracy. He said that only an autocratic government, in which the moral voice of the people was suppressed, could perpetrate such crimes against international law and humanity. He avowed that neutrality was no longer feasible or desirable where peace and freedom of peoples were menaced by autocratic government. Therefore, the only remedy was a peace founded upon a concert among democratic nations.

Some Realists had been saying the same thing ever since the *Lusitania* sank; however, when they talked about autocracy, they referred not only to the principle of autocracy but to the fact of German military power; when they talked about democracy, they were thinking not only of the ideal but, in particular, of the mutual political interests of Great Britain and the United States; and when they talked about a concert among democratic nations, they did not anticipate the end of power politics but rather the beginning of a larger political arrangement, through which America could secure its power and its vital interests. But Wilson was bound to dwell upon the spiritual aspects of America's cause, simply because he believed that it was the things of the spirit that gave the American mission its power. He was bound to stress the democratic basis of a concert of nations, because he believed, "Only free peoples can hold their purpose and their honor steady to a common end and prefer the interests of mankind to any narrow interest of their own."

Wilson would not taint America's mission with the suggestion of self-interest, for he believed that only in proportion as the nation was disinterested could it serve the rest of the world. Therefore, he declared that Americans

sought nothing material for themselves. They would fight only for the ultimate peace and liberation of others. Nor would he have the nation forsake
that magnanimity and self-control which it had exemplified during the trials
of neutrality. He pleaded that the war be conducted without rancor toward
the German people. America would fight only the selfish and irresponsible
German leaders. It would fight only for the privilege of all men, including
Germans, to be free. "The world must be made safe for democracy. Its peace
must be planted upon the tested foundations of political liberty."

Concluding his address, in solemn tones Wilson spoke again of the reluctance with which he had reached his fateful decision.

> But the right is more precious than peace, and we shall fight for the things which we
> have always carried nearest our hearts—for democracy, for the rights and liberties of
> small nations, for a universal dominion of right by such a concert of free peoples as shall
> bring peace and safety to all nations and make the world itself at last free. To such a task
> we can dedicate our lives and our fortunes, everything that we are and everything that
> we have, with the pride of those who know that the day has come when America is
> privileged to spend her blood and her might for the principles that gave her birth and
> happiness and the peace which she has treasured. God helping her, she can do no other.

Amid the orgy of rejoicing and congratulation that followed this pronouncement, Wilson stood pale and silent. He later remarked to his secretary,
Tumulty, "My message today was a message of death for our young men.
How strange it seems to applaud that."[44] Only a holy war could vindicate a
message so elevated and yet so tragic.

CHAPTER X

THE ROLE OF SELF-DEFENSE

1. The Significance of America's Motives for Intervention

WOODROW WILSON led the United States into war with the same altruistic passion that had pervaded his policy of neutrality. Although he failed to resolve the inconsistencies and incongruities of the nation's strict stand upon its neutral rights, he surmounted them, in his own mind, by fixing his vision upon the transcendent objectives of the American mission. Although he reached his final decision with great reluctance, he reached it with no lack of conviction or determination; nor was he troubled with gnawing doubts as to its present justification and ultimate vindication. But what of the nation as a whole? Did Woodrow Wilson speak the public mind? For what ends and with what motives did the American people enter the war?

From the standpoint of winning the war it probably made little difference whether Americans entered it to redress the balance of power, to vindicate their honor and rights, to make the world safe for democracy, or to achieve a democratic association of nations. But the public's motives made a vast difference as far as the aftermath of war was concerned, for the effect of America's participation upon its postwar role in world politics was, in large measure, determined by the reasons for which the nation intervened and fought.

America's intervention in World War I came not as an exhilarating breath of Manifest Destiny but rather as the sigh of exasperation punctuating a reluctant conclusion. The crusade of 1898, compared to its successor of 1917, had come naturally and painlessly. Its consequences, though they had seemed revolutionary to some and shocking to others, were very quickly reconciled with the popular attitude toward international relations. Those who felt that the crusade had been perverted were consoled by new vistas for the American mission revealed by the nation's ascendance to world-wide power and prestige. The war with Spain, though variously interpreted, was readily accepted as an inevitable stage of American progress. But World War I came to America from across the sea as an aberration of international society. Intervention came, not spontaneously, but in the wake of hesitations and doubts.

In the aftermath of World War I it became gradually more difficult for Americans to reconcile their intervention with their conception of America's proper role in world politics. As they measured their experience against

195

traditional attitudes, Americans, inevitably, drew a comparison between the reasons for intervention and its consequences; and the results of that comparison deeply affected their adjustment to the international environment.

This phenomenon is inexplicable except in terms of America's international innocence. When war became a fact to Europeans, it had become an anachronism to Americans. Until then the twentieth century had seemed like a happy continuation of the nineteenth; in other words, a beneficent era of material and cultural progress and the growth of international harmony and understanding, a wholly enlightened era of universal suffrage, international arbitration, equal rights, peace congresses, social legislation, and cooling-off treaties. A glow of great expectations lighted American skies, and the tender blossoms of domestic and international reform sweetened the air. In 1914 Andrew Carnegie and Nicholas Murray Butler were thinking about war in terms of peace palaces.

A people in such a pacific mood as this could not easily embrace war. Yet a people so proud would not pay the price of peace. A few years of neutrality demonstrated that moral optimism and the love of peace were no guarantee that peace would prevail. A few years of victory proved that America's choice of war had brought no clear assurance of the wisdom of intervention. It was this latter situation that revealed the true significance of the nation's reasons for its fateful decision.

For a nation so confirmed in peace and nonintervention as America only the most convincing and enduring reasons could have seemed valid in the aftermath of war. In hindsight, it seems that, given the circumstances after the war, only those reasons, only those ends and motives, which were of compelling national interest and which victory could have assured would have appeared worth the price of America's involvement in a European conflict. Self-defense might have been such an end, if the nation's security had been clearly threatened. The vindication of national honor was intangible and less convincing or enduring. Certainly, altruistic service to humanity was the most difficult of all ends to pursue or to achieve through warfare.

Obviously, the considerations which lead a people to undertake a war are seldom precise or rigidly logical. There is no attempt here to present a comprehensive analysis of the public's complex motivation. But self-defense, the national honor, and service to humanity are singled out because the way in which millions of American citizens responded to these ends holds a vital clue to the significance of that momentous experience in the nation's adaptation to its international environment.

This chapter is concerned with the first objective, self-defense, and, more particularly, with the preparedness movement, which led to unprecedented peacetime defense measures, since that movement relates so closely to the nation's attitude toward its security. If there is truth in Lippmann's thesis that the American people supported intervention because they intuitively understood that their self-preservation would be threatened by Germany's domination of the opposite shore of the Atlantic, one would expect to find evidence of this intuition in the evolution of the preparedness movement.

2. THE IMPLAUSIBLE POSSIBILITY

Laying aside the question of whether fear of a German victory was a decisive factor in American intervention, it is difficult to determine how seriously the nation considered even the possibility of a threat to American security. Certainly, this possibility must have seemed, at first, quite implausible, since it was not at all in accord with the traditional view of America's omnipotence and isolation. On the other hand, there was nothing inevitably static about the American attitude toward world politics.

As chapter VI illustrated, certain groups came to take a special interest in expounding the threat of a German victory to American security. The warnings of the preparedness advocates, the far-sighted analyses of responsible journalists and academic men, the sensational portrayals of the scare writers, and the popularized versions of German expansionist and militarist literature; all these sources of information and misinformation constituted a significant challenge to the nation's traditional belief in its invulnerability. However, the existence of this challenge is no indication, in itself, of the response of the American people as a whole.

It is reasonable to suppose that America's growing distrust of Germany's foreign policy, created by her submarine campaign, by her espionage within the United States, and by reports of the conduct of German troops, might have predisposed the public to believe the charge that the United States would be next on the list if Great Britain should succumb. However, a survey in any newspaper of the principal items that concerned Americans during 1914–17 would indicate that the issues which heightened popular distrust of Germany actually tended to divert public attention from considerations of national security. One can infer as much from the trend of the arguments of Theodore Roosevelt, of the *New Republic,* and of some of Wilson's advisers, who were themselves impressed by the German threat but who were forced to admit their inability to impress the public.

Perhaps the issue of security was clearest in the fall of 1914, when Roosevelt was pointing with alarm to the example of Belgium, and when Wilson himself seemed somewhat concerned over the consequences of a German victory.*

* On November 3, 1914, England's Ambassador Spring-Rice wrote Sir Valentine Chirol, "There is a distinct feeling of fear in the general public with regard to Germany and a belief

At any rate, the German Foreign Office felt at this time that official fears of a German threat were important enough to warrant a disavowal. In a note to the Department of State, dated September 3, 1914, Ambassador Bernstorff, repeating assurances which his predecessors Holleben and Sternburg had delivered a decade earlier, denied that Germany had any designs upon the Western Hemisphere: "I have the honor to inform your excellency that I am instructed by my Government to deny most categorically the rumors circulated by English agencies to the effect that Germany, in case she emerges victorious from the present war, intends to seek expansion in South America."[1]

The American reaction to this disavowal suggests that it need never have been made. Bernstorff's statement was ignored by the Department of State until Bernhard Dernburg, an unofficial German propagandist, referred to it in a speech in Newark, New Jersey, on October 24, 1914. Dernburg's speech and a subsequent interview in the *New York Times* were intended to assure the American public of the falsity of the rumors which Bernstorff had denied officially. In his disavowal he included North America and Canada and added, "Germany has not the slightest intention of violating any part or section of the Monroe Doctrine." His statement that Bernstorff had communicated such assurances to the Department of State led the *New York Times* to check on the matter. But, to the amazement of the *Times* reporter, he found officials at the Department of State completely ignorant of the note. Finally, after a search of the official files, the department discovered the note and released a paraphrase of it. And thus what would otherwise have been an insignificant disavowal of a rumor, received, for a few days, the publicity of an international incident.[2]

The American press seems to have been as puzzled by the disavowal as the Department of State. The fact that Germany considered the rumor important enough to disavow led some newspapers to examine the disavowals more closely. When they found that Dernburg's statement was more inclusive than Bernstorff's, Bernstorff had to allay suspicions by confirming his colleague's speech and interview. Then these curious sentences in Dernburg's address came to the attention of the press:

The fact that Canada has taken part in this struggle has opened up a new prospective to Americans. It is a wilful breach of the Monroe Doctrine for an American self-govern-

---

that if the Allies are beaten the turn of America would come next and come soon." Stephen Gwynn, ed., *The Letters and Friendships of Sir Cecil Spring-Rice* (Boston, 1929), II, 244. However, by April, 1916, Spring-Rice had altered this opinion. He informed Sir Edward Grey that "there is no widespread feeling of insecurity [in the United States], or of fear that such undefended riches are a great danger to the possessor. This fear, however, prevails very widely in thinking circles." *Ibid.*, II, 329.

ing dominion to go to war, thereby exposing the American Continent to a counterattack from Europe and risking to disarrange the present equilibrium.

Now Bernstorff had to make it clear that Germany would not try to grab Canada either, in spite of his belief that Canada had placed herself beyond the pale of American protection by sending troops to England to fight Germany. And, finally, the blundering Dernburg confirmed this interpretation.

Throughout this imbroglio there does not seem to have been any American fear of German actions that could remotely have warranted the anxious official disavowals. Some newspapers remained suspicious of Germany's intentions, but none saw any immediate danger. Most were inclined to view the matter as academic anyway. The disavowals were interpreted as the result of a bad conscience and an inability to understand the American people rather than as a justifiable attempt to remove serious fears from the public mind.[3]

3. The Preparedness Issue Is Raised

One gets the impression from scanning the newspapers during the neutrality years that the talk of a German or Japanese invasion was never taken very seriously by the complacently secure American public. Nevertheless, Germany had more than rumors to disavow, for there were groups in America intent upon asserting the threat of German invasion of the Western Hemisphere quite explicitly and categorically.

As chapter VI indicated, the single most prolific source of alarm was the advocates of military and naval preparedness, who were determined to arouse the nation to an awareness of its defenseless condition. The preparedness movement was a natural focus for such alarm, since, in deference to America's tradition of nonintervention and nonaggression, the principal justification for the expansion of the army and navy had to be found in "defense"; and the advocacy of defense obviously raised the question, Defense against whom? Although all those who approved of a stronger army and navy did not necessarily do so for reasons of national security, one would expect to find all who were truly apprehensive about the nation's security advocating preparedness. If the circumstances of the European conflict did arouse the instinct of self-preservation in the American people, an examination of the preparedness movement is a logical way to discover it.

In 1916 Woodrow Wilson himself took up the advocacy of military and naval expansion. Did this mean that the administration became converted to the thesis that America's security was endangered? Did the popular support of the military and naval appropriation bills of 1916 indicate a widespread apprehension over the consequences of a German victory? Certainly, if the

American people entertained any such apprehensions, instinctively or otherwise, they would have been revealed in the course of more than eighteen months of the debate over preparedness.

That debate was touched off in earnest in October, 1914, when the chairman of the House Committee on Military Affairs, Representative Augustus P. Gardner, a Republican from Massachusetts and Henry Cabot Lodge's son-in-law, delivered sensational charges regarding the condition of the nation's defenses and introduced a resolution calling for a public investigation of the military and naval establishments in order to determine whether the country was ready for war. Gardner prefaced his charges with this dramatic statement: "For a dozen years I have sat here like a coward, and I have listened to men say that in time of war we could depend for our defense upon our National Guard and our Naval Militia, and I have known all of the time that it is not so." He went on to explain why he thought that the nation's defenses were inadequate. Declaring that the American people could not continue to salve their consciences by believing that no one would dare attack the United States, he asked if anyone could doubt that Germany and Japan would be a threat to the Monroe Doctrine unless the United States were ready to fight for it.[4]

In a statement to the press on October 15, Gardner said that peace propaganda had blinded Americans to the facts of national insecurity, and he charged that those who knew the facts had withheld them. He said he could not understand "how any intelligent student of history could fail to see that we are impotent to defend ourselves and to enforce the Monroe Doctrine by moral suasion and financial might alone." Then he admitted that his views with respect to the European war were not neutral.

> I am entirely convinced that the German cause is unholy and, moreover, a menace to the principles of democracy. Furthermore, I believe that the god of battles will visit defeat upon the Germans. But no matter which side wins we must remember that since the beginning of time victorious nations have proved headstrong and high-handed.[5]

This opening blast of the preparedness campaign was representative of the views of its earliest sponsors. These men were mostly Republicans and strong opponents of the administration and of Woodrow Wilson especially. They were no friends of neutrality. They were the firmest supporters of Great Britain's cause and the most vociferous antagonists of Germany's aims and conduct in the war. Their bitter partisanship and militant partiality for one belligerent did not enhance the persuasiveness of their message of preparedness in the nation at large.

The *New York Times,* one of the first and most insistent advocates of preparedness among the press, commenting upon Gardner's speech, noted a growing feeling that the war was "getting nearer to us" and expressed its concurrence in the fear that a German victory might imperil the cherished Monroe Doctrine. But the *Literary Digest,* summarizing editorial opinion throughout the country, pointed out that many papers thought that Congressman Gardner was unduly alarmed. They thought that it was unlikely that any European power would be able or inclined to go to war for the next twenty-five years and that, even then, it would be virtually impossible for such a power or any combination of powers to launch a successful attack upon the Western Hemisphere, let alone the continental United States.[6]

But Gardner had raised an important question, and the preparedness advocates were determined that the nation should not ignore it. On December 2 Lodge followed suit with some startling charges of his own concerning the inefficiency of the Army and Navy.[7] On the same day the National Security League was organized by a group of prominent New Yorkers. George Haven Putnam and other speakers at the opening meeting pictured, in details which became the stock-in-trade of preparedness literature, an invasion of the United States after a crushing defeat of England.[8] On December 7 Lodge and Gardner both introduced resolutions calling for an inquiry into the whole subject of national defense.[9]

4. THE ISSUE IS JOINED

The nature of the early preparedness movement—its strong nationalist, pro-Ally, and anti-Wilsonian bias—made it almost certain that the administration would oppose it. President Wilson made front-page news when he ridiculed and denounced Gardner's views on October 19.[10] The day after the Congressional elections in November Colonel House, who had already made up his mind that the German threat necessitated military and naval expansion, approached the President on the matter of adopting precautionary measures of preparedness, but Wilson said that any such action would shock the nation and that "even if Germany won, she would not be in a condition seriously to menace our country for many years to come."[11] During the fall and winter of 1914-15 the President was thinking of peace, not war. He was looking for an opportunity to mediate between the belligerents, and he did not want to jeopardize the nation's neutrality by alarming the people or offending a belligerent. He felt that this was a time that called for self-control, and he feared that even a precautionary measure of preparedness might encourage the forces of nationalism and militarism and knock the nation off its even balance. Thus in his annual address to Congress, on December 8, he asserted, "No one who speaks counsel based on fact or drawn from a just and candid interpretation of realities can say that there is reason to fear that from any quarters our independence or the integrity of our territory is threatened." But he went further than this and stated that it was inconsistent with American principles to maintain a large standing army, for this would turn America into an armed camp and destroy the nation's "moral insurance against the spread of the conflagration." He saw no necessity of yielding to "nervous and excited" people. America's role, he said, was to stand aside and perfect its own ideals and institutions so that it might give disinterested service for lasting peace when the time came.[12]

Wilson's message only increased the determination of the preparedness advocates, but it won considerable support in Congress, the newspapers and periodicals, and among the general public, who sent many favorable letters and petitions to the President. Moreover, it set the stage for a debate upon fundamental principles. Once more, as in the case of the issue of empire and, on a smaller scale, the Taft-Knox arbitration treaties, the leaders of American opinion were aligning themselves in opposition to one another in response to a basic divergence in their attitudes toward international relations.

5. THE ISSUE IS BLURRED

Theodore Roosevelt was among the first to give voice to this underlying conflict. During 1914 he was preoccupied with the need for preparedness. After he satisfied himself that the administration would fail in its duty toward Belgium, he directed all his efforts toward bringing the American people to realize that what had happened to Belgium could happen to the United States, if Germany were to win the war and if the United States were to remain in its defenseless fool's paradise. But he was not content merely to set forth in calm, dispassionate language the defenselessness of the nation. His failure to persuade the people of their peril convinced him that the solution to the problem of preparedness lay deeper than reason. It lay within the character of the people, in their willingness to meet force with force instead of taking refuge in professions of altruism; for if Americans lacked the manly will to muster the material means to defend themselves against aggression, then all the peaceful sentiments, visions of brotherhood, all-inclusive arbitration treaties, and paper plans for international leagues would be powerless to protect them from the military might of an acquisitive foe.

As we have seen in chapter VII, the fundamental temperamental inclinations and philosophic convictions underlying Roosevelt's assertion of American insecurity became more and more explicit as he realized the full extent of his frustration at the hands of a public whose moral sense seemed to have been captured or drugged by a bogus idealism, as reprehensible as it was dangerous. Thus in his argument for preparedness the defense of righteousness and the preservation of the nation's virility and moral fiber came to supplant the mere protection of the United States and its strategic outposts as the principal objectives of military and naval expansion. This tendency to shift the debate from expediency to fundamental moral principles became more pronounced as German torpedoes began to claim American lives.

The opponents of preparedness were quick to recognize their old antagonists on a new field of battle. They were aided in their opposition by the public reaction against militarism and jingoism during the first months of the war. The preparedness advocates, they charged, were simply American militarists and imperialists in a new disguise. They were alarmists, who would involve the nation in foreign bloodshed in order to satisfy their lust for power and their hatred of the peace movement. Where was the threat to the American homeland? The warnings about a German invasion seemed to the anti-preparedness group like a wild pretense designed to whip up nationalistic hysteria. In their view America's strength lay not in her armed force but in the perfection of her institutions and the supremacy of her moral reputation; and nothing could be more damaging to America's moral reputation than her adoption of the expensive, undemocratic, and war-provoking military system that had plagued the Old World. Therefore, America should be thinking about how it could bring lasting peace to the world, not about how it could prepare for war.[13]

Secretary of State Bryan's Prayer Day address, October 4, 1914, opposed preparedness on the basis of ideals that were dear to Wilson's heart. Peace and preparedness for war, he said, were incompatible; for the threat of force leads to suspicion and war, and the exercise of force to gain a military victory arouses resentment in the defeated and militarism in the victor. America had a better way of dealing with nations, and that was on the basis of moral principles and the goal of peace.[14]

Such idealistic objections to strengthening the instruments of coercion carried all the more conviction because they were joined with a deep-seated complacency about America's invulnerability. In common with other opponents of preparedness, Bryan was contemptuous of strategic considerations, since he believed that the United States was perfectly isolated and omnipotent within its hemispheric shell. Colonel House, reporting a conversation with Bryan in November, wrote, "I found him in violent opposition to any kind of increase by the reserve plan. He did not believe there was the slightest danger to this country from foreign invasion, even if the Germans were successful. . . . He spoke with great feeling, and I fear he may give trouble."[15] The naïve patriotic sentiment behind Bryan's belief in American invulnerability was displayed when he assured a Baltimore audience in December,

"The President knows that if this country needed a million men, and needed them in a day, the call would go out at sunrise and the sun would go down on a million men in arms."[16]

In a similar vein, Andrew Carnegie, when asked his opinion on preparedness, expressed the view that, even if the United States could be invaded, Americans would have no trouble handling the enemy. "They would make themselves at home and, learning the advantages of staying with us, would become applicants for citizenship, rather than our opponents in warfare." If the invaders fought, most Americans owned arms and could shoot straight. If their liberties were threatened, the citizenry would rise up en masse.[17]

Against such complacency as this the mere repetition of the details of an hypothetical invasion made little headway. There was nothing in the nation's traditional attitude toward security or in its experience in world politics to suggest that America was in literal danger of invasion if Germany won the war. The most that can be said about the effect of the propagation of such fears is that they may have helped to induce a vague sense of uneasiness among the inhabitants of the East Coast concerning America's ability to meet all eventualities. A great many Eastern papers, while expressing no alarm and disavowing jingoism, called for a calm investigation of the nation's alleged defenselessness.[18] A *Literary Digest* poll in January, 1915, discovered that, while a majority of the more than four hundred newspaper editors polled throughout the nation thought that the nation's defenses were adequate in case of war, just as many were in favor of a prudent expansion of the Army and Navy.[19]

However, the heat generated by the early months of the preparedness debate was not conducive to prudence or to a calm appraisal of the facts. Because the debate touched upon fundamental principles, it raised a number of issues concerning the nature of force and morality in international relations, which had little to do with the hard facts bearing upon the nation's self-preservation. Actually, this debate had been going on in about the same form since the 1890's. The opponents of preparedness understood that the most vocal sponsors of military and naval expansion would have taken their stand regardless of whether there existed any new threat to the nation's security, for these martial-minded men were stalwarts of the movement that had been sedulously promoting American power for the past two decades. By the same token, the organizers of the preparedness movement—the men in the National Security League, the Army League, and the Navy League—knew that their opponents were merely the latest spokesmen for the legions of peace advocates, who had been their temperamental and ideological enemies since the Spanish-American War and before. Because of this circumstance a good deal of the preparedness propaganda was spent in opposing "pacifists," while much of the antipreparedness propaganda was devoted to denouncing "militarists."

The preparedness issue was further blurred by the fact that each side had to trim its sails to the winds of public opinion. The great majority of the people wanted to keep out of war. Consequently, the argument that the nation should prepare for war lacked popular appeal. For this reason the advocates of preparedness rather soft-pedaled their original warnings of potential invasion as the pacific sentiment of the people became manifest. Instead they argued that preparedness was the best assurance of peace. Roosevelt himself frequently stated this position, coupling it with a denial of the "ultrapacifist" assertion that lack of preparedness could prevent war. In his foreword to *America and the World War,* written in January, 1915, he stated the case this way: "Preparedness usually averts war and usually prevents disaster in war; and always prevents disgrace in war. . . . Unpreparedness has not the slightest effect in averting war. Its only effect is immensely to increase the likelihood of disgrace and disaster in war." When Lodge presented his resolution for an inquiry into the subject of national defense on January 15, the only reason he gave for building up the nation's defenses, except for a blunt assertion of the nation's defenselessness, was that preparedness was the best way of staying at peace.[20]

At the same time, men in political life, regardless of their distaste for preparedness extremists, could hardly fail to take note of the rising public pressure for, at least, some measure of defense. Wilson seems to have been inclined to take moderate precautions as early as the end of November, 1914.* In December the *New Republic,* which supported Gardner's resolution, made a significant suggestion. In its view, there was much to be said for a prudent preparedness, but it decried the more emotional arguments of the preparedness advocates. Therefore, the *New Republic* wanted to see the administration adopt the program in order to blunt the edge of the Republican sword. Since the agitation could not be suppressed, the editors suggested that the administration control it by giving it publicity and enlightening it.[21]

6. WILSON ADOPTS PREPAREDNESS

It is significant that the preparedness movement did not really become a popular movement until the administration adopted it. It is also significant that the movement's spurt in popularity during the spring and early summer of 1915 was a response to Germany's submarine warfare and a quickened

* In a conversation with House on November 25, 1914, Wilson agreed that the country should have a reserve army "but not a large army." Charles Seymour, *The Intimate Papers of Colonel House* (Boston, 1926, 1928), I, 300.

sense of patriotism rather than to a sudden fear of the consequences of a German victory.

President Wilson first turned his concentrated attention toward the matter of preparedness on February 8, 1915, four days after the German decree threatening to destroy Allied merchantmen within a war zone around the British Isles.[22] The first burst of popular enthusiasm for preparedness followed the news on May 8 of the sinking of the *Lusitania*. In the general indignation and patriotic fervor which this incident aroused, groups which had never before supported preparedness, notably growing numbers of the clergy, became its staunch advocates.[23] Others, who had approved of preparedness for some time, found their first opportunity for organizing the movement on a popular basis, appealing to patriotism and the new determination to uphold American rights.[24]

The growing popularity of preparedness was evidenced by the opening in August of Major General Leonard Wood's original civilians' voluntary military training camp at Plattsburg, New York, with a complement of twelve hundred business and professional men, old and young, representing a wide geographical distribution.[25] Similar camps were to spring up in Chicago, on the West Coast, and in other parts of the nation, with the general purpose of fostering a patriotic spirit, creating enthusiasm for national defense, and increasing the trained military reserve. Wilson, incidentally, heartily approved of these camps as aids to health and discipline and hoped that they would develop into a system of universal voluntary training.[26]

But in spite of the surge of preparedness sentiment after the *Lusitania* disaster, Wilson delayed his wholehearted support of the movement until he was satisfied that he could not reach a satisfactory settlement of the submarine controversy. Finally, on July 21, 1915—the day he sent the third note on the *Lusitania* issue, warning Germany that further acts of this sort would be regarded as "deliberately unfriendly"—he instructed his secretaries of the Army and Navy, Garrison and Daniels, to draw up definite plans for a "wise and adequate" preparedness.[27] On August 2 he started marshaling favorable legislative sentiment by writing outstanding leaders of the committees of Congress handling military and naval affairs; and soon he was meeting an unending train of individuals, delegations, and committees interested in preparedness.[28]

Judging from the circumstances in which Wilson launched his preparedness campaign—the growing enmity toward Germany and his inability to reach a settlement of the submarine controversy—it would seem that his chief purpose was to arm the country for a war which might be forced upon America in defense of its neutral rights. He may also have looked to preparedness to give him more leverage in securing American rights. And, perhaps, the *New Republic's* suggestion that he steal the thunder of the extremists and the Republicans carried some weight, especially as the election of 1916 approached.

It is also possible to attach some significance to the fact that House had been warning Wilson of the possibility of a German victory.[29] However, if Wilson was impressed by this threat, his private correspondence does not show it, and in his public pronouncements he was careful to disavow it. Thus in his address of November 4, 1915, in which he set forth his program for a trained citizen army, a moderately increased regular army, and a speeding up of naval expansion, he warned that all Europe was embattled and that, therefore, Americans should ask themselves "how far we are prepared to maintain ourselves against any interference with our national action or development"; but he also said, "No thoughtful man feels any panic haste in this matter. The country is not threatened from any quarter."[30]

Again, in his annual message on December 7, Wilson denied that the nation's security was in any specific way endangered. He would not alarm the people; he would keep the nation on an even balance so that it might serve the world in peace. National defense, he said, was at the front of his whole thought, and it was America's duty to protect its neighbors as well as itself from "all outside domination," as well as from violations of their rights; therefore, he was asking Congress to enact the measures recommended in the reports of the secretaries of the War and Navy departments. But, at the same time, he assured the nation, "I have had in my mind no thought of any immediate or particular danger arising out of our relations with other nations. . . . I am sorry to say that the gravest threats against our national peace and safety have been uttered within our own borders."[31]

In other words, President Wilson wanted to unite the country behind a preparedness program; he wanted to warn the people that he might not be able to secure American rights and still keep the nation out of war; and yet he wanted to free the whole issue of preparedness from passion, prejudice, and partisanship so that the nation might remain true to its mission of service to the rest of the world.

It was with these objectives in mind that the President undertook his preparedness tour through the Middle West in late January, 1916. Every speech on that tour was aimed at these objectives. Wilson scarcely mentioned the possibility of a threat to the nation's security, except to refute it. The danger he wanted the people to apprehend was the danger of war resulting from events upon the high seas. If America fought, it would be to vindicate the principles of right and liberty in the world, not to secure her own self-interest. As he said at Chicago on January 31,

> Therefore, what America is bound to fight for when the time comes is nothing more nor less than her self-respect. There is no immediate prospect that her material interests may be seriously affected, but there is constant danger, every day of the week, that her spiritual interests may suffer serious affront, and it is in order that America may show that the old conceptions of liberty are ready to translate themselves in her hands into conceptions and manifestations of power at any time that it is necessary so to transform them, that we must make ourselves ready.[32]

Even the threat to American rights from German submarines was moralized and generalized to an extent that logically refuted the urgency with which Wilson avowed it. Thus in Cleveland, on January 29, he urged haste in preparedness but added,

> I do not wish to leave you with the impression that I am thinking of some particular danger; I merely want to leave you with this solemn impression, that I know we are daily treading amidst the most intricate dangers, and that the dangers that we are treading amongst are not of our making and are not under our control, and that no man in the United States knows what a single day or a single hour may bring forth.[33]

David Lawrence, who accompanied Wilson on his tour, observed the public reaction carefully. The audiences cheered Wilson's fighting remarks. He appeared to gain the confidence of the people. They trusted him the more because they knew he was a man of peace. But Lawrence found something maddeningly vague about the nature of the menace against which Wilson was urging the nation to prepare. His speeches aroused the people's patriotism, and the people were willing to undertake precautionary measures of defense on his recommendation; but they could see no concrete menace to their interests. In Lawrence's view, the popular impression created by the tour seemed to be that there was some sort of real danger arising from the generally unsettled world conditions; that the nation was not prepared to meet this danger; and that the President would avoid militarism and do all he could to keep America out of the war.[34]

7. THE VAGUENESS OF PREPAREDNESS

The vagueness of the menace America was preparing to meet was understandable in view of a marked reluctance on the part of all but the most sensationalistic advocates of preparedness to speak clearly of the possibility of war, to identify the potential enemy, or discuss the specific imperatives of self-defense, lest their remarks be construed as alarmism or a desire for intervention. This reluctance was testimony to the success of the early antipreparedness movement in associating the argument for self-defense with militarism, war lust, and pro-Ally bias—an association, be it admitted, which vociferous advocates of preparedness said much to confirm.

The only case for preparedness that was concerned with specific military and political facts was so sensationalized and oversimplified that it actually discredited the rational case for self-defense and militated against further discussion of the concrete imperatives of security. The original preparedness advocates might have served both their cause and the American public better if they had not reduced the problem of national security to the problem of repulsing an attack upon the continental United States or adjacent areas. This approach to national security was neither plausible nor enlightening.

Preparedness must be more than the ability to resist an armed attack. It involves marshaling the necessary power in relation to the power of other nations to assure the fulfilment of strategic commitments and diplomatic objectives; and that is an exceedingly complex calculation. But even the problem of repulsing an attack cannot be defined by the tactical image of Bunker Hill, according to which a nation holds its fire until the whites of the enemy's eyes appear. In 1898 Mahan had taken note of the confusion in the public mind between defense in the political sense and defense in the military sense.

> A navy for defense only, in the political sense, means a navy that will only be used in case we are forced into war; a navy for defense only, in the military sense, means a navy that can only await attack and defend its own, leaving the enemy at ease as regards his own interests, and at liberty to choose his own time and manner of fighting.[35]

Many of the preparedness advocates understood this, but a realistic program of preparedness lacked the dramatic simplicity of figuratively snatching the musket from off the wall in order to avert aggression, and it was much more difficult to square with the American people's aversion to calculations of power politics and the anticipation of war.

On the other hand, the more dramatic argument placed a burden of proof upon its propagators; and, in the circumstances of World War I, mere assertion failed to carry conviction. The alarmists had cried "Wolf!" too often. Ever since the preparedness agitation of the 1890's, the opponents of military expansion had insisted that their antagonists point out from exactly what quarter the United States should expect an attack. Everyone admitted that the Army and Navy were for defense only; so against whom, they asked, should the nation prepare to defend itself? By thus limiting preparedness to defense from invasion and confining defense from invasion to the repulse of an actual attack upon the homeland, the opponents of preparedness defined national security so narrowly that only the direst circumstances could have logically evoked the instinct of self-preservation. But by tacitly accepting this definition through their own emphasis upon the hypothesis of invasion, the advocates of preparedness helped defeat their own cause. When the American people lost interest in the prospects of invasion, preparedness seemed to have no clear and compelling relation to the nation's self-interest, and the argument for self-defense gave way to generalities and irrelevancies.

In vain, the editors of the *New Republic* urged the preparedness advocates during the fall of 1915 to state their precise objectives. America had no reason to fear an invasion, they said; but the nation's security might, nevertheless, be seriously affected in other ways. Then what should America be prepared to defend and against whom? What are the German and Japanese ambitions? What is practicable for them? How far should the United States go in stopping them? How far should the nation go in backing up its various policies? Should we defend at all costs the Monroe Doctrine, Pan-Americanism, the Open Door in China, and British sea power? Would we regard a German protectorate in southern Brazil as a cause for war? These were the questions the *New Republic* kept asking. It considered Roosevelt's replies as inadequate as Wilson's. It beheld preparedness being ushered in upon a flood of evasions and platitudes. In vain the editors pleaded, "It cannot be repeated too often that the essence of preparedness is a definition of foreign policy. Unless a government knows what it is going to defend, it cannot be said to have a program of national defense."[36]

The disheartening aspect of the agitation for military preparedness, as the *New Republic* saw it, was not only that it lacked a clear conviction of America's international obligations, commitments, and opportunities but that it was animated by a kind of blind suspicion and panic.

Indeed, if there was panic in the spring of 1916, as the preparedness movement reached its peak, it seemed to be unrelated to any specific peril. But panic is too strong a word to describe the preparedness sentiment as a whole. Most of those who favored preparedness did so because moderate and trusted advice dictated this as a prudent policy rather than because they feared a hostile act or some immediate peril or because they entertained any well-reasoned concern for American security.[37]

At the Washington meeting of the National Security Congress in January, 1916, Mr. Coudert, delivering the keynote address, estimated that the average American did not really think that his country was in danger; and so he called for a campaign of education, asserting that American security depended on the preservation of the balance of power in Europe and that the British Navy was America's first line of defense. Another speaker won great applause when he warned of a postwar combination of Japan and England against the United States. But the other speakers, if they considered the reasons for preparedness at all, preferred to stress the vindication of American rights and the upholding of the bulwark of international law.[38]

By the summer of 1916 preparedness had been adopted by so many groups that it bore the aspect of a patriotic awakening more than a rational response to some vital and practical need. Preparedness had come to mean no more than common-sense alertness and willingness to defend one's country. Parades, flag-waving, patriotic exhortation, and fervent appeals for unity were, apparently, the most persuasive arguments the cause could produce.

Wilson's adoption of the movement had only served to infuse it with that vague amalgam of national honor and exalted purpose which characterized the administration's neutrality policy. And while the preparedness movement became broader under administration sponsorship, the opposition became narrower, as a nucleus of antipreparedness zealots—notably, Senator La Follette and Congressmen Tavenner, Hensley, Calloway, Witherspoon, Kitchin, Lindbergh, and Gray—charged that the whole program was simply another way to whip up war hysteria for the benefit of the munition manufacturers and war profiteers.[39]

All in all, there was little in the preparedness movement or its opposition to enlighten the nation on the fundamental bases of American security.

8. NAVAL PLANS AND DEBATES BEFORE LUSITANIA

But what about the specific defense programs, the recommendations of the Navy's General Board and of Secretary of the Navy Daniels, and the debate over the appropriation bills? These matters could not be decided in terms of general principles alone. Certainly, if the nation's security played a major role in America's relation to the European conflict, concrete political and military imperatives would have figured in the counsels of high strategy and in the debates over specific defense recommendations. Moreover, consistent with a long American tradition, expansion of the Navy was not regarded as bearing the same risks of militarism as the creation of a large standing army.

When the war broke out, the Navy's chief strategist was Rear Admiral Bradley A. Fiske, Aid for Operations.* No officer had taken a more consistent

---

* The nearest thing to a board of high strategy was the Navy's General Board, in existence since 1900. When Fiske, as a Captain, took his seat on the Board in October, 1910, he found that the Board had no war plans, only scattered information and suggestions. Although he was ignorant of the subject himself, he became head of a section on war plans. By 1914 the Navy still had no general staff. Rear Admiral Fiske, as Aid for Operations, was the only officer with remote pretensions to being a naval strategist; and, by his own admission, he was not fitted by training or experience for the position. Bradley A. Fiske, *From Midshipman to Rear-Admiral* (New York, 1919), pp. 477, 479, 530. On April 1, 1915, Fiske resigned as Aid for Operations because of his inability to persuade Secretary of the Navy Daniels of the need for greater pre-

and intense interest in co-ordinating naval strength with the overall objectives of foreign policy than he. Fiske had some positive ideas about what the size of the Navy should be and why. As early as 1910 he had decided that the Navy should be second to none. This view was not based on world strategy, of which he was largely ignorant at the time, but on the principle that the "probability of war between any two countries is least when their navies are equal in power." Beyond that, he was impressed with the predatory nature of the struggle among nations, and he was determined that the United States should not fall among the degenerate nations for lack of a large navy and a keen military spirit.[40]

In his autobiography, published after the war, Fiske said that in 1913 he and the higher naval officers realized that, although the French Navy was about the equal of the United States Navy, and the British Navy was much stronger, there were only two navies to fear, Germany's and Japan's—especially the German Navy, with its high efficiency, the concentration of national resources behind it, its strategic wisdom, and its abhorrent militaristic ideas.[41] Of course, there was nothing new about this fear of Germany and Japan. It had dominated American naval policy ever since the war with Spain. Accordingly, in 1913 the General Board of the Navy was still advocating the same program of naval expansion it had adopted ten years earlier, and it was sticking doggedly to its original estimate that the United States needed a navy "equal or superior to that of any probable enemy."[42]

Official fear of the German peril was, undoubtedly, sharpened by the outbreak of war in Europe. Fiske says that he and most of the high naval officers believed that Germany had gone to war on the basis of a deliberate calculation that the chances of victory were greatly in her favor. They believed that this calculation was accurate, and, knowing Germany's hatred of the United States, they thought that the situation ahead was one of "the greatest possible peril."[43]

On this basis Fiske drew up a memorandum, dated November 9, 1914, for Secretary Daniels in the vain hope of persuading him that the Navy was sadly unprepared. He called this memorandum the most important paper he ever wrote. Yet in view of his sense of urgency, Fiske was surprisingly vague about the exact nature of the threat which the Navy should prepare to meet, for he admitted that

even the most timid person can give no specific reason for anticipating war with any given country, at any given time.

It is true that I cannot specify the country with which war is most probable, nor the

paredness. When, due to Fiske's labors, the office of Chief of Naval Operations was created by the naval appropriation act for 1915, a man with no knowledge of, or interest in, strategy was appointed to that position. Fiske remained in hot water with Daniels until he retired on June 13, 1916. *Ibid.*, pp. 582, 584–5.

time, nor the cause. But my studies of wars in the past, and my observations of conditions at the present time, convince me that if this country avoids war during the next five years it will be accomplished only by a happy combination of high diplomatic skill and rare good fortune.*

Another representative of the Navy's General Board, Admiral Vreeland, had been somewhat more specific when he appeared before the House Naval Committee in connection with the hearings for an appropriation bill passed in June, 1914. Vreeland said then that the Board's recommendations were necessary to support the Monroe Doctrine, the Open Door policy in China, and the exclusion of Asiatics from the United States. He specified Germany and Japan as the most likely challengers of these policies. Although he admitted that the position of the United States seemed secure at the moment, due to its relative geographic isolation and the involvement of European powers in their own problems, he warned that America could not trust its security to the shifting alliances of Europe. But what disturbed him most was the possibility of Japanese reprisals against America's Pacific possessions, as a reaction to the West Coast's anti-Japanese policies.†

In the debates during April and May, 1914, on this same naval appropriation bill Representative Richard Pearson Hobson, a former naval officer and a long-standing champion of naval expansion, took the position of the General Board.‡ He made it clear that he considered Germany a menace, because she had a fleet that could destroy the American fleet, a powerful army, and a merchant marine capable of transporting that army across the Atlantic. Hobson, like Admiral Vreeland, placed no reliance upon the inhibiting effects of the European balance of power. America would have to rely exclusively upon her own power. Consistent with his position since the Russo-Japanese

* *Ibid.*, pp. 556–57. In various articles during 1915–17 Fiske argued that naval defense was not just defense against aggression but defense of trade routes and national policy, including the nation's reputation, honor, and prestige; that military and naval policy had paid too little attention to international and national circumstances; and that the United States needed a fleet on each ocean as strong as that of any nation with which America's policy might conflict. He was not much more specific than this, but he did make it clear that the Allies might not win and that Germany might then be a formidable menace. "Naval Preparedness," *North American Review*, CCII (November, 1915), 847–57; "Naval Policy," *ibid.*, CCIII (January, 1916), 63–74; "Naval Defense," *ibid.*, CCIII (February, 1916), 216–26; "The Navy Needs Strategy," *Independent*, LXXXIX (February 19, 1917), 301–2.

† *House Report*, No. 314, 66th Cong., 2d Sess. The General Board once more recommended a long-term naval program to include construction of 48 battleships by 1920 and based this recommendation on the need of supporting America's national policies and of resisting "the national policies of prospective challengers and the force they can bring against us." *Annual Reports of the Navy Department, 1913*.

‡ Hobson, who had played a distinguished part in the Spanish-American War, retired from the Navy in 1903 and became a Congressman from Alabama in 1907. After the war scare of 1907 he lectured and wrote frequently, portraying a coming war against Japan and England. See, for example, his series of articles in *Cosmopolitan*: XLIV (May, 1908), 584–93; XLV (June, 1908), 38–47; XLV (September, 1908), 382–87.

War, he regarded the Japanese Army and Navy as a serious threat to America's insular possessions in the Pacific and even to the Western Seaboard of the United States itself.[44]

Even though Hobson's conclusions about naval needs were accepted by some Republicans and big-navy Democrats, the nature of the Congressional debate on the appropriation bill indicates that few shared his reasoning.

A group of antipreparedness Democrats, including Hensley, Witherspoon, Buchanan, and Gray, ridiculed alarms of invasion, stressing America's impregnable position and pointing to the crippling distress of European and Far Eastern nations. They charged that the agitation for preparedness was sheer alarmism perpetrated by the Navy League, munitions manufacturers, financiers, and other groups with selfish interests.[45] Their thought was well summed up in the minority report of the House Naval Committee in February, 1913: "For the purpose of defending our country against attacks from any nation on earth we confidently believe that our Navy is amply sufficient, and for any other purpose we need no navy at all."[46]

Other Congressmen supported the administration's program, which was far more moderate than the General Board's recommendations.* They agreed with the antipreparedness group that the nation was in no danger from aggression, but they were anxious to keep the Navy at its same relative strength as a precautionary measure. A few, like Representative Williams, mentioned the need of supporting traditional American policies, such as the Monroe Doctrine and the Open Door.[47] It was this moderate group which prevailed. The act of June 30, 1914, authorized two battleships and a third, contingent upon the sale of two obsolete ships.

Nor did the authorization for 1915 reflect any alarm. In spite of Admiral Fiske's urgent memorandum of November 9 to Secretary Daniels, and the General Board's recommendation of four capital ships, and the House Naval Committee's virtual repetition of its previous report, Congress again followed Daniels' more economy-minded recommendation and, by the act of March 3, 1915, authorized two more battleships.[48]

In connection with the hearings and debates preceding this act, it is noteworthy that on December 8 and 9, 1914, Admirals Badger and Fletcher, much to Fiske's displeasure, testified before the House Naval Affairs Committee that the Navy was in a high state of preparedness and that the United States did not need to fear an invasion.[49] Although these men, of course, supported the program of the General Board, Fiske was disturbed by their sanguine approach; so through the co-operation of Representative Hobson, he presented

* Secretary Daniels asked for the usual two battleships plus eight destroyers and three submarines. *Annual Reports of the Navy Department, 1913.*

his own testimony on December 17 in order to correct the public impression.

Fiske's testimony received full coverage in the newspapers, since he was recognized as a capable and far-sighted man. His statements were even more newsworthy because they were diametrically opposed to the optimistic views of Badger and Fletcher. He said that it would take five years to bring the Navy up to an "effective condition," and he specified the Navy's weaknesses, including the entire absence of a naval staff with a general plan of national defense. However, he did not directly refute his colleagues' opinion that the United States was secure from an invasion. He told the Committee frankly that the American Navy was not the equal of Germany's in effective condition; he praised the efficiency of the German Navy frequently, drawing constant comparisons with the inferior United States Navy; and he warned that the end of the European war would bring changes no one could prophesy. But this was as close as he came to discussing what America was preparing to defend and against whom she was preparing to defend it. Perhaps he felt that it was not his part to delve into international political relations. But whether or not Fiske was inhibited by such restraints, the Committee quite obviously was; for the chairman, Representative Padgett, felt it necessary to warn his distinguished witness, at one point, that he could not permit the use of the name of any country in an invidious way or in a way that would cause criticism.[50]

In spite of the limited nature of his testimony, Admiral Fiske was of the opinion after the war that his statement, along with Congressman Gardner's dramatic pronouncement of October, 1914, was "probably the thing which gave the preparedness movement its first real start."[51] A more modest view might have led him to see in the actual events of the war a more powerful influence than the most persuasive words.

9. NAVAL PLANS AND DEBATES AFTER LUSITANIA

On May 7, 1915, the *Lusitania* was torpedoed, without warning, off the Irish coast. Until then none of the events in Europe, on the high seas, or in Asia had led either the General Board or the Secretary of the Navy to modify appreciably the naval plans which had been devised before the outbreak of the war in Europe; and the majority of Congress seemed content to follow the lead of the administration, on the assurance that the nation was no more seriously involved in foreign developments than when the war began. But on July 21, 1915, President Wilson, having sent his third *Lusitania* note to Germany, suggested to Secretary Daniels that he draw up "a wise and adequate naval program, to be proposed to the Congress at its next session."[52] In accordance with Daniels' request, the General Board drew up and submitted to him on July 30 a report, which went further than any of its previous recommendations, calling for a navy to be completed by 1925 "equal to the most powerful maintained by any other nation in the world."[53] The recommendations in this report were later revised to fit the more moderate request of the Navy department; and it was, substantially, this revised report which Secretary Daniels and President Wilson recommended to. Congress in the first week of December, 1915.

The important thing to note here is that the reasoning of the General Board reflected the same concern over the problem of maintaining neutral rights that motivated Wilson. In its report of November 9, 1915, the Board declared, "A navy strong enough only to defend our coast from actual invasion will not suffice. Defense from invasion is not the only function of the Navy. It must protect our sea-borne commerce and drive that of the enemy from the sea." Therefore, the Board concluded, "Our present Navy is not sufficient to give due weight to the diplomatic remonstrances of the United States in peace nor to enforce its policies in war."[54] In other words, the Board had broadened the objectives of its strategy from merely defending the nation's policies and its territory against the most probable enemies, Germany and Japan, to supporting the administration's determination to hold Germany "strictly accountable" and, at the same time, prepare the nation for war should the enforcement of neutral rights become incompatible with peace.

The one-year construction program authorizing five battleships but no dreadnoughts, which the House Committee on Naval Affairs agreed upon in May, 1916, and which the House approved on June 2, was not so ambitious as the administration's recommendations, since it was the result of a compromise between the Democrats and the little-navy men, aimed at preserving a semblance of party harmony on the eve of the national convention;* however, before this bill went before the Senate, the Democratic compromise was shaken by the Battle of Jutland, which appeared to demonstrate the battleship's superiority over the battle cruiser; consequently, Democratic leaders joined with the Republican minority in the Senate Naval Committee's report of June 30, 1916, in restoring the General Board's five-year program but telescoping it into three years.[55] On July 21, 1916, this bill, with some amendments, passed the Senate by a vote of seventy-one to eight. The House soon accepted this measure, over the protests of the little-navy Democrats, who denounced the abandonment of their compromise. On August 29, 1916,

---

* In the Committee five little-navy Democrats held the balance of power: Buchanan (Ill.), Calloway (Tex.), Connelly (Kan.), Gray (Ind.), Hensley (Mo.). However, they acquiesced in a program far exceeding their desires. Alex M. Arnett, *Claude Kitchin and the Wilson War Policies* (Boston, 1937), p. 95; *House Report*, No. 743, 64th Cong., 1st Sess.

President Wilson signed the most far-reaching naval appropriation act that preparedness advocates had ever dared hope for.[56]

No one could doubt that the passage of this unprecedented peacetime defense measure marked a great change in the nation's thinking since Representative Gardner introduced his resolution in October, 1914. Yet if the general acceptance of the act of 1916 was brought about by a new awareness of America's strategic dependence upon a British victory, the debates in the House and the Senate did not reflect the fact, for they failed to produce any arguments or reasoning that had not become commonplace since the summer of 1915.

The congressional opponents of preparedness cited Wilson's 1914 speeches against his present position. If the United States entered the armaments race, it would deprive the world of the services of the only peaceful, unselfish, self-possessed nation capable of bringing about peace and restoring health and sanity to the civilized world; preparedness was the surest incitement to war; an armaments program would saddle the people with a ruinous financial burden and would lead to domestic regimentation, militarism, and the loss of America's basic liberties. At the same time, these men insisted that they were not among those who believed in peace at any price. They would fight to defend the nation from aggression, and they would arm the nation if there were any serious chance that it might be attacked; but where, they asked, was the danger of invasion?

In the Congressional debate of 1916 it was not the advocates but the opponents of naval expansion who stressed considerations of American security. The United States, they said, was in no danger of attack; and they cited the testimony of high army and navy officials to prove it. Senator La Follette gave the most complete exhibition of this approach in his address on July 20, 1916.[57] He took note of all the sensational and lurid accounts of invasions of the United States that had been circulated in volumes of books and displayed in the newspapers and magazines. Then he asked whether the United States was really as defenseless as these accounts assumed. He was willing to support appropriations for coast and border defense, since that was truly defense and offered no temptation to war profiteers nor incitement to conquest. But he pointed out that General Weaver, chief of Coast Artillery and a member of the joint Army and Navy Board, had testified before the House Committee on Military Affairs a few months before that eleven thousand men added to the Coast Artillery would make American coasts impregnable to an attack from any source, and that General Nelson A. Miles, former commander-in-chief of the Army and Admiral Frank F. Fletcher, chief of the Atlantic Fleet, testifying before the same committee, had asserted that the lessons of Alexandria, Port Arthur, and the Dardanelles conclusively demonstrated that coast fortifications were more than a match for assaults by sea.

Nevertheless, if some nation could send an overwhelmingly powerful fleet to American shores, La Follette was willing to concede that it might make trouble if the American fleet were not equally powerful. So he considered the relative strength of the United States Navy and its potential adversaries. Again he cited Admiral Fletcher, this time in his testimony before the House Naval Affairs Committee in February, 1915. Admiral Fletcher had stated that there was but one navy superior to the American Navy, and that was England's, and that only the British Navy could defeat the American Navy. Rear Admiral Badger, testifying the same day, had admitted that, ship for ship, the United States Navy was superior to the German Navy. And yet, as La Follette construed Rear Admiral Knight's testimony before the House Committee in February, 1916, the General Board was committed to building a navy as large as England's, even though Admiral Knight himself had stated that England would probably have a much smaller navy after the war than at the beginning. Therefore, La Follette concluded, the United States would have the largest navy in the world at the end of the war; and the Board would commit the nation to this exorbitant program in spite of the fact that no preparedness advocate had even suggested that America should get ready for a war with England. If, on the other hand, the United States did expect a war with England, then La Follette was for fortifying the Canadian border in a hurry. But, under the existing circumstances, he could only conclude that professional navalists, the Du Pont Powder Company, and Bethlehem Steel were behind a campaign of panic designed to immerse the nation in a full-scale armaments program and a profiteers' war.

La Follette was only repeating what Congressmen Padgett, Stephens, Calloway, and Hensley had said in the House debates at the end of May.[58] After La Follette spoke, Senators Thomas, Vardaman, Clapp, and others said that they, too, would go the limit in defending the nation from invasion but that nobody worthy of consideration pretended that the United States was in any danger of that.[59]

No one was more intent upon driving this point home than Senator George W. Norris of Nebraska. In view of his position twenty years later, his fulsome protest to the naval appropriation bill makes interesting reading. On July 13 Norris rose to protest against the stream of propaganda from newspapers, the rostrum, the theater, moving-picture films, editorial columns, magazine articles, sensational books, the pulpit, the former President, and even the current President, spreading their "gloomy prophecies, forebodings, and warnings that in a day or an hour we may be overridden, subjected to conquest, and made the subjects and vassals of some conquering military host." He attributed the great part of this propaganda to the influence of war profiteers.[60]

On July 17 he noted that two Senators who supported the appropriation bill, Borah and Kenyon, had repudiated the notion that the United States was in danger of invasion, but he asserted that, the repudiation notwithstanding, this was "the scarecrow that has been used in every newspaper and in every magazine, from every rostrum and from many pulpits, to make the people of the United States believe that at the close of this war we would be in danger of absolute annihilation by some one or more of the powers now engaged in the war." He went on to say that after the current war the leading belligerent nations would be composed of women, cripples, and paupers, and that neither Germany nor any other nation would have the desire or the ability to cross the ocean and invade the United States. All the talk of invasion, he concluded, originated with men and institutions who stood to make money out of preparedness and the expenditures of war.[61]

Senator Norris most certainly exaggerated the claims of the preparedness advocates. He had caught them in an untenable position, and it was natural that he should exploit his advantage to the utmost. But, actually, the alarms of invasion, upon which he vented his sarcasm, had, by the summer of 1916, largely disappeared from preparedness propaganda. It is interesting that Hudson Maxim's name appeared frequently in the Congressional debate of 1916; but whereas not one preparedness supporter mentioned him, the antipreparedness group never tired of pointing out the absurdity of his book and the fact that Maxim was a munitions inventor and manufacturer.[62]

The speeches in support of the Army and Navy appropriations were conspicuous for their lack of any reasoned rebuttal to the ridicule and denunciation which the opposition showered upon the thesis that American security was endangered. No one rose to refute La Follette or Norris with an analysis of America's basic strategic interests. No one ventured to say that America's security depended upon the preservation of the European balance of power or the British Navy. No one suggested that the preservation of America's status in world politics depended upon anything besides its own sovereign, independent will and strength.

However, the preparedness movement had never been marked by a realistic appraisal of America's relation to its international environment. A more striking aspect of the preparedness speeches was the absence of any detailed descriptions of the bombardment of the East Coast and the capture of its industrial centers. If American security was mentioned at all, it was mentioned in general terms. If Germany was singled out as America's potential enemy, it was only by inference.

Senator Claude A. Swanson of Virginia, acting chairman of the Senate Committee on Naval Affairs, opened the Senate debate for the naval appropriation bill on July 13, 1916.[63] The necessity for an increase of the Navy was "immediate and urgent," he said. Naval supremacy means national pre-eminence. America needs a navy to protect its foreign commerce, on which its prosperity depends so heavily, against Great Britain and Germany alike. Then Swanson asked, "Are we foolish enough to believe that this Nation, which, with its vast wealth and unsurpassed possibilities—the object of envy and jealousy of other Nations—can be safe if we permit ourselves to become a fourth or fifth rate naval power?" What powers did he think would be envious and jealous? Germany, Russia, Japan, and Great Britain; all these nations, he said, had been guilty of predatory imperialism; and, consequently, the Philippines, American commerce, the Panama Canal, and the Monroe Doctrine were endangered. Why, in what way, and by whom he did not specify. However, he qualified his remarks by noting that Great Britain was not really a potential aggressor, since she maintained no standing army.

This was the extent of Senator Swanson's remarks about American security. The central point of his argument was that the United States needed a strong navy in order to give force to its diplomacy and maintain its prestige among nations. He drew a picture of American impotence if the United States should lack a navy second only to Great Britain's.

> Our foreign policies and intercourse will necessarily become timid and vacillating. The great affairs of the world affecting our interests will be regulated without consultation with us. We will then become suppliants, pleading for rights instead of boldly and courageously demanding them. It will mean the surrender of our great prestige. It will mean a distinct loss to the world of the great power possessed by this Nation for peace, justice, and liberty.

Senator Lodge seconded this view, remarking that the Senate bill would "be of more value to our peace than all the diplomatic notes that can ever be written.[64]

Senator Borah of Idaho, an ardent nationalist who had been more concerned about relations with Mexico than with Europe, agreed with Senator Swanson that the only way to make America's insistence upon its rights effective was to construct a powerful navy. On this general principle he cited a recent statement of the premier of Japan that diplomacy had to be backed by sufficient force. But he considered the premier's views, not as a threat, but as a practical precept all nations would do well to follow. In fact, he went out of his way to reject the theory that America's security was threatened by any particular nation. Like Swanson, he believed that the threat to American security was the general threat, arising from unforeseen, fortuitous circumstances, which a rich nation in a predatory world might expect, just on general principles. "Let us put aside all this idea of any particular nation planning an attack upon the United States. . . . But can we ignore the growth of nationalism, the intense spirit of nationality, the growth and the commercial ambitions of nations?" We are at peace now, he said; but our citizens have been drowned and our property seized at sea, and our honor has been affronted by the closing of the open door in the Orient. "No; we have not offended, but we have suffered incalculable loss in honor and in property. Weakness is an invitation to aggression, weakness is an invitation to war. As a people and as a Nation, we can not escape our responsibility."[65]

Senator Kenyon of Iowa spoke for the bill. But, like Borah, he confessed to being just generally alarmed, not specifically alarmed. He said that the people of Iowa had been visiting one another over the fence and asking just who was going to attack the United States, and they had got no convincing answer. His people, he said, were for a common-sense, reasonably adequate preparedness, but they weren't carried away with "alarming predictions that we are soon to be the theater of a great war." As he saw it, preparedness was like insurance, like a wise policy one takes out on general principles but with no specific danger in mind.[66]

Senator Gallinger said that he was supporting the army and navy bills solely in order to prepare America for all possible emergencies and not because he believed a war with any particular nation was imminent. Senator Jones made it clear that he was not voting for a strong navy out of any fear of aggression but simply because he wanted to insure a "peaceful respect for our just rights." Senator Brandegee said he did not know anything about a foreign invasion, but he still did not want to take any chances on the uncertain future.[67]

This was the substance of the entire debate upon the unprecedented naval appropriation act of 1916: a vague sense of danger from unforeseen circumstances; a patriotic desire to express America's prestige and self-respect; a determination to back up her diplomatic remonstrances; and a willingness to take precautionary measures so that the nation might give a good account of itself if, in spite of its good intentions, it got dragged into a war by circumstances beyond its control.

10. THE IMPACT OF PREPAREDNESS

Although no issue would seem to have concerned American security more directly than the issue of military preparation for defense, the preparedness movement, in reality, conspicuously failed to produce a dispassionate and realistic discussion of the fundamental bases of national self-preservation. It failed, fundamentally, because the circumstances of the war did not arouse any serious or widespread doubt about America's impregnable physical isolation and because they *did* arouse a strong concern for the nation's honor and self-respect. In general, the preparedness movement reflected the same sentiments, anxieties, ambitions, and uncertainties that characterized America's whole reluctant but steady drift into war. If Germany had seemed likely to win the war, if the British Navy had been crushed and the Continent of Europe overrun, perhaps then the preparedness movement would have constituted an education in the exigencies of power politics and survival; but, as it was, the movement actually amounted to miseducation, for, in deference to traditional American attitudes, both sides in the argument presented national security as something the nation could achieve, quite apart from its overall political policies and their relation to the stream of world politics, by arming a metaphorical fortress to resist an hypothetical assault. If the preparedness movement had any effect upon America's sense of security, it probably strengthened it, for the unprecedented defense measures that Congress finally adopted seemed to guarantee the invulnerability of the national fortress, even against the most powerful assailant.

There was little in the way America prepared militarily to indicate that she was prepared psychologically to assume the burden of intervention in a war so irrelevant to the instinct of self-preservation.

CHAPTER XI

WAR COMES TO AMERICA

1. The Perspective of Neutrality

THE development of the preparedness movement suggests that the circumstances of the European conflict had more effect on American public opinion than all the millions of words spent upon the question. The argument that a victorious Germany might invade the Western Hemisphere was bound to seem implausible when Germany was unable to conquer France and England. But the tragic sinking of the *Lusitania* was an incontrovertible fact. The American people would prepare to fight for their rights, but as for the threat to their security, they adopted a "show me" attitude.

Germany's submarine warfare might, nevertheless, have aroused the instinct of self-preservation which Lippmann perceived in retrospect, if the American people had been truly conditioned by their experience in world politics to respond to threats to the Atlantic Community. But that, distinctly, was not the case, for the great body of the nation had never known the fear of insecurity; it had not been touched by the discipline of adversity. Consequently, Americans approached the war in Europe with no familiar perspective of national interest, except the traditional policies of neutrality and nonintervention, which were based upon the assumption that the United States really had no vital interest at all in conflicts across the sea and could keep out of them if it wanted to.

In the American Creed the legal status of neutrality was enshrined as a moral principle and hence as a guide for all times and all circumstances. When President Wilson delivered his neutrality proclamation, he simply confirmed the popular belief that the current European conflict, like all the past conflicts, had arisen from purely European causes and would end in purely European consequences, and that the best thing for the United States to do was to conduct itself impartially and lend its moral prestige to the restoration of peace and sanity.

Yet, as Wilson well knew, neutrality was not simply an abstract principle, which a nation could follow without respect to the actions of other nations. Neutrality stood for a body of international law, more or less agreed upon, which not only imposed obligations but also granted rights. Therefore, even though America might remain faithful to its neutral obligations, if it insisted upon neutral rights which other nations were not prepared to grant, the very policy which was meant to preserve peace might draw the nation into war. From the first *Lusitania* note to the arming of American merchant vessels, the American people, as a whole, backed President Wilson in his insistence that Germany observe what the American government set forth as its just rights.

Although neutrality was posited upon America's indifference toward the fortunes of war, it was the fortunes of war, not America's legal impartiality, which determined the belligerents' willingness to observe American rights. However remote from the European conflict Americans might consider themselves, Europe could not ignore Americans, for the United States was a wealthy nation, determined to continue its commercial relations with the other side of the Atlantic, and the belligerents knew that the flow of American trade affected their very self-preservation. Under these circumstances neither belligerent stood to gain by observing a strict interpretation of American rights. Therefore, the ability of the United States to keep out of war depended, ultimately, upon the calculation which both belligerents made of the relative advantage of violating American rights as compared to the disadvantage of incurring American enmity. In the end, Germany preferred unrestricted submarine warfare to American neutrality, and, consequently, the United States was forced into the unenviable position of entering a foreign war to uphold a principle of national conduct that was based on the very premise that such a war could be of no vital interest.

In terms of national self-interest the issues of neutrality that faced America were simply: Is enforcing neutral rights rigidly against England worth the risk of a German victory? Is enforcing neutral rights rigidly against Germany worth the risk of a war with Germany? But to have framed the issue in this way would have meant the repudiation of neutrality and the surrender of national honor to expediency.

Moreover, few foresaw the unprecedented circumstances of submarine warfare. It was natural to try to apply conventional conceptions of neutrality at the outset. Yet once the United States had taken an official stand on a conventional interpretation, the American people proved that they preferred war to the dishonor of compromise.

Of course, the confusion in the public mind between wanting to keep out of war and demanding strict observance of American rights arose, basically, because Americans did not think in terms of alternatives. Their view of international relations was unclouded by such complexities. With innocent optimism they believed that they could eat their cake and have it too. Moreover, they lacked a central criterion, such as strategic interest, for discriminating among alternatives; and, being wedded to the illusion of isolation and omnipotence, they were contemptuous of the practical consequences of their national ideals and impulses. Without a realistic chart of the complex currents of national interests and power the nation was left to drift hazardously upon the turbulent waters of international politics, improvising its course as it went.

2. THE PERSPECTIVE OF INTERNATIONAL MORALITY

Americans might have been less emotionally entangled in the circumstances of the war if the issue of neutrality had been confined to the maintenance of legal rights; but Germany's submarine warfare violated America's sense of humanitarianism as well as its sense of honor. Having had little experience with the ravages of self-preservation upon international morality and having nurtured expectations of international morality scarcely warranted by the facts of world politics, the American people were appalled by the very existence of war and outraged by its breach of decency and humanity. Moreover, there was something peculiarly shocking and spectacular about sudden death by German torpedoes that was lacking in the no less poignant tragedy of starvation by British blockade.

America's moral indignation over German submarine warfare was heightened by a general impression of German lawlessness and guilt, which began to take form with the invasion of Belgium. It was not only the invasion of that neutralized nation that aroused Americans but, just as much, Germany's official alibi on the grounds of expediency. Chancellor Bethmann-Hollweg's reference to the Belgian treaty as "just a scrap of paper" and Von Jagow's explanation that the safety of the Empire had rendered the violation of Belgian neutrality necessary were taken as standing indictments of Germany's Machiavellian contempt for international morality. In America the invasion of Belgium was pre-eminently a moral question; and yet the Germans excused themselves in terms of military necessity.

Germany's continual failure to provide a moral pretext for acts of expediency betrayed a basic ignorance of American psychology. The incidents of the war that really aroused American hostility toward Germany were incidents that violated the public's humanitarian sentiments: the destruction of Louvain and Rheims, reports of Belgian atrocities, the shooting of Nurse Edith Cavell, the deportation of Belgian and French labor. Ambassador Bernstorff was one of the few German officials who understood the extent to which Americans judged international affairs from the standpoint of emotional values and sentiments of justice and morality. But he could never get his superiors to understand this. In his book about his ambassadorship he complained, "In Germany there was no understanding for the curious mixture of political sagacity, commercial acumen, tenacity and sentimentality, which goes to make up the character of the American people."[1]

Germany's violations of the laws of humanity were not, in themselves, sufficient provocation for American intervention, but the indignation which they aroused gave great moral assurance to America's strict interpretation of its neutral rights and made it possible to identify the nation's honor with the welfare of mankind.

3. THE "LUSITANIA" INCIDENT

In spite of Germany's violation of America's sense of national honor and international morality, the nation, as a whole, was very reluctant to go to war on these grounds. President Wilson was quite in harmony with public sentiment when he urged self-control. However, one suspects that for most Americans, especially during the first two years of the war, the basis of self-control was not so much an altruistic desire to serve the world as a practical desire to keep out of trouble. As long as the United States could discharge its obligations to the world merely by staying out of war and affording a beneficent example, altruism came easily; but Americans resisted every suggestion that they entangle themselves in a foreign struggle for the sake of humanity, just as they valued peace more highly than the vindication of neutral rights. Theodore Roosevelt called this cowardice, selfishness, and moral emasculation, but the great majority of Americans saw nothing reprehensible in the pursuit of such obvious and innocuous self-interest.

The public reaction to the sinking of the British ship *Lusitania* is an instructive example of America's practical pacifism. It was the *Lusitania* crisis that first aroused the nation to an awareness that the war concerned the United States as well as Europe. The loss of over a thousand lives, one hundred twenty-eight of whom were Americans, under such frightful circumstances came to the nation as an incredible reversal of the whole tide of civilization and moral progress, which had seemed about to sweep through the world before war broke out.

The American response was immediate and explosive. The *Literary Digest* observed, "Condemnation of the act seems to be limited only by the restrictions of the English language." The *New York Sun* thought that "no episode of the war has startled and aroused public opinion in this country in greater degree." The *Philadelphia Press* announced, "America is suddenly bought into the maelstrom of this gigantic war." The *New York Times* urged an official demand that "the Germans shall no longer make war like savages drunk with blood." The *New York Tribune* ominously declared, "The nation which remembered the sailors of the *Maine* will not forget the civilians of the *Lusitania*."[2] And the *Nation* exclaimed, "To speak of technicalities and the rules of war, in the face of such wholesale murder on the high seas, is a waste of time. The law of nations and the law of God have been alike trampled upon."[3] From the more nationalistic elements of the population came a torrent of epithets like "piratical," "dastardly," "abominable"; they called the incident "mass murder," "assassination," and "cold-blooded murder." But no group was more insistent upon placing Germany beyond the pale of civilization than the clergy.[4]

Ten days after the *Lusitania* disaster Ambassador Bernstorff reported to Chancellor Bethmann-Hollweg that Germany's propaganda in America had completely collapsed, and he pointed out that "another event like the present one would certainly mean war with the United States."[5] The excitement over the sinking was so great that Bernstorff had to remain in seclusion for several days afterward. When the propagandist Dernburg defended the German submarine commander's deed on the grounds that the *Lusitania* carried ammunition and munitions aboard, popular indignation became so great that Ambassador Bernstorff had no recourse but to advise him to leave the country voluntarily before he was deported.

However, indignation was one thing and action another. Roosevelt thought that it was "inconceivable that we should refrain from taking action on this matter, for we owe it not only to humanity but to our own national self-respect."[6] But his famous editorial "Murder on the High Seas" was 99 per cent invective and only one sentence worth of recommendation that the United States "act with immediate decision and vigor."[7] Most Eastern newspapers were satisfied to demand "quick and decisive action" or an "immediate accounting." The *New York Tribune,* after thinking the matter over, decided, "We shall not make war now to avenge those who have been murdered," but "we shall not continue to avoid war if the question becomes one of defending those who still live." Only a very few papers, such as the *Memphis Commercial Appeal,* the *Boston Transcript,* and the *Washington Times* went so far as to advocate a declaration of war if Germany failed to promise not to repeat such unlawful depredations.[8]

After the initial excitement wore off it was evident that the great majority of the people were as anxious as ever to keep out of war. There was a popular disposition to agree with the *Springfield Republican* that America's rights and dignity could be vindicated short of war and that, anyway, the nation was not prepared for war and could do more good as a neutral.[9] Among an imposing array of former Presidents, cabinet officers, and attorney generals, who were moved to proffer their advice, moderation was the key-note. Former President Taft and Vice-President Marshall doubted whether war would accomplish anything desirable. Taft shrewdly observed, "A demand that cannot survive the passion of the first days of public indignation and will not endure the test of delay and deliberation by all the people is not one that should be yielded to." No Congressman advocated war, though some recommended firm and decisive action that might have led to it.[10]

It was noteworthy that the Hearst papers, which had been the foremost purveyors of jingoism for years, showed great restraint concerning the *Lusitania* incident. Anglophobia and German sympathies and ties had something to do with this; but, beyond that, the papers could see no incentive for a war against Germany. War could only get the United States entangled in European power politics. A war against Mexico was one thing, but what could be accomplished by a war against Germany?

David Lawrence examined editorial comment carefully and concluded,

It is a singular thing that while a few people in the Eastern seaboard were clamoring for war, a careful examination of the editorials showed that out of a thousand compiled by telegraph in the three days after the *Lusitania* was sunk in May, 1915, less than one-half dozen indicated a belief that war should be declared.[11]

Secretary of Agriculture Houston, who was in southern California when the news of the disaster reached him, has described the public reaction in the West.

I found that the sentiment in the West was strongly with the President in his course. The war seemed out there to be very far away. Nobody was thinking about intervention either in Mexico or in Europe. The people were not seriously contemplating the possibility of our becoming involved in the war in Europe; but, at the same time, they wanted our rights safeguarded.[12]

The *Lusitania* affair was the occasion for a great patriotic revival. The American people were more united at this time than they had been since the war began. The Irish-American and German-American factions were, for the moment, subdued, though still convinced of German righteousness and British duplicity.[13] Yet, in the absence of some clear and compelling national interest at stake, there was no disposition to take hasty action that might involve the nation in "a war with which we have nothing to do, whose causes cannot touch us," as President Wilson had described it.[14] Whether the public would have exercised the same restraint if the *Lusitania* had been an American ship no one can say. Only two things were proved by the *Lusitania* incident: the American people wanted their right to travel safely on belligerent vessels upheld; they wanted to keep out of war. As a whole, they were willing to trust Woodrow Wilson to fulfil both wishes.

At the same time, the furor excited by the *Lusitania* outrage indicated that American self-control did not extend to that impartiality of thought which the President had counseled; for this event, like the invasion of Belgium, had the effect of establishing in American opinion a strong moral distinction between the Allies and Germany. Just as reports of German "barbarity" on land were to lend moral validity to the American case against Germany on the sea, so the violations of national rights and international morality on the high seas made the reports of inhumanity in Belgium and France seem more plausible. When the British passenger steamer *Falaba* was sunk on March 28, 1915, with the loss of over one hundred noncombatants, including one American, the *New York Times* observed that the event "tends to make the stories of other German atrocities credible."[15] The torpedoing of the *Lusitania* had the same effect; and the British, realizing this, rushed to completion and released, just five days after the event, the famous Bryce Report confirming German atrocities. The indignation over the *Lusitania,* coupled with Lord Bryce's high reputation in America, convinced many who had been skeptical before that the atrocity allegations were true. As the *New York Tribune* declared, "A civilized and neutral world . . . found it impossible to believe that the things reported in Belgium represented German deliberate and reasoned policy, but all such incredulity . . . sank with the *Lusitania.*[16]

America's growing moral indignation against German conduct, in turn, stiffened the popular insistence upon a strict observance of the neutral rights which the administration had asserted. More and more, the juristic uncertainties of neutrality were being resolved in that peculiar complex of nationalistic and idealistic fervor which had inspired the crusade against Spain.

4. WILSON FULFILS THE NATION'S DOUBLE WISH

By the time Wilson sent his first note of protest over the *Lusitania* sinking, the pattern of America's uneasy neutrality was set. From then on, America's ability to keep out of war depended upon Germany's conduct of her underseas warfare. America's agonizing approach to war became the story of a series of anxious fluctuations in the public temper between wanting to avoid all risk of war and wanting to vindicate the nation's rights and the rights of humanity, each fluctuation corresponding to another incident or to a diplomatic protest refused or accepted. With each fluctuation the public became less neutral in spirit. Yet each diplomatic position that was taken was taken in the name of neutrality, for neutrality stood for American rights as well as nonintervention.

Wilson's hesitations and doubts became the public's hesitations and doubts. Each new problem on the high seas was confronted with much legal disputation over whether or not the United States was really enforcing its rights neutrally. Always Wilson assured himself of public support before he committed the nation to another position. And so American lives, America's honor, and America's sense of international morality were all tied to the hazardous endeavor of telling one belligerent the conditions under which it could prosecute its warfare against the other, as well as telling both belligerents how their warfare must affect American lives and property on foreign as well as American ships.*

When President Wilson found it necessary, after Germany's unsatisfactory answer to his first *Lusitania* note, to send an even stiffer protest, insisting in the name of American rights and the rights of humanity that Germany stop her practice of torpedoing passenger liners without providing for the safety of the passengers, Secretary of State Bryan's discretion got the better part of his valor, and, on June 8, he resigned rather than become a party to what he regarded as an ultimatum that would provoke war. The American public was, in general, no more anxious for war than Mr. Bryan, but it was far less heedful of the consequences of the government's rigid policy. Bryan was showered with abuse and castigated as a coward and a traitor; Wilson was praised for taking a noble and forthright stand.

Four days before he resigned, Bryan wrote the President that an uncompromising demand upon Germany might result in war and that the people were against war. Wilson replied that he knew that "a great part of public opinion" was opposed to war, but he intimated that there was no sure way of carrying out "the double wish of our people, to maintain a firm front in respect of what we demand of Germany and yet do nothing that might by any possibility involve us in the war."[17] Nevertheless, he evidently believed that the chances of succeeding in this endeavor justified the risk; and most of the American people appeared to agree with him, if they seriously considered the risk of war at all.

American indignation was allowed to cool when the German government made a conciliatory reply to Wilson's second *Lusitania* note on July 8, 1915,[18] but it flared up again over disclosures of German espionage and sabotage in shipbuilding and munitions industries.[19] Yet as long as Wilson was able to grant the nation's "double wish," it seemed likely that manifestations of America's growing hatred and distrust of Germany would be confined to words.

The temper of the people rose once more on August 19, 1915, when a Ger-

---

* Before Germany declared unrestricted submarine warfare, only three American lives were lost on American ships as the result of submarine action, and these lives were lost on the tanker *Gulflight*, which was following British patrol boats and was, therefore, technically under convoy. Stephens to Secretary of State, May 3, 1915, *Foreign Relations, 1915, Supplement*, p. 378; Bryan to Page, May 6, 1915, *ibid.*, p. 381; Carlton Savage, *Policy of the United States toward Maritime Commerce in War* (Washington, D.C., 1926), II, 586.

man submarine commander, contrary to his instructions, sank the British passenger ship *Arabic,* killing two Americans. But when Bernstorff informed Secretary Lansing, on September 1, that submarine commanders had been instructed not to sink liners without warning and without safeguarding the lives of noncombatants, and when a few days later Germany disavowed the sinking of the *Arabic* and offered indemnity,[20] public opinion was quieted once more. Wilson's methods were, apparently, vindicated. The nation was heartened by another demonstration that its official representatives could, indeed, carry water on both shoulders.

Actually, the problems of neutrality had only been checked, not solved. In a tacit recognition of the difficulties of enforcing neutrality laws impartially, Lansing had proposed, in late January, 1916, that Great Britain discontinue its arming of merchant vessels in return for Germany's full compliance with conventional laws of visit and search. However, on the day Wilson returned from his preparedness tour, the British let it be known that they were strongly opposed to this *modus vivendi.*[21] On top of this blow, on February 10 Germany issued a memorandum stating that

enemy merchantmen armed with guns no longer have any right to be considered as peaceable vessels of commerce. Therefore, the German naval forces will receive orders, within a short period, paying consideration to the interests of the neutrals, to treat such vessels as belligerents.[22]

But how could a submarine commander distinguish an armed from an unarmed merchantman? Clearly, intensive submarine warfare under the conditions of this memorandum would destroy American neutrality. Yet the United States could not honorably avoid war at the price of accepting these conditions, even though Lansing's rejected *modus vivendi* with Great Britain was an admission that Germany had a good case as long as British ships were armed. So Lansing compromised and reinterpreted America's stand. To the press and the European governments he explained that the United States contended that belligerent merchantmen could arm, but "for the sole purpose of defense."[23]

According to this interpretation, Americans could travel on defensively armed vessels and expect to be granted the conventional rights of warning and provision for safety. At the same time, Germany's memorandum made it almost certain that submarines would attack these ships, and soon.

Congressional opponents of Wilson's neutrality policy sensed a new crisis in the offing. In order to save the United States from war Senator Gore and Representative McLemore, supported by Bryan and his followers in and out of Congress, introduced resolutions designed to prohibit Americans from traveling on armed belligerent merchantmen.[24] Senator Stone wrote a letter to Wilson denying the moral right, though not questioning the legal right, of citizens to risk the peace of the whole nation by traveling on armed belligerent vessels.[25]

This was the occasion for Wilson's famous reply, on February 24, that he could not accept the abridgment of the rights of American citizens in any respect, no matter what the cost, since the honor and self-respect of the nation were involved. "Once accept a single abatement of right, and many other humiliations would certainly follow, and the whole fine fabric of international law might crumble under our hands piece by piece."[26]

Through some shrewd domestic power politics Wilson succeeded in getting the resolutions tabled in the first week of March. The domestic crisis had passed, but the crisis on the high seas was closer than ever.

It is a singular fact that Wilson's reply to Senator Stone was generally applauded as a forceful assertion of American honor and idealism. The *Literary Digest* found, upon a careful examination, that the American press, divided into many camps on foreign policy generally, fell into line with "almost complete unanimity" in support of Wilson's stand. Any other course was regarded as "hauling down the flag" or "retreating under fire." Even in a city with such a large pro-German population as St. Louis the press expressed a willingness to go to war, if worst came to worst, in defense of American rights. There was a general disposition to put the issue on grounds of high principle, contrasting Wilson's position with one of base expediency.[27]

On the other hand, there was a good deal of support for the Gore-McLemore resolutions in Congress, both parties being pretty thoroughly split on the issue along geographical lines.[28] Undoubtedly, Senator Stone's letter to President Wilson reflected the doubts of a good many Americans of moderate opinion concerning the wisdom of entering a war in order to vindicate the right of American citizens to travel on armed belligerent vessels. But few chose to face the possibility of war seriously at the time. Moreover, the issue had passed beyond these narrow grounds into the shadowy realm of national honor and general ethical principles.

The dire consequences which Wilson's opponents prophesied seemed a good deal closer when the unarmed French steamer *Sussex* was torpedoed on March 24, 1916, with heavy loss of life and several Americans seriously wounded. This attack, coming as it did on a wave of new apprehensions and constituting a direct violation of Germany's pledge not to sink passenger liners without warning, aroused more indignation than any event since the *Lusitania* disaster. For a month a major diplomatic crisis seethed, with Lansing and House urging a break in relations and Wilson trying desperately to keep calm and organize a mediation effort. Finally, the administration was

pushed to a position one more step beyond "strict accountability." The note
that went to Berlin on April 18 stated flatly,

> Unless the Imperial Government should now immediately declare and effect an aban-
> donment of its present methods of submarine warfare against passenger and freight-
> carrying vessels, the Government of the United States can have no choice but to sever
> diplomatic relations. . . . This action the Government of the United States contemplates
> with the greatest reluctance but feels constrained to take in behalf of humanity and the
> rights of neutral nations.[29]

Once again Wilson had expressed the popular desire for a firm stand on
neutral rights and international morality, and once more he was right in
thinking that the people wanted to keep out of war. And again this dual
policy appeared to be vindicated when Germany acceded to American demands on May 4 and declared that orders had been issued that no more un-
resisting belligerent merchantmen were to be sunk without warning and
humanitarian precautions. It was true that the German note added that Germany would reserve "complete liberty of decision" in the event that the
United States failed to persuade the British government to "observe the rules
of international law" and that the United States replied that American rights
were not contingent upon the conduct of any other government;[30] but, in
the widespread relief that followed the German concession, these qualifications did not appear to mar Wilson's diplomatic achievement. Only German
submarines could do that.

During the nine months between the so-called *Sussex* pledge and Germany's announcement of unrestricted submarine warfare, on January 31, 1917,
the major diplomatic controversies were with Great Britain, not with Germany. The widespread resentment over the British black list and an accumulation of old and new grievances demonstrated that the American people did
not apply ethical criteria to Germany alone. Even the most pro-Ally journals
demanded that the United States take a firm stand against her strategic ally.
Although the possibility of war was not seriously considered, except in the
Hearst papers and in German-American and Irish-American quarters, the
diplomatic crisis approached the stage of a rupture in relations. Wilson told
House on July 23,

> I am, I must admit, about at the end of my patience with Great Britain and the
> Allies. . . . I am seriously considering asking Congress to authorize me to prohibit
> loans and restrict exportations to the Allies. . . . Polk and I are compounding a very
> sharp note. I may feel obliged to make it as sharp as the one to Germany on the sub-
> marine. . . . Can we any longer endure their intolerable course?[31]

Congress gave the President retaliatory powers against black-listed Americans and, on September 8, voted the largest naval bill ever passed by the

legislative body of a nation not at war. Wilson exclaimed in a moment of desperation, "Let us build a navy bigger than hers and do what we please."[32] After the war Lansing wrote in his *Memoirs* that America's relations with Great Britain would have strained to the breaking point but for the fact that British violations affected only American property, while German violations affected American lives.[33]

Wilson was now more convinced than ever that the only way out of the imbroglio of neutrality was to end the war through mediation. In his mind the negative goal of keeping out of war had always been sanctified by the higher purpose of America's mission of serving the world. By the summer of 1916 he had gained some influential support for the idealistic venture of bringing lasting peace to all nations.

However, as far as the mass of the American people was concerned, it seems probable that the negative aspects of nonintervention were still foremost. The Presidential campaign of 1916 was dominated by the claim, "He kept us out of war." This slogan originated in the Democratic convention as a result of Martin H. Glynn's keynote address. It was born in spontaneous enthusiasm. As Glynn celebrated the episodes throughout American history in which the United States had refused to fight even though its rights were violated, the convention broke into a tumultuous chant, punctuating the resurrection of each episode with, "What did we do?" And from Glynn, rapidly becoming intoxicated with his own oratory, would come the triumphant response, "We didn't go to war." It was a wild demonstration. William Jennings Bryan wept with emotion in the press gallery.[34]

There was nothing bogus about the sentiment of that day. The slogan was Democratic, but its sentiment was well-nigh universal. The Republican nominee, Charles Evans Hughes, could no more ignore its popularity than could the Democratic convention. "A vote for me is not a vote for war," he insisted. "It is a vote for lasting peace. It is a vote for the maintenance of American rights on land and sea, throughout the world."[35] Republicans and Democrats might rival each other in protesting their patriotic determination to secure American rights, but campaign orators were equally vehement in asserting their party's obsession for keeping the country out of the European catastrophe. Roosevelt might rant at this "moral cowardice," and Wilson might secretly regret the purely negative connotation of the Democratic slogan;* but the American people were neither so heroic as the Warrior nor so exalted as the Priest.

---

* Wilson felt that this slogan raised false hopes. To Secretary Daniels he confided, "I can't keep the country out of war. They talk of me as though I were a god. Any little German lieutenant can put us into the war at any time by some calculated outrage." Ray S. Baker, *Woodrow Wilson* (New York, 1927–39), VI, 258.

Yet there was nothing in the popular yearning for peace to suggest that Americans would forego those things that could not be had except by war, if circumstances beyond their control should make the choice between war and dishonor unavoidable. Eventually, Germany's resumption of unrestricted submarine warfare exposed the insubstantial basis of the nation's double wish and rapidly forced Americans to choose honor above peace. Because we have said that the ends and motives that led the American people into war shaped the nation's conduct during the war and afterward, it is important at this point to trace the development of some of those ends and motives during the uneasy prelude to Armageddon.

5. MILITANT IDEALISM

Although the American people were strongly attached to the ways of peace, there were signs that, if, in spite of their attachment, they should finally be forced to choose war, then war might yet come in the guise of a second crusade. For with each affront to its honor the nation had exhibited something of the patriotic pride and fervor that had avenged the *Maine*. And in the nation's mounting moral indignation toward Germany and its growing sense of altruistic mission there smoldered the same idealistic fervor that had liberated Cuba. As in 1898, it was moral indignation which lent this fervor its peculiar militancy and aroused the sort of antipathies that incite men to war.

We have already observed that the invasion of neutral Belgium, the destruction of Louvain and Rheims, reports of Belgian atrocities, the shooting of Nurse Edith Cavell, the deportation of Belgian and French labor, and German espionage and sabotage, as well as the inhumane circumstances of submarine warfare, created in the minds of many Americans a strong moral aversion toward Germany. This aversion was strengthened by the stubborn defense of German actions by German-American spokesmen, who were charged with practicing disloyalty and fomenting disunity during critical times.[36] Then, too, German wickedness seemed to be confirmed by the popularized exposés of the Machiavellian schemes of German ultranationalists. The despicable trio of Bernhardi, Nietzche, and Treitschke—more despised than feared—represented the moral depravity and the cynical contempt for international ethics which were believed to motivate the political and military rulers of the German people.

It is a significant commentary on the trend of the times that during World War I the doctrine that the international struggle for power is a civilizing influence, a manifestation of Darwinian evolution, became the focus of an ideological antagonism toward Germany. This was particularly ironic in view of the fact that it was America's ardent national egoists and her former imperialists who were most outspoken in the assertion of this antagonism. A circle of Roosevelt's admirers—General Wood, Elihu Root, Colonel Stimson, Senator Lodge, and others—and strong Anglo-Saxon patriots, like Ambassador Page and Colonel House, became America's most militant idealists.

These men were incensed at Germany's violations of American rights and the gentlemanly code of international ethics and decency, and their indignation was not inhibited by any timid years of the consequences of partiality; for they were no respecters of the fetish of neutrality; they believed that there could be no neutrality between right and wrong. In their view German policy was deliberately, unalterably, and by the very nature of Germany's rulers inhumane, autocratic, militaristic, expansionist, and utterly barbaric in its standards of international conduct. On the other hand, they were convinced that the preservation of American ideals, American interests, and civilization itself depended upon a British victory. Working together as proud and independent nations, the English-speaking peoples—"Anglo-Saxon" had fallen out of favor—could organize a peaceful, prosperous, and democratic world, they held; whereas, spiritually and practically, the defeat of one people would be a catastrophe for both.

According to the tenets of militant idealism, it was cowardly to postpone America's entrance into the war until Germany actually threatened American security or until the nation had been kicked and pushed and goaded into war as a final resort. Josiah Royce called Germany the "wilful and deliberate enemy of the human race."[37] Since Germany was as much an enemy of the human race after the sinking of the *Lusitania* as after the declaration of unrestricted submarine warfare, the natural inference was that a delay in intervention could only be explained by cowardice or moral myopia.

Militant idealism found its chief support among intellectuals, authors, publishers, and professional men, especially in the East: such men as Josiah Royce, Albert Bushnell Hart, George Louis Beer, Ralph Barton Perry, Lyman Abbott, Booth Tarkington, and George Harvey. These were men, by profession, peculiarly well equipped to expose German guilt and the ideological antipathy between Kultur and Western civilization.

James M. Beck's *The Evidence in the Case* (1914), subtitled *A Discussion of the Moral Responsibility for the War of 1914, as Disclosed by the Diplomatic Records of England, Germany, Russia, France, and Belgium,* became a textbook for militant idealists. By January, 1917, this book, which also appeared in serial form, had gone into its thirteenth printing. Beck was a lawyer, but his book, as the subtitle suggests, was as much a moral as a legal exposition. The central motif of *The Evidence in the Case* was the moral obligation of nations to justify their acts in the forum of the general conscience of mankind. Beck hauled Germany up before the court of Civilization and became one of the first and most influential Americans to pronounce an unqualified "Guilty"—a verdict which became a mainstay of America's second crusade and, after the war, the favorite target of the disillusioned.

Beck's second book, *The War and Humanity,* first printed in November, 1916, pronounced the verdict of guilt upon Woodrow Wilson as well. Beck charged that, largely because of Wilson's lack of vision and courage, the United States had failed in its responsibility to civilization, in its duty to cooperate with nations of "kindred ideals" and "substantially identical interests" for the defense of the peace of mankind. He made the moral basis of this indictment quite clear: "There is an everlasting right and an everlasting wrong about this stupendous war, and unless the right shall triumph a liberal civilization may perish in the world."[38] In the foreword of this tract Roosevelt wrote, "It is the kind of book which every self-respecting American, who loves his country, should read."

It was a simple matter for Beck and others to document the everlasting wrong from German sources. Ideologically, it was symbolized in the word "Kultur." German propaganda, with its customary inefficacy, instead of identifying Germany's cultural traditions with American traditions, seemed intent upon stressing the peculiar philosophical superiority of German Kultur, its greater profundity and intellectual purity. But it required no philosophical training for Americans to perceive something dangerously alien in a system of thought which ponderously theorized about the depth of the German soul and defined freedom in terms of duty.

Professor Hugo Münsterberg's *The Peace and America* (1915) typified the inefficacy of German propaganda. In this book Münsterberg paid his respects to American humanitarian and individualist ideals but implied that they were rather superficial and spiritually barren compared to the deeper meaning of German life. "To be a German," he explained, "means to be filled with the belief that the highest aim does not lie in the individuals and their states of happiness, but in the service to ideal values." In German Kultur "the word freedom is meaningless except as the counterpart of duty." Kultur, he explained, is the expression of a nation's soul, not the haphazard creation of individuals. Kultur stands for the capacity for theorizing about, and striving for, ideal ends; it is inseparable from the idea of the state. Münsterberg regretted the inability of Americans to comprehend the true meaning of Kultur, but he hoped that they would at least respect Germany for living up to the mission which she had received from the God of History.[39]

Obviously, the campaign for Kultur invited ideological counterattack.

The philosophical contentions of Germany's own sympathizers gave substance to the growing feeling that the European conflict was deeper than mere national rivalry. No wonder many concluded, with Wilbur Abbott, writing in the *Yale Review,* that "the war has been transformed from a trial of strength into a conflict of ideas and sentiments more far-reaching and significant than any possible manifestation of physical force."[40]

By all means, the most popular ideological counterattack delivered by the militant idealists was composed by William Roscoe Thayer, the eminent biographer of Cavour and Roosevelt. His *Germany Versus Civilization* was rushed to press by Houghton Mifflin in the spring of 1916 in the hope that it would become the book of the hour. It was destined for a large circulation and a wide influence. As the preface indicated, the purpose of *Germany Versus Civilization* was to assemble a body of "characteristic doctrines of the shapers of Prussian policy, from Frederick the Great to General Bernhardi, to remind the reader of the essential German elements underlying the Atrocious War." Thayer proceeded to trace the rise in Germany of the glorification of brute force and the doctrine of the survival of the fittest. Instances of German mendacity, cunning, and cruelty were all equated with deep-seated national traits and philosophical beliefs. Thayer fairly wallowed in the gory details of German atrocities. And the conclusion which all this led to was simply: "This war sprang as naturally from the German heart and will as a vulture springs from its nest."[41]

6. Pacific Idealism

Thayer unequivocally placed himself in the Roosevelt camp by denouncing Wilson for having brought humiliation and shame upon the nation. Wilson's silence in the face of the violation of Belgium and German atrocities and frightfulness, he charged, was tantamount to acquiescence in the doctrine that might makes right; that matter, not spirit, rules the universe. However, it would be a mistake to think that the idealistic basis for intervention propounded by Anglo-Saxon patriots and the nationalistic followers of Theodore Roosevelt was the exclusive property of any one group, no matter how jealous of its militancy that group might be. Rooseveltian righteous indignation was shared in good measure by the supporters of Wilson's high-minded policy of national self-control and altruism. Yet there were also important differences between the Rooseveltian idealists and the Wilsonian idealists—between the militant and what might be called the pacific idealists—and these differences were particularly significant in the development of that temperamental and philosophical antipathy which emerged full-blown in the great controversy over peace-making after America's crusade had ended.

Charles W. Eliot, former president of Harvard, was one of the first Americans to advocate intervention; yet his motives for intervention were more akin to Wilson's than to Roosevelt's. He and Wilson shared a great admiration for each other's views, and Eliot remained a supporter of Wilson's leadership throughout the war.* Eliot, who was eighty years old in 1914, wrote upwards of sixty articles on the war and related subjects between 1914 and 1920. In all of them the eighteenth-century liberal idealism of Wilson stands out.

In a letter to the President, dated August 6, 1914, Eliot proposed an offensive and defensive alliance between the United States and the Entente powers, including Japan and Italy, in order to enforce against Austria-Hungary and Germany "nonintercourse with the rest of the world by land and sea." He warned that a German victory would result in a perpetual threat to European peoples and, consequently, in an increased burden of armaments, and he added, "We shall inevitably share in these losses and miseries." However, he was as much impressed with the moral consequences as with the military consequences of a German victory. In violating neutral territory, Germany had committed a great wrong, he maintained; therefore, a German victory would be a victory for evil. The alliance he proposed was designed to punish Austria-Hungary and Germany "for the outrages they are now committing." He regarded it, not as a measure of national expediency nor as a stroke of vengeance, but as the institution of an international police method to replace the balance-of-power method; and he expected it to lead to the abolition of aggression, the reduction of armaments, and the establishment of "federal relations and peace among the nations of Europe."[42] Eliot presently withdrew his suggestion, on the grounds that all the facts were not known and that public opinion would not support the course he advocated, but the idealistic premise of his plan for intervention remained unchanged.[43]

Eliot, in common with many academic people, was very sensitive to the ideological issues of the war. He believed that the German doctrine of military necessity, the religion of valor, and the glorification of the state were the real causes of the war, and he was convinced that there could be no peace until they were banished through military defeat.[44] He never doubted that the fundamental issue of the war was whether autocracy or democracy should prevail. He supported official, legal neutrality, but he made it clear that "neutrality in our hearts is quite out of the question," for the war was one of militarism and imperialism against England and France, to whom America was indebted for her freedom and her faith in liberty under law. In his view

* Wilson had offered Eliot the ambassadorship to China and, when that was refused, the ambassadorship to Great Britain. Henry James, *Charles W. Eliot* (Boston, 1930), II, 228–29.

America was involved in the outcome of the war because her ideals were at stake. "We are an idealistic people. When our ideals are attacked and seem to be in danger, there is no people in the world that more promptly throws to the winds all material interests."[45] When the *Lusitania* sank, Eliot was as outraged as Roosevelt. With great feeling he wrote, "It is time for lovers of liberty and justice to cease to be merely lookers-on at the prodigious catastrophe. . . . Our flag should be somewhere in the trenches."[46]

From this time on, Eliot never doubted that intervention would come eventually. Nevertheless, he continued to support the administration's effort to keep the nation united and bring America into the war only on the highest possible grounds.

Supporters and opponents of Wilson, interventionists and noninterventionists, nationalists and internationalists, might hold different opinions about American policy, but they were in substantial agreement about the humanitarian and idealistic goals of the American mission; and Americans, as a whole, saw in Germany's conduct of the war and in German propaganda something alien and hostile to their ideals. The spokesmen for militant idealism were well-organized and vociferous; their energetic proselyting naturally set them apart from the nation as a whole. But the more pacific idealists—excluding the absolute pacifists—were not so far behind as their views upon neutrality and intervention suggested. It is not strange that Rooseveltian and Wilsonian idealists eventually joined together in April, 1917. Imperialists and subsequent anti-imperialists had combined in 1898.

There were signs of a new fusion of egoism with idealism in Wilson's gradual adoption of an attitude of righteous indignation toward Germany, an attitude he had hitherto scrupulously avoided. Roosevelt had seized the initiative in the battle for the vast reservoir of American idealism; but, one after another, his advanced views were adopted by the administration and by Americans in general. In Wilson's patient development of a moral basis for neutrality and, eventually, for intervention there were indications that the emerging crusade of democracy against autocracy would, like the preparedness movement, acquire new sponsors and broaden into a popular cause. The new sponsorship was bound to make a big difference in the quality of America's resurgent moral enthusiasm, a difference which was anathema to Roosevelt. In order to understand this important difference it is necessary to trace the process by which the leaders of Wilsonian idealism laid the moral basis for American intervention and, eventually, reconciled themselves to war.

If the pacific idealists lagged behind the militant idealists in their policy toward the European war, it was not because they were any less fervent disciples of the American mission but rather because they had more inhibitions concerning the use of force and violence. Consider the vanguard of the liberal reform movement: men like Waldo Frank, Walter Weyl, Ray Stannard Baker, Herbert Croly, Charles Beard, George Creel, and Frank Cobb, as well as some of the more conservative advocates of social and international melioration, such as Nicholas Murray Butler and Theodore Marburg, and even some emotional pacifists, like David Starr Jordan and William Jennings Bryan. These men were not, by temperament or intellect, opposed to a holy war; but, as members of that group of intellectuals and reformers who composed the self-appointed guardians of the idealistic conscience of America in the post-Rooseveltian era, they were bound to resort to force and violence only to achieve the highest ends and only after every resource of reason, good will, and compromise had been exhausted.

To these men it had seemed as though the second decade of the twentieth century would be an unprecedented period in the extension of reason and ethics throughout the sphere of international as well as domestic politics. In one way or another they had expected that love would gradually replace selfishness and coercion in human relations. They were themselves militant in the propagation of this gentle gospel, but they were repelled by the Rooseveltian brand of militancy because it seemed to them to be based upon alien premises. It seemed to exalt force, physical power, the military virtues, and the elements of struggle and conflict in human society as good things in themselves. It seemed out of tune with the times. Pacific idealists looked upon Roosevelt's passion for the vindication of American rights and ideals as impetuous and punitive. The way to peace and harmony, they protested, was through self-control and compromise. So they would purge themselves of hatred, subject their emotions to the discipline of reason, and look at all sides of the question. Vengeance was selfishness. If the American mission were to prevail, it would have to be free of all selfishness. National honor was held to be inadequate, in itself, as a motive for war, and futile as an objective of war. War for the vindication of neutral rights, especially where those rights rested upon uncertain legal precedents, seemed like fighting a duel—somehow ignoble, backward, and immature. It could never prove who was right or wrong nor advance the cause of humanity one iota.

Many of these pacific idealists were absorbed in the movement for domestic reform; consequently, they were haunted by the thought of the loss in personal rights, social betterment, and the respect for reason and truth which was bound to accompany war.* They were wary of the advantages which groups

* On the eve of his War Message to Congress Wilson told his friend Frank Cobb of the *New York World*, "Once lead this people into war, and they'll forget there ever was such a thing as

with special economic interests would reap during a war. Although during 1914–17 the chief impetus of the anti-munitions campaign came from pacifists and German-Americans, a good many non-pacifist liberals shared the suspicions of the earlier anti-imperialists that wars were largely the work of selfish economic interests, who were the sole beneficiaries of war's death and destruction.

Because of their inhibitions toward the exercise of violence and their mental reservations about the moral issues of the European conflict, pacific idealists were in desperate need of some positive, transcendent standard—something besides an idealized jealousy of national rights, a blind devotion to British aims, or an equally blind hatred of German autocracy and inhumanity—by which they could judge America's true relation to the European conflict. They found this standard in the abolition of all wars, in the establishment of a better world and a lasting peace.

7. Genesis of the Peace Controversy

There was no clearer manifestation of the underlying conflict beneath the surface unity of American idealism than the growing controversy over the organization of a lasting peace. It was largely the goal of a league to enforce peace that enabled Wilsonian idealists to reconcile themselves to intervention; but good Rooseveltians, having settled upon intervention for quite different reasons, became convinced that the scheme amounted to national emasculation and a menace to true idealism.

Through Wilson's use of the league idea, first, as a basis for mediating a peace without victory and, then, as a war aim, the whole matter became entangled with the issue of intervention. The league controversy became academic when Germany declared unrestricted submarine warfare, but it emerged later in the same form, only more intense, when the problem of planning peace arose. From the first, this controversy obscured the practical dictates of enlightened self-interest in the smoke of an irreconcilable conflict between divergent conceptions of individual and national conduct, which deprived the nation of realistic counsel on a matter of great practical importance from the standpoint of American ideals and American interests alike.

Charles Eliot's letter of August 6, 1914, was one of the first specific suggestions for the organization of a lasting peace that came to Wilson's atten-

tolerance. To fight you must be brutal and ruthless, and the spirit of ruthless brutality will enter into the very fiber of our national life, infecting Congress, the courts, the policemen on the beat, the man on the street." John L. Heaton, *Cobb of "The World"* (New York, 1924), p. 270.

tion after the outbreak of war. But a couple of weeks before this Hamilton Holt, editor of the *Independent*, had published a proposed constitution for a league of nations. And on August 16 Professor Irving Fisher of Yale presented, independently, a similar plan in a letter to the *New York Times*.[47] Such schemes were by no means new. Andrew Carnegie had proposed an association of nations as early as 1904; and Roosevelt, closely paralleling a plan previously outlined by Holt, had advocated a league of peace backed by force in his address accepting the Nobel Peace Prize at Christiana, Norway, in 1910.* Of course, similar plans had been projected by American and European thinkers for decades before the twentieth century.[48] However, with the outbreak of the European war in 1914, organized peace assumed a more immediate significance.

During the fall of 1914 both European and American interest in a league for peace rose rapidly. Roosevelt elaborated upon the plan he had suggested at Christiana. The New York Peace Society, of which Holt was an active member, held numerous discussions on the constitutional provisions of a league. Through the winter of 1914 until early April, 1915, this organization continued its work at a series of dinner conferences at the New York Century Club, in which Holt, Fisher, Taft, Theodore Marburg, A. Lawrence Lowell, and Frederick Lynch, among others, participated. Out of these conferences grew an organization called The League to Enforce Peace, organized officially on June 17, 1915. The League's program called upon the United States to join a league of nations binding the signatories to submit justiciable disputes to a tribunal and all other questions to a Council of Conciliation, and to join in applying economic and military sanctions against any member that committed an act of hostility against another member before the question at issue had been submitted for peaceful settlement.[49]

The League to Enforce Peace was, undoubtedly, the most important of the many peace organizations of the neutrality years and one which had a direct bearing upon Wilson's adoption of a league of nations as a war aim. During 1915 American labor and progressive groups, as well as British labor and German socialists, presented a number of schemes for achieving a lasting peace on the basis of disarmament, compulsory arbitration, democratic control of foreign policy, removal of trade barriers, freedom of the seas, and an international police force;[50] but none of these schemes received as much attention as the League's program, since none of them were sponsored by such an illustrious group nor by one so diversified in background and beliefs.

---

* Roosevelt's address was virtually the same as an editorial Holt had published several months before. Through the co-operation of Carnegie this editorial was transmitted to Roosevelt at Christiana. Ruhl J. Bartlett, *The League to Enforce Peace* (Chapel Hill, N.C., 1944), pp. 26-27.

The League contained leaders of the peace movement, such as D. S. Jordan and Frederick Lynch, as well as leaders of the preparedness movement, like James Beck and President Hibben of Princeton; supporters of Wilson, like Senator Williams of Mississippi, as well as his opponents, such as Lyman Abbott. Since the membership was weighted heavily toward the professional and business classes and included a number of men, like William Dudley Foulke and Booth Tarkington, with pro-Ally and nationalist leanings, those who scorned "pacifists," "mollycoddles," and "visionaries" could endorse this sound and sensible organization and remain perfectly respectable.

At the same time, the appeal of the idea of a league to enforce peace was by no means universal. Anglophobes and Germanophiles were repelled by the support which this scheme received from strong nationalists and Anglophiles. Pacifists opposed the use of force to fight force. At least two famous jurists, James Brown Scott and Elihu Root, were skeptical of the practicability of extending international sanctions to the political realm. However, the principal opposition to the idea of a league arose from the suspicions of a great many common Americans that a league would entangle the United States in the toils of European power politics, contrary to the traditional conception of national self-interest.

The league idea was, unquestionably, a challenge to the American tradition, and its advocates admitted it. Thus Taft, who was elected head of the League to Enforce Peace, stated on June 17, 1915, "We have got to depart from the traditional policy of this country . . . and assume certain obligations. . . ." We are "vitally interested in keeping war down" because we are, in modern circumstances, "likely to be drawn in ourselves."[51]

However, the strength of the league idea suffered not only from its opponents but from the differences among its supporters. Although the advocates of a league might be willing to renounce conventional isolationism, that renunciation meant different things to different advocates. To militant idealists a league to enforce peace was a means of protecting the supremacy of the great democratic powers over the have-not autocracies; it was an instrument of America's role as a great world power. It seemed to these men that, if there had been such a league—with its nucleus of Anglo-American power—when Germany invaded Belgium, Germany would have been condemned as an aggressor, and the United States would have rushed in to help the democracies punish the culprit, thereby performing its duty to humanity and protecting its own strategic interests at the same time, while avoiding all the shameful timidity and confusion of neutrality. But to the more pacific idealists a league of nations was the supreme expression of America's altruistic spirit of service to humanity, a means of replacing the outmoded diplomacy of the balance of power with the new, enlightened diplomacy, purged of national selfishness and the preoccupation with physical force.

As the European conflict continued, the differences between these two groups became sharper. Wilsonian idealists, unwilling to base American policy either on uncertain neutral rights or on the frank preference for one belligerent over the other, looked toward the league idea as a basis upon which the United States could mediate to end the war. But Rooseveltian idealists, intent upon vindicating American rights and the rights of humanity, considered a league of nations quite secondary to the immediate objective of securing the victory of democracy over autocracy. They insisted that a firm and courageous national policy was the indispensable condition of any practical international organization, and they looked upon the scheme to make a league the basis for negotiation or mediation as a cowardly and hypo- critical attempt to shirk a present moral obligation on the pretense of fulfilling an hypothetical future obligation.

We have already seen that by August, 1915, Roosevelt had come to the conclusion that advocacy of a league to enforce peace was inopportune as long as the nation failed to put righteousness above peace. Others were reaching the same conclusion. Senator Henry Cabot Lodge was one of these; but he continued to support the league idea conditionally until President Wilson publicly adopted a universal association of nations as a national aim.

In an address on June 9, 1915, Lodge said that the great fact of the day was unchained physical force. The question was how to bring about peace. Not by words or hopes, he answered. The problem was not to abolish physical force but to control it, and this required the substitution of the will of the international community for the will of individual nations. Lodge supported the principle of collective security, but not because he placed any faith in the altruism of nations. Selfishness, he asserted, is an attribute of human nature and nations alike, "but with this important difference, that in masses of men it is almost never controlled or conquered by the nobler emotions as it is very splendidly in the individual man." He further distinguished his views from those of the Wilsonian peace advocates by warning, "We cannot possibly succeed in any measure if we mix up plans for future peace with attempts to end this war now raging."[52]

Then on May 27, 1916, President Wilson, speaking before the first national annual assemblage of the League to Enforce Peace, delivered his own challenge to American isolation. As we have seen, he associated America's partnership in a universal association of nations, not with her own self-interest, but with a disinterested effort to lend the nation's moral prestige to the settlement of the war. Far from looking toward the preservation of a particular balance of power, Wilson's association of nations was intended to replace the balance of power system with a "new and more wholesome diplomacy" and to cast out all that selfishness from national relations which Lodge had said could almost never be controlled or conquered. And far from subordinating his plan for a league to a vigorous stand against Germany, Wilson aimed to subordinate his policy toward the belligerents to this one transcendent objective, which alone could give meaning to America's neutrality. America would remain impartial and magnanimous. With the causes and objects of the war she had no concern.[53]

Senator Lodge was on the same platform with Wilson that day, but when he spoke, his was a very different sort of speech. He commended the league idea as a "vision of a perhaps impossible perfection which has led humanity across the centuries." But he made it clear that this vision should not interfere with America's policy toward the war. At the outset he said,

> It is well, in understanding any great work . . . to know precisely where we stand; and I have been glad to learn that the League has laid down as a principle that it is not engaged in attempting to bring the war in Europe to an end, that its work lies beyond that war, for I have a somewhat deep impression that when the peace we all hope for comes, it will not be brought about by expeditions from the United States, nor by mass meetings and resolutions, no matter how admirable such resolutions may be.

In other words, no proposal for a league should interfere with the defeat of Germany.

Moreover, Lodge, like Roosevelt, was anxious that his endorsement of the league idea should not be interpreted as approval of a utopian internationalist position. The limit of voluntary arbitration had been reached, he said. In a veiled reference to the Taft-Knox arbitration treaties, against which he, Mahan, and Roosevelt had fought the good fight in 1911, he asserted that arbitration treaties which included questions that no nation would arbitrate, when the stress came, would retard the cause of peace and work vast mischief. Lodge further distinguished his position from that of the antimilitarist peace advocates by repeating the assertion of his speech in June, 1915, that an indispensable requisite of a league was force. Force behind the "will of the community" was as necessary as force behind the will of the nation. Both were essential to peace.[54]

Significantly enough for the future of the league idea, most of the speeches at the League convention were closer to Wilson's address than Lodge's in their general approach. The dominant note was America's moral obligation to break out of its isolation and come to the aid of the world. Clearly, even in the minds of these practical men of affairs the league idea sprang from a fervent spirit of altruism rather than from any broad conception of the imperatives of American power. Newton D. Baker, Wilson's secretary of war, expressed the prevailing sentiment.

> Why should America be specially concerned in this business? For one great reason. As things now seem, we have less to gain and more to give than any other nation in the world. It is because . . . America's ideals, or its ideal, is to be the leader of the human race in giving—in giving to mankind a new lease on life, new codes of liberty, new opportunities for justice.[55]

Theodore Marburg also defended the altruistic nature of a league to enforce peace.

> It is altruism which alone makes group action or co-operation possible, and co-operation has played a greater part in higher evolution than the individual qualities of fierceness and cunning. . . .
> To apply the principle of co-operation based on altruism to the society of nations, as it has already been applied within the state, is the aim and purpose of the League to Enforce Peace.

Marburg recognized the argument about entangling alliances as the weightiest argument against a league, but he denied that Washington would have opposed a league. The dominant trait in Washington was his sense of duty. Were he alive today would he not recognize the obligations of his country to fulfil a duty to the society of nations instead of taking advantage of its fortunate geographical position to shirk that duty? And Marburg made a prediction:

> America may on the surface appear a selfish nation but she has been stirred to her depth by ethical movements in the past and may be counted upon to rouse herself in similar fashion again. An appeal in a high cause involving sacrifice, even hardship and suffering, would go farther today than is dreamed of by the high priests of gain and ease and security.[56]

Marburg's exalted view of American opinion was, undoubtedly, encouraged by the growing popularity of the league idea. During the 1916 Presidential campaign both parties approved the guiding principles of the League to Enforce Peace, although neither party endorsed its program in detail. No prominent political figure dissented publicly from his party's approval of a future association of nations to guarantee peace. An analysis of editorial opinion which the League made concerning its meeting in May, 1916, showed that over 90 per cent of the editorials read favored a league, while the objection to the idea was negligible. By the end of 1916 America's participation in an association of nations after the war had won substantial support from leading journals, learned societies, students of international affairs, and well-informed, intelligent groups generally, though some like Charles Eliot, Roland Usher, and Walter Lippmann, believed that a league should be associated with an Anglo-American alliance.[57]

Until December, 1916, no prominent political figure of either major party, with the exception of Bryan, had taken an antileague stand. Bryan based his stand upon the pacifist argument against using force to fight force and upon his belief that membership in a league would entangle the nation in European quarrels and place American soldiers in a position to be ordered about by European monarchs.[58]

But was Bryan's stand really so different from the position of his countrymen? In spite of the apparent unanimity of internationalist sentiment, it is likely that a good many Americans who accepted the idea of a league, without really understanding its implications, shared Bryan's instinctive aversion toward foreign entanglements. Probably many more were simply indifferent toward the project. In assessing the public attitude toward American membership in a league, it is important to realize that, until after the war, the question was hypothetical and rather vague, as far as the great mass of Americans were concerned. In 1916 and 1917 being against a league was something like being against peace and a better world. Press comment was notable for its lack of detailed analysis. There was little attempt to inquire into just what measure of independence the nation would be required to sacrifice, and under what circumstances, if the United States actually became a participant in this idealistic scheme.

The issue of a league was not fully joined until the end of the war. Nevertheless, by December, 1916, it was clear from what source the most vocal opposition would arise. Not from Bryan, but from Roosevelt and Lodge and their militant compatriots. As might be expected, the spark that ignited the opposition was provided by that personification of altruism, Woodrow Wilson. On December 18, 1916, the President sent his note to the belligerents asking them to state the terms upon which they would agree to stop fighting and suggesting that the United States would co-operate in securing a lasting peace, including the establishment of a league of nations. To the strong nationalists this was the final proof that Wilson was using the ideal of eternal peace as a means of escaping America's present obligation to vindicate its honor and uphold the laws of humanity. Here was the most dangerous and outrageous effort yet to persuade Americans to shirk their obvious duty to throw the national might squarely into the struggle of democracy against autocracy.

When Senator Hitchcock introduced a resolution expressing Senate approval of Wilson's note, this became the signal for a concerted attack upon the league plan, with Senators Borah, Gallinger, and Lodge leading the way.[59] The burden of Lodge's argument was that a peace of righteousness was the only peace worth striving for, either for America's interests or the interests of humanity. Roosevelt joined the assault with characteristic violence in the February issue of the *Metropolitan*.

The *New Republic* sensed the rising opposition to the league movement and analyzed it in this manner:

It derives from pacifists who repudiate use of force even in the interests of international order, from militarists who refuse to seek peace even by means of possible coercion, and lawyers who resent any attempt to find a basis for international law except abstract right, recognized precedent and the voluntary consent of free and absolute sovereigns.[60]

The *New Republic* oversimplified the second class of opposition. "Nationalists" would have been a more accurate description than "militarists." What did men like Borah have in common with Lodge and Roosevelt? They were agreed in their opposition to the reduction of the nation's power of independent action, which was implied in America's membership in a league of nations. They were agreed in their opposition to the use of the league idea as a means of ending the war without vindicating American rights and assuring the victory of democracy over autocracy. Both groups were determined that no milk-and-water altruism should interfere with the nation's manly duty to serve righteousness. Both groups mouthed the same strictures against entangling the United States in European quarrels and abandoning America's sovereign right to determine its own immigration policy, defend the Monroe Doctrine, and control the disposition of its troops without foreign interference. Here, as a matter of fact, they spoke the same language as pacifist and noninterventionist isolationists, like Bryan and Senator Cummins. But there was a crucial difference in the meaning behind their commonplace asseverations.

For a quarter of a century Lodge and Roosevelt had been urging the abandonment of America's traditional isolation, whereas nationalists of the Borah variety had consistently opposed any deviation from America's conventional political relations with the rest of the world. The distinction lay in the fact that Lodge and Roosevelt meant by the abandonment of isolation the nation's assumption of a role of active intervention in world politics consistent with the Manifest Destiny of a great power. They welcomed limited entanglements in world politics as long as those entanglements were directed toward specific arrangements of mutual advantage which coincided with America's strategic interests and reinforced her status as a first-rate military power. In their judgment, membership in a league sponsored by internationalists and sentimental altruists like Wilson would produce the very opposite result.

On the other hand, Senator Borah, although emotionally in accord with the vigorous and independent assertion of American power in certain areas —Mexico, for example—remained, at the same time, unalterably opposed to promoting American power through political arrangements, especially with European or Asiatic nations. In this respect Borah was playing the role of Beveridge in 1898. Borah's isolationism sprang from an unreasoning xenophobia and a stubborn parochialism. Rooseveltian nationalism was grounded in a firm and consistent conception of political Realism. While Borah urged a narrowly nationalistic policy for America, he was shocked at the refusal of European powers to subordinate their own self-interest to universal moral principles. But Lodge and Roosevelt started with the premise that all nations consider their self-interest first and ideals second. After the war Borah demonstrated that his nationalism did not interfere with his faith in the efficacy of moral suasion in mitigating the competition among nations, but Realists trained in the school of Roosevelt and Mahan remained skeptical of the practicability or desirability of efforts to control the selfishness of nations by moral pronouncements.

Nevertheless, in the preliminary attack upon internationalism America's national egoists were, for all practical purposes, united. President Wilson's address to the Senate on January 22, 1917, his last desperate effort to end the war on the basis of a concert of nations and a "peace without victory," was promptly met with another barrage from the antileague forces. On February 1 Senator Lodge spoke. Confessing that mature consideration of the details of the league proposition had led him to change his mind on the subject, Lodge constructed a number of hypothetical cases in which Wilson's "glittering and glancing generalities" might, as a matter of practical consequence, contravene the vital interests of the United States; and he concluded that Americans had best ignore visionary schemes, commit themselves to nothing that was not in accordance with the realities of the international situation, and concentrate on building up the nation's military might.[61] These sentiments were echoed in the press.[62] Representative Augustus P. Gardner proved himself an ardent opponent of the league idea.[63] Henry Lane Wilson resigned as head of the Indiana branch of the League to Enforce Peace.[64] James M. Beck soon joined the nationalist defection.[65]

Yet the opposition had nothing specific upon which to direct its fire— nothing but an idea and an attempt at mediation. With the failure of Wilson's final effort to end the war, the league issue was pushed into the background. The battle lines between nationalism and internationalism had been drawn; the preliminary skirmishes had revealed the tactics that would be employed later; but the battle for public opinion would not be fought to a conclusion until the issue of peace became separate from the issue of war.

As for the significance of the peace controversy for America's entrance into the war, it clearly revealed the fundamental differences between the ends and motives of the two groups chiefly responsible for giving American intervention the aspect of a crusade; it exacerbated the deep-rooted antipathies between these groups and foreshadowed an irreparable schism in the crusade, under the stress of war and peacemaking. At the same time, the passions which it aroused further obscured the realistic case for intervention by distracting attention from the practical imperatives of American security.

8. UNRESTRICTED SUBMARINE WARFARE

Wilson believed that the American people had "responded nobly" to his message of January 22.[66] Certainly those who wanted to keep out of war, which included the great majority of the nation, approved of it as a sincere effort toward that end; but the issue that occupied noninterventionist minds in the next few months before America's entrance into the war was not the terms of peace or an association of nations but the intensified submarine warfare and its violation of American rights and the laws of humanity. The topic that filled the newspapers was not the league to enforce peace but shocking incidents on the high seas, new insults to the national honor, and anxious diplomatic exchanges.[67] The *New Republic* rejoiced at Wilson's announcement of a valid basis for armed intervention and a central objective of American foreign policy, transcending all the ephemeral confusions of neutrality. But though Wilson may have been able thus to sublimate American policy in his own mind, the American people as a whole were absorbed in the immediate issue of neutral rights. So now we return to the series of events that changed the nation from a neutral to a belligerent.

On January 31, 1917, the German high command announced its intention to wage unrestricted submarine warfare. In one blow this fateful decision demolished the whole frail basis upon which President Wilson had sought to grant the nation's "double wish" to uphold its rights and honor and still stay out of war. And yet it is a significant thing that neither the nation as a whole nor its leaders seemed capable of perceiving or willing to acknowledge this fact. Right down to the government's declaration that a state of war existed Americans viewed the European conflict with the same incongruous perspective of neutrality and nonintervention which they had held in 1914.

On February 3 Wilson went before Congress and said the only thing he could say: that the Government of the United States was severing relations with Germany because it had "no alternative consistent with the dignity and honor of the United States but to take the course which, in its note of the 18th of April, 1916, it announced that it would take. . . ." He stated his purpose of remaining at peace, but he warned that if Germany committed an "overt act," he would go before Congress and ask authority to use any means necessary to protect Americans in "their peaceful and legitimate errands on the high seas."[68] Wilson spoke the public mind. The country approved of the severance of relations with near unanimity; yet few wanted war in spite of the widespread indignation over Germany's repudiation of her *Sussex* pledge.

When Wilson went before Congress on February 26 to request authority to arm merchant ships, he requested it in the name of "armed neutrality" and disclaimed any intention of taking steps that "need lead" to war.[69] The Congressional debate on this request revolved about two questions: whether arming merchant ships was consistent with neutrality and whether it would lead to war. Both sides were united in their belief that neutrality and reducing the risk of intervention were the objectives desired. No one argued that armed neutrality was necessary to keep the Atlantic highway to the Allies open, and no one argued that armed neutrality was the best way to bring about an ultimate settlement of the war on the basis of a league to enforce peace.

When the House, fired by publication of the Zimmermann note, passed the armed-ship bill 403 to 14, and a group of eleven Senators, led by Norris and La Follette, filibustered the bill to death, even many pacifist journals agreed with the President that a "little group of wilful men had rendered the great government of the United States helpless and contemptible."[70] On March 12 Wilson announced that he was arming American merchant ships on his own authority.[71]

As America drifted into war, sucked into the maelstrom of a foreign conflict by the consequences of the very policy that stood for nonintervention, considerations of larger strategy were conspicuously absent from the public debate. By this time even those who understood the dependence of America's security upon the outcome of the war had become largely absorbed in promoting other objectives: the nation's honor and self-respect, the laws of international morality, or a permanent international organization.

9. America's Confidence in Allied Victory

The circumstances of the European conflict before Germany announced unrestricted submarine warfare had failed to evoke that widespread apprehension of American insecurity which Mahan and Einstein had seen as the necessary condition of a steady, far-sighted, realistic foreign policy. The events after Germany's announcement were no better calculated to arouse in Americans that instinct of self-preservation which Walter Lippmann and others attributed to them, in retrospect, on the eve of the nation's entrance into World War II.

In order to understand America's indifference toward the effect of the war upon its military security, it is important to realize that perhaps the most important circumstance that might have aroused widespread fear of the consequences of a German victory—namely, the likelihood of a British defeat—never became a serious consideration, even in the minds of America's amateur military experts.

At the outbreak of war the common estimate among both professional and nonprofessional military observers was that the European conflict would last from nine to eighteen months, with Germany, hemmed in by a wall of enemies, doomed to almost certain defeat.[72] The ease with which the German Army rolled through Belgium came as a shock, but with the subsequent stabilization of the war, most observers agreed with Frank H. Simonds, the George Fielding Eliot of World War I, that Germany's failure to crush France before Russia developed her full fighting efficiency had turned the war into a war of attrition and that the Allies' superior resources must eventually prove decisive. "Whatever is to happen now," said Mr. Simonds in the first week of December, 1914, "it is plain that France is not to be destroyed."[73] The specter of a Kaiser-dominated Europe had been laid to rest.

Thereafter, every German military success was interpreted as only a prolongation of the war of attrition, not as a threat of eventual victory. Summing up a year of war in August, 1915, a *Literary Digest* poll revealed that most editors saw a virtual stalemate, with the Allies likely to win after an indefinite period.[74] One year later some editors could discern an eventual complete triumph for the Allies, but others maintained that, while Germany would probably be defeated, she could not be conquered.[75]

In February, 1917, Frank Simonds, then associate editor of the *New York Tribune,* visited the battlefields in France and reported in a series of articles that the British Army was superior to its foe in material and morale and was finally advancing after two years of just hanging on.[76]

At the end of March, Rear Admiral Fiske was still sure that Germany had an even chance of winning and that, if she did win, her fleet would be in a position to cross the ocean to the American side; but he could find no one to agree with this estimate and, in fact, discovered that by merely expressing his opinion he created considerable irritation and ran the risk of being called pro-German.[77]

The intensification of Germany's submarine campaign during March, 1917, was regarded by most Americans as an act of desperation, induced by the

Allies' growing strength.[78] The full implications of the renewal of unrestricted submarine warfare, with its potentially disastrous military effect upon England, were not understood until after America entered the war. In the last month before intervention, the capture of Bagdad and the German withdrawal to the Hindenburg line were regarded as particularly good omens.

One can only speculate about the effect of a crushing military victory over France or a crippling submarine victory over Great Britain upon the American attitude toward the war. It seems likely that such a disaster would, at least in some measure, have revived all the old fears circulated about the German menace to the Western Hemisphere. If these fears had become general, American intervention might have been quite a different sort of phenomenon. But the plain fact is that this situation never came about and, so far as the great majority of Americans were concerned, never even seemed likely to come about.

10. THE ZIMMERMANN INCIDENT

In the few months preceding American intervention, only one incident seemed to Americans to have any direct bearing upon American security, and that was the publication on March 1 of the fantastic cable from the German Foreign Secretary, Zimmermann, to the German minister in Mexico. In this cable Zimmermann instructed the minister that, in the event of war with the United States, he should secure an alliance with Mexico on the basis of an understanding that Mexico would regain Texas, New Mexico, and Arizona and that he should also ask Mexico's provisional president, Carranza, to invite Japan to join the alliance. The British had intercepted Zimmermann's cable in the middle of January but, with that rare sense of timing displayed in the release of the Bryce atrocity report, they waited until the controversy over armed neutrality to reveal it to Ambassador Page. On March 4 Zimmermann naïvely admitted the authenticity of the revelation.[79]

Here was the first tangible evidence that Germany really had designs upon the Western Hemisphere. The fact that Zimmermann's instructions were predicated upon the outbreak of war between Germany and the United States over the submarine issue was generally overlooked in the excitement of the moment, except by German-American editors. If any event could have aroused America's instinct of self-preservation, it was the Zimmermann cable.

Wilson's official biographer, Ray Stannard Baker, has said, "No single, more devastating blow was delivered against Wilson's resistance to entering the war."[80] Lansing wrote in his *Memoirs* that when he showed Zimmermann's note to the President, Wilson was astounded and showed "much resentment."[81] However, Wilson's reaction was induced, not by any sudden fear that Germany threatened American security, but rather by bitter indignation over German duplicity. The fact that Zimmermann, as Lansing pointed out, had sent his note in code through the American Department of State under permission granted to expedite peace negotiations, which Wilson was desperately pursuing even at this late date, was profoundly disillusioning to the President; for this was irrefutable confirmation of his suspicion, which he had gained from reports of German subversive activities and intrigues in the United States, that the German government was cynical, mendacious, and congenitally perfidious in its dealings with other nations. On the basis of this revelation of iniquity he concluded that further efforts to bring about a peaceful settlement between the belligerents through negotiations with Germany were out of the question. And with the ruling out of peaceful settlement, Wilson's last hope for keeping the United States out of the war collapsed.[82]

The American people, as a whole, were every bit as aroused as Wilson. The almost universal indignation which this startling incident provoked probably had a greater effect in unifying the nation and preparing it for war than any of the previous submarine sinkings. The news of an intended German intrigue with Mexico brought the war home to the isolated citizens of the Midwest and Southwest as no event on the high seas could possibly have done. Even German-Americans, German sympathizers, Socialists, and pacifists had to admit their patriotic resentment at this evidence of German hostility.[83] Interventionists, of course, were jubilant. In a letter to Roosevelt, Senator Lodge predicted that publication of the Zimmermann note would "arouse the country more than anything that has happened"; it would "widen the breach with Germany and drive us toward the Allies," thereby forcing Wilson's hand.[84]

However, the public excitement does not seem to have reflected any feeling of insecurity. The danger of actual invasion by way of Mexico was generally treated by the press as hardly worth considering. The Zimmermann note was viewed chiefly as confirmation of German treachery and stupidity. The press expressed more indignation than alarm and more astonishment than indignation. Thus the *New York Evening Post* thought the note was an "inconceivable folly" and "the final proof that the German government has gone stark mad." It judged that the ultimate effect of the scandal would be to "argue the existence of an international madman, whom it is becoming increasingly an international duty to place under restraint."[85]

The *New Republic* wryly commented, "The reception by Congress and American opinion of the Zimmermann note to the Mexican government is characteristic of the unreality of the prevailing public attitude towards the problem of American foreign policy." In the *New Republic's* opinion the absurdity of the Zimmermann note had prevented the ordinary American from taking it seriously. The public classified the incident as a characteristic.example of Teutonic diplomacy. "But if it involved in American eyes the existence of any serious and lasting danger . . . if it implied the need of a change in the attitude of Americans towards their own foreign policy, no evidence of these implications has as yet been allowed to transpire."[86]

The *New Republic* was right. There was nothing in America's outburst of patriotism and moral indignation to alter the nation's profound sense of isolation from the political concerns of the rest of the world. If neutrality had failed to accomplish its purposes, the public did not imagine that this was because there was anything about America's position in world politics to make the premises of neutrality untenable; it was simply because a madman nation had run amuck and upset the normal processes of civilization.

11. America's Response to Wilson's War Message

In the end, a succession of "overt acts" during the middle of March, resulting in the loss of American lives on American ships, pushed both President Wilson and the American people beyond the limits of tolerance. With Wilson's stirring War Message on April 2 the logic of strict accountability was fulfilled. His concluding words paraphrasing Martin Luther, "God helping her, she can do no other," admirably expressed the popular mood. The nation was resolute in its course, but it had not really gone to war, as in 1898; rather the war had come to it, as the fateful consequence of traditional policies and unprecedented circumstances.

President Wilson felt compelled to go to war, and the American people were the more willing to follow him, because they sensed his reluctance to bow to the inevitable. Throughout America's uneasy neutrality this had been the crux of his leadership: his instinctive understanding of the people's "double wish" to enforce the nation's rights and yet keep out of war. However, in a larger sense, it is doubtful whether Wilson truly spoke the public mind in pronouncing the ultimate objectives of neutrality and intervention. This question is crucial in understanding the ultimate fate of his leadership.

America, as a whole, was pushed and kicked into war, from incident to incident. But Wilson's War Message was based on positive principles of national purpose, which transcended the agonizing confusions of neutrality. It was not just for the vindication of American rights that he was asking Congress to recognize that a state of war existed. In his mind American rights were inseparably bound up with the rights of all mankind and with the cause of democracy. He had consistently proclaimed that, if America fought, she would fight, not for her own selfish interests, but for the interests of all nations. He had reached the conclusion that the interests of all nations could only be served by "a steadfast concert for peace," maintained by "a partnership of democratic nations." In Wilson's mind the objectives of intervention sanctified its causes. Fundamentally, they were inseparable from its causes. They were the same objectives that had sanctified neutrality.

But was it too much to expect this exalted mood of the American people as a whole? Wilson's War Message was greeted in Congress with an overpowering burst of emotion and praise. It won almost unanimous acclaim from the nation. Yet some of his greatest messages were likely to mean different things to different men.

What did the call to war mean to the two groups who were intent upon making America's intervention a crusade? Pacific idealists and militant idealists were, apparently, united in their enthusiasm for the President's stirring pronouncement. Yet to perceive that this unity was deceptive, one had only to recall the ever-widening breach between nationalists and internationalists. Behind the common front of the American mission there existed a fundamental and long-standing conflict. America's most nationalistic patriots were entering the war to vindicate the same principles that Wilson avowed, but those principles were combined with a self-righteous bellicosity and a vindictive sense of national honor that repelled idealists who shared Wilson's temperamental and intellectual aversion to the free exercise of man's combative instincts. For militant idealists the national honor was a good and sufficient reason for intervention, especially when it coincided with the power interests of the nation. Universal ideals added zest to their fight but had no superior claims upon their consciences. But for pacific idealists, whose consciences were vexed with the stubborn inhibitions of love, gentleness, and reason, Wilson's exalted war aims were a psychological necessity. Nothing but the highest purpose could justify war for them. Nothing but a war to end all wars could consecrate American intervention. Out of great expectations in peace came great expectations in war; for if intervention could achieve a democratic and a peaceful world, then instead of bringing a sickening reversal of the advancing tide of civilization, war would be the very fulfilment of the material and ethical progress that seemed about to sweep over the world when the European aberration occurred.

President Wilson's War Message was a call to holy war and a call to break away from America's traditional self-sufficiency in its political relations with other nations. Both the militant and the pacific idealists accepted this call, though for somewhat different ends and motives. But what about the average American, who was neither so heroic nor so exalted?

In 1898 the American people had been knight-errants, rushing out to meet war on their own terms. With nationalistic and idealistic impulses converging in something approximating a spontaneous evangelistic revival, Americans had found themselves at war almost before they had had time to think about it. But it is a mistake to suppose that in April, 1917, the American people, as a whole, were moved by the same irresistible crusading fervor. Sidney Brooks, an astute English observer who had witnessed America's rush to war against Spain, found a striking contrast to the flag-waving and idealistic ferment of 1898. To him it seemed that the public mood was one of "grave satisfaction" and resignation.[87]

Americans had been content to follow Wilson's leadership through the perils of neutrality because he seemed able to uphold their honor and, at the same time, keep them out of war. When circumstances made this no longer possible, the people were resigned to following their President into war because they felt that he had tried every other decent alternative. As a whole, the nation was convinced that intervention was a moral act and that it ought to result in a better world; but, in April, 1917, America's decision was justified chiefly in terms of American rights.[88] The causes of intervention were not yet sanctified by Wilsonian objectives, except in the minds of those pacific idealists for whom utopia was a psychological necessity.

On the eve of intervention, the American people, as a whole, were by no means entirely convinced that the Allies were fighting for objectives which were compatible with the American mission, nor were they sure that any vital American interests were at stake, except the nation's honor and self-respect. One indication of this state of opinion is the fact that there was considerable sentiment for fighting a limited-liability war, fighting to force Germany to respect America's maritime rights and withdrawing from the war when this end was accomplished.[89]

At the same time, Americans did not consider intervention a selfish action. They agreed with President Wilson that the nation was seeking nothing material for itself—only the welfare of humanity. In a vague way, most Americans probably felt that they were fighting for the ideals of democracy against the principle of autocracy.[90] The Russian revolution made this thesis considerably more plausible. Sidney Brooks wrote, "America has entered the lists under the compelling power of her primal passion to serve and save the world at whatever cost to herself."[91] The New Republic admitted that America had nothing tangible to gain from the war, that all the tangible realities of the immediate situation counseled neutrality. "For the first time in history," it observed, "a wholly independent nation has entered a great and costly war under the influence of ideas rather than immediate interests."[92]

The *Philadelphia Public Ledger* caught the popular mood. It said that it was true that "the wanton destruction of a single American ship, the deliberate taking of a single American life, is a sufficient justification of exacting the penalty of the sword." But this motive was "nothing in comparison with the larger purpose." The larger purpose was crushing the menace of Prussianism to America's highest ideals. The *Public Ledger* insisted that America's purpose in the war was not selfish, and it rejoiced at the thought that now the nation had an opportunity to reveal its true idealism. "The war is our war because it is the war of humanity; not for ourselves, O Lord, not for ourselves, we join those who for all these weary months have been fighting it."[93]

In short, Americans believed that they had been forced into the war by Germany's violation of their rights on the high seas. They believed that their chief interest in fighting the war was the vindication of these rights. In a vague way, they also believed that they were fighting for humanity rather than for any selfish purpose. Yet the public mood was not one of crusade or self-sacrifice. There was no widespread enthusiasm for fighting the war for any reason—only resignation. Comparatively few were attracted by any tangible war aim, such as a league of nations. Comparatively few believed that intervention involved any break with America's traditional relations with the rest of the world. There was little in the public attitude toward the war in April, 1917, to indicate that Americans were prepared to fight a war on the terms of Wilson's War Message. This fact is of prime significance in understanding the fate of America's subsequent crusade.

12. CONGRESS AND THE WAR RESOLUTION

On the floor of Congress the speeches on the war resolution reflected the general public's attitude toward intervention. Nineteen Senators spoke for the war resolution, but not more than seven mentioned Wilson's international peace organization as a reason for fighting.[94] The great majority regarded intervention chiefly as a means of redressing violations of American rights on the seas, though a few also based their stand on the broader ground of democracy versus autocracy. Senator Lodge mentioned submarines and spies as the causes for war and asserted that what the United States wanted most from the war was the defeat of organized barbarity. Senator Borah made it quite clear that he was not voting for the war resolution out of sympathy for other nations or for any reason other than the vindication of American honor.

Suffice it to say now that there can . . . be but one sufficient reason for committing this country to war, and that is the honor and security of our own people and our own Nation. . . . I join no crusade. . . . I make war alone for my countrymen and their rights, for my country and its honor.[95]

In the House, seventy-eight addresses were made for the war resolution.[96] Considerably less than one third of these reflected a willingness to put the issue on the broad basis of achieving a more perfect international order. The chairman of the Committee on Appropriations and almost half of those who spoke for the resolution explicitly limited the scope of America's participation to retaliation for submarine depredations and other national insults. When the House Committee on Foreign Affairs reported the resolution for passage on April 5, it submitted a catalogue of acts that justified war, arranged under the following headings: Germany's conduct of sea warfare; intrigues in the United States, including bomb plots and espionage; indignities to Americans; other unfriendly acts, including the Zimmermann note.[97]

There was a general disposition among Congressmen, except on the part of the strong nationalists, to agree with Wilson that America was intervening for altruistic reasons, but Congressional professions of altruism were more the guise of national self-righteousness than the genuine expression of a spirit of self-sacrifice. Representative Ferris's remarks were typical:

In entering this unjust and inhuman war, ruthlessly thrust upon us by the Imperial German Government, we differ from all the rest. . . . We enter the war not for dollars, not for empire, not for conquest or hope of reward, but only for the preservation of our modest and undoubted right to be free, to be let alone, and only after an unholy war has been waged against us for more than two years. Could any nation enter a war so completely without selfishness and without guile? Ours is a war against crime, against murder, against autocracy, against militarism, against the overthrow of our freedom and our liberty, against imperialism; ours is a war for democracy, for justice, for freedom, for liberty, and that the republics of the world may endure and live.[98]

Noninterventionists argued that, since both belligerents had violated American neutrality, there was no cause to single out Germany as the enemy. They pointed to the horrors of war, both at home and abroad. They claimed that war profiteers were engineering the movement toward intervention.[99] But their principal argument, as in 1898, was that war would entangle the nation in the endless quarrels of European powers, contrary to American ideals, traditions and self-interest. Representative Reavis bespoke the depth of isolationist sentiment when he lamented, "Oh, my country, builded into an empire in your splendid isolation, you are at the parting of the ways, and I am powerless to prevent it."[100]

But more significant than the noninterventionists' appeals to isolationism was the complete absence of any direct challenge to this hoary tradition, even on the part of the most outspoken interventionists. From reading the Congressional speeches on the war resolution, one might conclude that no legislator believed that the European war was of any consequence to Americans except as it affected their right to travel unmolested upon the high seas. Representative Miller's disavowal of any deviation in America's traditional aloofness from world politics was typical:

> Gentlemen may further query whether or not the entrance into a war with the Imperial German Government means that we shall become entangled in European affairs. I say not so at all. As for myself, I propose to vote for the resolution that shall pledge this country to war not because of anything the entente powers are fighting for but to vindicate the right of America and to show the world that American life and property and sovereignty must be respected upon every sea and in every land [Applause]. Fear not the consequences when you know you are in the right, but like high-minded and brave men dare to go where duty calls.[101]

13. A JUDGMENT CONCERNING INTERVENTION

"Fear not the consequences when you know you are in the right." This would have made a fitting motto for America's intervention in World War I. On the part of some Americans, the motto would have represented bravado; on the part of others, altruism; for most it would simply have expressed a conditioned response to unforeseen circumstances. Few had calculated the effect of neutrality upon the nation's power position; fewer still were concerned with the expediency of intervention. Yet it was a dangerous oversimplification of the conditions of international politics to suppose that, in the long run, either universal ideals or the nation's self-interest could be achieved by ignoring these realities.

In the years after the war a great many Americans were embittered by the consequences of intervention and thoroughly convinced that intervention had been a terrible mistake. In retrospect, righteousness, honor, and the cause of world peace and democracy seemed inadequate motives for the grim sacrifices of war. The American mission, divorced from a conception of fundamental national self-interest, seemed to have been futile at best, false at worst; and the nation's scholars, journalists, and politicians set to work fixing the blame for intervention upon this group or that individual, as though to purge the nation of its guilt by indicting the selfishness, hypocrisy, or gullibility of a few.

To a certain extent the postwar mood was induced by the frustration of lofty expectations raised during the war. We shall examine this matter in the next two chapters. Yet, even Utopia might not long have compensated the nation for participation in a foreign war if Utopia had seemed a thing apart from the national advantage, for only the most compelling objectives, those closest to fundamental self-interest, could have completely justified intervention in retrospect.

If the American people had been more altruistic, they would have gladly accepted the sacrifices of war as the legitimate price of an idealistic enterprise. If they had been more egoistic, they would not have required such high ideals from war. If Americans had been more realistic, they might have tempered both their egoistic and idealistic inclinations with the discipline of enlightened self-interest and a soberer estimate of the role of morality in international relations. Then America's relation to the European conflict might have seemed, in the aftermath of the war, more consistent with compelling national ends and motives.

This does not mean that American intervention was a mistake. Such a judgment implies that the alternative of nonintervention would have served American ideals and interests better; and this we can never know. It is, at least, possible that German submarines would have succeeded in crippling Great Britain's military effort and reducing the British Isles to a state of helplessness. There was always that risk. And it is almost certain, if the Treaty of Brest-Litovsk is any indication, that a peace settlement in which Germany held the preponderance of power would have been infinitely more hostile to American ideals and interests than the severest critics of the Versailles Treaty claimed of that settlement. Allied victory guaranteed neither American ideals nor American interests, but at least it gave the nation the indispensable opportunity to achieve both ends through the establishment of a more peaceful and progressive international environment. Would nonintervention have been worth the risk of losing this opportunity?

If Woodrow Wilson erred, it was not because he led the United States into war but because he failed to do everything in his power to prepare the people to see their entrance into a foreign war as an act consistent with imperative principles of national self-interest, as well as with national ideals and sentiments. In fact, by stressing America's disinterestedness as a condition of her mission of bringing peace to the world, Wilson actually directed all the force of his leadership toward concealing what should have been the most compelling reason for American intervention.

If Americans, as a whole, supported intervention for insubstantial reasons, it was not because they were wrong in their idealism, their moral indignation, or their lively sense of national pride and honor; in the light of the international circumstances of 1914–17, there was justification for all these emotions. It was, rather, because they failed from the first to guide and restrain their aspirations and sentiments with a realistic view of national conduct and a prudent regard for the practical consequences of specific policies. For as a result of blind impulse and shortsightedness, their righteous indignation rested upon an uncertain legal case and an exaggerated ethical distinction between the belligerents, while their idealism dissipated itself in a self-righteous response to momentary passion. Americans, as a whole, were misguided in that they acted as though the complex task of reconciling the nation's self-interest with universal ideals could be simply and automatically achieved by satisfying certain emotional and temperamental proclivities in an unthinking response to the drift of events.

Armed intervention might well have been the wisest alternative from the long-run standpoint of American ideals and interests, but the great majority of the people did not choose war upon mature deliberation; they simply drifted into war, guided largely by impulses—some noble, some mean—with but a tenuous relation to broad and enduring national policy. Consequently, it is little wonder that the motives which led to war seemed inadequate in the perspective of peace, and that America's vaunted moral leadership revealed itself once more as the irresponsible outburst of a nation physically mature but emotionally and intellectually adolescent—a quick-tempered, good-hearted giant of a nation, moved by impulses it would later regret, undertaking commitments it would not fulfil, and never quite comprehending either the circumstances or the consequences of its erratic behavior.

Yet, lest the perspective of time distort our judgment of a different era, we shall do well to ponder the fact that each step that led to war was, in itself, consistent with the sentiments, beliefs, and policies which had evolved from America's previous experience in world politics; and that in the light of this experience each step was, at the time, a logical response to the unprecedented circumstances of an international conflict.

CHAPTER XII

THE SECOND CRUSADE

1. The Frustrated Crusade

THE way the American people fought World War I and the way they
made peace are two inseparable parts of the same frustrated crusade.
As in 1898, the impact of war wrought changes in America's crusade which
radically altered its entire aspect. Under the stress of war and with the approach of peace, an apparent fusion between egoistic and altruistic impulses
disintegrated in a conflict between divergent attitudes toward the nation's
role in international politics. America's pacific idealists, international reformers, and moral optimists reconciled themselves to violence by setting their
sights on the millennium. America's militant idealists and political realists
tried to counteract the lure of the millennium with the spirit of war, lest
altruism interfere with nationalistic goals. The controversy between these two
groups obscured the objects of enlightened self-interest, for which all factions
might have fought; it confounded the practical expedients of peacemaking,
upon which all might have agreed.

Because neither war nor peace seemed related to any enduring self-interest,
the motives which led to war were not adequate for the prosecution of war,
and the objects for which the nation fought were not sufficiently compelling
to sustain the break with isolation that was necessary for their fulfilment.
Consequently, the great mass of Americans thrilled at a glimpse of utopia,
and then, with the immediate object of victory achieved, lapsed back into
normalcy under the inertia of traditional conceptions of national self-interest
and conventional attitudes toward the outside world.

2. America Searches for a Reason to Fight

America began its second crusade with a spirit of resignation to the unavoidable task of vindicating American rights rather than with a spontaneous
burst of moral enthusiasm for waging the battle of humanity. Americans, as
a whole, did not enter the war for the objects that Wilson proclaimed in his
addresses of January 22 and April 2. Yet a nation so prone to judge international relations with an ethical yardstick and a nation so reluctant to entangle
itself in the world struggle for power could find little inspiration or satisfaction in fighting a war merely for the limited objective of vindicating American rights.

One indication that the motives which led to intervention would not suffice in war was a suggestion of bewilderment and a groping for explanations that crept into popular discussion of the war during the early months of American participation. The American people, having found themselves involved in a war begun and fought for reasons which they believed had nothing to do with their own tangible interests, now began to wonder how it had all happened and what it was all about.

Three weeks after the nation accepted the "challenge to all mankind," the *New Republic* observed that public opinion was curiously placid and unenthusiastic about the war. The people were loyally acquiescent; they had confidence in the President; but they still entertained a suspicion that something had been "put over" on them.[1] Several weeks later the Washington correspondent of the *New York Evening Post* reported that in all parts of the country he found "the opinion that apathy prevails, that there is not much genuine enthusiasm about the war, or the Liberty Loan, but that the people are responding more because of their traditional patriotism than a clear comprehension of what it is all about."[2]

The official explanation of intervention disavowed any hatred or rancor toward the German people and pledged the nation to eschew aggrandizement. At the same time, official and unofficial spokesmen rejected the notion that the United States was committed to the cause of the Allied Powers. So why were Americans fighting?

There was general agreement that the United States had intervened for its own reasons and would fight for its own ends. The *Topeka Capital* thought that America had entered the war "for special reasons, having nothing to do with the dynastic and nationalistic reasons actuating Russia, France, Italy, and England."[3] Oswald Garrison Villard's *New York Evening Post* expressed the opinion of many who had accepted intervention reluctantly when it stated,

It will not do to say that because Americans as a whole sympathize with the Allies, therefore they must lose their identity in a European alliance. Some say that its cause is ours. It may be. But we have never thought of going to war for that reason, and cannot now. If we take up arms against Germany it will be on an issue exclusively between that empire and this republic; and the republic must retain control of that issue from beginning to end.[4]

The *Nation*, another reluctant interventionist but a supporter of Wilson's moral leadership, also expressed the complete independence of America's purpose: "We have no selfish objects in the war. Conquests and indemnities we disclaim in advance. Our battle is solely for the law of nations and for the right of self-government." Therefore, it recommended that the United States withdraw from the war as soon as the original object of the war was achieved.[5]

However, the general tendency to believe that America should fight for its own ends was by no means matched by an agreement upon what those ends ought to be or how they could be attained. It is true that Wilson's phrase "the world must be made safe for democracy" achieved wide currency, but just what that meant in the way of concrete performance was left open to question. Did it mean a peace without victory, a negotiated peace for limited ends, or a crushing military defeat of Germany and a revision of the map of Europe? The one American who, above all others, was in a position to clarify this uncertainty was President Wilson himself.

3. WILSON EXPLAINS THE WAR

In the months following the tumultous welcome that Congress showered upon Wilson's War Message, the President scrupulously retained his sober mood of exalted purpose. He would allow no mean or petty selfishness, no unworthy passion, no hate nor vengeance to darken the higher counsel of service to humanity. Self-control and altruism had been the theme of his neutrality policy; they were equally the theme of his war policy.

Two weeks after his War Message the President delivered an appeal to the people. "There is not a single selfish element, so far as I can see, in the cause we are fighting for. We are fighting for what we believe and wish to be the rights of mankind and for the future peace and security of the world."[6] On May 12 he said, "We have gone in with no special grievance of our own, because we have always said that we were the friends and servants of mankind. We look for no profit. We look for no advantage."[7] In a Memorial Day address on May 30 he rejoiced that "in the providence of God America will once more have an opportunity to show to the world that she was born to serve mankind."[8] This religious sense of dedication was even more manifest in his address before the Confederate Veterans on June 5. Proclaiming the American mission, as hundreds of times before, Wilson conjured the people to envision the unfolding of God's majestic plan to use Americans as His chosen instrument to make liberty secure for all mankind, for God had made the nation strong in order to prove, not its selfishness, but its spirit of self-sacrifice.[9]

If this lofty purpose was the primary reason for fighting the war, had Wilson forgotten the loss of American lives on American ships and the long list of Germany's violations of American rights? In a rather heated letter to Congressman Heflin of Alabama, dated May 22, the President answered the critics who accused him of excessive vagueness in explaining the reasons

for war. As in his address of April 2, he drew a distinction between the causes
and the objects of intervention.

> It is incomprehensible to me how any frank or honest person could doubt or ques-
> tion my position with regard to the war and its objects. I have again and again stated
> the very serious and long continued wrongs which the Imperial German Government
> has perpetrated against the rights, the commerce, and the citizens of the United States.
> . . . No nation that respected itself or the rights of humanity could have borne those
> wrongs any longer.

"Our objects," he continued, "have been stated with equal clearness" in
the addresses of January 22 and April 2. "We have entered the war for our
own reasons and with our own objects clearly stated, and shall forget neither
the reasons nor the objects."[10]

Wilson's distinction between the reasons and objects of intervention was a
tacit recognition of the fact that he considered the immediate cause—that is,
the violation of American rights and honor—as, in itself, an inadequate
justification for war. He was no more willing to justify American intervention
than he had been content to press for strict accountability solely in terms of
vindicating purely national concerns. In both neutrality and war, only America's mission of bringing peace and democracy to the world elevated the
pursuit of American ends far enough above the level of selfishness to satisfy
Wilson.

As the war continued, Wilson's "objects" took precedence over his "reasons." This was to win for him the devout support of a vocal group of liberals,
intellectuals, and idealists and the determined opposition of America's strong
nationalists and militant Realists. It was to involve the great mass of Americans in a momentous crusade, the concrete implications of which they scarcely
comprehended.

Throughout 1917 Wilson's objects embellished his public pronouncements
as lofty expressions of American righteousness. But, although they received
general acclaim, they failed to inspire the nation with overwhelming enthusiasm for the war. There were signs that America wanted more than
sermons. If there was little with which one could disagree in Wilson's pronouncements, there was also little that one could solidly grasp. Ordinary
people seemed to demand something more concrete, something more down-
to-earth to fight for. There was a growing tendency to criticize the nation's
apathy, confusion, and lack of fighting spirit. There were demands that the
President assert a stronger leadership in order to rally American patriotism.
The strong interventionists and nationalists were particularly irritated by
Wilson's bland benevolence.

President Wilson seemed to make an effort to meet this situation in his Flag Day address on June 14. It was the most pugnacious statement of the reasons for intervention that he delivered during the entire war. Significantly enough, it was also one of his most popular addresses. There was nothing in this speech about making the world safe for democracy or dedicating the nation to the task of world peace. "It is plain enough how we were forced into the war," Wilson said; and he proceeded to denounce the "military masters of Germany" and their sinister conspiracy against the peace and security of democratic peoples, their flagrant violation of American rights and honor on the high seas and at home, the lies and hypocrisy of their propaganda concerning peace. "For us there is but one choice. We have made it. Woe be to the man or group of men that seeks to stand in our way."[11]

This fighting speech demonstrated Wilson's capacity for militancy. The nation responded to his Scotch combativeness. Yet it was not really his kind of speech. Roosevelt could have done it better. The effect soon wore off. When the President finally rallied American enthusiasm behind his leadership, it was on the basis of ideal goals which had been taking shape in his mind since the beginning of the European conflict. Just as Wilson had initiated a New Diplomacy, so he would lead the people in a new kind of war, one without hatred or bitterness, one for humanity, not just for the United States.

4. THE RESURGENCE OF EGOISM

Wilson based his moral leadership upon a mystic faith in the altruism of the people, but in the summer of 1917 it became increasingly evident that a powerful faction of the people was determined to wage war in the old way, for tangible and self-interested reasons first, and for universal ideals second. The *Literary Digest* of June 16 noted that there were journals and individuals of unquestioned loyalty "who feel that the official statement of our case, with its emphasis on noble and altruistic ideals, needs to be supplemented by a sharp reminder that this is for us a war of self-defense in which the very soul of our nation is at stake."[12]

Some who had warmly applauded Wilson's statement of American ideals in his War Message became disturbed when it appeared that the welfare of humanity might be stressed to the exclusion of practical self-interest and an unqualified victory over Germany. One such person was "Colonel" George Harvey, editor of the *North American Review*.

In May, 1917, Harvey, who had been Wilson's early political sponsor and was soon to become one of his bitterest political adversaries, had lauded the President's address as a "natural and logical sequence of the Declaration of Independence and the Emancipation Proclamation." He had held that the war was nominally for defense, since it was forced upon the nation by overt acts, but that, in the last analysis, "this war is a continuation of the three-centuries-old strife between the despotic spirit of the Old World and the free spirit of the New."[13]

However, Harvey had also believed that the way to vindicate the cause of democracy was to achieve a crushing military victory. Temperamentally, he had been in Roosevelt's camp. In fact, ever since the *Lusitania* incident his policy had been Roosevelt's rather than Wilson's. In the election of 1916 he had split with the administration because of what he regarded as its timidity in the face of national humiliation.

Therefore, it is not strange that, in the August issue of the *North American Review,* Harvey should have exclaimed, "Peace with complete victory! Peace with unconditional surrender! It is the only way—the only way of living, the only way of righteousness, the only way of mercy." He was dismayed by the lack of fighting spirit in the nation. "The predominant spirit even now is fidelity to the Government rather than to the cause." He warned that this attitude would have to be reckoned with later when American soldiers actually started dying on foreign battlefields and the old query as to why the United States should intervene in a European war arose again. He asserted that the only way to arouse the nation to meet this test was to fight the war on a straight nationalist basis.

It has seemed to us, having in mind the self-interest in human nature, that the most effective method of enlisting the full endeavors of our own people is by convincing them, first, of their own peril and, secondly, of what we believe to be the fact, namely, that if the war is to be won at all America must win it.[14]

Harvey's view was an omen of the same shift toward the aggressive and self-seeking impulses that had marked the imperialists' attitude toward the crusade against Spain. Once more the shock of war was intensifying the antipathy between an altruistic and self-assertive view of national conduct and revealing a fundamental schism among the proponents of the American mission.

The militant idealists of 1917 were on the defensive. They did not speak of the glories of violence, of war's beneficent influence upon human character and the progress of civilization. They did not conjure visions of a Manifest Destiny. They were defending the status quo now. But the temperamental and philosophical basis of their mounting antagonism toward the prophets of self-denial and sweet reasonableness was as evident as in 1898. The validity of universal ideals as a national goal was still, in their minds, contingent upon their coincidence with national self-interest. National benevolence and philanthropy were still valued only incidentally to the vigorous assertion of national power.

5. ROOSEVELT REPUDIATES WILSON'S WAR OBJECTIVES

Once more, in the private correspondence and public pronouncements of Theodore Roosevelt one can trace the shifting course of national egoism and militant idealism.

In chapter VII we observed the similarity between Wilson's War Message and Roosevelt's contemporaneous explanation of intervention, concerning both the causes and the objects of war, and, at the same time, the significant difference between the two men's acceptance of the final decision—Wilson solemn, exalted, yet oppressed; Roosevelt exultant and fervently bellicose. Under the stress of war it was the underlying difference between these two leaders which came to the fore.

Three days after Wilson's address Roosevelt wrote his British friend Arthur Lee, "If Wilson will now act in thoroughgoing fashion I shall back him to the limit of my power. I fear it is too late for us to do very efficient work; but thank God we are in, and are able to look men in the eyes without flinching!"[15]

In an article in the June issue of the *Metropolitan,* urging that American troops be sent to France immediately, Roosevelt wrote one of his last passages commending the President in any way.

Thank Heaven, we now have the right to hold up our heads, and look honorable men in the eyes without flinching. The President and the majority of Congress, without distinction of party, earned the gratitude of all self-respecting Americans by their attitude during the first week of April, 1917.

Now we must hit hard, Roosevelt continued. Let us have obligatory military service and conscription. Let us send an expeditionary force to help our comrades in arms. And, finally, let the average citizen get clearly in mind what this war is for. "Let us strive for the peace of justice and of international right." But let there be no peace, he said, until the objects of the war are obtained.[16] Roosevelt listed the peace terms for which the Allies should strive, in principle. They were remarkably similar to those of the subsequent Versailles Treaty, but, significantly, they concerned political and territorial settlements only.

In the July issue of the *Metropolitan* he was still considering the terms of a peace of righteousness, this time in greater detail. He stressed America's unselfish purpose.

The United States does not wish from Germany, Austria, or Turkey a foot of land or a dollar of indemnity. We are in this war partly because it had become impossible for a high-minded nation longer to submit to the intolerable outrages and injuries which for two years we had suffered from Germany; and partly because it was—as it long had been —our clear duty to take an active part in the war for democracy against autocracy, for right against wrong, for liberty against militaristic tyranny, for the cause of the free people against the despotic and oligarchic governments which deny freedom to the peoples.

Roosevelt admitted that it was impossible to devise a peace that would be entirely satisfactory from the standpoint of abstract justice, but substantial justice could be done, and the United States was in the best position to do it. There was little in this article with which Wilson could have disagreed; but the title, "The Peace of Victory for Which We Strive," was an omen of stormier days ahead.[17]

At the same time, Roosevelt's private correspondence expressed a deep and fundamental antagonism toward Wilson and what he stood for. Roosevelt was convinced that Wilson was a pacifist at heart and a selfish partisan and hypocrite into the bargain. He suspected that Wilson would try every way possible to get out of using violence. He despised the sonorous Wilsonian platitudes, and he thought it was the most colossal misfortune of the century that in a time of crisis the President of the United States should be a cold-blooded, unpatriotic rhetorician. He charged that as a result of Wilson's faltering and cowardly leadership Americans had entered the war without really knowing why. To Lord Bryce he wrote, scarcely two weeks after American intervention,

The perpetual talk and agitation by the International League to Enforce Peace, the announcements that we would welcome peace-without-victory, the hostile notes to England, the endless series, first of condemnatory notes to Germany and then of apologies to Germany, have resulted in the average man being completely puzzled. . . .[18]

Roosevelt's private opinion of Wilson's War Message was anything but favorable. It seemed to him that the only way it could be justified was by unstintingly condemning everything Wilson had done before, when he was spending two and one-half years dulling the American conscience and weakening the nation's moral fiber. To William Allen White he pointed out that there was more justification for going to war immediately after the sinking of the *Lusitania* than in April, 1917. He conceded that it was possible, though not proper, to make some kind of defense "for our going to war on the ground that we were fighting purely for our own interests and rights, and because after two years Germany still adhered to the position about which we had sent her an ultimatum two years previous."

But what is perfectly impossible, what represents really nauseous hypocrisy, is to say that we have gone to war to make the world safe for democracy, in April, when sixty days previously we had been announcing that we wished a "Peace without victory," and had no concern with the "causes or objects" of the war. I do not regard any speech as a great speech when it is obviously hypocritical and in bad faith; nor do I regard the making of such a speech of service to the world. I regard it as a damage to the cause of morality and decency.[19]

Roosevelt's revulsion from Wilson's persistent idealization of American intervention corresponded with his increasing dissatisfaction with what he considered the administration's half-hearted prosecution of the war. In his mind, winning the war came first; all other objectives depended upon victory. Above all, a sentimental attachment for lofty purposes should not be allowed to distract impressionable minds from the hard and practical dictates of righteousness. With mounting impatience he prodded the administration to fight a full-scale war and field an army of at least five million men. As in his campaign for preparedness, he became obsessed with the profound frustration of his militant idealism at the hands of an insidious form of pseudo idealism he was powerless to combat. His frustration was made doubly intense by Wilson's refusal to accept his offer to lead a Roosevelt Division in the field.

By the end of the summer of 1917 Roosevelt was bending all his energies toward arousing the American people to a fighting pitch, toward opening their eyes to the compelling national interests at stake. Now he said virtually nothing about peace terms or about the vindication of the principles of democracy. In an article entitled "Must We Be Brayed in a Mortar Before Our Folly Depart from Us?" he returned to his life-long theme of preparedness.

We cannot permanently hold a leading place in the world unless we prepare. But there is far more than world-position at stake. Our mere safety at home is at stake. . . . The probabilities are that the next time we fight a formidable foe we shall not again find allies whose interest it will be to protect us, and to shield us from the consequences of our feebleness and shortsightedness, as France and England have for six months—indeed for three years—been doing.[20]

Thus while Americans in general found increasing consolation in the thought that they were fighting the war to end all wars, Roosevelt was already thinking about the next war; for in his mind force always had been and, in the foreseeable future, would continue to be a persistent element of international relations, which men would ignore at their peril.

It was the basic elements of power and force in the current struggle that Roosevelt aimed to drive home to the American people in his tract *The Foes of Our Own Household,* which he completed in the fall of 1917. America was off on no crusade, he said. "We went to war because for two years the Germans had been murdering our unarmed men, women, and children, and had definitely announced their intention to continue the practice." America's object in the war was not to be defined in terms of any vague pronouncement about making the world safe for democracy. "First and foremost we are to make the world safe for ourselves. This is our war, America's war. If we do not win it, we shall some day have to reckon with Germany single-handed. Therefore, for our own sakes let us strike down Germany."

Recent technological advances in the art of warfare convinced Roosevelt that American isolation was less tenable than ever. He wanted the American people to understand

> that world conditions have changed and that the oceans and even the air have become highways for military aggression. . . . The exploits of the German U-boat off Nantucket last summer . . . showed that if Germany . . . were free to deal with us, the security that an ocean barrier once offered was annihilated. In other words, the battle-front of Europe is slowly spreading over the whole world.[21]

On September 20 Roosevelt set out upon a speaking tour of the West in order to take his message to the people. His speeches bristled with patriotism and bellicosity but said little about the war's ideal objectives. In fact, by way of depreciating these objectives, he seemed anxious to reassert the very reasons for intervention which Wilsonian idealists found most unsatisfactory. At Johnstown, Pennsylvania, he declared,

> We did not go to war to make democracy safe, and we did go to war because we had a special grievance. We went to war, because, after two years, with utter contempt of our protests, [during which] she had habitually and continually murdered our non-combatant men, women, and children on the high seas, Germany formally announced that she intended to pursue this course more ruthlessly and vigorously than ever. This was the special grievance because of which we went to war, and it was far more than an empty justification for going to war. As you know, my own belief is that we should have acted immediately after the sinking of the *Lusitania*.[22]

Clearly, the conception of war as vengeance for a grievance was more compatible with a warlike spirit than Wilson's view of war as an altruistic enterprise. It was consistent with Roosevelt's determination that the war should end in a complete victory, in an overwhelming show of force.

6. WILSON GIVES IDEALISTS A WAR PROGRAM: LASTING PEACE

As Roosevelt's war policy centered more and more upon an appeal to the fighting instincts and the basic imperatives of national power, President Wilson strove to place the war on an ever higher level of morality. On January 8, 1918, he went before Congress and, partly to restore the moral position of the Allies after Russian revolutionists had bared the Czar's archives, announced his memorable Fourteen Points, which soon became one of the most effective war programs in the history of modern nations.[23] Here, at last, was a neat formulation of the idealistic basis for a crusade.

Eight of the points applied to political and territorial settlements in specific

areas. These were quite similar to Roosevelt's peace terms of six months before; but the first five points expressed the ideal aspirations which had already
seized the imagination of liberal groups in England and the United States,
and in Germany as well, and which had even spread among revolutionary
groups in Russia and elsewhere: open diplomacy, freedom of the seas, the
reduction of economic barriers, the limitation of armaments, and the adjustment of colonial claims on a fair basis. The fourteenth point called for a
general association of nations to .guarantee the political independence and
territorial integrity of great and small nations alike; this was the point dearest
to Wilson's heart.

Wilson subsequently elaborated upon the Fourteen Points and added some
new points, but it was his original codification of the requirements of a better
world that captured the moral fervor of American idealists and became America's war program. However vague and subject to distortion and varied interpretation that program may have been, it had a tremendous impact upon
those who yearned for world reform and dreamed of the application of the
standards of individual conduct to international society. If war could realize
this vision, then it might truly merit the unqualified zeal of men imbued with
the gentle spirit of reason and good will.

It was Wilson's moral leadership, under the banner of the Fourteen Points,
that finally enabled pacific idealists to reconcile themselves completely to the
unpleasant fact of American participation in a world war. In a large measure,
it was this final reconciliation to war on the part of men imbued with a strong
liberal conscience and a deep-rooted aversion to naked power that consecrated
America's second crusade as an altruistic mission. Once these men became
convinced that America was going to fight a new type of war, a war to abolish
the old diplomacy of power politics, a war to end war, they dedicated their
intellects and their souls with unstinting devotion to Wilson's cause. From
their ranks came the most skilful, sincere, and enthusiastic propagators of
the thesis that America's prime purpose in the war was the disinterested
service of the rest of the world.

It is significant with what gusto America's most zealous domestic reformers
—people like Arthur Bullard, George Creel, Upton Sinclair, Samuel Hopkins
Adams, Ida Tarbell, and Will Irwin—threw themselves into the war for international reform. These were people who, at the outbreak of war in 1914,
had been full of the promise of American life and the religion of social progress. They had shared the feeling of many young liberal intellectuals, like
Francis Hackett, Van Wyck Brooks, and Waldo Frank, that the world was
witnessing the dawn of a cultural renaissance and a new era of human
freedom and creativeness, in which all might share the treasures of civilization.

The European war had come as a profound shock to these men of good will, for it seemed like a sudden reversal of the tide of progress and a refutation of their whole outlook upon human society. Ray Stannard Baker has recorded the sickening sensation which gripped him as the war came closer to America: "It seemed to me as we drifted steadily toward war that everything I had been interested in was threatened. All quiet inquiry, all the processes of reason, all sympathy of understanding, all the courtesies of cooperation in a peaceful world—all gone." Baker, like so many social meliorists, liked to think of himself as a "maker of understandings." He believed that ignorance and selfishness were the root of all evil. What the world needed was great mediators, great producers of common understandings—men of deep human sympathies, who could see both sides of a question, men who could produce a wider human sympathy. But what part could a maker of understandings play in a world torn by violence? "I could not help feeling that I was now facing a world in which 'men of my kind had no place, no useful service to perform."[24] This was Baker's state of mind when Wilson's program of lasting peace and international reform suddenly opened up a new channel for his reforming zeal and revived his hopes for humanity.

War is not only a great tragedy; it is sometimes a great opportunity. Only the opportunity for international reform made war bearable for many of America's pacific idealists. When one considers the strength of their inhibitions toward conflict and force, it is understandable that only the loftiest motives could have reconciled them to organized violence. It is no exaggeration to say that for the moral optimists of 1914 Wilson's war aims were a psychological necessity. Naturally, after America intervened these men were hypersensitive to every indication that the war might fall short of achieving these aims.

Of course, this was not true of all liberals and pacific idealists. The *New Republic* had taken a leading part in urging world peace as the basis for American intervention. One of its most influential editors, Walter Lippmann, subsequently had a major influence in the formulation of the Fourteen Points. As Secretary of The Inquiry, a group under the direction of House, which Wilson appointed in the fall of 1917 to prepare a program for peace, Lippmann was responsible for a large share of the abstract ideas which formed the basis of Wilson's war aims and which found their way into a number of Wilson's public speeches.[25] But Lippmann and the editors of the *New Republic* did not base their case for America's participation in the war solely upon Wilson's lofty objects. In their minds intervention was also a practical dictate of national expediency, justified upon grounds of enduring strategic interests; and they regarded membership in an international organization as a means of securing these strategic interests in a larger context.

After the United States intervened the *New Republic* continued to view the idea of a league, not as a dogma, but as a specific arrangement for controlling national power to the best interests of the United States.[26] Because the editors considered the plan for a league as a logical extension of America's reasons for entering the war, rather than as a moral compensation for that distasteful decision, they had no patience with those who, having been reconciled to war solely by the vision of international organization, became seized with doubts when the millennium failed to materialize according to schedule.

In an editorial on October 6, 1917, the *New Republic* joined the doubters in deploring the attempted perversion of America's cause at the hands of the nationalists and the lovers of violence, but it expressed its complete lack of sympathy with those who questioned the wisdom of the declaration of war against Germany on that account. The United States had entered the war because it anticipated the disastrous consequences of a German victory; the editors considered that subsequent events had thoroughly vindicated the wisdom of that calculation.[27]

In a later editorial, taking stock of the political and military changes that had come about during the year since Wilson's War Message, the *New Republic* concluded that interventionists had "abundant reason to congratulate themselves on their decision." The editors regretted the intolerance and hatred that accompanied America's war effort, but they were not disillusioned about intervention, for by that action the United States had prevented a German victory and thereby helped gain the opportunity for establishing a world organization, which might save the nation from future disaster.[28]

In its fusion of realism with idealism the *New Republic* was distinguished from its liberal confrere, the *Nation,* which had accepted intervention reluctantly and which became thoroughly reconciled to America's participation only after it received the assurance of Wilson's Fourteen Points that the war would result in a brave new world. Significantly, it was the *Nation* and not the *New Republic* which placed itself in the vanguard of disillusion when the New World order proved to be a continuation of the Old, after all.

Of course, there were also a few idealists who were never persuaded by Wilson's moral leadership that the glorious end might justify the dreadful means. Oswald Garrison Villard, the editor of the *New York Evening Post* and, after January, 1918, editor of the *Nation,* was one of these holdouts.[29] Randolph Bourne, a brilliant hunchback, who was to become a saint for disillusioned intellectuals after the war, was another.* These men—most of them

---

* Bourne died in 1918 at the age of 32. His articles for the avant-garde *Seven Arts* were posthumously gathered by James Oppenheim in Randolph Bourne, *Untimely Papers* (New York, 1919).

devout pacifists and democratic socialists—were repelled from the war chiefly by a sense of its futility and by an abhorrence of the repercussions of super-patriotism upon reason, decency, and the civil liberties of nonconformists.

As Bourne put it, "The whole era has been spiritually wasted." He charged that the intellectuals had sold their souls to all the rich and reactionary elements of society by abetting the war spirit in order to retain their influence with the nation. In his view the real enemy was War, not Germany. War was the absolute evil, with a will of its own, from which nothing good could result. The real arena of social conflict, he said, was among classes, not among artificial national units. Any idealism attached to the current war was sham and deceit. He pledged himself to purge the war of this deceit. "There is work to be done to prevent this war of ours from passing into popular mythology as a holy crusade."[30]

Bourne was a prophet a few years ahead of his time. For the great majority of liberal intellectuals, humanitarians, and social meliorists the splendor of Wilson's vision remained ample compensation for the seamy side of war—at least as long as the vision did not have to be translated into the realities of international politics. Their efforts in behalf of the war proved once more that a passion for peace and understanding, wedded to the instruments of violence, could produce a crusade of intense, if not lasting, force.

7. WILSON'S PROGRAM AND THE GENERAL PUBLIC

It was Wilson's program of international reform which set the tone of America's crusade. From his speeches the dynamic George Creel, whom Wilson appointed as head of the Committee on Public Information soon after intervention, and his devoted corps of liberal reformers and intellectuals fashioned the verbal magic that cast its spell upon all quarters of the world, elevating the American Messiah to a position of world leadership unprecedented in the annals of the presidency, and, finally, enchanting the German people themselves with the lure of the millennium.

Creel's moral offensive was equally ambitious in America. Five of the famous Red, White, and Blue pamphlets went over the million mark. Creel estimated that over one million of the ubiquitous Four Minute speeches were heard by four hundred million individuals during the eighteen months' life of the Committee on Public Information, while more than seventy-five million copies of war pamphlets, not counting the circulation given to them by the metropolitan dailies, state organizations, and private groups, found their way into American homes.[31]

The Committee's propaganda focused upon the moral issues of the war. A few pamphlets, such as *A War of Self-defense,* written by Secretary Lansing and Louis F. Post, emphasized the threat of German world domination to American security. Pan-German schemes were exposed once more in the *War Books,* written with the co-operation of many of Creel's academic assistants, and published at Princeton and the Universities of Wisconsin, North Carolina, Columbia, Chicago, and Illinois. But even these works were written in the context of German war guilt and depravity rather than in the vein of national expediency.

More typical was the reproduction of Franklin K. Lane's speech "Why We Are Fighting Germany," included in *The Nation In Arms,* in which he proclaimed, "The world of Christ . . . has come again face to face with the world of Mahomet, who willed to win by force"; or Baker's contribution to the same publication, in which he urged, "Never, during the progress of this war, let us for one instant forget the high and holy mission with which we entered it, no matter what the cost, no matter what the temptation"; or the assertion in *How the War Came to America,* largely the work of Arthur Bullard and approved by Lansing and Wilson, that with the Russian revolution the conviction "finally crystallized in American minds and hearts that this war across the sea was no mere conflict between dynasties, but a stupendous civil war of all the world."[32]

Through this program of holy war America's missionary fervor was aroused once more to the peak of 1898. Once more the nation looked beyond its shores, and out of the fullness of the American tradition of liberty and humanitarianism dedicated its wealth, its military power, and its prestige to the service of the rest of the world.

Yet it would be a mistake to suppose that this crusade, any more than its predecessor, reflected a concerted purpose on the part of the people as a whole to abandon the nation's relative isolation from the stream of world politics or to limit its sovereign independence in its relations with other nations. There is no reason to think that the great mass of Americans, in spite of their altruistic passion, seriously anticipated the sacrifice of a standard of national conduct so firmly established as the tradition of isolation and self-sufficiency for the sake of alleviating the sufferings of foreign peoples.

It is true that Wilson's announcement of the Fourteen Points was received with enthusiasm throughout the country. Hamilton Holt's magazine, the *Independent,* believed that the President had "articulated . . . the very conscience of the American people."[33] The *Literary Digest* reported almost universal approbation of Wilson's address. However, the nation's press virtually ignored the league issue; it was preoccupied with the territorial terms. Apparently, as when John Hay announced the Open Door principle, the American public was basking in the sunshine of its own righteousness, drinking in the gratifying spectacle of the United States advising the unenlightened nations how to straighten out their affairs; but if there was a general desire to undertake any concrete political commitments on behalf of Wilson's pronouncements, the press did not reveal it.

Wilson's mystic faith in his identity with the common people of America was encouraged by the obvious popularity of his war leadership. He never seems to have doubted that the people shared—or soon would share, when they completely understood the matter—his own opinion of the supreme importance of America's participation in a league of nations. Because he was convinced that the people were essentially moral and unselfish, and because he believed that international organization was, at bottom, a moral issue, he was filled with a certain naïve assurance that the great mass of Americans were as fervently and consistently altruistic as he and, therefore, equally attached to his program of international organization.

Perhaps he was right, but it is necessary to recall that while America was at war the league remained a rather vague aspiration, except on the part of those who made international organization their special concern, like the members of the League to Enforce Peace, or those among the band of devout liberals who could reconcile themselves to the fact of war only by saturating their minds in schemes for everlasting peace. There was nothing in the way America's idealistic war program was presented to the nation to produce any more solid attachment to the fourteenth point than was manifested toward Wilson's "steadfast concert for peace" at the time of America's decision to enter the war.

Furthermore, President Wilson intended that this supreme war aim should remain vague until it came time to make peace. During the winter of 1917–18 he took no official steps to start public discussion on the proposed league, lest that divert the people's attention from the war effort and lead to a precise formulation of the fourteenth point, which he might have to oppose later. The demand for a league plan that followed his proclamation of the Fourteen Points led him to ask House to discuss the subject with eminent American advocates, but even then the President remained unwilling to stimulate discussion on constitutional details, for fear that such discussion might ripen into controversy. Even in the summer of 1918, in spite of House's advice that he ought to announce some specific plan so that opinion could crystallize around it, the President blocked public discussion of details and methods because he saw grave dangers in stirring up national sentiments that might endanger solidarity against Germany.

Those who made international organization their special concern continued to publicize the idea and develop its details. The proposals of the League to Enforce Peace continued to elicit an impressive body of favorable comment from political figures, the general public, and the press. In June, 1918, the *New Republic* could observe with satisfaction, "Men who at first sneered at a world made safe for democracy now believe in it without reservation."[34] Yet general approval of a theoretical organization to preserve peace was not the same thing as actual acceptance of the commitments of a specific league of nations.

As long as winning the war remained the immediate, tangible objective in the public mind, the league idea flourished, principally, as a general aspiration for the end of all wars and as an expression of the righteousness of America's cause rather than as a deliberate and reasoned choice of a revolutionary program of participation in world affairs. In fact, American enthusiasm for a league was, in large part, enthusiasm for a world in which the nation could escape a recurrence of its present involvement in the toils of world politics. To this extent the desire for a league arose from the very sentiments that made acceptance of new international commitments unlikely.

Something of the vagueness of the public's understanding of the fourteenth point is reflected in the nature of the publicity campaign of the League to Enforce Peace. In order to identify itself with the war effort and distinguish itself from the "peace-at-any-price" groups the League went out of its way to conform to the requirements of the popular war spirit. Thus the slogan of the League's big national convention in the middle of May, 1918, was "Win the War for Permanent Peace." In the keynote address Taft said that the convention was called to "sound the trumpet of stern implacable war to the end," and speaker after speaker warned against a premature peace. The meeting was reported under such headings as "War to Death Taft's Demand of Peace League," "Peace League to Urge Victory First," and "Carry on War till Victorious Peace Is Forced on Huns." Some editors singled out the league plan for comment, both adverse and favorable; but the emphasis in the press, as in the convention, was upon complete victory.[35]

Like the preparedness campaign, the campaign for a league of nations, as it grew in popularity, broadened in scope and tended to merge with the general stream of patriotic sentiment. While the war was yet to be won, the aim of a league to enforce peace gained strength as a kind of sublimation of the immediate and tangible goal of victory. Yet this very basis of strength would prove a source of weakness when the immediate goal of victory no longer existed. The way in which the league was popularized as a war aim ill prepared the general public to take a strong and consistent stand in the debate between nationalism and internationalism that soon raged around the Versailles Treaty.

8. Nationalism Versus Internationalism Again

As we saw in the last chapter, the nationalist opposition to the league idea revealed its tactics in the debate over Wilson's appeal to the belligerents of December 18, 1916. The developing struggle with the internationalists was largely suspended while America was at war, except for the nationalists' depreciation of altruistic war aims and their insistence that the promotion of peace terms should not interfere with the achievement of a complete and unconditional victory. However, as the war came to a close and the prospect of a peace settlement on the basis of the fourteenth point became distinctly probable, the debate was revived.

In addresses on July 4 and September 27, 1918, President Wilson made it clear that he considered some sort of international organization essential for the preservation of a peace settlement.[36] Senator Lodge, speaking in the name of the Republican party on the floor of the Senate, made it equally clear that he considered an unconditional surrender of Germany far more important than the establishment of any league to enforce peace.[37]

In July former Senator Albert J. Beveridge and Theodore Roosevelt agreed to wage an all-out battle on the issue of nationalism versus internationalism. "Wilson has hoisted the motley flag of internationalism," wrote Beveridge. "That makes the issue, does it not? Straight Americanism for us. There is both sense and sentiment in that." Roosevelt replied, "You understand exactly how we feel."[38] And through his articles in the *Kansas City Star* and the *Metropolitan* he took his case to the public.

There was nothing new in Roosevelt's plea for nationalism against internationalism. His arguments were the same arguments he had been broadcasting for two decades. They were applied to the league proposition with perfect consistency. "The cult of internationalism," he exclaimed, "is the cult of a doctrine of fatal sterility." This cult had great vogue among clever intellectuals and the superficially cultivated, he admitted; but it inevitably emasculated its sincere votaries. Every civilization worth calling by that name had to be built upon a spirit of intense nationalism. Roosevelt brandished his virile metaphor once more: Promiscuity in patriotism is as unwholesome as promiscuity in domestic relations. "Within our national limits I distrust any man who is as fond of a stranger as he is of his own family; and in international matters I even more keenly distrust the man who cares for other nations as much as for his own."[39] Logically, one might well wonder what this argument had to do with an international organization that was not even on paper yet. But more than logic was involved in Roosevelt's profound revulsion from the altruistic, self-denying idealism, which, he suspected, was at the bottom of the league agitation. Accordingly, he was putting the nation on its guard.

Although he anticipated the worst kind of league, Roosevelt was still not prepared to denounce the idea absolutely. In the fall of 1918 he had repudiated the Fourteen Points as a basis for peace, but he continued to think that a league might be useful, providing that it was set up in such a way that it would not interfere with vital national interests or distract the public's attention from the pressing necessity of maintaining an adequate preparedness program.[40]

Senator Lodge took the same view. In a letter to Beveridge, written December 3, he said that he thought it would be a mistake to meet the league proposition with a flat denial, since no one could quarrel with the purpose of a league —that is, the preservation of world peace. But, as in his address of February 1, 1917, he stressed his opinion that everything depended on the details and their practical consequences. If the league involved "control of our legislation, of our armies and navies, or the Monroe Doctrine, or an international police, and that sort of thing, then our issue is made up, and we shall win."[41]

One can admit that this approach was conceived as a stratagem of debate and an instrument of personal spite and partisan advantage and still recognize that it was also based upon a view of international relations which both Lodge and Roosevelt had held long before antipathy toward Wilson and a desire to reinstate the Republican party in the coming Congressional elections became a consideration. Moreover, Lodge's subsequent use of the league issue for partisan purposes fails to demonstrate any sinister erection of expediency above principle, for Lodge—and those, like Roosevelt, who agreed with him— simply never looked upon the league idea as an urgent moral principle. In Lodge's mind benevolence, magnanimity, and morally impeccable institutional arrangements counted for little in international relations unless they coincided with the realities of national self-interest. An Anglo-American rapprochement and the steadfast maintenance of American power was what really interested him. If a league to enforce peace were consistent with this goal, he would favor it, from the standpoint of national welfare and the advancement of Western civilization as well. But if a league involved a reduction rather than an extension of American power and independence—as he suspected that it would under the sponsorship of international altruists like Wilson—then he would regard it as not only useless but positively pernicious.

The ensuing controversy between nationalism and internationalism cannot be assessed in terms of logic alone, for much of the emotion which it generated arose from underlying temperamental and philosophical antipathies, such as we have seen develop from the turn of the century. But to reduce these fundamental antipathies to personal and partisan differences is to mistake a particular manifestation of a continuing conflict in the American attitude toward international relations for the conflict itself.

Actually, the international organization established by the treaty of Versailles was neither as idealistic as President Wilson claimed nor as contrary to American power and independence as Lodge and Roosevelt asserted; but because the issue of American membership in the League of Nations involved principles of national conduct that touched the very roots of man's adaptation to his human environment, the objective merits of this controversy, as in the case of the controversies over neutrality and preparedness, became obscured and distorted under the stress of a deeper struggle within the human soul. It is a familiar phenomenon in personal relations: A comparatively narrow practical difference between individuals becomes exaggerated out of all proportion by an underlying conflict of principles and prejudices.

This study is not concerned with the complex details of the debate over the League, with the intricate parliamentary maneuvers and the welter of personal and partisan prejudices that led to the repudiation of the Versailles Treaty. These matters are important, but more important for an understanding of the role of ideals and national self-interest in American foreign relations is an analysis of the continuing struggle between an egoistic and an altruistic view of national conduct, which underlay the frustration of America's second crusade.

9. The Egoistic Defection From Wilson's Program

Woodrow Wilson viewed the making of peace as a fulfilment of the purpose for which America had waged war, and he relied upon the common people of America, with their tremendous resources of idealism, to support his plans for peace with the same zeal they had spent upon war. On the day of the Armistice, November 11, 1918, he told a joint session of Congress that victory was no mere military decision, no mere relief from the trials of war, but a divine vindication of universal principles and a call to greater duties ahead.[42] Two days before he sailed for the Paris peace conference he proclaimed the continuation in peace of America's disinterested service to humanity during war: "We are about to give order and organization to this peace not only for ourselves but for the other peoples of the world as well, so far as they will suffer us to serve them. It is international justice that we seek, not domestic safety merely."[43]

Wilson forgot—if, indeed, he ever realized it—that America, as a whole, had not entered the war in the spirit of altruism; that there was implicit in American intervention no acceptance of revolutionary international commitments; that the nation's war-born enthusiasm for a world made safe for democracy and the end of all wars gained a good part of its inspiration from a simple desire to lick the Hun and stay out of future trouble. However fervent America's belief in the righteousness of its cause may have been, the general approval of Wilson's war aims implied no eagerness to sacrifice traditional modes of national conduct for the sake of other nations and peoples.

Nevertheless, one cannot deny that the American people had come to believe that their war was a crusade for a freer, more democratic, and more peaceful world. This vague aspiration would somehow have to be fulfilled in order to justify the sacrifices of war. For by the time the German Army was defeated, the principal reasons which had justified intervention in April, 1917—the maintenance of neutral rights and the vindication of national honor —had all but disappeared from popular discussion. The war had been fought for a different set of reasons from those that had led to intervention; and these reasons, however imperfectly conceived, raised expectations of a nature that could not be satisfied by mere military victory.

Wilson counted upon the fundamental altruism of the people to bridge the gap between the League and tradition. But with the strongest basis for popular idealism removed by victory, it seems likely that only some persuasive appeal to fundamental national self-interest could have sustained America's crusade into the period of peacemaking. Yet Wilson, by his very nature, could appeal only for an even greater subordination of self-interest to moral principle.

Wilson insisted that the League of Nations was pre-eminently a moral conception, an organization to turn the "searching light of conscience" upon wrong and aggression wherever it might be contemplated.[44] It followed from his faith in the moral sense of the masses that the American people were bound to embrace this plan once they understood its lofty nature. Therefore, he expounded its transcendent idealism in the confidence that Americans would prefer the interests of mankind to all other interests. While this approach made American membership in an international league seem less and less compelling to the great body of Americans as war-born idealism subsided, it positively assured a mounting hostility toward the project on the part of Realistic national egoists like Roosevelt and Lodge.

Although Wilson was not ignorant of the practical national advantages to be gained through membership in a league, his whole nature rebelled at a frank acknowledgment of expediency as a basis for national action. He preferred to emphasize the universal moral principles that bound men together as human beings rather than the fine adjustments of self-interest among nations, which might disintegrate into violent jealousies with a slight change of circumstance. Consequently, he presented the League as a substitute for the balance-of-power system, not as a supplementation or extension of it. As he told an English audience on December 30, "If the future had nothing for us but a new attempt to keep the world at a right poise by a balance of power, the United States would take no interest, because she will join no combination of power which is not the combination of all of us."[45]

Roosevelt, on the other hand, took just the opposite view. In his opinion it was folly to join a concert of nations that did not reflect the actual power situation. As far as he was concerned, both practical and idealistic considerations pointed to the wisdom of an Anglo-American alliance. On November 19 he wrote Arthur Lee that he had become more convinced than ever that "there should be the closest alliance between the British Empire and the United States."[46] To George Haven Putnam, who had solicited his membership in the English-Speaking Union, he wrote,

I regard the British Navy as probably the most potent instrumentality for peace in the world. . . . Moreover, I am now prepared to say what five years ago I would not have said. I think the time has come when the United States and the British Empire can agree to a universal arbitration treaty.[47]

In one of his last editorials Roosevelt declared that he strongly shared the feeling that there should be some kind of international league to prevent a recurrence of war, but he warned his readers not to be deceived by sham idealism, by high-sounding and meaningless phrases, such as those embodied in the Fourteen Points. Let us face the facts, he wrote. The first fact is that nations are not equal. Therefore, let us limit the league to the present Allies and admit others only as their conduct warrants it. Let us specifically reserve certain rights from the jurisdiction of any international body. America should be very careful about promising to interfere with, or on behalf of, "impotent or disorderly nations and peoples outside this league" where they lie "wholly outside our sphere of interest." Roosevelt concluded with a plea for universal military training.[48]

Actually, Roosevelt's conception of a peace settlement as one phase of a continuing accommodation of power was as remote from the popular view as Wilson's vision of the selfless submerging of national sovereignty in a community of interest. Both views involved a serious break with traditional conceptions of America's relation to world politics. However, in his strong assertion of national prerogatives Roosevelt was joined by parochial nationalists, such as Borah and Beveridge, who were unalterably opposed to all involvements in power politics, including those for limited national ends, on the grounds that nothing that happened overseas could be of enough concern to the United States to warrant contaminating the nation by association with the evil balance-of-power system. While Lodge and Roosevelt had never been opposed to joining an international organization that would redound to the national interest, Beveridge and Borah were convinced, as a matter of principle, that the national interest and membership in a league were mutually contradictory. But, whatever their differences, both groups were agreed that American interests came first; and, if only for this reason, Wilsons' persistent association of the League with altruism proved as repelling to Realistic as to parochial nationalists.

Moreover, the President's moralistic approach gave the nationalists a distinct tactical advantage in the debate over the terms of America's membership in the League; for if America's entrance into the League of Nations were purely a philanthropic gesture, then there was strength in the argument that the nation ought to be able to determine, independently of others, the proper extent of its own generosity. On this basis Lodge argued for his reservations to the League Convenant. In an address before the Senate on February 28, 1919, he accepted Wilson's contention that American participation in the League would be almost wholly for the benefit of others and asserted that, therefore, the United States had a right to limit the sacrifice of its sovereignty as it pleased.[49] On August 12 he argued, "Surely it is not too much to insist that when we are offered nothing but the opportunity to give and to aid others we should have the right to say what sacrifices we shall make and what the magnitude of our gifts should be."[50]

Senator Borah had presented the same thesis of limited philanthropy the week before.

I may be willing to help my neighbor, though he be improvident or unfortunate, but I do not necessarily want him for a business partner. I may be willing to give liberally of my means, of my council and advice, even of my strength or blood, to protect his family from attack or injustice, but I do not want him placed in a position where he may decide for me when and how I shall act or to what extent I shall make sacrifice.[51]

If the majority of the nation were willing to grant philanthropy a greater scope than Borah, it was not because they were more idealistic but simply because they were less apprehensive of the sacrifice demanded of them.

10. The Idealistic Defection from Wilson's Program

In urging the nation to sustain its crusade at a wartime pitch and subordinate its own interests to the interests of mankind Wilson greatly overestimated the idealism of the great majority of his countrymen; but there was at least one group of Americans as altruistic as he, and this was that small but articulate band of liberals and intellectuals in the vanguard of the nation's pacific idealists, which had long constituted itself as a sort of guardian of the American conscience. These men yeqrned for the fulfilment of America's crusade with that passion for perfection which obsessed the prewar anti-imperialists and peace advocates. In a sense, their very self-respect depended upon the achievement of Wilson's goals, for nothing much short of those goals could have vindicated their personal concessions to the war spirit. Unfortunately, their exalted aspirations were not balanced by a comprehension of the rigid limitations upon altruism in international relations. It is not strange that this group of ardent idealists should have become the most bitterly disillusioned in the 1920's.

The sources of disillusionment were apparent before the completed draft of the Versailles Treaty was made public, for it became obvious almost from the start of the Paris peace conference that most of the Fourteen Points—which, contrary to the opinion of many idealists, was a unilateral statement of general principles by Woodrow Wilson and not a contract signed by the Allies—would be carried out only imperfectly, if at all. The idealists who had given Wilson his strongest support were the first to be shocked by the inevitable deviations from his war aims amid the post-armistice reassertion of nationalism throughout the world.

Wilson's astounding pinnacle of world leadership in November, 1918, represented the triumph of Wilson the Conqueror, not Wilson the Peacemaker. The Armistice filled Wilson with a sober anticipation of great world responsibilities, but hundreds of thousands of his own countrymen were merely exultant over the vanquishing of the Hun and the end of the trials of war. In view of the disillusionment of the 1920's and 1930's, it is interesting to recall that the great majority of Americans in the autumn of 1918 had no doubts whatsoever that Germany was guilty of perpetrating the war and ought to be punished accordingly. If Americans were worried about the peace terms, it was because they feared that the settlement would be too soft, not too tough.[52]

Abroad the spirit of vengeance was, quite naturally, even more intense. And one had but to read the front page of the newspapers to discover that the Fourteen Points had no more abolished the national egoism of foreigners than of Americans. Winston Churchill, then British Minister of Munitions, announced that the League of Nations could be no substitute for the supremacy of the British fleet and should not interfere with Great Britain's retention of the German colonies or the conquered parts of Turkey. Lloyd George won a sweeping victory in the general elections on the issue of "Hang the Kaiser and make the Germans pay the cost of the war." French patriots were talking of reconstructing Central Europe in accordance with French interests. Italian patriots were talking about acquiring the Dalmatian Coast and control of the Adriatic. Leaders of all nations were advancing their territorial and financial claims. Evidently, hundreds of millions of peoples of conflicting hopes and ambitions regarded Wilson as the Messiah of their special national concerns and theirs only.

In January the wily French Premier, Clemenceau, who had privately ridiculed Wilson for claiming four more points than the Lord Himself, shocked American idealists and overjoyed the Chamber of Deputies when he unequivocally asserted, "There is an old system of alliances called the Balance of Power—this system of alliance, which I do not renounce, will be my guiding thought at the Peace Conference."[53]

These revelations, supplemented by additional evidence at the peace conference that Wilson's New Diplomacy had failed to transform the world, had a devastating effect upon the moral optimism of the most ardent apostles of the American mission. Their early defection, and not the nationalist assault, was the real beginning of the general repudiation of America's second crusade that swept the nation in the 1920's; for it was they, and not the nationalists, who were chiefly responsible for associating American intervention with altruistic goals, and it was they who first became disillusioned with their handiwork.

11. THE "NATION" BECOMES DISILLUSIONED

One can trace the early course of disillusionment in the pages of the *Nation*. Thoroughout the war the *Nation* had followed Wilson's lead in seeking a basis for a truly liberal peace. Like the English Liberal press, it had urged the statesmen of the world to proclaim a clear formulation of war aims in accordance with Wilson's lofty objectives. By January, 1918, the editors began in earnest to advocate discussion of peace terms in preparation for the reconstruction of the world when the proper time should arrive. In Wilson's declaration of the Fourteen Points they recognized the principles for which they had stood year in and year out. They denounced the demands for unconditional surrender, led by Lodge and Roosevelt, as manifestations of that very Junkerism against which America was supposed to be fighting.

However, with the approach of Armistice the *Nation* became very much concerned over the resurgence of national passions, no longer concealed by the moralistic battle dress of war. With dismay it observed the Allied statesmen ceasing to talk ideals and settling down to the old game of getting as much for their nations as they could. It was sorely disappointed by Wilson's withholding of the German peace note from publication on the grounds that the note was propaganda, and it grew indignant over his communication of the Armistice terms to Vienna and Berlin before they were revealed to the American people. For did not the Fourteen Points pledge the statesmen of the world to observe open diplomacy? The *Nation* considered Wilson's statement to the effect that open diplomacy prohibited secret agreements, not secrecy in negotiations, a mere attempt to explain away a shocking relapse into old-style power politics.

Then came the worst blow of all: Wilson's premature announcement of a new three-year naval construction program. In the *Nation's* opinion this could only mean that the President was deliberately discarding "the most vital principle of all the fourteen peace terms, disarmament." And the editors warned him that his present policy was jeopardizing the very objective for which the nation had entered the war.[54]

By the end of December the *Nation* was unable to see a single indication that the coming peace settlement was intended to be a "people's settlement." It was thoroughly alarmed at Clemenceau's statement to the Chamber of Deputies. Here was fresh proof that the representatives of the old-style diplomacy of aggrandizement and intrigue were conspiring to create another Congress of Vienna. The editors warned that America would not join any scheme to further the ambitions of European and Asiatic politicians.[55]

On February 22, 1919, the *Nation,* while refraining from outright opposition to the League Covenant or peace treaty, declared that the time had come to say that the peace conference had consistently ignored the spirit and principles of liberalism and that the League of Nations was, so far, no more than an old-style alliance for old-fashioned purposes, just one more instrument for the maintenance of the economic and political status quo.[56]

By the middle of March the editors were completely disgusted at the dominance of the forces of selfishness and reaction in the preparation of the constitution of the League.

If anyone ever really imagined that the proposal of a league of nations would bind together the spokesmen of the nations in unity of sentiment regarding the problems which confronted them, or repress the schemes of calculating selfishness which the years of war had stimulated, he must by this time have been undeceived.[57]

One week later, the *Nation* took a position of unqualified opposition to the Covenant as long as it remained an integral part of the peace treaty. The editors had no objection to the treaty's surrender of national sovereignty; what they condemned was the terms of the settlement which the surrender was intended to enforce. It considered the terms that Wilson brought back at the end of February not even a step in the right direction. "It has no quality or characteristic which essentially differentiates it from treaties that have hitherto bound the European states into competitive and predatory groups."

What the *Nation* wanted was world economic and social reform and the inauguration of that new kind of diplomacy which Wilson had preached. Instead, Wilson was asking America to swallow an organization of financial imperialism—a reference to the absence of guarantees for free trade. "What we have is a calm, arrogant, and ruthless formulation of a plan of world-domination by the five conquering powers. . . ." In short, Mr. Wilson had seduced liberal opinion with his talk of open diplomacy, freedom of the seas, freedom of trade, disarmament, and the rights of small nations in order to betray it to its enemies.[58]

The *Nation* was thoroughly disillusioned by the time it witnessed the end of the peace conference in a final series of cynical and undemocratic compromises over Fiume, Shantung, and the Saar Valley. It is interesting to observe that the only move of Wilson's that the editors found worthy of applause in the final weeks of the conference was his disastrous appeal to the reason and morality of the Italian people over the heads of their nefarious diplomatic representatives concerning the Fiume controversy. "For once President Wilson has struck out well in Paris. . . . A ray of truth has illumined the fog of hypocrisy and cant which has concealed the land-grabbing going on in the name of democracy and the war to end war." The editorial admitted that Wilson's appeal might wreck the conference, but at least he spoke the truth and spoke directly to the public opinion of the world.[59] Wilson's appeal did not wreck the conference. It did, however, cause the Italian delegation to quit Paris; and, at one blow, it converted the American Messiah into the world's great villain in the eyes of the outraged Italian masses.

In its condemnation of the peace settlement the *Nation* reflected the sentiments of Oswald Garrison Villard, who became its chief editor, in January, 1918. Villard's uncompromising idealism, his doctrinaire perfectionism and utopianism, spawned under the tutelage of Schurz and Godkin, was to play a large role in postwar disillusionment and in the paralysis of national action during the turbulent events preceding World War II. In his single-minded, obsessive zeal for the right above everything else he was the embodiment of that intense crusading fervor which made a virtue out of ignoring expediency. Villard, who had never reconciled himself to intervention, became a leader of those who had reconciled themselves only by virtue of utopian expectations. He was among the first influential idealists to proclaim that the failure of the peace meant the failure of the war and that the failure of this war meant the futility of all wars.

It would have been one of the most remarkable events in history if the peace conference had lived up to Villard's standards. Early in January, 1918, he set forth in the pages of the *Nation* the general principles of peace upon which liberal-minded men ought to agree: immediate and total disarmament of all nations; establishment of free trade and the abolition of all protective tariffs; assurance of the principle of no government without consent; and the establishment of an international parliament and an international court to consider all issues, including those affecting national honor. Villard acknowledged that his prescription might seem too idealistic, but he avowed, "Sane men everywhere have a right to hitch their wagons to stars as never before. Can we not all agree that if none of these four principles is accepted when the war ends, then the unparalleled sacrifices of this war will have been largely for nothing?"[60] It was a natural and a short step from this position to his view, expressed at the end of April, 1919, that the failure at Paris was "a far-reaching test of the value of war as the creator of moral values."

Can war be cured by more war, or is it to be cured by frankly trying to apply the doctrines of Christianity and the brotherhood of man? This is the question which is to be answered at Paris. Beside it the new Holy Alliance misnamed the League of Nations sinks into insignificance.[61]

12. AMERICANS FAVOR THE LEAGUE BUT NOT ITS OBLIGATIONS

By the time President Wilson returned to Paris, on March 14, 1919, after presenting the first draft of the League Covenant to his countrymen, the egoistic and the idealistic opposition was already poised to spring upon the completed draft, which the President introduced into the Senate arena on June 9, 1919. But it would be a mistake to suppose that the majority of the American people were antagonistic toward the work at Paris and Versailles. It seems probable that they were strongly in favor of it.

A *Literary Digest* poll of newspaper editorial opinion, published on April 5, 1919, asked the question, "Do you favor the proposed League of Nations?" Seven hundred and eighteen replied "Yes"; 181, "No"; and 478 gave conditional answers.* Among the papers with a large circulation, the great bulk of the unconditional opposition was represented by the Hearst chain. The opponents of the League criticized its alleged impracticality and the softness of its leading advocates. They charged that the League would involve America in foreign quarrels and destroy the Monroe Doctrine, while depriving the nation of its sovereignty. Advocates of the League stressed its idealism, portray-

* *Literary Digest,* LXI (April 5, 1919), 13 ff. This poll also showed that the great majority of Democratic, Republican, and Independent papers favored the League, with the bulk of those conditionally favoring it being Republican; that in each geographical region the sentiment was favorable; and that in no one state was there an opposing majority.

ing it as a continuation of America's humanitarian crusade and charging that its rejection would destroy America's reputation for idealism and make a mockery of the war.

Evidence from other sources indicates that organized labor and the farm organizations were almost solidly behind the League. The majority of the Protestant clergy and educational leaders favored it.[62] Typical of the sentiment among these latter two groups was the resolution endorsed by the World Alliance for International Friendship, an international group of churchmen:

> The World Alliance contends that the principles of justice and brotherhood apply to the action of nations no less than of individuals; and as a consequence, general human interests should take precedence of special national interests, and a nation no less than an individual must recognize that it lives as a member of a larger whole.[63]

The opponents of the League realized that it commanded widespread support. Senator Lodge, writing in 1925, recalled that in May, 1919, "the great mass of the people, the man in the street," wanted the treaty ratified "as quickly as possible."

> What I may call the vocal classes of the community, most of the clergymen, the preachers of sermons, a large element in the teaching force of the universities, a large proportion of the newspaper editors, and finally the men and women who were in the habit of writing and speaking for publication, although by no means thoroughly informed, were friendly to the League as it stood and were advocating it.[64]

However, Lodge did not think that the general approval of the League was matched by a comprehension of its actual provisions or its practical implications; and he believed that if the people understood these things, they would be much less favorable toward the idea. Accordingly, he made a bargain with the irreconcilable Borah to attack the League by questioning its details. Borah agreed to support the introduction of Lodge's amendments and reservations but made it quite clear that he would vote against the treaty even if it were amended.[65]

This stress on the details and the actual working of the League was an approach which Lodge had taken ever since his speech on February 1, 1917; it was entirely consistent with his long-standing objections to all-inclusive arbitration treaties. In this case, political tactics conformed with sincere conviction. Lodge's position on the League was similar to that of Elihu Root, whose integrity has never been reproached. Root was certainly one of America's most learned and effective advocates of the peaceful settlement of international disputes, but he had declined to join the League to Enforce Peace because he doubted whether the American people would live up to the actual obligations of a league, no matter how strongly they might approve the plan on general principles. In July, 1919, Root agreed that the great majority of Americans wanted the Versailles Treaty with the League ratified at once, but he opposed the treaty, as long as it lacked certain reservations, because he believed that the people did not really understand the practical workings of the League and would not make the necessary sacrifices of sovereignty and isolation if an actual case of aggression arose under its provisions.[66]

Public opinion is a nebulous thing, but it does seem plausible that, in this instance, Lodge and Root were shrewder judges of the public attitude toward the League than President Wilson. In the long run, the question that had to be answered was not so much whether the general public would accept American membership in such an eminently idealistic organization but whether they would live up to its revolutionary obligations—whether they would fulfil its implied responsibility for a continuing interest and participation in international affairs, which might only indirectly affect American interests. There was little in the development of the American attitude toward world politics before World War I or during it to suggest that the nation as a whole accepted the League in this fuller sense.

The remarkable thing about the final phase of the debate on the League, which began with Wilson's return from Paris in the spring of 1919, was not that the United States failed, in the end, to join the League but that it failed in spite of the fact that a large majority of the Senate and probably of the nation at large wanted to participate in an international organization of some kind, which, under certain conditions, would commit the United States in advance to join with other nations in coercing an aggressor.

In spite of the crafty delaying and harassing tactics within the Senate, the jealousy of Senatorial prerogative, the depth of partisan feeling, and the bitterness of personal antipathies; in spite of the complexity of the issues and the campaign of deliberate obfuscation; in spite of President Wilson's tragic collapse at Pueblo, Colorado, on September 25, virtually removing him from office for several months; but, above all, in spite of the long and stubborn national tradition of political isolation and sovereign independence; still 85 per cent of the Senators voting on the Versailles Treaty on November 19, 1919, were willing to accept American membership in the League of Nations, some with reservations and some without.* And, although the treaty failed to pass, because those who wanted some reservations and those who wanted none would not combine against those who opposed any league at all, organized public sentiment was so strongly in favor of some kind of league that

---

* The vote on the treaty with fourteen reservations was 39 yeas to 55 nays. Forty-two of the nays were "noninterventionist" Democrats; 13 were "irreconcilable" Republicans. A motion to approve the treaty without reservations was defeated 38 yeas to 53 nays. William S. Holt, *Treaties Defeated by the Senate* (Baltimore, 1933), pp. 294–98.

three months later the Senate was forced to reconsider its decision and resume the debate. On March 19, 1920, again 85 per cent of those voting on the treaty were willing to accept membership in some sort of league; and an actual majority of 49 to 35, seven short of the necessary two-thirds majority, voted for the treaty with reservations.*

Nor was there any great practical difference between the League with reservations and the League without them. Notwithstanding Wilson's insistence that Lodge's fourteen reservations constituted a "nullification" of the whole treaty, the machinery of the League could, undoubtedly, have operated as effectively with these reservations as without them.[67] Many of the Democratic Senators who supported the League realized this and were anxious to break the parliamentary deadlock by accepting the reservations. Herbert Hoover, former President Taft, and William Jennings Bryan, among others, urged the President to abandon his uncompromising position of all or nothing; but Wilson was, evidently, more willing to compromise with the troublesome peacemakers at Versailles than with the intractable treaty makers in Washington. Ironically, the President's own confidential reservations, which he gave to Senator Hitchcock to use as he saw fit, were substantially the same as Lodge's reservations relating to Article X, the Monroe Doctrine, domestic questions, and withdrawal from the League.[68]

The United States came remarkably close to entering the League. Yet it would be rash to infer from this fact that Americans were eager to embrace a new conception of their political relations with the rest of the world. One indication to the contrary was the extraordinary placidity with which they accepted the return to normalcy under the Harding administration.

The election of 1920 was by no means the "solemn referendum" on the League issue which Wilson had called for. There were many issues besides American membership in the League. Important members of both parties said that a vote for their candidate would be a vote for the League. Harding's position was so platitudinous and ambiguous as to defy logical analysis. If the tremendous Republican pluralities showed anything about the American attitude toward international responsibilities, they showed that the people were growing increasingly indifferent toward them; in other words, returning to their normal state. Their crusading energy had played out; they were tired of Wilsonism; they wanted a change. However, if the results of the election were inconclusive, the public's unprotesting acquiescence in America's subsequent

---

* Twenty-three of the nays, all Democrats, approved of the treaty without reservations. They joined with 12 "irreconcilables" to deprive the treaty of its two-thirds majority. Of the yeas, 21 were Democrats, 28 Republicans. *Ibid.*, pp. 300–302.

repudiation of the League and its withdrawal from political contact with the Old World was more significant, for these developments showed that the general approval of the League's objects was not rooted in the kind of sound comprehension of compelling national interests which gives stability to ideals.

Perhaps the shock of America's withdrawal could have been mitigated had the United States been a member of the League. And even if the nation had not been willing to live up to its obligation to help enforce peace, one can argue that membership in the League was a wiser alternative than non-membership, since America's very presence on the League Council might have given that body the courage and foresight to check by measures short of coercion the disastrous chain of consequences which blew up in the face of the Western world in 1939. But the point here is that, whether the United States joined the League or not, the task of American leaders—though it may well have been a hopeless task—was to stiffen the nation's moral purpose with a sense of responsibility for the practical consequences of ideals—above all, the consequences for America's own security and material welfare. Yet, as in the controversy surrounding American neutrality and intervention, it was this vital element of political realism that was most conspicuously absent from the debate over the Versailles Treaty. Those who were most actively concerned with the nation's selfish interest wasted their efforts in an impulsive and myopic assertion of nationalist xenophobia. Those who most clearly understood the imperatives of power politics were absorbed in ideological warfare with the proponents of altruistic idealism. Those who were most intent upon realizing the vision of a world prospering under the guidance of Christian ethics were ignorant or contemptuous of the intricate and intractable obstacles in the path of perfection.

13. Wilson's Case for the League

President Wilson's leadership, while morally above reproach, seemed to strike precisely the note of exalted altruism that was least likely to create a realistic appreciation of the larger political consequences of America's membership in the League.

The constant theme of his post-Armistice addresses urging the nation to join the League of Nations was America's moral responsibility for fulfilling the idealistic object of her intervention. But the more he depicted the League as an embodiment of American ideals, the more he disillusioned those idealists who expected perfection. The more fervently he appealed for selfless service to the rest of the world, the more he antagonized the champions of American nationalism. The more he urged the nation to maintain its crusade with un-flagging energy, the more weary Americans grew with a cause which appeared to demand so much and promise so little tangible in return.

Wilson's address at Boston, on February 24, 1919, upon his first return to the United States set the keynote. He said that American idealism had injected a whole new spirit of confidence and hope in Europe and that the world was on the threshold of a new age, in which nations would understand one another. And this was all due to the power of ideals. "Speaking with perfect frankness in the name of the people of the United States I have uttered as the objects of this great war ideals, and nothing but ideals, and the war has been won by that inspiration." America was the hope of the world, he said; and if she withdrew into a narrow and selfish isolation, she would bring despair and blackness to the homes of the world.[69]

In his address at New York City, on March 4, on the eve of his departure for the peace conference Wilson went so far as to defend European statesmen as converts to American idealism. If they were once cynical, they had changed now, he said.[70]

Speaking on Memorial Day, May 30, at Suresnes Cemetery in France he recognized that there were faint stirrings of the old order trying to reassert itself, but he had no doubt that the great tide in human affairs was running forward, that this was an age which "rejects the standards of national selfishness that once governed the counsels of nations and demands that they shall give way to a new order of things in which the only questions will be, 'Is it right?' 'Is it just?' 'Is it in the interest of mankind?'"[71]

When the President presented the Versailles Treaty for ratification to the Senate, on July 10, he explained that it was simply the realization of the objects for which America had entered the war. Americans had entered, not because their material interests were directly threatened, but because they saw freedom and right jeopardized by autocracy. As the nation had fought for no selfish interest, so it had sought nothing for itself in the peace settlement—only the restoration of right and the assurance of liberty for all peoples. "Shall we or any other free people hesitate to accept this great duty? Dare we reject it and break the heart of the world?" American isolation ended twenty years ago, Wilson declared. America was a world power whether it wanted to be or not; and the only question was whether she would accept or reject the moral leadership offered her. In a stirring passage infused with the Wilsonian faith in the power of spiritual conceptions the President concluded,

The stage is set, the destiny disclosed. It has come about by no plan of our conceiving, but by the hand of God who led us into this way. We cannot turn back. We can only go forward, with lifted eyes and freshened spirit, to follow the vision. It was of this that we dreamed at our birth. America shall in truth show the way. The light streams upon the path ahead, and nowhere else.[72]

Yet as Senator Lodge tied up the treaty in committee, waiting for the slump in idealism to take hold of the nation, as the hearings wore on and the League opposition grew increasingly determined, Wilson was forced to conclude that only a direct appeal to the people could arouse their idealism sufficiently to force the Senate to fulfil the nation's obligation to humanity. He may also have realized that moral appeals would not be enough. Certainly the addresses he delivered on his famous tour of the West in September reflected a new sensitiveness to his critics' depreciation of Wilsonian idealism.

In several speeches he argued for the League on the basis of national self-interest, though this was obviously distasteful to him. He would preface his arguments with statements like, "If you do not want me to be too altruistic, let me be very practical";[73] or, "Very well, then, if I am to compete with the critics of this League and of this treaty as a selfish American, I say I want to get in as quick as I can";[74] or, "I do not like to put the thing on that plane, my fellow countrymen, but if you want to talk business, I can talk business."[75] Then he would warn his audience that America's abstention from the League would create the commercial conflict and international rivalry that might drag the United States into another war; or that if America stood apart from the rest of the world, it would have to support a standing army and run the risk of militarism; or he would point out that American industry would gain much from the nation's membership on the Reparations Commission, which would consist of members who wanted to get American markets.[76]

However, it was not Wilson's nature to apologize for his idealism; and he was, by his own admission, reluctant to argue on the basis of self-interest. More typical was his statement at Sioux Falls, South Dakota: "Sometimes people call me an idealist. Well, that is the way I know I am an American. America, my fellow citizens . . . is the only idealistic Nation in the world."[77]

When Wilson spoke this way, he spoke from the depths of his faith in the force of morality among the common people of America. At Tacoma, Washington, he explained why he would not argue for the treaty on the lowest level of material advantage: "I believe in my heart that there is hardly a man in America, if you get really back of his superficial thoughts, who is not man enough to be willing to make the sacrifice to underwrite civilization."[78] Wilson could say no less than this and remain consistent with the principles of his War Message and his subsequent enunciation of America's war aims. In his mind America had entered the war unselfishly, she had fought the war unselfishly, and it would be a betrayal of her mission to seek anything selfish from the peace.

Thus at Billings, Montana, he urged Americans not to forget what their gallant youth had died for. "For the redemption of America? America was not directly attacked. For the salvation of America? America was not immediately in danger. No; for the salvation of mankind. It is the noblest errand that troops ever went on."[79] At Coeur D'Alene, Idaho, he insisted that America had sent its soldiers across the seas "not because we thought this was an American fight in particular, but because we knew that the purpose of Germany was against liberty, and that where anybody was fighting liberty it was our duty to get into the contest."[80] And at Los Angeles, on September 20:

My friends, we did not go to France to fight for anything special for America. We did not send men 3000 miles away to defend our own territory. We did not take up the gage that Germany had thrown down to us because America was being specially injured. America was not being specially injured. We sent those men over there because free people everywhere were in danger and we had always been, and will always be, the champion of right and of liberty.[81]

14. THE IDEALISTIC REJECTION OF VERSAILLES

By insisting that acceptance of the Versailles Treaty was essential to fulfil America's whole purpose in entering the war, Wilson seemed to be asserting, in effect, that intervention could be justified only if America achieved the loftiest objectives in peace. It was precisely this belief that became the basis for postwar disillusionment with American intervention. America, it was said, had fought to save the world, but the world, lapsing into its wicked habits, had rejected American generosity and subjected its savior to a campaign of vilification and slander; therefore, America had been played for a sucker; American beneficence had been turned to the evil advantage of selfish and unenlightened forces. Never again! This sullen and peevish paranoia gained its original impetus from the more creditable moral indignation of idealists who had staked their reluctant support of the war upon the expectation of achieving the full measure of Wilson's Fourteen Points.

The Versailles Treaty, in the perspective of a second effort at settling a world conflict, seems now much less iniquitous than it seemed in the light of the disappointed hopes following World War I; and it is right that it should. Certainly, Woodrow Wilson's role in drafting that treaty was admirable and sometimes skilful, barring a few blunders and considering the almost insuperable obstacles beyond his control, or for that matter beyond the control of any of the much-maligned statesmen and politicians at the peace conference.[82] In any case, no peace is achieved with the signing of a document. The preservation of peace is a continuous process and an arduous one. Wilson understood this, and he was aware of the treaty's imperfections; but he regarded the League machinery as the instrument through which these imperfections might be eliminated.

Nevertheless, it was true that the treaty was a bundle of compromises, and in world politics and international reform American idealists were far less tolerant of compromise than in the sphere of domestic politics and national reform. Their intolerance of the half-loaf of Versailles was sharpened by their anticipation of Wilson's whole loaf; and Wilson heightened their dissatisfaction by insisting that the treaty was, in principle, the whole loaf, even though he himself had obviously been willing to accept many half-loaves during the hectic negotiations of the treaty.

Only jilted lovers could have reached the depths of bitterness and disappointment expressed in the *Nation's* editorial of May 17, 1919, "The Madness at Versailles." This editorial, which Villard later called the most prophetic editorial that ever appeared in the *Nation* or any other journal, took a position which eventually became commonplace but which was in advance of the liberal press at the time.[83] "In the whole history of diplomacy," it charged, "there is no treaty more properly to be regarded as an international crime than the amazing document which the German representatives are now asked to sign." And it delivered this extraordinary recrimination upon Wilson:

> The one-time idol of democracy stands today discredited and condemned. His rhetorical phrases, torn and faded tinsel of a thought which men now doubt if he himself ever believed, will never again fall with hypnotic charm upon the ears of eager multitudes. The camouflage of ethical precept and political philosophizing which for long blinded the eyes of all but the most observing has been stripped away, and the peoples of the world see revealed, not a friend faithful to the last, but an arrogant autocrat and a compromising politician.[84]

When the treaty came before the Senate, the *Nation* cared little whether the League Covenant had reservations or no reservations. It preferred complete rejection to the dishonorable compromise represented by the peace terms. When the treaty was defeated, the *Nation* rejoiced, even though it regretted the narrow, nationalistic arguments responsible for its defeat.

The *New Republic* also advocated rejection of the treaty, but it is significant that it did not succumb to the bitterness toward Wilson nor the deep disillusionment with the war that seized the *Nation*. After considerable hesitation, the editors found that they could not in good conscience or with regard for America's own interests support a treaty that would breed class struggles, hostile alliances, and new wars. Yet they did not take their disappointment over the peace settlement as a cause for repudiating their support of American intervention or for condemning war as an absolute evil. The *Nation* attributed the *New Republic's* failure to denounce American intervention to pride in authorship. In the *Nation's* view it was inconsistent to uphold American intervention and yet bemoan the fact that war did not achieve liberal objectives, for "whenever liberalism strikes hands with war it inevitably goes down. . . . For war and liberalism to lie down together anywhere, at any time, with any excuse, means only one thing—disaster to liberalism."[85] That the editors of the *New Republic* did not reach this disastrous conclusion should be attributed as much to the realistic considerations which led them to advocate intervention as to their pride of authorship.

The *New Republic* reached the peak of its circulation during the war but sank rapidly afterwards. The *Nation* did not approach a quarter of its liberal brother's peak until 1918, but by November, 1919, it had far surpassed the *New Republic's* largest circulation.[86] The comparative prosperity of these two journals was indicative of the trend of American idealism.

15. THE EGOISTIC REJECTION OF VERSAILLES

The *Nation's* view of the war came to dominate liberal thought in the next two decades. Yet it was not the repudiation of intervention or warfare that motivated the principal opposition to the Versailles Treaty in the Senate. It was, rather, a resurgence of national egoism, abhorrent to the liberal idealists who had hitched their wagon to Wilson's star.

It is significant that Wilson's controversy with his nationalist opponents in the Senate should have revolved about Article X of the League Covenant, in which the members of the League pledged themselvs to protect each other from external aggression. It seems likely that the Versailles Treaty would have passed had Wilson been willing to accept reservations to this provision, but Wilson took the position that Article X was the "heart" of the Covenant and insisted that the Senate would have to accept the heart without reservaion or reject the entire treaty. The nationalist opposition was quite willing to agree with the President's estimate of the importance of this article, for this enhanced the plausibility of the nationalists' thesis that the League would amount to a superstate ordering American soldiers about in foreign lands to suppress purely foreign quarrels.

Actually, Article X set forth no specific measures for enforcing its obligation to oppose aggression but only stated that "the Council shall advise upon the means by which this obligation shall be fulfilled." Wilson himself said, time and again, that the article was not legally binding but only permissive. Then why, if it carried no legal obligations, was it so vital to the peace of the world? Wilson's answer was that it expressed a supreme moral principle; and he contended that, since moral obligations took precedence over legal obligations, it was the most binding sort of pledge that honorable nations could make. Thus, once more, he declared his indomitable faith in the power of ideals. In his mind Article X represented one of those spiritual conceptions, transcending the material elements of life, which underlie all the truly great advances of civilization.

It was precisely this moralizing about matters of great practical consequence which so antagonized the hard-headed Lodge, for embedded deeply in his unyielding mind was the belief that the affairs of nations moved according to self-interest, not moral principles. Since his fight against the Taft-Knox arbitration treaties he had grown increasingly alarmed about attempts to substitute lofty ideals and felicitous expressions of altruism for the hard requirements of national power. Article X, like the Taft-Knox treaties, seemed to commit the United States to general international obligations without adequate guarantees that these obligations would redound to America's benefit; and, as in 1911, Lodge thought that one of the best ways to correct this deficiency was to assure the Senate the power to pass upon each practical application of the general obligation. This he attempted to accomplish with a reservation denying any obligation under Article X to undertake military or economic coercion unless, in a particular case, Congress so provided.[87] This reservation was no more than a statement of what would actually happen anyway in a given circumstance, but in Wilson's mind it constituted a nullification of Article X because it vitiated a great moral principle.

Of course, personal spite and partisan passion also played their part in the position of Lodge and the "strong reservationists," but this fact should not be allowed to conceal the operation of a long-standing antipathy based upon fundamentally divergent notions of international relations. And here one must differentiate between the position of a man like Borah, who opposed Article X out of a simple parochialism and xenophobia, and the position of Lodge, whose opposition stemmed from solid intellectual conviction, grounded in political Realism, and not merely from militant national egoism. It is interesting to note that Lodge, George Harvey, and a number of other Realists approved of the specific entanglement embodied in the French Security Treaty, which pledged the United States and Great Britain, pending the effective establishment of the League of Nations, to come to the aid of France in case of an attack by Germany.[88] Wilson himself had granted this treaty in return for France's promise to give up her claim to the German Rhineland, among other things. Yet he did not feel that it embodied any great ideal, and he would not promote it as a measure of practical self-interest. In fact, it was only after a great clamor from his senatorial foes that he submitted the pact to the Senate, nineteen days after submitting the Versailles Treaty, contrary to the explicit terms of the fourth article, which required that the two treaties be submitted simultaneously.

In the case of Article X and the French Security Treaty, as in other matters of war and peace, Wilson's inveterate habit of placing all measures on the highest possible moral ground, coupled with his tendency to treat idealism and self-interest as mutually exclusive ends, merely widened the breach between him and his nationalist opponents, whereas the practical difference between them, in terms of the concrete consequences of specific provisions, was comparatively slight.

16. Futility of the League Controversy

In the futility of the controversy over the Versailles Treaty there was something symbolic of the immaturity of America's conduct in international relations. After all, the underlying antipathies which divided Wilson and the reservationists seem unimportant when measured against the practical consequences of America's rejection of the League. It is difficult to see how either the United States or humanity profited from the failure to reach a compromise on a pragmatic basis. Whether the Versailles Treaty had reservations or not, America's position in world politics was made no more secure by her withdrawal from the potential center of collective security and her rejection of the best instrument of an Anglo-American accord; and, on the other hand, America served the material and spiritual welfare of mankind no better by withholding her force and her moral reputation from the world's best hope for the reconstruction of peace.

And was not the position of the irreconcilable nationalists and the irreconcilable idealists equally futile? Senator Borah would not sacrifice the nation's freedom of action for the sake of international philanthropy, but would he have sacrificed America's long-run self-interest for the sake of a meaningless national sovereignty? Oswald Garrison Villard rejected the Versailles Treaty out of impatience with imperfection, but how much perfection did the world attain by the Senate's refusal to accept the half-loaf?

In the complex environment of international relations neither self-interest nor universal ideals are attained by impulse alone. Both objects require a realistic assessment of the practical consequences of alternative policies; and that assessment cannot be made on the basis of an inflated sense of national pride, a xenophobic fear of contamination, a doctrinaire insistence on perfection, or an exaggerated notion of the efficacy of moral principles in composing international conflict.

No matter what decision America had made concerning its relations with the rest of the world, it could not have escaped the consequences of that decision. That was one of the penalties of becoming a world power. Therefore, it should have been the first principle of both self-interest and idealism to decide upon America's relation to the League only in the light of the actual political consequences of membership or nonmembership. With regard to these consequences Lodge and Wilson were far closer to agreement than they could ever have been on grounds of doctrine, personality, or party politics.

It must be said that President Wilson's leadership throughout the period of war and peacemaking, though it was eternally right in its moral objectives, could not have been deliberately calculated to defeat its own ends more surely; for by exhorting his countrymen to subordinate their self-interest to abstract moral standards and the welfare of the rest of the world, Wilson demanded an impossible and an unnecessary performance, encouraged the postwar repudiation of the very objects he sought, and obscured the one basis upon which a more realistic view of national conduct could have been created, a basis which might have recommended itself to nationalists and internationalists, egoists and idealists alike. That basis was enlightened self-interest.

Nevertheless, it would be a serious distortion of the evolution of America's international conduct to imply that President Wilson could have done much to create a popular awareness of the realistic basis for judging the League issue; for the whole climate of opinion resisted any such awareness, and Wilson did not have it within his power to work any fundamental change in the American attitude toward world politics, even though he might well have secured American membership in the League of Nations. If an appeal to altruism merely intensified the nation's shocked innocence and the tenacity of its desire for isolation, what self-interested motives could have inspired a realistic awareness of the political consequences of national action? Not the urge to assert American power aggressively; Americans had rejected this motive soon after their first crusade. Not the instinct of self-preservation, for the circumstances of international relations simply did not press upon the United States in such a way as to excite fear for survival.

World War I demonstrated once more the power of America's faith in its ideals. The abiding aspiration for world peace and international harmony, for democracy and the elimination of tyranny, for the promotion of humanitarianism and material welfare, for the abolition of oppression and poverty among all peoples; these ideals were no flimsy rationalization of war-born patriotism; they were rooted too solidly in American tradition. Moreover, the rest of the world generally recognized the strength and the sincerity of American idealism and for this reason welcomed American leadership as a breath of hope and enlightenment in the troubled society of nations. In spite of the bitterness toward Woodrow Wilson and America, which festered in the unwholesome environment of postwar Europe, the United States had enjoyed an unparalleled reputation for idealism among foreign peoples; America's desertion of its crusade in 1919–20 was a severe blow to them.

Could it be that ideals which carried such weight in the world as these were incompatible with America's vital interests? On the contrary, the course of events in the period between two world wars suggests that there was a vast area in which American ideals and American interests coincided; indeed, in which they were indispensable to one another. The popular realization of this fact and the will to act upon it realistically was born in the adversity of a second world war. The interim of precarious peace between the crusade for democracy and the fight for survival was a fitting prelude to this transformation.

PART III

SUMMARY

THE aftermath of the second crusade, like the aftermath of the first, gave eloquent testimony to the fleeting and insubstantial quality of American altruism, as an unstable union of universal idealism and nationalistic egoism, lacking the balance wheel of political realism and a consciousness of fundamental self-interest, disintegrated under its own centrifugal energy. Once more the forbidden fruits of war turned bitter in the mouths of a people whose innocent conscience would permit them to taste neither the sweetness of idealism nor the solid texture of self-interest after they had whetted their appetite upon the first eager bite. Again American idealism turned back upon itself, as though to purge itself of its evil association with war. But this time the poignancy of remorse and disenchantment was heightened by the paucity of the crusade's material and spiritual rewards in proportion to the magnificence of the idealistic hopes it had raised and the seeming enormity of its sacrifices, both tangible and intangible.

The ritual of flagellation by which Americans discredited their abortive crusade left idealism still more ineffectual and politically irresponsible and placed realism in lower repute than before. The resulting combination of wishful utopianism and impulsive idealism was particularly manifest in popular attempts to safeguard an uncertain peace by limiting armaments and outlawing war—essentially attempts to banish international discord through the moral pressure of public opinion alone and without regard for conflicts of national power and interests. The danger and futility of such attempts was illustrated by the nation's failure to come to grips with the unpleasant realities of the struggle for power in the Far East.

Postwar disillusionment was a poor preparation for dealing with conflicts of power in the interwar period; nevertheless, by depreciating altruism and the strict preservation of the nation's legal rights and honor as motives for active intervention in international affairs, it created a climate of opinion conducive to a new regard for the demands of national expediency. This climate of opinion, together with the pressure of revolutionary events across the seas in the late 1930's and early 1940's, led a growing body of Americans to find in the increasingly plausible assertion that their very security was endangered by the destruction of the world balance of power a frankly self-interested basis for undertaking a measure of participation in the arena of world politics more consonant with America's extensive material and moral commitments.

This new popular fear and consciousness of the impact of world politics upon the nation's self-preservation, born in the revolutionary circumstances preceding America's intervention in World War II and perpetuated under the adversity of a continuing power struggle, constitutes a major transformation in America's attitude toward its international environment.

CHAPTER XIII

THE AFTERMATH OF ARMAGEDDON

1. THE MOOD OF DISILLUSIONMENT

TO THE friends of international organization and the advocates of a fuller American participation in the affairs of the world the 1920's have always seemed like a period of dark reaction, like a sharp break in the steady progress of America's dealings with the outside world and a reversion to something peculiarly primitive and unenlightened. Especially in the glow of the San Francisco conference, the aftermath of Versailles seemed like a period barren of constructive vision and intelligent foresight. One remembers this period for the cynical manipulation of President Harding by the hard-bitten anti-League cabal, Harding's opportunistic equivocation on the League issue, followed by his announcement that the League was "as dead as slavery," and the government's failure for months to so much as open official mail from Geneva. One remembers the complacency, the partisanship, the superpatriotism, the self-righteous recrimination of foreign peoples, the shortsighted economic nationalism, and everywhere the dead hand of Normalcy.

Yet in less conspicuous respects the post-Wilsonian decade was really a continuation of prewar trends toward a broader international outlook. A strong body of internationalists kept their faith in the League and worked quietly to educate the American people to a more cosmopolitan view of foreign policy. The organized peace movement continued to expand, though its prescriptions for peace were, as usual, multifarious. By 1926 some twelve hundred organizations for the study of international questions had been established, whereas there had been scarcely one hundred and twenty in 1914.[1] And gradually the government itself had to recognize that the League existed and that much of the work it performed might affect the welfare of the United States. In August, 1921, the Department of State consented to write letters in reply to an accumulation of unopened League communications. By 1922 the government was sending "unofficial observers" to attend League conferences, where they might even go so far as to participate in the debates. Distinguished Americans, like Elihu Root and John Bassett Moore, devoted their time and intelligence to the World Court. Through participation in a series of disarmament conferences outside the League the nation demonstrated its continuing interest in developments beyond its own borders and tacitly acknowledged that the United States was not a fortress walled off from chaos.

309

Of course, if one assumes that America's participation in World War I signified a general abandonment of traditional policies, then the postwar decade constitutes a startling reaction to that sudden transformation; but, as a matter of fact, the war against Germany does not seem to have penetrated any deeper into fundamental attitudes toward international relations than the war against Spain. If one assumes that there was something basic and substantial about the surge of popular interest in foreign affairs during wartime, then the Harding-Coolidge era is a great reversal in the cosmopolitan trend of public opinion; but, actually, it seems more accurate to hold that indifference toward foreign affairs and absorption in domestic and private affairs is the normal state of public opinion and that only the pressure of some vital immediate interest or some compelling long-run interest can fix public attention upon the remote and esoteric game of diplomacy for even a short time. The interest excited by World War I was immediate victory, not permanent security.

Nevertheless, when all this is admitted, the fact remains that a great many ordinary Americans, as well as a number of sensitive and trained observers, got the impression at the time—and the impression has stuck—that the nation was passing through some sort of psychological transformation, variously described as a "slump in idealism" or "disillusionment." Scott Fitzgerald said, "We are tired of great causes," and President Harding turned this observation into a prescription when he declared, "America's present need is not heroics but healing; not nostrums but normalcy; not revolution but restoration."

George Creel, writing an impassioned defense of Wilson in 1920, found the slump in idealism so catastrophic as to be incomprehensible. In his opinion, it was not just a natural relaxation of taut nerves, a let-down from high emotionalism. The slump had become an obsession.

> The day of the Armistice America stood on the hilltops of glory, proud in her strength, invincible in her ideals, acclaimed and loved by a world free of an ancient fear at last: today we writhe in a pit of our own digging, despising ourselves and despised by the betrayed peoples of the earth. Instead of unity a vast disintegration, instead of enthusiasm an intolerable irritation, instead of fixed purpose a strange and bewildering indecision.[2]

One might expect Creel to take a particularly dismal view of the aftermath of Armageddon, but his observation suggests an important fact about disillusionment: It was more of a mood, a form of spiritual malaise, than a rational attitude. In some it took the form of disappointment over the frustration of high hopes, others a bitter disenchantment with the hopes themselves; but in the majority of Americans both of these sensations were overlaid with a dulling apathy and a pervasive sense of bewilderment and loss of purpose. Something had gone wrong. The war just didn't make much sense. One would prefer to forget the whole thing; and yet the patriotic frenzy, the Wilsonian ideals, the stark fact of death and personal loss, the parades, conscription, then the trenches, the ubiquitous war posters and war songs and war slogans, and the whole incongruous upheaval in the normal course of affairs—these things had happened and the memory of them could not be erased.

2. THE INITIAL POSTWAR REACTION

The initial American reaction to the war was not one of bitterness or of renunciation. There was no widespread disposition to doubt the wartime thesis that America had intervened to secure a more peaceful and democratic world through the defeat of autocracy. If during the Harding era there was any well-defined attitude toward the late crusade, it was one of indifference.

American literature showed signs of groping for a new interpretation, but even here there were few indications, at first, that the war had left a lasting impression. The novelist Robert Herrick observed at the end of 1921 that literature was at dead center, because ever since the peace conference America had been in a spiritual coma. "Literature like life no longer seems to have an unhesitating conviction about anything." He complained how little impact the war had left upon the imaginative life of mankind.

> It is as if the war had never been, as if by tacit agreement the war was to be considered a bore, a mistake not to be mentioned in public except casually. . . . It is a phenomenon worth pondering. Three years after the bloodiest conflict known to mankind . . . one may go into almost any theatre . . . one may buy almost any magazine or book on the stalls, and except for an occasional remote allusion to happenings in the years of interregnum it is impossible to guess that anything momentous has happened to the world, to life itself since 1914.[3]

As one reads through the newspapers and periodicals of the postwar decade, one is struck by the absence of comment upon the most highly advertised war in history. The issues of the day were not war and peace but prohibition, jazz, the Ku Klux Klan, the Big Red Scare, Sacco and Vanzetti, the length of skirts, Teapot Dome, the Scopes "monkey trial," and Al Capone.

Under the pall of widespread apathy toward international matters, the nation gave free rein to its egoistic impulses. The phenomenon of superpatriotism known as One Hundred Percent Americanism—partly a holdover from the war-born zeal for conformity and partly an attempt by conservatives to get back in the saddle—constituted one of the more unseemly movements that rushed into the vacuum left by the dissolution of the Wilsonian issues. One

Hundred Percent Americanism, as propagated by such organizations as the Daughters of the American Revolution, the American Security League, and the American Legion, was especially concerned with forcing American life into a reactionary social, economic, and political mold; but in its efforts to discredit liberal and cosmopolitan ideals and reassert the superiority of distinctly American behavior, purged of all foreign influence, in its bombastic identification of patriotism with contempt for foreign nations, this movement was an extreme manifestation of the introverted and exclusive national egoism that dominated America's postwar relations with its former associates in battle.

However, the One Hundred Percent Americans did not repudiate America's participation in the war; they only repudiated the objects for which Wilson said the war had been fought, as though, having won a decisive victory over Wilsonism, they were determined to erase the last taint of altruism and crusading ardor from the public consciousness in order to emphasize the magnitude of their victory. It was an ironic commentary upon the demoralization of the times that the proud, forward-looking nationalist strain, which had once heralded America's entrance into world politics as the inexorable manifestation of a boundless mission, should finally be betrayed to the vigilantes of a peevish parochialism by its obsessive enmity toward the movement which had so long denied it moral leadership.

Yet, as far as the public at large was concerned, it is fair to say that the initial nationalist attack upon Wilsonism aroused little popular enthusiasm. Americans didn't want to be bothered with any further moral effort, but neither were they given over to a sullen yearning to destroy all of Wilson's works. The general public was especially slow to repudiate its support of the recent war as an idealistic crusade. An incident in the spring of 1921 illustrates the point.

On May 19, 1921, George Harvey, the self-styled "passionate patriot," who had been awarded an ambassadorship at the Court of St. James for his services in the famous smoke-filled room, took the occasion of his first public utterance in England to arouse a furor in America. Speaking at a dinner tendered to him in the great dining hall of Hotel Victory, Ambassador Harvey announced, at the outset, that he had come to London as an "unalloyed American." He said that Americans didn't mind being called idealists. "But," he added, "we have come to realize quite sharply during the last few years that ideals only too often resolve into illusions, and illusions we have found to be both dangerous and profitless." And this brought him to the point. Until recently, he said, the impression was prevalent that the United States went into the war to save humanity.

Not a few remain convinced that we sent our young soldiers across the sea to save this Kingdom and France and Italy. That is not the fact. We sent them solely to save the United States of America, and most reluctantly and laggardly at that. We were not too proud to fight, whatever that may mean. We were afraid not to fight. That is the real truth of the matter.[4]

Although the purpose of Harvey's remark was to dispel any illusion that the United States might yet be beguiled into the League and, especially, to lay the moral basis for insisting upon Europe's payment of her debts to the United States, the American public took it as an affront to their idealism and patriotism—an interpretation which certainly would not have occurred to them in April, 1917. Gold-star mothers, veterans' organizations, and various patriotic groups were particularly incensed. There were even attempts to impeach Harvey or withhold his salary. Harvey's friendly biographer has declared, "I should doubt if ever a speech of any ambassador, or for all that of any public man was ever made the target for so much reviling and verbal mud-slinging."* The war might be ignored and considered a bore, but, apparently, no large segment of public opinion—in 1921 at least—had reached the conclusion that Europe had taken advantage of American idealism and played the nation for a sucker.

3. The Liberal Attack on Intervention

In the early postwar years those who set out to convince their countrymen that the war was a mistake were, for the most part, men who had held the same view while the war was being fought. Villard's *Nation* was amused at the popular indignation over Harvey's statement; it had long since concluded that American intervention sprang from selfish motives, and it pronounced itself delighted at this calm overriding of Wilsonian bunkum.[5] But, strictly speaking, Villard was not disillusioned, since, from his own point of view, he had never really shared the illusions that were alleged to have victimized more gullible liberals. The same could be said of agrarian radicals like La Follette and social intellectuals like the author Scott Nearing. The only difference from wartime was that now those who thought as they did could speak out more freely.

However, what gave the postwar era its distinct air of disenchantment was the fact that, gradually, the anti-interventionist views of these liberal and radical nonconformists took root in the minds of the liberals and intellectuals

---

* Willis F. Johnson, *George Harvey* (Boston, 1929), p. 299. For the public reaction to Harvey's remarks see the *Literary Digest*, LXIX (June 18, 1921), 10–12; *New York Times*, June 5, 1921. Some Republican dailies approved of the speech. It received full official approval before Harvey left the country; President Harding wrote a laudatory letter after Harvey spoke. Johnson, *op. cit.*, pp. 302–4. Two weeks later Secretary Hughes was wildly cheered when he injected into a speech a defense of the idealistic purpose of intervention. *New York Times*, June 16, 1921.

who had come to terms with the war. This latter group, in turn, proved to be America's most effective propagator of disillusionment. Its views upon American intervention and war in general dominated an entire postwar generation, becoming the common currency of all those who were determined never again to be led to slaughter by an excess of idealism.

The crux of the liberal attack upon American intervention was the assertion, in one form or another, that all the evils of the war were the result of misguided idealism. This view came to be accepted by the great majority of Americans, irrespective of their political and social outlook, but it burned most fiercely, at first, among those who were most acutely conscious of the adverse effect of war upon civil liberties and social and economic reform. Idealists who had joined Wilson's crusade as a sort of extension of domestic reform on a world-wide plane were understandably bitter about the wartime repression of nonconformists and the postwar resurgence of reactionary doctrines and practices. In their disillusionment and remorse some of these men decided that the ideal purposes of intervention had been corrupted by political opportunists and bigoted nationalists; others concluded that the existence of an ideal purpose in the first place was only an illusion cultivated by propagandists and international reactionaries. All agreed that the nation had been misled by virtue of its naïve idealism.

The views of Harold Stearns are representative of the early disillusionist school of young liberal intellectuals. Stearns was one of those who had opposed intervention from the first. Those liberals who had come to terms with the war accorded his views all the more respect because they now appeared in the light of a brilliant foresight vindicated by history.

Stearns voted for Wilson because he had kept America out of war; he entered the ranks of the disillusioned when Wilson became the spokesman for intervention. During the dark days of the war about the only remarks that struck Stearns as intelligent came from the rebellious pen of Randolph Bourne. He never had anything but contempt for those liberals who hoped for something good to come out of violence. To him the war was a reversal rather than an advancement of the Wilsonian ideals. Only by isolating himself from the war could he bear its repression and barbarity.[6]

After the war Stearns was more certain than ever that liberal idealism and force could never mix. He presented this idea in a book called *Liberalism in America: Its Origin, Its Temporary Collapse, Its Future* (1919).

The true liberal is skeptical of coercion no matter for what purpose it is used; he doubts the permanency of any results achieved by it. . . .

The root of liberalism, in a word, is hatred of compulsion, for liberalism has the respect for the individual and his conscience and reason which the employment of coercion necessarily destroys.[7]

The trouble with liberals during the war, he wrote, was that they forgot this principle and abdicated their critical faculty in order to retain some influence upon the course of events. Liberal idealists had been powerless to stem the tide of intolerance and bigoted chauvinism because of one central weakness: a pernicious habit of overlooking the actual consequences of wartime idealism in their frantic pursuit of utopia.

It can be seen that there was implicit in Stearns's interpretation of the failure of idealism a chastened conception of the practical limitations imposed by political realities. However, the chief conclusion that emerged from his critique was not that men of lofty purpose ought to be guided by a more realistic view of the relative efficacy of self-interest and idealism in international relations but, rather, that they should avoid all reliance upon force, on the theory that force inevitably corrupts true idealism.

4. The Revisionists

Stearns's attack upon the idealistic basis of intervention was duplicated on an historical level by a growing number of publicists, journalists, and scholars, whose works soon became the documentary text of liberal disillusionment. The attack was two-fold: on the one hand, the suggestion that intervention was a mistake, which the nation could have avoided and should have avoided; and, on the other hand, the assertion that the Allies had not fought for idealistic reasons and that Germany was no more responsible for the outbreak of war than other nations. Frequently, these two aspects of revisionist history were joined in the same work; but it was the latter aspect which received the most attention during the 1920's, partly because it was not until the 1930's that the vital source material concerning American intervention, the official documents and the private papers of key statesmen, were opened to the public.[8]

The earliest historical attack upon the Wilsonian interpretation of American intervention was John K. Turner's *Shall It Be Again?* (1922), which went through four printings and may have sold as many as eight thousand copies.[9] In this book Wilson was portrayed as the supreme villain, as a hypocritical political opportunist who lured the people into war on idealistic pretenses and then betrayed them by squelching democracy at home and engineering at Paris and Versailles an imperialistic alliance of the victors instead of a peace without victory. In Turner's opinion none of the reasons which Wilson gave for war were justifiable, least of all the promotion of peace and democracy, which was by its very nature incompatible with war. Consistent with his socialist and muckraking background, he attributed intervention to the machinations of Wall Street and the special economic interests.

In deflating the war's idealistic reputation, Turner drew upon the postwar writings of European liberals, such as Francis Neilson, Philip Gibbs, and

Georges Brandes, who had exposed the fallacies and exaggerations of Allied propaganda about German atrocities and German militarism.[10] These revelations tended to reduce all the belligerents to the same level of wickedness and thereby undermine the idealistic basis of the war allegedly fought for democracy against autocracy. Much the same purpose was served by the scholarly revisions of the thesis of German war guilt. These revisions were made possible by the fact that revolutionary governments in Russia, Germany, and Austria, anxious to discredit the regimes they replaced, published secret diplomatic documents containing some embarrassing evidence that all was not black and white in the prelude to Armageddon. The writings of European revisionists, especially the writings of British liberals, like Neilson, Gooch, and Morel, had a marked influence upon the course of American scholarship.[11]

In 1920 and 1921 Professor Sidney B. Fay, fully exploiting the German and Austrian revelations of 1919 for the first time, wrote a series of articles in the *American Historical Review* which aroused the world's scholars to reconsider the orthodox interpretation of war guilt, largely taken for granted since James Beck's tract of 1914. With the publication of the Russian documents and the failure of the British to make similar publications until 1926, and the French until 1928, there arose a group of writers in Europe and America who demanded a revision of the war-guilt clause, Article 231, in the Versailles Treaty; and a host of historians, few of whom displayed Professor Fay's fidelity to dispassionate scholarship, plunged into the task of proving, in one way or another, the ubiquity of self-interest and the dearth of idealism in the affairs of the great nations.

Frederick Bausman, a State of Washington jurist with a loathing for France, saw in the revelation of documents about Franco-Russian relations proof that the war had arisen from a conspiracy between France and the Court of St. Petersburg and that Germany had entered only reluctantly and in self-defense. Although the major portion of his book *Let France Explain* (1922) was occupied with a revision of the orthodox view of German war guilt, drawing heavily upon the French revisionists, it was evident that, in his mind, revision was no mere academic exercise but an instrument for condemning American intervention.

Bausman recalled the innocent good will and the high hopes with which America had entered the war, and he decried the idealistic illusions upon which they were based. Americans, he asserted, had entered the war in the spirit of pure altruism, but the nations they undertook to save had turned out to be more culpable than the nations they fought against.

It was not America we were saving; not one in a thousand believed we were ourselves in danger. It was England that we would aid, France that should not die.

Not since the Crusades has a soldiery gone forth with a purpose so high. . . . Not one American in a thousand, I say again, felt that we were in danger, not one in a thousand doubted that we could defend this continent against a victorious Germany.[12]

In *Facing Europe* (1926) Bausman elaborated upon Allied perfidy, this time not excluding Great Britain from his incriminations. By 1926 he was chafing under a new cause of disillusionment: Europe's resentment toward the United States over the war debt issue. America, which had given unstintingly and unselfishly of her men and money, was, apparently, to be rewarded by the contempt and ingratitude of her beneficiaries. Consequently, *Facing Europe* was aimed directly at explaining the cause of America's misguided generosity. Bausman placed the chief blame upon Allied propaganda, Allied deception, and Wilson's gullibility.

In the same year Professor Harry Elmer Barnes, a colleague of Fay's at Smith College, presented *The Genesis of the World War: An Introduction to the Problem of War Guilt* (1926), the first comprehensive book-length statement of the revisionist view of war guilt. The book was scholarly in that it took account of the secret documents and monographic material published since 1917, but throughout there ran a note of impassioned disillusionment, which deprived it of the calm balance of Fay's work.

In the introduction Barnes got his *mea culpa* off his chest. He confessed that he had been thoroughly pro-Ally and had accepted completely the conventional Entente mythology until he was awakened by Fay's articles. The rest of the book was written in the spirit of making amends for this error and guarding against its recurrence.

If we can but understand how totally and terribly we were "taken in" between 1914 and 1918 by the salesmen of this most holy and idealistic world conflict, we shall be the better prepared to be on our guard against the seductive lies and deceptions which will be put forward by similar groups when urging the necessity of another world catastrophe in order to . . . "crush militarism," "make the world safe for democracy," "put an end to all further wars," etc.[13]

Barnes wiped the stain of guilt off Germany and smeared it on France and Russia, who were depicted as co-conspirators in a gigantic plot to recover Alsace-Lorraine and the control of the Straits, respectively.

In a chapter devoted directly to the question of how the United States got "taken in" Barnes placed the burden of the blame on the pressure of pro-Ally bias, Entente propaganda, and American financial interests. These influences, he contended, had prevented the United States from enforcing its neutral rights equally against England and Germany and had, thereby, placed Germany in a position in which retaliation by unrestricted submarine warfare became necessary for survival.

In 1929, C. Hartley Grattan, one of Barnes's students, wrote a scholarly and generally sober expansion of this theme, with special emphasis upon economic ties and Allied propaganda. However, in spite of its title, nowhere in *Why We Fought* did Grattan produce an explanation for American intervention. Like most revisionist historians his real interest seemed to be what America did not fight for and why she should not have fought at all. Ten years later Grattan explained that he had only intended to show that America's entrance into the war was not a simple black-and-white matter, but by that time he was painting intervention in jet black strokes and enjoying a far greater audience than when he wrote his less polemical account of 1929.[14]

Historical revisionism, like the liberal attack upon American intervention, was an inseparable part of postwar disillusionment. Its proponents were, generally, men of tender conscience, pacific temperament, and liberal outlook, men who had supported the war—if they had been able to reconcile themselves to it at all—with the expectation that it would result in the fulfilment of Wilson's visions. To them the failure of the millennium meant the futility of the war.

One gets the distinct impression that revisionists were as much concerned with their own guilt in bringing about this failure as with the guilt of the belligerents, for there runs throughout their writings an unmistakable thread of confession and self-deprecation, concealed only by the eager acceptance of some scapegoat, be it Woodrow Wilson, propaganda, European statesmen, or the war profiteers. The pages of the *New Republic* and the *Nation* during the twenties stand out as an historical Wailing Wall where the penitent revisionists lamented their sins and sought forgiveness.

In retrospect it would seem that the penitent, however disillusioned they may have been by the consequences of the war, were not really repudiating their idealism or even injecting a note of realism. Actually, they were seeking desperately to bolster their moral sentiments by purging them of all impurities. Revisionists did not revise their basic utopian premises about international society. On the contrary, they cast realism into lower repute than ever and placed even greater reliance upon the efficacy of reason and morality in resolving international conflict. The very nature of their eager search for the cause of the recent war and the person or persons responsible for it bespoke an assumption that war might yet be exorcized if only a sufficient weight of intellect could be brought to bear upon the problem.

5. THE DEBUNKERS

The depreciation of idealism as a motive for war was only one manifestation of a national mood of disparaging and debunking ideals in general. This mood was zealously promoted by frustrated liberals and intellectuals, who would ordinarily have been in the vanguard of reform.

The most conspicuous aspect of the debunking mood was the literary revolt of young intellectuals from orthodox manners, tastes, and pretensions. Some of this literature was inspired directly by a revulsion from war—Dos Passos' *Three Soldiers* and Hemingway's *A Farewell to Arms,* for example; but most of it was dedicated to a more oblique assault upon American wartime idealism, an assault upon the sham, the hypocrisy, and the vulgarity underlying the accepted standards of virtue and respectability in all aspects of American society. Sinclair Lewis, F. Scott Fitzgerald, E. E. Cummings, Edmund Wilson, Matthew Josephson, and the other members of that iconoclastic clan which Gertrude Stein called the "lost generation" were by no means a homogeneous group, but they had one thing in common: a passionate desire to expose the spiritual poverty and the hollow pretense behind conventional professions of idealism.

It is important to realize that their urge to disparage idealism arose not from cynicism or even pessimism but from their own inveterate moral sentiments. Their writings might take the form of cold-blooded objectivity, realism, or nihilism, they might dwell interminably upon the ugliness and depravity of human nature; but always there was a strong undercurrent of disappointed idealism. The lost generation, like the revisionists and the other apostles of disillusionment, wanted to restore, not to destroy, America's blunted enthusiasm for the liberal and humanitarian values. All that it intended to destroy were the sentimental illusions and the corruptions of self-interest which had led idealism astray. The literary devastators of the 1920's were squarely in line with the social protestants and muckrakers of the Progressive Era, except that they were more tired and less constructive. Their apparent cynicism was really inverted idealism, a crusade against crusading.

It is significant that the debunkers found their most enthusiastic audience among the traditional generators of idealism, the youth of the nation and particularly the youth in college. Throughout the campuses of America student idealists struck the new pose of nihilism and toughness. A copy of Henry L. Mencken's deliciously irreverent *Mercury* magazine was their badge of sophistication. Mencken enjoyed an immense prestige among the disillusioned youth by virtue of his flippancy toward all the traditional forms of idealism, which their self-discredited elders had embraced. He ridiculed the refined cosmopolitanism of liberals and the flag-waving patriotism of the philistines with the same impartial sarcasm. All idealism was "bilge" to him, and that included do-gooders, progressives, and reformers, as well as One Hundred Percent Americans and boosters.

Yet it takes an idealist to become disillusioned, and it was the disillusioned who idolized Mencken. Certainly, much of the appeal of Mencken's icono-clasm can be attributed to the fact that it afforded weary and guilty idealists a means of registering social protest, while, at the same time, they avoided the effort and embarrassment of advocating constructive measures. Through the pages of the *Mercury* one might burn with moral indignation, even though one felt betrayed by ideals. By this sort of literary flagellation the disillusioned regained their sense of self-righteousness.

There was something profoundly soul-satisfying in all forms of debunking. The economic interpretation of war allowed the postwar generation to pin its own sense of guilt upon others and, at the same time, provided it with a devastating instrument for puncturing its own inflated ideals (or ideologies, as they were now called) as a kind of ritual of penance to relieve the pressure of moral responsibility. Modern psychology served the same purpose. By an imaginative use, or misuse, of its "scientific" jargon and techniques one might discover base motives in the noblest actions and thoughts, even as the literary iconoclasts found a certain nobility in the most animalistic behavior. The emerging study of semantics, later popularized by Stuart Chase in *The Tyranny of Words* (1938), like the dissection of wartime propaganda, dis-closed the relativity and deceptiveness of absolute beliefs and strong convic-tions and seemed to suggest that subtle conditioning or self-interested manip-ulation, rather than the clear insight of honest conscience, was responsible for moral enthusiasm.

Yet even among the most devout debunkers there was a strong element of idealism and moral optimism underlying the surface hardness and in-souciance. Few assumed that the selfishness and meanness which the his-torians, intelligentsia, psychologists, and semanticists uncovered were an im-mutable feature of human nature. The unexpressed assumption was, rather, that the very recognition of the hidden evil in man would prove to be his salvation, since human nature was basically reasonable and moral. This was precisely the utopian idealism that had underlaid anti-imperialism, the peace movement, and Wilson's crusade, although the sophisticates of the aftermath of Versailles would not dare to admit it.

Perhaps because the debunking mood struck hardest at articulate young in-tellectuals and middle-class liberals, who were, traditionally, the backbone of idealism, it exerted an influence disproportionate to the numbers of its active exponents, but even this core of disillusionment had begun to disintegrate by the end of the 1920's. As the novelty of disparagement wore off, insurrection gave way to resignation, and resignation gradually gave way to the con-structive reassertion of liberal and humanitarian principles. The *Mercury* reached its peak circulation in 1927 and then steadily declined. At the same time, college students grew bored with their counter-crusade and, around 1930, began discarding the pose of indifference and acquiring a social and political conscience.[15] In the Autumn of 1928 Henry S. Harrison noted in the *Yale Review* that most of the literary devastators had already lost interest in the movement.[16] Harold Stearns, who had edited a famous symposium on the degeneracy of the postwar United States, called *Civilization in the United States* (1922), and then dramatically left the country to become the idol of Montparnasse, grew tame, saddened, and homesick and finally returned to his native land to try to reconstruct his ideals and build a new life.[17] Malcolm Cowley has described the pathetic frustration, hysteria, and bewilderment of such self-exiled intellectuals in the late twenties.[18] In the thirties the liberal intelligentsia who had retained their self-respect took up the offensive for idealism once more.[19] Slowly, cautiously, shell-shocked reformers ventured out of the spiritual ruins of disillusionment to meet the challenge of a host of depression-born issues. Gradually, embittered missionaries regained their confidence and compassion as the lure of new endeavors softened their disappointment over old ones.

The debunking movement was intellectually superficial and emotionally immature. It deprecated the outward manifestations of selfishness but failed to illuminate the inward compulsions. In a childish exhibition of wounded pride and guilt it feigned cynicism in order to conceal sentimental idealism. The extreme manifestations of disillusionment which it fostered were soon corroded by their own acid. And yet the movement left an unmistakable scar upon the American attitude toward international relations. Americans never completely regained their confidence in the old symbols of internationalism and altruistic diplomacy. They never quite recovered their assurance that America's mission should be one of magnanimous service to the rest of the world.

6. POSTWAR IDEALISM

In 1932 Walter Lippmann took note of a profound spiritual bewilderment and demoralization among Americans, in which the individual trusted nobody and nothing, not even himself, and believed nothing but the worst of everybody and everything.[20] This was certainly hyperbole if he meant his observation to apply to the entire nation. At no time during the interwar period was America without an influential body of forthright and consistent advocates of a vigorous and constructive American participation in projects for world peace. On the other hand, by the tone and content of these advocates' appeals one can discern their alienation from the rest of the nation.

Manley O. Hudson, a professor of international law at Harvard and a member of the legal section of the League Secretariat, went directly to the pages of the *Nation* to defend the League—not as a panacea, but as the only practical hope for achieving the ideals for which the *Nation* stood. He delivered this biting judgment upon the League's liberal opponents:

> They have allowed themselves to be jockeyed by the disillusionists of the war, the disappointments of the peace, and the discouragements of American politics into strange fellowship with isolationists, superpatriots, and ultraconservatives. Living still in the orgy of their peace pessimisms, they are emotionally disposed to find the League a symbol of power abused, of force rampant, and of greed triumphant. Without a knowledge of the three years' record and of what the League has actually become, they are still dominated by the a priori fears of what it might be and by the bogies of their 1919 legalisms.[21]

Elihu Root, who had taken a leading role in framing the famous Statement of the Thirty-one declaring that a vote for Harding would be a vote for the League, somewhat plaintively insisted in the magazine *Foreign Affairs,* in April, 1925, that

> our people really do desire to contribute towards the preservation of peace and the progress of civilization throughout the world. We do not wish to be selfish and cynical and indifferent about the welfare of the rest of the world. . . . We really have ideals about human progress and we wish to stand for them.[22]

In December, 1929, when Root acknowledged an award by the Woodrow Wilson Foundation for his fatherhood of the World Court, he was a good deal sharper in his comments. He denounced America's petty and vindictive isolation from the League and defended the League and the Court for "rendering the best service in the cause of peace known to the history of civilization; incomparably the best."

> We have allowed insensate prejudice, camouflaged by futile phrases to appear, but falsely to appear to represent the true heart of the American people, with all its idealism, with its breadth of human sympathy, with its strong desire that our country should do its share for peace and happiness and noble life in the world.

Root could only pray that Americans might be delivered from these "evils visited upon us by a hateful and contentious spirit."[23]

Yet if the American people appeared to have deserted their mission, the trouble was not, as Root implied, in their hearts. Idealism remained a strong force in the American attitude toward international relations. The nation's very repudiation of its crusade was largely idealistic in its origin. Moreover, idealists did not long remain content asserting themselves purely negatively. Once more they dedicated themselves to the peace movement, this time with the added incentive of preventing a recurrence of world war. The postwar peace movement was, in fact, stronger and more determined than the prewar peace movement. If it did not lead to the measure of participation in international relations which Hudson and Root desired, it was not because Americans were lacking in human sympathy or in the desire to spread peace and happiness throughout the world but because, more than ever before, the ideal of peace was divorced from the political realism required to make peace effective. More than ever, peace was seen as merely the avoidance of war rather than as a continuous process of political accommodation.

As soon as Harding was elected the *Nation* started promoting its own peace program to take the place of Wilson's. In the issue of November 17, 1920, it urged Harding to call a third Hague conference, to be attended by all nations, large and small, victors and vanquished, in order to consider the codification of international law, the outlawry of war, the creation of a statute permitting the Hague Court to pass on all international disputes, universal and immediate disarmament, the remaking of the Versailles Treaty, and the nationalization in each country of every munitions and armaments industry.[24] Throughout the 1920's the *Nation's* prescription for peace consisted in the outlawry of war, complete disarmament, a world court with universal compulsory jurisdiction, and a parliament of all nations, which would achieve an equitable distribution of the world's supply of raw materials and abolish the grievances of exploited races and classes everywhere.

As for the League, as far as the *Nation* was concerned, it was still cursed with the original sin of the Versailles Treaty. For a year the *Nation* said the League was dead and rejoiced at each bit of evidence that the pronouncement was true. When the League's membership increased from forty-two nations to fifty-two, the editors grudgingly admitted that its humanitarian activities merited American support and conceded that its political and legal activities might be all right for Europe, but this is as close as they came to a reconciliation. Evidently, the *Nation* was willing to hold out indefinitely for the whole loaf as a matter of principle.

In its emphasis upon the outlawry of war and complete disarmament the *Nation* was quite in harmony with the general premise of the postwar peace movement that force was never a legitimate instrument of national policy and that war and armaments, which were presumed to lead to war, were evil in themselves. The same premise was reflected in the work of the various peace organizations and in the research of individual students of international relations. Whether or not they favored American membership in the League, they tended to equate peace with international government and war with power politics, as though power, being evil, and peace, being good, the two were mutually exclusive.[25]

Associated with this view of peace and power was the belief that, since peace is largely a matter of moral conduct, the best way to achieve it is to get men into the proper frame of mind. The belief that peace is a state of mind, a belief which pervaded the prewar peace movement, seemed to have been confirmed by the postwar revelations exaggerating the influence of wartime propaganda. Liberals were now particularly wary about any manifestation of the "war spirit," as though a pacific spirit were all that was needed to avoid the toils of international conflict. The *Nation* was so sensitive about this bogy that it seriously advocated eradicating the very thought of war. "Words for peace are very well. But what we must have in addition is a burning, an unconquerable, an undeviating hatred of war, any war for whatever reason. When war becomes unthinkable, then, and then only, is peace assured."[26]

Something of the same theory of peace by incantation was behind the concentration of peace organizations upon creating what Nicholas Murray Butler called the "international mind" through the promotion of international intercourse and the gathering together of people of different nationalities upon the basis of common interests—a noble purpose but hardly, in itself, a solution for conflicts of power and interest.

The *Nation's* idea about making war unthinkable seemed to underlie the postwar publicity campaign to make peace as glamorous and heroic as preparedness and war. Using all the devices of slick advertising, peace advocates held antiwar demonstrations on Armistice Day, organized a coast-to-coast "Peace Caravan," distributed colored peace lithographs for billboards, obtained a commercial sponsor for a weekly program, campaigned against toy soldiers, and established an organization called "World Heroes," dedicated to publicizing and rewarding acts of outstanding courage performed in the routine course of everyday life.[27]

The tendency to renounce war as an absolute evil was, as one might expect, especially pronounced among those who had been most fervently idealistic during the war and most guilty about their fervor afterwards. This was particularly true of Protestant Church leaders. Typical was the public atonement made by the Chicago Federation of Churches, representing six hundred and fifty churches and fifteen denominations: "In humble penitence for past mistakes and sincere repentance for our want of faith and devotion to the ideals of the Kingdom of God . . . we declare ourselves as unalterably opposed to war."[28] Samuel McCrea Cavert, the general secretary of the Federal Council of Churches, expressed a similar view.

I am disillusioned as to the causes of war. I now see that the war arose chiefly as the result of deep-rooted economic competition to control the raw materials and markets of the world. . . . I have come slowly but clearly to the conclusion that the Church, in its official capacity, should never again give its sanction to war or attempt to make war appear as holy.[29]

With all the uniformity of deviationists at a communist trial Raymond Fosdick, Rabbi Stephen S. Wise, Frederick Lynch, and other prominent churchmen, one after the other, recanted their sin of sanctioning war. In the spring of 1931 answers to questionnaires sent out to fifty-three thousand clergymen of more than a dozen denominations indicated that 62 per cent believed that the churches of the United States should go on record as refusing to sanction or support any future war. Fifty-four per cent were prepared to state that they would personally take this position.[30]

The average American citizen did not find it necessary to go through contortions of self-accusation in order to restore the purity of his conscience, but he tended to agree with the churchmen that war could be abolished if enough people would realize how evil it was and swear never to become involved in it again. In the common American view World War I became transmuted into war in general. Since World War I had proved to be a futile delusion, it seemed that all wars must prove equally futile and deluding. Since America had been dragged into World War I because of idealistic illusions and a misguided sense of national honor, it seemed to follow that the nation could avoid future wars by guarding against idealistic distinctions and a resurgence of the war spirit.

Nicholas Murray Butler, long a leader in the peace movement, was simply voicing what passed for common sense when, in 1920, he stated his belief that a peace society, pure and simple, had become an anachronism, since the whole world, save for its lunatic fringe, was committed to the cause of peace.[31] One can judge the extent to which this sort of antiwar sentiment swept the nation by the fact that Butler, who had outraged liberals in 1917 by dismissing faculty members at Columbia for sending a protest to Congress over America's participation in the war, took the occasion of Armistice Day, November 11, 1931, to condemn war without qualification and demand that governments abolish armies and navies and consign the implements of war to museums.[32]

7. POSTWAR REALISM

In this climate of opinion political realism was thoroughly stifled. Those who called themselves realists were only disillusioned. In 1928 Norman Thomas observed, "We are learning to substitute realism for romanticism in facing the problem of war and peace." But he thought that one of the most hopeful signs of this was Secretary of State Kellogg's proposal for multilateral treaties outlawing war. He found realism, above all, in the new understanding of war itself. War had been stripped of its glory and revealed for all its dull, horrible, primitive reality. Unlike twenty years ago students now knew all about militarism, imperialism, and propaganda. They knew that "wars are not fought in a pure passion for some clearly seen ideal but rather in a wild emotional orgy in which the main ingredients are fear and hate." Mr. Thomas saw further evidence of realism in the new recognition of the utter inability of war to achieve the ideals it nominally seeks, and he also pointed to a new awareness of the true causes of the late war and American intervention—that is, the causes which the revisionists had discovered.[33]

Norman Thomas's disillusionment may have been a step toward realism, but his inability in the thirties to recognize the greatest threat to American security in a century and a half suggests that his conception of reality left out some important elements.

In the aftermath of World War I the realistic appraisal of the imperatives of power in American foreign relations was more rare and more unpopular than ever before. Very few who had anything good to say about power were saying it publicly. And those who did, clearly revealed their isolation from the main stream of public opinion.

H. H. Powers continued to urge the masterful peoples—that is, the Anglo-Saxons—to assert their mastery lest they lose out in the struggle for international power. The war impressed him anew with America's responsibility for taking up the burden of world leadership as world power shifted from Great Britain to the United States.[34] But even before the peace settlement he was decrying the quixotic and self-righteous attitude which made Americans unsympathetic toward the material interests of Great Britain; he attributed this defect to the fact that "so far as the popular consciousness is concerned, we entered the war for other than the compelling reasons of national safety which actuated our Allies."[35]

Paul Scott Mowrer, a young war correspondent in the Balkans and France, who had embraced the Wilsonian ideals during the war, reached the conclusion after the war that a favorable world balance of power, particularly a strong British Navy and French Army, was essential to a stable peace.[36] He reread Washington's Farewell Address and took to heart its warning not to trust any nation to act consistently from any motive but its own interest, but he admitted his inability to persuade his friends to think in terms of national interests. "We had not been trained that way. We preferred to think with our feelings. To some staunch Wilsonians, it was almost indecent to mention interests—selfish, grasping. It lowered us, they sensed, from our high moral plane to the level of the other nations."[37]

In 1921, after a tour of the Balkans, he wrote *Balkanized Europe: A Study in Political Analysis and Reconstruction,* in which he applied the principle of the balance of power to the Balkans and argued that the United States was involved in the international politics of that region whether it wanted to be or not. The title caught on, and "balkanized" became a common expression. The reviews were unanimously favorable. But the book sold only five thousand copies.[38]

Mowrer set to work harder than ever to find some universal principle that governed or should govern the conduct of nations. He could discover none save the balance of power. This principle seemed to break through all the confusing sentiments and ideals of international relations and clarify the obscurities of statecraft. Mowrer sought to embody his thoughts on the balance of power in a treatise, but he called the project off when Harper & Brothers' publishers concluded that the subject was too unpopular.[39] In 1924 E. P. Dutton and Company published *Our Foreign Affairs: A Study in National Interest and the New Diplomacy,* but the sales were small.

In *Our Foreign Affairs* Mowrer pleaded for a more realistic view of international relations. No nation, he asserted, was to be trusted beyond its own interests. Sentiment was fickle, but "nations which act upon interest are sure of themselves." Echoing the thoughts of Richard Olney, he contended, "What is dangerous to the world is not that nations should act reasonably, in accordance with their interests, but that they should act unreasonably, at the dictation of the reforming instinct, or of some megalomaniac dream."[40]

In Mowrer's view internationalism would succeed to the extent that nations found interests in common; for mutual self-interest, not ideology, was the surest foundation of international good will. As for the problem of aggression, the balance of power—or the natural tendency of states to combine against potential aggressors—remained the "only known means of exercising preventive restraint upon the possible aggressor." This would be true, he said, whether or not there were a League of Nations.

Mowrer argued that World War I had profoundly transformed the international position of the United States, so that the nation's interest required an active participation in world politics and world organization. However, like H. H. Powers, Mowrer was distressed by the feeling of moral superiority, on the one hand, and the fear of entangling alliances, on the other, which prevented the American people from seeing their true interest in international co-operation. He charged that Americans, "except for a few individual statesmen, and unlike most other peoples," had never "learned to think rationally and objectively, in terms of our situation and our interests."[41] He believed that a conflict between sentiment and interest had caused a paralysis of American policy. The only solution that he could suggest was to bring the nation's sentiments into line with its long-run interests through the process of public education and the public-spirited efforts of an educated elite, devoted to the objective study and debate of international politics and economics.

Whether education, apart from international circumstances, would be sufficient in itself Mowrer did not say. Significantly, he believed that the United States had never been more secure.[42] If the United States became insecure, would education enable Americans to recognize the circumstance and deal with it? In that case, Mowrer evidently thought that instinct would suffice. In a passage anticipating Walter Lippmann's thesis, he contended that America had entered the late war out of an instinctive response to the tendency of nations to combine against potential aggression. "So sure and subtle is the operation that it determines the conduct even of peoples who are unconscious of it, and who think they are immune from its magnetism—for example, the American people."[43]

After 1920 and for the following decade Walter Lippmann himself was silent about the instinct of self-preservation. However, in 1919 he was still defending his wartime position concerning America's dependence upon the balance of power in Europe and the Atlantic. Although Lippmann had left the peace conference, where he had been attached to House's staff, in dismay over Allied intervention in the newly-created Soviet Union, he defended the League in an essay, which the *New Republic* printed as a supplement in March, 1919, as "a constitution of common action adopted by the stable powers in a period of unpredictable change," as a sort of communications center for the new world order, whose nucleus was a British and American entente or "pool of power." As historical sanction for his plea for a recognition of America's deep political interest in the maintenance of British sea power and the balance of power on the Continent, Lippmann asserted that there had been no difference in principle between Theodore Roosevelt and Woodrow Wilson on the question of intervention; both men, he said, had made the decision only when German aggression reached the world's ocean highways and struck at the basis of Anglo-American naval mastery.[44]

In December, 1919, Lippmann again contended that a working partnership with British sea power was the indispensable basis of a liberal peace, this time taking as his point of departure an unfavorable review of Harold Stearns's *Liberalism in America*.[45] He observed that in 232 pages of criticism of the attitude of prowar liberals Stearns never once examined the threat of Germany's submarine campaign to American security, and he asserted that this threat alone was sufficient justification for American intervention.* He went on to deny the thesis of Bourne and Stearns that the failure of the peace

---

* Stearns had cited Lippmann's anonymous editorial "The Defense of the Atlantic World" as an example of the specious justifications whereby liberals reconciled themselves to the war, but he had not presented any reasons for this opinion. Harold E. Stearns, *Liberalism in America* (New York, 1919), pp. 113-4.

was inevitable, and he charged that one reason for the failure was a defect in liberalism which Stearns exemplified: the naïve avoidance of the practical task of organization and administration in the desire to remain above such sordidly practical matters.

After this thrust Lippmann wasted no more words defending his forgotten thesis or countering liberal revisionism. As a member of the *New York World* staff in 1921 and as head of the editorial page of that paper from 1923 to 1931, he did not expand upon his views concerning an Anglo-American nucleus of power. Like most editorial writers, he became more and more absorbed in domestic politics and national affairs; and the recent war seemed to slip out of focus.

In his *Public Opinion* (1922) he was by no means sure why Americans had fought the war. He considered Ambassador Harvey's statement in May, 1921, quite presumptuous. Now all that he could be sure of was that "a war was fought and won by a multitude of efforts, stimulated, no one knows in what proportion, by the motives of Wilson and the motives of Harvey and all kinds of hybrids of the two."*

Not until aggression reared its head once more did Lippmann return to his thesis of America's strategic interest in the Atlantic Community. Not until another world war loomed on the horizon did he come to see America's participation in World War I as a popular response to the instinct of self-preservation, which he had despaired of arousing at the time.

A comment which Lippmann directed at Sir Halford J. MacKinder's seminal study in geopolitics *Democratic Ideals and Reality* (1919) might well apply to his own case:

The facts being inconceivably rich are capable of almost any kind of grouping and selection. So grouped and so selected they will support almost any cause, and their support is valuable for they seem to put it behind the momentum of all human experience. History is rewritten by each nation for every important occasion.[46]

8. THE IMPACT OF THE DISILLUSIONISTS

There were many sources of popular disillusionment: shock, disappointment, guilt, and injured pride. Disillusionment expressed itself in many different ways: self-deprecation, withdrawal, nationalism, and the search for scapegoats. But all forms sprang from the belief that the common people had entered and fought the war primarily for idealistic reasons, and all forms led to a determination that this should never happen again.

It is impossible to determine with any assurance exactly what influence the

* Lippmann, *Public Opinion* (New York, 1922), p. 194. In 1926 Lippman wrote, "In the period of neutrality Wilson saw more clearly than any living man what the country really wanted." Lippmann, "The Intimate Papers of Colonel House," *Foreign Affairs*, IV (April, 1926), 386.

propagators of disillusionment exerted in creating this popular outlook. The causes of American intervention did not become a burning issue until the late 1930's, when another world war threatened to erupt. However, it seems fair to say that the general impression, which became the commonplace conviction of the 1930's, that the war had not been worthwhile, that American altruism had somehow been betrayed, took root in the public mind during the 1920's. This impression was undoubtedly promoted by the disillusionists. But, on the other hand, it seems likely that it would have arisen anyway under the impact of circumstances that affected all Americans, intellectuals and nonintellectuals alike.

An altruistic enterprise which brought neither material nor spiritual reward and even resulted in substantial sacrifices, both tangible and intangible, was bound to seem futile, if not pernicious, in the long run. No nation would have regarded it differently.

Peace not only failed to bring about a new era of international reform, it produced a harvest of social and political unrest, an armaments race, and a general revival of international tension. Since Americans had come to look upon the war almost exclusively as a crusade to end all wars and to create a peaceful and democratic world order, it is no wonder that they reached the conclusion that the war had "solved nothing."

Actually, in comparison with other nations America had sacrificed relatively little in the war. American expenditures and European buying produced unprecedented industrial expansion and prosperity. America's death toll was slight. By contrast, the European powers suffered staggering losses in men, shipping, buildings, and economic dislocation. But it was chiefly in relation to the reasons for which Americans thought they had fought that their sacrifices seemed exorbitant. A war for self-defense would have justified such sacrifices many times over; but a war for the Wilsonian ideals, although a compelling purpose when victory was the immediate object, seemed like a far less compelling reason for sacrificing the boys in Europe when the battle was over.

The human sacrifices of war were later magnified by a body of literature which stressed the horror and the stultification of battle. The dull, grim trench warfare of World War I held little of the romance and heroism of the Spanish-American War. The dashing captains of Richard Harding Davis were gone forever. A translation of Erich Remarque's *All Quiet on the Western Front,* which portrayed with trance-like detachment the loathsome details of life in the trenches, became the most popular war book in America. Books like Barbusse's *Under Fire,* Dos Passos's *Three Soldiers,* Hemingway's *A Farewell to Arms,* and Lawrence Stalling's gory pictorial record, *What Price Glory,* reduced war to its lowest level of brutality and suffering and, by implication, affirmed what many soldiers had concluded from their personal experience, that war is a great leveler, the absolute evil, beside which all idealistic distinctions pale into insignificance. In the avidity with which traditionally happy and optimistic Americans devoured morbid literature there is a suggestion of the masochistic urge that sometimes seizes guilty consciences. A nation which was deeply shocked by the *Lusitania* incident could not easily absolve itself from responsibility for joining with such patriotic elation in the sickening tragedy which Remarque depicted.

The American people found cause enough for disillusionment in the material and human sacrifices of the war and in the failure of the peace, but the peculiarly bitter resentment with which they came to view their crusade arose, principally, from the ingratitude of its supposed beneficiaries. If the material and spiritual sacrifices of America's altruistic adventure brought no tangible compensation, it seemed as though disappointed and bewildered crusaders might at least be granted the reward of gratitude.

There was no single greater cause of international resentment and bitterness than the debt controversy. The devastated European nations could not understand the kind of magnanimity which moved a smug and rich America to demand its pound of flesh so soon after pledging itself to the service of others, especially when the chief means of repayment was blocked by a rising American tariff wall. Americans, on the other hand, could not tolerate European slander of Yankee ways so soon after the nation had saved these foreigners from autocracy and given them a chance to mend their ways.

Nothing could have more clearly revealed the subtle element of egoism in the American mission than the popular reaction to European criticism. American altruism had always been sustained by a sense of pride in the nation's unequaled moral reputation. Now even that was being challenged by the very people who were supposed to appreciate it the most. From this sense of injured pride there arose the common feeling that Uncle Sam had been played for a sucker, that unscrupulous power-politicans, propagandists, or some other devil had taken advantage of American idealism to lure the nation into war for wicked purposes. The persistent postwar sucker tradition seems to have summed up all those adolescent fears and embarrassments of unrequited love that commonly seize young and impulsive innocents.

The active propagators of disillusionment merely emphasized in a more scholarly or philosophical context the conclusions about wartime idealism which the general public would probably have reached independently in response to the impact of postwar events upon exaggerated and unstable idealistic impulses. However, the disillusionists' influence upon American foreign policy was more subtle than a mere intensification of anti-crusade and anti-internationalist sentiment. It must be remembered that the disillusionists were idealists. Their most eloquent spokesmen were schooled in the prewar tenets of moral perfection and the abhorrence of force as an absolute evil. The demoralization of American idealists, traditionally an exceedingly influential group in the nation's life, could not help but exert a tremendous influence upon America's international conduct during the whole interwar period, if only because the nation was thereby deprived of the moral leadership it might otherwise have experienced.

The orgy of self-accusation whereby liberals made amends for their indulgence in idealism during the war created a sort of paralysis of moral judgment among idealists, which prevented them from beholding the mote in their brother's eye in their obsession with casting out the beam from their own. When they were subsequently faced with an international evil far more virulent and menacing than any they had previously imagined, they were thrown into doubt and confusion. They dared not think that their own nation was right and another wrong when they remembered all the death and barbarity, the wholesale deceit and repression, which these very moral distinctions had brought upon the world in the recent war. Besides, how could one be sure of right and wrong when the weight of objective research had demonstrated that all value-judgments were relative to conditions and circumstances and all idealistic enthusiasm subject to the distortions of propaganda and self-deception?

Of course, this sort of anguished speculation bore much less weight among average citizens than among the self-conscious and conscience-stricken idealists who absorbed the full shock of disillusionment. But in one form, at least, the moral paralysis of the disillusionists seized almost all groups, and that was the inability to countenance the resort to coercion or war for idealistic ends. Americans, in general, were embarrassed by their exhibition of moral fervor during World War I. It was as though they had made a hasty and unseemly show of emotion on a false assumption and discovered the facts of international life too late to retract the mistake. The response to this experience was a well-nigh unanimous "Never again!" Thereafter, every national move was measured against the possibility of its dragging America into another war; and since it was believed that the nation had entered the last war on idealistic grounds, Americans were on their guard against undertaking commitments on the basis of strong moral positions toward the affairs of other nations. Their wariness was tested to the utmost by the events of the thirties and forties.

CHAPTER XIV

PEACE WITHOUT POWER

1. The Fear of War

IN THE postwar years America's disillusionment with the application of force to idealistic ends reinforced the utopian belief, cultivated by idealists in the placid prewar atmosphere, that the exercise of national power was antithetical to the achievement of peace and that war could be abolished by eliminating the competition for power. Consistent with this sanguine assumption, the search for peace in the fateful interim between two world wars was characterized by attempts to deprive nations of the instruments of coercion and to exorcize war by declarations of principle.

However, behind this simple approach to the problem of international conflict there was little of the old confidence that war, like the duel, had become obsolete; the bouyant optimism that infused American idealism before the war never returned. Peace advocates like Mr. Butler might rejoice because the whole world wanted peace and war was unthinkable, but their anxiety to halt the armaments race and outlaw war refuted the complacent assumption that peace was merely a state of mind. In fact, much of the passion for peace was the obverse side of a fear of war, stimulated, in part, by the nation's revulsion from its participation in World War I. This fear was not so much the fear of an immediate war or of a particular war, arising from specific, well-defined conflicts of national interests, as it was the fear of war in the abstract, of war as an absolute evil, which men must banish from the earth lest the United States find itself, once more, sucked into the hideous maelstrom of world conflict.

Unfortunately, this generalized fear did not inspire a proportionate regard for the real sources of war. Rather it tended to obscure them by focusing attention upon war's obvious and dramatic aspects, upon its wickedness as an instrument of national policy and its dependence upon instruments of violence, almost to the exclusion of the complex conflicts of power that lie at the roots of war. Moreover, it made the avoidance of war rather than the achievement of the national interest the indispensable requirement of foreign policy, while blinding men to the fact that these two objects might be irreconcilable. And so the task of composing particular national conflicts in a manner consistent with the national interest was swallowed up in the general problem of either avoiding or eliminating armed conflict, as though the problem of war and peace were something abstracted from the painful process of political adjustment among nations. America's role in the Washington Conference, the Peace of Paris, and the attempt to check Japanese aggression in Asia in the thirties illustrates the deficiencies of this approach to world politics.

2. ALIGNMENTS OF POWER AND INTERESTS

To the American people as a whole the Washington Conference of 1921 signified the end of a costly and dangerous naval race and the beginning of a new era of international amity, brought about by means of mutual agreements on the limitation of armaments; but to the statesmen of the great powers it meant something more than this; it signified an attempt through both military and political agreements to stabilize the competition for power in the western Pacific. The significance of the Washington Conference for America's adjustment to its international environment is revealed in the interaction of popular sentiment and power politics.

The Washington Treaties grew out of the political rivalry of Japan, Great Britain, and the United States. This rivalry took the form of a three-cornered race in naval construction, but it went much deeper than the ambitions of navalists; it had its origins in a shifting distribution of world power. From the standpoint of America's interests the most threatening aspect of the postwar distribution of power was the greatly enhanced strength of Japan and the growing influence of Japanese imperialists upon national policy. The destruction of German power in the Pacific and the virtual withdrawal of Russia, France, and Great Britain from Asia left the United States as the only obstacle to Japanese hegemony over East Asia; but the United States was in a poor position to stop Japanese imperialism. As the result of a wartime expedient and the pressures of peacemaking Japan had acquired a permanent mandate over the whole chain of islands which had belonged to Germany—the Marshalls, Carolines, and Marianas.* These possessions, flanking America's line of communications for a thousand miles from Hawaii to Guam, the Philippines, and the China Coast, gave Japan naval dominance in the west-

---

* In the fall of 1914 Great Britain invoked the Anglo-Japanese Alliance and invited Japan to take possession of Germany's Pacific possessions "temporarily" as part of a plan to relieve British commerce from the paralyzing effect of Germany's strong cruiser squadron. At the peace conference the Japanese, fortified by a secret pledge from Great Britain to support Japanese claims to all German colonies north of the equator in return for Japanese support of British claims south of the equator, gained formal possession of these archipelagoes as the administrator of a mandate. The Department of State and informed students of naval strategy were fully aware of the strategic implications of Japan's eastward expansion, but the American press, on the whole, either ignored or belittled the danger; and Wilson was far more concerned with the moral aspects of Japan's aggressions in Shantung. Harold and Margaret Sprout, *Toward a New Order of Sea Power* (2d ed.; Princeton, 1943), pp. 34–38, 88–94.

ern Pacific, a position roughly similar to America's dominance of the Caribbean after 1900. Thereafter, the rights and interests of other nations in this region, including the United States, would depend primarily upon the good will and tolerance of Japan.

There was every indication that Japanese policy would not be distinguished by these tender qualities. Japanese expansionists had indicated their designs on China by presenting, during the war, the notorious "twenty-one demands." After the war they had prodded their statesmen to drive bargains that confirmed Japanese succession to all German rights and possessions in the Pacific and the Far East north of the equator and had then set about extending and consolidating their position in Shantung, tightening their grip on southern Manchuria, making inroads in the Russian sphere of influence in northern Manchuria, and even plotting the conquest of the maritime province of Siberia.

Moreover, Japan's attitude toward the United States was anything but friendly. America's outspoken assertion of the Open Door against Japan's notorious twenty-one demands on China in 1915, President Wilson's revival of the four-power consortium in 1917 against Japanese economic penetration in China, and the frustration of Japanese designs by the presence of American troops in Siberia from 1918 to 1920 irritated Japanese expansionists. At the peace conference the United States' opposition to Japan's succession to German rights in Shantung, her dogged wrangling over Japanese possession of a tiny cable center, the Island of Yap, and Wilson's failure to support a clause affirming racial equality in the League of Nations clearly marked the United States as an antagonist. Irritation turned to hostility with the postwar revival of anti-Japanese agitation on the West Coast, Washington's increasing opposition to the Anglo-Japanese Alliance, due for renewal in 1921, and the Navy department's widely publicized plans for building a total of more than fifty capital ships.

The shift of power toward Japan in the western Pacific seriously jeopardized America's position in the Far East, but influential naval and civilian officials and a vocal section of the press were determined to continue supporting American claims and possessions in this region, even if it meant building a navy strong enough to lick Japan in her own waters. In the face of this prospect the Japanese were not willing to surrender their dominant position; yet all but the most incorrigible militarists were inclined to avoid the tremendous drain on the government's revenue by joining in an international limitation of armaments that would preserve the status quo, providing someone else would take the initiative.

As for the British, they were in no position to afford the great financial outlay that would be required to preserve naval equality with the United States, and they recognized that a three-way naval race would be disastrous for British interests in the Pacific and for the Anglo-American entente, which seemed more essential than ever in Britain's war-weakened condition. On the other hand, considerations of pride and the external relations of the Empire forbade the British government either to surrender first place on the sea to the United States or to beg or threaten the United States as a means of instituting negotiations for naval limitation. British statesmen and navalists were painfully aware of the fact that the war had boosted the American Navy from a poor third among naval powers to a rank second only to England's.

Only the United States, by virtue of its superior economic and military potential and its relative continental security, was in a position to initiate an international conference to limit naval construction. In the United States, as in Japan and Great Britain, there was a mounting desire for just such a conference; but there was also a determined opposition to any armaments agreement as long as Great Britain maintained the Anglo-Japanese Alliance, which had become a source of distrust and suspicion with the mounting postwar antagonism between Japan and the United States. Yet Japan would not agree to naval terms acceptable to the United States without the political support which the Alliance provided, and Great Britain was reluctant to abandon its long-standing agreement with Japan unless Japan and the United States could agree on limitation.

In the meanwhile, the precarious alignments of national power and interests operated in such a way that the United States, Great Britain, and Japan each had dominant power in its own sphere of influence, and yet each had interests within the strategic sphere of one or both of the other powers. In this situation any attempt on the part of one power to protect its interests outside its own sphere by naval or military expansion would inevitably provoke counter moves by the other powers, and any attempt of one power even to assure its continued superiority within its own dominant sphere of influence by purely military means would be interpreted as a threat to the interests of the nations with an inferior strategic position in that region. Clearly, there could be no military solution of this problem unless it was based upon a political settlement—upon an adjustment of national interests and power relations.

3. The Disarmament Movement

The immediate impetus for the political and military settlement achieved at the Washington Conference was provided by the pressure of American public opinion, but the American public was generally ignorant of the larger political implications of the international turmoil which the conference sought to compose. The American people were not interested in power politics, but they were highly disturbed by the nation's expanded naval program and thoroughly frightened by the prospect of an all-out naval race with Japan and Great Britain. "Disarmament"—more accurately, the limitation of armaments—seemed like the most direct, as well as the most idealistic method of striking at the source of their anxiety.

Behind the disarmament movement, which gathered momentum so rapidly during the winter of 1920–21, were all the sentiments and assumptions that had moved American idealists since the turn of the century. The proponents of disarmament argued that large navies were the archaic devices of power politicians, professional navalists, and profiteers, which led inevitably to militarism, imperialism, and continual warfare at the expense of the great mass of peace-loving peoples. They observed that the nation had just fought a war against militarism and autocracy and avowed that America's true course lay not in embracing these Old World doctrines but rather in leading the way to a new era in which men would be free from the scourge of armaments and organized violence. The idealistic aspects of disarmament were given particular prominence by two of the cause's most ardent group advocates: the women's organizations, which were highly conscious of demonstrating the beneficent influence of the newly-acquired women's vote, and the churches, which were eager to regain their leadership in the peace movement.[1]

Americans found equally persuasive reasons for disarmament on grounds of self-interest. Rumors of an American-Japanese war, fears of another world war, filled war-weary Americans with apprehension when they anticipated the consequences of a wild naval competition. The pugnacious chauvinism of the Hearst press and the preparedness preaching of the big-navy advocates, which had once rallied great patriotic enthusiasm, now only exacerbated public apprehension.

A pervasive theme throughout the whole disarmament campaign was the necessity of avoiding the onerous tax burden and probable bankruptcy which an expanded armaments program would entail. In this respect the disarmament movement was an expression of the general postwar depression sentiment for cutting back governmental expenditures to peacetime levels and returning to normalcy. This theme was dominant in the arguments of business and conservative groups, but it was seldom omitted from the altruistic and humanitarian appeals of liberals, reformers, and evangelists.

Finally, disarmament advocates had a powerful argument in their appeal to America's abiding sense of isolation. What foreign menace, they challenged, requires building a navy second to none? The implication of this rhetorical question was twofold: No purpose but continental self-defense could justify naval expansion; there was no conceivable threat to the American continent.

The agitation for arms limitation became a full-fledged movement in December, 1920, as the result of two developments: The Navy department presented a huge building program, which threatened to touch off accelerated naval developments in Great Britain and Japan, and Senator Borah assumed leadership of the limitation cause by sponsoring a congressional joint resolution requesting the President to open negotiations on the subject with Great Britain and Japan.[2]

Within two weeks after the introduction of Borah's resolution the disarmament movement had gathered irresistible momentum throughout the country, gaining recruits from virtually all sectors of the population—not only from reformers, women's organizations, the churches, and youth but also from respected military men like General Bliss and General Pershing, conservative financial journals, the preparedness-conscious *Boston Transcript,* and even from the big steelmakers and the labor unions, both of which would sacrifice much immediate financial gain through retrenchment.[3] By the spring of 1921 the surge of hope and faith that swelled up in the nation had assumed the proportions of a mammoth revival meeting. Only President Harding and his advisers and the big-navy majority in the Senate Naval Committee, aided and abetted by Senator Lodge, stood in the way of a reduction of armaments and an American call for international negotiation; and, one by one, the government's hastily improvised dikes against naval retrenchment were being swept away in the flood of public sentiment.

This astonishing development of public pressure, together with the British government's announced intention of assuming the initiative itself if the United States failed to call a conference within four days, finally prodded Washington into action.[4] On July 8 the State Department dispatched a tentative proposal for an arms conference to the governments of Great Britain, France, Italy, and Japan.[5]

4. THE WASHINGTON SETTLEMENT

The Washington Conference opened in the most dramatic and, probably, the most effective manner possible when, on the morning of November 12, 1921, Secretary of State Hughes stunned the unsuspecting delegates with an audacious detailed proposal that the United States, Great Britain, and Japan halt construction of capital ships for ten years and scrap other battleships built or building so that the three powers would be left with a ratio of 5-5-3, respectively. With this unorthodox stratagem Hughes captured the imagination of the world and stirred up a wave of popular enthusiasm, in his own country and abroad, which mere statesmen were powerless to ignore. Hughes's skill as a publicist, as well as a diplomat, had a great deal to do with the fact that the Washington Conference became the first armaments conference to achieve more than a juggling of statistics and a spate of generalities.

In the three principal treaties that resulted from the negotiations at Washington, military and political provisions were interdependent. By the terms of the Five Power Naval Treaty the United States, Great Britain, Japan, France, and Italy agreed to a ten-year naval holiday, during which no new capital ships were to be built, and accepted a ratio of 5-5-3-1.75-1.75, respectively, in capital ship tonnage. In addition, they agreed to limit the total tonnage of aircraft carriers and the size and armament of capital ships, aircraft carriers, and cruisers.

These naval provisions were accepted by Japan only because of the insertion of Article XIX, which pledged the signatories not to build any new fortifications or naval bases in the Pacific.* From the standpoint of the security of America's vulnerable line of communications to the Far East the construction and fortification of bases in Guam and the Philippines would have been extremely important; military and naval experts were unanimous in this opinion. However, Japan was understandably opposed to a fixed naval ratio as long as a powerful competitor was free to build up bases within Japan's sphere of influence in the western Pacific, threatening her local dominance and, hence, jeopardizing the security of her home islands and the execution of her plans for hegemony in eastern Asia. Moreover, in the view of American statesmen the risk of precipitating a disastrous naval race with Japan if the United States did not accept Article XIX seemed especially unwarranted, considering the opinion of virtually all observers, including the big-navy advocates, that Congress would never consent to spend the vast sums required to build or fortify bases in Guam and the Philippines anyhow.[6]

The Five Power Treaty made it possible, in the end, for statesmen to overrule purely military considerations in favor of a long-run political settlement in the Far East, the first requirement of which was the avoidance of an armaments race among the three great naval powers of the world.

Just as the acceptance of naval limitations depended upon Article XIX, so the agreement on Article XIX depended upon the Four Power Treaty.[7] The American delegation, in harmony with a strong current of opinion in the na-

---

* There were certain exceptions to this provision; they included the Hawaiian and Aleutian islands.

tion, was firmly opposed to accepting the status quo in Pacific bases and fortifications as long as the Anglo-Japanese Alliance existed; but the Japanese were not willing to abrogate the Alliance and thereby lose its moral support against American pressure in the Far East, and the British were not willing to antagonize their Oriental ally in order to appease their Occidental friend. This political stalemate was resolved by agreement upon the Four Power Treaty, which specifically superseded the Anglo-Japanese Alliance. By the terms of this treaty a bilateral pact was transmuted into a multilateral pledge whereby the three great naval powers and France agreed to respect each other's rights in insular possessions in the Pacific and to consult each other in case those rights should become the subject of a controversy or the object of a threat by an outside power.

The Four Power Treaty cleared the way for further accommodation of Far Eastern questions, which, in turn, had much to do with the willingness of the American delegation and the American Senate to accept naval limitations.[8] According to the Nine Power Treaty all the nations represented at Washington obligated themselves to observe the Open Door principle and respect the territorial integrity of China. This was the most sweeping affirmation of that cherished American principle ever made. As in the case of its original promulgation, it was suggested by the British but left to American initiative to propose. The conference also achieved acceptable compromises on the controversies concerning the Island of Yap, Shantung, and the withdrawal of Japanese troops from Siberia.

Taken as a whole, the Washington Treaties probably represented the best practicable settlement of the naval competition and the underlying political controversies which accompanied the postwar shift in power in the Far East. However, this settlement, like all international settlements, was just an incident in a continual process of political accommodation. It did not supplant the competition for national power; it simply set a pattern for moderating and regularizing that competition. It did not transform the basic relations among nations; it registered existing facts about those relations.

In effect, the Washington Treaties recognized the superior power of Japan, Great Britain, and the United States within their respective spheres of influence. Article XIX of the Five Power Treaty may have made the defense of America's Pacific line of communications more difficult than before, but it did not basically change existing power relations. Only a tremendous armaments and fortifications development—one far more ambitious than any American naval official had proposed—could have possibly overcome the relative impotence of the United States in the western Pacific.

The Five Power Naval Treaty did not permit the United States to build up the power necessary to enforce the Open Door principle and the territorial integrity of China, which had been reaffirmed by the Nine Power Treaty; but the United States did not possess that power before the conference either, and it is not clear how this situation could have been altered as long as China herself remained weak and divided. From the time of Hay's original announcement of the Open Door policy no American statesman had ever contemplated its enforcement; the Five Power Treaty did not change this situation.

The Four Power Treaty contained no provision for the enforcement of its terms; it did not obligate its signatories to do anything more than consult one another. Yet it represented the maximum commitment to which the contracting powers were willing to bind themselves; and, no matter what its provisions had been, this treaty could have induced its signatories to co-operate no further than they were willing to co-operate in specific political circumstances. The effectiveness of the Four Power Treaty, like the effectiveness of the other treaties, depended upon mutual trust and good will, which it had played a key role in creating at Washington.

The mere ratification of the Washington Treaties did not guarantee a Far Eastern settlement; it simply set forth terms upon which the signatories might seek a settlement through continual adjustment and compromise. Clearly, the whole balance of power and configuration of interests which these treaties embodied might be upset if Japan, or any other nation, should set out to destroy the status quo. Therefore, from the standpoint of America's self-interest, and the interests of world peace as well, the achievement of a Far Eastern settlement within the framework of the Washington Treaties demanded an unremitting effort through all the resources of diplomacy, backed by adequate national power and the willingness to use it, to preserve the spirit of amity created by the conference and to keep Japan satisfied with the military and political status quo. And if this effort should prove unavailing, then the United States might still legally construct a formidable fleet of submarines, cruisers, and aircraft carriers capable of waging a far ranging *guerre de course;* and she held a powerful card in Japan's crucial dependence upon America's markets and raw materials.

Ultimately, the power to support the Washington Treaties and to take countermeasures if Japan violated them depended upon collaboration between the two powers which had a common interest in maintaining the status quo in the Far East, the United States and Great Britain. Together these nations could marshal considerable naval power in the western Pacific and control the vital marine highways which sustained the industry and military power of Japan. However, the ability of these nations to take effective parallel action depended upon the preservation of a balance of power on the continent of Europe that would permit Great Britain to maintain her dominance of the vital sea routes through the English Channel, the Mediterranean, and into the Atlantic. An Anglo-American entente, providing it were willing to take quick and forceful action, might successfully meet a challenge to the balance of power in either Europe or Asia, but it could scarcely afford a simultaneous challenge from both quarters; and in either case the failure of one member to take decisive parallel action would spell disaster for both.

5. POPULAR VIEW OF THE WASHINGTON SETTLEMENT

Inevitably, the Washington Treaties had defects. One of them, the failure to extend the limitations on capital ships to cruisers, auxiliary ships, and aircraft, became manifest soon after the Treaties went into effect. But no defect could have been nearly as harmful to American interests and the cause of peace as the failure of the American people to see that these treaties were only the imperfect beginning of a continuing political accommodation and not the perfect consummation of man's desire to be rid of war. The limitation of armaments would be futile if it were not supported by a persistent effort to balance and mitigate the conflicts of national power and interests that led to the accumulation of armaments in the first place. Yet the American people, on the whole, were indifferent to the underlying political basis of the Washington settlement. They were preoccupied with the dramatic success of disarmament. Miraculously, the Treaties seemed to have broken the deadly chain of armaments, taxes, bankruptcy, and war. This achievement was regarded as a triumph *over* power politics, not a triumph *of* power politics.

The public mood of relief and exaltation was created at the opening of the conference by Secretary Hughes's astonishing address, telling each power just how many ships it should scrap. Senator Borah pronounced this "the first great triumph of open diplomacy." All groups of Americans were overwhelmed with admiration and high hopes. The clergy was ecstatic. And foreign comment was almost equally enthusiastic.[9] Overnight Hughes seemed to have elevated the United States once more to the active role of missionary among heathens.

This mood was maintained after the Washington Treaties had been concluded. Hughes gave voice to America's and the whole world's rebirth of confidence in peace when he told the closing session of the conference, "This Treaty ends, absolutely ends, the race in competition of naval armament. At the same time it leaves the relative security of the great naval powers unimpaired. . . . We are taking perhaps the greatest forward step in history to establish the reign of peace."[10] The American press spoke in superlatives of a reconstructed world and a new epoch. The *New York Times* predicted that sea power would decline in importance and that the world's business would henceforth be carried on without great navies to guard it.[11] Amid this all but universal acclaim, virtually the only voices of dissent came from the chauvinistic Hearst press, most naval experts, and a few students of world politics;* and these dissenters were either ignored or roundly denounced for militarism. Villard's *Nation* could not be denounced for militarism. On rigid idealistic grounds it remained dissatisfied with anything but complete abolition of armaments;[12] but most Americans, being more prone to take the wish for the fact, were less demanding of perfection; they were too eager to believe that the ominous menace of naval rivalry had finally been put to rest.

Yet, because America's emotional appreciation of the achievement at Washington was largely undisciplined by a rational comprehension of the real conditions for peaceful settlement, popular enthusiasm soon gave way to indifference and, in some cases, disillusionment when the intractable realities of world politics failed to substantiate the nation's naïve faith in the magic of disarmament. An indication of the insubstantial basis of the nation's enthusiasm for disarmament is the fact that the only important opposition to the Washington Treaties was directed at the crucial political implications of the Four Power Treaty and especially at Article II, which provided that, if a signatory's rights were threatened by the aggressive action of an outside power, all the signatories would "communicate with one another . . . in order to arrive at an understanding as to the most efficient measures to be taken . . . to meet the exigencies of the particular situation."

The Four Power Treaty became the subject of a major parliamentary battle, consuming about two hundred pages of the Congressional Record.[13] The most impassioned attack was led by the League "irreconcilables" Borah, Johnson, and Reed, who once again sprang to the defense of nationalism versus internationalism, charging that the Washington Conference had been turned aside from the limitation of naval armaments to the execution of a new alliance, an insidious "quadruple alliance," which, like the League of Nations, would entangle the United States in the toils of an alien balance of power in order to serve the selfish designs of predatory nations and secret financial

* For the Navy's verdict on the conference see Sprouts, *Toward a New Order of Sea Power*, pp. 266–71. Raymond Buell was typical of those scholars who criticized the Washington agreements for their lack of positive sanctions and their weakness against Japanese imperialism. However, three years later he concluded that he had underestimated the moral strength of world opinion. *The Washington Conference* (New York, 1922), pp. 238–41, 310–14; *Problems of the Pacific* (Boston, 1925), p. 33. Walter Lippmann hailed Hughes for stopping the drift into a ruinous war; but after Japan took advantage of her dominance in the western Pacific to make war on the United States, he denounced the conference as "exorbitant folly." *New York World*, January 29, 1922; *U.S. Foreign Policy* (Boston, 1943), pp. xii, 40.

344 IDEALS AND SELF-INTEREST IN AMERICA'S FOREIGN RELATIONS

interests. Senator Borah, who had been the prime mover in the public agitation for the conference, looked upon the Four Power Treaty as "trans-
ferring to the Pacific the old system of political groupings which has tormented and tortured Europe for three hundred years." He pointed with
alarm to the similarity between Article II of the Four Power Treaty and
Articles X and XI of the League Covenant, and he suggested that the provision for consultation concealed a secret agreement between the United States
and Great Britain.[14]

Some of the supporters of the League also objected to the political implications of the Four Power Treaty, but not on narrowly nationalistic grounds.
Senator Hitchcock, who had directed the fight for ratification of the Versailles Treaty, declared that the Four Power Treaty was just the sort of entangling alliance which the League had been designed to prevent. Whereas
the League was an association of many nations to guarantee peace and justice
for all, the Four Power Treaty was an alliance in the old balance-of-power
tradition between a few nations to maintain their hold on certain Pacific
islands. In Hitchcock's opinion this sort of limited military alliance would
provoke counteralliances and, perhaps, lead to aggression and war. Like the
"irreconcilables," he conjured up the dire consequences of America's commitment in the event of a Russian attack upon southern Sakhalin Island or some
other Japanese possession.[15]

Senator Lodge, whom Hughes had shrewdly included in the American
delegation and to whom he had given the honor of presenting the Four Power
Treaty to the conference, now found himself defending the treaty before the
Senate and the country against many of the same arguments he himself had
used to fight Article X. As a member of the American delegation to the conference and a frequent adviser of Secretary Hughes, Lodge was quite aware
of the considerations of national power and self-interest which the Washington Treaties embodied. With a good deal of justice he could have defended
them on this basis; and he would have been defending no more than the sort
of limited political arrangement for a specific strategic gain which he and
Roosevelt and Mahan had always supported. But, in deference to the public
distaste for power politics, Lodge followed Hughes's approach by completely
side-stepping the realistic grounds for the Washington settlement and, instead,
bending all his energies to exalting its idealistic blessings and minimizing its
practical obligations. He vigorously denied that the Four Power Treaty was
marred by any of the features of an alliance, and he repeatedly emphasized
the absence of any obligation to enforce its provisions. Before the Senate he
concluded his case for the Washington Treaties with a stirring plea for the
fulfilment of America's moral leadership.

We called this conference. We proposed the treaties, agreements, and declarations in which the conference culminated. Are we now to stumble and fall at the threshold of the understanding which we designed and brought to fulfilment? Are we to sink back into a sullen solitude, a prey to dark suspicions, a hermit nation armed to the teeth and looking forward always to wars as inseparable from the existence of mankind upon the earth? . . . The United States has never permitted failure or defeat to be written in her history. She will not permit it now. Under her lead a beginning has been made to secure the world's peace in the coming years. Let us not blight or wither this new hope.[16]

This speech did not appease the League "irreconcilables," who referred to it variously as a "poor paraphrase of the language Woodrow Wilson used," "unconscious cerebration," and just plain "plagiarism."[17] They declared that if the Four Power Treaty was as harmless as Lodge said it was, then it was also worthless, and the United States should not, on the strength of it, reduce its armaments and give up the right to build and fortify bases.

Lodge's depreciation of the treaty's obligations did not meet with the favor of all its supporters either. Even before the Senate debate the *New York Times* had called Article II "a clumsy paraphrase of Article X of the Covenant" and caustically observed, "Mr. Lodge and other enemies of the League covenant have undertaken a deal of explaining to make it appear that under Article II the use of power is not provided for. Their protestations are futile. The use of power is implied quite as clearly in the new treaty as in the old."[18]

In the end, Lodge's cause was victorious; the treaty passed the Senate with the help of a superfluous reservation affirming his negations by stating that there was no "commitment to armed force, no alliance, no obligation to join in any defense." The Four Power Treaty surmounted its opposition because the irreconcilables were not numerous enough and because most of those who thought that it was a poor substitute for the League preferred to have some sort of agreement on armaments limitation rather than none at all. However, from the debate that preceded the passage of this treaty it is clear that its proponents did no more than its opponents to enlighten the American people about the real conditions for the settlement of the postwar political and military competition which the conference had attempted to mitigate. The American people were thoroughly entangled in world-wide conflicts of national power and interests; but they were ignorant of the unpleasant consequences of this fact, and no one who wanted the United States to accept the Washington Treaties dared breathe this awful truth.

With a spontaneous burst of relief, hope, and enthusiasm, occasioned by the international limitation of armaments, the nation had regained the thrill of being the moral leader of the world. Yet the thrill was based largely on wish and fancy divorced from the hard substance of international politics; and such leadership as the American people, as a whole, exercised was politically ignorant, irresponsible, and short-lived. The transient thrill afforded by the Washington Conference was a miserable preparation for the test of political leadership provided by the ominous events that undermined the Far Eastern settlement a decade later.

6. OUTLAWING WAR

The Pact of Paris, signed on August 27, 1928, by representatives of the United States and fourteen other nations, was the perfect expression of the utopian idealism which dominated America's attempts to compose international conflicts and banish the threat of war in the interwar period. This pact sought to end warfare by making it illegal.

Behind the Pact of Paris was the idea of devising international laws against war instead of continuing to accept laws recognizing war as a legal condition. This idea was originally promoted by Salmon O. Levinson, a wealthy, civic-minded Chicago lawyer, who started publicizing the phrase "outlawry of war" in 1918 as a rather picturesque way of expressing a popular aspiration encouraged by Wilson's war to end war. During the early 1920's the idea of outlawry made little progress, except among a small, distinguished group of idealists, whom Levinson enlisted in the cause. However, outlawry gave promise of a bright future when Senator Borah, who always had an open mind for peace schemes which did not involve force or political entanglements, was persuaded—but not without difficulty—to introduce Senate Resolution 441 on February 13, 1923. This resolution was, in effect, the complete Levinson program. It called for a universal treaty to make war a public crime under the law of nations and bind every nation to punish its own "war breeders or instigators or war profiteers." It also called for a comprehensive code of international law and a world court with "affirmative" jurisdiction over purely international controversies.

In spite of Borah's powerful faculty for bringing public sentiment to bear upon national policy, his resolution for outlawry attracted little public attention until growing international friction, the rise of great power rivalry in the construction of cruisers, submarines, and smaller craft, and the utter failure of the Geneva Disarmament Conference of the summer of 1927 to alleviate this ominous situation deflated public confidence in the magic of disarmament and disposed anxious taxpayers to look to other measures for help. But public sentiment might still not have been translated into an international agreement if Aristide Briand, the French foreign minister, had not made outlawry a practical concern of statesmen by proposing on April 6, 1927, in an address aimed directly at the American people, that France and the United States outlaw war between them. The Pact of Paris, like the Washington Treaties, was the result of a strange interaction of popular sentiment and power politics.

In Briand's mind an outlawry agreement with the United States was a means of enlisting American power and prestige in the service of France's continental security. By gaining America's assurance that she would never go to war against France, Briand hoped to strengthen the series of bilateral nonaggression pacts with which he had been encircling Germany since the World War, for it would be greatly to France's advantage to have this assurance should France have to go to war under the terms of her various defensive agreements. Ironically enough, Briand's proposal had the active support of influential Americans, who, far from viewing outlawry as a bilateral nonaggression alliance, envisioned it as the basis for reconstructing a collective security system. In fact, one of these men, James T. Shotwell, a professor at Columbia University and a director of the Carnegie Endowment for International Peace, wrote Briand's speech and persuaded him to deliver it.[19]

Briand's proposal was generally ignored and then forgotten until Nicholas Murray Butler, President of the Carnegie Endowment and Columbia University, wrote a letter on April 25, 1927, to the New York Times calling attention to Briand's proposal. Butler succeeded in arousing considerable Senatorial interest, but not from Senator Borah, who smelled an old-style alliance. President Coolidge and Secretary of State Kellogg maintained a studied silence and began thinking of ways to head off Shotwell's and Butler's amateur diplomacy, which threatened to force their hand. However, it soon developed that Briand's proposal, with the help of Butler's letter and the failure of the Geneva Disarmament Conference, had united the American peace movement, both pro-League and anti-League factions, and set off another tidal wave of public sentiment, like the one that had swept the reluctant Harding administration into the Washington Conference. By the fall of 1927 Senator Borah had caught up with his followers, and peace leaders were clamoring for action on his resolution. It was evident that the government would have to take some positive official stand on outlawry, but it remained determined not to fall into Briand's trap.

The way was finally cleared for official action by invention of the happy device of multilateralizing the suggested outlawry pact. This idea appealed strongly to Borah and gave great solace to the irascible Secretary Kellogg. Borah now glowed with enthusiasm for a pact which he considered an "incalculable contribution" to the security of nations, and Kellogg actually began to believe that a multilateral treaty renouncing war would be a great boon to mankind.[20] The peace organizations redoubled their activity.

On December 28, 1927, Kellogg formally suggested to the French government that the contemplated bilateral pact be expanded to include the other great powers. Now it was Briand who tried to wriggle off the hook. But it was no use; after three months of diplomatic maneuvering the self-ensnared Foreign Minister accepted Kellogg's proposal in principle. After another considerable delay fifteen powers sent their plenipotentiaries to Paris, where the Kellogg-Briand Pact, as it was popularly known in the United States, was finally signed. Subsequently, every sovereign state, except three South American republics, adhered to it.

What was this Pact of Paris, which was so widely hailed as a document of revolutionary importance? The Pact of Paris simply declared that its signatories renounced war as an instrument of national policy and agreed that international conflicts should be settled only by pacific means. It contained absolutely no obligation for any nation to do anything under any circumstances. The contracting powers did not even attempt to deal with the turbulent political conflicts, which threatened to produce the war that the Pact sought to exorcize with a general proscription. Moreover, just to make sure that outlawry would be meaningless, Secretary Kellogg officially interpreted the renunciation of war as "an instrument of national policy" as excluding wars resorted to under the "inalienable right of self-defense." Great Britain later stipulated that in her case the right of self-defense included "certain regions of the world the welfare and integrity of which constitute a special and vital interest for our peace and safety." The United States ratified the treaty with a similar reservation applying to the region covered by the Monroe Doctrine. France explained that "an instrument of national policy" did not refer to wars undertaken collectively under previous treaties or the League Covenant.

On January 15, 1929, the Senate voted its approval of the Kellogg Pact by a count of eighty-five to one. This vote fairly represented the magnitude of the treaty's popularity in the nation as a whole. However, the basis of popular approbation was just as insubstantial and unrealistic as the basis upon which the nation had embraced the Washington Treaties, and America's statesmen and politicians had done nothing to temper the public's extravagant expectations with the discipline of cold reason.

President Coolidge, addressing a capacity crowd in Wisconsin, in August, 1928, encouraged the people in their blind exultation by assuring them,

Had an agreement of this kind been in existence in 1914, there is every reason to suppose that it would have saved the situation and delivered the world from all the misery which was inflicted by the great war. . . . It holds a greater hope for peaceful relations than was ever before given to the world.[21]

The *Boston Herald* expressed the same mood: "It is a thing to rejoice over, it is superb, it is magnificent. We should sing the *Te Deum Laudamus.*"[22]

The public paid little attention to the interpretive notes and reservations with which the contracting powers accepted the Pact; and it is little wonder, since the proponents of the treaty represented them as being completely inconsequential. Kellogg maintained, with dubious accuracy, that they were in no way a part of the Pact and could not be considered as reservations. Senator Borah said that the so-called reservations were no more than expressions "of a personal opinion, I presume largely for local use."[23]

As the benefits of this treaty were maximized, its obligations were proportionately minimized. Testifying before the Senate Committee on Foreign Relations, Kellogg stressed the fact that the United States was under absolutely no obligation to apply sanctions, to come to the help of any power, or to do anything at all except abstain from using war as an instrument of national policy.[24] Borah, in his defense of the treaty before the Senate, was quite emphatic in stating that there was no obligation, express or implied, to apply coercive or punitive measures to a violator.[25]

It is not clear just how much solid conviction underlay the popular rejoicing over a treaty which promised so much but asked so little. It is certain that many Senators approved it with skepticism. Senator Reed called it an "international kiss." Senator Swanson thought that the wars of self-defense excluded from the operations of the treaty by Secretary Kellogg's interpretation were "as limitless as the imagination or the ambition of nations may desire" and covered "almost any war that has occurred in the last century," but he supported the treaty as a "noble gesture."[26] Senator Carter Glass announced that he would vote for the treaty for the simple reason that he thought its defeat would be a bad thing psychologically; but, with more candor than most of his colleagues, he put the people of Virginia on notice that he was not simple enough to suppose that it was "worth a postage stamp in the direction of accomplishing permanent international peace"; and for the nation as a whole he proclaimed a notable judgment.

I say that all the people all the time for nearly the last ten years have been fooled. They are going to be fooled now by a so-called peace pact that, in the last analysis, is one of the many devices that have been contrived to solace the awakened conscience of some people who kept the United States out of the League of Nations; and, whether it was so intended or not, it is going to confuse the minds of many good and pious people who think that peace may be secured by polite professions of brotherly love.[27]

The American people were indeed fooled, but mere Senators could hardly be expected to have disabused them of their illusions by bucking the flood of petitions and letters which beseeched votes for a treaty against international sin. The American people were too profoundly fooled to be enlightened by Senatorial words or votes. No argument except the argument of events could have transformed the fundamental approach toward international relations that misinformed the nation's anxious search for peace without power. Only an extraordinary course of events capable of shaking the American people's complacent confidence in its insulation from the shocks of world-wide power conflicts could have induced the public to pay heed to the troublesome necessities of force and political accommodation in the pursuit of national ends.

Underlying the popular sentiment for outlawing the abstract evil of war was a widespread assumption that international conflicts could be settled and peace secured through international declarations and the pressure of world opinion alone, without respect to force and the other distasteful devices of power politics. This sanguine assumption was sustained, in turn, by the nation's confidence that, no matter what happened in the sphere of international relations across the seas—whether, for instance, nations conducted their affairs in accordance with the Briand-Kellogg Pact or not—the United States' own self-interest would not be endangered in any event. It was this false sense of isolated security that encouraged that distinctive combination of moral enthusiasm and political irresponsibility which has too often characterized America's excursions into world politics and which was expressed to perfection in the Pact of Paris.

7. THE MANCHURIAN INCIDENT POSES SOME PROBLEMS

The Pact of Paris was a self-denying pledge, which asked nothing of its signatories except that they recognize the moral principle of renouncing war as an instrument of national policy and as a means of settling disputes. The Washington Treaties contained specific political and military agreements which bound the contracting powers to observe the terms of a balance of power in the Far East. On the night of September 18, 1931, Japanese armies began overrunning southern Manchuria. This "Manchurian Incident," as the Japanese chose to call it, was a direct challenge to the Pact of Paris and the Washington Treaties; as such it presented the United States with both a moral and a political problem.

As the Japanese armies continued their forcible occupation of strategic cities and towns throughout all Manchuria it became evident that, whatever might be Japan's special economic and political rights and vital interests in this area—and they were extensive—her method of securing them against Chinese pressure constituted a violation of the Kellogg-Briand Pact. So the United

States was confronted with the moral problem: What does one do when another signatory of a self-denying pledge violates that pledge? Is one nation justified in setting itself up as judge of another's morality? Even though Japan had violated the Kellogg-Briand Pact, the moral issue was not crystal clear. Basically, the issue was between the security of Japan's political and economic interests, many of which had been sanctified by treaty, and China's aspiration to obtain complete national independence in an area over which she held juridical sovereignty. The exceedingly complicated historical background of this conflict never warranted the simple assumption that here was a case of Japanese aggression versus Chinese self-defense. The Lytton Commission, which thoroughly and objectively investigated the origins of the Manchurian Incident, made this very point.[28]

The political problem with which Japan's action confronted the United States was even less susceptible to easy resolution. The Washington Treaties had recognized the dominant power of Japan, Great Britain, and the United States within their respective spheres of influence; but the success of the whole Washington settlement, with its interdependent agreements, depended upon the good will and mutual trust of its signatories; and this good will and trust rested, in turn, upon the validity of the assumption, of particular concern to the United States in relation to the Nine Power Treaty, that the contracting powers would not attempt to overthrow the status quo with respect to the interests and rights of other nations within their dominant spheres. The emergence in Japan of a powerful group of militarists and ultra-nationalistic politicians, who seemed bent upon incorporating East Asia into a greater Japanese Empire, posed a distinct threat to the status quo in China; the Nine Power Treaty promised to be the first victim of what Japanese expansionists referred to as their Monroe Doctrine for Asia.

Rising Chinese nationalism, the resurgence of Russian power, and the closing of foreign markets by the erection of trade barriers like America's Smoot-Hawley tariff were rapidly conspiring to supplant Japan's so-called "friendship" policy toward China with a "positive" policy. No one could foresee with any certainty what this "positive" policy would mean for America's position in the Far East. If it meant the violation of the Open Door, the United States had been faced with that situation before and had never considered it important enough to warrant more than a protest or the refusal to recognize offending treaties. But nations were growing more interdependent with the extension of political influence and the advance of communications and transportation technology, so that a given action at a remote spot on the globe which, formerly, would have impinged upon America's self-interest in only a minor way might now have repercussions of major importance. Thus the

Manchurian Incident might mean more than the violation of China's territorial integrity and a restriction upon America's commercial opportunities there; it might mean the first step in a general imperialist drive, which would endanger the security of America's Pacific possessions and the whole balance of political and military power which the Washington Treaties were designed to preserve. Even so, the United States had to be particularly cautious and shrewd in choosing the means of checking adverse developments in the Far East, for every move that could be made to seem hostile to Japan would be used by the militarists to reduce the domestic power of the moderates and enhance their own influence; already America's high tariff barriers and the 1924 immigration act excluding Orientals had built up a reservoir of ill will, which Japanese nationalists were busily exploiting.

The moral and the political problems facing the American people were inextricably entangled. In spite of the complexity of the rights and wrongs of Japan's military actions in Manchuria, it could be argued, with considerable justice, that the United States was morally obligated to protest Japan's violation of the Kellogg-Briand Pact and the Nine Power Treaty or even to impose some sort of sanction against Japan in order to uphold the principle of peaceful settlement and the sanctity of treaties. But this moral position would become dubious, to say the least, if it actually failed to restrain Japan and, in fact, played into the hands of the militarists. No nation would be justified in taking a stand for international morality which, in its actual consequences, only aggravated the evil situation the nation sought to remedy. No nation would be justified in blindly supporting general principles of international conduct in far quarters of the globe if, in supporting them, it jeopardized its own vital interests and even its territorial security. However, if Japan's actions not only contravened international morality but also, directly or indirectly, endangered interests for which the American people would have preferred to fight rather than forfeit, then the nation should have been prepared to undertake strong measures, not excluding coercion and force, as a less objectionable alternative to sacrificing fundamental ideals and vital interests. On the other hand, if the United States had no more to lose from Japan's violation of the Kellogg-Briand Pact and the Nine Power Treaty than equal commercial opportunity in an area in which American trade was relatively small, then, regardless of the consequences for international morality, the nation should have been willing to content itself with ordinary diplomatic devices and an exercise of force and coercion limited to relatively unprovocative measures, such as the strengthening of the Navy within legal limits. In any case, the decisive factor in the choice among the various alternatives available to the United States should have been a rational consideration of the concrete effect of that policy choice upon America's long-run self-interest—above all, upon America's security.

As a matter of fact, neither the American government nor the American people approached the Manchurian Incident in this manner. What actually happened was that the nation took a vigorous moral stand against Japan's actions without regard for the actual consequences and, at the same time, remained unwilling to back up this stand with political commitments or the exercise of national power, since Japan's threat to international morality did not seem to endanger fundamental national interests. The result was something like the reverse of Theodore Roosevelt's maxim about talking softly and carrying a big stick. Once more America assumed a moral position that was politically irresponsible. The measures the nation was willing to undertake to support its policy proved pitifully inadequate to achieve the goals it sought, while the public was encouraged to depreciate this inadequacy in accordance with the wishful supposition that world opinion alone could alter basic power conflicts.

8. DIPLOMACY BY CONDEMNATION

Secretary of State Henry L. Stimson took the lead in shaping American policy toward Japan's incursions in Manchuria. He rapidly made up his mind that Japan was chiefly responsible for this disturbance, that she had violated the Kellogg-Briand Pact and the Nine Power Treaty, and that this situation was a vital concern of all the major signatories of these treaties, including the United States. In his view the United States was concerned because its self-interest was involved and because basic moral principles were at stake.[29]

As for America's self-interest, Stimson foresaw Japanese militarism causing direct damage to American trade in China; but more important in his mind than any immediate damage to American trade was the damage to American prestige; for it was his conviction that, ultimately, all of America's material interests in this region, present and future, depended upon the prestige which the United States enjoyed by virtue of its traditional support of China's territorial and administrative integrity. Like so many American missionaries, traders, and statesmen since the dawn of America's interest in the Orient, Stimson was profoundly moved by a vision of a potentially united, powerful, peace-loving, democratic China acting as a dominant, stabilizing influence in the whole Far East and transacting a huge trade with its historic friend and protector, the United States. He held that the United States could not afford to abandon Chinese sovereignty and independence to Japanese aggression and exploitation, for if America lost China's friendship or if China were dominated by a militaristic and aggressive regime or converted into such a regime by Japanese exploitation, the whole future of the United States in the Far East would be ruined. Moreover, he believed that there was a distinct possibility that a struggle between China and Japan might not only destroy America's potentially profitable relations with China but even endanger America's territorial possessions.

Stimson did not differentiate precisely between national self-interest and supranational ideals in his deliberations about American policy toward the Far Eastern disturbance. In his mind national self-interest coincided so perfectly with ideal principles in this situation that there was no cause to weigh these considerations separately and balance one against the other. However, it is clear from the tone and the context of Stimson's pronouncements, as well as from his own explanation of his attitude, which he presented in his book *The Far Eastern Crisis* in 1936, that moral considerations were uppermost in his mind. In his book he summed up the chain of events following the Manchurian Incident in this significant manner: "The history of the Sino-Japanese controversy of 1931 is the record of the arraignment, the trial and the condemnation of a great power for the violation of certain new standards of conduct aimed at preventing international aggression."[30]

Stimson was not willing to base American policy on any narrow, immediate national interest, such as the protection of commercial rights, when great moral issues were at stake. He saw Japan's attack upon China primarily as a sin against international order and stability, as a denial of the theory of the Kellogg Pact and a blow at the whole postwar treaty structure. He believed that Japan was thereby striking at the foundation of a system of collective security, upon which, ultimately, the enlightened self-interest of the United States and all other nations depended. Stimson's convictions about the immorality of Japan's actions gained poignancy by virtue of his strong sympathy for the Chinese people and China's ancient culture, which he regarded as the only firm basis in the Orient for the development of the ideals of Christian civilization.

The principal method which Secretary Stimson employed for dealing with Japan's international sin was collective condemnation backed by the moral force of world opinion. To this end he enunciated a policy of diplomatic nonrecognition. On January 7, 1932, he addressed an identic note to Japan and China stating, with reference to Japan's action in Manchuria, that the United States "does not intend to recognize any situation, treaty, or agreement which may be brought about by means contrary to the covenants and obligations of the Pact of Paris."

Stimson, who, like Hay, regarded co-operation with Great Britain as the touchstone of America's foreign policy, was unsuccessful in his efforts to get the British Foreign Office to take a similar stand, but he did not give up hope of securing parallel action. When Japanese troops clashed with Chinese forces at Shanghai, where British interests were far greater than in Manchuria, he was instrumental in arranging parallel American and British protests to Japan. These protests, combined with surprising Chinese resistance, may have helped induce Japan to withdraw from Shanghai; to Stimson, at any rate, this eventuality was proof of the power of Anglo-American co-operation and world opinion.[31]

He was unable to follow up this success with a joint British and American representation to Japan in terms of the Nine Power Treaty, but on February 23, 1932, after the Japanese had launched a major attack, he decided to deliver another unilateral protest, this time by means of a letter to Senator Borah. In this letter he reviewed the history of the Open Door policy, reaffirmed the Nine Power Treaty and the Kellogg-Briand Pact, declared that the United States would stand by these treaties, called attention to his previous proclamation of the nonrecognition doctrine, and invited the nations of the world to follow that example.[32] Eventually, this vigorous moral stand received something of the color of the collective condemnation Stimson had always sought when, in March, 1932, the League of Nations Assembly unanimously adopted a resolution which incorporated almost verbatim his nonrecognition doctrine.

The position Stimson set forth in his original nonrecognition note and in his letter to Borah became the basis of American policy toward Japan right down to Pearl Harbor. Later—too late, in fact—Franklin Roosevelt's administration combined this policy with restrictions on the export of certain materials essential to the Japanese war effort; and, at the last moment, it froze Japanese assets in the United States, thereby virtually cutting off all exports to Japan. But these measures, coming at a time when Japanese imperialism had gone too far to stop or withdraw, only hastened the blow that began the Pacific war. Before the American government resorted to these last-ditch measures it consistently eschewed the imposition of sanctions against Japan. It resisted public pressure to restrict the export of oil, scrap iron, and other materials which sustained the Japanese military machine. It scrupulously avoided political commitments with other nations and even refused requests from China, Great Britain, and France to act as a mediator. The most that it would contribute toward collective action was to refrain from interfering with measures that other nations might take.

9. DILEMMA OF ENDS AND MEANS

In dealing with Japanese expansion in the 1930's the United States relied upon mobilizing the moral force of nations through collective condemnation.

Therefore, the success of American policy depended, largely, upon the effectiveness of constant reiterations of principle and a succession of earnest remonstrances. In retrospect it would seem that this combination of moral chastisement and the rejection of any commitment to coercion or collective action was the most ineffective means possible for achieving the desired end. It did not strengthen any treaties or vindicate international morality; it did not protect America's interests in the Far East; it did not avoid war. It actually worked to defeat all these objectives by arousing Japanese resentment, fixing conditions for a settlement which the Japanese could never meet, and, at the same time, displaying a weakness which encouraged the radical elements in Japan to pursue their imperialist ambitions.

Of course, there is no assurance that the early use of coercion or the threat of coercion would have protected American interests and ideals any better. Perhaps the signatories of the Nine Power Treaty could have forced Japan and China to settle their dispute peacefully in 1937 when Japan was relatively weak and absolutely dependent upon these powers for the supplies to operate its military machine; and, even later, collective sanctions combined with the sending of America's Pacific fleet to Singapore to join Britain, France, and Holland in the defense of important possessions might have provided diplomacy with the requisite power to achieve a satisfactory settlement. Ideally, force should have been combined with measures that would have given Japan a sense of economic and political security. However, at any time, coercion would have carried the grave risk of open warfare, in which the United States would have borne the major share of the fighting. Moreover, no effort at collective coercion could have succeeded unless the United States had been willing to take the lead in organizing it. As at the Washington Conference, the United States, by virtue of its latent power, the nature of its commitments in the Far East, and its relative continental security, was the logical power to take the initiative in a political and military settlement. Diplomacy combined with military strength might still have failed as completely as collective condemnation and military weakness. But the important thing to note here is that this alternative was never seriously considered until Japan was entrenched in China and in a position to drive southward into the strategically crucial areas of Southeast Asia and the Dutch East Indies.

Of course, there were practical reasons for eschewing sanctions and collective action, just as there were moral reasons for pursuing a policy of nonrecognition. There was the hope that steady Chinese resistance would eventually cause Japan to tire and withdraw. There was the fear, in some quarters, that compulsion might bring a sudden political collapse within Japan, throwing the nation into the hands of the Communists and leaving the way open to Russian expansion into Manchuria. Most important, there was the well-

grounded opinion that attempts to coerce Japan might play into the hands of
Japanese militarists and destroy any influence of the moderate elements. But
beneath all such reasoning there was a profound emotion: a great fear of
becoming involved in another war, the same fear of war and the weapons
of war which had underlain the attempts to limit armaments and outlaw
war. Therefore, even when the failure of appeals to world opinion, when the
failure of diplomatic conciliation and protest by themselves, became obvious,
and though it became evident that America's very stand on the Nine Power
Treaty and the Kellogg Pact could not be supported by diplomatic protests
alone, the shapers of America's foreign relations were reluctant to face the
dreaded alternative of combining diplomacy with force or the threat of force.

The kind of dilemma which this aversion to force created for men of high
principle and intelligence is illustrated in the diary of Joseph C. Grew, the
American ambassador to Japan from 1932 through 1941.[33] Throughout his
ten years in Japan Grew was torn between contradictory conclusions. On
the one hand, he suspected that only force could restrain Japanese expansion;
but, on the other hand, he feared that force and even moral condemnation
would enable the militarists to gain support for new adventures. He repeatedly expressed the hope that a policy of nonintervention might bring a
moderate policy to the fore, but from time to time he was also moved to observe that the Japanese were incurably expansionist and could never be dissuaded from realizing their long-cherished ambition of hegemony in East
Asia.

Ambassador Grew struggled hard to reconcile his dim view of Japanese
motives with his abhorrence of force. Thus when Japan resigned from the
League in February, 1933, after the League-sponsored Lytton report had
called for the restoration of Manchuria to China, Grew wrote that he was
convinced that diplomatic pressure and the moral obloquy of the world had a
negligible effect upon the Japanese, except to strengthen their determination.
So he asked himself: If moral ostracism is ineffective, how else can the United
States implement the Kellogg Pact, the League Covenant, and all the other
peace machinery, upon which the sanctity and stability of treaties everywhere
depend?

> Certainly not by force of arms, which would be contrary to the very principle for
> which the Kellogg Pact stands. The great war to end wars has signally failed in that
> particular purpose. If other world wars are the only method of protecting our peace
> structure, then we had better abandon that structure here and now, because civilization
> itself will be in jeopardy.

He reasoned that severance of diplomatic relations, an arms embargo, or an
economic and financial boycott would probably be ineffective. So what was
left? The only solution that he could offer was the theoretical one of diag-

nosing and curing the disease of aggression before the disease materialized.[34]

Grew felt keenly the incongruity of the ambitious moral ends and the meager practical means of American Far Eastern policy. He perceived the ironic contradiction between these means and their probable consequence. In his diary entry on December 1, 1939, he tried to clarify his thoughts on this incongruity and contradiction. In shaping the course of the United States in the Far East, he theorized, the government should have in mind two distinct considerations: the principles of America's international policy—that is, respect for treaties and international morality—and a "sense of realism which takes cognizance of the existence of objective facts." According to principle, he believed that the United States was committed to uphold the Nine Power Treaty; and yet he foresaw that "nothing in international affairs can be more mathematically certain . . . than that Japan is not going to respect the territorial and administrative integrity of China, now or in the future, has not the slightest intention of doing so, and could be brought to do so only by complete defeat."

So here the nation was faced with the eternal problem of reconciling principle with realism. What should be done about it? Grew concluded that to compromise with principle was unthinkable. At the same time, he was more certain than ever that sanctions would lead to war, and he could not countenance running the risk of war except in defense of the nation's sovereignty.[35] This reasoning may have clarified the contradictions perplexing Mr. Grew, but it certainly did not resolve them, for now he had determined that he would not compromise on principles of international peace and morality, which he recognized could be attained only by war; and yet, equally for the sake of peace and morality, he would not approve the coercive measures necessary to defend those principles, because he believed that their defense did not justify the risk of war.*

Secretary of State Stimson perceived the same dilemma that troubled Ambassador Grew. Shortly after he had sent his famous letter to Senator Borah insisting on the maintenance of China's independence and integrity he wrote in his diary, "At present it seems to me that if Japan keeps up this attitude in which she now is, we are shaping up an issue between the two great theories

* After Prince Konoye, in a statement delivered in August, 1940, unequivocally defined Japan's New Order as including "Greater East Asia," Grew came to the conclusion that, because of the threat of this policy to American security, the United States ought to impose sanctions to back up its diplomacy, even at the risk of war, on the theory that this course involved less risk to American interests than a continuation of a course of laissez-faire. Yet he continued to believe that the United States could achieve its ends and still remain at peace with Japan; for, to the last, he placed his faith in the possible but improbable proposition that the United States could negotiate a settlement with Japan without sacrificing the principles of the Open Door. For Grew's cogent defense of his position, written from the perspective of 1951, see Walter Johnson, ed., Joseph C. Grew, *Turbulent Era* (Boston, 1952), II, chap. xxxiv.

of civilization and economic methods." Japan's determination to exploit China's markets by force would, in the long run, be frustrated by Chinese resistance. "But in the meanwhile, there will be presented a very sharp issue with our policy in the Pacific . . ." And Stimson prophesied, "During the course of that rivalry it is, in my opinion, almost impossible that there should not be an armed clash between two such different civilizations."[36]

Stimson shared Grew's intimations of the frightful consequences of America's rigid stand on the sanctity of treaties, and he was no more willing to compromise principles on that account; but, unlike Grew, he was, from the outbreak of the Manchurian Incident, quite willing to have the United States utilize political means of a strength commensurate with its ambitious ends—whether because he rated the effectiveness of coercion higher or the risk of war lower, or both, is not clear. Stimson never considered nonrecognition alone as an adequate means to support the goals of American policy, although from the perspective of 1947 he found his optimism about the efficacy of moral pressure appalling. He believed that public opinion could be made "one of the most potent sanctions of the world" if the people of the world had the will to make it effective; but he regarded nonrecognition as only a first step in that direction, and he argued—privately when in office and publicly when out of office—that America's position demanded the coercive power of embargoes or sanctions as well as the moral pressure of nonrecognition. From Stimson's point of view the chief limitations upon a more vigorous policy arose not from his own inhibitions about the use of force but rather from the deep-rooted inhibitions of the general public in America and the other democratic nations.[37]

In retrospect, it would seem that the prevailing current of public opinion was, in fact, the major limitation operating upon all American policy makers, upon those who were content to swim with the stream as well as upon those who wanted to swim against it or divert it into different channels.

10. POPULAR LIMITATIONS UPON POLICY

The limitations which the state of public opinion imposed upon American policy took immediate and tangible form in the person of President Hoover, who, with respect to the fundamentals of American foreign policy, was not only the official spokesman of the nation but also the actual spokesman for the views of the great mass of citizens. Like most of his countrymen, President Hoover combined a firm allegiance to the Open Door principle with a strong aversion to using force or political commitments to back it up, while he reconciled the disparity between ends and means with the wishful supposition that stubborn Chinese resistance and the moral pressure of world opinion would suffice to bring the aggressor to book. Above all, he was determined that the United States should make no political agreement that would commit it to a future course of action or to the use of force, for he was convinced that this would be the road to another world war; and he believed that nothing less than a direct threat to the liberty of the American people could justify the sacrifice of American lives. He formed these views soon after the eruption of the Manchurian crisis and never wavered from them thereafter.[38] Nor did the American people.

The American people, as a whole, were slow to pass judgment on Japan until she extended her military operations from Manchuria, where rights and responsibilities were obscure, to Shanghai and other parts of China, where the issue appeared to be aggression versus self-defense.[39] After January, 1932, America's traditional sympathy for China and her hatred of militarism and autocracy became increasingly important factors in the popular attitude toward Far Eastern policy. The public was generally enthusiastic about Stimson's nonrecognition note and his letter to Borah. The press, with the exception of some of the more isolationist papers, which detected warmongering and dangerous meddling, hailed these pronouncements as great acts of enlightened statesmanship in the tradition of John Hay's original proclamation of the Open Door doctrine.

However, the widespread applause for bold statements of principle did not indicate proportionate enthusiasm for bold action. It indicated moral indignation and a desire to assert America's moral leadership, but these sentiments developed quite apart from the fear of war, which dominated the nation's approach to the Far Eastern crisis. Thus many newspapers coupled condemnation of Japanese aggression with fervent pleas that the United States keep out of war no matter what Japan did. They did not want the United States to police the world, and they saw no reason to run the risk of losing American lives in order to save China from Japan. As one paper put it, "The American people don't give a hoot in a rain barrel who controls North China." Senator Borah, who was among the earliest to denounce Japan's action as a violation of international law, took the lead in opposing a boycott and all other forms of intervention in the Far Eastern dispute. The *Nation* and the *New Republic* both condemned the Japanese bombing of Shanghai and declared that this sort of thing would have to stop if peace were to be safeguarded, but they warned that America's interests did not justify shedding American blood. The mounting public indignation made them more concerned than ever about avoiding warlike measures. They advised withdrawing from China altogether.

It is true that almost from the outbreak of the Manchurian crisis there were always a few small but vocal groups calling for sanctions and embargoes. Perhaps the most influential of these was a group of academic men and publicists led by President Lowell of Harvard. Lowell became convinced by events in Manchuria and Shanghai that official protests and public opinion alone would not restrain the use of armed force; in fact, he believed that Stimson's nonrecognition policy, unsupported by action, was the policy most likely to result in war.[40] In a petition to President Hoover, delivered a few days before the release of Stimson's letter to Borah, he urged the government to signify to the League of Nations that the United States would concur in economic measures it might take to restore peace.[41] Within a week five thousand civic leaders from all parts of the country had signed petitions modeled on this one.[42]

Yet it is not likely that the advocates of coercion were any more aware of the troublesome matter of political consequences than the opponents of coercion. Both groups were largely politically irresponsible. Lowell understood better than most of his followers the danger of combining weak measures with a strong moral stand, but he said little if anything about the considerable dangers involved in coercion. He seemed to think that an economic boycott would quickly put an end to the Manchurian disturbance, and that that would be all there was to it.[43] This facile assumption played a great part in enabling the supporters of Lowell's position to reconcile their fear and abhorrence of armed force with their strong desire to uphold the sanctity of treaties and international morality. Thus among the most enthusiastic advocates of embargoes were the churches, peace organizations, and even pacifist-minded journals like the *Christian Century,* which were also the most vigilant wardens of America's determination to keep out of war.[44] The results of a poll taken among Protestant Church-members indicated that a great majority favored backing up nonrecognition with an embargo on loans and war supplies in co-operation with the League, but that an equal majority advocated withdrawing American warships and marines and endorsed the flat statement, "We should refuse to be drawn into war with Japan."[45]

This blind indifference toward the military and political consequences of a morally-inspired position was even more manifest when the original minority support of embargoes became a popular movement. As Japanese troops extended their conquests and Japanese planes rained death on helpless Chinese civilians, there emerged during 1939 and 1940 a strong movement for cutting off shipments of oil, scrap iron, and other materials indispensable to Japan's military machine. But this popular sentiment for embargoes was formed, in large part, without regard for the effect of embargoes on Japan's military actions or for America's ability to deal with such actions; and those who were concerned with these difficult considerations did precious little to inform the general public about them. At a time when the framers and executors of American policy were preoccupied with weighing a number of decisive considerations bearing directly upon American security—such as the strategic importance of the Dutch East Indies and the Malay Peninsula, the military and economic position of Japan, the probable effect of sanctions upon Japanese policy, the possibilities of negotiation, the relation of events in Asia to the security of the Atlantic, and the state of America's military preparedness—the government's public assertion and explanation of American policy was largely comprised in Secretary of State Hull's pious reiterations of general principles of international conduct.

With respect to the whole series of developments following the Manchurian Incident there is, of course, no assurance that American interests or ideals would have been better served even if the American public had been thoroughly alert to the complex ramifications of Far Eastern policy and thoroughly prepared to undertake the wisest diplomatic, economic, political, and military measures. It is quite possible that nothing the United States might have done could have prevented the power conflict between Japan and the United States from erupting into a military struggle before Germany was disposed of; and it is even possible that it was better for the United States to clash with Japan when it did. The point here is that a whole area of relevant calculations and actions in the realm of power politics, which might have enabled the nation to promote its fundamental ideals and self-interest more effectively in the long run, was virtually ruled out of consideration by the prevailing American approach to international relationships; that is, by a politically ignorant and irresponsible moral impulsiveness, a utopian view of the problem of mitigating international conflict, and a blind aversion to war and the instruments of war as absolute evils abstracted from the conflicts of power and national self-interest which lead to war.

There was no simple dichotomy of wise rulers and a naïve populace; for, in general, the official shapers of foreign policy, though better informed of the details of international relations, shared much the same attitudes toward world politics as the general public. Those who did not wholeheartedly share these attitudes might have enlightened the citizenry somewhat had they been less anxious to make their arguments conform to popular predispositions, but probably no amount of reasoning or persuasion could have substantially altered the fundamental limitations upon American Far Eastern policy imposed by the state of the public mind. For, in the last analysis, nothing but the argument of events could have led the American people to act upon a realistic appraisal of the complexities of reconciling ideals with national self-interest as long as the nation basked in its traditional assurance that events in the Far East had no vital bearing upon essential American interests. This assurance persisted until the concurrence of the fall of France with disastrous events in Asia convinced the mass of Americans that Japanese expansion was a threat to their own independence and territorial integrity as well as to China's. The folly of trying to make peace without a reasoned regard for considerations of national power and self-interest began to be apparent only when the fear of aggression became stronger than the fear of war.

CHAPTER XV

THE NEW ISOLATIONISM

1. What Made the New Isolationism "New"?

IN THE history of American foreign relations the 1930's stands out as the period in which isolationism reached its zenith. Certainly it was never a more lively issue. Never was isolationism more heatedly defended in practice or more vehemently denounced in name. Yet it would be a mistake to interpret the intensity of isolationist sentiment during these years as marking a fundamental change in America's attitude toward the outside world. Its basic motivation was the old desire to keep the political affairs of the United States as independent as possible from the affairs of other nations. Its basic premise was the old belief that America's most vital interests, the things worth fighting for, could not be destroyed by events beyond the seas.

The isolationism of the thirties was distinguished from the isolationism of other periods not by the number of its adherents but by the number of its opponents. Isolationism was more passionate and more vociferous because it was more controversial. More than at any time in previous American history, isolationists were forced to defend their fundamental premises in the forum of public opinion.

Of course, isolationism reached this state of controversy because of events, not just because of words. It became a crucial issue because the rapid acceleration of international conflict throughout the world reopened the whole question of America's relation to foreign quarrels less than twenty years after the war to end all wars. The juxtaposition of sudden anxiety over revolutionary new events with well-established attitudes toward past events wrought a tremendous disturbance in conventional patterns of thinking about America's relation to its international environment. In response to these new events the new isolationism took the form of a reassertion of antiwar sentiment, feeding upon the bitter memory of intervention in World War I. Disillusionment with Wilson's crusade pervaded isolationist thought and dominated isolationist arguments to such an extent that it became almost impossible to debate America's policy toward World War II without taking a position on intervention in World War I. Consequently, all the smoldering thoughts and emotions stirred up by World War I were like so much heat added to the fire of the new controversy, and all the events of World War II were reflected in the afterglow of the last conflagration.

In its antiwar sentiment the new isolationism had overwhelming popular support. A Gallup poll in April, 1937, disclosed that 64 per cent of those questioned regarded America's participation in World War I as a mistake. A poll published in November, 1939, found three principal causes given for intervention: 34 per cent believed that America had been the victim of propaganda and selfish interests, 26 per cent believed that America had had a just and unselfish cause; only 18 per cent thought that the nation had entered the war for her own safety.[1]

On the twentieth anniversary of America's entry into World War I, the Emergency Peace Campaign, a new coalition of peace advocates, launched its "No Foreign War Crusade" in a nation-wide radio broadcast. The names of the six Senators and fifty Representatives who had voted against war with Germany were entered in the *Congressional Record* with a solemn tribute. Eleven of the twenty-six survivors gathered at a private dinner in their honor and were later extolled by Congressmen at a special reception. George W. Norris, the only surviving dissenter in the Senate, was sought out for more newspaper interviews than at any other period in his public career. His colleagues, who had fiercely opposed him on the war question, did not begrudge him his public vindication.[2]

This was the nation's frame of mind as it anxiously watched the approach of a second Armageddon.

2. THE NYE COMMITTEE INVESTIGATION

One mark of the extent to which the experience of World War I impressed itself upon the American attitude toward international relations in the thirties was the fact that all the arguments against unneutrality and intervention which were made during 1914–17 were repeated during 1935 to 1941. However, some arguments received so much greater emphasis as to amount to altogether new arguments; and, of course, all arguments, new and old, were affirmations of the purported lesson of history that America's intervention in 1917 had been a disastrous mistake.

The most influential of the newly emphasized arguments held that wars are caused by war profiteers. This thesis gained great popularity as a result of the sensational activities of a special Senate committee established in 1934 to investigate the munitions industry. Although the committee was ostensibly concerned with developing regulatory procedures, under the chairmanship of the extreme isolationist Senator Gerald P. Nye it staged a series of command performances by bankers and armaments manufacturers, notably J. P. Morgan and the four Du Pont brothers, which were designed to prove that these "merchants of death" had inveigled the United States into World

War I. Long before the Nye Committee issued its final report a score of journalists, scholars, and politicians, with Nye himself in the vanguard, had broadcast this thesis throughout the land. They found a receptive audience.

This simple economic—or, more accurately, mercenary—interpretation of historical causation was especially popular among domestic reformers, who held financial corruption and predatory business practices responsible for the depression; but countless others with no particular animus toward free enterprise welcomed it as an explanation for an otherwise inexplicable war, as well as a convenient scapegoat for a sense of guilt over their own share in the bloodshed. In effect, Senator Nye's munitions investigation turned the revelations of revisionist scholars into a popular orthodoxy. It had a direct impact upon America's foreign relations in that it convinced many lawmakers that one of the best ways to avoid war was to legislate against economic entanglements; but, in a more general way, it drove the final nail in the coffin of Wilsonian idealism. As Charles Beard observed in 1939, with that strange fusion of scholarship and pamphleteering which he purveyed in these years,

By disclosing the secret methods and the economic backgrounds . . . of the Wilson regime, the Nye Committee injected realistic knowledge into the consideration of dynamic forces shaping foreign policies. Whatever the final verdict of that shadowy tribunal called 'history' might be, the popular idea of Wilson as the pure idealist who went to war for the sole purpose of saving democracy was shattered beyond repair. Could 'the universal philanthropy' of 'the great moral crusade' launched in 1917 ever again present the same aspects to that part of the public which sought knowledge and did any thinking?[3]

By implanting this sort of "realistic knowledge" in American thinking the Nye Committee probably provided the single most convincing argument in the whole arsenal of arguments that sustained the isolationism of the thirties.

3. The New Neutrality

With the outbreak of the Italo-Ethiopian crisis in May, 1935, there loomed the threat of a new world war, and the causes of American intervention in the last one assumed an immediate significance. America's answer to this threat was the so-called neutrality laws of 1935, 1936, and 1937, which were designed to prevent the nation from committing the mistakes which were presumed to have led it into World War I.

The influence of the Nye Committee was clearly reflected in the provisions prohibiting loans and the sale or transport of munitions to the belligerents. Congress was unwilling to go so far in preventing a repetition of 1917 as to embargo shipments of raw materials to the belligerents, but it did take the precaution of stipulating in the 1937 law that such commodities as the President should list would have to be paid for upon delivery and taken away from the United States in the buyer's ship; this "cash-and-carry" plan was limited to two years.

An even more remarkable deviation from the neutrality policies of 1914–17 was the deliberate renunciation of neutral rights in the name of neutrality through a provision in the 1935 law making travel on belligerent ships the citizen's own risk, and a provision in the 1937 law making such travel illegal.

In all these acts Congress, contrary to the wishes of Franklin Roosevelt and the State Department, denied the President the authority to discriminate against the aggressor nation.

As in 1914–17, the case for neutrality rested on the isolationist assumption that America's only vital interest in a foreign conflict was to keep out of it; but in the argument for the "New Neutrality," as it was called, this assumption was reinforced by the conviction that American intervention in 1917 had been an unmitigated tragedy, which could have been avoided if the Wilson administration had only taken a wiser legal stand. However, the big difference between American neutrality in the 1930's and during 1914–17 did not really lie in a greater respect for international law but in the fact that the American people, in order to keep out of war, were willing and even eager to surrender traditional legal rights, like the right to travel on belligerent ships, which they had entered a war to uphold, as a point of national honor, in 1917. As events actually developed, the new neutrality legislation did not keep America out of another war; but it did permit the nation to enter that war on grounds of national self-interest more fundamental and compelling than the defense of its honor and rights amid the vicissitudes of warfare on the high seas. And this made a tremendous difference in the evolution of America's attitude toward world politics, for it permitted the nation, as a whole, to understand for the first time the extent to which its security was involved in events across the seas.

4. THE NEW REVISIONISM

The resurgence of isolationist and neutrality sentiment after 1935 was both a cause and an effect of a new burst of historical revisionism, touched off by Walter Millis's highly readable *Road to War* (1935) and directed primarily at a reinterpretation of American intervention.

Millis's book profited greatly from the widespread interest in the sinister causes of war, which the Nye Committee stirred up. *Road to War* made much of the influence of foreign propaganda and America's economic ties with the Allies and relied heavily upon wit and sarcasm to depreciate idealistic considerations in American intervention. Nowhere did Millis commit himself to a clear explanation of why America had taken the road to war, but the lesson which he drew was clear enough to any reader atune to the times: the United States had gained nothing by entering the war; it could have stayed out of the war if it had been genuinely neutral.* If the reader could not perceive that this book was written with an eye to preventing the nation from repeating its blunder of 1917, the jacket blurb proclaimed an account of "the Frenzied Years of 1914–17 when . . . a peace-loving democracy, muddled but excited, misinformed and whipped to frenzy, embarked upon its greatest foreign war. . . . Read it and blush! Read it and beware! Read it and renew your youth!"

The blunders of 1914–17 received more technical treatment in such books as Professors Borchard's and Lage's *Neutrality for the United States* (1937). This book sprang from the conviction that the United States had been forced into the war through legal obtuseness and the distortion of true neutrality by moral judgments.

Some of Borchard's and Lage's legal criticisms were cogent. Those directed at the Wilson administration's policy toward armed merchantmen were virtually unanswerable. However, like the rest of revisionist literature, this scholarly work completely ignored the possible military consequences of nonintervention. In accordance with the overwhelming opinion of the time, the authors took it for granted that, since war was always a bad thing, America could have had nothing to gain from participating in the last one. From this assumption it was easy to draw the lesson: Keep out of all future wars. On the basis of this assumption Borchard and Lage trusted national policy to "an honest intention to remain aloof from foreign conflict, a refusal to be stampeded by unneutral propaganda, a knowledge of the law and a capacity to stand upon it, meeting emergencies and problems not romantically but wisely."[4]

Considering the tone and context of Millis's and Borchard's and Lage's scholarship, one can understand why postwar historical revisionism became heavy ammunition for isolationists when the outbreak of another European war revived the controversy over America's relations with foreign belligerents. More than a few historians acknowledged the relevance of their scholarship to the renewed debate by coming down from their ivory towers to take a personal part in the movement to stem the advance of what C. Hartley Grattan called "the deadly parallel."[5]

---

* In a more scholarly and little-known article published in the same year Millis examined the confused jumble of motives, conflicting economic and psychological influences, and innumerable variables and concluded, "The facts of the period from 1914 to 1917 are complex enough to support almost any theory of historical causation that may apply to them, at the same time they are obstinate enough to resist almost any theory of how the ultimate entanglement could have been prevented." Walter Millis, "Will We Stay Out of the Next War: How We Entered the Last One," *New Republic,* LXXXIII (July 31, 1935), 323–27.

5. Liberal Isolationism

Since the isolationism of the thirties drew so much of its inspiration from disillusionment with American intervention in 1917, it was natural that a great part of the original impetus behind the popular desire to remain aloof from the European and Asiatic conflicts should have arisen from the chief purveyors of disillusionment; that is, from the liberal and intellectual idealists, who were desperately anxious to depreciate idealistic motives for national action.

As disillusionment sprang from lofty aspirations and excessively tender consciences rather than from a cynical or narrowly egoistic spirit, so liberal isolationism reflected a kind of inverted idealism rather than a selfish nationalism or a mean and petty spirit. It was ironic that these gifted debunkers should have supplied the intellectual ammunition for the hard core of parochial isolationism and ultranationalism, with whom they had little in common besides a fear of war.

In their attitude toward Fascist aggression liberal isolationists were troubled by a characteristic ambivalence. On the one hand, they were shocked by a direct challenge to international peace and democracy incomparably greater than the Kaiser's Germany had ever imposed; but on the other hand, they were obsessed with the purpose of purging their minds of moral distinctions, for fear of deceiving themselves once more into violating their most sacred principles of reason, tolerance, and good will. They dared not burn themselves again by playing with idealistic fire, and yet they could not ignore the highly inflammable conduct of the rising totalitarian nations.

It was natural that liberal isolationists should have tried to escape this dilemma by minimizing the importance of moral distinctions in international affairs. Their consciences were indebted to their intellects for discovering that moral distinctions were always deceptive. This conclusion was seemingly confirmed by a wealth of debunking literature, which for a decade or more had subjected idealistic pretensions to sharp historical and sociological analysis, until an intelligent person felt a little ridiculous about forming absolute moral judgments concerning foreign nations—at least, if those judgments were the kind that might lead to another war. Strip the cloak of propaganda and ideology off international relations, and the assumption was that one would always find the same old familiar pattern of self-seeking diplomacy. One nation was as bad as another—or, at least, all were bad enough so as to preclude any practical distinctions among them.

When the editors of the *New Republic's* twenty-fifth anniversary number asked Stuart Chase what kind of America he hoped his grandchildren would enjoy in 1975, he replied that he would want them to live in a world of "ideological immunity," so that they might "think straight." In his view it was impossible to rationalize nations into ideological camps. Behind the ideological smoke there was always rampant nationalism. Chase wanted Americans to be tough-minded. An ideology, he said, was just an "emotional attachment to a noise." It seemed to him that the generation which could dissipate these verbal ghosts with the help of scientific analysis and semantics would have made such a tremendous advance that it could resolve the paradox of need amid plenty and banish war forever.[6]

Of course, Stuart Chase did not come near to achieving ideological immunity himself, as one can readily discover by reading his popular exposition of semantics, *The Tyranny of Words* (1936). Yet it was possible for idealists like Chase to acquire a kind of localized moral anesthesia in the area of international relations through a variety of attitudes and poses which tended to belittle the evils of fascism while magnifying America's own deficiencies and the deficiencies of the democratic nations.

Liberal isolationists leaned over backward to be fair and objective and broad-minded about Hitler's progressive modification of the map of Europe. They would not be swayed by the superficial appearance of things. Instead they would approach the matter in the light of historical perspective and their knowledge of the economic and psychological causes of international maladjustment. Thus many liberals found themselves agreeing with Hitler that Germany's rearmament, her reoccupation of the Rhineland, and the annexation of Austria were justifiable responses to the injustice of the Versailles settlement. They explained Fascist excesses as the consequence of the reactionary, shortsighted, and selfish diplomacy of the world war victors. They saw the aggressiveness of the Rome-Berlin Axis as a manifestation of the natural acquisitiveness of "have-not" nations, pressing against the iniquitous status quo preserved by the "have" nations. All nations were presumed to go through this stage. The British and the French had simply gone through their expansionist phase at an earlier period in history; they deserved no moral commendation for being the first to satiate themselves on the fruits of empire.

It is, perhaps, characteristic of moral perfectionists to lose all perspective about the object of their disillusionment. Certainly, it was a common tendency of the disenchanted liberals of the thirties to distort their moral perceptions beyond all reason by concentrating upon the defects of the democratic powers and dwelling upon the evils of the past, while seeking extenuating circumstances for Fascist conduct and minimizing the present danger. Thus Harry Elmer Barnes, writing in 1939, was so militantly disillusioned that he condemned Woodrow Wilson as the foremost autocrat in the world, compared with whom the Kaiser was but a "timid and retiring old gentleman." As for the present apportionment of guilt, Barnes thought that Great Britain was ruled by an arrogant, selfish group "even less interested in humanity and social justice than the Fascist leaders." At another time in 1939 he wrote, "There are not a few who prefer the forthright brutality and aggression of a Hitler to the smug double-crossing and sanctimonious hypocrisy of Britain's umbrella bearer."[7]

The conscience-striken liberal was often spared the necessity of making war-provoking moral judgments by the subtlety of his intellect, which permitted him to look beyond the external manifestations of military power to discern the complex realities of underlying "forces." In accordance with this kind of insight, the danger of fascism in literal terms of military aggression was dismissed as a superficial approach to the real danger of social and economic maladjustment, which had, presumably, caused the rise of fascism in the first place. One could not check Fascist aggression except by dealing with its fundamental causes. Thus Kirby Page, one of the more prolific disillusionist writers, declared, "It would be a fatal mistake to assume that Hitler and Mussolini are the most ominous threats to world peace and that our primary task is to overthrow these dictators. Far more are they products than causes."[8] By this reasoning the defects of democracy seemed to excuse the evils of fascism, since the democracies, the "have" powers, could not escape their responsibility for having contributed to the kind of environment which brought forth Fascist excesses.

On the assumption that the historical causes of Hitler and Mussolini were more important than Hitler and Mussolini themselves, some held that the problem of fascism could be met only by alleviating the internal tensions and the inequities of the status quo which impaired the international environment; but since, as a practical matter, there seemed to be little chance of international reform in the thirties, liberals could console themselves with the thought that they were combating world-wide fascism by perfecting democracy at home.

The comforting theory that domestic reform was a substitute for diplomacy gained credence through the findings of a school of liberal thought preoccupied with the domestic economic sources of foreign policy. Thus Stuart Chase argued that the policy of pushing American trade had caused American intervention in 1917, which, in turn, had caused economic dislocation and the postponement of domestic reform; and he concluded from this argument that by remaining relatively self-sufficient and refraining from blindly pushing exports the United States could avoid unnecessary entanglement in international affairs and concentrate on solving its many social and economic problems at home.[9] The implication of this line of reasoning was that by concentrating upon the solution of domestic problems Americans could avoid the toils of power politics.

Another propounder of this thesis was one of America's most renowned political scientists and historians, Charles A. Beard. Even after World War II had ended and isolationism had virtually lost its claim to intellectual respectability, Beard continued to spell out in great detail and with impressive scholarship his belief that the real motives for America's intervention in world politics stemmed more from domestic sources than from what went on outside the borders of the United States.

Beard had been an enthusiastic interventionist in 1917 and a strong advocate of Wilsonian internationalism throughout the war. He had held that American isolation was an illusion, already outmoded by the great multiplication of the nation's material and moral ties with the rest of the world. Yet in the 1930's he established himself as the champion of "continentalism" and one of the most persuasive opponents of Wilsonian internationalism.[10]

As early as 1934 Beard was devising a new conception of national interest, one more in accord with domestic social and economic progress than with what he regarded as the conventional pattern of expanding international trade, large naval expenditures, and foreign adventures. When he wrote *The Idea of National Interest* (1934) he thought he detected the fragments of this new conception in Franklin Roosevelt's policies and measures, the central idea of which he stated in the following manner: "By domestic planning and control the American economic machine may be kept running at a high tempo supplying the intranational market without relying primarily upon foreign outlets for 'surpluses' of goods and capital."[11]

In *The Open Door at Home* (1934) Beard presented a fuller statement of his evolving philosophy of national interest. The chief animus of his analysis was toward internationalism, which he saw as a program of escape from economic crisis, rationalized in terms of muddle-headed philanthropism. Reflecting upon the causes of American intervention in World War I, he reached the conclusion that the probability of the United States becoming involved in another war varied in direct proportion to the foreign economic interests possessed by American nationals. In his opinion public control of foreign trade and a limited exchange of goods would eliminate a powerful incentive for going to war. His own program of national interest looked toward a comprehensive planning and control of national resources, skills, foreign trade, and financial transactions in order to create a stable and productive economy, instead of relying upon "wasteful, quixotic, and ineffectual extension of interests beyond the reach of competent military and naval defense."[12]

In *The Devil Theory of War* (1936) Beard showed himself very much impressed by the Nye Committee's revelations. He rejected the notion that the Committee's findings proved what caused the war, but he did reach the conclusion that they pointed out the economic pressures which made war possible.

In *America in Midpassage* (1939), the third volume of his monumental history *The Rise of American Civilization,* written jointly with his wife, Beard spent over twenty pages elaborating "the economic interests, pressures, stresses, and strains amid which the diplomacy of the Wilson administration was waged and its foreign policies were formulated" and left the reader with the unavoidable impression that, if these pressures were not the only cause of American intervention, they were at least one cause without which there would probably have been no war.[13]

In this same work Beard further expounded the doctrine of continentalism, as opposed to collective internationalism. He represented the policy of the League of Nations and collective security as the mere rationalization of a "world image," which envisaged the unification of all nations according to Victorian free-trade standards as a means of relieving the strains of the domestic economy and doing good deeds abroad. He asserted that the continentalists, whom he was careful to distinguish from isolationists, were more realistic, since they understood that the inefficient distribution of wealth at home was the primary force in the rivalry of nations and since they eschewed middle-class evangelistic efforts to denationalize the world and abolish surpluses through free trade. Continentalists, said Beard, did not repudiate international co-operation.

> What they objected to was lecturing other nations, constantly stirring up, in effect, warlike emotions, and using the power of the United States to force any scheme of politics or economy on other peoples. They especially opposed, as distracting and dangerous to domestic life, the propagation of the idea that any mere foreign policy could in any material respect reduce the amount of degrading poverty in the United States, set American economy in full motion, or substantially add to the well-being of the American people. Foreign policy, they held, could easily be made the instrument to stifle domestic wrongs under a blanket of militarist chauvinism, perhaps disguised by the high-sounding title of world peace.[14]

Considering the strength of Beard's preconceived notions about the motives of internationalists, it is not strange that he was unable to discern in the mounting European conflict any moral or material reason for the United States to be interested in the outcome. He believed that the United States was geographically impregnable and economically virtually self-sufficient; and, as far as he could tell, one belligerent was on about the same moral level as another. He was convinced that those who thought that the United States had a vital interest in the foreign quarrel were either the victims of mis-guided philanthropism or the tools of economic self-interest.[15] Thus he neatly fitted his antagonists into his ingenious, self-contained pattern of analysis and avoided the painful task of judging events by their external appearance or accepting the motives of those with whom he disagreed at face value.

In his isolationist tract *Giddy Minds and Foreign Quarrels* (1939) Beard implied that President Roosevelt's shift from a concentration upon domestic affairs to a concentration upon foreign affairs was a result of his failure to solve America's economic crisis by purely national means. He represented Roosevelt's desire to quarantine aggressors as a policy of reforming Europe and Asia, forcing upon alien peoples, whose circumstances the United States was powerless to modify, a utopian formula for permanent economic welfare. Having devised this image of Roosevelt's foreign policy, Beard easily disposed of it as quixotic and based upon false notions of the national interest.

In *A Foreign Policy for America* (1940) Beard elaborated upon his doctrine of continentalism and, undistracted by the superficial appearance of a German sweep across the continent of Europe, focused his intellect upon the under-lying economic motives of those who claimed that events abroad vitally con-cerned the United States. He concluded that interventionists who wanted to modify the neutrality laws to help the Allies were moved by the same deluded internationalism that had impelled Wilson's crusade. Fortunately, the world image of the great mass of Americans was less subtle than Charles Beard's image of Americans.

One powerful factor in the preoccupation of liberal isolationists like Beard with domestic reform and the shortcomings of democracy was the pessimistic belief, born, in part, of the bitter memory of wartime repression of civil liberties, that American democracy would inevitably perish by its own sword if it undertook another war. It was thought that war, preparedness for war, or, in the extreme view, even the anticipation of war, would arouse base passions of fear and hatred, which would undermine the fine structure of liberal and humane values sheltering the frail institutions of free men. This self-conscious reasoning tended to distract attention from the obvious military developments taking place outside the United States.

George Soule, an editor of the *New Republic,* writing in 1939, explained America's military preparedness program as a response to "a subjective need to find an outlet for our frustrated aggression." In his mind aggression was subjective, not objective; the peril was internal, not external.

If we let loose our whole energy in hating the foreign enemy and preparing to defeat him on the field of battle, we shall overlook the more subtle but equally real danger of becoming like him ourselves. We shall fail to take the necessary steps at home to preserve and fulfil the democracy we are so eager to fight for. It is easier to be willing to die for a cause than to understand it and to live well for it.

Defense against totalitarian enemies merely by hating or fighting them is a regressive process; it is a concealed imitation of the enemy. Here lies the real peril.[16]

According to this same theory, John Dos Passos, as late as September, 1940, drew the following lesson from the fall of France: "The danger that threatens us most is not from across the Atlantic; it is the danger that comes from poor thinking and incomplete organization at home."[17]

Some idealists went so far as to agree with Norman Thomas that America would not only sacrifice its social and economic progress and its civil liberties by going to war but that it would probably turn into an imperialist power and succumb to a conscious or subconscious imitation of Fascist success.[18]

Oswald Garrison Villard combined a fear that America would inevitably lose her democracy in war with a stubborn conviction that force could never accomplish anything and that war would always hurt the victors as much as the vanquished. This was obviously a difficult position for a man so deeply dedicated to the democratic principles threatened by world fascism. The British and French capitulation to Hitler at Munich was a profound shock to Villard. His first reaction was to denounce Prime Minister Chamberlain for consenting to the dismemberment of Czechoslovakia. He held that the European democracies should have stood together and refused to bow to Hitler's will. But did he mean that France and Great Britain should have been prepared to use force? Did he think that they were better able to preserve their democracy in a war than the United States? Villard stopped short of embracing this paradox. He hastily added, "I am as resolute against war as I ever was."[19] Later he sadly submitted to the logic of his underlying premise:

I never dreamed that I could feel so badly about a bad peace as I do about the settlement of Munich. But now it has come back to me that like all other pacifists I have repeatedly said that those who believe that war must be avoided at all costs must be prepared to suffer grievous injustice and wrong. . . . The Czechs have obeyed the Biblical injunction, "Resist not evil," and they are paying the price.[20]

In his fear of force and his sense of democracy's guilt and weakness Villard was closer to Chamberlain than he suspected.

Perhaps the only convincing answer to the self-conscious doubts that paralyzed an important section of liberal opinion in the face of an unprecedented threat to the ideals they cherished was the one Theodore Roosevelt had given in 1915 in reply to a request that he address the American Sociological Congress on "the effect of war and militarism on social values." The most important thing to remember, he had written to the Congress, was that "if an unscrupulous, warlike, and militaristic nation is not held in check by the warlike ability of a neighboring nonmilitaristic and well-behaved nation, then the latter will be spared the necessity of dealing with its own 'moral and social values' because it won't be allowed to deal with anything."[21] But it was a characteristic of liberal isolationists—indeed of all isolationists—that they refused to believe that the United States was seriously endangered by the course of the European or Asian conflict.

Norman Thomas charged that the warnings about America's insecurity, voiced by President Franklin Roosevelt and others, were an hysterical attempt "to evade the certain and tragic consequences of our entry into this war by concentrating attention on the less certain dangers to us of a Hitler victory."[22]

Stuart Chase wrote that, even if England, France, and Russia were wiped out, the United States would be in no danger from foreign aggression. He didn't bother to analyze this hypothesis. "I apologize for wasting your time in this discussion," he wrote. "It would make an admirable topic for debate in an insane asylum." Chase approved an adequate defense for staving off an invasion, but he would not spend one dollar for any other military purpose. "Our task, so far as one can scan the future today, is to hold the new western front."[23]

Charles Beard based his foreign policy on the assumption that America's security would be threatened only by an actual attack upon the continental United States.[24] In *Giddy Minds and Foreign Quarrels* (1939) he said that only one circumstance would make foreign affairs of any vital concern to the United States: "Not until some formidable European power comes into the western Atlantic, breathing the fire of aggression and conquest, need the United States become alarmed about the ups and downs of European conflicts, intrigues, aggressions, and wars."[25] While Beard continued to maintain that he was advocating George Washington's policy of promoting the defensive security of the United States, as opposed to the quixotic attempt of the World Imagists to right the wrongs of Europe, he consistently failed to detect any threat to American security in the course of events beyond America's continental borders.

Oswald Garrison Villard believed that the United States could safely disarm, since it was beyond danger of attack through the air, on the surface of the water, or below it.[26] The outbreak of war in Europe failed to change this estimate. Writing from London in September, 1939, he assured his readers that there was no need for an increase of American arms. "Actually, from the purely military point of view the security of the United States has been increased by the outbreak of war. And the longer war continues, the safer the

United States will be, if it ever was in danger. For with each day the exhaustion of the contestants will become greater."[27]

In *Our Military Chaos* (1939) Villard proved to his own satisfaction that the United States was absolutely secure from a military standpoint because she was impregnable from attack by either Germany or Japan. He devoted a special chapter to the bogy of a Japanese invasion, in which he declared, "Of all the defense impostures and delusions the worst is that a war with Japan is physically possible."[28]

After his return from Europe in January, 1940, he expressed the opinion that the United States was more impregnable than ever: "Even if Hitler should win this war, Europe would be prostrate for years, and a victorious Hitler would be surrounded by enemies who would welcome his getting embroiled in a war with the United States."[29]

6. THE FORTRESS CONCEPT

The same assumption of American impregnability underlay the position of all those who believed that the most important objective of American foreign policy was to avoid the risk of becoming a participant in a foreign conflict, whether or not they arrived at this belief through liberal premises.

Among isolationists and noninterventionists during the period preceding World War II the fortress concept of American strategy was an explicit, not merely an implicit assumption; for by the nature of the arguments opposing them these groups were forced to spell out their view of the effect of international military and political developments upon the nation's security. This was a very significant circumstance, for it meant that the debate over a series of crucial issues, such as the revision of the embargo on munitions and the passage of the Lend-Lease Act, turned, in large part, upon a controversy over national expediency which events in Europe and Asia clearly decided in favor of the interventionists and internationalists.

The assumption that the United States was an impregnable fortress protected by two gigantic moats was particularly evident in the thinking of conservative isolationists, for these men did not feel called upon to garnish their appeals to national egoism with quite so many broadly idealistic professions. It was not the welfare of humanity or social and economic reform that excited their urge to keep America isolated but rather a desire to continue business as usual under a thriving free enterprise system and a nationalistic urge to keep America's independent will untrammeled by the will of other nations. Therefore, they found it intellectually and temperamentally more congenial to frame their arguments in terms of unadorned national expediency.

The more responsible conservative opponents of the foreign policy of the Roosevelt administration, such as former President Hoover and Senators Taft and Vandenburg, as well as the ultranationalist and Anglophobic type of isolationist, manifested a deep-seated emotional bias against involving America's independent destiny in the toils of European politics. This emotional bias was reflected in a constant stress upon freedom of national action, as though that were a state of affairs subject to choice, which Americans might readily achieve if they would only get back to the good old patriotic virtues. Yet these men did not frame their arguments in terms of sheer xenophobia; to a large extent they argued in terms of national self-interest; so that, as far as logic was concerned, their opposition to administration policy seemed to be based largely on a divergent conception of America's strategic interests.

Conservative isolationists represented themselves as the practical, hard-headed advocates of America's cold self-interest, as opposed to the muddle-headed romanticists and international do-gooders, who were said to be driven by a messianic desire to practice social and economic reform on faraway peoples and save the world for democracy all over again. They naturally found that the most practical, hard-headed object they could advocate was America's own security, which they spoke of as the liberty of the American people. However, they were confident that this object was assured by natural geographical advantages, if only Americans would keep out of foreign entanglements by confining their efforts to the good of America first and by concentrating upon developing the nation's superior economic system.

These men were willing to send a certain amount of material aid to the forces fighting fascism, just in order to demonstrate America's ideological affinity with France and Great Britain and the general correspondence of her interests with the interests of all democracies; but they were unwilling to support the transfer of destroyers, the occupation of Iceland, lend-lease, or other measures which carried too great a risk of involving America in war; and if, by some chance, America's security were jeopardized, then they thought that the United States had best keep its valuable resources for its own independent use instead of lavishing them on a lost cause.

The crux of this view, as its proponents repeatedly stated, was the belief that the nation's self-preservation depended solely upon its own defensive power protecting the Western Hemisphere and not upon the British Navy or the balance of power on the continent of Europe. Consequently, even if Europe fell to Hitler and the British Navy were captured or destroyed, which was held unlikely, the presumption was that America could survive, walled off from the world in her impregnable continental fortress.

Thus Herbert Hoover, arguing against President Roosevelt's decision to convoy lend-lease shipments between the United States and Iceland, urged the nation to face the hard facts and realize that it would be folly to aid Great Britain at the price of American intervention. He reasoned that the nation was unprepared, militarily or psychologically, for a war, and he pointed out that if Britain fell and the United States were in the war, American boys might be saddled with the impossible task of invading Nazi-controlled Europe three thousand miles away. In addition to these practical difficulties of waging war there was, of course, the bloodshed, the loss of liberty, bankruptcy, and increased government control that invariably accompanied total war.

But were not all these disadvantages and horrors preferable to the consequences of a Nazi victory? Hoover did not confront the alternative directly, but his answer was contained in the basic assumption of his whole policy: "The potential might of this nation is the strongest thing in this whole world. . . . That strength is always here in America. The defense of the United States is not dependent upon any other nation. America cannot be defeated."[30] As he said on another occasion, the Western Hemisphere was protected by a "moat of three thousand miles of ocean on the east and six thousand miles on the west," which constituted a virtually insurmountable military barrier.[31]

Senator Taft's arguments against Roosevelt's foreign policy were based on this same strategic outlook. Thus, in condemning the President's decision to send troops to Iceland without Congressional approval, Taft explained that he detested Hitler and wanted to extend aid to England in every manner short of war but that he found himself unalterably opposed to any Presidential attempt to arrogate Congressional authority to intervene in the war by military or naval action. Not only was this unconstitutional, in his view, but as a matter of national policy it was disastrous; for if Americans allowed their emotions and sympathies to draw the United States into the European war, they would be involved in that war "year after year"; and even if Hitler were finally crushed, the United States would be faced with the task of policing Europe and maintaining the balance of power for years to come. Therefore, the United States should content itself with sending "countless airplanes" to the British in the hope that they might at least secure a negotiated peace, "better than England could now secure, but probably with a Hitler dominant on the Continent."

But what if Hitler gained control of the whole Atlantic Community? Would not the United States eventually have to restore the balance of power for its own security? And if so, wasn't it better to defend the lifeline to England, even at the risk of war, while England still stood? Senator Taft's answer was, evidently, "No." His reason was the same as Hoover's.

> I believe that the peace and happiness of the people of this country can best be secured by refusing to intervene in war outside of the Americas, and by establishing our defense line based on the Atlantic and Pacific oceans. I believe that the difficulty of attacking America across those oceans will forever prevent any such attack being even considered, if we maintain an adequate defense on the sea and in the air. I believe that air power has made it more difficult, not easier, to transport an army across an ocean, and that conquest must still be by a land army.[32]

The fortress concept appeared throughout isolationist literature and speeches. It was a major tenet of the America First Committee, which became the leading isolationist organization in the fall of 1940. Thus General Robert E. Wood, the chairman of this organization, argued that, no matter what befell England or the Continent of Europe, the United States could survive by building up its defenses and guarding a line running from Greenland to Trinidad and, possibly, down to a base in Brazil, which would present an impregnable front to an invader.[33]

Charles A. Lindbergh, a leading speaker at America First rallies, repeatedly declared that the United States could not possibly win a war against Germany in Europe and that every disadvantage America would have in invading Europe would make a European invasion of America impossible. Why, he asked, should America entangle her destiny with European ambition, rivalry, and caprice when she could build an impregnable military and commercial position within her own continental bastion?[34] As late as 1941 he was expressing the view that the United States was in no danger as long as it did not waste its planes and equipment on the doomed British.

No matter what other arguments isolationists might employ, no matter what their underlying motives might be, their whole position rested upon a basic assumption about American security, which became quite explicit and increasingly the focus of public attention as the balance of power in Europe shifted toward the Axis powers. This circumstance was simply a reflection of the crucial importance of considerations of national expediency in the formation of public opinion toward the European war. It was a significant contrast with the course of debate in 1914–17, not only because of its immediate consequences for the program of aid to America's Atlantic partner but also because of its long-run implications for America's attitude toward world politics.

CHAPTER XVI

THE NEW REALISM

I. REINHOLD NIEBUHR

THE elements of a new political realism in America's outlook upon its international environment began to appear even before the pressure of international events aroused the nation's instinct for survival. In the 1930's, as at the turn of the century, the increasingly overt manifestations of conflict in international society, the disintegration of old patterns of conduct and the emergence of new patterns, began to impress sensitive minds with the importance of power in human relations. This impression was reinforced by a similar process of conflict and disintegration in domestic society, following upon the heels of the depression.

One barometer of the changing outlook was the writings of Reinhold Niebuhr, one of America's most distinguished Protestant leaders and a seminal thinker in the philosophy of human relations. As a young clergyman Niebuhr, like many utopian idealists, had seen the shattering of Wilson's new world order as a failure of liberalism itself. The fatal defect of liberalism, he wrote in June, 1919, had been its "gray spirit of compromise." It had not been sufficiently fanatical to move the world out of its beaten track. Niebuhr drew the lesson which Harold Stearns proclaimed: When liberalism compromises with the old order, the old order invariably wins. He concluded, "We need something less circumspect than liberalism to save the world."[1]

In the 1920's Niebuhr was thoroughly disillusioned with crusades for democracy and the ways of peacemakers; he was painfully conscious of the pretense and self-deception which had afflicted wartime idealism. In 1923 he wrote,

Gradually the whole horrible truth about the war is being revealed. Every new book destroys some further illusion. How can we ever again believe anything when we compare the solemn pretensions of statesmen with the cynically conceived secret treaties? Here was simply a tremendous contest for power between two great alliances of states in which the caprice of statesmen combined with basic economic conflicts to dictate the peculiar form of the alliances.[2]

At this time the chief conclusion Niebuhr drew from his disillusionment was the one he expressed in his diary after his return from a trip through Europe: "This is as good a time as any to make up my mind that I am done with the war business. . . . I hope I can make that resolution stick."[3] However, by 1932 he had progressed beyond a simple attitude of renunciation and was groping for a constructive philosophy of human society, based upon a realistic insight into both class conflict and national conflict. In *Moral Man and Immoral Society* (1932) he displayed a new disposition to accept as a permanent condition of mankind the limitations upon morality and the persistence of power in group relations. The trouble with moralists, he now believed, was not their willingness to compromise with perfection but their inability to recognize the prevalence of imperfection, imposed by the stubborn resistance of group egoism to moral and rational suasion.

> They regard social conflict either as an impossible method of achieving morally approved ends or as a momentary expedient which a more perfect education or a purer religion will make unnecessary. They do not see that the limitations of the human imagination, the easy subservience of reason to prejudice and passion, and the consequent persistence of irrational egoism, particularly in group behavior, make social conflict an inevitability in human history, probably to its very end.[4]

Niebuhr now saw the hypocrisy of idealists as the inevitable attribute of all collective activity, springing from the inability of the human spirit to make its collective life conform to its individual ideals. Now he looked upon force as something idealists should recognize as a permanent feature of society. "The limitations of the human mind and imagination, the inability of human beings to transcend their own interests sufficiently to envisage the interests of their fellowmen as they do their own makes force an inevitable part of the process of social cohesion."[5]

The implication Niebuhr drew from this perception was not that idealism was futile but that idealism enmeshed in the illusions and sentimentalities of the Age of Reason was incapable of coping with the mounting injustices and brutality of man's increasingly interdependent collective life, both within and among nations. Reason and love were inadequate by themselves to resist injustice. Social justice could never be achieved unless men used power to combat group egoism. The role of conscience and reason in the tortuous process of trying to salvage universal ideals from group egoism was only to qualify and mitigate, not to abolish, the inevitable power struggle among human collectives.

As the disintegration of international society continued unabated, Niebuhr became preoccupied with the perplexing fusion of universal ideals and self-interest in national behavior. Every nation, he observed, pursues its own power and prestige in competition with other nations, but, at the same time, every nation claims that its primary loyalty is to universal values. He concluded that the claim to idealism was not necessarily wholly spurious, but that no nation could be truly altruistic. "No nation is ever true to the cause which transcends its national life," he wrote, "if there is not some coincidence between the defensive necessities of that cause and the defensive requirements of the national organism."[6]

In *Christianity and Power Politics* (1940) Niebuhr directed his realistic critique at Christian pacifism, charging that the kind of moral paralysis purveyed in the name of moral purity by such advocates of neutrality and pacifism as the *Christian Century* amounted to a sentimentalized distortion of the profoundest Christian insight, the doctrine of original sin, which avers an irreducible minimum of egoism in all human behavior. The judgment of foreign affairs, he asserted, was being clouded by moral absolutists, who measured political realities according to purely ideal possibilities and, consequently, created an attitude of irresponsibility and cynicism in estimating the present danger. He delivered this harsh indictment of his Church:

> The Christian Church of America has never been upon a lower level of spiritual insight and moral sensitivity than in this tragic age of world conflict. . . . If modern churches were to symbolize their true faith they would take the crucifix from their altars and substitute the three little monkeys who counsel men to "speak no evil, hear no evil, see no evil."[7]

2. The Revival of Moral Fiber

Niebuhr's realistic critique of liberal idealists, and of Christian pacifists in particular, was just one manifestation of a general movement in America to revive the nerve and restore the determination of idealists in the face of an unprecedented world-wide challenge to democratic and humane principles. It is important to understand that these new Realists were moved, not by a self-assertive egoism or by cynicism, but by a desperate awareness of the unpleasant conditions imposed upon the pursuit of traditional ideals. Unlike the disillusionists, the new Realists were not motivated by a guilt-laden desire to repudiate embarrassing moral distinctions and soothe tender consciences for alleged misdeeds. They were inspired, rather, by an urgent desire to stiffen the nation's moral fiber and strengthen the popular will to resist power with power in order that the cherished values of the American mission might be preserved.

Because the Fascist challenge to the values of freedom and brotherhood was, pre-eminently, a challenge of sheer force, the liberal revival of the thirties took the form of a reaction from utopianism and a discovery of the importance of power in international relations. The revival was, in fact, a kind of disillusionment with disillusion. Liberal revisionists charged that the exaggerated expectations of moral perfectionists had subjected the nation to a wave of cynicism, self-doubt, and moral apathy, which rendered men of good will incapable of coping with the hard facts of the real world. Therefore, they sought to purge liberalism of its utopian proclivities and inject it with a more realistic view of the persistence of self-interest and power in all group relations. As one writer paradoxically put it, they sought the "deflation of American ideals."[8]

Some of the earliest efforts to restore America's idealistic energy were in the nature of moral exhortations; but these exhortations were markedly distinguished from those of twenty years before by their frank recognition of the imperatives of power in international relations and the exigencies of sheer defensive national self-interest. This distinction grew apace with the mounting urgency of democratic survival.

One of the earliest and most persuasive tough-minded reaffirmations of ideals in American foreign policy was the much-discussed *We or They* (1937), written by Hamilton Fish Armstrong, editor of the magazine *Foreign Affairs*. The crux of Armstrong's thesis was that the authoritarian and liberal systems of life were basically irreconcilable and that America's welfare was fatally dependent upon the welfare of the other democracies. With great vigor and earnestness he expounded the moral and cultural gulf between the free nations and the Fascist nations. He doubted whether these two groups could indefinitely survive on a live-and-let-live basis.

However, Armstrong was not satisfied with the simple assertion, heard so often during 1914–17, that virtue could never tolerate evil. He was keenly aware that the peril of autocracy was pre-eminently the peril of military and economic force, threatening not only democratic ideals but the democratic nations themselves. He saw Fascist aggression as a problem in power politics, not just a moral issue. Accordingly, he believed that the answer to the Fascist threat was neither a holy war nor a passive reliance upon moral pronouncements. Instead, he called for the maintenance of routine diplomatic relations and, at the same time, a general mobilization—economic and military, as well as moral—against the dictatorships. He was reluctant to anticipate the ultimate resort to war; he hoped that this evil eventuality might be postponed and, ultimately, avoided by the development of hostilities among the Fascist nations. However, he was ready to face one dreadful conclusion which the disillusionists were determined to escape: "Our fathers won their liberties by force, in three centuries of struggle. Programs of action to take these liberties away by force give notice that we must be ready at some point to reply in kind."[9]

Lewis Mumford, writer and lecturer, proclaimed the we-or-they theme with equal moral fervor but directed his exhortations more pointedly toward fellow liberals who, like himself, had fallen under the spell of Randolph Bourne's romantic defeatism. In the spring of 1938 he chose the pages of the *New Republic* to deliver a blast at liberal passivism, which reverberated throughout the liberal domain for months afterward.[10] He charged the editors of the *New Republic* with maintaining a disastrous state of apathy and wishful thinking toward the threat of fascism and declared that "the ultimate treason of the intellectual is to place his credulous wishes above fact and truth, merely because the facts are repugnant, or because the situation they point to cannot be changed without heroic action." Like Niebuhr, he found the trouble with liberalism in its inability or unwillingness to confront evil head-on and accept coercion as an alternative to conversion.[11] Fascism, he declared, was "codified and co-ordinated barbarism." Only a militant democracy could cope with the challenge of fascism. As a practical means of coping with it Mumford recommended economic and political nonintercourse with Germany, Italy, and Japan, and the expansion of the Navy.

However, Mumford did not base his case for militant democracy on moral and ideological grounds alone. He made it clear that Americans should be concerned with the cancerous expansion of fascism, not because they wanted to save the world but because they wanted to save themselves. He merely hoped that, in the end, saving America might also prove to be Europe's salvation. In his mind, the world-wide threat of fascism was the threat of external power. It could not be checked by internal reform alone. Ultimately, it could be checked only by the sole means the Fascists recognized as valid: superior military strength, backed by a more concentrated moral purpose.

In *Men Must Act* (1939) Mumford expanded upon these ideas. In much the same manner as Armstrong, he pictured the survival of free states and the self-aggrandizement of Fascist states as fundamentally irreconcilable.

> In short: there is now no conceivable limit to Fascist aggression until the world is made over in the Fascist image. For the only security of fascism against the ever-rising, ever-recurrent forces of civilization is to reduce mankind as a whole to its own state of barbarism. In the face of this fact a policy of wishful waiting on the part of democracies is a policy of submission. To arrive at a peaceful adjustment of this kind of conflict is impossible; the best one can hope for is the stalemate of armed hostility, continued in existence until the weaker side disintegrates.[12]

Mumford was somewhat vague about the exact nature of the Fascist menace to the United States. He repudiated the notion of military invasion but seemed to fear internal subversion and disintegration and the threat of air attack. However, he left no doubt about his belief that the very survival of American democracy was at stake and that the single aim of American policy should be to make the United States impregnable to fascism.

An equally urgent plea for a democracy with spine and nerve enough to survive was delivered by Max Lerner under a title which quickly became a popular slogan, *It is Later Than You Think* (1938). Lerner's thesis was that democratic power was necessary to combat nondemocratic power. Liberalism, he declared, had to become more than broad-mindedness; it had to become confident and aggressive; it had to seize the instruments of power, realizing that power was neither good nor bad in itself but that it could be used to achieve socially acceptable goals without corrupting the user.

In *Ideas Are Weapons* (1940), *Ideas for the Ice Age* (1941), and numerous essays Lerner urged the New World to resume the ideological initiative by organizing the world on the basis of a real democratic revolution, but he never neglected to admonish democratic idealists to be tough-minded and unsentimental about human nature. He did not believe in the capacity of liberalism to triumph unaided by force and organization. The trouble with the liberal intellectuals in World War I, he thought, was that they had underestimated the egoism of nations; they had sought to enact their program through sheer force of ideas. He urged liberals to stop fearing force and power as absolute evils and start accepting them as means to an end. Whether such means would brutalize men would depend, he thought, not on the means but on the men.

Lerner, like many liberals, got a new insight into the pervasiveness of power in international relations when the Nazi-Soviet pact in 1939 demonstrated that even the ideology-conscious Russians followed the dictates of national advantage—and with a ruthlessness that came as a shock to many of those who had desperately hoped that the Communist experiment might be the true exponent of the tradition of international reform betrayed by Woodrow Wilson. "The discovery shocked most of us," Lerner explained, "not because we underrated the force of power politics but because we had overrated the compulsion of ideologies. We had assumed that the Soviet Union would cleave to its doctrine or perish; and it has preferred to suspend its doctrine."[13]

Realizing the strength of the compulsion of self-interest in international politics, Lerner was not dazzled by the demands of perfection. Although he called upon America to lead a world democratic revolution, he never forgot that democracy's first task was the task of surviving. As he wrote in July, 1941, when he had already reached the conclusion that the United States would have to become a belligerent,

There is one usable principle which, I fear, many of my friends in groups that have been fighting for real democracy have forgotten; that is, that first things in our world are the imperatives of survival against fascism. . . . Machiavelli, who was clear-eyed and unsentimental before he was anything else, never tired of repeating that in politics men must choose between varying degrees of what they dislike.[14]

By the time France fell under the power of the Nazi legions American liberals had largely recovered their nerve and their confidence and had once more resumed the ideological offensive, abandoned in the aftermath of Wilson's crusade.[15] Liberals, to a large extent, took the lead in urging joint action against the Fascist nations.[16] They strongly repudiated the mystical defeatism Anne Morrow Lindbergh preached in her strange little book, *The Wave of the Future* (1940), wherein she represented the great Fascist surge as part of an elemental revolution in the affairs of men, which the democracies were incapable of resisting, and dismissed fascism's evil excesses as merely "the scum on the wave of the future."

At the same time, the aroused liberals of the thirties, unlike the militant idealists of World War I, were not militant because they wanted to assert the manly virtues, flex the national muscles, or wreak vengeance upon the wicked. Their moral fiber was steeled to the overriding purpose of survival. They went out of their way to avoid the kind of national self-assertion which Theodore Roosevelt had avowed. The days of the righteous crusade were long ended. Consequently, they were generally opposed to Henry Luce's *The American Century* (1941), which urged Americans to exert the full impact of their influence in order to make the twentieth century the "American Century." Luce envisioned America's role as a dynamic leader of world trade, as the global distributor of technical and artistic skills, as the Good Samaritan dedicated to the task of feeding the world's hungry and destitute, and as the repository and chief propagator of the ideals of civilization. Although he explicitly disavowed any intention of advocating the imposition of American institutions on the rest of the world, liberals were wary of his missionary capitalism, of the overtones of crusade, and the ominous references to the assertion of American power, as though that were something good in itself or something biologically imperative. They were inclined to regard Luce's brand of exhortation as a discordant echo of Manifest Destiny. Only the defensive necessities of democracy and, especially, of American democracy, could move them to run the risk of war by arraying force against force. That was their legacy from the last crusade.

3. The Transition to Liberal Interventionism

The decisive influence of the fear of American insecurity in the shift of liberal opinion from a passive attitude to an active disposition to aid Great Britain and France, even at the risk of American intervention, is registered in the pages of the *Nation* and the *New Republic*.

The *Nation* was quick to react to Fascist aggression. In the early 1930's it consistently supported a policy of collective security and advocated concerted action against Japan, Italy, and then Germany. It believed that the Pact of Paris had made the doctrine of neutrality an anomaly, and it disagreed strongly with the *New Republic's* policy of withdrawing from Europe.[17] However, the editors based their early support for collective security on the supposition that it might prevent a war, into which the United States would almost certainly be drawn, rather than upon a clear conception of the dependence of American security upon the security of the nonaggressive nations.[18] Moreover, the *Nation* was opposed to the use of military force or the threat of force on the principle that force corrupted the user and encouraged war, the absolute evil. Its program for preventing war consisted in the perfection of international organization, the mobilization of world opinion, and economic sanctions.[19] In 1937 this program was supplemented by a recommendation that the President be empowered to lift a mandatory embargo on munitions, loans, credits, and basic war materials if a majority of the signatories of the Kellogg Pact found that one country had attacked another in violation of the Pact.[20]

Until it occurred to the editors that America's own security was threatened by Fascist aggression they would condone only "defensive" armaments. They opposed President Roosevelt's greatly expanded naval program in 1938 on the grounds that it was aggressively militarist and threatened Japan. They noted that the ships authorized were for offensive warfare and that there were no appropriations for coastal defense.[21] Collective security, they declared, could never be built on the basis of military preparedness and military sanctions. They proposed as an alternative program joint economic action to aid China, a disarmament conference, and a new fight on the depression, by means of public works rather than battleships.[22]

The peace at Munich came as a great shock to the *Nation,* as to all liberals. For the capitulation of the democracies forced the editors to consider seriously for the first time the validity of an unexpressed assumption underlying their whole position: that Great Britain and France would not submit to Nazi force. An editorial in the issue of October 22, 1938, speculated upon the effect of a British collapse on American security. It wondered if the United States would not be left to fight alone if she failed to co-operate with those whose cause was so fundamentally her own. The editorial even admitted that armed preparedness was beginning to look like the lesser of two gross evils.[23]

When war finally erupted in September, 1939, the *Nation* hoped for an Allied victory because a victorious Hitler would endanger America's interests. At the same time, it hoped that the United States would be able to stay out of the war. However, in a significant break with the orthodox revisionist interpretation of the causes of American intervention, the editors predicted that, if the nation did enter the war, it would not be because of its undoubted economic, emotional, and moral stake in Allied victory but because the nation feared the consequences of a German victory.[24]

The *Nation* continued to support a policy of discriminating against the aggressor nations in the shipment of American goods and armaments as a means of keeping the country out of war, but now it based this policy on the grounds that by aiding Great Britain and France America would indirectly protect its own security, for which, in the absence of such aid, it would have to go to war later. Arguing for the repeal of the Neutrality Act, an editorial in the middle of September, 1939, reasoned,

> Defeat for the Allies would seriously undermine American security. It would bring Hitler and Hitlerism to our very door. Realistically analyzed, our choice is not between aiding or not aiding Britain; it is whether we are to send ample material aid now or by restricting this aid increase the likelihood of sending men later.[25]

A week later Freda Kirchwey recommended that the United States keep out of the war as long as it could without sacrificing its own interests but added, "Only one circumstance would weaken this determination: if England and France faced defeat by Germany, the United States would almost certainly decide to go to war."[26]

After the invasion of Norway and Denmark the *Nation* frequently discussed the effect of a Nazi victory upon American security. Now it based its policy of aid to the Allies almost entirely on grounds of self-interest. It criticized President Roosevelt for explaining the government's program of aid too much in terms of sympathy for the victims of Nazi aggression instead of as an integral part of America's own defense. But it took heart from this observation: "The belief that sheer self-interest should persuade this country to help the Allies in every way possible 'short of war' is beginning to spread."[27]

In the June 15 issue the editors publicly swallowed the unpalatable dose of universal military training, so impressed were they with the demand of new conditions upon old dogmas.[28]

Another sign of the pressure of new conditions was Villard's resignation in the last of June because of differences with the editorial board. In his farewell editorial Villard declared that he had always regarded war as the sum of all villainies, and he delivered a parting warning that the course the editors were pursuing would ultimately end all social and political progress.[29]

By the time Villard resigned, France had fallen, and the editors believed that the principal issue for American foreign policy was preventing a German victory, not keeping out of the war. As far as Freda Kirchwey was concerned, the United States was already at war with Germany and had been for years, and the means which the nation should take to prosecute the war was only a matter of expediency.[30]

The *New Republic* was slower than the *Nation* to conclude that America's security was threatened by events in Europe but quicker to erect America's own selfish interest as its exclusive guide for foreign policy. While the *Nation* was proposing the repeal of the neutrality laws in order to aid the democracies; the *New Republic* was advocating more stringent laws. The editors opposed sending aid to England and France because they were afraid that this would involve the United States in war. Moreover, they did not consider the "have-not" nations worthy of support, since they were not truly democratic. If we must save the British Empire, they cried, "let us make the decision in terms of hard skepticism and not because of an ideological crusade."[31]

As the war clouds gathered over Poland in September, 1939, the *New Republic* had a premonition of the hard, skeptical basis upon which it might reverse its policy. In the September 6 issue the editors speculated upon the possibility of a British and French defeat. The prospect of the destruction of the British Navy and a Nazi conquest of the New World, they noted, "may be only a nightmare, but it will affect many people, and there is just enough substance in it to supply food for a greatly strengthened interventionism." On the strength of this apprehension the *New Republic* was willing to amend the Neutrality Act so as to place the sale of munitions under a cash-and-carry provision and thereby help the Allies while preserving legal impartiality.[32]

The editors still refused to contemplate the use of American force—although they supported British and French resistance—on the principle that the evil of fascism could not be fought by physical means. However, even on this issue they changed their minds when they became convinced that America's survival, not just the survival of the Allies, was threatened. Apparently, the danger of fascism did not become physical in their minds until it encompassed the United States.

Thus in the spring of 1938 the *New Republic* opposed Lewis Mumford's "Call to Arms" chiefly on the grounds that the action he proposed failed to deal with the real danger of fascism. "What constitutes the real danger from fascism? Is it a danger of being conquered by force of arms? No considerable opponent of fascism has yet been subdued by this means. Certainly the United States is in no conceivable danger from military conquest."

This estimate of the Fascist menace spared the editors the necessity of examining their general principle that fascism could be combatted only by removing its causes. Until this estimate was revised it was possible to assume that the United States "will not go Fascist if it strengthens its own democracy and remains at peace."[33]

The editors did not take long to make that important revision after Denmark and Norway fell under the Nazi Blitzkrieg. In the issue of April 22, 1940, George Soule wrote, "It has been a tacit assumption of American thinking that Germany would lose the war. Though in words the question of her possible victory has often been raised and answered, we have never before really believed in it." Now, he declared, the United States must face the consequences of a Hitler victory point-blank. He considered the possibility of armed invasion fantastic, but he anticipated a heavy burden of preparedness to keep totalitarians out of bases from which they might strike.[34]

For the moment the *New Republic* resisted the logic of intervention, but even before Hitler unleashed his troops upon the Lowlands, the editors concluded that the question of intervention was, after all, academic, for the United States was already at war, and the big problem that faced the nation was how to prevent Germany from winning the war. They could only insist that the decision to send troops should be based, not on moral slogans, but on the strict question of American defense.[35]

4. THE EXPERTS DISCOVER POWER

In their growing emphasis upon America's defensive self-interest the *Nation* and the *New Republic* simply registered the power of the hard facts of the international environment to cut through the veil of doubt and disillusionment which had clouded the American, and, to a peculiar degree, the American liberal's outlook upon world politics since 1919. A similar process took place in the minds of those who made it their business to study and teach and publicize international relations. This process was marked by a new emphasis on the factor of power in international relations and a new concern for the political and military conditions of American security.

One manifestation of the discovery of power during the 1930's was a shift in the focus of scholarly interest from the institutional structure and what international relations ought to be to the configuration of power and what world politics actually is.[36] Thus Frederick L. Schuman prefaced his monumental *International Politics,* published in 1933, with the statement that his approach would be "that of *Realpolitik,* characterized by Machiavellian detachment and an earnest effort to delve beneath phraseology to underlying realities."[37] Of course, detachment frequently meant the concealing of value judgments in analytical terminology, but the new emphasis upon the conflict of interests and the competition for power was, nevertheless, a

significant reflection of the actual course of international events and a har-
binger of a new realism in the American attitude toward the outside world.

Another sign of the realistic trend of scholarship was an increasing attention
to the influence of objective, relatively immutable factors in man's environment upon the conduct of nations. Geographical factors attracted special attention.[38] The German preoccupation with geopolitics had a considerable
effect upon the rise of a native American school of geopoliticians in the late
thirties.[39]

Industrious students revived the writings of the great exponents of power
politics. Machiavelli became the subject of a number of monographs, essays,
personal portraits, and even full-length biographies. The ideas of one of the
earliest modern geopoliticians, Sir Halford J. MacKinder, came to light.
America's own exponent of *Realpolitik,* Alfred Thayer Mahan, received a
more lively interest than he had enjoyed since Theodore Roosevelt's presidency.

Esther C. Brunauer, speaking before the annual meeting of the Academy
of Political and Social Science in July, 1941, took notice of the new line of
thought developing in scholarly discussions of the international scene. "Have
you noticed," she asked her colleagues, "how much more often we hear the
word 'power' in these discussions than we used to?" It seemed to her that
this new emphasis had suddenly appeared in 1939 and 1940, as if by spontaneous combustion.

But there was no mystery about this phenomenon. The sudden awareness
of power was, above all, a response to the immediate crisis. The intellectual
impact of this crisis was, quite naturally, most conspicuous in the writings
about America's foreign relations. Students and publicists of American foreign policy, regardless of their estimate of the precise impact of the international conflict upon American interests, found it increasingly difficult to ignore
power politics and considerations of American security as they witnessed the
systematic subjugation of Europe.

One of the first writers in the thirties to recognize the dependence of American security upon the balance of power in Europe and Asia was Livingston
Hartley. Hartley's influence upon American opinion was probably negligible,
but his views are important as an indication of the developing transformation
in the American outlook.

In *Is America Afraid?* (1937) Hartley announced his aim of presenting a
new concept of American foreign policy. This concept was really a restate-
ment of the strategic bases of American survival propounded by a score of
statesmen, scholars, and politicians during the age of Mahan. On the basis
of an analysis of the relative power ratios among the great nations of Europe

and the Far East, according to their population, area, resources, productive capacities, and their geographical situation, Hartley concluded that if either of these areas were to become consolidated under a dominant power, the United States would face an almost hopeless task in maintaining its security. In his view the conquest of the British Commonwealth would strike a particularly disastrous blow at America's strategic position in the Atlantic and the Pacific. An armed clash might not occur for a generation, but the nation would have to be on a war footing in preparation for the inevitable.

Hartley proceeded to set forth exactly which actions would be practicable under various future contingencies. His general conclusion was that cold self-interest dictated, in the first place, American intervention in some form to check German expansion and prevent Japan from overrunning China and, in the second place, closer relations with the Soviet Union, as long as its policy remained oriented toward defense rather than world revolution.

In *Our Maginot Line* (1939), written before the invasion of Poland, Hartley considered at greater length the threat of German and Japanese expansion, stressing, particularly, America's strategic dependence upon the maintenance of British sea power in the Atlantic, the preservation of the balance of power on the continent of Europe, and the prevention of hostile penetration of South America. Hartley's analysis was distinguished by its deliberate concentration on self-defense divorced from ethical and ideological considerations. This approach did not imply that moral principls were unimportant; it was designed simply to set forth the elements of American foreign policy according to the lowest common denominator upon which all citizens could agree, while avoiding all the conflicting sentiments and emotions excited by idealistic considerations. As Hartley explained,

> It is clear that the basis for the defensive policies of a democracy is the support of all of its people all of the time. For this reason it seems wisest to consider our defensive problem not in the light of principles upon which Americans may divide, but in the light of national interests toward which Americans should be unanimous.[40]

This same lowest-common-denominator approach was apparent in the writings of observers of foreign policy who did not share Hartley's interventionism. Isolationists were wont to rest their case for limiting aid to the beleaguered democracies upon arguments demonstrating America's defensive security. They frequently cited the conclusions of George Fielding Eliot's *The Ramparts We Watch* (1938) as evidence for their assertion that America's security could be protected by an army capable of defending American shores and overseas possessions.

Through a detailed consideration of America's strategic position and military requirements Eliot reached the conclusion that the United States could depend primarily upon its Navy for defense. In 1938 he anticipated no threat from Germany or Japan that would require the United States to intervene in a foreign conflict; however, he did not commit himself on future developments.[41]

In 1944 Eliot wrote that his 1938 estimate had been based on the belief that there existed in Europe and Asia a reasonable balance of power, "and that the security of the United States could best be assured by the maintenance of powerful offensive armaments based largely on sea and air strength, coupled with a foreign policy of complete freedom of action." But he explained, as many others had foreseen,

> The possibility of finding security in such a policy vanished when the collapse of France destroyed the balance of power in Europe, and, in its results, in turn destroyed the balance of power in Asia. When France went down, the involvement of this nation in the struggle against totalitarianism became instantly inevitable.[42]

The logic of events forced Eliot to reconsider his view of American intervention, but just as important as his changed strategic estimate in causing this reconsideration was his consistent premise that American foreign policy should be geared to the imperatives of survival. It was this premise that underlay his whole attempt to get the American people to pay more attention to military policy and power politics. "The first necessity," as he put it, "is for completely realistic thinking, for the banishment of altruism and sentiment, for single-minded attention to the national interests."[43]

Hanson Baldwin, military editor of the *New York Times* and another strategist cited as an authority by isolationists because of his support of a moderate defense plan and his opposition to armed intervention abroad, was as thorough as Eliot in exploring the strategic requirements of the defense of the Western Hemisphere. He considered the talk of a direct invasion of the United States in the event of a German victory as nothing but a bogy designed to scare the nation into an ill-conceived defense program.[44] However, he anticipated that a British defeat would be disastrous to American interests, and he thought that even an invasion of the continental United States would be possible if the enemy got bases in the Western Hemisphere.[45] Like Eliot, Baldwin made his recommendations contingent upon the persistence of certain factors in the power equation, and, like Eliot, he also set forth the general policy that, no matter what course of action the nation took, it should take it "primarily upon the cold, hard bedrock of common sense and national interest."[46]

The writers upon military and strategic matters during the crisis years before Pearl Harbor differed in the details of their analyses and their recommendations. Some, like Major General Hagood, thought that the nation could obtain continental immunity from invasion "by an expenditure not greater than the average cost of the army during the ten years preceding the depression."[47] Others, like Hanson Baldwin and George Fielding Eliot, thought that hemispheric defense was adequate protection. Analysts like Max Werner, Fletcher Pratt, Fleming MacLeish, and Cushman Reynolds believed that some affirmative action beyond continental or hemispheric defense was imperative.[48] But all were united in stressing the importance of a cool, calm calculation of the requirements of self-preservation as the first principle of American foreign policy. Most of them found it necessary to discuss America's security in relation to the balance of power overseas, whether or not they considered the current balance a menace.

This realistic approach toward America's foreign relations did not necessarily lead to the conclusion that America's first line of defense was the French Army or the British Navy; but, as the German forces scored one startling success after another, many of those who sought an affirmative American policy toward the rampant chaos of fascism became convinced that America's self-preservation, the basic principle of foreign policy upon which all citizens could agree, was inextricably involved in the shifting distribution of power in Europe and Asia.

Edward Mead Earle of the Institute for Advanced Study at Princeton University was one of the most persistent and effective advocates of this view of American security among academic men. As early as the spring of 1938 he began appealing for an inquiry into the basic assumptions of America's military policy, for in his view national defense was one of the primary responsibilities of statesmanship and should not be left to a policy of drift and improvisation.[49]

Earle's search for a definite criterion of national security looked beyond America's geographical circumstances and the size of her army and navy and found through historical analysis that American security depended, in large part, on the fact that no power or coalition had ever enjoyed unquestioned supremacy on the Continent of Europe or in its adjoining seas. In an article in the *New Republic* in November, 1939, he hazarded an historical judgment which was to receive great publicity through Walter Lippmann's writings. Wilson's policies in 1914–19, he said, were a continuation of the power politics inherited from Wilson's predecessors, who had seen Germany as the disturber of the balance of power in Europe. The United States had intervened in 1917 because a German victory seemed likely and American statesmen had wanted to guard the nation's security and trade. Earle was not prepared to say that the United States should intervene again to support the European balance of power, but he did recommend reasonable measures short of war for supporting the British Navy and the French Army.[50]

In articles throughout 1940 and 1941 Earle elaborated upon his view of American intervention in 1917 and pleaded for a reasoned and systematic consideration of the historic military and political foundations of American security.[51] In the security of the United States, he asserted, lay the standard for a sound and consistent policy toward the European conflict. He took issue with the parochial conception of national security as continental defense. America's security, he declared, was relative to her moral, political, and strategic commitments and to the balance of power in Europe and the Far East; it was not just a product of her geographic position. He pointed out that the Nazi technique of aggression involved flanking maneuvers, economic pressure, subversion, and psychological warfare, not just head-on military assault.[52] He reasoned that America's strategy should be predicated upon a defense in depth, with the security of France and Great Britain the first line, British sea power in the Atlantic the second, to be defended at all costs, and bases protecting Latin America the third line.[53]

All these views were embodied in his tract for the times, *Against This Torrent* (1941), in which he pointed to the peril of a Nazi victory and warned that the United States should be ready to use its economic power, diplomatic resources, and, if necessary, its naval and military establishments to strike at Hitler before the opportunity was lost. "Nor should we be swayed by cynicism in interpreting our experiences of 1917 to 1919," he added. "We entered the last war primarily to defend our interests as we saw them—because we felt then, as we feel now, that the defeat of Great Britain would involve so serious a threat to our strategic position that we could not run the risk of continued neutrality."[54]

This same combination of special pleading and historical interpretation was the theme of *The Atlantic System* (1941), written by Forrest Davis, a rewrite man and slick-paper journalist by trade but not an unscholarly historian. Davis went back to the Forefathers to trace the rise of the Anglo-American community of interests, and he erected Mahan as the supreme strategist of this Atlantic System. In a chapter called "The First Battle of the Atlantic" Davis stated that the United States had entered the war in 1917 for the sake of the strategic advantages Mahan had expounded. Although he produced no substantial evidence to show that the American people or their leaders were motivated by an instinct for self-preservation, he asserted,

On April 2, 1917, the blockade issue became academic. The U-boat record, while dramatic, seems little more than incidental to the basic war cause, which, as it has appeared here, was the possible loss of control-of command-of the Atlantic. . . . The United States took up arms in the last analysis because it seemed likely that without American intervention the scepter of the Atlantic would pass from the hands of the English-speaking peoples into those of a stranger.[55]

So positive was Davis that the United States had intervened for the sake of its own self-interest that he declared, "We may now scarcely doubt that our aim would have been the same had the enemy been a republic or a constitutional monarchy."[56]

In the concluding chapters Davis clearly showed that the purpose of his exposition was to demonstrate that in 1941 the defense of the Atlantic world had once more become an historical imperative. In his mind the full weight of history sanctioned intervention.

> For the immediate future America's course is plainly chartered. An all-out military partnership with Great Britain and her Allies is a minimum condition of our survival as a great, liberal power. . . . Under "the law of the opposite shores," the United States cannot tolerate the establishment of a hostile sea power on the European side of the Atlantic. In the fall of 1941 it was apparent that our government did not propose to tolerate it. The clock had struck with the fall of France. The exact hour in which our full force would be engaged in the struggle could not be foretold. That it would be so engaged could not be doubted.[57]

5. Genesis of the Lippmann Thesis of Intervention

The most skilful and the most influential exponent of the Atlantic Community thesis of American security was Walter Lippmann. Like Edward Mead Earle and Forrest Davis, Mr. Lippmann combined history with his polemics. At the beginning of Part Two we noted his retrospective interpretation of America's entrance into World War I as a self-interested response to Germany's threat to the Atlantic lines of communication. The origins of this interpretation, which Lippmann presented in 1941 and after, appear clearly in the circumstances preceding World War II.

As early as 1937 Lippmann had begun to detect an historical parallel between America's response to the current international situation and her action in 1917. Reflecting upon the Neutrality Act of 1937 in an article in *Foreign Affairs,* he observed that, in spite of Congress's intention of avoiding the economic ties which were alleged to have drawn the nation into the war on England's side in 1917, it had just passed a law which, in the event of another war, would effectively integrate the American economy with British sea power and British finance, since Great Britain alone had the money and means to utilize the "cash-and-carry" provision.[58] This paradox suggested to him that there existed an inexorable tendency of American foreign policy to follow the prescribed path of inescapable interest, that somehow the logic of America's conscious minds was not the logic that determined her behavior.

"It is as if some kind of overriding necessity, some deep necessity in the very nature of the world as it is, had compelled men to reinforce the British connection when they thought they were severing it."[59]

This mystical insight and the editorials of the *New Republic* were about the only substantiation of his thesis of intervention that Lippmann ever attempted, unless one assumes that the mere similarity between American action in 1941 and 1917 proves identical motivation. However, Lippmann the publicist and prophet was always prior to Lippmann the historian. His analysis of the past was really a speculation about the future. He believed and he hoped that past experience decreed that if British naval supremacy were to collapse under attack by Germany in the North Atlantic, by Italy in the Mediterranean, and by Japan in the western Pacific, Americans would not remain indifferent, regardless of their present intentions. "In the final test," he concluded, "no matter what we wish now or now believe, though collaboration with Britain and her allies is difficult and often irritating, we shall protect that connection because in no other way can we fulfill our destiny."[60]

Whatever one may think of Lippmann's history, one must grant the accuracy of his prohecy; and no one worked more effectively to fulfil that prophecy than Lippmann himself. Chiefly through his syndicated column in the *New York Herald Tribune,* which billed him as "The Great Elucidator," Lippmann, after 1939, consistently pointed with alarm to the world-wide revolutionary menace of expanding fascism. After the fall of France he became certain that England and the British Navy were America's first line of defense. At first, he advocated a policy somewhere between isolationism and interventionism. In an article in *Life,* July 22, 1940, he suggested economic and political nonintercourse with the Axis, but he also held that the nation's main concern should be "to save the United States and not be drawn into the vortex of European barbarism."[61] However, as the German threat to the Atlantic increased, he became much less concerned about intervention than about preventing a German victory. By the time he wrote the lead article in *Life,* April 7, 1941, entitled "The Atlantic and America," he considered the United States already in the war, for all practical purposes.

This article clearly demonstrated the close connection between history and policy in Lippmann's thinking. As we observed in chapter VI, "The Atlantic and America" was largely devoted to the contention that the United States intervened in World War I when, and only when, Germany's threat to wrest control of the other side of the Atlantic from Great Britain endangered American security. However, Lippmann did not fill seven full-page columns of a popular picture weekly for the sake of an academic historical exposition. He plainly indicated that his eagerness to set the record of 1917 straight was inspired by his concern for the present. Starting from the premise that the United States was already in the war, Lippmann asserted that the principal cause of intervention in 1941 and in 1917 was one and the same, and he suggested that if Americans could understand the real explanation for both interventions, "We shall, I believe, see clearly why and how we went so wrong the first time that we now have to do the work all over again a second time."[62] By presenting the real explanation for America's interventions as self-preservation, Lippmann could argue that America was not really repeating foolish mistakes of 1914–17, as the cynical postwar distortions of history might have led one to suspect, but was, instead, repairing the error of 1919–20, when the English-speaking peoples abandoned the Atlantic Community, which they had fought the war to preserve. In other words, said Lippmann, the nation had lost the peace because it did not remember why it had gone to war. Therefore, if the people could see through the philanthropic visions of Wilson and the equally false revisionism of the postwar historians and grasp the real cause of intervention, it would follow, he hoped, that they would recognize their present need for joining forces with Great Britain and maintaining the Anglo-American entente as a nucleus of the peace to come.

The function of Lippmann's historical thesis becomes clear when one considers the extent to which Americans were conditioned to look at the events of 1935–41 through the disillusioned eyes of the postwar historians of 1914–17. At a time when every argument for a vigorous American foreign policy was likely to be met by the charge that it was a repetition of the misguided thinking that had led to the disaster of 1917, it behooved those who felt that America's fortunes were bound up with the fortunes of the powers resisting fascism either to justify intervention in World War I or else to distinguish the present situation from the past. Lippmann's thesis accomplished both objectives. By circumventing the orthodox explanations of the intervention of 1917 it dissociated that experience from its postwar stigma and made it more acceptable to a generation disillusioned with crusades. By focusing the explanation of intervention in 1941 upon strategic considerations instead of moral, economic, or legal factors it distinguished the situation confronting America in 1941 from the postwar interpretation of 1917. By identifying the cause of both interventions as the same cause Lippmann placed the sanction of history behind a clear and compelling standard of national self-interest at a time when there was a widespread feeling, sedulously cultivated by isolationists, that the United States, in contrast to the determined Axis nations, lacked a clear and consistent foreign policy.

If the interpretation of the actual role of national self-preservation in American intervention which was presented in Part Two is correct, then we must conclude that the propagandistic value of Lippmann's thesis exceeded its service to the study of history. But in this history-conscious era what men think about the past is frequently more important than the past itself.

6. "1939 Is Not 1917"

Not all those who advocated an affirmative foreign policy in the years preceding Pearl Harbor were convinced, with Walter Lippmann, of the wisdom of America's participation in World War I; but they were, nevertheless, moved to demonstrate that the present situation was quite dissimilar from the revisionist descriptions of the situation in 1914–17. The manner in which they demonstrated the dissimilarity was a mark of the nation's new regard for·considerations of national power and self-interest.

There were many dissimilarities between the two prewar periods to which one could point. The enormity of the actual Fascist crimes against humanity, for example, far surpassed the fabricated atrocities charged to the Kaiser's troops in Belgium. Hitler's challenge to democratic and Christian principles was direct, arrogantly proclaimed, and ruthlessly organized. The worst things that William Roscoe Thayer ever said about Kultur could not begin to describe the psychopathic rantings of Herr Goebbels or Hitler. There was nothing remotely comparable in the Germany of World War I to the systematic Jewish persecutions of the Third Reich.

Yet it was not these differences which the co-operationists and the interventionists stressed but rather the relatively greater impact of facism upon America's selfish interests. Thus I. F. Stone, writing in the *Nation,* found the difference between 1937 and 1914 in the fact that the Atlantic was no longer the barrier it had once been and that fascism was a very tangible threat to the survival of democracy, whereas in 1914 German imperialism had threatened only British and French imperialism.[63]

Walter Millis, one of the revisionists to revise his view of America's relation to European quarrels under the impact of Nazi aggression, did not specifically repudiate his interpretation of American intervention in *Road to War;* but he was at pains to explain that 1939 was not 1914, and he warned that an uncritical rehearsal of the facts about American intervention in 1917 might leave the nation unprepared for the new situation. In an article in *Life,* November, 1939, he said that the United States had entered the war in 1917 for many reasons but that the people had been moved by relatively minor considerations. But 1939 was different, he thought, because the nation was inured to the horrors of war and far less susceptible to the tug of moral indignation. The people were facing the European conflict much more deliberately, soberly, and realistically. The neutrality laws would prevent them from rushing in to preserve trade profits or to prevent Germany from using an inhumane weapon of warfare. And the biggest distinction of all between the two periods was that in 1939 the major question that faced the United States was not how to keep out of war but how to keep out of war for any reason short of a threat to American security. He averred that the nation faced a situation of "considerably greater potential menace to its material interests, its way of life and its national safety than was the situation in 1914." Consequently, if America did go to war, it would go "because larger reasons seem to make it imperative that the United States should attempt to decide the struggle."*

Such attempts to distinguish the past from the present would have carried little weight with the American public had not unmistakable distinctions appeared with appalling regularity in the front pages of the daily newspapers and the hourly radio newscasts and interpretations. By the end of 1940 it was evident to the news-conscious American public that the whole scope and technique of warfare had changed to such an extent that national security no longer was assured by mere freedom from military invasion. The novel and highly publicized techniques of economic aggrandizement, subversion, and psychological warfare, not to mention new weapons and unorthodox concepts of military strategy, made conventional standards of legal, geographic, and military security seem strangely irrelevant. In the late thirties and early forties America's reading public was flooded with articles and books conveying the revolutionary nature of Fascist warfare.[64] Every article and book, but, even more clearly, every instance of Nazi aggression, was a blow to the illusion that World War II was just a repetition of World War I.

Dorothy Thompson, who became a columnist in 1936 and within two years built up a clientele of 140 newspapers with a circulation of 7,500,000, was one of the earliest and most vehement publicists to warn Americans about the revolutionary methods of total warfare and to declare that the German aim was nothing short of a total redistribution of world power and a complete reorganization of the world. For example, in her column on September 18, 1939, she asserted that analogies with 1914–18 were completely irrelevant.

It is a revolutionary war. Its object is not to effect reasonable adjustments which will give greater justice to nations suffering from a lack of raw materials and commercial outlets. Its object is to change the whole structure of human society, to destroy all existing Western forms of political and economic organization. . . .[65]

* Walter Millis, "1939 Is Not 1914," Life, VII (November 6, 1939), 75 ff. See also Millis's noteworthy mea culpa, "The Faith of an American," published originally in Zero Hour (New York, 1940). In a book review in 1934 Millis expressed skepticism about the thesis that British propaganda had drawn the United States into World War I, and he distinctly repudiated the conspiratorial thesis as applied to a parallel between 1914–17 and 1939. "Propaganda for War," Southern Review, V (Autumn, 1939), 201–10.

Such alarming testimony would have been easier to discount as warmongering or a repetition of the hysteria of 1917 if it had not been for the fact that much of it came from the public statements of the masters of Fascist strategy themselves. But the most important factor in distinguishing the late thirties and early forties from 1914–17, the really decisive factor in determining the credibility of the foreign menace to America's vital interests, was less what was said than what was done. In the last analysis, it was the grim record of events in Europe and Asia in the years preceding Pearl Harbor that convinced the American people that their very survival was involved in events beyond the ocean barriers. This conviction was the popular foundation for the emergence of the new Realism.

CHAPTER XVII

THE DISCIPLINE OF ADVERSITY

1. The Transformation of American Opinion

THE period of international upheaval from the attack on Ethiopia to Pearl Harbor is a revolutionary period in America's adaptation to its status as a world power, for in this period the pressure of world politics radically altered America's conventional assumptions about its security. For the first time since the days of the French Alliance and the War of 1812 the great body of Americans came to understand that their most fundamental interest, national self-preservation, was at stake in the course of world politics.

The response of the American people to the surge of Fascist aggression was a product of their observation of the actual impact of aggression abroad, of their traditional attitudes toward foreign affairs, and of their interpretation of America's intervention in World War I.

The words and deeds of the totalitarian and Fascist leaders were a profound shock to the nation's humanitarian and idealistic sensibilities. Americans were almost unanimous in their moral condemnation of the Axis nations; and when war with the democracies broke out, the overwhelming majority wanted the aggressors defeated. At the same time, the nation's traditional desire to remain isolated from the toils of world politics, sharpened by its belief that intervention in the last war had been a great mistake, made Americans reluctant to act partially, lest this involve them in another foreign controversy. Nevertheless, as it became clear from Fascist incursions elsewhere that foreign aggression was a tangible threat to American security, Americans became willing to modify their isolation and even run the risk of war in order to aid those still resisting aggression.

Although idealistic preferences were a major motive in America's strong desire for an Allied victory, it was national self-interest in its lowest common denominator, self-preservation, that brought the nation to the point of wanting an Allied victory more than it feared involvement in war. It was primarily the circumstances of the war that aroused America's instinct for survival and a new concern for the imperatives of national power; but calculations of national expediency would not have counted so heavily in American conduct had not disillusionment with World War I made the nation wary about acting upon moral distinctions, violations of neutral rights, and affronts to the national honor. When the disturbing events of the late 1930's and early 1940's revived the debate over intervention and isolation, the most convincing arguments turned not upon American rights or American honor or even American ideals, but rather upon an interpretation of the practical requirements of America's fundamental self-interest.

From Italy's cynical invasion of Ethiopia to Japan's treacherous attack upon Pearl Harbor the American people were regularly bombarded with newspaper and radio reports of national lawlessness and inhumanity far surpassing the invasion of Belgium, the shooting of Nurse Edith Cavell, or the sinking of the *Lusitania*. Yet public opinion displayed an amazing calmness in the face of totalitarian depredations. This was partly due to the fact that the Neutrality Acts largely precluded incidents directly affecting American citizens, but equally important was the popular determination to avoid the emotional reactions which were believed to have propelled the nation into war in 1917. Thus when Japanese aviators bombed the United States gunboat *Panay* in December, 1937, under circumstances suggesting deliberate provocation, there was a momentary burst of indignation in the land, but it did not approach the dimensions of the massive reaction to the *Maine* or *Lusitania* incidents. Far more Americans continued to want the United States to withdraw entirely from China in order to avoid such incidents than wanted the government to force respect for American rights.[1] The very regularity with which the totalitarian powers violated the conventional standards of international law and decency tended to accustom Americans to lower moral expectations. By 1941 Americans were hardened cynics compared to the innocent days when the explosion of the *Maine* rocked the nation.

The people, as a whole, were far less susceptible to the pressure of impulse and far more deliberate in the pursuit of national self-interest than in 1914. At first, self-interest seemed to lie in isolation and nonintervention, but as Americans read the hard lesson of survival in the fate of Europe, the great majority became convinced that their own survival was inextricably bound up with the interest of Great Britain and France in preventing German domination of Europe. This remarkable transformation in the American outlook might not have come so readily had not the overwhelming majority of the nation felt that America's practical advantage coincided with a compelling moral purpose; but it was the international flux of power, not the dictates of morality, that proved to be the decisive factor in the actual course of action which the nation adopted.

At first, America's determination to stay out of foreign disputes was strengthened by the belief that foreign disputes could not seriously affect American self-interest. The neutrality legislation of 1935–37 was an expression of this belief. As long as Americans retained this complacent assumption, they might become morally and emotionally committed to the cause of the free nations, but they would continue to reject any material commitment or the remotest suggestion of one. Thus when President Franklin Roosevelt delivered his famous Quarantine Speech at Chicago on October 5, 1937, calling for the "peace-loving" community to impose a "quarantine" upon the spreaders of international anarchy and proclaiming America's interest in that purpose, the nation exhibited an intense alarm over this ambiguous suggestion that the United States participate in common action with parties to a foreign conflict, and the isolationists seized the opportunity to set up a great cry against warmongering in the White House. Secretary of State Hull declared in his *Memoirs* that the adverse reaction to Roosevelt's startling pronouncement set back the administration's educational campaign by six months.[2]

The initial effect of the outbreak of war in Europe in September, 1939, was only an increased popular determination to keep America isolated from foreign turmoil. The American people were far better prepared to pursue this goal in 1939 than in 1914. War came as no great surprise to the American people, although there had been a general disposition to wish away the unpleasant prospect of that occurrence. The underlying skepticism of the American people about the chances of peace is indicated by the fact that even in 1937 two-thirds of those polled believed that there would be another world war.[3] From the time of the Munich concession in September, 1938, until the invasion of Poland a year later Americans lived in an atmosphere of crisis. They were kept in a constant state of excitement and apprehension by the dramatic disembodied voice of the radio relating incredible events in a matter-of-fact tone. Therefore, when war finally did erupt, the nation had thoroughly steeled itself to playing the unedifying role of neutral spectator at the mortal contest between totalitarian and democratic nations.

Until the trend of military events in Europe seemed to endanger American security, the debate over America's relation to the European conflict skirted around the vital issues of national expediency and revolved around conventional arguments about neutrality and nonintervention. Thus in the summer and autumn of 1939, both before and after the outbreak of war in Europe, the heated debate over revision of the Neutrality Act so as to permit shipment of arms to potential and actual victims of aggression took the devious form of a dispute over the definition of neutrality, with the opponents of revision arguing that repeal of the arms embargo would be an unneutral change in the rules of the game to help one side against the other and the supporters contending that the existing policy was unneutral because it was a reversal of traditional practices of international law and served to throw American influence on the side of the aggressors. Both sides argued that its method was the best way to keep the nation out of war, one side claiming that war trade with the Allies would bring a repetition of the fatal process which the Nye Committee had exposed, the other side replying that to deny the instruments of war to the democracies would encourage the aggressors to make war and help them to wage it successfully, thereby increasing the risk of America's involvement.

The irrelevance of much of the debate over neutrality was accentuated by the fact that the act of 1939, which was finally passed on November 3, had little relation to neutrality anyway, as neutrality was known in conventional international law. The provision for cash and carry on the shipment of arms and the provision establishing prohibited danger zones were related to neutrality only in the special American sense of legislation designed to prevent intervention in foreign wars.

Nevertheless, there ran beneath the surface sound and fury of the neutrality debate an unmistakable undercurrent of controversy over the fundamental issue of the effect of a German victory on American security. Many observers in Washington reported that the real arguments were heard repeatedly in private conversations, with the repealists contending that Germany had to be defeated for America's own interests and the anti-repealists expressing their unwillingness to trust Roosevelt with enough discretion to drag the country into war.[4]

Perhaps greater candor on the part of the administration in explaining the dependence of American security upon the flow of vital materials to Great Britain and France might have encouraged a sounder approach to the issue of repealing the arms embargo; but neither President Roosevelt nor Secretary of State Hull had confidence in the ability of candor to achieve the administration's immediate legislative object, whereas they well knew the risks of arousing Congressionl alarm and opposition. It should be remembered that the President's ability to aid the democracies depended directly upon what Congressmen did and only indirectly upon what the general public thought; and in the matter of transforming America's traditional foreign policy Congress consistently lagged behind the public.

In order to assess the relative wisdom of candor and circumspection in the process of committing the United States to the defense of the democracies it is important to note that in the fall of 1939 there was no widespread fear either in Congress or among the general public that Germany would win the war or that, winning it, she would threaten American security. The crucial significance of this consideration was demonstrated by Senator Henry Cabot

Lodge, Jr., the grandson of Wilson's antagonist, when he spoke before the Senate in October, 1939, in opposition to repeal of the arms embargo. After recognizing that what the advocates of repeal really wanted was to help England and France so that the United States would not have to fight the war if those powers fell, Senator Lodge gave his own hard-headed reasons for disagreeing with this position.

> I submit that the chances of England and France being defeated are slim indeed. The choice seems to be between a defeat of Germany on the one hand and a stalemate on the other. I further contend, however, that even if Germany were victorious and desired to conquer the United States, she never could do so. . . . Fortunately, our national safety is not at stake.[5]

The great majority of the American people agreed with Lodge's political and military estimate. Until the course of events in Europe changed this estimate, any mere assertion of the German threat, however forcefully and candidly delivered, was likely to strike the skeptical as alarmism rather than prudence. It was likely to strike an increasingly recalcitrant and suspicious Senate as a Rooseveltian exaggeration prompted by ulterior motives.

In any event, less than a year after the revision of the Neutrality Act startling developments in the European war had rudely shattered the public's confidence in the complacent estimate Lodge expressed. By the winter of 1940 the American people were far more interested in enabling the democracies to win by all measures short of American intervention than in hewing to an abstraction called neutrality. In the spring of 1940 the government began abandoning, step by step, the last vestiges of neutrality. It continued to justify its policy on legal grounds, largely in deference to the isolationist minority in Congress, but the great majority of the nation understood that the central issue facing the nation was security, not legality. This transformation in American opinion was a direct result of the German invasion of Denmark and Norway in April, 1940, and the subsequent fall of the Netherlands, Belgium, Luxemburg, and, finally, France.

When Germany overran Norway and Denmark, William Allen White, who had deserted the ranks of the disillusioned to become a leader in the movement to revise the Neutrality Act, decided that it was time to organize a committee that would consolidate public opinion and induce Congress to arm Great Britain as a measure of American defense.[6] By the end of April, White and Clark Eichelberger had organized the Committee to Defend America by Aiding the Allies, a name which admirably expressed the nature of the American response to the ominous shift of power in Europe. Within several weeks this organization became one of the most influential organs of public opinion. Through a nation-wide campaign it agitated for amendment of the neutrality legislation and for the adoption of a nonbelligerent status. One faction within White's committee, the Century Group, was so alarmed by the German threat to American security that it advocated a declaration of war.[7]

The ease with which Nazi dive-bombers and tanks broke through the French line at Sedan and outflanked the whole Maginot Line—that cherished symbol of defensive impregnability—at first stunned the incredulous American public and then terrified them with the realization that Germany had suddenly achieved domination of western Europe. American columnists and radio commentators now began the grim game of speculating about Hitler's next move, calculating air distances and relative military strengths and anxiously inquiring into the strategic significance of Greenland, Iceland, the Azores, and a score of less-known places which had to be looked up in atlases and located on globes. The great mass of Americans now called loudly for all aid short of war for the hard-pressed democracies and made frantic demands for large-scale preparedness. As one newspaperman observed, "Revolution seems not too strong a word for the change in American thought from belief in security to dread of tomorrow."[8]

The public opinion polls tell the story of rising American apprehension. In the middle of September, 1939, about 82 per cent of Americans polled expected the Allies to win; 7 per cent thought Germany would win; 11 per cent were undecided. But in the middle of May, 1940, these figures had changed to 55 per cent, 17 per cent, and 28 per cent respectively. By the end of July only 43 per cent expected England to win, while 24 per cent believed that a German victory was more likely, and 27 per cent were undecided.[9] These figures become more significant when one considers that by July half of those polled were convinced that, if Germany and Italy defeated England, they would start a war against the United States sometime within the next ten years.[10] In July 69 per cent believed that a German victory would affect them personally, whereas in March only 47 per cent had held this view.[11] Seven out of ten believed that Germany would try to get control of the South American countries.[12]

But what did Americans intend to do about the Fascist threat? They intended to build up America's military establishment and take measures to protect the Western Hemisphere; these objectives were as popular among isolationists as among interventionists. Moreover, all but the irreconcilable isolationist minority were prepared to give considerable aid to the Allies, even though they understood that this meant an increased tax burden and a risk of becoming involved in the war. However, no sizeable group would even consider the proposal that America enter the war. After the invasion of the Lowlands Americans became far more skeptical about the ability of the

United States to stay out of the European conflagration, and the percentage of those who thought that the United States ought not to stay out more than tripled as compared to October, 1939; but not until the spring of 1941, when the majority believed that the United States was already in the war for all practical purposes, did more than 20 per cent approve of a declaration of war against Germany and Italy and the dispatch of American troops and naval units abroad;[13] and at no time before Pearl Harbor did the Gallup poll find more than 24 per cent in favor of a shooting war.

This is not surprising. The thought of declaring war was always repugnant to the American people; it was especially repugnant after America's intervention in World War I, which a substantial proportion of the nation continued to consider a disastrous mistake.[14] At a time when isolationists argued that those who favored the government's program of aid to Great Britain were leading the country into another futile crusade, the defenders of that program found themselves denying this fact almost by habit. They stressed the argument that helping Great Britain fight the Axis powers at the present was the best way for the United States to avoid fighting them in the future, but they tended to side-step the awkward question of what the nation should do if the Allies seemed likely to lose.

Opponents of the administration's foreign policy were forever pointing to the fact that the polls consistently showed that at least 80 per cent of the nation were opposed to entering the war, but this figure was a misleading index of the public's attitude toward the European conflict. More revealing was the fact that in May and June, 1940, 36 per cent of the nation believed that it was more important to help England win the war, even at the risk of being drawn into the conflict, than to keep the United States out of the war. After the fall of France the percentage rose steadily until it became a substantial majority in the spring of 1941.[15] According to a July, 1940, poll, 73 per cent thought that the United States should do everything possible to help England except go to war. Although at this time only 13 per cent were in favor of armed intervention, 50 per cent said they would approve of armed intervention if they were sure that Germany would try to attack the United States after England were defeated.[16]

The pattern of opinion in the spring and summer of 1940 indicates that the decisive factor that moved Americans to extend aid to the democracies was America's own security. Not until the invasion of the Lowlands and the fall of France convinced most Americans that it was more important, from the standpoint of national self-interest, to help England win the war than to keep out of it themselves could the administration get widespread popular support for measures short of war. Thereafter, America's willingness to aid Great

Britain fluctuated according to the threat of Nazi domination of Europe, until the winter of 1940, when it became clear that the United States would probably have to join the fight itself; and then America's desire to help England fluctuated according to the people's estimate of England's ability to withstand the Nazi assault.[17]

Thus the trend of American interventionism was a direct response to the circumstances of the European conflict as they appeared to impinge upon tangible interests. The people did not even act on the anticipation of emergencies, but only on their actual occurrence. They were skeptical. They had to be shown. Only after the successful invasion of Norway was there a noticeable increase in America's desire for a larger army. Only after the invasion of the Lowlands were a majority sufficiently aroused to favor conscription of a limited nature.[18] Not until Hitler was astride most of the Continent of Europe did most Americans decide that the United States ought to do everything it could to help England, short of entering the war.

2. Franklin D. Roosevelt

The circumstances of the war largely set the pattern of America's attitude toward foreign events. Nevertheless, as in the period of 1914–17, it was primarily the Chief Executive who defined the terms of debate, rationalized the people's choices within the framework of their basic emotional and intellectual responses to the international environment, and translated opinion into specific actions. In estimating the impact of the upheaval in Europe and Asia on the evolution of America's foreign relations one must weigh heavily the factor of Franklin D. Roosevelt. Yet one cannot properly assess the influence or the quality of his leadership except in terms of the public pressures he shaped and was shaped by.

In some ways President Roosevelt was a spiritual descendant of Woodrow Wilson. There can be no doubt that he was deeply impressed with America's moral responsibility for promoting peace, democracy, and a better way of living throughout the world. Like Wilson, he was profoundly stirred by humanitarian sympathies. Perhaps Harry Hopkins struck at one root of Roosevelt's complex nature when he told Robert Sherwood,

> You and I are for Roosevelt because he's a great spiritual figure, because he's an idealist, like Wilson, and he's got the guts to drive through against any opposition to realize those ideals. Oh—he sometimes tries to appear tough and cynical and flippant, but that's an act he likes to put on, especially at press conferences. . . . You can see the real Roosevelt when he comes out with something like the Four Freedoms. And don't get the idea that those are any catch phrases. *He believes them!* He believes they can be practically attained.[19]

Roosevelt spoke from the heart when, in a tribute to Wilson at his birthplace in Virginia, on May 4, 1941, he avowed the "unyielding strength of things of the spirit" and declared that "physical strength can never permanently withstand the impact of spiritual force."[20]

At the same time, there was a streak of pragmatism in Roosevelt that saved him from Wilson's extravagant moral expectations. There was a subtlety of nature and a temporizing quality which allowed him to accept the half-loaf. Moreover, he was keenly aware of the practical failure of Wilson's lofty objectives and determined to avoid a repetition of his mistakes.[21]

Roosevelt had a grasp of the stuff of world politics, a respect for the imperatives of power, which Wilson never attained or sought. He was a sailor and an amateur geographer from his youth. He encountered the works of Mahan at the age of fourteen. When he declared that America's isolation had passed forever, as he frequently did, he was thinking in terms of the dependence of American security upon foreign naval bases and upon the vital sea lanes into the Atlantic and not merely in terms of the spiritual interdependence of peoples. It may be that by contemporary sophisticated standards of wisdom in *Realpolitik* Roosevelt was woefully ignorant. Certainly, his early pronouncements about foreign policy indicate that he, like almost all the rest of the nation, was blind to the full implications of the rise of fascism. His fondness for the Navy and his lively interest in the role of sea power were not matched by a clear and comprehensive conception of power politics or by a sound grasp of the role of the great land masses. He preferred to improvise and play by ear when it came to rendering the strange polyphony of international politics; he had little patience with the complexities of notation or the principles of composition. Nevertheless, Roosevelt's relatively enlightened view of the realities of international relations did enable him to perceive one fact of immense importance, and that was the fact that the domination of either Europe or Asia by a hostile and aggressive power would be a disaster for America's hemispheric security.

This conception of American security dominated Roosevelt's thinking about foreign policy during the critical years before Pearl Harbor. It is true that, time and again, he justified specific measures designed to check Fascist aggression on grounds suggesting that nothing was dearer to his heart than keeping America strictly neutral and free of foreign entanglements and wars; but what Roosevelt thought and what Roosevelt felt compelled to say in order to get his program enacted were frequently two different things. After the adverse public reaction to his famous Quarantine Speech in 1937 he was extremely careful to say nothing that might deprive him of a sufficient number of Congressional votes to support each successive step whereby he circumvented the restrictions of neutrality and threw the weight of the nation behind the Allied cause. A major Congressional reversal, he felt, would have been a disastrous blow to Allied resistance when the fate of democracy and America's own survival hung in the balance.

Roosevelt, like his cautious Secretary of State, Cordell Hull, was acutely conscious of the force of traditional attitudes toward American foreign policy and, perhaps, too little aware of the transformation of the American outlook being wrought under the impact of revolutionary circumstances. Consequently, he defended America's step-by-step involvement in the world struggle for power too much in terms of neutrality, nonintervention, and altruism at a time when these traditional considerations were becoming increasingly irrelevant to the real issues which troubled the American public. Thus in order to appease an isolationist minority he muddled the public's perception of the hard-headed case for American aid to the anti-Fascist powers and weakened its will to act upon that perception. Whether this was an inevitable result of necessary domestic political expediency is another matter.

Yet there can be no doubt that Roosevelt himself, as well as his advisers, understood the nature of the Fascist threat to American security, though he may have underestimated its magnitude; and there can be no doubt that he publicly declared—especially after the invasion of the Lowlands—the solid, selfish basis for America's interference in the shifting balance of power across the seas, though he may have impaired the effectiveness of his declaration with appeals to outmoded conceptions of American policy.

At an early date Roosevelt perceived the threat of Fascist aggression to America's self-interest. He publicly recognized this threat in his Quarantine Speech in October, 1937. Referring to the Japanese aggression in China and suggesting that this reign of terror might undermine the very basis of civilization, he warned Americans,

If those things come to pass in other parts of the world, let no one imagine that America will escape, that America may expect mercy, that this Western Hemisphere will not be attacked and that it will continue tranquilly and peacefully to carry on the ethics and the arts of civilization.[22]

However, the American public scarcely noticed this appeal to national self-interest in its general displeasure over a speech which it regarded as a gratuitous Wilsonian attempt to assume a moral obligation for other people's affairs. Americans would not give credence to warnings such as Roosevelt delivered, especially when the nature of the Fascist menace was left unspecified, until the threat to American security was driven home by the fall of France. Moreover, it must be admitted that, in its general tenor, the Quarantine Speech was more of a moral exhortation than an appeal to national self-interest. At this time Roosevelt was not primarily concerned with defending America by giving material aid to the democracies; he was thinking in terms of halting the disintegration of international peace and order by throwing the weight of American opinion behind some sort of collective diplomatic action based upon commonly-agreed moral principles. The Quarantine Speech, like Stimson's pronouncements of the nonrecognition doctrine, was primarily an expression of this purpose.[23]

After the Quarantine Speech Roosevelt spoke of the totalitarian menace in less alarming terms, and he was careful to reassure the nation that American policy was governed by opposition to political or military commitments and by noninterference in foreign quarrels. However, in his own mind, these objects seemed to be increasingly jeopardized by the trend of world politics. After the Munich settlement he concluded from military and political information he received that the position of Great Britain and France was perilous and that, therefore, for the sake of its own security, the United States urgently needed to strengthen its front line of defense in Europe. By the spring of 1939 the President and his advisers were convinced that war in the near future was distinctly probable and that this war might be disastrous for the United States. He shared the prevalent view that the British and French would win such a war; therefore, he was unwilling to contemplate American armed intervention. However, he was wary enough of the possibility that the Allies might lose the war to conclude that America's best hope of staying out of it lay in preventing war from ever occurring.[24]

With these considerations in mind Roosevelt advocated revising the neutrality legislation so that the American government could let the aggressors know that it would give unstinted material support to the democracies. If war should break out after all, he thought that revision would still be the best way of keeping America out, because it would enable the democracies to win. In an effort to get Congressional support for revision Roosevelt conferred with a number of House leaders in May, 1939, and told them his position quite frankly, spelling out in specific military detail the danger of German and Japanese penetration of South America in the event that war broke out and the British Navy were seized or put out of action. However, when a neutrality bill embodying a watered down version of his ideas on revision ran into Congressional opposition, Roosevelt and Hull were somewhat more circumspect in defending it. They stressed keeping America out of war far more than bolstering America's first line of defense. This was partly a result of domestic political expediency and partly a result of Roosevelt's resistance to the unpleasant conclusion that war might break out regardless of any legislation passed by Congress and that Great Britain and France might actually lose the war.

The bill was blocked in the Senate, despite the fact that a majority of the nation supported revision, largely because Borah and many other Senators were confident that war would not break out and suspected that revision was a device to serve Roosevelt's personal ambitions and his secret desire to intervene in foreign conflicts.[25] Roosevelt might have overcome Senatorial objections to neutrality revision if he had stressed the prevention of a European war less and aid to the democracies for the sake of American security more; but it must be remembered that at a time when there was a great deal of wishful thinking—especially in Congress—that war would not break out, the disposition to reject alarms about the Fascist threat to American security would probably have been even stronger than the tendency to discount warnings about the possibility of war.

Hitler's invasion of Poland confirmed Roosevelt's worst fears. With the Allies in virtual control of the Atlantic, only the existing neutrality legislation deprived them of the American goods they needed to defend themselves. So once more he sought revision of the arms embargo, convinced that the real issue was more urgent than ever. Nevertheless, he and his Secretary of State still took the position that it was folly to discuss aid to the democracies in connection with neutrality legislation, except as such aid could be represented primarily as a means of keeping America out of war. Accordingly, the supporters of the administration's Pittman Bill, taking their cue from Roosevelt and Hull, said little about the necessity of aiding the democracies for the sake of American security; instead they argued that neutrality revision was more compatible with "real" neutrality and more likely to keep the country out of war than the existing legislation. They contended that the new "cash-and-carry" provision, the very epitome of the isolationist view that the country had to keep out of war at almost any cost, would bring the United States business and still avoid the risk of involvement. Under the limitations imposed by these legislative tactics it is little wonder that the whole debate over neutrality appeared to turn upon conceptions of international law and the best way to keep America out of war.[26]

The passage of the Pittman Bill may have been a vindication of Roosevelt's legislative tactics, but it did not register a Congressional or popular verdict on the real apprehensions which had led the President to seek revision. Actually, the winter months of "phony war" that followed the passage of this bill made such apprehensions seem quite implausible. Among military men and laymen alike the comforting view spread that the Allies were bound to win the war; consequently, there was much less disposition to consider the potential Fascist threat to American security.

Roosevelt's uneasiness about the domestic political situation restrained him from attempting to counteract the growing complacency, but his own anxiety was not allayed by the lull before the storm. It was his well-founded anxiety which led him to send Under Secretary Sumner Welles to Europe in January, 1940, in a desperate effort to head off the impending all-out offensive upon the Western powers. Like Wilson, Roosevelt sought to end a war he was afraid America could not escape; but the Welles mission, unlike the House mission, was motivated by fear of a very specific menace to America's self-interest. As Roosevelt told Welles, he believed that, if war continued, one of two major dangers would be inevitable.

The first: a victory by Hitler would immediately imperil the vital interests of the United States. The other: an eventual victory of the Western powers could probably be won only after a long and desperately fought contest which would bring Europe to total economic and social collapse, with disastrous effects upon the American people.[27]

The utter failure of Welles's mission to discover any basis for peace shattered Roosevelt's last illusions about the possibility of forestalling the forthcoming holocaust in Europe, but he was quite unprepared for the swift Nazi victories in Norway, Denmark, the Low Countries, and France. This startling development had much the same effect on Roosevelt as on the rest of the country, but the basic policy objectives for dealing with it had already been established: hemispheric defense, the survival of Great Britain, and the safety of the Atlantic sea lanes. What took place in administration policy now was an intensification of effort and an acceleration of pace and, along with these changes, a more frank and explicit public recognition of the paramount importance of national security in America's relation to the foreign struggle.

On May 16 the President asked Congress for an expanded armament program, including the astounding goal of fifty thousand planes a year. He justified his request on grounds of the threat to American security. With specific details he elaborated—and undoubtedly exaggerated—that threat in terms of the flying times to various points in the Western Hemisphere from Greenland, the Azores, the Cape Verde Islands, and other strategic bases. From the developments of the last few weeks he drew the lesson that "the possibility of attack on vital American zones" made it essential that the nation have "the physical, the ready ability to meet those attacks and to prevent them from reaching their objectives." The major part of his appeal was concerned with hemispheric defense, which was popular in all quarters; but he did not neglect to repudiate the isolationist view by stating that effective defense required a strategy of attack upon bases and lines of supplies and communications far from American shores. Moreover, he made it clear that he considered the defense of England and France an integral part of the defense of the United States, and he warned that American defense needs should not take priority over the needs of these countries.[28]

Roosevelt expressed this concept of defense more forcefully in his address at Charlottesville, Virginia, on June 10, in which he repudiated the illusion that "we of the United States can safely permit the United States to become a lone island, a lone island in a world dominated by the philosophy of force" and unequivocally announced, "We will extend to the opponents of force the material resources of this nation."[29] With this declaration of policy the President positively rejected the fortress concept of national defense, which had pervaded the preparedness agitation of 1915–17 and dominated isolationist thinking at all times. With this declaration he also rejected the defeatist arguments of men like Charles Lindbergh and Ambassador Joseph Kennedy, who said that France and England were incapable of defending themselves and urged the nation to abandon them and concentrate on arming the United States exclusively.

During the presidential campaign of 1940 this bold theme was muted, to say the least, as Roosevelt, badgered by his isolationist opponents, competed for the antiwar vote with assurances that he would never send the boys into foreign wars and with ambiguous declarations that the purpose of defense was simply self-defense.* Nevertheless, Roosevelt's actions bespoke a continuing interest in maintaining America's European and Asiatic lines of defense, for during the three months preceding the election he achieved the enactment of America's first peacetime conscription law, transferred fifty overage destroyers to Great Britain in return for British bases in the Western Hemisphere, and tightened the embargo on the shipment of war materials to Japan.

With the election safely over Roosevelt felt free to get the nation back to the business of helping England to survive. It was Great Britain's critical financial and material position in the fall and winter of 1940 that moved him to evolve the historic lend-lease device, which was introduced into Congress in January, 1941, and finally approved after a bitter debate on March 11, 1941. Roosevelt first announced the basis for this ingenious legislation in a Fireside Chat on December 29. In this speech he proposed that the United States should become nothing less than "the great arsenal of democracy," and he

---

* Franklin D. Roosevelt, *The Republic Papers and Addresses of Franklin D. Roosevelt, 1940* (New York, 1941–50), pp. 464, 488; *New York Times*, September 8 and 14, 1940. Roosevelt qualified his antiwar pledges, in his own mind, with the escape clause in the Democratic platform, "except in case of attack," but he did not always mention this qualification, because he thought that it was too obvious. See his address on October 30, 1940, and his subsequent explanation. Roosevelt, *Public Papers, 1940*, p. 517; Robert E. Sherwood, *Roosevelt and Hopkins* (New York, 1948), p. 191.

pointed again to the danger of an Axis attack on the Western Hemisphere if Britain were crushed. True, he did not neglect to say that his sole purpose in converting America into the arsenal of democracy was to keep America at peace, but he made it clear that the greatest threat to American peace was not aid to Great Britain but the likelihood of German aggression upon the United States in the event that such aid failed to check aggression on the opposite shore of the Atlantic.[30]

On the face of it, Roosevelt's idea of turning the nation into an arsenal of democracy was the most extreme interpretation of the American mission, in terms of a tangible commitment, ever suggested by anyone charged with the conduct of America's foreign affairs. Woodrow Wilson had never even conceived of so bold a scheme as this. And yet the idea was readily accepted by the general public and, in due course, enacted into law. One may grant the force of sympathy and idealism in achieving this result but still reach the unavoidable conclusion that it was the instinct of self-preservation, not missionary fervor, that moved the nation to respond to Roosevelt's revolutionary suggestion.

President Wilson spurned appeals to national expediency as unworthy of American idealism, but Roosevelt struck one of the most crucial and effective blows for American ideals in the twentieth century by avowing its integral relation to the nation's selfish advantage. And yet the real difference between Franklin Roosevelt's and Woodrow Wilson's achievements lay not in their personal temperaments but in the temper of the nation, which both men reflected so accurately in their time.

3. THE LEND-LEASE CONTROVERSY

In effect, the Lend-Lease Act, which authorized the President to aid any nation "whose defense the President deems vital to the defense of the United States," committed the United States to the military defeat of Germany. The passage of H.R. 1776 marked America's complete abandonment of neutrality and its assumption of a nonbelligerent status. The public discussion, the hearings, and the Congressional debates on this momentous bill, while revealing a certain popular reluctance to face the full logic of nonbelligerency, nevertheless reflected a widespread comprehension of the broad concept of self-defense which underlay it. It was on the basis of this concept that Americans reached the series of crucial decisions which gradually converted the nation into a virtual cobelligerent.

The opponents of H.R. 1776 charged that it would lead straight to war. Convoys would be the next step, then shooting, then full-scale war. They called it a "blank check" and expressed their unwillingness to trust President

418 IDEALS AND SELF-INTEREST IN AMERICA'S FOREIGN RELATIONS

Roosevelt with the authority; some suggested that this was a "dictatorship bill" as well as a war measure. Variations upon this theme, many of them beyond the bounds of reason, were delivered by ultranationalists and Roosevelt haters, like Hearst and McCormick, by Anglophobes and anti-Semites, such as Father Coughlin, Elizabeth Dilling, Gerald L. K. Smith, and Senator Reynolds, and by those like Charles Lindbergh, former Ambassador Kennedy, and Representative Clare Hoffman, who wanted a negotiated peace and were confident that America could do business with the Axis.

The core of the isolationist position was what it had always been: the assumption that an Axis victory would not jeopardize America's vital interests to an extent worth taking additional risks of intervention to prevent; the assertion that the measures of foreign aid which the administration proposed would lead to war, either through rashness or by design. In accordance with this position, isolationists maintained that even if Germany consolidated its hold on the Continent of Europe and conquered Great Britain in her island home, the United States could get along well enough within the impregnable ramparts of the Western Hemisphere; and, anyway, why, they asked, rush to adopt costly and dangerous measures, bound to plunge America into war, on the basis of hysterical speculation about the future? Wait and see what the Germans will do; then there will be plenty of time to take appropriate countermeasures; that was their advice.

A great portion of the hearings on lend-lease was consumed in the efforts of administration opponents to get various witnesses to admit that the continental United States was in no immediate danger of a hostile assault. It would seem that they often went to great lengths to ignore the real conditions of defense in order to make their point. For example, the House minority report, which supported aid to Great Britain on grounds of sympathy rather than self-defense, made much of the assertion that the naval and·military experts before the hearing committee had agreed that the nation was in no danger of attack;[31] whereas, in actual fact, these experts had only said that that there was no danger of an immediate attack in force. The report chose to overlook the fact that Secretary of the Navy Knox, Secretary of War Stimson, Rear Admiral Yarnell, and General Pershing had all testified that the United States would be in very great danger of attack—perhaps in immediate danger of air assault—if the British Isles should fall or if the British Navy should be captured or destroyed.[32]

The administration supporters in Congress followed the President's lead in disavowing any intention of involving the nation in war and protesting that the bill was, in fact, the best assurance of peace, since it would keep the war on the other side of the ocean. They preferred not to discuss the circumstances under which the United States should enter the war in order to prevent the potential assault on the Western Hemisphere. What if England were conquered? They said they would meet that situation when it arose.

Obviously, presenting lend-lease as a peace measure involved some logical difficulties. Senator Taft perceived this when he pressed Senator Barkley to explain why, if a Nazi attack on the United States would be the inevitable result of the fall of England, the United States was not logically bound to enter the war immediately to prevent that disaster. He said that if he believed this result were inevitable he would advocate intervention himself. But Senator Barkley refused to fall into the trap of supporting complete intervention or none at all.

> What I am undertaking to say is that those of us who support the pending measure believe that the safest and surest way for the United States not to be compelled to be involved in war is to give such aid as will enable the countries which are now fighting Hitler to win. I cannot be a sufficiently accurate prophet to be certain that under no circumstances in the future will we go to war; but I am certain that if England wins we shall be less likely to be required to go to war than if Hitler wins.[33]

It is true that the exigencies of countering isolationist charges made most proponents of lend-lease less than frank in acknowledging the full logic of their position.* Like over 60 per cent of the population at this time, they probably believed that it was more important to help England win than to keep America out of war, but as long as England seemed likely to win they did not feel called upon to profess this hypothetical preference at the risk of confirming isolationist suspicions that they were interventionists. Nevertheless, there can be no doubt that they understood the nature of America's interest in the European conflict in the same way that Roosevelt and his advisers understood it.

Although Representative Luther A. Johnson defended lend-lease as a peace measure, it was a peace measure in his terms only because it checked the danger of Nazi invasion by preserving the British Navy's control of the Atlantic Ocean. He would meet the isolationists on the narrowest national grounds, which they themselves insisted upon. "On one proposition we must agree before we can consider this bill from any angle. This country is in danger. If the United States is not in danger there is no need, no justification even, for a consideration of this bill. . . ."[34]

On the same grounds, Senator Norris, the living symbol of opposition to

---

* One exception was the fiery Senator Pepper, who declared, "Call it war or do not call it war—lay it down as a premise, America will not let England fall to Hitler. If the action now proposed will not save England, we will save it anyway. Watch American opinion and see if what I say is not true." *Cong. Rec.,* 77th Cong., 1st Sess., p. 1058.

intervention in World War I, became one of the most active supporters of lend-lease. Norris never repudiated his position in World War I; but, as he wrote in his autobiography, he believed that the circumstances in 1941 were quite dissimilar, since the Axis plan of aggression and conquest "constituted a direct threat to the safety and security of the United States."[35] Throughout the winter and spring of 1941 Norris argued that lend-lease was the best assurance of peace, because the more aid the United States gave England, the more likely England was to win; whereas if England lost, he fully expected Germany to wage ruthless economic warfare upon the Americas and, eventually, launch a military attack, with the aid of her despotic allies.[36] Twenty-five years before, no one had more persistently heaped ridicule upon this thesis than Senator Norris. In the end, Norris resisted every argument against isolation but the argument of events.

4. After Lend-Lease

After the passage of Lend-Lease the United States was virtually a belligerent. Americans were still reluctant to concede the full logic of H.R. 1776; but, in practice, they acknowledged it by approving each successive step—the military occupation of Greenland and Iceland, the freezing of German and Italian assets, convoys, the arming of merchantmen, and, finally, shooting war—whereby the United States committed itself to the defeat of the Axis.

Some who granted the dependence of American security upon the survival of Great Britain refused to go as far as the administration in fighting the battle of the Atlantic. The great majority of Americans were opposed to armed intervention. Perhaps they hoped that England would finally win without American intervention; or, perhaps, they simply could not bring themselves to come any closer to the irrevocable step which had caused so much misery a quarter of a century before. William Allen White, for example, drew the line of acceptable intervention short of convoys and carrying contraband into belligerent waters. In his mind these were war measures, and he believed that war would defeat the end for which his Committee was organized; he feared that armed intervention would bring on "a thirty year conflict."[37] The *New York Times* wisely observed after White's resignation from his Committee early in January, 1941, "Like the rest of us he had no doubt been pulled two ways—toward doing everything possible to beat Hitler and toward doing nothing that will get us into war."[38] For all Americans the attempt to reconcile these two compelling purposes required a perplexing compromise, which, because of the strength of the motives involved, was bound to defy the dictates of cold, hard reason. Something of the perplexed state of public opinion is suggested by the fact that in June, 1941, the Gallup poll revealed that, although less than one-quarter of the nation favored intervention, four-fifths believed that the United States was already in the war for all practical purposes.[39]

The United States was, indeed, in the war—and for many practical purposes the public did not even suspect. Six months before the attack on Pearl Harbor the United States and Great Britain were exchanging top secret scientific information, pooling their military intelligence, co-operating closely on security matters, and exchanging military and technical specialists. Damaged British warships were being repaired in American shipyards. R.A.F. pilots and aircrews were being trained in the United States. American-British staff talks, begun in Washington at the end of January, 1941, were proceeding with the formation of a joint grand strategy.

After the passage of the Lend-Lease Act there were some, notably Secretary of War Stimson, who thought that President Roosevelt should display a more candid and energetic leadership, abandoning the pretense of nonbelligerence and nonintervention and openly adopting whatever measures were expedient for the preservation of British power, without regard for isolationist sensibilities.[40] But Roosevelt had based American policy toward the European conflict on the lowest common denominator, self-defense; and in his estimation the general public and Congress drew the line of justifiable self-defense short of the all-out measures Stimson recommended and would continue to do so until Nazi depredations on the high seas seemed to warrant those measures, step by step, for the defense of the Atlantic supply line. Moreover, Roosevelt seems to have shared much of the ambivalence and wishful thinking that prevented most Americans from frankly embracing the dreaded alternative of armed intervention. He perfectly well perceived the vital necessity of defeating Hitler's military machine, but he was also determined to keep America out of war. Consequently, he was able to convince himself that the democracies would win with American aid short of war, even though the military advice he received frequently pointed to the opposite conclusion.[41]

The administration's struggle to obtain extension of the Selective Service Act in July and August, 1941, and its passage in the House by the narrow margin of one vote suggest that Roosevelt was moving as fast as Congressional and public opinion would permit. Nevertheless, one cannot know what the public and the Congressional reaction would have been had the President frankly disabused the American people of their hope of staying out of the war and forthrightly appealed to the nation, in terms of its own self-interest, to adopt all measures, defensive or otherwise, to resist German aggression.

To a certain extent, Roosevelt's policy at this time, like Wilson's in 1915–17, rendered American action dependent upon the belligerents' interference or lack of interference with American rights and honor rather than upon the dictates of American security, despite the President's intention of not permitting "incidents" to become a cause of war. As it happened, the Japanese attack on Pearl Harbor spared America the opportunity of ascertaining whether Germany, possibly in collaboration with Japan, would attack the Western Hemisphere in the event that Great Britain were crushed. But Roosevelt's conduct of foreign policy might now deserve a harsher judgment if the Japanese had moved southward into the Dutch East Indies instead of bombing Pearl Harbor and if Hitler had restrained his submarines from attacking American ships along the supply route to England, for then the Axis powers might well have succeeded in stalling off American intervention until they could have handled America alone. And if, on the other hand, after a long series of incidents on the high seas, the nation had finally been kicked into war as in 1917, might not Americans once more have suffered unprecedented sacrifices for reasons which would have seemed woefully inadequate in retrospect?

This latter possibility, at least, seems quite implausible; for, as this chapter has sought to demonstrate, the great majority of the American people were convinced that German domination of the opposite shore of the Atlantic and German destruction of the British Navy would have a disastrous effect upon America's own security. The nation's aroused instinct for survival was the assurance that 1941 would not follow the course of 1917 in American opinion. The shifting balance of power after the fall of France aroused that instinct long before the battle of the Atlantic reached the shooting stage. Consequently, most Americans realized that it was because of a very real menace to their own interests and not because of the machinations of war profiteers, the deceit of British propagandists, or even, primarily, because of an urge to promote democracy and freedom, that they had assumed the risk of war.

And it must be acknowledged that in the public's prompt and clear-sighted recognition of the true nature of the Fascist menace and in its ready adoption of the means to combat it President Roosevelt's leadership played a decisive role. In a sense, both his success in securing the Lend-Lease Act and his near-failure in the bare passage of Selective Service vindicated his step-by-step method. He realized that his greatest single asset was the course of events. With the battle of the Atlantic approaching a crisis he had good reason to be confident that a policy of patience and admonition would be rewarded.

After the passage of Lend-Lease the exigencies of American security were more prominent than ever in Roosevelt's public pronouncements. For example, in his radio address on May 27, 1941, proclaiming an unlimited national emergency, he spelled out once more the exact nature of the peril facing the United States; he spelled it out in terms of island bases, ocean lanes, and air routes.[42] "The pressing problems that confront us are military and naval problems," he said. "We cannot afford to approach them from the point of view of wishful thinkers or sentimentalists. What we face is cold, hard fact."

Our whole program of aid for the democracies has been based on hard-headed concern for our own security and for the kind of safe and civilized world in which we wish to live. Every dollar of material that we send helps to keep the dictators away from our own hemisphere, and every day that they are held off gives us the time to build more guns and tanks and planes and ships.

Again he repudiated the isolationist strategy of defense. In considerable detail he applied the lesson of Nazi conquest in Europe to the defense of the Western Hemisphere. He warned that the attack on the United States could begin with the domination of any base that menaced American security. "Our Bunker Hill of tomorrow may be several thousand miles from Boston."

"The deadly facts of war compel nations, for simple self-preservation, to make stern choices," he declared; and then he outlined America's defense strategy once more in terms of the program set forth at Charlottesville.

First, we shall actively resist wherever necessary, and with all our resources, every attempt by Hitler to extend his Nazi domination to the Western Hemisphere, or to threaten it. We shall actively resist every attempt to gain control of the seas. We insist upon the vital importance of keeping Hitlerism away from any point in the world which could be used and would be used as a base of attack against the Americas.

Second, from the point of view of strict naval and military necessity, we shall give every possible assistance to Britain and to all who, with Britain, are resisting Hitlerism or its equivalent with force of arms. Our patrols are helping now to insure delivery of the needed supplies to Britain. All additional measures necessary to deliver the goods will be taken. Any and all further methods or combinations of methods, which can or should be utilized, are being devised by our military and naval technicians, who, with me, will work out and put into effect such new and additional safeguards as may be needed.

There was nothing equivocal about this address. Nor was it based upon the kind of military gossip and nationalistic distrust that inspired so much of the fear of German, Japanese, and Russian intentions in the first two decades of the twentieth century. The President's warnings were based upon sound professional advice, which, in turn, was based upon strategic calculations of the most detailed and objective sort.

An example of such calculations is the document Robert Sherwood has reproduced, called the "Joint Board Estimate of United States Over-all Production Requirements," dated September 11, 1941, and signed by the Chiefs of Staff General Marshall and Admiral Stark.[43] This comprehensive military estimate, as Sherwood states, "was the result of two years of wartime deliberation by Marshall, Stark, and their staffs, and of upwards of a year of exchanges of information and opinion by the British and American staffs working together in secret and unofficial but highly effective co-operation." The Joint Board's statement of the major national objectives related to military policy reveals the scope of America's vital strategic interests.

. . . preservation of the territorial, economic and ideological integrity of the United States and of the remainder of the Western Hemisphere; prevention of the disruption of the British Empire; prevention of the further extension of Japanese territorial dominion; eventual establishment in Europe and Asia of balance of power which will most nearly ensure political stability in those regions and the future security of the United States; and, so far as practicable, the establishment of regimes favorable to economic freedom and individual liberty.

Significantly, the Board decided, "These national policies can be effectuated in their entirety only through military victories outside this hemisphere, either by the armed forces of the United States, by the armed forces of friendly powers, or by both." On the basis of an analysis of probable German and Japanese strategy it reached the conclusion that "the principal strategic method employed by the United States in the immediate future should be the material support of present military operations against Germany, and their re-enforcement by active participation in the war by the United States while holding Japan in check pending future developments." This was the basic strategy of global war which the United States followed for the next four years. It was based upon geographic, economic, and political factors which prevailed at the turn of the century and which are as relevant to America's power position today.

Strategic considerations were foremost in Roosevelt's mind during the months before Pearl Harbor. In his thoughts during 1941, he forms a striking contrast to Woodrow Wilson in 1917. Roosevelt was probably as sincerely dedicated to America's mission of world peace and freedom, as profoundly convinced in the cause of international organization, as Wilson; but his thinking reflected the temper of his times, and in 1941 he was absorbed in the nation's immediate task of self-preservation rather than in the problem of preventing future wars. Moreover, Roosevelt, along with the nation at large, had already decided upon what basis America would intervene, if intervention should become necessary. That basis was America's security, such an obvious and compelling object that affirmations of altruism and declarations of ideal visions of the future seemed almost irrelevant.

Roosevelt's frame of mind is illustrated by his refusal during the dramatic meeting with Winston Churchill aboard the *Augusta* in August, 1941, to consider as urgent the need for reaching a decision about the nature and scope of a postwar international organization. Although the Atlantic Charter, which resulted from this meeting, announced the broad terms of a system of collective security for the preservation of the peace yet to be won, and although Roosevelt clearly believed that its principles were the foundation for a free and a secure world, he was determined to consider first things first and was, therefore, reluctant to distract the American public from the primary object of winning the war by taking a stand on matters which would revive bitter memories of the League of Nations and Wilson's abortive crusade.[44]

Roosevelt intuitively sensed the temper of public opinion, and he gave voice to it. The public was guided neither by altruism nor by a hair-trigger sense of national honor. Americans were impatient with nebulous generalities and wary of impulsive indignation. Too much was at stake. The atmosphere was grim and tense, not exhilerating. There was no spirit of high adventure; no exaltation. When American security was at stake, it was enlightened self-interest that called the tune. Roosevelt was literally correct when he wrote on July 17, 1941, for the 1940 volume of his *Public Papers,* "Our policy is not based primarily on a desire to preserve democracy for the rest of the world. It is based primarily on a desire to protect the United States and the Western Hemisphere from the effects of a Nazi victory upon ourselves and upon our children."[45]

Franklin Roosevelt was determined to avoid a repetition of Woodrow Wilson's tragic failure, but he was no more willing than Wilson to embrace the methods of his distant cousin Theodore. Looking back on the period between the passage of Lend-Lease and the attack on Pearl Harbor from the vantage point of 1946, Henry Stimson thought that his old friend Theodore would have handled the crisis of 1941 better than Franklin.

> T. R.'s advantage would have been in his natural boldness, his firm conviction that where he led, men would follow. He would, Stimson felt sure, have been able to brush aside the contemptible little group of men who wailed of "warmongers," and in the blunt strokes of a poster painter he would have demonstrated the duty of Americans in a world issue.[46]

Probably there were wiser courses of leadership available to President Roosevelt than the ones his own distinct brand of political intuition led him to choose, but adopting the blunt strokes of the Rough Rider was not one of them. The age of Franklin Roosevelt was no more congenial to the ways of the Warrior than to the ways of the Priest. In 1941 the American people were neither heroic nor exalted. They were sober and anxious. The mood marked America's passing from the age of innocence. Whether it meant maturity only the continuing discipline of adversity could reveal.

CONCLUSION

CONCLUSION

G REAT changes in the way a nation thinks and acts come like the tide. They come gradually, almost imperceptibly, in a series of surges and recessions, unevenly, like the waves on a shore. But they come steadily and surely, so that if one fixes one's attention upon a landmark along the changing shoreline, one can measure the advance in the course of time, just as Thucydides observed the tide in the thoughts and behavior of Athens.

If one fixes one's attention upon the ways in which men orient themselves to their international environment, it is apparent, I think, in the perspective of the half-century since the United States became a fully conscious world power, that the American attitude toward world politics has changed so greatly as to have been virtually transformed. If one views this transformation as part of the process by which the nation has adapted itself to its status as a world power, it becomes clear, in the light of the historical interpretation presented in this study, that such a revolutionary trend in the nation's outlook must have very significant implications for America's foreign relations in the current power struggle.

The transformation in the American outlook during the crisis years preceding Pearl Harbor consisted chiefly in the fact that, for the first time since the nation had become a world power, the great majority of the American people came to understand that their everyday lives were seriously affected by what happened beyond the seas. For the first time the great mass of Americans reached the conclusion that the nation's vital interests could be jeopardized by shifts in the distribution of international power in foreign areas, especially in western Europe and the North Atlantic.

The chief source of this recent national awakening to the dependence of America's welfare upon events abroad has been the mounting fear since the beginning of World War II that the maintenance of America's democratic institutions and the preservation of America's territorial integrity are seriously threatened by the restless surge of aggressive and antidemocratic powers outside the Western Hemisphere.

If the analysis of the sources of America's international conduct which this study has presented is correct, then the recent popular fear of American insecurity is the necessary condition for the development in the national outlook of that element of political realism so vital to America's adaptation to its status as a world power and so conspicuously absent during the prosecution and aftermath of both the Spanish-American War and World War I.

The importance of the development in America of a more realistic approach to foreign relations should be apparent from the view of international realities which this study has endeavored to expound and apply. According to this view, a nation's achievement of either universal ideals or strictly national goals depends upon its making an accurate estimate of the configuration of world power and an objective calculation of the most effective means to an end. Since, in the present stage of international relations, the effective means to a national end remains, essentially, the exercise of independent national power, it is folly to expect national selflessness or sheer impulse to promote either national welfare or the welfare of humanity. On the contrary, selflessness or impulsiveness, by blinding reason to the practical conditions of national power and the specific consequences of national actions, may achieve untold international mischief and even jeopardize a nation's survival.

This basic condition of international society applies to all nations, whether their citizens realize it or not. Consequently, a nation which fails to base its actions upon the realities of international politics is doomed to impotence, at the least, and suicide, at the worst.

Surveying America's foreign relations in the light of the realities of international politics, one must conclude that the United States escaped suicide during the first thirty years or so of the twentieth century because of a fortunate configuration of circumstances rather than because of the wisdom or maturity of her international outlook. Thanks to America's relative isolation, her security was not directly or seriously threatened by shifts in international power. Thanks to her strategic dependence upon nations with similar traditions and ideals, popular sentiment and impulse coincided with the nation's long-run political and strategic interest in resisting adverse changes in the distribution of power in Europe and the Atlantic Community.

On the other hand, because the American people, as a whole, were ignorant of the political and strategic grounds of their survival, because they were innocent of the real limits upon the efficacy of impulse and moral sentiment in international relations, the United States was not fortunate enough to escape the evils of an ineffective and unstable foreign policy. Because conventional preconceptions about the wickedness or irrelevance of world politics and the omniscience and saintliness of America's international outlook were not tested by the harsh imperatives of survival, Americans acted upon the basis of expectations that could not be fulfilled, undertook commitments they would not honor, plunged themselves into bewilderment and disillusionment, and drifted about aimlessly, without chart or compass, upon the strange currents of international politics.

Americans, like all other peoples swayed by patriotic pride in a consciousness of kind and a unique history and mission, have never been consistently true to their ideals if the translation of those ideals into reality has required an important sacrifice of the national self-interest, as they have conceived it. America, like all other nations, has acted with positive and responsible idealism only when the great mass of the citizenry has been convinced that ideals and self-interest coincided. This has been a psychological fact of immense significance in America's adaptation to its status as a world power. Many Americans urged the nation to embrace the responsibilities of world leadership as a moral duty, but only when circumstances seemed to demand an abandonment of political isolation on the grounds of expediency did the nation, as a whole, accept responsible participation in world affairs commensurate with its status as a world power. Only when America's idealistic pretensions were subjected to the discipline of adversity did the nation begin to conduct its foreign relations according to a more realistic view of international society. It is the perplexing intrusion of international politics upon America's very sense of self-preservation that provides the basis for that painful but necessary transition from fitful adolescence to self-possessed maturity.

In the light of this interpretation of the underlying sources of American conduct, one can readily discern a process of national maturing, according to which the American people, under the impact of two crusades and a war for survival, have gradually adapted their conduct of foreign relations to the realities of international society.

During the international upheavals at the turn of the century and in the period 1914–17 this process of maturing was marked by a heightened concern among certain individuals and groups for the impact of international politics upon American power. True, that concern was not shared by the nation as a whole, and even among most of its chief propagators it did not represent a clear and calm political realism. Nevertheless, the American reaction to two crusades, and, particularly, the widespread disillusionment with the second one, did lay the psychological foundation for a more realistic response to the circumstances of a third upheaval.

Under the pressure of Fascist aggression there arose, in response to an aroused instinct of self-preservation, a new popular respect for the exigencies of power politics, a more sober view of the penalties of impulsiveness, and, in some quarters, an attempt to formulate a conception of American idealism more in accord with the hard facts of human nature and international life, more responsible to the practical consequences of national conduct.

With the perpetuation and intensification of the struggle for international power since World War II the trend toward political realism has become increasingly apparent. Among politicians, statesmen, and scholars there has been a mounting emphasis upon the imperatives of power in international relations. Among ordinary citizens defensive self-interest has become the determining incentive for national action. The astounding growth of America's willingness to take an active part in world politics, the amazing speed with which Americans have junked old concepts of neutrality and readily entangled their affairs in political and military arrangements with other nations, deliberately adopting extensive world-wide commitments unthinkable a short while ago; these developments reflect a widespread recognition of the exigencies of survival. They may also signify the emergence of a more stable and effective foreign policy.

2. INSECURITY DOES NOT ASSURE REALISM

The fear of national insecurity is the indispensable condition for the growth of political realism, but it is not realism itself.

Only a cursory examination of the history of America's foreign relations during the last ten years reveals that the trend toward political realism has been uneven and uncertain. There can be no assurance that its pace will be equal to the revolutionary rate of change in America's international environment.

The public confusion and uproar about such matters as the Yalta Agreement and America's relations with China's Kuomintang suggest that the nation was permitted to embrace ideal expectations not in accord with the hard facts of international politics or the demands of national expediency.

Most Americans, including the best-informed men in positions of great responsibility, were slow to perceive and reluctant to believe the true nature of Soviet Russian expansion and its implications for American security. America's disastrous demobilization in the face of Russia's drive into the war-created power vacuums in Asia and Europe reflected a widespread illusion that victory over such a menacing foe would automatically mean the end of ruthless power conflicts, the end of America's time of troubles.

The American people are still prone to anticipate a standard of perfection in international diplomacy that exceeds the bounds of real possibilities. American leaders are still prone to seek approval of expedient compromises by muting the aspects of imperfection and appeasing the popular longing for easy and palatable solutions to essentially insoluble problems. The temptation to subordinate reason to wish grows as the people become increasingly anxious about their national and personal security.

Americans have learned much from recent experience with power politics, but their basic inexperience manifests itself in a tendency to draw extreme lessons from their disillusionment. Thus an extravagant faith in the ability of the United Nations Organization to resolve power conflicts now shows signs of giving way to an exaggerated depreciation of the United Nations as an instrument of peace and security. America's bitter discovery of the limitations upon the ordinary means of suasion and diplomacy in dealing with Russian power may lead to an unrealistic reliance upon military force or psychological warfare. From the disastrous failure of the nonaggressive powers to combine to check the aggressive powers in the thirties some now draw the dangerous conclusion that all peace-loving nations must join in resisting aggression anywhere in the world, regardless of the particular dictates of national power and security.

Those who interpret the lesson of history as the compensating for one extreme with another at least show the wisdom of recognizing that there is no escape from the trials of power politics. But there are others who view these trials as purely the result of blundering or treason, on the assumption that everything in the world that goes wrong for America must be America's fault. This illusion is the obverse side of the fatuous belief that the United States is omnipotent and can, accordingly, arrange the terms of its entanglement to suit itself.

Behind the popular impatience with international reality there is a gnawing desire to withdraw from the troublesome arena of world politics and return to an age of innocence. Basically, most Americans resent the existence of foreign relations. They would be glad to let the rest of the world go its own way if it would only go without bothering the United States. But Americans sense that they are bound to participate in the sordid society of nations for the sake of their own survival. Thus only the fear of insecurity makes their burden of world responsibility, their material and human sacrifices, seem bearable, while the very intensity of this fear heightens their yearning for withdrawal. It is a cruel dilemma which requires a nation to entangle itself in world affairs in order to escape them. Under this circumstance it is natural that the scapegoat, the easy way out, should become more and more attractive; that the troublesome imperatives of survival should become obscured by a compulsive yearning to retire to a nonexistent idyl of carefree ease and comfort.

Thus common facts of psychology, as well as the nation's traditional habits of foreign conduct, suggest that, while the transformation in the American attitude may alleviate some previous difficulties, it will also raise some new problems and exacerbate some old ones, which will seriously hamper the nation's adaptation to the real conditions of its international environment; for, manifestly, the fear of insecurity may, in fact, lead to a dangerously unrealistic state of mind and confound the free operation of clear, objective reason. Men can be panicked by fear; they can be paralyzed. Fear can make men domineering; it can make them submissive. It can even make them stubbornly complacent, when they try to wish it out of existence. There is more than one way to escape from the fear of insecurity; and what makes escape attractive is that each method can be taken in the name of national security; for security, like danger, takes many forms, and anxious minds will tend to perceive the form that best suits their predispositions.

In the future it seems likely that the great debates on American foreign policy will be argued, not in terms of the existence of a foreign menace, but in terms of the nature and magnitude of the menace and the strategy of combatting it. This emphasis was already apparent in the isolationist debates preceding World War II. But, in spite of the rational exterior, beneath the surface of these arguments there will seethe the same sentiments and impulses which have always shaped the American attitude toward international politics. So the danger for the future is not that America will fail to recognize the threat to its security but that it will lack the patience and wisdom to take a sufficiently broad, far-sighted, and imaginative view of the threat to confront it effectively. Patience, wisdom, imagination, and foresight are qualities which call for strong nerves. America's nerves have never been tested by prolonged international tension.

It is not altogether fortunate that the threat which has aroused and sustained America's instinct for survival has been envisioned, primarily, as a threat of direct military aggression. True, the nation's preoccupation with the fear of hostile military force, which is rooted, ultimately, in the mental image of an hypothetical attack upon American soil, has resulted in constructive measures which might not otherwise have been taken; but this simple view of reality has also fostered a certain superficial and erratic quality in America's international outlook. As in 1939–41, America's willingness to act internationally has tended to fluctuate in response to the tension of the immediate situation. For example, it is doubtful whether the Marshall Plan could have survived Congressional scrutiny but for the timely pressure of Soviet Russian force; yet the Marshall Plan was based upon economic and psychological considerations which would have been urgent regardless of the temporary flux of potential military power. The fate of universal military training seems to depend primarily upon the momentary level of popular fear; yet the plan for universal military training is based upon a long-term calculation of the distribution of international power, which is valid or invalid regardless of the size of the daily headlines.

A half-century of controversy over military preparedness has demonstrated that Americans insist upon visualizing national power in concrete terms. That is natural, because it is easy. But, in the long run, the crucial elements of power may exert a subtle, steady pressure—like the pressure of psychological, economic, and political factors—which will severely tax the ordinary citizen's powers of perception. The greater the international tension, the more difficult imaginative perception becomes.

One of the most important elements of national power is diplomacy, for diplomacy is the instrument which gives direction to all the other elements of power and applies them to the complex procedures whereby one nation communicates with another. But the average American still tends to regard diplomacy as one of the black arts, by means of which the high priests of the frock-coated clan confound the simple and direct purposes of the ordinary citizen. The more conspicuous the elements of international conflict become, the more suspicious the ordinary citizen grows concerning the occult dealings of the diplomatic masters of his destiny. The more conspicuous the elements of force, the more impatient he becomes with the delicate, devious negotiations and compromises, which are the essence of diplomacy. At the same time, the instruments of force, the weapons, the planes, the bombs, become more and more the accepted criteria of national power and the military leaders more and more the shapers of national policy.

3. The Increased Need for Realism

Thus the very circumstances which are the potential source for the growth of a new realism in the American attitude toward foreign affairs are circumstances which make realism more difficult. These circumstances promise to grow more difficult yet, as the power struggle between the Russian-dominated and non-Russian–dominated worlds is prolonged, as popular anxiety increases, patience runs out, and nerves grow taut. At the same time, these are also the circumstances that make political realism an absolute prerequisite for American survival.

Since World War II the international contest for power has become polarized between the East and the West. The era of a multiplicity of great powers, engaging in ever-shifting alliances and alignments, which had begun to vanish even before World War II, has given way to an era of two dominant power centers, balanced only by the unstable equilibrium of an all-out competition for supremacy. Along with the passing of the old era there has also passed the circumspection and caution, the limited objectives and moderate aspirations, which characterized traditional balance-of-power diplomacy. The buffers, buttresses, and neutralizing elements that diffused and dispersed international tensions when the world was inhabited by many power centers have vanished with the ascension of two hostile giants irrevocably committed to a "cold war." The possibilities of what Henry Adams called "McKinleyism" have now been completely and, probably, eternally precluded by the process of combination which both of the Adamses and H. H. Powers foresaw.

With the polarization of international conflict America's position as a world power has been revolutionized. Formerly, the great international struggles for power were centered in Europe; the United States was involved in European chaos only indirectly. But now the United States, as one of the two non-European power centers, is directly and inextricably involved in power contests throughout the world; and the nations composing America's strategic bulwark in western Europe are frequently concerned with these contests only indirectly through their dependence upon American strength. One obvious result is that the United States has lost what remained of her freedom to act or not to act without suffering the consequences. Now every international move that the American government makes, indeed every failure to move, bears directly upon the nation's own security, prestige, and general welfare.

Clearly, this situation exacerbates the perplexing conflict between America's longing to withdraw from world responsibility and her anxious apprehension of the real conditions for survival. It heightens the emotional strains, the nervous drain, the distortions of reason, the wishful thinking, the impatience with reality, which have accompanied America's rising preoccupation with force and self-preservation. Yet just because the interests of the United States are so inextricably entangled in world politics, a realistic approach to the relation of the means to the ends of national policy has become indispensable for sheer self-preservation. Because the United States is now one center of a polarized international society, the train of consequences resulting from a given American action has become not only more directly related to American survival but also immeasurably more complex and far-reaching. Consequently, the nation must conduct its foreign relations in accordance with a farsighted and imaginative calculation of the practical effect of its actions upon American interests, if only because the pitfalls and penalties of impulsiveness and unrealistic expectations are so greatly magnified.

The revolutionary circumstances of America's world position not only complicate the nation's problems of calculating its own interests but thrust upon it the problems of leading a coalition of nations, each of whose interests are intricately entangled with American interests and yet not identical with either America's interests or the interests of the other members of the coalition. When Theodore Roosevelt and Woodrow Wilson urged their countrymen to assume world leadership, the United States could choose—though it had less choice than most Americans supposed—whether it would lead or just drift, and it did not have to worry about the effect upon its own security in any immediate or direct way. But world leadership is unavoidable now, since America must assume the responsibilities of the head of a coalition for the sake of its own self-preservation.

Obviously, under this circumstance the possibilities of vexing differences with other nations are multiplied immensely. The temptation to lapse into sullen xenophobia or petulant self-righteousness must be correspondingly greater. At the same time, the consequences of excessive national pique or pride and of all those manifestations of intolerance in which Americans have traditionally indulged themselves with impunity become magnified far beyond the bounds of ill feeling. Compromise and tact become prerequisites of survival, not just canons of good taste. America's maturity and poise in its foreign relations, just as clearly as planes and tanks, become indispensable elements of national power.

Clearly, the attainment of national maturity and poise demands a large measure of rationality and objectivity in the attitude of the American people toward the outside world. A consistent rationality and objectivity, in turn, presupposes a realistic comprehension of the fundamental political conditions for the preservation of America's essential national interests.

4. The Mounting Contradictions between Ideals and Self-interest

A great part of the difficulty as well as the necessity of realistic world leadership arises from the fact that the current polarized power conflict is not only a relentless struggle between divergent national interests but also an uncompromising contest between competing ideologies.

As this study has sought to demonstrate, ideal goals are not obtained in the real world of conflicting national purposes by moral fervor alone but only by a pragmatic calculation of the means to an end, by a rational anticipation of the actual consequences of a given action. But because international society is morally and institutionally imperfect, it is inevitable that the effective means for the achievement of even the loftiest ends will frequently fall far short of ideal standards; therefore, the wise conduct of foreign relations must involve a continual series of compromises with perfection.

A nation that was truly isolated from the ordinary concerns of international society could avoid most of these compromises by contenting itself with self-defense. But a nation that seeks to alter the course of international relations for ideal purposes or a nation whose self-interest depends upon events beyond its own borders avoids compromising its principles only at the ultimate sacrifice of its ideals or its self-interest or both.

By the same logic, the more a nation's position in world politics depends upon the actions of other nations, the more compromises it will have to accept. Because the United States, by virtue of its gigantic power, has been thrust into an inescapable position of world leadership, it will, inevitably, face more and more decisions in which it must compromise its ideals in the short-run in order to achieve them in the long-run, just as it must sacrifice something of its immediate material welfare and independence of action in order to preserve them ultimately.

The more conscious of the need for defending and promoting its ideals America becomes, the more acute this dilemma will grow. Since the current power struggle takes the form of an ideological contest, Americans will be constantly perplexed by the task of reconciling the immediate demands of national expediency with the traditional principles of the American mission. They will be plagued, as never before, by the seeming inconsistency between their ideals and their actions. In the long run America's power interest may correspond to its ideal goals. That would seem to be the lesson of the last two wars. But in the short run the imperfection of international society confronts men of good will with the most unpalatable contradictions between self-interest and universal ideals, contradictions which they can ignore only at the ultimate sacrifice of both ends.

These contradictions will appear in different forms to men of different temperamental and philosophical predispositions. Liberal idealists and international reformers, who seek to spread liberty, equal opportunity, and material progress throughout the world, will find that these worthy objects depend, first of all, upon the survival of the United States and its allies; and, realizing this, they will be forced to put the exigencies of power politics ahead of their moral sensibilities. Similarly, if they want to pursue their ideals effectively, they must base American aid to foreign peoples primarily upon the power advantage of the United States and only secondarily upon humanitarian considerations. They must, at times, support reactionary and antidemocratic regimes with arms and money. They must even put themselves in the position of resisting with force the misguided proponents of a social revolution, which arises, in large part, from basic human aspirations which the American mission itself claims to fulfil.

Conservative idealists, who share the humanitarian sentiments, some of the political principles, but few of the fervent economic and social beliefs of their liberal brethren, men who are little concerned with reforming the status quo but unalterably opposed to communism and all its works, will be faced with the fact that effective opposition to communism may require negotiating and temporizing with Communist states, granting them certain concessions, and even aiding them with arms and money if they stray from the Russian power center; for the long-run interests of the anti-Communist bloc may absolutely depend upon all these distasteful compromises.

As a crescendo of international conflict magnifies the consequences of each national decision, America's problem of reconciling its ideals with its self-interest comes close to being a life-or-death matter. With the multiplication of contradictions between ideals and self-interest, the problem grows infinitely more complex. Balancing a present loss against a future gain is always a difficult operation for a nation. When the operation requires compromising one's principles in order to promote them, it doubly strains man's limited reason and imagination. When reason and imagination are subjected to the pressure of a persistent and pervasive power struggle, clearly, international circumstances have conspired to put a premium upon American maturity.

Men naturally seek to avoid the task of reconciling contradictions between their reason and their desire, even if they fear the consequences of a failure to reach an effective compromise; for, as we have suggested, fear itself may weaken and distort reason, while impelling unreasoning desire to wrap itself in rational camouflage. Under the present impact of world politics upon the American outlook, as under the circumstances of 1914–17, the practical task of reconciling national expediency with universal ideals will be confounded by temperamental and philosophical biases and antipathies, even though divergent opinions may be couched largely in terms of America's self-interest.

Those idealists who yearn to believe that the world is governed by reason and morality and who are repelled by irrational conflict, undisciplined emotion, and the crude resort to physical force, may underestimate the sheer military threat of organized communism in their preoccupation with its social, moral, or intellectual roots. They will probe beneath its aggression and violence and perceive that these are but the outward symptoms of a social revolution transcending national conflict. They will examine history and discover that these external manifestations are the result of a spiritual wound which the West itself has inflicted or, at least, failed to heal. Accordingly, some may obscure the contradictions between their ideals and the unpleasant dictates of expediency by supposing that America's interests and the interests of humanity depend far less upon the negative policy of opposing force with force than upon a positive program of social and economic reconstruc-

440 IDEALS AND SELF-INTEREST IN AMERICA'S FOREIGN RELATIONS

tion, an ideological counteroffensive, and a variety of devices to pacify or convert the misguided masses under Communist rule.

On the other hand, national egoists who are scornful of attempts to mitigate international conflict by rational suasion and by altering the international environment, as well as those whose political philosophy leads them to an obsessive hatred and fear of communism, and those whose visceral reactions predispose them to regard the forceful and independent assertion of strictly American objectives as the end-all and be-all of foreign relations, may tend to oversimplify the sources of communism, to comprehend Communist power almost solely in terms of internal subversion, cruel repression, and military force, or to equate America's defense with an inflexible opposition to communism in all forms, everywhere, and at all times. They will ignore the contradictions between their hatred of communism and the real exigencies of power politics by equating the disruption of Communist ideology with the resistance to Russian imperialism.

Associated with this latter group will be a host of irresponsibles, motivated chiefly by their antipathy toward the liberal, intellectual position; and, allied with them, will be the parochial nationalists and xenophobes, for whom opposition to communism is simply an expression of their special brand of superpatriotism, a manifestation of hostility toward an alleged internal threat, corresponding closely to the exigencies of domestic politics but bearing only a nominal relation to the imperatives of international politics.

According to their particular prejudices and predilections, a variety of groups, each exhibiting its own species of unrealism, will be tempted to disregard the inevitable contradictions between the practical dictates of American policy and their emotional inclinations by envisaging American interests in a way better calculated to gratify their desires in the short run than to achieve them in the long run. Beneath the rational exterior of the running debate upon American policy the underlying antipathies among these groups will rub against each other, confounding reason with the heat of passion and distracting popular attention from the practical conditions of fundamental self-interest, upon which all groups might agree. The verbal symbols of this process of obfuscation will be words like "appeaser" and "isolationist," rather than "mollycoddle" and "militarist," but the end result, as during 1914–19, could well be a national policy of drift and impulse, undisciplined by a comprehension of the complex circumstances of the real world.

5. REALISM REQUIRES REASON FOCUSED UPON SELF-INTEREST

A widespread political realism remains the indispensable balance wheel of America's foreign relations, but there is no formula for attaining it, no final solution or magic key to the problem. There is the hope, however, that America's public officials—above all, the President—and America's political and intellectual leaders will have the wisdom to discover and the ability to communicate—while the great majority of the nation has the ability to appreciate and the fortitude and patience to follow—the dictates of clear, calm, unencumbered reason. For it will take a courageous respect for reason to penetrate the web of fear and hope that distracts anxious minds from the true conditions of self-preservation; it will take reason to fix the nation's attention upon the trying exigencies of world leadership.

The focus of reason must be America's own enlightened self-interest—above all, America's self-preservation—not only because all other objects depend upon this one but also because national security commands a steady and a compelling respect from the great mass of the American people. It is an indispensable object, and all patriots agree that it is indispensable. Therefore, national security lends itself to rational discussion, relatively free of the temperamental and philosophical antipathies which hover about the more intangible objects, such as national ideals and national honor.

Skeptics may disparage the power of reason to govern the actions of a democratic people, and one could endlessly debate this point in general terms. But the fact remains that it was, pre-eminently, an appeal to popular reason which finally transformed America's attitude toward its political relations with the rest of the world, in spite of all contrary preconceptions and emotional inclinations. The history of the last decade has shown that when the American people are convinced that their vital interests are at stake, reason is a more persuasive guide to policy than either wish or impulse. There is a strong element of pragmatic common sense in the American people. It needs only to be informed to be effective.

6. REALISM MUST PERCEIVE THE INTERRELATION OF IDEALS AND SELF-INTEREST

If the United States is to have a stable and effective foreign policy, neither egoism nor altruism must interfere with the rational, objective assessment of the real long-run conditions of American self-interest; but this does not mean that Americans should forsake their traditional idealism and relapse into cynicism or moral apathy, any more than that they should renounce their self-esteem. It does not mean that American foreign policy should be guided solely by the goal of self-preservation. This is neither necessary nor desirable. America's task is to be realistic in its view of the actual conditions of international politics without sacrificing its allegiance to universal ideals as an ultimate standard of conduct.

In the Introduction it was contended that idealism and self-interest need not be mutually exclusive in international relations, any more than in personal relations. They should be and are, in fact, complementary. In our everyday life we take it for granted that society gains most when idealism and self-interest coincide. The common slogans that appeal for ethical conduct among individuals recognize this bit of wisdom: Honesty is the best policy; Crime doesn't pay; Drive carefully, the life you save may be your own.

Certainly, there is a vast area of international relations in which the universal ideals of peaceful settlement, humanitarianism, individual liberty, and the extension of material progress coincide with America's selfish advantage. The turbulent events of the last half-century—for instance, America's experience in resisting Fascist aggression—have repeatedly demonstrated this truth. In the great majority of the decisions which face the United States in its relations with the outside world, as in countless commonplace decisions confronting individuals in their personal relations, it is not a question of choosing between idealism or self-interest but of combining the two.

Therefore, having urged the necessity of a realistic cognizance of the imperatives of power politics in America's approach to its international environment, this essay must affirm that the calculation of national advantage without regard for the interrelation of ideals and self-interest is not only immoral as a national end but unrealistic as a means to an end. It is unrealistic because such a restricted view of the ends and motives of nations cannot comprehend the real conditions under which nations can hope to achieve their ends by reconciling national self-interest with universal ideals. It fails to comprehend these conditions because it does not perceive that the pursuit of national self-interest without regard for universal ideals is self-defeating, because it misjudges human nature, and because it ignores the interdependence of expediency and principle.

7. SELF-INTEREST WITHOUT IDEALS IS SELF-DEFEATING

Fundamentally, there is no justification for ideals beyond the ideals themselves. They are matters of faith, not empirical propositions. But, if one assumes the worth of the Christian-liberal-humanitarian ideals, as this essay does, then it is relevant to understand that the calculation and pursuit of national self-interest without regard for universal ideals is not only immoral but self-defeating. Any assessment of the conditions for achieving a nation's international ends which ignores this fact is unrealistic.

If one believes that the enrichment of the individual's life, and not the aggrandizement of the state, is the ultimate goal of politics, if one believes that the object of survival is not mere breathing but the fulfilment of the liberal and humane values of Western civilization, then the preservation and the promotion of American power and interests cannot be an end in itself; it is but a means to an end. This is not just a theoretical consideration. It has practical implications for the conduct of America's foreign relations, and for her domestic affairs too, in the present time of troubles.

National security, like danger, is an uncertain quality; it is relative, not absolute; it is largely subjective and takes countless forms according to a variety of international circumstances. Under the complex circumstances of a world-wide power conflict the bounds of self-preservation are vastly extended, until there is scarcely any aspect of foreign policy that does not involve the nation's safety. Under the impact of persistent fear and tension national security becomes even more protean and nebulous, so that the notion of self-defense tends to become absorbed in the notion of self-assertion, and the assertion of national pride, honor, prestige, and power tends to become an end in itself. But when the preservation or aggrandizement of national power becomes an end in itself, the search for security will have defeated its very purpose; for according to the values which America professes to exemplify, power is meaningless unless it is a means to some ultimate goal.

If American power becomes an end in itself, American society, no less than international society, will suffer; for unless American security is measured by ideal standards transcending the national interest, it may take forms that undermine the moral basis of all social relations. If the Christian, humanitarian, and democratic values, which are the basis of America's social and political institutions, are valid at all, they are as valid outside American borders as within. Consequently, if they cease to compel respect in America's foreign relations, they will, ultimately, become ineffective in her domestic affairs. The resulting destruction of America's moral fiber through the loss of national integrity and the disintegration of ethical standards would be as great a blow to the nation as an armed attack upon her territory.

I do not mean that the standard of conduct in America's internal affairs varies in direct proportion with her standard in foreign relations. Clearly, this is not the case, for the relative anarchy of international society imposes severe limitations upon human morality, which, fortunately, do not apply to relations among groups and individuals within the structure of American society. Nevertheless, since the validity of the moral and ethical principles which form the bonds of American society is derived from their universal applicability, it would be unrealistic to suppose that the American people can maintain the vitality of these principles within their national borders while they are allowed to languish outside. If national self-interest becomes an all-consuming end in America's outlook upon international relations, it will necessarily jeopardize the strength and stability of liberal and humane values within the United States.

Woodrow Wilson and other American idealists understood the profound moral and psychological bond between America's international and her national behavior. Their mistake was in confusing what was ideally desirable with what was practically attainable. To expect nations to conform to the moral standards obeyed by groups and individuals within nations is not only utopian but, as Theodore Roosevelt asserted, ultimately destructive of both universal principles and the national advantage. But it is equally true that to reduce what is ideally desirable to what is practically attainable is to deprive the popular conscience of a standard of moral judgment which is indispensable to the progress and stability of all social relations, whether within or among nations. This is the moral dilemma posed by the impact of man's egoism upon his desire for perfection. In the past, American Realists have been too prone to ignore this dilemma by investing the unpleasant realities of national egoism with the character of normative principles.

Men who would be idealistic and realistic at the same time could better afford to ignore the moral incongruities of international politics if they lived in an environment which permitted them to achieve all their goals simultaneously without compromising one goal in terms of another. But, actually, the complexity of international relations absolutely precludes this circumstance. Thus national security pursued without relation to ideal goals may lead to the sacrifice of individual freedom, social progress, and other transcendant values which make security worth having in the first place. It follows that, unless Americans constantly relate their pursuit of national security to a hierarchy of universal values, they will, ultimately, drive out of their national, as well as their international conduct, those moral qualities which are as indispensable to national welfare as character is to personal welfare.

This is no academic proposition, for as America's foreign relations grow more complex, there will be a natural tendency to resolve moral dilemmas and contradictions by ignoring them or by rationalizing them out of existence. When the exigencies of national power conflict with universal principles, patriots will tend to reconcile the two goals by identifying American interests with the interests of humanity. This identification will be all the easier, and a lot more dangerous, by virtue of the fact that the interests of free peoples everywhere are to such a large extent dependent upon the interests of the United States. Self-deception and self-righteousness reign supreme in matters of international morality, and Americans are by no means immune. Thus under the stress of "cold war" America's moral fervor could become little more than a thin rationalization of a self-defeating preoccupa-

tion with American security, just as the crusading ardor of American imperialists once sanctified an urge for national power.

It is quite unlikely that Americans will again set out on the kind of crusade
they embraced in either 1898 or 1917, but unless they manifest a firm allegiance
to positive ideal goals that are something more than a rationalization of
immediate impulses, they may well be tempted to indulge in a different sort of
crusade, which would be equally abortive and far more disastrous than either
of America's previous crusades. In this crusade Americans would be absorbed
in the negative purpose of opposing communism.

A nation on the defensive, a nation preoccupied with preserving its security,
naturally views its foreign policy in terms of opposing the enemy. The intensification of ideological warfare and the mounting threat of subversion and
military force may lead many Americans to equate the resistance to communism with the transplanting of American institutions and America's economic system abroad, while committing the nation as a whole to a compulsive opposition to anything and everything that appears to encourage the
spread of communism or to alter the status quo. This negative crusade would
be rationalized in terms of traditional American ideals and the exigencies of
survival, and this rationalization would be largely justified; but hatred and
fear would be its dominant motive; a stupefying hatred and a paralyzing fear
would determine its consequences. And this crusade, compared to its two
predecessors, would be far less restrained by isolationist inhibitions.

A realist must recognize that a crusade like this would undermine
America's ideals as well as her material interests; for communism cannot be successfully opposed by making foreign relations conform to a rigid
ideological pattern, and the complex nature of international relations forbids
impulsive solutions to intractable problems of power. If the American people
become so transfixed by their fears of communism that they forget what
they are for in their obsession with what they are against; if the only standard
of national conduct they demand of their leaders is that every national act
manifest a moral judgment against communism, regardless of the consequences; if they reduce the American mission to a dead-level anticommunism;
then they will, in large measure, abdicate control of their own affairs according to their own purposes and, instead, render national policy the haphazard
product of a series of shortsighted responses to the actions of others. Superficial ideological consistency is a formula for disaster.

Yet it would be equally unrealistic to ignore or depreciate the moral issues
in foreign relations in an effort to concentrate upon the practical requirements
of national self-interest. This essay has taken the position that a rational
calculation of the imperatives of American power is needed to moderate and

guide the nation's idealistic impulses; but it would be foolish to suppose that a concern for America's power interest could, by itself, suffice to check the impulsiveness of American foreign policy; for it is, to a large extent, that very concern which, under the stress of continual fear, tends to distort reason and destroy moderation. Once more the lesson is clear: unless national self-interest is sought within the context of ultimate moral values transcending both egoistic and idealistic impulses, it must be self-defeating. Unless contemporary Realists in seeking to counter utopianism take into account the interdependence of ideals and self-interest in international relations, they will spread little enlightenment by opposing one kind of oversimplification with another.

8. HUMAN NATURE DEMANDS THAT IDEALS SUPPLEMENT REASON

It should not be supposed that recognizing the role of ideals in giving direction and purpose to the pursuit of national self-interest is purely an intellectual operation; it requires a sympathetic appreciation as well as a rational calculation of national ends. We have held that reason without moral purpose is incapable of resisting the tendency of national self-interest to become an end in itself, since only moral purpose can hold man's incurable egoism subordinate to the universal values which give self-interest meaning. But only an idealistic nation could fully appreciate this truth.

A view of international relations which imagines that nations can in the long run achieve a stable and effective foreign policy solely by a rational calculation of the demands of national self-interest is based upon an unrealistic conception of human nature, for it is certainly utopian to expect any great number of people to have the wit to perceive or the will to follow the dictates of enlightened self-interest on the basis of sheer reason alone. Rational self-interest divorced from ideal principles is as weak and erratic a guide for foreign policy as idealism undisciplined by reason. No great mass of people is Machiavellian, least of all the American people. Americans in particular have displayed a strong aversion to the pursuit of self-interest, unless self-interest has been leavened with moral sentiment.

A genuine realist should recognize that the transcendent ideals expressed in the traditional American mission, no less than America's fundamental strategic interests, are an indispensable source of stability in America's foreign relations. The vitality and the persistence of the liberal strain of American idealism—whether manifested in anti-imperialism, the peace movement, internationalism, the search for disarmament, or anti-fascism—is evidence of this fact. However naïve or misguided the proponents of this central strain of American idealism may have been during the last half-century, they have,

nevertheless, tenaciously preserved its vital core, which constitutes its universal validity; and their continual reassertion of that vital core of moral
purpose—a reassertion kindled by a lively conscience and a profound faculty
for self-criticism—has been one of the strongest, most consistent, and most
influential aspects of America's international conduct. If American idealism
has, at times, been an unsettling influence upon foreign policy, it is because
it has lacked the discipline of political realism; but this is largely due to
America's relative isolation and security in the past, not to any fatal antithesis
between realism and idealism. One can well imagine American idealism
being moderated by a less utopian view of international politics—indeed signs
of this development are already apparent—but a steady and effective foreign
policy devoid of moral appeal is scarcely conceivable.

If the present international tension puts a premium upon a rational comprehension of the thrust of national power and self-interest in world politics,
it equally demands an unwavering devotion to ideal ends transcending the
national interest in order that reason be given direction and purpose. For
example, we have observed that, according to a realistic view of international
relations, the American people must be prepared to compromise their ideals
in the short run in order to preserve and promote them in the long run.
We have stated that compromise will become increasingly necessary, the
longer the polarized power struggle persists; and that, therefore, the need
for clear, calm reason will become correspondingly great. However, unless
the people realize that reason is only the instrument for effecting compromises
and not the standard for judging their effectiveness, some anxious citizens, in
their growing concern for the national security, may become so habituated to
compromise that they will lose sight of the ideal criteria of judgment which
determine whether a compromise achieves its purpose. They may blindly
settle upon the half-loaf or reject the loaf altogether, when three-quarters of
the loaf is available. As fear may constrict ideals to an inflexible pattern,
reason may so continually stretch ideals to suit expediency that they will
lose all shape and elasticity. The end result will be the same: the undermining
of that idealistic element of stability in foreign relations, which reason alone
cannot supply.

We have said that the test of political realism in the future will be not so
much the nation's realization that its security is threatened as its ability to
take a sufficiently broad, far-sighted, and imaginative view of the threat to
confront it effectively. The danger is that the American people will ignore or
underestimate the subtle forms of power—the intangible psychological and
political influences, the devious pressure of diplomacy—because of their preoccupation with the obvious show of sheer military force; and that, because

they view the threat of power too narrowly, they will meet it inadequately. But what can induce the people to take a sufficiently broad view of their self-defense? Fear is more likely to exaggerate the overt forms of power than to stimulate an awareness of the subtle forms. A strictly rational concentration upon America's self-interest may lead to an equally narrow view of the real requirements of security. Too mean a spirit of national egoism breeds contempt for the great variety of motives that move men's minds; therefore, it leads men to misjudge a factor of power basic to all other factors: the psychological factor, the popular will.

A preoccupation with expediency leads men to seek the minimum risk and effort in the expectation of a limited return; it dulls imagination and saps initiative. A purely selfish attitude tends to confine attention to those manifestations of power which bear directly and immediately upon the national interest; it tends to obscure those positive, constructive measures which cope with the basic social and psychological conditions behind such manifestations. Rational self-interest, by itself, fails to inspire boldness or breadth of vision. It may even corrode the national faith and paralyze the will to resist. In a sense, the collapse of France was the collapse of pure rational expediency, as expressed in the popular slogan "Why die for Danzig?" It is no accident that those American isolationists in the period preceding Pearl Harbor who were most insistent that the United States shape its foreign relations strictly according to its selfish interests were also the ones who were most blind to the real requirements of American self-interest, and the least willing to take measures that recognized the dependence of American security upon the survival of Great Britain and France; whereas those idealists who were most sensitive to the Fascist menace to Western culture and civilization were among the first to understand the necessity of undertaking revolutionary measures to sustain America's first line of defense in Europe.

In other words, a realistic conception of human nature must recognize that national egoism unenlightened by idealism may lead men to view America's self-interest too narrowly to achieve or preserve security itself, for idealism is an indispensable spur to reason in leading men to perceive and act upon the real imperatives of power politics. It limbers the imagination and impels men to look beyond the immediate circumstances of the power struggle. It places the status quo in the perspective of ultimate goals. It frees the reason to examine broadly and perceptively the variety of means for adjusting the instruments of national purpose to the ever-changing international environment. Idealism illuminates the basic human aspirations common to all people and thus sharpens men's insight into the psychological sources of national power. It excites the human sympathies which inspire men to enlarge the area of mutual national interest among peoples sharing common values. Idealism is the driving force, the dynamic element, which can dispel the inertia of habit and move men to adopt the bold, constructive measures necessary for surmounting the present crisis and the crises beyond. In the long run, it is the only impulse that can sustain the people's willingness to make the personal and national sacrifices that are indispensable for sheer survival.

9. The Expediency of Idealism

A true realist must recognize that ideals and self-interest are so closely interdependent that, even on grounds of national expediency, there are cogent arguments for maintaining the vitality of American idealism.

Ideals are as much an instrument of national power as the weapons of war. All manifestations of national power, including the threat of coercion, operate by influencing the thoughts and actions of human beings, whether by frightening them or by converting them. Since men are motivated by faith and moral sentiment as well as by fear and the instinct of self-preservation, the strength of America's moral reputation and the persuasiveness of the American mission are as vital a factor in the power equation as planes, ships, and tanks. One has only to recall the consequences of the rise and fall of America's moral reputation during and after World War I to understand the force of American idealism among foreign peoples.

The persuasiveness of the American mission is especially significant under the present circumstances, when the competition of ideologies is such a conspicuous feature of the power struggle between the Russian and the American orbits and when the effectiveness of American policy depends so heavily upon winning the moral and intellectual allegiance of vast numbers of people in the throes of social and nationalistic revolution. If in the eyes of millions of people living in underdeveloped areas of the world the United States ceases to stand for a positive and constructive program of social and material progress, if American ideals no longer mean anything beyond smug generalities and hypocritical rationalizations of selfish national advantage, then all the wealth and military power the United States can muster will not render these people an asset to the free world. If the nations within the Western Coalition conclude that America has lost all passion for improving the lot of common people for the sake of the people themselves, if they believe that Americans have lost interest in the vision of world peace in their overriding concern for their national self-interest, then no display of shrewd power politics will win for the United States the popular trust and admiration which American leadership requires.

Moreover, no coalition can survive through a common fear of tyranny without a common faith in liberty. If the leader of the Western Coalition ceases to sustain that faith, then who will sustain it? Because the United States is unavoidably thrust into a position of global leadership, her standards of conduct must, inevitably, have a great influence in setting the moral tone of international relations in general. Consequently, it behooves America to conduct its foreign relations in a way that will encourage the kind of international environment compatible with its ideals and interests.

That kind of environment cannot exist apart from a widespread respect for the universal ideals of peace, brotherhood, and the essential dignity of the individual. To perceive this one has but to imagine the unmitigated anarchy that would ensue if every nation identified the interests of all nations with its own interests and pursued its own independent security as a self-sufficient end without relation to universal goals; for if every nation made expediency its sole guide in foreign relations, and if every nation anticipated that every other nation was motivated solely by the improvement of its own welfare, the only bond among nations would be the concurrence of their interests. But there is no automatic harmony of interests among nations, and unadorned reason is a weak instrument for achieving the tolerance and fair play indispensable to a contrived harmony. If national self-interest were the sole standard of conduct common to nations, an improvement in the power position of one nation would set off a wave of distrust among the rest; and, eventually, the pressure of international conflict would loosen what moral and ethical restraints man has succeeded in placing on his collective behavior; international society would disintegrate into a Hobbesian state of anarchy. In the light of this prospect, it is apparent that America's moral leadership is an indispensable instrument of her survival.

We may admit the expediency of America's reputation for idealism, but we should not imagine that America's ability to gain the moral and intellectual allegiance of foreign peoples is merely a problem in the technique of propaganda. To be sure, skilful propaganda can make a vast difference in the effectiveness of America's leadership. American ideals must be interpreted with resourcefulness and imagination, according to the particular needs and aspirations of different peoples. But, no matter how clever American propaganda may be, if it is not consistent with American actions, it will be of little value as an instrument of policy and may well alienate its intended converts. At the same time, the actions of the United States must, in the long run, reflect the actual state of American opinion; for no foreign program, least of all one of international benevolence, will survive long in a democracy if it is contrary to public opinion, and it would be extremely unrealistic to expect Americans to support such a program for its propagandistic worth if they did not also believe in its moral worth. It follows that a sincere and widespread devotion to positive ideals of human betterment is a prerequisite for effective propaganda, for Americans cannot pretend to be idealists without being truly idealistic. American idealism cannot be exported like American machinery and weapons. The United States is a democracy, and, therefore, official propaganda, in its broad outlines, must be believed to be effective. Otherwise, it will be undermined at home, foreign peoples will see that it is undermined, and American idealism will be marked down as deception and hypocrisy. Therefore, genuine conviction becomes necessary in order to sustain the appearance of idealism demanded by sheer national expediency. It is fortunate for the survival of democratic government that this paradox exists.

10. To Mature and Yet Stay Young

The history of America's conduct of foreign policy and the trend of world politics in the last half-century demonstrate that America desperately needs a more rational, a more realistic approach toward her relations with the rest of the world. At the same time, the facts of human nature and the requirements of a foreign policy capable of holding the allegiance of the American people and the respect of foreign peoples point to the necessity of a robust faith in the universal ideals traditionally embodied in the American mission. An idealistic policy undisciplined by political realism is bound to be unstable and ineffective; political realism unguided by moral purpose will be self-defeating and futile.

Of course, the success or failure of America's foreign policy will always be determined, in the first instance, by a series of practical decisions, more or less improvised to meet circumstances as they arise; but, unless these decisions conform to America's fundamental hierarchy of values among egoistic and idealistic ends and to the conditions for reconciling these ends, they will, in the long run, place foreign policy at the mercy of the international environment and dissolve the very standards of success or failure which make improvisation worthwhile.

Whether, in the next half-century, the United States will achieve a more stable and effective balance of its self-interest with the universal moral and ethical principles it has traditionally espoused depends, ultimately, upon the character of the American people—upon their moral determination and their rationality, upon their patience, humility, and adaptability. Taken as a whole, the record of the foreign relations of the United States during the last half-century is more promising when judged from the standpoint of American character than when judged by the conventional tenets of statesmanship.

One judges an adolescent by his potentialities, by his ability to learn from experience, as well as by the standards of mature wisdom. After all, the United States is young in terms of its experience with the adversities of international politics. Only since the fall of France, in 1940, has the nation, as a whole, experienced a real threat to its self-preservation, the kind of threat which the older nations of Europe have had to live with for over a century. Yet ever since the United States became a fully-conscious world power a considerable number of Americans have had the foresight and imagination to perceive the true measure of America's international commitments and responsibilities. And since the fall of France the great majority has shown a remarkable readiness to adapt America's international conduct to revolutionary circumstances and virtually transform her traditional relations with the other nations of the world.

At the same time, America's devotion to ideals transcending its own interests has, in spite of self-righteousness and erratic fluctuations in moral enthusiasm, remained the substance of a strong and profound popular conscience. In the course of two crusades and a war for survival America's sense of mission has lost much of its youthful buoyance, but, on the other hand, it has gained a certain soberness and humility, which enhance its stability.

The American people have shown an ability to grasp the hard realities of world leadership and yet retain the moral enthusiasm nourished during isolation and innocence. No people has had to grow old so fast. The nation is still in transition. But for one who takes a cue from the confidence which Americans traditionally place in themselves, there is reason for hoping that the United States is one nation that will mature and yet stay young.

NOTES

NOTES

NOTES TO INTRODUCTION

1. Thucydides *The Peloponnesian Wars* ii. 40.
2. *Ibid.* v. 89, 105.
3. Carlton J. H. Hayes, *Essays on Nationalism* (New York, 1941), chap. iv.

NOTES TO CHAPTER I

1. Clara E. Schieber, "The Transformation of American Sentiment towards Germany, 1870–1914," *Journal of International Relations*, XII (July, 1921), 51–55.
2. The following account of the Samoan crisis is based upon George H. Ryden, *The Foreign Policy of the United States in Relation to Samoa* (New Haven, 1933).
3. George T. Davis, *A Navy Second to None* (New York, 1940), p. 81. An amusing account of how Assistant Secretary of the Navy Theodore Roosevelt handled this panic appears in Roosevelt to Bonaparte, August 1, 1905, Elting E. Morison, ed., *The Letters of Theodore Roosevelt* (Cambridge, 1951), IV, 1295.
4. Davis, *op. cit.*, p. 83.
5. Alfred T. Mahan, *The Influence of Sea Power upon History, 1660–1783* (Boston, 1890), pp. 26–27, 82–83. A good summary of Mahan's doctrine of sea power appears in Harold and Margaret Sprout, *Toward A New Order of Sea Power* (Princeton, 1940), chap. i.
6. William D. Puleston, *Mahan* (New Haven, 1939), p. 129.
7. For Mahan's influence abroad see *ibid.*, pp. 107–9, and William E. Livezey, *Mahan on Sea Power* (Norman, Oklahoma, 1947), pp. 58 ff.
8. Harold and Margaret Sprout, *The Rise of American Naval Power, 1776–1918* (Princeton, 1946), p. 205.

9. *The Interest of America in International Conditions* (Boston, 1910), p. 168.
10. *The Problem of Asia and Its Effect upon International Policies* (Boston, 1900), p. 187.
11. *The Interest of America in Sea Power, Present and Future* (Boston, 1898), p. 243.
12. *Ibid.*, p. 245.
13. *Ibid.*, p. 51.
14. *Ibid.*, p. 212.
15. *Ibid.*, pp. 156–57.
16. *Ibid.*, chap. i.
17. *Ibid.*, chap. ii.
18. *Problem of Asia*, pp. 29–30.
19. *Interest of America in Sea Power*, p. 121.
20. *Ibid.*, p. 122.
21. *Ibid.*, p. 233.
22. *Lessons of the War with Spain and Other Articles* (Boston, 1899), p. 110.
23. *Interest of America in Sea Power*, p. 156.

NOTES TO CHAPTER II

1. *Foreign Relations, 1897*, p. xv.
2. Julius W. Pratt, *Expansionists of 1898* (Baltimore, 1936), p. 211.
3. *Ibid.*, pp. 22, 232–316.
4. Alfred T. Mahan, *Retrospect and Prospect* (Boston, 1902), pp. 48–49.
5. Pratt, *op. cit.*, chaps. ii, iii, v.
6. Henry F. Pringle, *Theodore Roosevelt* (New York, 1932), pp. 175–76.
7. Roosevelt to Root, April 5, 1898; Roosevelt to Bacon, April 8, 1898, Elting E. Morison, ed., *The Letters of Theodore Roosevelt* (Cambridge, 1951), II, 813, 814.
8. Roosevelt to Lodge, June 12, 1898, *ibid.*, p. 842.
9. Claude G. Bowers, *Beveridge and*

the Progressive Era (Boston, 1932), pp. 68–70.

10. *Ibid.*, pp. 153–54.

11. Henry Cabot Lodge, *Selections from the Correspondence of Theodore Roosevelt and Henry Cabot Lodge* (New York, 1925), I, 44–45.

12. Stephen Gwynn, ed., *The Letters and Friendships of Sir Cecil Spring-Rice* (Boston, 1929), I, 326.

13. Pringle, *op. cit.*, p. 167.

14. Roosevelt to Anna Cowles Roosevelt, May 8, 1898, *Letters of Theodore Roosevelt*, II, 829.

15. Quoted in *Cong. Rec.*, 55th Cong., 2d Sess., App., p. 573.

16. Address of January 4, 1899, printed in *United States Imperialism* (pamphlet collection in Widener Library, Harvard University).

17. Alfred K. Weinberg analyzes and documents this shift of emphasis in *Manifest Destiny* (Baltimore, 1935), pp. 296, 309 ff. Typical imperialist arguments in support of McKinley's decision to annex the Philippines appear in *Cong. Rec.*, 55th Cong., 3d Sess., pp. 287–97, 838, 1451, 502–3.

18. Thomas A. Bailey, *A Diplomatic History of the American People* (3d ed.; New York, 1946), p. 520.

19. James K. Eyre, "Japan and the American Annexation of the Philippines," XI (March, 1942), 55–71; "Russia and the American Acquisition of the Philippines," *Mississippi Valley Historical Review*, XXVIII (March, 1942), 539–62.

20. *Cong. Rec.*, 55th Cong., 3d Sess., p. 960.

21. Weinberg, *op. cit.*, p. 313.

22. Richard Olney, "Growth of Our Foreign Policy," *Atlantic Monthly*, LXXXV (March, 1900), 293.

23. See, for example, Alfred T. Mahan, "The Transvaal and the Philippines," *Independent*, LII (February 1, 1900), 290.

24. Roosevelt to Coudert, July 3, 1901, *Letters of Theodore Roosevelt*, III, 105.

25. Representative anti-imperialist arguments appear in *Cong. Rec.*, 55th Cong., 3d Sess., pp. 93–96, 493–502, 922, 1064–67, 1070, 1297, 1384–88, 1445–50, 1532.

26. *The Conquest of the United States by Spain* (Boston, 1899), p. 25. This was an address delivered on January 16, 1899, and circulated widely in pamphlet form.

27. William M. Gibson, "Mark Twain and Howells: Anti-Imperialists," *New England Quarterly*, XX (December, 1947), 435–70; Fred H. Harrington, "The Anti-Imperialist Movement in the United States, 1898–1900," *Mississippi Valley Historical Review*, XXII (September, 1935), 211–30; "Literary Aspects of American Anti-Imperialism, 1898–1902," *New England Quarterly*, X (December, 1937), 650–67.

28. Richard Olney, "International Isolation of the United States," *Atlantic Monthly*, LXXXI (May, 1898), 577–88. Delivered as an address at Harvard University, March 2, 1898.

NOTES TO CHAPTER III

1. William J. Bryan, *Speeches of William Jennings Bryan* (New York, 1909), II, 47.

2. Quoted from McKinley's instructions advising the peace commissioners to acquire cession of the Philippines, issued on September 16, 1898. *Sen. Doc.*, No. 148, p. 7.

3. A. Whitney Griswold, *The Far Eastern Policy of the United States* (New York, 1938), p. 42.

4. Lionel M. Gelber, *The Rise of Anglo-American Friendship* (New York, 1938), pp. 30–32.

5. Hay to Lodge, July 27, 1898, recounts German schemes communicated by Spring-Rice, A. L. P. Dennis, *Adventures in American Diplomacy, 1896–1906* (New York, 1928), p. 98. For the effect of these reports upon the decision to retain the Philippines see Charles S. Olcutt, *William McKinley* (Boston, 1916), pp. 11, 111, 135, and Griswold, *op. cit.*, p. 31.

6. Lester B. Shippee, "Germany and the Spanish-American War," *American Historical Review*, XXX (July, 1925), 754–57.

7. Jeanette Keim, *Forty Years of German-American Political Relations* (Philadelphia, 1919), pp. 218–19. The same

could be said of the Russian, Italian, and French press.

8. Griswold, *op. cit.,* p. 20.

9. Hay to White, September 24, 1899, William Roscoe Thayer, *The Life and Letters of John Hay* (Boston, 1915), II, 221.

10. Alfred T. Mahan, *The Interest of America in Sea Power, Present and Future* (Boston, 1898), pp. 107–34.

11. *Ibid.,* p. 34.

12. *Ibid.,* p. 112.

13. Tyler Dennett, "The Future in Retrospect, Mahan's *The Problem of Asia,*" *Foreign Affairs,* XIII (April, 1935), 414.

14. Mahan, *The Problem of Asia and Its Effect upon International Policies* (Boston, 1900), pp. 164–65, 167.

15. Tyler Dennett, *John Hay* (New York, 1933), chap. xxvii, "McKinleyism."

16. Gelber, *op. cit.,* pp. 89–93.

17. Adams to Hay, December 16, 1900, Worthington C. Ford, ed., *Letters of Henry Adams* (Boston, 1930–37), II, 307.

18. Henry Adams, *The Education of Henry Adams* (Boston, 1918), pp. 423–27.

19. *America's Economic Supremacy* (New York, 1900) stresses economic determinism; *The New Empire* (New York, 1902) leans toward geographical determinism.

20. *America's Economic Supremacy,* pp. 22, 26.

21. *Ibid.,* chap. ii. This chapter was originally published as an article in February, 1899. It seems likely that Brooks was responsible for Henry's interest in the competition with Russia in Asia. During 1897–98 this new interest was the central feature of Henry's correspondence with John Hay. William A. Williams, "Brooks Adams and American Expansion," *New England Quarterly,* XXV (June, 1952), 217–32.

22. Powers, "The Ethics of Expansion," *International Journal of Ethics,* X (April, 1900), 288–306.

23. "The War as a Suggestion of Manifest Destiny," *Annals of the American Academy of Political and Social Science,* XII (September, 1898), 192.

24. *International Journal of Ethics,* X, 305; *Annals,* XII, 186.

25. *Annals,* XII, 190.

26. Richard Olney, "International Isolation of the United States," *Atlantic Monthly,* LXXXI (May, 1898), 577–88.

27. Griswold, *Far Eastern Policy,* pp. 96, 104.

28. Seward W. Livermore, "American Naval-Base Policy in the Far East, 1850–1914," *Pacific Historical Review,* XIII (June, 1944), 129.

29. Alfred Vagts, *Deutschland und die Vereinigten Staaten in der Weltpolitik, 1890–1906* (New York, 1935), II, 1188; Dennis, *Adventures in Diplomacy,* p. 364; Roosevelt to Lodge, June 16, 1905, Elting E. Morison, ed., *The Letters of Theodore Roosevelt* (Cambridge, 1951), IV, 1230, 1232.

30. For Roosevelt's contemporary description of his attempts to persuade the belligerents to talk peace see Roosevelt to Lodge, June 16, 1905, *Letters of Theodore Roosevelt,* IV, 1221–33. For an analysis of Roosevelt's futile efforts to bend European politics to the purposes of peacemaking see Griswold, *op. cit.,* pp. 95–132.

31. Edward H. Zabriskie, *American-Russian Rivalry in the Far East* (Philadelphia, 1946), chaps. vi, vii.

32. Tyler Dennett, *Roosevelt and the Russo-Japanese War* (New York, 1925), pp. 165 ff.

33. *Ibid.,* pp. 90, 148, 152; Roosevelt to Lyman Abbott, June 22, 1903, *Letters of Theodore Roosevelt,* III, pp. 500–501.

34. Joseph B. Bishop, *Theodore Roosevelt and His Time* (New York, 1920), I, 477.

35. Allan Nevins, *Henry White* (New York, 1930), pp. 267–68; Gelber, *Rise of Anglo-American Friendship,* p. 255.

NOTES TO CHAPTER IV

1. Thomas A. Bailey, "Dewey and the Germans at Manila Bay," *American Historical Review,* XLV (October, 1939), 76–77.

2. Tyler Dennett, *John Hay* (New York, 1933), p. 218.

3. See Carnegie's advocacy of an An-

glo-Saxon federal republic as set forth in "A Look Ahead," *North American Review*, CLVI (June, 1893), 685–710.

4. Carl Schurz, "The Anglo-American Friendship," *Atlantic Monthly*, LXXXII (October, 1898), 433–40.

5. Claude G. Bowers, *Beveridge and the Progressive Era* (Boston, 1932), pp. 68–70.

6. *Ibid.*, p. 70.

7. Hay to John .W. Foster, June 23, 1900, Dennett, *Hay*, p. 333.

8. *Ibid.*, pp. 291–95.

9. A. Whitney Griswold, *The Far Eastern Policy of the United States* (New York, 1938), p. 83; Seward W. Livermore, "American Naval-Base Policy in the Far East, 1850–1914," *Pacific Historical Review*, XIII (June, 1944), 123–24.

10. A. L. P. Dennis, *Adventures in American Diplomacy, 1896–1906* (New York, 1928), chap. xix.

11. Winston B. Thorson, "American Public Opinion and the Portsmouth Peace Conference," *American Historical Review*, LIII (April, 1948), 439–64.

12. Roosevelt to Lodge, June 3, 1905, Henry Cabot Lodge, *Selections from the Correspondence of Theodore Roosevelt and Henry Cabot Lodge* (New York, 1925), II, 134–35.

13. Roosevelt to Taft, August 21, 1907, Henry F. Pringle, *Theodore Roosevelt* (New York, 1931), pp. 408–9.

14. Henry Adams to Brooks Adams, February 7, 1901, Harold D. Cater, comp., *Henry Adams and His Friends* (Boston, 1947), p. 504.

15. A useful table of naval rankings, based on relative tonnages, according to figures of the Office of Naval Intelligence, appears in George T. Davis, *A Navy Second to None* (New York, 1940), p. 171.

16. Von Bülow to Von Holleben, December 28, 1898; Von Holleben to Von Bülow, December 31, 1898, *Die Grosse Politik der Europaischen Kabinette, 1871–1914* (Berlin, 1922–27), XV, 95–97; Earl S. Pomeroy, "American Policy Respecting the Marshalls, Carolines, and Marianas, 1898–1941," *Pacific Historical Review*, XVII (February, 1948), 43–53.

17. The Japanese war scare of 1907 is a case in point. Thomas A. Bailey, *Theodore Roosevelt and the Japanese-American Crisis* (Stanford, 1934), chap. xi; Pringle, *op. cit.*, chap. x; M. A. DeWolfe Howe, *George Von Lengerke Meyer* (New York, 1919), pp. 370–71.

18. Alfred T. Mahan, *The Problem of Asia and Its Effect Upon International Policies* (Boston, 1900), pp. 197–98.

19. Dexter Perkins, *The Monroe Doctrine, 1867–1907* (Baltimore, 1937), chap. v; Clara E. Schieber, "The Transformation of American Sentiment Towards Germany, 1870–1914," *Journal of International Relations*, XII (July, 1921), 65–67.

20. Speck Von Sternburg, "The Phantom Peril of German Emigration and South American Settlements," *North American Review*, CLXXXII (May, 1906), 641–50.

21. Alfred Vagts, *Deutschland und die Vereinigten Staaten in der Weltpolitic, 1890–1896* (New York, 1935), II 1738, 1947.

22. Charles C. Tansill, *The Purchase of the Danish West Indies* (Baltimore, 1932), pp. 392 ff.

23. *Ibid.*, pp. 418–19.

24. *Ibid.*, pp. 452–53.

25. Davis, *A Navy Second to None*, p. 141.

26. Alfred Vagts, "Hopes and Fears of an America-German War, 1870–1915," *Political Science Quarterly*, IV (March, 1940), 53–76. Vagts was unable to determine to what extent these discussions were part of a hostile scheme or merely an aspect of the customary calculation of all possible eventualities.

27. Vagts, *Deutschland und die Vereinigten Staaten*, II, 1427–1537, *passim*. Vagts's exhaustive study, based on archival documents, concludes that the German jingoes exercised no control over the policies of the Chancellor and the Foreign Office.

28. Lodge, *Selections*, I, 485, 487, 494; Pringle, *op. cit.*, p. 288.

29. Theodore Roosevelt, *The Works of*

Theodore Roosevelt (Mem. ed.; New York, 1925), XVII, 185.

30. Roosevelt to Spring-Rice, November 1, 1905, Stephen Gwynn, ed., *The Letters and Friendships of Sir Cecil Spring-Rice* (Boston, 1929), II, 10.

31. *Foreign Relations, 1903*, p. 275.

32. Annual message, December 6, 1904, Roosevelt, *Works*, XVII, 299; Perkins, *Monroe Doctrine*, chap. vi.

NOTES TO CHAPTER V

1. Claude G. Bowers, *Beveridge and the Progressive Era* (Boston, 1932), p. 143.

2. William J. Bryan, *Speeches of William Jennings Bryan* (New York, 1909), II, 49.

3. Annual message, December 2, 1902, Theordore Roosevelt, *The Works of Theodore Roosevelt* (Mem. ed.; New York, 1925), XVII, 175.

4. Annual message, December 3, 1906, *ibid.*, pp. 450–51.

5. Annual message, December 6, 1904, *ibid.*, pp. 297–98.

6. William D. Puleston, *Mahan* (New Haven, 1939), p. 217.

7. Annual message, December 5, 1905, Roosevelt, *Works*, XVII, 346–47; cf. address to the Naval War College, June, 1897, *Proceedings of the United States Naval Institute*, XXIII (1897), 447 ff.

8. Frederick Lynch, *Personal Recollections of Andrew Carnegie* (New York, 1920), p. 156.

9. David S. Jordan, *Imperial Democracy* (New York, 1899), p. 36.

10. Bryan, *Speeches*, II, 222–23.

11. Eliot, *The Road Toward Peace* (Boston, 1915), pp. 10–15.

12. Burton J. Hendrick, ed., *Miscellaneous Writings of Andrew Carnegie* (Garden City, N.Y., 1933), II, 237. Carnegie was not an absolute pacifist; his plan for a League of Peace, which he tried to sell to the Kaiser in 1907, included an armed force to compel obedience. Hendrick, *The Life of Andrew Carnegie* (Garden City, N.Y., 1932), II, 309–10.

13. David S. Jordan, *America's Conquest of Europe* (Boston, 1913), p. 2.

14. Roosevelt, *Works*, XVIII, 410–27.

15. *Ibid.*, p. 411.

16. William S. Holt, *Treaties Defeated by the Senate* (Baltimore, 1933), pp. 230–35; Philip C. Jessup, *Elihu Root* (New York, 1938), II, pp. 270–77; Henry F. Pringle, *The Life and Times of William Howard Taft* (New York, 1939), II, 741–55.

17. *Outlook*, XCVIII (May 20, 1911), 97–98.

18. Roosevelt to Lee, August 22, 1911, Jessup, *Root*, II, 274.

19. William T. R. Fox, "Interwar International Relations Research: American Experience," *World Politics*, II (October, 1949), 68–69.

20. Puleston, *Mahan*, p. 301.

21. Alfred T. Mahan, *The Interest of America in International Conditions* (Boston, 1910), p. 81.

22. Puleston, *Mahan*, pp. 321–23.

23. *Outlook*, CIX (January 13, 1915), 85–86.

24. Lewis Einstein, *American Foreign Policy* (Boston, 1909), p. 16.

25. "The United States and Anglo-German Rivalry," *National Review*, LX (January, 1913), 736–50.

26. For biographical material see Clare Boothe's introduction to Homer Lea, *The Valor of Ignorance* (New York, 1942).

27. *Ibid.*, p. 11.

28. Alfred T. Mahan, *Armaments and Arbitration or the Place of Force in the International Relations of States* (New York, 1912), chap. vi.

29. William C. Askew and J. Fred Rippy, "The United States and Europe's Strife, 1908–13," *Journal of Politics*, IV (February, 1942), 71–73; *Messages and Papers of the Presidents*, Bur. of Nat. Lit. ed., XVI, 7667, 7783–84.

30. Edward H. Zabriskie, *America-Russian Rivalry in the Far East* (Philadelphia, 1946), pp. 144 ff.; A. Whitney Griswold, *The Far Eastern Policy of the United States*, chap. iv.

31. Dexter Perkins, *Hands Off* (Boston, 1941), chap. iii; Samuel F. Bemis, *The Latin American Policy of the United States* (New York, 1943), pp. 161–66.

32. Harley Notter, *The Origins of the Foreign Policy of Woodrow Wilson* (Baltimore, 1937), p. 228.

33. Ray S. Baker and William E. Dodd, *The Public Papers of Woodrow Wilson* (New York, 1927), III, 92–93; Ray S. Baker, *Woodrow Wilson* (Garden City, N.Y., 1925–27), IV, 421.

34. *New York Times*, March 12, 19, 1913; statement to foreign governments, March 18, 1913, *Foreign Relations, 1913*, p. 170.

35. Baker and Dodd, *Public Papers*, III, 64–69.

36. Lodge to Roosevelt, July 22, 1905, Lodge, *Selections*, II, 160.

37. Bemis, *Latin American Policy*, p. 194.

NOTES TO CHAPTER VI

1. A *Literary Digest* poll in November, based on the replies of 367 editors throughout the country, found that 105 favored the Allies, 20 favored the Germans, and 242 were impartial. *Literary Digest*, XLIX (November 14, 1914), 939.

2. *Ibid.* (August 15, 1914), pp. 256–57.

3. Walter Lippmann, "The Atlantic and America: The Why and When of Intervention," *Life*, X (April 7, 1941), 85.

4. *Ibid.*, p. 87.

5. Lippmann, *U.S. Foreign Policy* (Boston, 1943), p. 37.

6. *Ibid.*, p. 33.

7. *U.S. War Aims* (Boston, 1944), pp. 41–48, 42.

8. "What Program Shall the United States Stand for in International Relations?" *Annals of the American Academy of Political and Social Science*, LXVI (July, 1916), 60–70; cf. Lippmann in the *New Republic*, V (January 29, 1916), 334–35.

9. Edward H. Buehrig, "Wilson's Neutrality Re-examined," *World Politics*, III (October, 1950), 16–18. In his covering letter Lippmann stated that he was speaking also for Herbert Croly and that his memorandum was prepared in consultation with Colonel House.

10. "The World Conflict in Its Relation to American Democracy," *Annals of the*

American Academy of Political and Social Science, LXXII (July, 1917), 1–10.

11. *Ibid.*, p. 10.

12. *The Stakes of Diplomacy* (2d ed.; New York, 1917), p. xxi.

13. *The Stakes of Diplomacy* (New York, 1915), p. 111.

14. *New Republic*, V (December 25, 1915), 195–96.

15. *New Republic*, V (February 20, 1915), 60; (April 20, 1915), pp. 247–48.

16. *Ibid.*, III (May 15, 1915), 24.

17. *Ibid.*, IV (July 31, 1915), 322–24. Angell's plan was presented in the same issue, "A New Kind of War," pp. 327–29. The *New Republic* had previously mentioned international control of the sea in II (April 24, 1915), 293, and III (April 15, 1915), 24.

18. *Ibid.*, V (November 13, 1915), 27.

19. *Ibid.* (November 20, 1915), pp. 56–58; VI (March 18, 1916), 167–69.

20. *Ibid.* (April 22, 1916), pp. 303–5.

21. Ray S. Baker and William E. Dodd, *The Public Papers of Woodrow Wilson* (New York, 1927), IV, 184–88.

22. *New Republic*, VII (June 3, 1916), 102–4.

23. *Ibid.*, X (February, 10, 1917), 33, 36–38.

24. *Ibid.* (March 17, 1917), pp. 181–82.

25. *Ibid.* (March 31, 1917), pp. 248–49.

26. Washington, "The United States and Anglo-German Rivalry," *National Review*, LX (January, 1913), 736–50.

27. "The War and American Policy," *ibid.*, LXIV (November, 1914), 357–76.

28. Beer, "The War, the British Empire, and America," *Forum*, LIII (May, 1915), 548–66; "America's Part Among Nations," *New Republic*, V (November 20, 1915), 62–64; "America's International Responsibilities and Foreign Policy," *Annals of the American Academy of Political and Social Science*, LXVI (July, 1916), 71–91.

29. Adams, "America's Obligation and Opportunity," *Yale Review*, V (April, 1916), 474–83.

30. Hart, *The War in Europe* (New York, 1914); *New York Times*, December 27, 1914; "Shall We Defend the

Monroe Doctrine?" *North American Review*, CCII (November, 1915), 681–92; "Preparedness," *National Economics League Quarterly*, I (February, 1916), 3–4.

31. Hart, *The Monroe Doctrine* (Boston, 1917), pp. 399–403.

32. Hart, "Please, Mr. President," *New York Times Magazine*, February 11, 1917.

33. "Neutrality, Armed Neutrality, and War," *ibid.*, March 4, 1917.

34. H. H. Powers, *America Among the Nations* (New York, 1917), p. 11.

35. *Ibid.*, pp. 272–73.

36. Usher, "Our Inconsistent Foreign Policy," *New Republic*, III (May 29, 1915), 89–90.

37. *The Winning of the War* (New York, 1918), pp. 276–77.

38. Usher, "The Significance of Victory," *North American Review*, CCIX (January, 1919), 49. The idealistic context of Usher's observation is indicated by his statement, "Our true influence must be moral, and the true greatness of the United States in the future will come from the fact that our situation enables us to espouse the idealistic even at the cost of our material interest."

39. Usher, *The Story of the Great War* (New York, 1919), chap. xxx.

40. The English edition of *Germany and the Next War* was first published in London in 1912. In 1914 it was republished in London and New York and subsequently appeared in several different additions. Its sequel, *How Germany Makes War* (New York, 1914), was less well known. Albert J. Beveridge, in Germany to collect material for a series of articles during 1914, found upon independent investigation that only six thousand copies of Bernhardi's first book had been printed and not all of those sold. Albert J. Beveridge, *What Is Behind the War?* (Indianapolis, 1915), p. 169.

41. Hearst's International Library, in addition to publishing the regular edition of this book, also distributed a cheaper edition at sixty cents a copy or ten copies for five dollars.

42. For example, Cleveland Moffett, *A*

Romance of Disaster and Victory (New York, 1916); Julius W. Muller, *The Invasion of America* (New York, 1915); J. Bernard Walker, *America Fallen! The Sequel of the European War* (New York, 1915); Howard D. Wheeler, *Are We Ready?* (Boston, 1915).

NOTES TO CHAPTER VII

1. Hermann Hagedorn, *The Bugle That Woke America* (New York, 1940), pp. 8–9.

2. Hermann Freiherr Von Eckardstein, *Lebenserinnerungen und Politischen Denkwürdigkeiten* (Leipzig, 1921), p. 175; quoted in Hagedorn, *op. cit.*, p. 9.

3. Theodore Roosevelt, "The World War: Its Tragedies and Its Lessons," *Outlook*, CVII (September 23, 1914), 169–78.

4. See letters to Spring-Rice, Kipling, Sir Edward Grey, on October 3, 1914; to Kipling, November 4, 1914; to Von Sturm, December 2, 1914; to Dr. Dernberg, December 4, 1914, *Roosevelt Collection* (Widener Library, Harvard University); Joseph B. Bishop, *Theodore Roosevelt and His Time* (New York, 1920), II, 370–73; Russell Buchanan, "Theodore Roosevelt and American Neutrality, 1914–1917," *American Historical Review*, XLIII (July, 1938), 777; cf. letters to J. Medill Patterson and George E. Miller in early 1915, Hagedorn, *op. cit.*, pp. 64–65; conversation on September 5 with E. A. Valkenberg and William D. Lewis, *ibid.*, pp. 17–18.

5. *New York Times*, November 8, 1914.

6. *Ibid.*, November 29, 1914.

7. Bishop, *Roosevelt*, II, 374–75.

8. Roosevelt, "The Need of Preparedness," *Metropolitan*, XLI (April, 1915), 68.

9. Bishop, *Roosevelt*, II, 376.

10. H. J. Whigham, "The Colonel As We Saw Him," *Metropolitan*, XLIX (March, 1919), 5.

11. Roosevelt, "Murder on the High Seas," *ibid.*, XLII (June 1915), 3; cf. Hagedorn, *op. cit.*, p. 70.

12. Ray S. Baker and William E. Dodd,

The Public Papers of Woodrow Wilson (New York, 1927), III, 321.

13. Roosevelt, "Good Americans Should Support Mr. Hughes," *ibid.*, XLV (December, 1916), 14.

14. George S. Viereck, *Spreading Germs of Hate* (New York, 1930), pp. 255–56.

15. Roosevelt, *The Works of Theodore Roosevelt* (Mem. ed.; New York, 1925), XIX, 5.

16. Hagedorn, *op. cit.*, p. 64.

17. From *Fear God and Take Your Own Part* (New York, 1916) in Roosevelt, *Works*, XX, 450.

18. Hagedorn, *op. cit.*, p. 88.

19. Roosevelt to Selous, December 4, 1914, *Roosevelt Collection.*

20. Roosevelt to Kipling, October 3, 1914, *ibid.*

21. Bishop, *Roosevelt*, II, 407.

22. *New York Times*, October 11, 18, 1914; "Utopia or Hell," *Independent*, LXXXI (January 4, 1915), 13–17.

23. Roosevelt, "Peace Insurance by Preparedness against War," *Metropolitan*, XLII (August, 1915), 64; cf. "Awake and Prepare," *ibid.*, XLIII (January, 1916), 12.

24. Baker and Dodd, *Public Papers*, IV, 184–88.

25. Bishop, *Roosevelt*, II, 417.

26. Roosevelt, "The League to Enforce Peace," *Metropolitan*, XLV (February, 1917), 15.

27. Roosevelt, *Works*, XX, 526; John J. Leary, *Talks with T. R.* (Boston, 1920), p. 333.

28. Bishop, *Roosevelt*, II, 419–20.

29. Henry C. Lodge, *Selections from the Correspondence of Theodore Roosevelt and Henry Cabot Lodge, 1884–1918* (New York, 1925), II, 503.

30. Baker and Dodd, *Public Papers*, V, 6–16.

31. Roosevelt to Bryce, April 19, 1917, and Roosevelt to Porter, June 6, 1917, *Roosevelt Collection.*

32. Roosevelt, "Now We Must Fight," *Metropolitan*, XLV (May, 1917), 4.

33. "The Peace of Victory for which We Strive," *ibid.*, XLVI (July, 1917), 24.

NOTES TO CHAPTER VIII

1. "The Atlantic and America," *Life* X (April 7, 1941), 87.

2. Page to House, September 22, 1914, Burton J. Hendrick, *Life and Letters of Walter H. Page* (New York, 1922), I, 334.

3. Page to Wilson, September 6 and October 15, 1914, *ibid.*, III, 139, 162–64.

4. See, for example, Page to A. W. Page, November 6, 1914, *ibid.*, I, 350.

5. *Ibid.*, II, 152–54.

6. Page to Lansing, October 15, 1914, *Foreign Relations, 1914, Supplement*, pp. 248–49.

7. Hendrick, *Page*, I, 324–43.

8. Page to House, January 2, 1914, *ibid.*, pp. 282–83.

9. Page to House, October 11, 1914, *ibid.*, p. 342.

10. Page to Doubleday, May 29, 1916, *ibid.*, II, 137.

11. Page to A. W. Page, March 25, 1917, *ibid.*, pp. 217–21.

12. *Ibid.*, p. 211.

13. *Ibid.*, pp. 274–75.

14. *Ibid.*, p. 18.

15. Charles Seymour, *The Intimate Papers of Colonel House* (Boston, 1926, 1928), I, 433; cf. Page to House, June 29, 1917, Hendrick, *Page*, II, 147–48. In an analysis of English opinion with respect to America's action on the *Lusitania* incident Page implied that only by entering the war could America save her respect in English eyes; he pointed out that intervention would end the war quickly and give the United States a voice in the peace settlement. Page to Bryan, May 8, 1915, *Foreign Relations, 1915, Supplement*, pp. 385–86. However, Hendrick says that Page believed that a diplomatic break would have been sufficient to end the war. Hendrick, *Page*, II, 216.

16. Hendrick, *Page*, II, 5.

17. Page to House, July 21, 1915, *ibid.*, p. 26. In an undated letter to House, probably written in August, Page reiterated his belief that such an incident was only a question of time. *Ibid.*, p. 16.

18. *Ibid.*, p. 26.

19. Page to Wilson, November 24, 1916, *ibid.*, pp. 190-95.

20. Page to Alderman, June 22, 1916, *ibid.*, p. 144.

21. Page to Houston, April 1, 1917, *ibid.*, p. 227.

22. Seymour, *House*, I, 285; George S. Viereck, *The Strangest Friendship in History* (New York, 1932), p. 187.

23. Seymour, *House*, I, 209-10, 297.

24. *Ibid.*, II, 84-85.

25. House to Polk, October 11, 1915, *ibid.*, p. 85.

26. *Ibid.*, pp. 100-101.

27. House to Page, August 4, 1915, Ray S. Baker, *Woodrow Wilson* (New York, 1927-39), V, 371-72.

28. House to Wilson, February 9, 1916, Seymour, *House*, II, 164.

29. *Ibid.*, pp. 201-2.

30. Harley Notter, *The Origins of the Foreign Policy of Woodrow Wilson* (Baltimore, 1937), p. 467.

31. Hendrick, *Page*, II, 2.

32. House to Wilson, May 9, 1915, Seymour, *House*, I, 433-34.

33. House to Wilson, April 25, 1916, Edward H. Buehrig, "Wilson's Neutrality Re-examined," *World Politics*, III (October, 1950), 6.

34. These memoranda appear in Robert Lansing, *War Memoirs of Robert Lansing* (Indianapolis, 1935).

35. *Ibid.*, p. 101.

36. *Ibid.*, pp. 19-21.

37. Lansing to Wilson, August 24, 1915, *ibid.*, pp. 44-45.

38. *Ibid.*, pp. 102-4.

39. Lansing to Wilson, March 27, 1916, Carlton Savage, *Policy of the United States toward Maritime Commerce in War* (Washington, D.C., 1936), II, pp. 468-70.

40. Lansing, *Memoirs*, pp. 208-9.

41. Lansing to Wilson, February 2, 1917, *ibid.*, pp. 591-92.

42. Lansing to Wilson, March 19, 1917, *Foreign Relations, the Lansing Papers, 1914-1920*, I, 626-28.

43. Lansing to House, April 4, 1917, *ibid.*, p. 636.

44. Robert Lansing, "America's Future

at Stake," *A War of Self-Defense* (1917); cf. address on July 29, 1917, reproduced in *Current History*, VI (July-September), 455-59.

45. Gerard to Bryan, February 26, 1915, *Foreign Relations, 1915, Supplement*, p. 17.

46. Seymour, *House*, II, 28.

47. James W. Gerard, *My Four Years in Germany* (New York, 1917), p. 252.

48. Gerard to Lansing, October 25, 1915, *Foreign Relations, the Lansing Papers, 1914-1920*, I, 665.

49. Gerard to House, November 2, 1915, Seymour, *House*, II, 81.

50. Gerard to Lansing, February 25, 1916, *Foreign Relations, 1916, Supplement*, p. 179.

51. Gerard to Lansing, May 7, 1916, *ibid.*, p. 262.

52. Gerard to Lansing, May 8, 1916, *ibid.*, p. 264.

53. Gerard to Lansing, February 4, 1917, *Foreign Relations, 1917, Supplement 1*, p. 114.

54. *Foreign Relations, the Lansing Papers, 1914-1920*, I, 675-700.

55. Gerard, *My Four Years in Germany*, pp. x-xi.

56. For more evidence of Wilson's advisers' prudence about the German threat toward American security see statements concerning the views of the following men: Henry Van Dyke, Minister to the Netherlands: Van Dyke to Wilson, September 14, 1914, Tertius Van Dyke, *Henry Van Dyke* (New York, 1935), pp. 329-30. Franklin K. Lane, Secretary of the Interior: Oswald G. Villard, *Fighting Years* (New York, 1939), p. 296; A. W. Lane and L. H. Wall, eds. *Letters of Franklin K. Lane, Personal and Political* (Boston, 1922), p. 234; *Literary Digest*, LIV (June 16, 1917), 1834-35. David F. Houston, Secretary of Agriculture: David F. Houston, *Eight Years with Wilson's Cabinet* (New York, 1926), I, 230, 236, 248.

NOTES TO CHAPTER IX

1. Ray S. Baker, *Woodrow Wilson* (New York, 1927-39), V, 333.

2. Wilson to House, February 20, 1915, Charles C. Tansill, *America Goes to War* (Boston, 1938), p. 449.

3. Baker, *Wilson*, VI, 129, 150. For earlier differences between Wilson and House see *ibid.*, V, 312–13.

4. A. W. Lane and L. H. Wall, eds., *Letters of Franklin K. Lane, Personal and Political* (Boston, 1922), p. 175.

5. Baker, *Wilson*, V, 157.

6. Spring-Rice to Grey, September 3, 1914, George M. Trevelyan, *The Life and Letters of Sir Edward Grey* (Boston, 1937), pp. 355–56.

7. Harley Notter, *The Origins of the Foreign Policy of Woodrow Wilson* (Baltimore, 1937), p. 422.

8. Charles Seymour, *The Intimate Papers of Colonel House* (Boston, 1926, 1928), I, 299–300.

9. For example, see Wilson's address at Cincinnati, October 26, 1916, Ray S. Baker and William E. Dodd, *The Public Papers of Woodrow Wilson* (New York, 1927), IV, 377–78.

10. Robert Lansing, *War Memoirs of Robert Lansing* (Indianapolis, 1935), p. 172.

11. Notter, *op. cit.*, pp. 113, 129, 133.

12. Baker and Dodd, *Public Papers*, II, 294.

13. *Ibid.*, I, 404.

14. *Ibid.*, II, 80–81; cf. *ibid.*, I, 420 ff.; II, 149–50; Woodrow Wilson, "The Significance of American History," *Harper's Encyclopedia of United States History* (New York, 1901), I, xxiv.

15. Baker and Dodd, *Public Papers*, II, 298–99, 401.

16. *Ibid.*, III, 371.

17. *Ibid.*, pp. 147–48.

18. *New York Times*, August 4, 1914.

19. *Foreign Relations, 1914, Supplement*, pp. 547–51.

20. Baker and Dodd, *Public Papers*, III, 158–59.

21. Seymour, *House*, I, 292–93.

22. Joseph P. Tumulty, *Woodrow Wilson as I Know Him* (New York, 1921), pp. 230–31.

23. Baker and Dodd, *Public Papers*, III, 224–27.

24. Baker, *Wilson*, V. 74.

25. Baker and Dodd, *Public Papers*, III, 302–7.

26. Bryan to Gerard, February 10, 1915, *Foreign Relations, 1915, Supplement*, pp. 98–99.

27. In his conversation with Stockton Axson in August, 1914, Wilson said, "I am afraid something will happen on the high seas that will make it impossible for us to keep out of the war." Baker, *Wilson*, V, 74. House recorded in his diary a conversation on September 30, 1914, in which Wilson, commenting on his account of Mahan's problems before the War of 1812 in *History of the American People*, expressed his opinion that that war "was started in exactly the same way as this controversy is opening up." Seymour, *House*, I, 303–4.

28. *Official German Documents Relating to the World War* (New York, 1923), II, 1133–35, 1153, 1260–61, 1319, 1321.

29. Baker and Dodd, *Public Papers*, III, 321.

30. *Ibid.*, pp. 133–34.

31. Bryan to Gerard, *Foreign Relations, 1915, Supplement*, pp. 393–96.

32. Wilson to Bryan, April 22, 1915, Carlton Savage, *Policy of the United States toward Maritime Commerce in War* (Washington, D.C., 1936), II, 468–70.

33. Lansing to Gerard, June 9, 1915, *Foreign Relations, 1915, Supplement*, pp. 431–32.

34. Wilson to Stone, February 24, 1916, *Foreign Relations, 1916, Supplement*, pp. 177–78.

35. Baker and Dodd, *Public Papers*, III, 127; cf. addresses on January 22 and 31, 1916, *ibid.*, IV, 8, 63.

36. *Ibid.*, IV, 432.

37. Wilson to Bryan, June 7, 1915, Merle Curti, "Bryan and World Peace," *Smith College Studies in History*, XVI (April–July, 1931), 211; addresses at Pittsburgh, Cleveland, Milwaukee, Chicago, and Des Moines, January 29, to February 1, 1916, Baker and Dodd, *Public Papers*, III, 31, 44, 48, 60, 75–76.

38. Baker and Dodd, *Public Papers,* IV, 184–88.

39. *Foreign Relations, 1916, Supplement,* pp. 97–99.

40. Baker and Dodd, *Public Papers,* IV, 407–14.

41. *Foreign Relations, 1916, Supplement,* pp. 259–60.

42. Lansing to Gerard, April 18, 1916, *ibid.,* p. 234.

43. Baker and Dodd, *Public Papers,* V, 6–16.

44. Tumulty, *Wilson,* p. 256.

NOTES TO CHAPTER X

1. Bernstorff to Secretary of State, September 3, 1914, *Foreign Relations, 1914, Supplement,* pp. 87–88.

2. The whole incident is related in the *New York Times,* October 25, 1914.

3. *Literary Digest,* XLIX (November 7, 1914), 871–83.

4. *H. J. Res.* No. 372; *Cong. Rec.,* 63d Cong., 2d Sess., p. 16694.

5. *Cong. Rec.,* 63d Cong., 2d Sess., p. 16747.

6. *Literary Digest,* XLIX (October 31, 1914), 836.

7. *New York Times,* December 3, 1914.

8. *Ibid.,* December 2, 1914.

9. *Sen. J. Res.* No. 202. The resolution was tabled. Debate began on January 15, 1915.

10. *New York Times,* October 20, 1914.

11. Charles Seymour, *The Intimate Papers of Colonel House* (Boston, 1926, 1928), I, 298.

12. Ray S. Baker and William E. Dodd, *The Public Papers of Woodrow Wilson* (New York, 1927), III, 224–26.

13. The preparedness and antipreparedness positions are well represented in a bound collection of pamphlets in Widener Library, Harvard UUniversity: *Pamphlets on National Defense, 1904–1917.*

14. *New York Times,* October 5, 1914.

15. Seymour, *House,* I, 300.

16. Merle Curti, "Bryan and World Peace," *Smith College Studies in History,* XVI (April–July, 1931), 233.

17. *New York Times Magazine,* December 6, 1914.

18. *Literary Digest,* XLIX (December 12, 1914), 1159–61.

19. *Ibid.,* L (January 23, 1915), 137–38. The coastal editors were most alarmed. Opinion was evenly divided in the interior sections.

20. *Cong. Rec.,* 63d Cong., 3d Sess., pp. 1601–10.

21. *New Republic,* I (December 5, 1914), 3; (December 12, 1914), p. 3.

22. Ray S. Baker, *Woodrow Wilson* (New York, 1927–1939), VI, 8.

23. Ray H. Abrams, *Preachers Present Arms* (Philadelphia, 1933), chap. ii.

24. Ralph B. Perry, *The Plattsburg Movement* (New York, 1921), p. 26.

25. *Ibid.,* p. 32. Wood was a close friend of Roosevelt and an active proponent of preparedness since 1908. Hermann Hagedorn, *Leonard Wood* (New York, 1931), II, 131–33, 150–51; chap. vii.

26. Perry, *op. cit.,* p. 3; *New York Times,* August 6, 1915.

27. Baker, *Wilson,* IV, 8; *New York Times,* July 24, 25, and September 3, 1915.

28. Baker, *Wilson,* IV, 9; *New York Times,* August 6, 1915.

29. House to Wilson, June 16, 1915, Harley Notter, *The Origins of the Foreign Policy of Woodrow Wilson* (Baltimore, 1937), p. 431; House to Wilson, July 14, 1915, Seymour, *House,* II, 19.

30. Baker and Dodd, *Public Papers,* III, 384–92.

31. *Ibid.,* pp. 410–12, 423.

32. *Ibid.,* pp. 68–69.

33. *Ibid.,* p. 42.

34. David Lawrence, *The True Story of Woodrow Wilson* (New York, 1924), pp. 158 ff.

35. Alfred T. Mahan, "Current Fallacies Upon Naval Subjects," *Harper's New Monthly Magazine,* XCVII (June, 1898), 44–45.

36. *New Republic,* V (November 20, 1915), 55.

37. *Literary Digest,* LII (March 11, 1916), 617 ff.

38. *Proceedings of the National Security Congress*, Washington, January, 1916.

39. See, for example, Tavenner's analysis, December, 1915, of the connection between the Navy League and high finance and war industry. *Cong. Rec.*, 64th Cong., 1st Sess., pp. 272–93; App. pp. 860–67; cf. pp. 8812, 8868, 11330, App. 1313.

40. Bradley A. Fiske, *From Midshipman to Rear-Admiral* (New York, 1919), pp. 487, 490.

41. *Ibid.*, p. 528.

42. *Annual Reports of the Navy Department, 1900*, p. 32.

43. Fiske, *op. cit.*, pp. 547, 548.

44. *Cong. Rec.*, 63d Cong., 2d Sess., pp. 7147, 7380.

45. *Cong. Rec.*, 63d Cong., 2d Sess., pp. 7020, 7042, 7052, 7218, 7219, 7282, 8107.

46. *House Report*, No. 1557, Part II, 62d Cong., 3d Sess., p. 4.

47. *Cong. Rec.*, 63d Cong., 3d Sess., pp. 7048–52.

48. *Annual Reports of the Navy Department, 1914; House Report*, No. 1287, 63d Cong., 3d Sess.

49. House Naval Affairs Committee, *Hearings on Estimates for 1915*, 63d Cong., 2d Sess., pp. 463–570, 504 ff., 536 ff., 546 ff.

50. Fiske, *op. cit.*, pp. 563–65; *New York Times*, December 18, 1914.

51. Fiske, *op. cit.*, p. 664.

52. Wilson to Garrison, July 21, 1915, Baker, *Wilson*, VI, 9; Wilson to Daniels, July 21, 1915, *U.S. Naval Institute Proceedings*, XLI (September–October, 1915), 1654.

53. *Annual Reports of the Navy Department, 1915*, p. 73.

54. *Ibid.*, pp. 73–74.

55. Harold and Margaret Sprout, *The Rise of American Naval Power, 1776–1918* (Princeton University, 1946), pp. 338–41; *Senate Report* No. 575, 64th Cong., 1st Sess.

56. For its provisions see *U.S. Statutes at Large*, XXXIX (1917), 616, 617.

57. *Cong. Rec.*, 64th Cong., 1st Sess., pp. 11330–36.

58. *Ibid.*, pp. 8785–87, 8799–8804, 8805–7, 8867–69, 8812–13. When the Senate's amended bill returned to the House, the little-navy men took a final fling at ridiculing the thesis that America's security was endangered. *Ibid.*, pp. 12672–74, 12685–86, 12697.

59. *Ibid.*, pp. 11161–67, 11204–6.

60. *Ibid.*, p. 10934.

61. *Ibid.*, pp. 11185–89.

62. *Ibid.*, pp. 8812, 8823, 8871–72.

63. *Ibid.*, pp. 10922–26.

64. *Ibid.*, p. 10926.

65. *Ibid.*, pp. 11171–74.

66. *Ibid.*, pp. 11178–80.

67. *Ibid.*, pp. 11178, 11209, 11377–78.

NOTES TO CHAPTER XI

1. Johann H. Bernstorff, *My Three Years in America* (New York, 1920), p. 30.

2. *Literary Digest*, L (May 15, 1915), 1133–34.

3. *Nation*, C (May 13, 1915), 527.

4. *Literary Digest*, L (May 22, 1915), 1218–19.

5. Bernstorff, *op. cit.*, p. 30.

6. Joseph B. Bishop, *Theodore Roosevelt and His Time* (New York, 1920), II, 376.

7. Theodore Roosevelt, "Murder on the High Seas," *Metropolitan*, XLII (June, 1915), 3.

8. *Literary Digest*, L (May 22, 1915), 1197–99.

9. *Ibid.*, p. 1198.

10. *Ibid.*, pp. 1201–2.

11. David Lawrence, *The True Story of Woodrow Wilson* (New York, 1924), pp. 197–98.

12. David F. Houston, *Eight Years with Wilson's Cabinet* (New York, 1926), I, 132.

13. *Literary Digest*, L (May 22, 1915), 1200–1201.

14. Annual message, December 8, 1914, Ray S. Baker and William E. Dodd, *The Public Papers of Woodrow Wilson* (New York, 1925–27), III, 226.

15. *New York Times*, March 29, 1915.

16. *Literary Digest*, L (May 29, 1915), 1257–59.

17. Bryan to Wilson, June 4, 1915, Merle Curti, "Bryan and World Peace," *Smith College Studies in History*, XVI (April–July, 1931), 211.

18. Gerard to Secretary of State, July 8, 1915, *Foreign Relations, 1915, Supplement*, pp. 463–66.

19. The disclosures began in March and reached a peak on August 15 with the capture of the German agent Dr. Albert's brief case and on September 8 with the recall of the Austrian Ambassador Dumba. Frederic L. Paxson, *American Democracy and the World War: Pre-War Years, 1913–1917* (Boston, 1936), pp. 262–73.

20. Bernstorff to Secretary of State, September 1, 1915, and October 5, 1915, *Foreign Relations, 1915, Supplement*, pp. 530–31, 560.

21. Telegram from Grey to Spring-Rice, February 3, 1916, left at State Department, February 4, *Foreign Relations, 1916, Supplement*, pp. 158–59. On March 23 and 24, 1916, the Allies issued a formal rejection. *Ibid.*, pp. 211–13.

22. Gerard to Secretary of State, February 10, 1916, *ibid.*, pp. 163–66.

23. Secretary of State to Diplomatic Officers in European Countries, February 15, 1916, *ibid.*, p. 170.

24. McLemore's resolutions appear in *Cong. Rec.*, 64th Cong., 1st Sess., pp. 2756, 2958. Gore's concurrent resolution appears in *ibid.*, p. 3120.

25. Stone to Wilson, February 24, 1916, *Current History*, IV (March, 1916), 15–16.

26. Wilson to Stone, February 24, 1916, *Foreign Relations, 1916, Supplement*, pp. 177–78.

27. *Literary Digest*, LII (March 11, 1916), pp. 625–27. The German-American and the Hearst press were exceptions to the general rule. Some papers indorsed Wilson's stand but thought that Americans should voluntarily refrain from taking passage on armed ships.

28. *Ibid.*, (March 18, 1916), p. 697. The great part of the support for these resolutions came from Midwestern Congressmen.

29. Lansing to Gerard, April 18, 1916, *Foreign Relations, 1916, Supplement*, p. 234.

30. Gerard to Secretary of State, May 4, 1916, *ibid.*, pp. 257–60; Lansing to Gerard, May 8, 1916, *ibid.*, p. 263.

31. Charles Seymour, *American Diplomacy During the World War* (Baltimore, 1934), pp. 76–77.

32. Diary entry, September 24, 1916, Charles Seymour, *The Intimate Papers of Colonel House* (Boston, 1926, 1928), II, 316.

33. Robert Lansing, *War Memoirs of Robert Lansing* (Indianapolis, 1935), p. 111.

34. Ray S. Baker, *Woodrow Wilson* (New York, 1927–1939), VI, 250–53, 257; Walter Millis, *Road to War* (Boston, 1935), p. 318.

35. *New York Times*, November 1, 1916.

36. Clifton J. Child, *The German-Americans in Politics, 1914–1917* (Madison, Wisconsin, 1939); Carl Wittke, *German-Americans and the World War* (Columbus, Ohio, 1936).

37. Address delivered at Tremont Temple, Boston, in 1916 and printed as a pamphlet, *The Duties of Americans in the Present War*.

38. James M. Beck, *The War and Humanity* (2d ed.; New York, 1917), p. xiv.

39. Hugo Münsterberg, *The Peace and America* (New York, 1915), pp. 69, 77, 83.

40. Wilbur C. Abbott, "Germany and Prussian Propaganda," *Yale Review*, IV (July, 1915), 664–65.

41. William Roscoe Thayer, *Germany Versus Civilization* (Boston, 1916), p. 104.

42. Eliot to Wilson, August 6, 1914, Seymour, *House*, I, 287–89.

43. Eliot to Wilson, August 20, 1914, *ibid.*, pp. 290–91. In letters to the *New York Times* during the fall of 1914 Eliot continued to denounce Germany's war practices and her ideological depravity, and he warned of the consequences of a German victory. Charles W. Eliot, *The

Road toward Peace (Boston, 1915), pp. 80–128.

44. Eliot, "American Views on the War," *The Prime Cause of the War* (London, 1914). This view is clearly expressed in Eliot's letters to the *New York Times* and to Jacob H. Schiff during the winter of 1914. Eliot, *The Road toward Peace*, pp. 129–50.

45. Address on October 15, 1914, Eliot, *The Road toward Peace*, pp. 105, 111.

46. Edward H. Cotton, *The Life of Charles W. Eliot* (Boston, 1926), p. 359.

47. Hamilton Holt, "A Basis for a League of Peace," *Independent*, LXXIX (July 20, 1914), 83–84; *New York Times*, August 16, 1914.

48. Ruhl J. Bartlett, *The League to Enforce Peace* (Chapel Hill, N.C., 1944), pp. 3–28. Merle Curti, *Peace or War, The American Struggle, 1636–1936* (New York, 1936), p. 238. For the European background of the league idea see Florence Wilson, *The Origins of the League Covenant* (London, 1928), pp. 126 ff.

49. Bartlett, *op. cit.*, pp. 30–40.

50. Randolph S. Bourne, comp., *Towards an Enduring Peace,* (New York, 1916).

51. *Taft Papers on the League of Nations* (New York, 1920), p. 51.

52. Henry C. Lodge, *War Addresses, 1915–1917* (Boston, 1917), pp. 23–48.

53. Baker and Dodd, *Public Papers,* IV, 184–88.

54. *Enforced Peace: Proceedings of the First Annual National Assemblage of the League to Enforce Peace, Washington, May 26–27, 1916* (New York, 1916), pp. 64–167.

55. *Ibid.*, p. 127.

56. *Ibid.*, pp. 129, 136.

57. Bartlett, *op. cit.*, pp. 60, 63–66, 69.

58. Curti, "Bryan and World Peace," *op. cit.*, pp. 224–25. Bryan gave the fullest exposition of his antileague stand in his debates with Taft in December, 1916, printed as a pamphlet, *World Peace* (New York, 1917).

59. *Cong. Rec.*, 64th Cong., 2d Sess., pp. 736–37, 791–97, 892–97. A substitute

for the Hitchcock resolution, endorsing only Wilson's request for peace terms, was finally passed on January 15, 1917.

60. *New Republic,* IX (January 6, 1917), 255–57.

61. *Cong. Rec.*, 64th Cong., 2d Sess., pp. 2364–70.

62. *Literary Digest,* LIV (February 10, 1917), 324–25.

63. Bartlett, *op. cit.*, p. 81.

64. Cedric Cummins, *Indiana Public Opinion and the World War: 1914–1917* (Indianapolis, 1945), p. 239.

65. *Ibid.*, pp. 86–87.

66. Wilson to Seabury, January 25, 1917, Baker, *Wilson,* VI, 431.

67. H. Schuyler Foster, Jr., "Charting America's News of the World War," *Foreign Affairs,* XV (January, 1937), 311–19.

68. *Foreign Relations, 1917, Supplement 1*, pp. 109–12.

69. Baker and Dodd, *Public Papers,* IV, 428–32.

70. *Current Opinion,* LXII (April, 1917), 229–31. The House debate on this bill appears in *Cong. Rec.*, 64th Cong., 2d Sess., pp. 4563, 4636–92, 4858–60, 4876–4912, 4914–17, 4988–5020.

71. Savage, *Maritime Policy,* II, 577–80.

72. *Literary Digest,* XLIX (August 15, 1914), 255; (August 22, 1914), pp. 289–90; (October, 1914), p. 616.

73. *Ibid.*, (December 12, 1914), p. 1163.

74. *Ibid.*, LI (August 14, 1915), 281–84.

75. *Ibid.*, LIII (August 12, 1916), 340–42.

76. *Current History,* VI (April–June, 1917), 120.

77. Bradley A. Fiske, *From Midshipman to Rear-Admiral* (New York, 1919), pp. 635–37.

78. *Literary Digest,* LIV (March 10, 1917), 608.

79. Burton J. Hendrick, *Life and Letters of Walter H. Page* (New York, 1922), III, 336 ff.; Page to Secretary of State, received February 24, 1917, *Foreign Relations, 1917, Supplement 1*, p. 147.

80. Baker, *Wilson,* VI, 474.

81. Lansing, *Memoirs,* pp. 227–28.

82. Baker, *Wilson*, VI, 497.

83. *Literary Digest*, LIV (March 17, 1917), 687–90; (March 10, 1917), p. 607.

84. Lodge to Roosevelt, March 2, 1917, Henry C. Lodge, *Selections from the Correspondence of Theodore Roosevelt and Henry Cabot Lodge, 1884–1918* (New York, 1925), II, 499.

85. *Current Opinion*, LXVI (April, 1917), 233–34.

86. *New Republic*, X (March 10, 1917), 151–53.

87. Sidney Brooks, "Impression of America at War," *North American Review*, CCV (April, 1917), 673–82.

88. Russell Buchanan, "American Editors Examine American War Aims and Plans in April, 1917," *Pacific Historical Review*, IX (September, 1940), 253–65.

89. *New York Times*, March 21, 22, 1917; *Literary Digest*, LIV (March 3, 1917), 538–39.

90. *Literary Digest*, LIV (April 14, 1917), 1043–46.

91. Brooks, "Impressions of America at War," *loc. cit.*, p. 681.

92. *New Republic*, X (April 14, 1917), 308–10.

93. *Literary Digest*, LIV (April 7, 1917), 966.

94. *Cong. Rec.*, 65th Cong., 1st Sess., pp. 200–254.

95. *Ibid.*, p. 253.

96. *Ibid.*, pp. 305–412.

97. *Current History*, VI (April–June, 1917), 214–22.

98. *Cong. Rec.*, 65th Cong., 1st Sess., p. 393.

99. Senators Norris and La Follette laid particular emphasis on this contention. For a refutation see Alice M. Morissey, *The American Defense of Neutral Rights, 1914–1917* (Cambridge, 1939), pp. 194–97.

100. *Cong. Rec.*, 65th Cong., 1st Sess., p. 357.

101. *Ibid.*, p. 328.

NOTES TO CHAPTER XII

1. *New Republic*, X (April 21, 1917), 334–36.

2. *Current Opinion*, LXIII (July, 1917), 5.

3. *Ibid.*, LXII (May, 1917), 302.

4. *Ibid.*, p. 302.

5. *Nation*, CIV (April 26, 1917), 480.

6. Ray S. Baker and William E. Dodd, *The Public Papers of Woodrow Wilson* (New York, 1925–27), V, 22.

7. *Ibid.*, p. 33.

8. *Ibid.*, p. 53.

9. *Ibid.*, pp. 54–57.

10. *Ibid.*, p. 47.

11. *Ibid.*, pp. 60–67.

12. *Literary Digest*, LIV (June 16, 1917), 1834–35.

13. George Harvey, "The Call to Arms," *North American Review*, CCV (May, 1917), 642; "For Democracy and Freedom," *ibid.*, p. 650.

14. George Harvey, "Unconditional Surrender: the Only Way," *North American Review*, CCVI (August, 1917), 177–87.

15. Roosevelt to Lee, April 5, 1917, *Roosevelt Collection* (Widener Library, Harvard University).

16. Theodore Roosevelt, "Put the Flag on the Firing Line," *Metropolitan*, XLVI (June, 1917), 7 ff.

17. Roosevelt, "The Peace of Victory for Which We Strive," *ibid.*, XLVI (July, 1917), 24 ff.

18. Roosevelt to Bryce, April 19, 1917, *Roosevelt Collection*.

19. Roosevelt to White, August 3, 1917, *ibid.*

20. *Metropolitan*, XLVI (September, 1917), 5 ff.

21. Theodore Roosevelt, *The Works of Theodore Roosevelt*, (Mem. ed.; New York, 1925), XXI, 10–11, 12, 4.

22. Joseph B. Bishop, *Theodore Roosevelt and His Time* (New York, 1920), II, 436.

23. Baker and Dodd, *Public Papers*, V, 155–62.

24. Ray S. Baker, *American Chronicle* (New York, 1945), pp. 298–301.

25. Charles Seymour, *The Intimate Papers of Colonel House* (Boston, 1926, 1928), III, 171; James T. Shotwell, *At the Paris Peace Conference* (New York,

1937), p. 4. The Inquiry included George Louis Beer, David Hunter Miller, Isaiah Bowman, Shotwell, and Dr. Mezes, House's brother-in-law.

26. *New Republic*, XI (July 7, 1917), 260–61.

27. *Ibid*. (October 6, 1917), pp. 254–57.

28. *Ibid.*, XIV (March 30, 1918), 248–51.

29. Oswald G. Villard, *Fighting Years* (New York, 1939), pp. 327 ff. To Villard the staffs of the *Nation* and the *Evening Post* seemed almost wholly prowar.

30. Randolph Bourne, *Untimely Papers* (New York, 1919), p. 45.

31. George Creel, *How We Advertised America* (New York, 1920), pp. 94, 114.

32. Many of the C.P.I. pamphlets are reproduced in *Current History* and the *New York Times*. Many are gathered in the bound volumes of World War I propaganda in Widener Library, Harvard University.

33. *Independent*, XCIII (January 19, 1918), 89–92.

34. *New Republic*, XV (June 22, 1918), 221.

35. Ruhl J. Bartlett, *The League to Enforce Peace* (Chapel Hill, N.C., 1944), pp. 93–95.

36. Baker and Dodd, *Public Papers*, VI, 231–35, 253–61.

37. *Cong. Rec.*, 65th Cong., 2d Sess., pp. 11160, 11171.

38. Beveridge to Roosevelt, July 14, 1918, Claude G. Bowers, *Beveridge and the Progressive Era* (Boston, 1932), p. 498; Roosevelt to Beveridge, August 14, 1918, *ibid.*, p. 498.

39. Theodore Roosevelt, "Don't Spread Patriotism Too Thin," *Metropolitan*, XLIX (July, 1918), 6 ff.

40. *Kansas City Star*, October 17 and 30, 1918, in Roosevelt, *Works*, XXI, 417, 420–23; Roosevelt to Beveridge, October 16, 21, 31, 1918, Bowers, *Beveridge*, pp. 499–500.

41. Lodge to Beveridge, December 3, 1918, Bowers, *Beveridge*, p. 500.

42. Baker and Dodd, *Public Papers*, V, 294–302.

43. Annual message, December 2, 1918, *ibid.*, p. 312.

44. Address at the University of Paris, December 21, 1918, *ibid.*, p. 330.

45. *Ibid.*, pp. 352–53.

46. Roosevelt to Lee, November 19, 1918, *Roosevelt Collection*.

47. Roosevelt to Putnam, December, 5, 1918, *ibid*. In reply to Putnam's solicitation, Roosevelt wrote that he was in sympathy with the objects of the English-speaking Union but could not take a position on the board.

48. Theodore Roosevelt, "The League of Nations," *Metropolitan*, XLIX (January, 1919), 9 ff.

49. *Cong. Rec.*, 65th Cong., 3d Sess., pp. 4520 ff.

50. *Cong. Rec.*, 66th Cong., 1st Sess., p. 3783.

51. *Ibid.*, pp. 3911–15.

52. *Literary Digest*, LIV (November 23, 1918), 12–13; (December 28, 1918), pp. 11–12. In May, 1919, the press, in the main, approved of the terms of the treaty with Germany as just and merciful, considering the magnitude of her offense, and emphatically denied the German charge that they violated the Fourteen Points. *Ibid.*, LXI (May 17, 1919), 11–15; (May 24, 1919), pp. 9–13; (May 31, 1919), pp. 15–16.

53. *Literary Digest*, LX (January 11, 1919), 9–11.

54. *Nation*, CVII (November 9, 1918), 544.

55. *Ibid.*, CVIII (January 11, 1919), 37.

56. *Ibid.* (February 22, 1919), p. 268.

57. *Ibid.* (March 15, 1919), p. 384.

58. *Ibid.* (March 22, 1919), pp. 416–17.

59. *Ibid.*, CVI (January 3, 1918), 8–10.

60. *Ibid.* (May 3, 1919), p. 676.

61. *Ibid.* (April 26, 1919), pp. 646–47.

62. Bartlett, *op. cit.*, pp. 130–31.

63. *Literary Digest*, LXI (April 12, 1919), 30.

64. Henry C. Lodge, *The Senate and the League of Nations* (New York, 1925), pp. 146–47.

65. *Ibid.*, p. 147.

66. Philip C. Jessup, *Elihu Root* (New

York, 1938), II, 374 ff.; Bartlett, *op. cit.*, pp. 43, 131.

67. Thomas A. Bailey presents a fair and penetrating analysis of the Lodge reservations in his *Woodrow Wilson and the Peacemakers* (New York, 1947), II, 154 ff.

68. *Ibid.*, pp. 172, 387–94.

69. Baker and Dodd, *Public Papers*, V, 432–40.

70. *Ibid.*, p. 450.

71. *Ibid.*, p. 505.

72. *Ibid.*, pp. 537–52.

73. *Ibid.*, p. 640.

74. *Ibid.*, p. 640.

75. *Ibid.*, VI, 55.

76. *Ibid.*, V, 625, 635–39.

77. *Ibid.*, VI, 52.

78. *Ibid.*, p. 176.

79. *Ibid.*, p. 104.

80. *Ibid.*, p. 139.

81. *Ibid.*, p. 324.

82. A balanced exposition of this view of Wilson's accomplishments at Paris is set forth in Paul Birdsall, *Versailles Twenty Years After* (New York, 1941), and Bailey, *op. cit.*, I.

83. Villard, *Fighting Years*, p. 458.

84. *Nation*, CVIII (May 17, 1919), 778–80.

85. *Ibid.*, CXI (November 3, 1920), 489.

86. Villard, *op. cit.*, p. 361.

87. *Cong. Rec.*, 66th Cong., 1st Sess., p. 8773.

88. Bailey, *op. cit.*, II, 7–8.

NOTES TO CHAPTER XIII

1. Merle Curti, *Peace or War* (New York, 1936), p. 273.

2. George Creel, *The War, The World, and Wilson* (New York, 1920), p. 99.

3. *Nation*, CXII (December 7, 1921), 658–59.

4. Willis F. Johnson, *George Harvey* (Boston, 1929), p. 297.

5. *Nation*, CXII (June 1, 1921), 777.

6. Harold E. Stearns, *The Street I Know* (New York, 1935), pp. 141 ff.

7. Harold E. Stearns, *Liberalism in America* (New York, 1919), pp. 10–11.

8. Richard W. Leopold, "The Problem of American Intervention, 1917: Historical Retrospect," *World Politics*, II (April, 1950), 407.

9. *Ibid.*, p. 408.

10. George Brandes, *The World at War* (New York, 1917); Philip Gibbs, *Now It Can Be Told* (New York, 1920); Francis Neilson, *How Diplomats Make War* (New York, 1916).

11. Selig Adler, "The War-Guilt Question and American Disillusionment, 1918–1928," *Journal of Modern History*, XXIII (March, 1951), 8–9.

12. Frederick Bausman, *Let France Explain* (2d ed.; London, 1923), pp. 63–64.

13. Harry E. Barnes, *The Genesis of the World War* (New York, 1926), p. 682.

14. C. Hartley Grattan, *The Deadly Parallel* (New York, 1929), p. 21.

15. James Wechsler, *Revolt on the Campus* (New York, 1935), pp. 21 ff.

16. Henry S. Harrison, "Last Days of the Devastators," *Yale Review*, XVIII (Autumn, 1928), 88–103.

17. Stearns, *The Street I Know*, pp. 370 ff.; *Rediscovering America* (New York, 1934).

18. Malcolm Cowley, *Exile's Return* (New York, 1934), chap. vii.

19. Henry Steele Commager, *The American Mind* (New Haven, 1950), pp. 266 ff.

20. Walter Lippmann, *Interpretations, 1931–1932* (New York, 1932), p. 27.

21. Manley O. Hudson, "The Liberals and the League," *Nation*, CXVI (April 4, 1923), 383–84.

22. Elihu Root, "Steps Toward Preserving Peace," *Foreign Affairs*, III (April, 1925), 352.

23. *New York Times*, December 29, 1929.

24. *Nation*, CXI (November 17, 1920), 549–50.

25. William T. R. Fox, "Interwar International Relations Research: The American Experience," *World Politics*, II (October, 1949), 74 ff.

26. *Nation*, CXXXIII (July 22, 1931), 79.

27. Curti, *Peace or War*, pp. 274–75;

Dixon Wecter, *The Age of the Great Depression, 1929–1941* (New York, 1948), p. 306.

28. Ray H. Abrams, *Preachers Present Arms* (Philadelphia, 1933), p. 235.

29. *Ibid.*, p. 236.

30. *Nation*, CXXXII (May 6, 1931), 494.

31. Carnegie Endowment for International Peace, *Yearbook 1920* (Washington, 1921), p. 174.

32. Nicholas M. Butler, *Looking Forward* (New York, 1932), pp. 315–17.

33. Norman Thomas, "Advances in the Quest for Peace," Kirby Page, ed., *Recent Gains in American Civilization* (New York, 1928), chap. iv.

34. Powers, *The American Era* (New York, 1923); "Independence or Civilization," *Harper's*, CXXXV (February, 1925), 249–62; "Amenities and Responsibilities," *Harper's*, CXXXIX (April, 1927), 466–73; *America and Great Britain* (New York, 1918).

35. *The Great Peace* (New York, 1918), chap. xx, p. 322.

36. Mowrer, *The House of Europe* (Boston, 1945), pp. 269, 278, 358.

37. *Ibid.*, p. 360.

38. *Ibid.*, p. 390.

39. *Ibid.*, pp. 618–21.

40. Mowrer, *Our Foreign Affairs* (New York, 1924), p. 49.

41. *Ibid.*, p. 18.

42. *Ibid.*, pp. 66, 187.

43. *Ibid.*, pp. 254–56.

44. Walter Lippmann, *The Political Scene* (New York, 1919), pp. 32, 42, 48.

45. *New Republic*, XXI (December 31, 1919), 150–51.

46. *Ibid.*, XIX (July 30, 1919), 424.

NOTES TO CHAPTER XIV

1. Charles L. Hoag, *Preface to Preparedness* (New York, 1941), pp. 89 ff., 100 ff.

2. *Cong. Rec.*, 66th Cong., 3d Sess., p. 310.

3. Hoag, *op. cit.*, pp. 42–47, 73 ff., 114 ff.; Harold and Margaret Sprout, *Toward a New Order of Sea Power* (2d ed.; Princeton, 1943), pp. 114 ff.

4. Sprouts, *op. cit.*, p. 120.

5. *Foreign Relations, 1921*, I, 18.

6. Sprouts, *op. cit.*, pp. 175–76. Merlo J. Pusey, *Charles Evans Hughes* (New York, 1951), II, 476–77.

7. Sprouts, *op. cit.*, p. 172.

8. *Ibid.*, pp. 253–54.

9. Pusey, *Hughes*, II, 473.

10. Sprouts, *op. cit.*, p. 256.

11. *Ibid.*, pp. 271–74; Winston B. Thorson, "Pacific Northwest Opinion on the Washington Conference of 1921–1922," *Pacific Northwest Quarterly*, XXXVII (January, 1946), 109–27. Thorson believes that newspaper editors in the Pacific Northwest were enthusiastic but not unqualifiedly optimistic.

12. *Nation*, CXIII (November 9, 1921), 520; (December 7, 1921), p. 638; CXIV (January 11, 1922), 33; (March 8, 1922), p. 275; (March 22, 1922), p. 330; (April 5, 1922), p. 383.

13. *Cong. Rec.*, 67th Cong., 2d Sess., pp. 3232 ff., 3408 ff., 3555 ff., 3606 ff., 3776 ff., 3787 ff.

14. *Ibid.*, pp. 3787 ff.

15. *Ibid.*, pp. 3232–37.

16. *Ibid.*, p. 3552.

17. *Ibid.*, p. 3606.

18. *New York Times*, December 12, 1921.

19. Briand's motives and Shotwell's part in Briand's address are explained in Robert H. Ferrell, *Peace in Their Time* (New Haven, 1952), pp. 71 ff.

20. *Ibid.*, pp. 164–65, 168.

21. *New York Times*, August 16, 1928.

22. *Literary Digest*, XCVIII (September 8, 1928), 6.

23. Ferrell, *op. cit.*, pp. 192–93, 207.

24. *Ibid.*, p. 241.

25. *Cong. Rec.*, 70th Cong., 2d Sess., pp. 1063–66.

26. *Ibid.*, pp. 1186–89.

27. *Ibid.*, p. 1728.

28. A. Whitney Griswold, *The Far Eastern Policy of the United States* (New York, 1928), pp. 402–4.

29. Henry L. Stimson, *The Far Eastern Crisis* (New York, 1936), pp. 88–90, 233–42.

30. *Ibid.*, p. 242.

31. Henry L. Stimson and McGeorge Bundy, *On Active Service in Peace and War* (New York, 1948), p. 242.

32. *Ibid.*, pp. 249–54.

33. Joseph C. Grew, *My Ten Years in Japan* (New York, 1944).

34. *Ibid.*, pp. 75–80.

35. *Ibid.*, pp. 299–305.

36. Stimson and Bundy, *op. cit.*, p. 255.

37. *Ibid.*, pp. 244–45, 258, 260–62.

38. See, for example, his statement to his Cabinet in December, 1931, Ray L. Wilbur and Arthur M. Hyde, *The Hoover Policies* (New York, 1937), pp. 600–1.

39. For American opinion about the Sino-Japanese War see Eleanor Tupper and George E. McReynolds, *Japan in American Public Opinion* (New York, 1937), pp. 284 ff.

40. *New York Times*, January 8, 1933.

41. *Ibid.*, February 18, 20, 1932.

42. *Ibid.*, February 26, 1932.

43. A. Lawrence Lowell, "Manchuria, the League, and the United States," *Foreign Affairs*, X (April, 1932), 351–68; *New York Times*, January 8, 1933.

44. *Literary Digest*, CXI (December 5, 1931), 3–4; CXII (March 19, 1932), 21–22.

45. *New York Times*, March 5, 1932.

NOTES TO CHAPTER XV

1. *Public Opinion Quarterly*, V (Fall, 1941), 477.

2. *New York Herald Tribune*, April 7, 1937.

3. Charles A. and Mary R. Beard, *America in Midpassage* (New York, 1939), p. 421.

4. Edwin Borchard and William P. Lage, *Neutrality for the United States* (New Haven, 1937), p. 350.

5. C. Hartley Grattan, *The Deadly Parallel* (New York, 1939).

6. Stuart Chase, "Ideological Immunity, 1975," *New Republic*, CI (November 8, 1939), Part II, 80–86.

7. Paul C. French, ed., *Common Sense Neutrality* (New York, 1939), pp. 12–13.

8. Kirby Page, *Must We Go To War?* (New York, 1937), p. 36.

9. *The New Western Front* (New York, 1939). A similar thesis is argued in Clark Foreman, *The New Internationalism* (New York, 1934), and Jerome Frank, *Save America First* (New York, 1938).

10. Walter Millis, *Road to War* (Boston, 1915), p. 429; Bernard C. Borning, "The Political Philosophy of Young Charles A. Beard," *American Political Science Review*, XLII (December, 1949), 1175–76; Charles A. Beard, "A Call Upon Every Citizen," *Harper's Magazine*, CXXXVII (October, 1918), 655–56; Frederic A. Ogg and Charles A. Beard, *National Governments and the World War* (New York, 1919), p. 589. Beard appears to have turned against the League after 1918. His isolationism stemmed, in the first instance, from a disgust with international politics rather than from a repudiation of America's intervention in 1917. Selig Adler, "The War-Guilt Question and American Disillusionment, 1918–1928," *Journal of Modern History*, XXIII (March, 1951), 8–9.

11. Charles A. Beard and G. H. E. Smith, *The Idea of National Interest* (New York, 1934), p. 552.

12. Charles A. Beard and G. H. E. Smith, *The Open Door at Home* (New York, 1934), chaps. vi, x, pp. 269, vii.

13. Beards, *America in Midpassage*, pp. 401–22.

14. *Ibid.*, p. 455.

15. Beard, "We're Blundering into War," *American Mercury*, CLXXXIV (April, 1939), 388–89.

16. *New Republic*, XCIX (May 17, 1939), 37–38.

17. *Boston Transcript*, September 25, 1940.

18. Norman Thomas, "Why Our Country Should Stay Out of War," N. Schoonmaker and D. F. Reid, eds., *We Testify* (New York, 1941), p. 208.

19. *Nation*, CXLVII (September 24, 1938), 299; (October 1, 1938), p. 325.

20. *Ibid.* (October 15, 1938), p. 381.

21. *The Works of Theodore Roosevelt*

(Mem. ed.; New York, 1925), XX, 264.

22. Thomas, "Why Our Country Should Stay Out of War," *op. cit.,* p. 206.

23. Chase, *The New Western Front,* pp. 167, 173. This was written before Germany invaded Poland.

24. *The Open Door at Home,* p. 261.

25. *Giddy Minds and Foreign Quarrels* (New York, 1939), p. 74.

26. *Nation,* CXLVII (July 30, 1938), 110; CXLVIII (March 11, 1939), 295.

27. *Ibid.,* CXLIX (September 23, 1939), 324.

28. Oswald G. Villard, *Our Military Chaos* (New York, 1939), p. 69. This book was finished just before the invasion of Poland, but in the foreward Villard stated his opinion that the outbreak of war made no difference in his conclusions.

29. *Nation,* CXLX (January 13, 1940), 47.

30. Herbert Hoover, "The Immediate Relation of the United States to This War," Schoonmaker and Reid, *We Testify,* pp. 3–12, 12.

31. *New York Times,* February 2, 1939.

32. Robert A. Taft, "Shall the President Make War without the Approval of Congress," Schoonmaker and Reid, *We Testify,* pp. 215–29, 215.

33. Robert E. Wood, "America's Foreign Policy Today," *ibid.,* pp. 107–19.

34. Charles A. Lindbergh, "A Letter to Americans," *ibid.,* pp. 63–81; *New York Times,* October 31, April 23, 1941.

NOTES TO CHAPTER XVI

1. *New Republic,* XIX (June 14, 1919), 218.

2. *Leaves from the Notebook of a Tamed Cynic* (New York, 1929), p. 42.

3. *Ibid.,* p. 48.

4. *Moral Man and Immoral Society* (New York, 1932), p. xx.

5. *Ibid.,* p. 6.

6. "Ideology and Pretense," *Nation,* CXLIX (December 9, 1939), 645–46.

7. *Christianity and Power Politics* (New York, 1940), pp. 33–34.

8. Edgar Kemler, *The Deflation of*

American Ideals (Washington, D.C., 1941).

9. Armstrong, *"We or They"* (New York, 1937), p. 102.

10. Mumford, "Call to Arms," *New Republic,* LXXXXV (May 18, 1938), 39–42.

11. This view is spelled out in greater detail in Mumford's "The Corruption of Liberalism," *ibid.,* CII (April 29, 1940), pp. 568–73, and in an essay written in March, 1941, at the request of Reinhold Niebuhr, reprinted as "The Aftermath of Utopianism" in Mumford, *Values for Survival* (New York, 1946).

12. *Men Must Act* (New York, 1939), pp. 74–75.

13. Max Lerner, "Revolution in Ideas," *Nation,* CXLIX (October 21, 1939), 435–37; cf. Reinhold Niebuhr, "Ideology and Utopia," *ibid.* (December 9, 1939), pp. 645–46, and Frederic L. Schuman, "Machiavelli in Moscow," *New Republic,* CI (November 29, 1939), 158–60, and *ibid.* (December 27, 1939), p. 290.

14. Lerner, "American Leadership in a Harsh Age," *Annals of the American Academy of Political and Social Science,* CCXVI (July, 1941), 119.

15. For other examples of liberal militancy see Waldo Frank, "Our Guilt in Fascism," *New Republic,* CII (May 6, 1940), 603–8; Frank, *Chart for Rough Water* (New York, 1940); Archibald MacLeish, *The Irresponsibles* (New York, 1940).

16. As early as the spring of 1938 the *Nation* reported that over nine thousand replies to a questionnaire sent to a representative selection of liberals indicated that only one-sixth subscribed to an isolationist policy, as opposed to some form of collective security. Eighty-one per cent of those favoring joint action against aggressors placed their faith in economic sanctions; about 60 per cent favored a threat of collective armed resistance. *Nation,* CXLVI (May 7, 1938), 522–23.

17. *Nation,* CXXXVI (May 31, 1933), 597; CXXXVII (November 1, 1933), 499; CXLIV (February 20, 1937), 200.

18. *Ibid.,* CXLI (September 4, 1935),

256–57; (November 6, 1935), p. 524; CXLVI (January 1, 1938), 733.

19. *Ibid.*, CXXXVII (October 4, 1933), 368.

20. *Ibid.*, CXLIV (February 27, 1937), 228–29.

21. *Ibid.*, CXLVI (February 5, 1938), 141.

22. *Ibid.* (February 19, 1938), pp. 200–201.

23. *Ibid.*, CXLVII (October 22, 1938), 396–97.

24. *Ibid.*, CXLIX (September 9, 1939), 260–61.

25. *Ibid.* (September 16, 1939), pp. 281–82.

26. *Ibid.* (September 23, 1939), p. 307.

27. *Ibid.*, CXL (June 1, 1940), 665–66.

28. *Ibid.* (June 15, 1940), p. 724.

29. *Ibid.* (June 29, 1940), p. 782.

30. *Ibid.* (June 22, 1940), pp. 743–44.

31. *New Republic,* C (August 30, 1939), 89.

32. *Ibid.* (September 6, 1939), pp. 116–17.

33. *Ibid.*, LXXXXV (May 18, 1938), 32–33; cf. CII (February 12, 1940), 198–99.

34. *Ibid.*, CII (April 22, 1940), 525–26.

35. *Ibid.* (May 6, 1940), p. 591; CIII (July 8, 1940), 46–47.

36. William T. R. Fox, "Interwar International Relations Research: The American Experience," *World Politics,* II (October, 1949), 77–79; Grayson Kirk, *The Study of International Relations in American Colleges and Universities* (New York, 1947).

37. *International Politics* (New York, 1933), p. viii.

38. For example, Nicholas J. Spykman, "Geography and Foreign Policy" *American Political Science Review,* XXXII (February, 1938), 28–50; (April, 1938), 213–36; Derwent Whittlesey, *The Earth and the State* (New York, 1940).

39. Robert Strausz-Hupé, *Geopolitics* (New York, 1942), pp. 119–25.

40. Livingston Hartley, *Our Maginot Line* (New York, 1939), pp. 10–11.

41. Eliot, *The Ramparts We Watch* (New York, 1938); G. F. Eliot and R. E. Dupuy, *If War Comes* (New York, 1937). In "The Impossible War with Japan," *American Mercury,* XLV (September, 1938), 16–25, Eliot presented the view that a war between the United States and Japan and a Japanese attack upon Hawaii were impossible.

42. Eliot, *Hour of Triumph* (New York, 1944), p. vi.

43. Eliot, *The Ramparts We Watch,* p. 13.

44. Baldwin, *Defense of the Western World* (London, 1940), pp. 69, 75; chap. ii. In 1939 Baldwin called Hartley an alarmist; Hartley replied; Baldwin repeated his charge. *New York Times Book Review* (April 9, 1939), p. 19; (May 7, 1939), p. 19.

45. *Defense of the Western World,* pp. 42, 75.

46. *Ibid.*, p. 43.

47. Johnson Hagood, *We Can Defend America* (Garden City, N.Y., 1937), p. 86.

48. Max Werner, *Battle for the World* (New York, 1941); Fletcher Pratt, *America and Total War* (New York, 1941); Fleming MacLeish and Cushman Reynolds, *Strategy of the Americas* (New York, 1941).

49. Earle, "American Military Policy and National Security," *Political Science Quarterly,* LIII (March, 1938), 1–13.

50. "The Future of Foreign Policy," *New Republic,* CI (November 8, 1939), Part II, 86–94. Earle revised his interpretation of American intervention after World War II. "A Half-Century of American Foreign Policy: Our Stake in Europe, 1898–1948," *Political Science Quarterly,* LXIV (June, 1949), 182.

51. "National Security and Foreign Policy," *Yale Review,* XXXII (Spring, 1940), 444–60; "National Defense and Political Science," *Political Science Quarterly,* LV (December, 1940), 481–95.

52. "The Threat to American Security," *Yale Review,* XXX (Spring, 1941), 454–80.

53. "American Security—Its Changing Conditions," *Annals of the American Academy of Political and Social Science,* CCXVIII (November, 1941), 186–98.

54. *Against This Torrent* (Princeton, 1941), pp. 61-62.

55. Forrest Davis, *The Atlantic System* (New York, 1941), p. 245.

56. *Ibid.*, p. 249.

57. *Ibid.*, p. 339.

58. Walter Lippmann, "Rough-Hew Them How We Will," *Foreign Affairs*, XV (July, 1937), 587-94.

59. *Ibid.*, p. 590; cf. Lippmann, "Britain and America: The Prospects of Political Co-operation in the Light of Their Paramount Interests," *Foreign Affairs*, XIII (April, 1935), 363-72.

60. "Rough-Hew Them How We Will," *op. cit.*, p. 594.

61. "The Economic Consequences of a Germany Victory," *Life*, IX (July 22, 1940), 65-69.

62. "The Atlantic and America: The Why and When of Intervention," *Life*, X (April 7, 1941), 85.

63. I. F. Stone, "1937 Is Not 1914," *Nation*, CXLV (November 6, 1937), 495-97.

64. For example, translations and excerpts from *Mein Kampf;* Hermann Rauschning, *The Revolution of Nihilism* (New York, 1939); Edmund Taylor, *The Strategy of Terror* (Boston, 1940); Otto D. Tolischus, *They Wanted War* (New York, 1940); Max Werner, *Battle for the World* (New York, 1941).

65. *New York Herald Tribune,* September 18, 1939.

NOTES TO CHAPTER XVII

1. *Literary Digest,* CXXIV (December 25, 1937), 11; *Fortune,* XVII (April, 1938), 109.

2. Cordell Hull, *Memoirs of Cordell Hull* (New York, 1948), I, 544 ff.

3. Jerome S. Bruner, *Mandate from the People* (New York, 1944), p. 19. Bruner's conclusions about public opinion are based on careful analysis of the findings of the principal opinion polls.

4. See, for example, Kenneth G. Crawford, "Shadow Boxing in Washington," *Nation,* CXLIX (October 14, 1939), 403-4.

5. *Cong. Rec.*, 76th Cong., 2d Sess., p. 250.

6. Walter Johnson, *The Battle Against Isolation* (Chicago, 1944), p. 64.

7. William L. Langer and S. Everett Gleason, *The Challenge to Isolation, 1937-1940* (New York, 1952), pp. 506-7.

8. Laurence Greene in the *New York Post,* June 7, 1940.

9. *Public Opinion Quarterly,* IV (September, 1940), 390, 550.

10. *Ibid.*, V (Fall, 1941), 478; Thirty-four per cent disagreed with this estimate; 11 per cent did not know what to think.

11. *Ibid.* (June, 1940), p. 390.

12. *Ibid.*, IV (September, 1940), 391.

13. *Ibid.*, V (June, 1941), 326; (Fall, 1941), p. 482.

14. As late as April, 1941, 39 per cent thought that intervention had been a mistake; 43 per cent did not; 18 per cent did not know. *Ibid.* (Fall, 1941), p. 477.

15. *Ibid.*, p. 481.

16. *Ibid.*, IV (September, 1940), 391, 390.

17. Bruner, *op. cit.*, pp. 22-26.

18. *Public Opinion Quarterly,* IV (September, 1940), 405-6.

19. Robert E. Sherwood, *Roosevelt and Hopkins* (New York, 1948), p. 266.

20. Franklin D. Roosevelt, *The Public Papers and Addresses of Franklin D. Roosevelt, 1941* (New York, 1941-50), pp. 151-52.

21. Sherwood, *op. cit.*, p. 227.

22. Roosevelt, *Public Papers, 1937*, p. 408.

23. Langer and Gleason, *op.. cit.*, pp. 18 ff.

24. *Ibid.*, pp. 47, 51.

25. The best accounts of the first attempt to gain neutrality revision are *ibid.*, pp. 136 ff., and Basil Rauch, *Roosevelt from Munich to Pearl Harbor* (New York, 1950), pp. 114 ff.

26. For a full account of the second attempt at neutrality revision see Langer and Gleason, *op. cit.*, pp. 218 ff., and Rauch, *op. cit.*, chap. vi.

27. Sumner Welles, *The Time for Decision* (New York, 1944), p. 73.

28. Roosevelt, *Public Papers, 1940*, pp. 198-205.

29. *Ibid.*, pp. 259 ff.

30. Roosevelt, *ibid.*, pp. 633–44.

31. *House Report*, No. 18, Part II, p. 1.

32. *Hearings before the House Committee on Foreign Affairs*, 77th Cong., 1st Sess.

33. *Cong. Rec.*, 77th Cong., 1st Sess., p. 1040.

34. *Ibid.*, pp. 496–99.

35. George W. Norris, *Fighting Liberal* (New York, 1945), pp. 191–92, 196, 392.

36. *Cong. Rec.*, 77th Cong., 1st Sess., pp. 1975–77.

37. Johnson, *op. cit.*, p. 182.

38. *New York Times,* January 4, 1941.

39. *Public Opinion Quarterly,* V (Fall, 1941), 477, 482.

40. Henry L. Stimson and McGeorge Bundy, *On Active Service in Peace and War* (New York, 1948), pp. 372 ff.

41. Langer and Gleason, *op. cit.*, pp. 495, 514, 533–34, 539.

42. Roosevelt, *Public Papers, 1941,* pp. 181–94.

43. Sherwood, *op. cit.*, pp. 410–18.

44. Sumner Welles, *Where Are We Heading?* (New York, 1946), pp. 3 ff.

45. Roosevelt, *Public Papers, 1940,* p. xxx.

46. Stimson and Bundy, *op. cit.*, p. 326.

INDEX

INDEX

PHOENIX BOOKS
in Political Science and Law